EXPERIMENTS IN
PERSUASION

SOCIAL PSYCHOLOGY

A series of monographs, treatises, and texts

Edited by

Leon Festinger
Department of Psychology
Stanford University
Stanford, California

and

Stanley Schachter
Department of Social Psychology
Columbia University
New York, New York

EXPERIMENTS IN
PERSUASION

EDITED BY

Ralph L. Rosnow and **Edward J. Robinson**

Department of Psychology   *Communication Research Division*
Temple University   *Boston University*
Philadelphia, Pennsylvania   *Boston, Massachusetts*

ACADEMIC PRESS   New York and London   **1967**

ACADEMIC PRESS INC.
111 Fifth Avenue, New York, New York 10003

United Kingdom Edition published by
ACADEMIC PRESS INC. (LONDON) LTD.
Berkeley Square House, London W.1

LIBRARY OF CONGRESS CATALOG CARD NUMBER: 67-29743

PRINTED IN THE UNITED STATES OF AMERICA

To Mimi and Priscilla

Preface

Our purpose in compiling this book was to present a general introduction to the literature in one of the major areas of specialization in experimental social psychology — persuasion. We found our task to be both exhilarating and frustrating. It was exhilarating in that by exposing ourselves to the growing literature on persuasion, we were able to share the excitement that is a concomitant of scientific discovery. There is a burgeoning literature on this subject, a literature which reflects many new insights about human behavior and communication. But we also found our task frustrating. Like a passenger on a fast-moving train who tries to describe at any given moment aspects of the scene outside, we found that aspects in our field seemed to move so quickly that it was difficult to capture them completely. New ideas, qualifications of earlier findings, reports of programmatic research on theoretical constructs — all of these continued to accumulate at such a rapid pace that a major part of our job was one of constant reformulation and updating.

We are grateful to Academic Press for their interest and encouragement throughout the preparation of this work. We also benefited greatly from the comments of our colleagues, particularly Herbert Greenwald who gave so freely of his time. Robert Lana read the entire manuscript, and we want to thank him for his valuable criticisms. We are likewise obliged to the authors and publishers who permitted us to reprint their work. For their assistance in the preparation of the bibliography and the final manuscript, thanks are due Arthur Goldman, Jane Goldberg, and Linda Clausen. Our writing was facilitated by grants to the first author from the National Institute of Mental Health (MH-11972-01) and the National Science Foundation (GS-1375); preparation of the manuscript was supported by the Boston University Communication Research Center. To our wives, Mimi and Priscilla, we are especially indebted. They were a constant source of understanding, assistance, sympathy, encouragement, and patience throughout the two years of this collaborative effort.

RALPH L. ROSNOW
EDWARD J. ROBINSON

Boston, Massachusetts
June, 1967

L. A.H. Robson

Contents

CONTENTS

CONTENTS

CONTENTS

Introduction

A young woman about twenty years of age, already a heavy smoker, volunteers to participate in a research study. She is told by the experimenter that the aim of the study is to examine two important problems about the human side of medical practice: how patients react to bad news and how they feel about a doctor's advice to quit an enjoyable habit like smoking. She is asked to imagine that the experimenter is a physician who has been treating her for a bad cough that was not getting any better and that this is her third visit to his office, during which she will learn the results of X rays and other medical tests that were carried out previously. The experimenter then outlines five different scenes and asks her to act them out, role-playing each one as realistically as possible.

The first scene, he tells her, takes place in the physician's office. While awaiting the doctor's diagnosis, she is to express her thoughts aloud—her worry, her feelings about whether or not to give up smoking. The second scene is her confrontation with the physician. He will tell her that he has identified a small malignant mass. She will be encouraged to ask questions but will be told that there is only a moderate chance for success from surgery for this condition. In the third scene, she will express aloud her thoughts and feelings about the bad news, while she overhears the physician in the background phoning for a hospital bed. The fourth scene is her conversation with the physician concerning the details of her imminent hospitalization. He will tell her that, because chest surgery requires such a long time to heal, she should expect to be in the hospital for at least six weeks. In the final scene, the physician will raise questions about the woman's history of smoking and will ask if she is aware of the relationship between smoking and cancer. He will stress the urgent need for her to stop smoking immediately and will encourage her to speak freely about the difficulties she expects in trying to break her smoking habit.

This description is a condensation of an actual situation, devised by Irving L. Janis and Leon Mann, to study under controlled conditions the effectiveness of emotional role-playing in modifying habits and attitudes about smoking.[1] What would you guess were their findings?

---

[1] The Janis and Mann study is reprinted in its entirety later in this volume, pp. 361–367.

Do you think that emotional role-playing appreciably influenced the young woman's attitude toward smoking? What do you think the effect of role-playing was, if any, on her belief that smoking causes lung cancer? Do you think that her vicarious experience may have heightened her fear that personal harm might result from smoking? What of her willingness to give up smoking? Would you guess that this experience subsequently influenced her smoking habits?

Emotional role-playing has been viewed by some as a process of unintentional self-persuasion. When a person is constrained to extemporaneously defend a position or to play a role that is contrary to his private beliefs (or his public behavior), one effect of that experience may be to modify those beliefs. Hence, if a member of the John Birch Society were to find himself engaged in a debate where he was obliged to defend the position that Red China should be admitted to the United Nations, might he not persuade himself of the reasonableness of what was previously an anathema? Similarly, if, for the sake of expediency, a politician were convinced that he must publicly take a stand in support of civil rights and open housing, positions which were diametrically opposite to his private beliefs, might not his public counterattitudinal advocacy influence his personal beliefs on the subject?

Obviously, such subtle situations as these do not reflect typical, everyday experiences. Our daily encounters with persuasion and propaganda usually are more direct and to the point. Think again of the young woman who was a subject in Janis and Mann's experiment. It is likely that, on her way to the research institute, she encountered innumerable undisguised persuasive appeals, specifically intended to strengthen her smoking habit by bolstering her existing attitude. If she drove to her destination, she may have turned on her car radio and heard the ubiquitous Kent[2] jingle, or perhaps she traveled by bus and was confronted by a poster carring the familiar slogan "L.S./ M.F.T."[3] She probably passed at least one billboard reading "Winston tastes good—like a cigarette should."[4] If she read the morning newspaper or skimmed through a popular magazine, she would have found numerous other persuasive appeals: "Pipe Tobacco in a Filter Cigarette,"[5] "Us Tareyton smokers would rather fight than switch!"[6],

---

[2] © P. Lorillard Co.

[3] © American Tobacco Co.

[4] © R. J. Reynolds Tobacco Co.

[5] © American Tobacco Co.

[6] © American Tobacco Co.

etc.[7] The young woman was bombarded by persuasion from all sides.

PERSUASION: ATTITUDE VERSUS OPINION

This book is about persuasion. It embraces the study of persuasiveness, on the one hand, and persuasibility, on the other. It is also about attitudes and opinions—how they are formed and how they can be strengthened or weakened.

Webster's defines persuasion as an act "of influencing the mind by arguments or reasons."[8] English and English regard persuasion as "the process of obtaining another's adoption of a course of action, or his assent to a proposition, by an appeal to both feeling and intellect."[9] Fotheringham conceives of persuasion as "that body of effects in receivers, relevant and instrumental to source-desired goals, brought about by a process in which messages have been a major determinant of those effects."[10] All of these definitions are acceptable and, for the most part, concise.

By contrast, it is not as easy to define succinctly the concepts "opinion" or "attitude," the distinction between which is blurred as

---

[7] Had the young woman been cognizant of such things when she was a child, she might now recall countless other slogans and symbols associated with similar persuasion campaigns from the past: Marlboro's introduction in 1956 of the rugged-looking he-man idol, his tatooed hand holding a filter cigarette in an attempt to counter the feminine image of the previously red filter Marlboro; Viceroy's reference, in their early 1950s' advertisements, to a *Reader's Digest* article on the deleterious effects of smoking— thereby implying Viceroy's stand on the side of health. And, although our young woman is not old enough to have encountered personally many earlier cigarette persuasion campaigns, her parents certainly will recall Johnny's stepping out of thousands of store windows, in the late 1930's and early '40's, to the clarion "Call for Philip Morris" (©Philip Morris Inc.), and, several years before this, Lucky Strike's slogan ("Consider Your *Adam's Apple!!* Don't Rasp Your Throat With Harsh Irritants. Reach for A LUCKY Instead." (© American Tobacco Co.), possibly even the World War I era campaign slogan "I'd walk a mile for a Camel" (© R. J. Reynolds Co.). A fascinating account of this subject is Tyler, W. D. A gallery of American advertising—100 years of creative progress reviewed. *Advertising Age*, 1964, Dec. 7, **35**, No. 49, Sect. 2, pp. 99 ff.

[8] Quoted by permission from *Webster's Third New International Dictionary*, copyright 1966 by G. & C. Merriam Co., publishers of the Merriam-Webster Dictionaries.

[9] Quoted from English, H. B., & English, A. C. *A comprehensive dictionary of psychological and psychoanalytical terms.* New York: Longmans, Green, 1958. P. 385. By permission of David McKay Co., Inc.

[10] Quoted from Fotheringham, W. C. *Perspectives on persuasion.* Boston: Allyn & Bacon, 1966. P. 7. By permission of the author and the publisher.

a result of their all too often having been used interchangeably in the literature on persuasion. Unfortunately, both concepts have become laden with diverse connotative meanings. In this volume we shall think of opinions as verbal responses. Sometimes they are the antecedents of behavior, in which case they can be thought of as independent variables ("My doctor's opinion is that I should stay home, take two aspirins, and go right to bed."). More often, however, opinions are dependent variables, or the consequences of stimuli ("I believe that the doctor is correct, so I'll stay home."). Where opinions are concrete, "attitude" is abstract. Attitudes are hypothetical constructs. The term "attitude" denotes the organization in an individual of his feelings, beliefs, and predispositions to behave as he does. Opinions, being verbal responses, can be measured directly. Attitudes can only be inferred.

Attitudes are made up of three principal components which can vary in their complexity—*affect, cognition,* and *behavior.*[11] The affective component is a function of the individual's emotional response to social stimuli (How does he *feel* about foreigners? Does he like them, or does he dislike them?). The cognitive component is a function of the individual's knowledge of the social stimuli (What does he *believe* to be true of foreigners—specifically, and in general?). The behavioral component is a function of the individual's tendencies toward action relevant to the social stimuli (Given the opportunity, what would he *do* for, or to, foreigners?).

GENERALITY OF LABORATORY SOCIAL RESEARCH

This book focuses upon specific theoretical, empirical, and methodological problems in persuasion and considers the efforts that have been made in laboratory social situations to find the solutions to these problems. In the main, however, it is concerned with the processes influencing attitude and opinion change. Most of the papers reprinted here and the findings that are discussed reflect one specific methodological approach to the study of persuasion. They are *experimental* in nature. All emphasize a strict control of the independent and dependent conditions in persuasion and attitude change.

How much confidence can we have in the generality of such laboratory findings to "real life"? One answer—to which we subscribe—is provided by Hovland, Janis, and Kelley:

---

[11] Katz, D., & Stotland, E. A preliminary statement to a theory of attitude structure and change. In S. Koch (Ed.), *Psychology: A study of a science.* Vol. 3. *Formulations of the person and the social context.* New York: McGraw-Hill, 1959. Pp. 423–475.

It is presumptous, of course, to expect all problems to be amenable to investigation in this fashion. Nor can all propositions concerning communication and opinion change be submitted to experimental test at the present time. . . Even when a controlled analytical experiment shows a given factor to be significantly related to communication effectiveness, the question still remains as to the generality of the relationship. For example, experimental results may show that a communication designed to induce people to volunteer for civilian defense activities is more effective when fear-arousing appeals precede rather than follow the action recommendation. Would the outcome be the same in the case of a different topic? Or a different type of communicator? Or another medium? Or a different type of audience? Or a different type of recommended action? The solution to these problems lies, of course, in replication with strategic variations. The first experiment to test a general hypothesis is capable only of showing that the hypothesis holds true under the conditions represented in the experiment. It is necessary to carry out further investigations of the same hypothesis under carefully selected conditions, assigning different values to the supposedly irrelevant factors. Only in this way can one ultimately determine whether or not the hypothesis is a valid generalization and, if so, whether it requires specification of limiting conditions.[12]

PLAN OF THE BOOK

This book is divided into five sections, following the traditional Smith, Lasswell, and Casey formula:[13] "*Who* (source) says *what* (message) to *whom* (recipients) through which *medium* (channel) with what *effect*." In each section the principal findings of experimental research on attitude and persuasion are considered as they relate, respectively, to each of the five components of this formula.

Part I summarizes the literature on prestige suggestion, reviewing the effect on the potency of a communication of both relevant and objectively irrelevant aspects of the communicator's credibility, and the influence on attitude of positive and negative source factors.

In Part II the message is considered. The effects of one-sided and two-sided communications are contrasted. The question is raised whether, in two-sided communication, the first or the last argument has the advantage. Emotional versus rational propaganda are compared in an interesting field experiment where voting behavior constitutes the dependent variable. Finally, experimental research is introduced dealing with the influence on attitude of verbal threat, fear arousal, and coercion.

---

[12] Quoted from Hovland, C. I., Janis, I. L., & Kelley, H. H. *Communication and persuasion.* New Haven, Conn.: Yale Univer. Press, 1953. Pp. 5–6. By permission of H. H. Kelley and the publisher.

[13] Smith, B. L., Lasswell, H. D., & Casey, R. D. *Propaganda, communication, and public opinion.* Princeton, N. J.: Princeton Univer. Press, 1946.

Part III focuses upon the recipient. Discussed are both inherent and induced factors related to gullibility. Methods of heightening resistance to persuasion are enumerated. The question of self-persuasion and the role of active versus passive participation, problems alluded to earlier, are discussed here in detail, as are the motivational processes invoked in persuasion.

The channel, or means, of communication is the subject of Part IV. The potential catalytic function of this variable is described, with emphasis placed on the distinction between the mass media, specialized channels of communication, and face-to-face confrontation.

Part V comprises the effects of persuasion. The questions raised here relate to the magnitude of the impact of a communication (How much attitude change should a message demand if it is to have the greatest effect?), the persistency of that impact (How long-lasting is its effect?), its diffusion, or repercussion, onto other stimuli, and, lastly, an introduction to some of the principal sources of artifact in research on persuasion and attitude change.

FOCUS

Much of the research considered here reflects the influence of two imposing figures from social psychology—Carl I. Hovland (1912–1961) and Kurt Lewin (1890–1947).

Beginning after the Second World War, Carl I. Hovland and his associates at Yale University initiated a program of research whose impressive aim was to improve our understanding of the human psychological processes by studying the effects of communication on attitudes and behavior.[14] The idea for that program had its inception during the war when Hovland and his colleagues carried out their now well-known experimental investigations of the effectiveness of the United States military training and indoctrination films.[15]

An important parallel development in communications research was the career of Kurt Lewin—a student of Gestalt psychology, an eminent theoretician and teacher at Stanford, Cornell, the University of Iowa, and the Massachusetts Institute of Technology.

Over the years, Hovland, Lewin, their associates, and their students continued to provide valuable insights into the nature of the psy-

---

[14] Hovland, C. I., Mandell, W., Campbell, E. H., Brock, T., Luchins, A. S., Cohen, A. R., McGuire, W. J., Janis, I. L., Feierabend, R. L., & Anderson, N. H. *The order of presentation in persuasion.* New Haven, Conn.: Yale Univer. Press, 1957. P. *v.*

[15] One of those experiments is reprinted later in this volume, Pp. 71–97.

chological processes through their careful, extensive, systematic research and theory in communication. It is their pioneering work which shaped many of the ideas reported here. Their orientation provides the focus of this book.

PART I

SOURCE

The potency of any persuasive appeal depends on the nature of its content, the quality of its presentation, the credibility of its source, recipients' perceptions of its intent, and a host of other factors. We shall begin by examining one of these factors — credibility.

One probably would predict that if a communication were attributed to a source that were highly respected, its impact would be greater than if it were attributed to an untrustworthy source. This would be common sense — the assumption being that of *prestige suggestion*. Presumably, the value ascribed to the communication would be determined by communicatees' perceptions of the credibility of the source. Highly valued communications — those emanating from a respected, capable source — would be the most influential. Whether or not that assumption is correct is one of the questions we shall probe here.

Other questions about source credibility involve more subtle relationships and appear not to lend themselves so easily to simple intuitive analysis. Consider the following four well-known adages:[1]

"Clothes make the man," *but* "You can't make a silk purse out of a sow's ear."

"Absence makes the heart grow fonder," *but* "Out of sight, out of mind."

Although common sense lends to all four an air of psychological credibility, when we pair each adage with its logical opposite it becomes obvious that common sense is not infallible. Similarly, many questions can be raised relevant to the factor of source credibility for which intuition alone cannot confidently be relied upon to provide the correct answers.[2] For example, why are some speakers perceived as highly trustworthy by some people, yet, at the same time, untrustworthy by others? Are the long-range effects of source credibility any different than the immediate effects? Is a negative communicator ever more effective than a positive communicator?

---

[1] Krech, D., Crutchfield, R. S., & Ballachey, E. L. *Individual in society.* New York: McGraw-Hill, 1962. P. 3.

[2] It is a common belief, for instance, that tall people, because they give an appearance of more authority than short people, have greater persuasive power. The experimental evidence does not support this conclusion. Baker and Redding have found that tall people are not necessarily any more persuasive than short. Although physical stature may not affect persuasiveness, physical attractiveness does. Mills and Aronson find that a physically attractive communicator will influence opinion more than one who is unattractive, even when the audience has been made aware of the communicator's persuasive intent. Baker, E. E., & Redding, W. C. The effects of perceived tallness in persuasive speaking: An experiment. *J. Communication*, 1961, **12**, 51–53. Mills, J., & Aronson, E. Opinion change as a function of the communicator's attractiveness and desire to influence. *J. Pers. soc. Psychol.*, 1965, **1**, 173–177.

Before attempting to answer these questions, let us first consider some of the major variables which determine credibility. Sherif, Sherif, and Nebergall note that "credibility and like terms do not represent attributes of communicators; they represent judgments by the listeners. ... There is no such animal as a perfectly credible communicator, although there may be a few persons willing to accept absolutely anything some other special person says."[3] Whether or not a communicator is credible depends on the point of view of the recipient of his communication. To paraphrase an old saying, *credibility is in the eye of the beholder.*

Certainly, however, there are verbal[4] and nonverbal cues[5] to which an audience can respond which may influence its perceptions of a communicator. For example, the "expert" often *sounds* as though he knows what he is talking about. He exudes an air of self-confidence and authority. Yet, his authoritativeness usually seems to vanish when he discusses matters outside his immediate area of expertise or defends a position inconsistent with his beliefs. One explanation for this effect is implied in the "consistency hypothesis" — discussed in detail in a later section (pp. 298 ff.). Here, however, we can note that when a speaker is placed in a psychologically inconsistent position, where his public behavior is counter to his private beliefs, the consistency hypothesis predicts that he would experience psychological discomfort. Often, the discomfort tends to be manifested unwittingly in some overt, observable act to which an audience can respond. Hence, when an otherwise credibly perceived communicator defends a position not his own, he may stumble over his words, show uneasiness, "hem"

---

[3]Quoted from Sherif, C. W., Sherif, M., & Nebergall, R. E. *Attitude and attitude change.* Philadelphia, Pa.: W. B. Saunders, 1965. Pp. 201–202. By permission of M. Sherif and the publisher.

[4]Markel, N. H., Meisels, M., & Houck, J. E. Judging personality from voice quality. *J. abnorm. soc. Psychol.*, 1964, **69**, 458–463. Bem, D. J. An experimental analysis of self-persuasion. *J. exp. soc. Psychol.*, 1965, **1**, 199–218.

[5]Brouwer, M. J., & Lissenburg, D. Stereotypen over heilssoldaten. In M. Mulder (Ed.), *Mensen, groepen, organisaties: Speurwerk in de sociale psychologie.* Vol. 1. Assen, Netherlands: Van Gorcum, 1963. Pp. 311–329. Iverson, M. A. Personality impressions of punitive stimulus persons of differential status. *J. abnorm. soc. Psychol.*, 1964, **68**, 617–626. Thompson, D. F., & Meltzer, L. Communication of emotional intent by facial expression. *J. abnorm. soc. Psychol.*, 1964, **68**, 129–135. Ekman, P. Differential communication of affect by head and body cues. *J. Pers. soc. Psychol.*, 1965, **2**, 726–735. Rosenfeld, H. M. Instrumental affiliative functions of facial and gestural expressions. *J. Pers. soc. Psychol.*, 1966, **4**, 65–72.

and "haw," and in general lose his air of authority, and his persuasiveness along with it. [6]

Another important variable influencing source credibility is implied in findings by Thomas Ewing and Walter Weiss. Ewing observed that acceptance of a communication from an unknown or ambiguous source is increased if at the beginning of the message there is the claim that the communicator's position is consistent with that of the audience. [7] Weiss found that by agreeing with the views of an audience on one issue, he was better able to persuade the audience on other issues. [8] Apparently, we are significantly influenced by communicators with whom we can identify—those whose personal beliefs seem not unlike our own. "I can trust him; he believes in the same things I do." [9]

Furthermore, when people think that a communicator sincerely likes them, they may make the assumption that he cares about their welfare and that whatever he asks them to do is probably in their

---

[6] Greenberg and Tannenbaum find that when a writer is given information which attacks his beliefs, he makes more grammatical errors, takes longer to write the message, and exhibits similar behavior, as might be predicted from the consistency hypothesis. Bettinghaus and Preston obtained somewhat the same results and a correlation between this type of behavior and what Rokeach has termed "closed-mindedness." Greenberg, B. S., & Tannenbaum, P. H. Communicator performance under cognitive stress. *Journ. quart.*, 1962, **39**, 169–178. Bettinghaus, E. P., & Preston, I. L. Dogmatism and performance of the communicator under cognitive stress. *Journ. quart.*, 1964, **41**, 399–402. Rokeach, M. *The open and closed mind.* New York: Basic Books, 1960.

[7] Ewing, T. N. A study of certain factors involved in changes of opinion. *J. soc. Psychol.*, 1942, **16**, 63–88.

[8] Weiss, W. Opinion congruence with a negative source on one issue as a factor influencing agreement on another issue. *J. abnorm. soc. Psychol.*, 1957, **54**, 180–186.

[9] One variation of this statement might read, "I can trust him; he uses the same amount of paint that I do." Brock, in an imaginative field experiment, found that customers in the paint department of a large retail store were influenced more by a salesman who told them that he used about the same amount of paint as they did, compared to a salesman whose magnitude of paint consumption was not like the customers'. A more recent experiment by Berscheid also emphasizes the importance in social influence of the recipient's perceptions of the similarity or dissimilarity of his own beliefs with those of the communicator. Berscheid has found that when a belief, presumably shared by the communicator and communicatee, is relevant to the persuasive communication, even greater opinion change results than when the shared belief is irrelevant to the communication. Similarly, when a belief relevant to the communication is not shared by the communicator and the communicatee, less opinion change results than when the nonshared belief is irrelevant to the communication. Brock, T. Communicator-recipient similarity and decision change. *J. Pers. soc. Psychol.*, 1965, **1**, 650–654. Berscheid, E. Opinion change and communicator-communicatee similarity and dissimilarity. *J. Pers. soc. Psychol.*, 1966, **4**, 670–680.

self-interest. The more they think he likes them, probably the more susceptible they will be to his arguments.[10] However, if the source's motives are held suspect by the audience, he may be perceived as less fair, less honest, and even a poorer communicator than one who is perceived as impartial.[11]

It also has been observed that age can play an important part in determining whether a communicator is influential. Duncker found that young children are more likely to be influenced about food preferences by an older child,[12] and Berenda noted a similar relationship in a length-judging task.[13] Interestingly, these findings have been cited in support of the contention that age may be important insofar as it is a characteristic of the recipients rather than of the communicator.[14]

Among the many other possibilities that have yet to be explored in the laboratory is whether the various personality factors which establish qualities of leadership in an individual also determine his credibility as a communicator.[15]

Having noted some of the relevant findings regarding credibility, we now consider three important experiments on the subject. The papers which follow explore different aspects of source credibility. The first focuses upon the commonsense assumption that the credible source is also the more persuasive. The second paper tests a prediction derived from cognitive dissonance theory that a negative communicator can be more influential than a positive communicator. The third paper probes the influence on the potency of a communicator's presentation of an objectively irrelevant aspect of his credibility.

[10] Mills, J. Opinion change as a function of the communicator's desire to influence and liking for the audience. *J. exp. soc. Psychol.*, 1966, **2**, 152–159.

[11] Hovland, C. I., & Mandell, W. An experimental comparison of conclusion-drawing by the communicator and by the audience. *J. abnorm. soc. Psychol.*, 1952, **47**, 581–588.

[12] Duncker, K. Experimental modification of children's food preferences through social suggestion. *J. abnorm. soc. Psychol.*, 1938, **33**, 489–507.

[13] Berenda, R. W. *The influence of the group on the judgments of children.* New York: King's Crown Press (Columbia Univer.), 1950.

[14] Hovland, C. I., Janis, I. L., & Kelley, H. H. *Communication and persuasion.* New Haven, Conn.: Yale Univer. Press, 1953. P. 49.

[15] These leadership factors are enumerated and discussed elsewhere; cf. Stogdill, R. Personal factors associated with leadership: A survey of the literature, *J. Psychol.*, 1948, **25**, 35–71. Gibb, A. Leadership. In G. Lindzey (Ed.), *Handbook of social psychology.* Vol. 2. *Special fields and applications.* Reading, Mass.: Addison-Wesley, 1954. Pp. 877–920. Bass, B. M. *Leadership, psychology, and organizational behavior.* New York: Harper, 1960. Hare, A. P. *Handbook of small group research.* Glencoe, Ill.: Free Press, 1962.

Prestige Suggestion

In a well-known and widely read review on the effects of the mass media, Hovland observed that most of the early work on prestige suggestion customarily dealt with the characteristics of the communicator and his role in society.[1] Typical of those early studies was one by Arnet, Davidson, and Lewis, in which attitude statements were presented to graduate students for their opinions before and after the statements were attributed to a credible source. Their results seem to be dictated by common sense. The student's own positions on each item changed in the direction attributed to the credible source.[2]

A finding by Bowden, Caldwell, and West is like the one of Arnet and his colleagues. Statements proposing solutions to the economic problem of an appropriate monetary standard for the United States were more often approved when the source of the statements was identified as an educator or a businessman, less often when the source was identified as a minister.[3] Disclosure of the credibility of the source had a facilitative effect inasmuch as the credibility was relevant to the communication. Common sense tells us that educators and businessmen, because of their training and professional experience, are more reliable sources of information on matters of finance than ministers. Hence, a finding by Kulp comes as no surprise. Graduate students in education respected the opinions of professional educators and social scientists more than the opinions of laymen when the opinions had to do with social and political questions.[4]

---

[1] Hovland, C. I. Effect of the mass media of communication. In G. Lindzey (Ed.), *Handbook of social psychology.* Vol. 2. *Special fields and applications.* Reading, Mass.: Addison-Wesley, 1954. P. 1071.

[2] Arnet, C. E., Davidson, H. H., & Lewis, H. N. Prestige as a factor in attitude change. *Sociol. soc. Res.,* 1931, **16,** 49–55.

[3] Bowden, A. O., Caldwell, F. F., & West, G. A. A study in prestige. *Amer. J. Sociol.,* 1934, **40,** 193–204.

[4] Kulp, D. H. Prestige as measured by single-experience changes and their permanency. *J. educ. Res.,* 1934, **27,** 663–672.

Certain people, of course, seem highly influential almost regardless of the issues involved. In broadcasting, for example, male communicators seem much more authoritative than females. A President, a Pope, or a Prime Minister might appear equally sincere, authoritative, and persuasive to some people whether he were advocating an excise tax on babies or arguing the injustices of war.

The experiment which follows, by Walter Weiss and Carl I. Hovland, focuses on the influence of source credibility in persuasive communication. In this experiment, Hovland and Weiss attribute identical communications to highly trustworthy sources and to sources perceived as untrustworthy. The immediate impact of source credibility is striking in the resulting differences in opinion change. The delayed effects are even more dramatic. Initially, subjects discount information from untrustworthy sources. With the passage of time, however, they tend to disassociate the content from its source. As their original skepticism fades, the untrustworthy material becomes more acceptable to them. "Lies," in fact, seem to be better remembered than "truths."

Reprinted from Public Opinion Quarterly, 1951, Vol. 15, pp. 635–650, by permission of W. Weiss and the publisher.

The Influence of Source Credibility on Communication Effectiveness*

BY CARL I. HOVLAND AND WALTER WEISS

A<small>N</small> important but little-studied factor in the effectiveness of communication is the attitude of the audience toward the communicator. Indirect data on this problem come from studies of "prestige" in which subjects are asked to indicate their agreement or disagreement with statements which are attributed to different individuals.[1] The extent of agreement is usually higher when the statements are attributed to "high prestige" sources. There are few studies in which an identical communication is presented by different communicators and the relative effects on opinion subsequently measured without explicit reference to the position taken by the communicator. Yet the latter research setting may be a closer approximation of the real-life situation to which the results of research are to be applied.

In one of the studies reported by Hovland, Lumsdaine and Sheffield, the effects of a communication were studied without reference to the source of the items comprising the opinion questionnaire. They found that opinion changes following the showing of an Army orienta-

---

* This study was done as part of a coordinated research project on factors influencing changes in attitude and opinion being conducted at Yale University under a grant from the Rockefeller Foundation. (See Hovland, C. I., "Changes in Attitude Through Communication," *Journal of Abnormal and Social Psychology*, Vol. 46 (1951), pp. 424-437.) The writers wish to thank Prof. Ralph E. Turner for making his class available for the study.

[1] See e.g. Sherif, M., "An Experimental Study of Stereotypes," *Journal of Abnormal and Social Psychology*, Vol. 29 (1935), pp. 371-375; Lewis, H. B., "Studies in the Principles of Judgments and Attitudes": IV. The Operation of "Prestige Suggestion." *Journal of Social Psychology*, Vol. 14 (1941), pp. 229-256; Asch, S. E., "The Doctrine of Suggestion, Prestige, and Imitation in Social Psychology." *Psychological Review*, Vol. 55 (1948), pp. 250-276.

tion film were smaller among the members of the audience who believed the purpose of the film was "propagandistic" than among those who believed its purpose "informational."[2] But such a study does not rule out the possibility that the results could be explained by general predispositional factors; that is, individuals who are "suspicious" of mass-media sources may be generally less responsive to such communications. The present study was designed to minimize the aforementioned methodological difficulties by experimentally controlling the source and by checking the effects of the source in a situation in which the subject's own opinion was obtained without reference to the source.

A second objective of the present study was to investigate the extent to which opinions derived from high and low credibility sources are maintained over a period of time. Hovland, Lumsdaine and Sheffield showed that some opinion changes in the direction of the communicator's position are larger after a lapse of time than immediately after the communication. This they refer to as the "sleeper effect." One hypothesis which they advanced for their results is that individuals may be suspicious of the motives of the communicator and initially discount his position, and thus may evidence little or no immediate change in opinion. With the passage of time, however, they may remember and accept *what* was communicated but not remember *who* communicated it. As a result, they may then be more inclined to agree with the position which had been presented by the communicator. In the study referred to, only a single source was used, so no test was available of the differential effects when the source was suspected of having a propagandistic motive and when it was not. The present experiment was designed to test differences in the retention, as well as the acquisition, of identical communications when presented by "trustworthy" and by "untrustworthy" sources.

PROCEDURE

The overall design of the study was to present an identical communication to two groups, one in which a communicator of a generally "trustworthy" character was used, and the other in which the communicator was generally regarded as "untrustworthy." Opinion ques-

---

[2] Hovland, C. I., A. A. Lumsdaine and F. D. Sheffield, *Experiments on Mass Communication.* Princeton: Princeton University Press, 1949, pp. 101f.

tionnaires were administered before the communication, immediately after the communication, and a month after the communication.

Because of the possibility of specific factors affecting the relationship between communicator and content on a single topic, four different topics (with eight different communicators) were used. On each topic two alternative versions were prepared, one presenting the "affirmative" and one the "negative" position on the issue. For each version one "trustworthy" and one "untrustworthy" source was used. The topics chosen were of current interest and of a controversial type so that a fairly even division of opinion among members of the audience was obtained.

The four topics and the communicators chosen to represent "high credibility" and "low credibility" sources were as follows:

	"High Credibility" Source	"Low Credibility" Source
A. *Anti-Histamine Drugs*: Should the anti-histamine drugs continue to be sold without a doctor's prescription?	*New England Journal of Biology and Medicine*	Magazine A* [A mass circulation monthly pictorial magazine]
B. *Atomic Submarines*: Can a practicable atomic-powered submarine be built at the present time?	Robert J. Oppenheimer	*Pravda*
C. *The Steel Shortage*: Is the steel industry to blame for the current shortage of steel?	*Bulletin of National Resources Planning Board*	Writer A* [A widely syndicated anti-labor, anti-New Deal, "rightist" newspaper columnist]
D. *The Future of Movie Theaters*: As a result of TV, will there be a decrease in the number of movie theaters in operation by 1955?	*Fortune* magazine	Writer B* [An extensively syndicated woman movie-gossip columnist]

* The names of one of the magazines and two of the writers used in the study have to be withheld to avoid any possible embarrassment to them. These sources will be referred to hereafter only by the letter designations given.

In some cases the sources were individual writers and in others periodical publications, and some were fictitious (but plausible) and others actual authors or publications.

The "affirmative" and "negative" versions of each article presented an equal number of facts on the topic and made use of essentially the same material. They differed in the emphasis given the material and in the conclusion drawn from the facts. Since there were two versions for each topic and these were prepared in such a way that either of the sources might have written either version, four possible combinations of content and source were available on each topic.

The communication consisted of a booklet containing one article on each of the four different topics, with the name of the author or periodical given at the end of each article. The order of the topics within the booklets was kept constant. Two trustworthy and two untrustworthy sources were included in each booklet. Twenty-four different booklets covered the various combinations used. An example of one such booklet-combination would be:

Topic	Version	Source
The Future of Movie Theaters	Affirmative	Fortune
Atomic Submarines	Negative	Pravda
The Steel Shortage	Affirmative	Writer A
Anti-Histamine Drugs	Negative	New England Journal of Biology and Medicine

The questionnaires were designed to obtain data on the amount of factual information acquired from the communication and the extent to which opinion was changed in the direction of the position advocated by the communicator. Information was also obtained on the subject's evaluation of the general trustworthiness of each source, and, in the after-questionnaires, on the recall of the author of each article.

The subjects were college students in an advanced undergraduate course in History at Yale University. The first questionnaire, given five days before the communication, was represented to the students as a general opinion survey being conducted by a "National Opinion Survey Council." The key opinion questions bearing on the topics selected for the communication were scattered through many other unrelated ones. There were also questions asking for the subjects' evaluations of the general trustworthiness of a long list of sources, which included the critical ones used in the communications. This evaluation was based on a 5-point scale ranging from "very trustworthy" to "very untrustworthy."

Since it was desired that the subjects not associate the experiment with the "before" questionnaire, the following arrangement was devised: The senior experimenter was invited to give a guest lecture to the class during the absence of the regular instructor, five days after the initial questionnaire. His remarks constituted the instructions for the experiment:

"Several weeks ago Professor [the regular instructor] asked me to meet with you this morning to discuss some phase of Contemporary Problems. He suggested that one interesting topic would be The Psychology of Communications. This is certainly an important problem, since so many of our attitudes and opinions are based not on direct experience but on what we hear over the radio or read in the newspaper. I finally agreed to take this topic but on the condition that I have some interesting live data on which to base my comments. We therefore agreed to use this period to make a survey of the role of newspaper and magazine reading as a vehicle of communication and then to report on the results and discuss their implications at a later session.

Today, therefore, I am asking you to read a number of excerpts from recent magazine and newspaper articles on controversial topics. The authors have attempted to summarize the best information available, duly taking into account the various sides of the issues. I have chosen up-to-date issues which are currently being widely discussed and ones which are being studied by Gallup, Roper and others interested in public opinion.

Will you please read each article carefully the way you would if you were reading it in your favorite newspaper and magazine. When you finish each article write your name in the lower right hand corner to indicate that you have read it through and then go on to the next. When you finish there will be a short quiz on your reaction to the readings.

Any questions before we begin?"

The second questionnaire, handed out immediately after the booklets were collected, differed completely in format from the earlier one. It contained a series of general questions on the subjects' reactions to the articles, gradually moving toward opinion questions bearing on the content discussed in the articles. At the end of the questionnaire there was a series of fact-quiz items. Sixteen multiple choice questions, four on each content area, were used together with a question calling for the recall of the author of each of the articles.

An identical questionnaire was administered four weeks after the communication. At no prior time had the subjects been forewarned that they would be given this second post-test questionnaire.

A total of 223 subjects provided information which was used in some phase of the analysis. Attendance in the history course was not mandatory and there was considerable shrinkage in the number of students present at all three time periods. For the portions of the analysis requiring before-and-after information, the data derived from 61 students who were present on all three occasions were used. Thus for the main analysis a sample of 244 communications (four for each student) was available. Since different analyses permitted the use of differing numbers of cases, the exact number of instances used in each phase of the analysis is given in each table.

RESULTS

Before proceeding to the main analyses it is important to state the extent to which the sources selected on *a priori* grounds by the experimenters as being of differing credibility were actually reacted to in this manner by the subjects. One item on the questionnaire given before the communication asked the subjects to rate the trustworthiness of each of a series of authors and publications. Figure 1 gives the percentages of subjects who rated each of the sources "trustworthy."

FIGURE 1
CREDIBILITY OF SOURCES

TOPIC	SOURCE	N	PERCENT RATING SOURCE AS TRUSTWORTHY
ANTI-HISTAMINES	*NEW ENGL. J. BIOL. & MED.*	208	94.7%
	MAGAZINE A	222	←—5.9%
ATOMIC SUBMARINES	OPPENHEIMER	221	93.7%
	PRAVDA	223	←—1.3%
STEEL SHORTAGE	*BULL. NAT. RES. PLAN. BD.*	220	80.9%
	WRITER A	223	17.0%
FUTURE OF MOVIES	*FORTUNE*	222	89.2%
	WRITER B	222	21.2%

The first source named under each topic had been picked by the experimenters as being of high credibility and the second of low. It will be observed that there is a clear differentiation of the credibility in the direction of the initial selection by the experimenters. The differences between members of each pair are all highly significant (t's range from 13 to 20). The results in Figure 1 are based on all of the subjects present when the preliminary questionnaire was administered. The percentages for the smaller sample of subjects present at all three sessions do not differ significantly from those for the group as a whole.

Differences in perception of communication of various audience sub-groups. Following the communication, subjects were asked their opinion about the fairness of the presentation of each topic and the extent to which each communicator was justified in his conclusion. Although the communications being judged were *identical*, there was a marked difference in the way the subjects responded to the "high credibility" and "low credibility" sources. Their evaluations were also affected by their personal opinions on the topic before the communication was ever presented. Audience evaluations of the four communications are presented in Table 1. In 14 of the 16 possible comparisons the "low-credibility" sources are considered less fair or less justified than the corresponding high credibility sources. The differences for the low credibility sources for the individuals initially holding an opinion different from that advocated by the communicator and those for the high credibility sources for individuals who initially held the same position as that advocated by the communicator are significant at less than the .004 level.[3]

EFFECT OF CREDIBILITY OF SOURCE ON ACQUISITION OF INFORMATION
AND ON CHANGE IN OPINION

Information. There is no significant difference in the amount of factual information acquired by the subjects when the material is attributed to a high credibility source as compared to the amount learned

[3] The probability values given in the table, while adequately significant, are calculated conservatively. The two-tailed test of significance is used throughout, even though in the case of some of the tables it could be contended that the direction of the differences is in line with theoretical predictions, and hence might justify the use of the one-tail test. When analysis is made of *changes*, the significance test takes into account the internal correlation (Hovland, Sheffield and Lumsdaine, *op. cit.*, pp. 318ff.), but the analyses of cases of post-communication agreement and disagreement are calculated on the conservative assumption of independence of the separate communications.

when the same material is attributed to a low credibility source. Table 2 shows the mean number of items correct on the information quiz when material is presented by "high credibility" and "low credibility" sources.

TABLE 1

EVALUATION OF "FAIRNESS" AND "JUSTIFIABILITY" OF IDENTICAL COMMUNICATIONS WHEN PRESENTED BY "HIGH CREDIBILITY" AND "LOW CREDIBILITY" SOURCES AMONG INDIVIDUALS WHO INITIALLY AGREED AND INDIVIDUALS WHO INITIALLY DISAGREED WITH POSITION ADVOCATED BY COMMUNICATOR

A. PER CENT CONSIDERING AUTHOR "FAIR" IN HIS PRESENTATION*

	High Credibility Source		Low Credibility Source	
Topic	Initially Agree	Initially Disagree (or Don't know)	Initially Agree	Initially Disagree (or Don't Know)
Anti-Histamines	76.5%	50.0%	64.3%	62.5%
Atomic Submarines	100.0	93.7	75.0	66.7
Steel Shortage	44.4	15.4	12.5	22.2
Future of Movies	90.9	90.0	77.8	52.4
Mean	78.3%	57.9%	60.5%	51.9%
N=	46	76	43	79

B. PER CENT CONSIDERING AUTHOR'S CONCLUSION "JUSTIFIED" BY THE FACTS**

	High Credibility Source		Low Credibility Source	
Topic	Initially Agree	Initially Disagree (or Don't know)	Initially Agree	Initially Disagree (or Don't Know)
Anti-Histamines	82.4%	57.1%	57.1%	50.0%
Atomic Submarines	77.8	81.2	50.0	41.2
Steel Shortage	55.6	23.1	37.5	22.2
Future of Movies	63.6	55.0	55.6	33.3
Mean	71.7%	50.0%	51.2%	36.7%
N=	46	76	43	79

* Question: Do you think that the author of each article was fair in his presentation of the facts on both sides of the question or did he write a one-sided report?

** Question: Do you think that the opinion expressed by the author in his conclusion *was* justified by the facts he presented or do you think his opinion *was not* justified by the facts?

Opinion. Significant differences were obtained in the extent to which opinion on an issue was changed by the attribution of the material to different sources. These results are presented in Table 3. Subjects changed their opinion in the direction advocated by the communicator in a significantly greater number of cases when the material was attributed to a "high credibility" source than when attributed to a "low credibility" source. The difference is significant at less than the .01 level.

TABLE 2

MEAN NUMBER OF ITEMS CORRECT ON FOUR-ITEM INFORMATION QUIZZES ON
EACH OF FOUR TOPICS WHEN PRESENTED BY "HIGH CREDIBILITY" AND "LOW
CREDIBILITY" SOURCES. (TEST IMMEDIATELY AFTER COMMUNICATION)

Topic	Mean Number of Items Correct			
	High Credibility Source		Low Credibility Source	
Anti-Histamines	(N=31)	3.42	(N=30)	3.17
Atomic Submarines	(N=25)	3.48	(N=36)	3.72
Steel Shortage	(N=35)	3.34	(N=26)	2.73
Future of Movies	(N=31)	3.23	(N=30)	3.27
Average	(N=122)	3.36	(N=122)	3.26
Per cent of items correct		84.0		81.5
Pdiff. M.			.35	

TABLE 3

NET CHANGES OF OPINION IN DIRECTION OF COMMUNICATION FOR SOURCES
CLASSIFIED BY EXPERIMENTERS AS "HIGH CREDIBILITY" OR "LOW
CREDIBILITY" SOURCES*

Topic	Net percentage of cases in which subjects changed opinion in direction of communication			
	High Credibility Sources		Low Credibility Sources	
Anti-Histamines	(N=31)	22.6%	(N=30)	13.3%
Atomic Submarines	(N=25)	36.0	(N=36)	0.0
Steel Shortage	(N=35)	22.9	(N=26)	−3.8
Future of Movies	(N=31)	12.9	(N=30)	16.7
Average	(N=122)	23.0%	(N=122)	6.6%
Diff.		16.4%		
Pdiff.		<.01		

* Net changes = positive changes *minus* negative changes.

From Figure 1 it will be recalled that less than 100 per cent of the subjects were in agreement with the group consensus concerning the trustworthiness of each source. The results presented in Table 3 were reanalyzed using the individual subject's own evaluation of the source as the independent variable. The effects on opinion were studied for those instances where the source was rated as "very trustworthy" or "moderately trustworthy" and for those where it was rated as "untrustworthy" or "inconsistently trustworthy." Results from this analysis are given in Table 4. The results, using the subject's own evaluation of the trustworthiness of the source, are substantially the same as those obtained when analyzed in terms of the experimenters' *a priori* classification (presented in Table 3). Only minor shifts were obtained. It appears that while the variable is made somewhat "purer" with this analysis this advantage is offset by possible increased variability attributable to unreliability in making individual judgments of the trustworthiness of the source.

TABLE 4

NET CHANGES OF OPINION IN DIRECTION OF COMMUNICATION FOR SOURCES JUDGED
"TRUSTWORTHY" OR "UNTRUSTWORTHY" BY INDIVIDUAL SUBJECTS.

Topic	*Net percentage of cases in which subjects changed opinion in direction of communication*			
	"Trustworthy" Sources		*"Untrustworthy" Sources*	
Anti-Histamines	(N=31)	25.5%	(N=27)	11.1%
Atomic Submarines	(N=25)	36.0	(N=36)	0.0
Steel Shortage	(N=33)	18.2	(N=27)	7.4
Future of Movies	(N=31)	12.9	(N=29)	17.2
Average	(N=120)	22.5%	(N=119)	8.4%
Diff.		14.1%		
Pdiff.		<.03		

RETENTION OF INFORMATION AND OPINION IN RELATION TO SOURCE

Information. As was the case with the immediate post-communication results (Table 2), there is no difference between the retention of factual information after four weeks when presented by high credibility sources and low credibility sources. Results in Table 5 show the mean retention scores for each of the four topics four weeks after the communication.

TABLE 5

MEAN NUMBER OF ITEMS CORRECT ON FOUR-ITEM INFORMATION QUIZZES ON EACH
OF FOUR TOPICS WHEN PRESENTED BY "HIGH CREDIBILITY" AND "LOW
CREDIBILITY" SOURCES (RECALL FOUR WEEKS AFTER COMMUNICATION)

Topic	*Mean Number of Items Correct*			
	High Credibility Source		*Low Credibility Source*	
Anti-Histamines	(N=31)	2.32	(N=30)	2.90
Atomic Submarines	(N=25)	3.08	(N=36)	3.06
Steel Shortage	(N=35)	2.51	(N=26)	2.27
Future of Movies	(N=31)	2.52	(N=30)	2.33
Average	(N=122)	2.58	(N=122)	2.67
Per cent of items correct		64.5		66.7
Pdiff.		.46		

Opinion. Extremely interesting results were obtained for the retention of opinion changes. Table 6 shows the changes in opinion from immediately after the communication to those obtained after the four-week interval. It will be seen that compared with the changes immediately after the communication, there is a *decrease* in the extent of agreement with the high credibility source, but an *increase* in the case of the low credibility source. This result, then, is similar to the "sleeper effect" found by Hovland, Lumsdaine and Sheffield.[4] The results derived from Tables 3 and 6 are compared in Figure 2, which shows the changes in opinion from before the communication to immediately afterwards and from before to four weeks afterwards.

The loss with the "trustworthy" source and the gain with the "untrustworthy" source are clearly indicated. A parallel analysis using the individual's own evaluation of the source credibility (similar to the method of Table 4) showed substantially the same results.

TABLE 6

NET CHANGES OF OPINION FROM IMMEDIATELY AFTER COMMUNICATION TO FOUR WEEKS LATER IN DIRECTION OF "HIGH CREDIBILITY" AND "LOW CREDIBILITY" SOURCES

Topic	High Credibility Source (A)	Low Credibility Source (B)	Difference (B-A)
Anti-Histamines	(N=31) −6.5%	(N=30) +6.7%	+13.2%
Atomic Submarines	(N=25) −16.0	(N=36) +13.9	+29.9
Steel Shortage	(N=35) −11.4	(N=26) +15.4	+26.8
Future of Movies	(N=31) −9.7	(N=30) −6.7	+3.0
Average	(N=122) −10.7%	(N=122) +7.4%	+18.1%
Pdiff.			.001

Retention of name of source. One hypothesis advanced for the "sleeper effect" involved the assumption that forgetting of the source would be more rapid than that of the content. This is a most difficult point to test experimentally because it is almost impossible to equate retention tests for source and for content. It is, however, possible to make a comparison of the retention of the name of the source where the subjects initially agreed with the source's position and considered the communicator a "trustworthy" source, and those where they disagreed and considered the source "untrustworthy." Data on this point are presented in Table 7.

[4] *Op. cit.*

TABLE 7

RECALL OF SOURCE IMMEDIATELY AFTER COMMUNICATION AND AFTER FOUR WEEKS

	Trustworthy Source		Untrustworthy Source	
	Individuals initially holding position advocated by communicator	Individuals not initially holding position advocated by communicator	Individuals initially holding position advocated by communicator	Individuals not initially holding position advocated by communicator
Recall				
Immediately after communication	93.0% (N=43)	85.7% (N=77)	93.0% (N=43)	93.4% (N=76)
Four weeks after communication	60.5 (N=43)	63.6 (N=77)	76.7 (N=43)	55.3 (N=76)

FIGURE 2.

"RETENTION" OF OPINION. CHANGES IN EXTENT OF AGREEMENT WITH POSITION ADVOCATED BY "HIGH CREDIBILITY" AND "LOW CREDIBILITY" SOURCES.

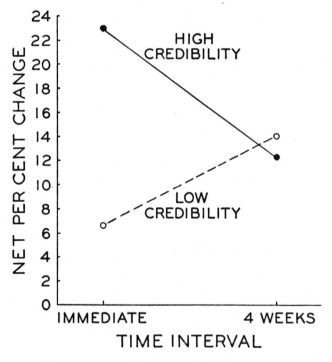

No clear differences are obtained immediately after the communication, indicating comparable initial learning of the names of the different sources. At the time of the delayed test, however, there appears to be a clear difference in the retention of the names of "untrustworthy"

sources for the group initially agreeing with the communicator's position as compared with that for the group disagreeing with the communicator's position ($p = .02$). Since the "sleeper effect" occurs among the group which initially disagrees with an unreliable source (but subsequently comes to agree with it), it is interesting to note that among this group the retention of the source name is poorest of all. Too few subjects were available to check whether retention was poorer among the very subjects who showed the "sleeper effect," but no clear-cut difference could be seen from the analysis of the small sample.

DISCUSSION

Under the conditions of this experiment, neither the acquisition nor the retention of factual information appears to be affected by the trustworthiness of the source. But changes in opinion are significantly related to the trustworthiness of the source used in the communication. This difference is in line with the results of Hovland, Lumsdaine and Sheffield, who found a clear distinction between the effects of films on information and opinion.[5] In the case of factual information they found that differences in acquisition and retention were primarily related to differences in learning ability. But in the case of opinion, the most important factor was the degree of "acceptance" of the material. In the present experiment, this variable was probably involved as a consequent of the variation in source credibility.

The present results add considerable detail to the Hovland-Lumsdaine-Sheffield findings concerning the nature of the "sleeper effect." While they were forced to make inferences concerning possible suspicion of the source, this factor was under experimental control in the present experiment and was shown to be a significant determinant of subsequent changes in opinion. In terms of their distinction between "learning" and "acceptance," one could explain the present results by saying that the content of the communication (premises, arguments, etc.) is learned and forgotten to the same extent regardless of the communicator. But the extent of opinion change is influenced by both learning and acceptance, and the effect of an untrustworthy communicator is to interfere with the acceptance of the material ("I know what he is saying, but I don't believe it"). The aforementioned authors suggest that this interference is decreased with the passage of time, and at a more

[5] *Ibid.*

rapid rate than the forgetting of the content which provides the basis for the opinion. This could result in substantially the same extent of agreement with the position advocated by trustworthy and by untrustworthy sources at the time of the second post-test questionnaire. In the case of the trustworthy source, the forgetting of the content would be the main factor in the decrease in the extent of opinion change. But with an untrustworthy source the reduction due to forgetting would be more than offset by the removal of the interference associated with "non-acceptance." The net effect would be an increase in the extent of agreement with the position advocated by the source at the time of the second post-communication questionnaire. The present results are in complete agreement with this hypothesis; there is a large difference in extent of agreement with trustworthy and untrustworthy sources immediately after the communication, but the extent of agreement with the two types of source is almost identical four weeks later.

The Hovland-Lumsdaine-Sheffield formulation makes forgetting of the source a critical condition for the "sleeper" phenomenon. In the present analysis the critical requirement is a decreased tendency over time to reject the material presented by an untrustworthy source.[6] This may or may not require that the source be forgotten. But the individual must be less likely with the passage of time to associate spontaneously the content with the source. Thus the passage of time serves to remove recall of the source as a mediating cue that leads to rejection.[7]

It is in this connection that the methodological distinction mentioned earlier between the procedure used in this experiment and that customarily employed in "prestige" studies becomes of significance. In the present analysis, the untrustworthy source is regarded as a cue which is reacted to by rejection. When an individual is asked for his opinion at the later time he may not spontaneously remember the position held by the source. Hence the source does not then constitute a

[6] In the present analysis the difference in effects of trustworthy and untrustworthy sources is attributed primarily to the *negative* effects of rejection of the untrustworthy source. On the other hand, in prestige studies the effects are usually attributed to the *positive* enhancement of effects by a high prestige source. In both types of study only a difference in effect of the two kinds of influence is obtained. Future research must establish an effective "neutral" baseline to answer the question as to the absolute direction of the effects.

[7] In rare instances there may also occur a change with time in the attitude toward the source, such that one remembers the source but no longer has such a strong tendency to discount and reject the material. No evidence for the operation of this factor in the present experiment was obtained; our data indicate no significant changes in the evaluation of the trustworthiness of the sources from before to after the communication.

cue producing rejection of his position. In the usual "prestige" technique, the attachment of the name of the source to the statement would serve to reinstate the source as a cue; consequently the differential effects obtained with the present design would not be expected to obtain. An experiment is now under way to determine whether the "sleeper effect" disappears when the source cue is reinstated by the experimenter at the time of the delayed test of opinion change.

Finally, the question of the generalizability of the results should be discussed briefly. In the present study the subjects were all college students. Other groups of subjects varying in age and in education will be needed in future research. Four topics and eight different sources were used to increase the generality of the "source" variable. No attempt, however, was made to analyze the differences in effects for different topics. Throughout, the effects of the "Atomic Submarine" and "Steel Shortage" communications were larger and more closely related to the trustworthiness of source variable than those of the "Future of Movies" topic. An analysis of the factors responsible for the differential effects constitutes an interesting problem for future research. A repetition of the study with a single after-test for each time interval rather than double testing after the communication would be desirable, although this variation is probably much less significant with opinion than with information questions. The generality of the present results is limited to the situation where individuals are experimentally exposed to the communication; i.e. a "captive audience" situation. An interesting further research problem would be a repetition of the experiment under naturalistic conditions where the individual himself controls his exposure to communications. Finally for the present study it was important to use sources which could plausibly advocate either side of an issue. There are other combinations of position and source where the communicator and his stand are so intimately associated that one spontaneously recalls the source when he thinks about the issue. Under these conditions, the forgetting of the source may not occur and consequently no "sleeper effect" would be obtained.

SUMMARY

1. The effects of credibility of source on acquisition and retention of communication material were studied by presenting identical content but attributing the material to sources considered by the audience

to be of "high trustworthiness" or of "low trustworthiness." The effects of source on factual information and on opinion were measured by the use of questionnaires administered before, immediately after, and four weeks after the communication.

2. The immediate reaction to the "fairness" of the presentation and the "justifiability" of the conclusions drawn by the communication is significantly affected by both the subject's initial position on the issue and by his evaluation of the trustworthiness of the source. Identical communications were regarded as being "justified" in their conclusions in 71.7 per cent of the cases when presented by a high credibility source to subjects who initially held the same opinion as advocated by the communicator, but were considered "justified" in only 36.7 per cent of the cases when presented by a low credibility source to subjects who initially held an opinion at variance with that advocated by the communicator.

3. No difference was found in the amount of factual information learned from the "high credibility" and "low credibility" sources, and none in the amount retained over a four week period.

4. Opinions were changed immediately after the communication in the direction advocated by the communicator to a significantly greater degree when the material was presented by a trustworthy source than when presented by an untrustworthy source.

5. There was a *decrease* after a time interval in the extent to which subjects agreed with the position advocated by the communication when the material was presented by trustworthy sources, but an *increase* when it was presented by untrustworthy sources.

6. Forgetting the name of the source is less rapid among individuals who initially agreed with the untrustworthy source than among those who disagreed with it.

7. Theoretical implications of the results are discussed. The data on post-communication changes in opinion (the "sleeper effect") can be explained by assuming equal *learning* of the content whether presented by a trustworthy or an untrustworthy source but an initial resistance to the *acceptance* of the material presented by an untrustworthy source. If this resistance to acceptance diminishes with time while the content which itself provides the basis for the opinion is forgotten more slowly, there will be an increase after the communication in the extent of agreement with an untrustworthy source.

The Persuasive Negative Communicator

The sleeper effect obtained by Hovland and Weiss, in the preceding study, was replicated by Weiss in a later experiment where he was able to control for differential initial learning of the communication.[1] Kelman and Hovland have observed that it is possible to reduce the likelihood of the sleeper effect simply by reminding the audience of the source's high or low credibility.[2]

The Hovland-Weiss credibility-opinion change relationship has also been replicated—by a former student of Weiss, Tong-He Choo, using a communication asserting no causal relationship between cigarette smoking and lung cancer,[3] and cross-nationally by Arthur H. Hill at the University of Melbourne using a dozen different topics and Australian high school students as subjects.[4] The consistent finding thus far is that the more persuasive communicator is the one whose expertise, experience, or social role establishes him as a credible source of the information presented.

More recently, however, it has been observed that *when* a source is identified can be as important as *how* he is identified. Theodore Husek conducted an experiment where twenty-minute talks promoting favorable attitudes toward concepts relating to mental illness were directed at groups of high school students by a speaker who was identified as an ex-mental patient. The talks were more effective when this presumably negative information about the speaker was introduced at the end, and least effective when it was presented at the beginning. In fact, no mention of the information was better than mentioning it too soon.[5,6]

---

[1] Weiss, W. A 'sleeper' effect in opinion change. *J. abnorm. soc. Psychol.*, 1953, **48**, 172–180.

[2] Kelman, H. C., & Hovland, C. I. 'Reinstatement' of the communicator in delayed measurement of opinion change. *J. abnorm. soc. Psychol.*, 1953, **48**, 327–335.

[3] Choo, T. Communicator credibility and communication discrepancy as determinants of opinion change. *J. soc. Psychol.*, 1964, **64**, 65–76.

[4] Hill, A. H. Credibility, discrepancy and latitude of communication as dimensions of dissonance influencing attitude change. *Australian J. Psychol.*, 1963, **15**, 124–132.

[5] Husek, T. R. Persuasive impacts of early, late, or no mention of a negative source. *J. Pers. soc. Psychol.*, 1965, **2**, 125–128.

[6] Based on Rokeach's conceptualization of dogmatism, Powell has studied the rela-

Nevertheless, the mere fact that a communicator is perceived negatively does not always mean that his capacity to influence must suffer. Philip Zimbardo, basing his speculation on *cognitive dissonance theory*,[7] has taken the position that sometimes the negative communicator can be even more influential than the positive communicator. Its rationale lying in the consistency hypothesis, dissonance theory would maintain that a person who has been made to experience psychological discomfort as a result of his having been pressured to engage publicly in behavior contrary to his beliefs has available several alternative solutions for alleviating his discomfort. One possibility is to alter his private beliefs, bringing them into line with his public behavior. Zimbardo hypothesizes that when behavior is in response to a negative communicator, greater discomfort is experienced than when it is in response to a positive communicator. Hence, where only some minimal attitude adjustment may be needed when the communicator is perceived positively, a greater attitude adjustment would be needed with a negative communicator.[8] This would imply that the traditional finding of communicator credibility increasing the effectiveness of persuasive communication may not always hold true.[9] Zimbardo's analysis leads to a prediction diametrically opposite to the usual credibility finding.[10]

An attempt was made recently by Ewart Smith to test experimentally Zimbardo's dissonance hypothesis. Smith's study is particularly interesting primarily because of the novel experimental situation which he used. Army reservists were persuaded to eat fried grasshoppers![11] Although Smith's findings seem to confirm the dissonance

tionship between open- and closed-mindedness and the ability to respond differentially to the source and to the message. Powell finds that the more open a person's belief system, the better able he is to act upon information on its own merits and independent of the positiveness or negativeness of the source. Powell, F. A. Open- and closed-mindedness and the ability to differentiate source and message. *J. abnorm. soc. Psychol.*, 1962, **65,** 61–64. Rokeach, M. *The open and closed mind.* New York: Basic Books, 1960.

[7] Festinger, L. A *theory of cognitive dissonance.* Stanford, Calif.: Stanford Univer. Press, 1957. Cognitive dissonance theory is discussed in greater detail in Part III, pp. 300 ff.

[8] Zimbardo, P. G. Involvement and communication discrepancy as determinants of opinion conformity. *J. abnorm. soc. Psychol.*, 1960, **60,** 86–94.

[9] Somewhat the same implication is raised in findings by Powell, F. A. Source credibility and behavioral compliance as determinants of attitude change. *J. Pers. soc. Psychol.*, 1965, **2,** 669–676.

[10] A similar prediction is proposed by Brehm, J. W., & Cohen, A. R. *Explorations in cognitive dissonance.* New York: Wiley, 1962. P. 111.

[11] Smith, E. E. The power of dissonance techniques to change attitudes. *Publ. Opin. quart.*, 1961, **25,** 626–639.

hypothesis, Zimbardo has pointed out several methodological complications in the experiment which make the results somewhat difficult to interpret.[12] In the paper that follows, Zimbardo, Matisyohu Weisenberg, Ira Firestone, and Burton Levy describe an investigation which grew out of Smith's experiment, and which also was designed to test Zimbardo's dissonance hypothesis.

----

[12] Zimbardo, although impressed by the ingenuity of Smith's experiment, is critical of several aspects of the design and execution as they are elaborated in Smith's longer progress report, viz. Smith, E. E. *Methods for changing consumer attitudes: A report of three experiments.* Tech. Rep. PRA 61–2 to Quartermaster Food & Container Inst. for the Armed Forces, 1961. For example, Zimbardo questions Smith's manipulation of source positiveness-negativeness:

> The negative communicator was formal, cool, official, stiff, ordered rather than requested, etc. Such a role is standard operating procedure in the army and might go unnoticed as being "negative." In fact, it would be interpreted as the experimenter performing his job efficiently. On the other hand, if someone who is given official authorization to perform research during an army reserve meeting is permissive, smiling, says "Call me Smitty," tells the men to relax and enjoy themselves, etc., he will be quite unusual in this context, so much so that he might be regarded with suspicion ("What's he after?"), or with less seriousness (thus less attention, etc.).

Quoted by permission of Zimbardo, P. G. A critical analysis of Smith's 'grasshopper' experiment. A report from the Exp. Soc. Psychol. Lab., Univer. Coll. of N. Y. U., Dept. of Psychol., May, 1964. P. 7. Additional criticisms are enumerated in the Zimbardo *et al.* paper reprinted here.

Reprinted from Journal of Personality, 1965, Vol. 33, No. 2, pp. 233–255, by permission of Philip G. Zimbardo and Duke University Press.

Communicator effectiveness in producing public conformity and private attitude change[1]

Philip G. Zimbardo, Matisyohu Weisenberg, Ira Firestone, and Burton Levy

One of the most widely held generalizations in social psychology is that the effectiveness of a persuasive communication is increased if its source is "credible." The early research by Hovland and Weiss (1951) and by Kelman and Hovland (1953) which gave substance to this conclusion has recently been extended to demonstrate the efficacy of credible communicators even when the amount of change advocated is extreme (Aronson, Turner, & Carlsmith, 1963).

Credibility has been defined traditionally in terms of communicator attributes which are perceived by the audience as relevant to the topic being communicated. Two of its major components which have been experimentally manipulated are the communicator's ability and his motives for personal gain, or what Hovland, Janis, and Kelley (1953) term "expertness" and "trustworthiness," respectively. However, positive and negative source traits which bear no objective relevance to the topic of the communication can also be effective in modifying attitudes toward its conclusions.

The potent effect of such irrelevant communicator characteristics has long been utilized in practical influence situations outside the laboratory: by lawyers aware of the importance of

1. This research was supported in part by a grant from the Quartermaster Food and Container Institute for the Armed Forces, QM Research and Engineering Command, U.S. Army (Project No. 7X95-01-001) and in part by funds from the National Science Foundation (Grant No. G24114). The views or conclusions contained in this report are those of the authors, and are not to be construed as necessarily reflecting the views or endorsement of the Department of Defense. Acknowledgment is due to Lt. Colonel J. L. Dell'omo, who made available officers and army reservists from the Patterson Army Reserve Center (Bronx, New York). We are also indebted to Len Dworkin and Kathy Rees, whose intelligent assistance contributed in an important way to this research project.

dress and demeanor of their client upon jury attitudes, by advertisers sensitive to the "topic-free" nature of a sexy communicator, and more recently by politicians interested in creating an image by appropriate "packaging" of irrelevant traits.

That irrelevant aspects of communicator credibility are important determinants of attitude change has been shown empirically in a study in which the race of a communicator influenced the acceptance of a speech which extolled the virtues of arithmetic to sixth-grade students (Aronson & Golden, 1962).

Such objectively irrelevant characteristics are of great importance in interpersonal communication situations in which attitude change is often mediated by a host of physical, social, and psychological traits of the influencing agent. For example, it is well known that the attitudes and behavior of the uncommitted voter are more affected by personal influences, such as friends and relatives, than by formal communication media. One of the reasons why these personal relationships may be effective, according to Lazarsfeld, Berelson, and Gaudet (1944), is that they often accomplish their behavioral goal without first instilling conviction. Thus one respondent in their study reported, "The lady where I work wanted me to vote. She took me to the polls and they all voted Republican, so I did too." Such a person would, if asked, be likely to defend his voting decision in terms of attributes of the influencing agent which are irrelevant to the political issues at stake. Thus it appears that both relevant and irrelevant aspects of communicator credibility may at times operate in the same direction—to increase the probability of accepting a persuasive communication.

Let us consider whether this conclusion can be generalized to a situation in which the respondent is not uncommitted, but rather has a definite stand, and the communicator attempts to induce a behavioral change rather than merely a modification of opinion. If pressure is put on a person to engage in behavior discrepant with his relevant attitudes and values, then obviously the extremity of this pressure to comply is a determining factor in what the person will do. If it is too weak, he will not comply and his attitudes will remain unchanged, while if it is too strong, he will comply publicly, but likewise his private attitudes should remain stable. If the overt compliance can be completely justified in terms of its instrumental nature to the rewards and punishments controlled by the communicator, then there is no further need to adjust one's attitude to this discrepant behavior. But as the probability of compliance approaches a value of .5 in a given population, then it becomes increasingly likely that characteristics of the communicator which are essentially irrelevant to the content of the behavior will be used as justification as, for example, "I did it because he's a nice guy."

If, on the other hand, a person complies to the inducement of a negative communicator, i.e., someone disliked, clearly he cannot rationalize the discrepant behavior by invoking the personal characteristics of the communicator as justification. Zimbardo (1960) has suggested that such a person should be likely to change his attitudes to bring them in line with his behavior. Such a prediction is derived from the theory of cognitive dissonance (Festinger, 1957) which states that the dissonance produced by overt behavior which does not follow from one's relevant attitudes is inversely proportional to the amount of justification supporting performance of the discrepant act.

Since denial of the overt behavior is constrained by social reality, an alternative mode of dissonance reduction is to modify one's private attitudes to make them consonant with the public behavior. Actually two sets of attitudes are amenable to change: attitudes toward the communicator and attitudes toward the topic or subject of the behavioral act.

Bettelheim (1943) tells us that many Nazi officers who were extremely negative in their treatment of prisoners, often inducing them to engage in behavior quite contrary to their values, eventually came to be admired. The prisoners insisted that these officers "hid behind their rough surfaces a feeling of justice and propriety." However, this type of communicator attitude change, or identification with the aggressor, demands conditions of high fear and dependency.

When these conditions are not present, but the communicator is still a dominant, salient feature of the situation, then public compliance to a negative communicator should produce greater dissonance than compliance to a positive communicator. If attitude change is the major dissonance-reducing mechanism utilized, then the general hypothesis which can be experimentally tested is that public compliance to a negative communicator (compared to a positive one) will result in greater attitude change in the direction indicated by the overt behavior.

Recently this derivation was tested by Smith in an interesting experiment in which army reservists were induced to eat a food they highly disliked—fried grasshoppers—under varied communicator conditions. His results were quite dramatic: the positive communicator produced almost complete public conformity—everyone ate, but they didn't change their attitudes. The negative communicator, on the other hand, could induce only half the men to conform publicly and eat a grasshopper, but those who did, changed their attitudes a great deal—in fact, they ended up mildly liking grasshoppers.

Unfortunately, the conclusions to be drawn from Smith's brief published article (1961b) are not supported by his complete technical report (1961a). Numerous artifacts of design, execution, and analysis raise serious questions of the validity of his results. It is necessary to mention several of these features[2] in order to clarify part of the research design and methodology used in the present study.

The most serious problem is the sampling unit and the conditions of testing employed by Smith. Although 20 Ss were run within each communication condition, they were tested in two groups of 10 each. Moreover, the Ss, who knew each other, sat around a large table and could interact freely before, during, and after the novel request by a stranger to eat a grasshopper. In such a situation it is obvious that social contagion effects and group pressures play the major role in determining conformity behavior. Since extraneous and uncontrolled sources of pressure may operate uniquely in each sample, influencing eating and attitudes quite independently, a priori predictions cannot be made for the effects of communicator credibility. The present test of the dissonance derivation demands that attitude change

2. A more thorough analysis of Smith's research is available by writing to the senior investigator.

be a consequence only of the initial attitude, a private decision, and the characteristics of the communicator.

A second problem is that all Ss received what amounts to a persuasive speech about the need for a mobile army, the need to eat unusual survival foods, and the need to study attitudes and reactions toward eating grasshopper. They received this speech after the experimenter began to play his role as a positive or negative communicator, but *before* he measured their initial attitudes toward grasshopper. As would be expected, the initial attitudes of the men in the positive communicator condition were much more favorable than those in the negative condition. This initial position bias leaves the results open to explanation in terms of relative scale distance available for change, as well as to regression effects, since there is no "true" control group. Thus it is necessary to isolate the measurement and manipulation phase of this research.

Finally, the manipulation of communicators, while statistically significant, produced an extremely positive communicator for one condition but a very positive communicator in the other. This is in part because all of the "negative" communicator's role behaviors are standard operating procedure for army officers or authorities. In any case, differences the manipulation may have produced cannot even be determined, since they are evaluated by a single Likert-type rating to the loaded statement: "The experimenter was friendly and courteous"—a nonanonymous rating made in the presence of the E himself. Therefore, careful operational analysis of the communicator's role behavior and of the assessment of his credibility is crucial.

The goals of the present research then, were to study the effects of irrelevant source factors upon behavioral conformity and attitude change, and by so doing, to test several derivations from dissonance theory relating justification for acceptance or rejection of public compliance with attitude change. Finally, a replication of the group-interaction condition was included for purposes of comparison and in order to permit appraisal of the social contagion effects upon public and private conformity.

METHOD

General Design

Attitudes toward eating a highly disliked food—fried grasshoppers—were measured before and immediately after an inducement to eat the food by a communicator who adopted a friendly, positive role for half the Ss and an unfriendly, negative role for the others. Some Ss were tested in freely interacting group conditions, while others were individually isolated from their group during testing. For some of the isolated Ss a money incentive for eating the grasshoppers was used as a second possible source of justification.

Subjects

A total of 243[3] Ss were tested in these studies, 175 experimental and 68 control Ss. Of this number, 50 were recruited from the introductory psychology class at University College of New York University as part of a course requirement. In the group-interaction replication 72 Ss were used from an army reserve base adjacent to the campus of New York University, while the third study used 121 army reservists from this same center. The reserve Ss, who were all privates and corporals, were only a few years older than the college sample, but roughly equivalent in educational background.

Procedure

The communicator. Since the person selected to be the communicator (B.L.) was Brigade Commander of the New York University ROTC, his "true" positive and negative traits could be determined by means of an alleged officer-rating survey; 53 members of the college ROTC rated him, as well as several other officers on a 6o-item adjective check list.[4] This trait profile served as the basis for establishing a set of positive and negative role behaviors.

Having determined from the officer-rating survey those personality traits which the communicator possessed, a set of behaviors was developed which would operationally define a positive or negative communicator by emphasizing certain traits and concealing others. For both positive and negative conditions the communicator had to be perceived as possessing a number of positive traits necessary for effective execution of the experiment. That is, we wanted all Ss

3. Fifteen Ss had to be eliminated from attitude change analyses because of incomplete or unreliable rating data, or because they had previously eaten grasshopper as part of an army survival program (nine were from the positive communicator condition, while six were from the negative, and all were from the reserve group).

4. The adjective check list was taken from Gough's list as presented by Newcomb in *The Acquaintance Process.* New York: Holt, Rinehart and Winston, 1961. Pp. 279-280.

to have the same regard for the "scientific" worth of the experiment, to attend closely to all phases of the experiment, and to take the study seriously. Thus, the communicator had to be seen by all Ss as conscientious, capable, well organized, concerned about the reactions of the Ss, and industrious. In addition, it was important not to evoke hostility in the Ss in either condition. However, in the negative condition he should be perceived as someone personally unpleasant, a person one would not want to know, work with, or work for. This perception was guided by actions which would make him snobbish, demanding, tactless, bossy, cold, and hostile to others, among other things.

The communicator interacted with his "assistant" according to a prearranged script in which, for the positive condition, he gave politely phrased requests to the assistant, called him by his first name, responded to a "mistake" by the assistant with equanimity, and in general was considerate and pleasant. But at all times it was clear he was the E and in control. Perception of the negative communicator, however, was largely directed by his quite formal interaction with the assistant, whom he always referred to by his last name, ordered about, with whom he was exacting and somewhat annoyed and irritated. When the assistant mistakenly brought in the "wrong" experimental food, a tray of eels, the E, who was in the process of talking to the Ss in his most pleasant manner, suddenly blew up and said, "Oh, dammit, can't you remember the schedule? That food is for the next group . . . . Let's get with it and hurry up about it!" As the assistant left, somewhat embarrassed, the E shrugged his shoulders disgustedly, then caught himself short, reversed his role behavior in front of the Ss, apologized for the interruption, and proceeded again in the same tone as previously.

The effectiveness of these role variations in producing differential perceptions of the communicator as well as our measuring instruments were first tested in our laboratory with a college sample. Then army reservists were tested under conditions similar to Smith's, maximizing group contagion effects, with communicator variations as the only independent variable. Finally, other army reservists were tested under conditions of minimal group influence, with communicator, incentive, and pretesting experience manipulated.

College study. The procedure for the college sample was generally similar to that used for the army Ss, with the exception that the rationale was in terms of the relation of physiological and intellectual reactions to food deprivation and to eating behavior. We had attempted to manipulate level of hunger, but this manipulation was not effective as measured by self-report scales or by any of the measures used in the study. Thus the only variable to be considered here is communicator variations for moderately hungry Ss.

Army studies. In order to minimize the possibility that Ss would become aware of our procedures and deceptions, the entire experiment was run on three consecutive nights during which different reserve units met. The group-interaction study (replication of Smith) was run the first night, while half the Ss in all treatments were run on each of the other two nights. Ss were randomly assigned to conditions and the running order of conditions was approximately counterbalanced within and between test nights.

Approximately 100 Ss were brought to a large lecture hall, where one of us (P.G.Z.) was introduced as a civilian liaison from the Quartermaster Corps interested in some aspects of food preferences. Ss then completed a nine-point attitude scale[5] of degree of liking of a wide range of food items, among them fried grasshopper. Experimental Ss were sent to an adjoining room, while control Ss were sent either immediately or after a delay period to a third room, where they completed a post-attitude scale, without any intervening manipulation. There was no contact between Ss who had completed the experiment and those waiting their turn to begin.

The communicator (previously described to the Ss as "the experimenter in charge") and his assistant were dressed in lab coats, while those measuring pre- and post-attitudes were differentiated by being dressed in suits. In the group-interaction conditions about 10 Ss sat around a large table in full view of each other and the E. In the separated-individual conditions, the same number of Ss was tested simultaneously, but interaction was minimized by partitions between them.

Differences in role behavior commenced as soon as the Ss entered the experimental room. After the Ss completed a hunger and eating habit questionnaire, heard a spiel about the needs of the new mobile army, and witnessed the assistant's "mistake," a plate with five fried grasshoppers was placed in front of each of them as the E was saying:

"Before asking you to eat the experimental food, *I* want to make it clear that this part of the experiment is *voluntary*, and no one has to eat these fried grasshoppers if they don't want to. However, for the purposes of the study, *I* would like you to try at least one and preferably to eat all on the plate. In order to get as many people as possible to try one, *I* will pay, right now, fifty cents to each person who eats one." (Pause) "Take a moment to decide. *I* will place the money next to each plate. Those of you who are willing to try the grasshopper, please indicate it by pulling the plate and money toward you. Those of you who are unwilling to even give it a try, leave the plate and money where they are and raise your hand to indicate you

5. This hedonic scale, which was anchored at every point with verbal labels from "like extremely" to "dislike extremely" has a reliability coefficient of .96 (Peryam et al., 1960).

don't want to eat any. All right now, go ahead and eat." Obviously, money was not mentioned in the no-incentive condition.

Control Groups

On the group-interaction night, one before-after control was run with 25 Ss, while on each of the other nights, two control groups were run with approximately 10 Ss in each. One control received the hunger questionnaire and same mobile army spiel prior to their second attitude rating; one control got neither of these treatments, while the other two controls got one or the other treament. Since there were no differences between any of these groups which even approached significance, they were combined for comparison with the experimental treatments. To assess the possible effects of premeasure sensitization on the relation of the manipulations to the post-measure, half of the individually tested army Ss got a premeasure on grasshopper as well as other survival and usual foods, while half got a premeasure which did not include grasshopper or most of the survival foods.

The final ratings, which were made in a third room, were in the absence of the "experimenter-communicator." The assistant of the civilian liaison told the Ss that he wanted to evaluate various aspects of the experiment and get more information from them. At this time the experimental Ss completed:

1. a post-measure of attitudes toward a number of foods,
2. a measure of willingness to endorse eating grasshopper,
3. checks on the experimental conditions of choice, pressure, etc.,
4. and finally, several indexes of evaluation of both the communicator and his assistant.

RESULTS AND DISCUSSION

Public Conformity: Eating

Approximately 50 per cent of the Ss in each condition in the three subsamples accepted the inducement to eat a grasshopper. Thus none of the experimental treatments had an effect upon the frequency with which grasshoppers were eaten nor upon the amount eaten (a mean of about two grasshoppers per eater in each condition).

This result is in clear contrast to Smith's data (1961a) which indicate that over 90 per cent of the men ate grasshopper in every condition except the negative-communicator condition. The validity of the results of the present study is attested to by the following related findings. Although all Ss accurately perceived that they had little choice in whether or not to come to the experiment (they were not volunteers), nevertheless, they reported having a high degree of choice in whether to eat the experimental food. There were no group differences on either of these measures, but the difference between the perception of the lack of choice to participate and the free choice to eat was highly significant for all comparisons ($p < .001$). In addition, it should be noted that the Ss felt that the communicator did not exert much direct pressure upon them to eat. Thus the decision to eat was determined not only by experimental situational pressures, but also by the men's food preferences. It should be noted that the aversiveness of grasshopper was established by comparative ratings of it and a number of other unusual foods like snake, octopus, eel, etc. It was rated most negative among 10 such foods by an additional sample of 217 college students; fewest Ss had tried it, and 57 per cent said they would not try it!

Finally, a recent Quartermaster Corps study (Peryam et al., 1960) showed that food preference and acceptance were highly correlated (as high as .77). In conclusion, therefore, the extent of public conformity observed in the present study is what one would expect from the conditions of inducement, choice, and food preference operating here. This is not meant to imply that eating behavior cannot be influenced by differences in communicator credibility, but that it was not affected given the specific manipulations employed.

It may be instructive at this point to examine the reasons given for eating or avoiding grasshopper. The major reason given by 76 per cent of the eaters was "for curiosity to see what it was like." In fact, eaters tended to characterize themselves as "the kind of person who tries new and unusual foods" more so than did the noneaters ($F = 5.83$, $df = 1, 72$, $p < .05$). Other reasons for eating grasshopper were to help the army's survival program, to help the E, and not to appear different from the other guys in the group. Among those refusing to eat, 44 per per cent said that "it looked bad," 39 per cent said they weren't hungry enough, while 10 per cent expected it to taste bad. Miscellaneous other reasons were religious and personal reactions against the E.

The college Ss were asked to list all the things they thought about when they considered eating grasshoppers. Below are some of the negative cognitions they associated with this food: ugly, greasy appearance, slimy, shiny, charred, repulsive, squirming, eyes, wings, dirty, rat feces, might hurt me, burned them as a child, biology laboratory, graveyard, and not kosher.

Private Conformity: Attitudes toward Grasshopper

Contagion effects. It was postulated that the procedure used by Smith (1961) was not ideal for testing the dissonance hypotheses because of the uncontrolled social-contagion effects likely when a freely interacting group of army reservists is presented with such a unique situation. In the present study, these effects were recorded directly by two independent observers as well as on tape. Among the college Ss who were run four at a time in completely separated cubicles, there was almost no interaction at any time. In the eight army groups tested under conditions which increased privacy and minimized interaction, there was no talk at all in six of them (although some slight laughter at times), and a slight disturbance by only one S in each of the other two groups.

In contrast, the incidence of interaction, influence attempts, and contagion were marked in the four groups of army reservists tested under conditions similar to Smith's. In general, there was a great deal of laughter and giggling when the grasshoppers were presented. Typical of the comments were: "Their eyes are

Table 1. Mean attitude change as a function of communicator, and eating (for group-interaction army Ss).

			N	Eaters	Noneaters
COMMUNICATOR	Positive	1st Sample (a)	10	.00	−.60
		2nd Sample (b)	12	1.75	.38
		Mean		+.78	.00
	Negative	1st Sample (c)	9	2.50	−.71
		2nd Sample (d)	9	.22	none
		Mean		+.64	−.71

Note.—"Sample" refers to a group of Ss tested simultaneously.

adorable," "They taste like shrimp," "They make me sick," "What's the money for, a bribe?" and "Here's your tail money, buddy." Most of the men talked before, during, and after the eating experience.

The effects of communicator credibility upon attitude change for this group condition are presented in Table 1.

The conclusions to be drawn from this table appear to be contradictory. Considering only the first samples, the negative communicator produced much more change than did the positive one—an exact replication of Smith's finding. However, the data for the second sample within each communicator condition are exactly opposite, indicating greater effectiveness of the positive communicator. Over-all, there is no main effect of communicator.

This confusion is readily resolved by examination of the nature of the interaction which occurred. In the two samples (b and c) in which eaters changed their attitudes markedly, the majority of the group did not eat, while in the other two samples when the majority of the group ate, there was little or no attitude change. Justification in terms of group pressure may have minimized the need to change one's attitude, while deviation from the group norm would be expected to increase the dissonance from eating, and hence the attitude change. Of special interest are the two samples in the negative-communicator treatment, where in one (sample c) the first man to taste the food said, "I can't eat them, they taste like shit, I'm nauseous," while in the other sample (sample d), an eater turned to a noneater and shouted out that he was a coward. Every man in this condition then ate. Clearly then, "social atmosphere" influenced both public conformity and private attitude change, but not in any way predictable from the between-group treatment effects. It remains for future investigation to turn this source of confounding into a legitimate independent variable.

Dissonance Effects

Table 2 presents the major set of attitude change data in terms of net proportion of Ss who change in the direction desired against those who change in the opposite direction. This measure, derived from Hovland, Lumsdaine, and Sheffield (1949) is

Table 2.   Mean net proportion of attitude change as a function of eating and communicator (for college and army Ss in separated testing conditions).

		Positive communicator					Negative communicator		
Eaters (50 per cent)	(N)	Direction of change (+)	(−)	Net change (per cent)	Eaters (45 per cent)	(N)	Direction of change (+)	(−)	Net change (per cent)
College	(12)	42	33		College	(14)	57	7	
Army	(8)	38	38		Army	(6)	83	17	
Total	(20)	40	35	+5		(20)	65	10	+55
Noneaters					Noneaters				
College	(12)	8	25		College	(12)	8	25	
Army	(8)	0	22		Army	(12)	0	15	
Total	(20)	5	24	−19		(24)	4	20	−16
Net effect				+24					+71

Control group (N = 68), net change = +10 per cent.

for Ss in both the college and army samples who were tested under conditions permitting an evaluation of the dissonance hypotheses.

The pattern of results is similar and quite clear for both college students and army reservists. While a net proportion of 60 per cent of those who eat the unpleasant food change their attitudes to like it more, 34 per cent of those who refuse to eat show a boomerang effect, liking it even less ($p < .01$). Among those who eat, the negative communicator is much more effective in changing attitudes in the desired direction (55 per cent) than is the positive communicator (5 per cent). Among those who do not eat there is a slightly greater boomerang effect produced by the positive communicator. The difference in the net proportion of change as a function of communicators is statistically significant (C.R. = 2.00, $p < .05$).

If the data are analyzed according to magnitude of change (mean scale distance), the results are similar to those obtained with the frequency measure of change. For each of the three subsamples in this study eaters changed a greater amount than did noneaters (combined over subsamples, $F = 12.13$, $p < .001$).

It should be noted that although the initial attitudes of eaters toward grasshopper (6.7) were more favorable than were those of the control group (7.4), which in turn were more favorable than those of noneaters (7.7), these differences did not approach significance. There were no differences in initial attitude position between communicator or incentive conditions.

While the mean change for the control group was +.3 units, it was +.6 for the positive-communicator eaters, and twice as much, +1.2 for the negative-communicator eaters. While the positive communicator condition is not different from the control group (by a Duncan Multiple Range Test), the negative communicator produced significantly greater change ($p = .02$). Although noneaters in both conditions changed to dislike grasshopper even more, the boomerang effect by the positive-communicator Ss (mean $= -.2$) is not different from the control mean, while that of the negative-communicator Ss (mean $= -.4$) is significant ($p < .05$).

Table 3. Mean attitude change as a function of communicator incentive and eating (for separated army Ss).

Incentive		Communicator	
		Positive	Negative
50 cents	Eaters	.66	1.75
	Noneaters	.00	.00
None	Eaters	.40	2.01
	Noneaters	−1.20	−.86 (N = 37)

Table 3 presents attitude change means for the separated army Ss with and without a monetary incentive. Neither the main effects of communicator, incentive, or their interaction is significant. This is due in part to the small cell size in several of the eater groups ($n < 5$). The following results are therefore presented as only suggestive for future validation.

If we collapse across incentive conditions and perform a Duncan Multiple Range Test on the four remaining groups, the negative-communicator eaters are significantly different from the positive-communicator eaters ($p < .05$) and even more significantly different from either of the noneater groups ($p < .01$). The same analysis including the incentive condition revealed that the negative-communicator eaters without monetary incentive were significantly different ($p < .01$) from all the noneater groups as were their money counterparts and they approached a statistically significant difference from the positive-eater groups ($p < .10$). The difference between eaters and noneaters is greatest when there is least justification—a negative-communicator and no monetary incentive. However, even under incentive conditions the negative communicator produces a greater change than does the positive. Finally, it should be noted that again, as predicted, greatest negative change should be in response to refusing to accept the request from a positive communicator. That this should occur more for no-money than money conditions is contrary to our expectations, except that for many Ss the fifty cents was almost a negative incentive—a bribe.

Attitude Change: Endorsement

Another way of looking at the effects of the communicator variable on private acceptance is by means of a specially devised measure of the extent to which S was willing to endorse or recommend grasshoppers to other soldiers. Such a measure, it is felt, is a more stringent yet more valid test of communicator effectiveness, since it involves a public commitment to one's attitude, less anonymity, and greater consequences to the individual soldier.

After completing the post-attitude questionnaire, the army reservists were told that it was the job of this research team to prepare a manual to be used by men about to enter a survival course. They were informed that: "We feel that one of the best understood, most honest and effective techniques is to prepare a report in which the actual information and statistics are supplemented by personal endorsements by men like yourselves who have had some direct experience with the food." They were then given an endorsement release form which presented six quotations pertaining to eating grasshoppers. The quotations were arranged and labeled in order from "strongest endorsement" through "weak endorsement" to "no endorsement," and were prefaced by an introduction which stated that the respondent authorizes use of his name to be associated with the statement he has signed. For one of the six statements S had to write in the name of the food he ate, his signature, and date. The endorsements varied from: "I've tried (the food) personally, found it to be very tasty, and would certainly recommend it" to "If you try eating (the food) as I did, you'll find that they're not so bad, in fact they had no taste at all."

Among those army Ss who ate at least one grasshopper, there is a significant degree of association between their post-experimental attitudes and their level of endorsement. Of those with con attitudes 94 per cent give a weak endorsement, while 88 per cent of those with pro attitudes give a strong endorsement. The majority (66 per cent) of those with moderate attitudes tend to give weak rather than strong endorsements (chi-square = 16.76, $df = 2$, $p > .001$; $C = .48$).

The results obtained by using this measure show a correspondence with those presented previously; 37 per cent of those in the negative-communicator condition give strong endorsements, while only 11 per cent do so in the positive condition. Furthermore, by far the greatest amount of attitude change in any cell is the change of more than two scale units for negative-communicator Ss who give a strong endorsement. This mean degree of attitude change increases to 2.5 units for Ss who accept more than the minimal inducement, i.e., eat more than one grasshopper. Unfortunately, these results are not statistically significant because of the relatively small sample size left after eliminating all those who did not eat or refused to endorse the food. However, the measure appears to offer some validity for the hedonic attitude scale, and the pattern of results complements those obtained by frequency and scale distance measures of private acceptance of the experimental food.

In passing it should be mentioned that there is a weak but consistent generalization effect of attitude change toward grasshopper upon other survival foods. While changes in grasshopper attitudes are unrelated to changes in nonsurvival foods, the generally positive change for grasshopper eaters is reflected in group positive changes on 9 of 12 comparisons of other survival foods for both army and college Ss. Similarly, the negative change for noneaters is mirrored by group negative changes on 9 of 12 comparisons. This effect is more consistent for the negative than the positive-communicator condition.

Pretest Sensitization

A group of Ss was run without first asking their attitudes toward grasshopper and the other survival foods. They did receive a pretest but it included only usual army foods to be evaluated. This was done in order to assess the sensitizing effect of mentioning grasshopper and survival foods on attitudes. Although a t-test on post-grasshopper attitudes for Ss with and without the grasshopper pretest did not yield significant results ($t = 1.30$, $p < .20$), nevertheless, there is a consistent effect of this treatment. The effect of the pretest made post-attitudes toward grasshopper more negative in six of eight groups (and in one by as much as 2.0 scale units). Thus it appears that pre-exposure to the specific issue of eating grasshoppers and the general issue of survival foods increased negative reactions toward each. This in part could be observed from comments of derision made by a few of the men in the pretest condition. Since the no-pretest Ss were physically separated from the pretest Ss, they were not influenced by such comments or by personal anticipatory reactions to the thought of eating the foods.

Communicator Credibility

The positive communicator is perceived as having more positive traits and an absence of negative ones (on the adjective check list), while the negative communicator is characterized by a greater number of negative traits and a lesser degree of positive traits. In the college sample, the positive communicator was seen as having more positive traits than the negative communicator ($F = 17.96$, $p < .001$) and also as having fewer of the negative traits ($F = 8.18$, $p < .001$). The same effect holds for both the group-interaction and separated army Ss on total score, as well as for individual analyses of positive and negative traits, the F values for each comparison being greater than 10.0 ($p < .001$).

Thus the experimental variations in the role behavior of the communicator were accurately perceived by the Ss, while the nonvariable behavior of the assistant was also perceived veridically, i.e., no difference in the two communicator conditions. Moreover, there is no difference between the communicator and the assistant under positive conditions, while there is under negative conditions, the communicator in all cases being perceived as a more negative person ($F = 15.05$, $p < .001$).

On another measure, Ss in the negative condition indicated they "probably would not like to work with," and "probably not hire as an experimenter" the person who was their E. Under positive conditions, E was rated significantly more favorably ($p < .001$), the same as was the assistant under both communicator conditions.

A somewhat different way of assessing the effectiveness of the manipulation is to compare 12 of the communicator-trait evaluations given by those who evaluated him outside of the experimental situation (ROTC students) with those by the experimental Ss. While the nonexperimental sample ranks "calmness" as the communicator's most salient trait, it is ranked identically in the positive experimental condition, but ranked eighth in the negative condition. In like manner, being "bossy" is ranked ninth for the ROTC sample, is a more salient trait for the negative condition (fourth-ranked) but less salient for the positive condition (eleventh).

Since our interest is as much in specifying source factors which are important in controlling attitude change, as in merely testing the dissonance derivations, it is not enough to note that our manipulations were effective in such gross terms. Therefore, Table 4 presents the 22 personality traits on which the Ss evaluated the communicator, and which we tried in our induction to modify. The traits are arranged in rank order from smallest to largest difference between the ratings of the positive and negative communicators.

The first seven traits are ones we attempted to hold constant in order to insure that the E would have the attention of the Ss

Table 4. Mean rating of communicator traits (averaged over all Ss).

Rank Order	Trait	Communicator		p Values
		Positive	Negative	
1.	Conscientious	1.3	1.2	
2.	Capable	1.3	1.2	
3.	Well organized	1.5	1.3	
4.	Concerned about your reactions	1.0	.7	p = n.s.
5.	Industrious	1.3	1.0	
6.	Hostile to you	1.3	1.0	
7.	Efficient	1.7	1.4	
8.	Clear-thinking	1.4	.8	
9.	Fair-minded	1.1	.5	
10.	Egotistical	.2	−.4	
11.	Insincere	.8	.2	p < .05
12.	Hostile to others	1.3	.7	
13.	Mature	1.4	.7	
14.	Genuinely interested in you	.2	−.5	
15.	A cold person	.2	−.7	
16.	A warm person	.0	−1.0	
17.	Courteous to you	1.7	.7	
18.	Snobbish	1.0	−.2	p < .01
19.	Calm	1.5	.3	
20.	Demanding	1.0	−.2	
21.	Bossy	.4	−.9	
22.	Tactless	1.2	−.2	

Note.—Scores can range from +2.0 to −2.0, negative scores being unfavorable.

and be viewed as equally competent ("expert") in both conditions. There are no differences on these traits. The last eight traits are the ones we explicitly tried to manipulate, and we were quite successful in creating two different personalities—well beyond the .01 level (by multiple *t*-tests). The middle set of traits shows smaller but still significant differences ($p < .05$) between the two conditions. These traits are also linked in direct or indirect ways to the experimental induction.

The positive communicator does not possess any of the negative traits, is rated high on being calm, courteous, mature, clear-thinking, and is neither tactless nor hostile to others. However, he is seen as affectively neutral, being neither cold nor warm. The perception of him as not being geniunely interested in the Ss individually is an accurate one, since he always tested the men in groups and could not respond to the subjects on a personal, individual level. His ratings on the traits of "bossy" and "egotistical" can likewise be attributed to the planned instructions, which included constant references to what *he* wanted them to do, and constant requests put to the assistant and the Ss to perform various tasks.

The picture of the negative communicator is quite different. While he is no different than the positive communicator in possessing those traits necessary for the effective execution of the experiment, he is not a warm person, is primarily bossy, tactless, demanding, snobbish, not genuinely interested in the subject, egotistical, and somewhat insincere and not very calm. It appears, therefore, that this scale was quite sensitive to the subtle as well as the gross aspects of our manipulation of communicator traits.[6]

One final point to be made is that within the negative condition the eaters did not view the communicator more favorably than did the noneaters on even a single trait; in fact, noneaters felt he was more capable ($t = 2.16$, $p < .05$), and more industrious ($t = 2.07$, $p < .05$) than did eaters. For the positive communicator, there were differences between eaters and noneaters on four traits, but on each of these eaters felt the communicator was more positive than did noneaters. He was fairer ($t = 2.24$, $p < .05$), less egotistical ($t = 2.22$, $p < .05$), more genuinely interested in them ($t = 1.97$, $p = .05$), and more mature ($t = 1.82$, $p < .10$).

Thus eaters under negative communicator conditions changed their attitudes toward the object of their induced public behavior —eating fried grasshoppers—but did not develop more favorable attitudes toward the communicator, while positive-condition eaters did not change their attitudes much, but did tend to justify their eating in terms of irrelevant, personal communicator characteristics.

Conclusions and Implications

The present study indicates that a communicator who advocates public compliance to behavior discrepant from a person's attitudes and values can also influence attitude change, without

6. This instrument is also highly reliable, as shown by the internal consistency coefficient of .90 obtained in this study (using Cronbach's alpha, 1951).

specifically communicating persuasive arguments and conclusions. Those who accept the inducement change in the desired direction, while those who do not comply often show boomerang effects—adopting more extreme attitude positions. This attitude change following public compliance (predicted by the theory of cognitive dissonance) is greater when the behavior cannot be as readily justified in terms of communicator characteristics, i.e., when the communicator is negative rather than positive. Thus source factors which are on an irrelevant dimension of communicator credibility may operate in interesting and nonobvious ways.

These findings may have considerable generalizability, since there were no differences in the pattern of results for college and army reserve samples, and our army reserve sample appears to be comparable to regular army Ss used in related research.[7] The results of this research also raise provocative questions about the operation of social contagion effects in group-participation decision-making. According to the present analysis, the operation of strong group pressures to conform should serve as justification for conformity and thus minimize the extent of private acceptance. In fact, attitude change may be greatest when the individual is put in the position of behaving in a manner not only contrary to his own initial values, but also to the group majority.

Although the manipulation of the communicator was quite successful in creating two different "personalities," it remains for future research to evaluate the relative efficacy of specific individual communicator traits, e.g., "hostility," especially as they interact with complementary or divergent traits of the audience.

Finally, the magnitude of the results obtained here, when contrasted with the relatively weak effects observed in the earlier studies on communicator credibility, leads one to speculate whether this change might not even be more permanent than in those studies where the initial differences vanish on subsequent

7. A number of the foods rated by our Ss were used because they represented foods which were found to be highly disliked, liked, or neutral in a large-scale normative study of food preferences of men in the regular army (Peryam et al., 1960). For each of five comparable foods the means and variances of our army reserve sample were the same as those obtained with regular army soldiers (whose educational and geographic backgrounds were quite variable).

testing. It might be that in standard influence situations, the perceptual associations are between communicator and content of his communication—both external to the S—while in the situation described in our study the association is between the communicator and the S's own behavior—and thus the perceptual response is stronger and the attitude change made of sterner stuff.

SUMMARY

Communicator characteristics which were objectively irrelevant to the topic of communication were studied in their relationship to behavioral compliance and to subsequent attitude change. Both college students and army reservists were induced to eat a highly disliked food, fried grasshoppers, by a communicator whose positiveness and negativeness were experimentally varied. Although public conformity was unrelated to communicator differences, private attitudes were significantly influenced. Those who complied with the request from a negative communicator increased their liking of grasshoppers (as a food) significantly more so than did those exposed to a positive communicator. Non-compliance was associated with boomerang effects in which grasshoppers became even more disliked. Under conditions which maximized group interaction marked variability occurred between groups within the same condition as a consequence of social contagion phenomena. The results support a dissonance theory analysis of communicator characteristics as a source of justification in forced compliance situations.

REFERENCES

Aronson, E., & Golden, B. W. The effect of relevant and irrelevant aspects of communicator credibility on opinion change. *J. Pers.*, 1962, **30**, 135-146.

Aronson, E., Turner, Judy, & Carlsmith, J. M. Communicator credibility and communication discrepancy as determinants of opinion change. *J. abnorm. soc. Psychol.*, 1963, **67**, 31-36.

Bettelheim, B. Individual and mass behavior in extreme situations. *J. abnorm. soc. Psychol.*, 1943, **30**, 417-452.

Cronbach, L. J. Coefficient alpha and the internal structure of test. *Psychometrika*, 1951, **16**, 297-334.

Festinger, L. *A theory of cognitive dissonance.* Evanston, Ill.: Row, Peterson, 1957.

Hovland, C. I., Lumsdaine, A. A., & Sheffield, F. D. *Experiments on mass communication.* Princeton: Princeton Univer. Press, 1949.

Hovland, C. I., & Weiss, W.   The influence of source credibility on communication effectiveness.   *Publ. Opin. Quart.*, 1951, **15**, 635-650.

Hovland, C. I., Janis, I. L., & Kelley, H. H.   *Communication and persuasion.* New Haven: Yale Univer. Press, 1953.

Kelman, H. C., & Hovland, C. I.   "Reinstatement" of the communicator in delayed measurement of opinion change.   *J. abnorm. soc. Psychol.*, 1953, **48**, 327-335.

Lazarsfeld, P. F., Berelson, B., & Gaudet, Hazel.   *The people's choice.*   New York: Columbia Univer. Press, 1944.

Peryam, D. R., Polemis, Bernice W., Kamen, J. W., Eindhoven, J., & Pilgrim, F. J.   *Food preferences of men in the U.S. Armed Forces.*   Publication of the Quartermaster Food and Container Institute for the Armed Forces, Chicago, 1960.

Smith, E. E.   Methods for changing consumer attitudes: A report of three experiments.   *Technical Report to Quartermaster Food and Container Institute for the Armed Forces* (PRA 61-2), 1961. (a)

Smith, E. E.   The power of dissonance techniques to change attitudes.   *Publ. Opin. Quart.*, 1961, **25**, 626-639. (b)

Zimbardo, P. G.   Involvement and communication discrepancy as determinants of opinion conformity.   *J. abnorm. soc. Psychol.*, 1960, **60**, 86-94.

"Irrelevant" Source Characteristics

There is a substantial body of research emphasizing the importance of shared beliefs and of the congeniality of ideas in social influence.[1] We noted earlier the finding that a communicator sometimes is more persuasive simply because he has been introduced as one who shares some of the audience's beliefs.[2]

What if, instead of a belief, the audience and the communicator did *not* share some other socially influential characteristic, for example, race? Would a Negro communicator be any less, or any more, effective than a Caucasian if the audience consisted only of Caucasians? It has been found that people are more influenced by a communicator who "practices what he preaches." His sincerity is less apt to be questioned. Hence, a Caucasian communicator arguing for civil rights is more persuasive when he is shown interacting with Negroes than when he is shown interacting only with other Caucasians.[3]

But what of the situation where race is not logically relevant to the communication? Can an objectively irrelevant aspect of a communicator's credibility influence the potency of his presentation? This is the intriguing problem alluded to by Zimbardo *et al.* in their introduction to the study reprinted in the preceding section and explored in depth by Elliott Aronson and Burton W. Golden in the paper that follows.

---

[1] Back, K. W. Influence through social communication. *J. abnorm. soc. Psychol.*, 1951, **46**, 9–23. Burnstein, E., Stotland, E., & Zander, A. Similarity to a model and self-evaluation. *J. abnorm. soc. Psychol.*, 1961, **62**, 257–264. Stotland, E., Zander, A., & Natsoulas, T. Generalization of interpersonal similarity. *J. abnorm. soc. Psychol.*, 1961, **62**, 250–256. Brock, T. C. Communicator-recipient similarity and decision change. *J. Pers. soc. Psychol.*, 1965, **1**, 650–654. Rokeach, M., & Mezei, L. Race and shared belief as factors in social choice. *Science*, 1966, **151**, 161–172. Byrne, D., Clore, G. L., Jr., & Worchel, P. Effect of economic similarity-dissimilarity on interpersonal attraction. *J. Pers. soc. Psychol.*, 1966, **4**, 220–224.

[2] Weiss, W. Opinion congruence with a negative source on one issue as a factor influencing agreement on another issue. *J. abnorm. soc. Psychol.*, 1957, **54**, 180–186.

[3] Kraus, S. Modifying prejudice: Attitude change as a function of the race of the communicator. *Audio-Visual Communication Rev.*, 1962, **10**, 14–22.

Reprinted from Journal of Personality, 1962, Vol. 30, No. 2, pp. 135–146, by permission
of Elliott Aronson and Duke University Press.

The effect of relevant and irrelevant aspects of communicator credibility on opinion change[1]

ELLIOT ARONSON AND BURTON W. GOLDEN

Several experiments have demonstrated the operation of a so-called prestige factor on the effectiveness of a communication. That is, a given communication has been shown to induce a greater change in the opinions of an audience if attributed to a source having high credibility than if attributed to a source having low credibility. Credibility has usually been defined in terms of the expertness and/or the trustworthiness of the source (Hovland, Janis, & Kelley, 1953). Thus, if a communicator is in a position to know what he is talking about and is not in a position to profit personally by misleading his audience, he has been shown to be most effective in influencing opinion change.

Research in this area has typically involved manipulating variables of communicator credibility which are quite relevant to the content of the persuasive communication. Some studies have employed variables which were of general relevance, e.g., intelligence, responsibility, honesty, sincerity, etc. (Arnett, Davidson, & Lewis, 1931; Kulp, 1934). Other studies have employed variables which were relevant specifically to the content of the communication. Thus, audiences have been exposed to a communication from "J. Robert Oppenheimer" about the feasibility of an atomic submarine (Hovland & Weiss, 1951); a communication by a juvenile court judge about juvenile delinquency (Kelman & Hovland, 1953); a communication about health insurance by the Surgeon-General of the United States (Haiman, 1949), etc.

But what about positive or negative aspects of a communicator

[1] This research was supported by a grant from the Harvard University Laboratory of Social Relations. The authors wish to express their appreciation to Mr. Stephen Graham and Mr. Larry Schiff for their help, and to Miss Mary B. Loftus of the Revere Public School System for her kind cooperation.

that bear no objective relevance to the topic of the communication? If a communicator were highly credible, would an objectively irrelevant personal characteristic have a bearing on the effectiveness of his communication? For example, if a Nobel prize-winning physicist were lecturing on nuclear physics, would he be less effective if he were a poor basketball player? Would his impact be different if he were fat or thin, sloppy or neat, ugly or handsome, Negro or white? By neglecting to consider irrelevant aspects of communicator credibility, studies in this area have unwittingly implied that audiences are composed of people who are responsive solely to objectively relevant aspects of a communicator. This implication is consistent with Asch's assertion that individuals generally make use of their ability to understand the objective character of a social situation, and thus act in keeping with its rational requirements (Asch, 1952). It would be of some interest to determine whether or not this implication is valid.

This discussion is based upon the assumption that some attributes of a communicator are of greater objective relevance than others. But the term "relevance" is somewhat ambiguous, and hence difficult to define in an unequivocal a priori manner. Thus, in the above illustrations we have made certain implicit assumptions which should be spelled out more clearly. For example, we assumed that, in the case of a person delivering a lecture on physics, being a Nobel prize winner is more relevant than being a Caucasian. But suppose that the communicator is a Negro and that a member of the audience holds the firm belief that most Negroes are stupid. If this were the case, it might be argued that, for this member of the audience, the skin color of the communicator is of great relevance—one does not allow oneself to be influenced by stupid people. Suppose, however, that the audience were given objective proof that this Negro communicator's IQ was 170. When confronted with such evidence, it would be difficult for a member of the audience to hold the belief that this Negro is stupid. In an objective sense the communicator's skin color is of minor importance. Similarly, if the members of the audience were informed that the Negro communicator was a Nobel prize winner, or a physicist doing brilliant work for the government, they would be forced to accept this as evidence of his credibility. The communicator's credentials would seem to be too solid to allow him to be written off as "just another stupid Negro." When faced with compelling evidence such as this, a prejudiced listener (i.e., one who believed most Negroes to be stupid) might maintain his general stereotype, but it seems apparent that he would be forced to accept this particular Negro as an exception to the rule. It is our contention that, in this situation, most members of an audience, though acknowledging this Negro's obvious intelligence, would be less persuaded by a Negro expert than by a Caucasian expert. In short, they would be responding to objectively irrelevant aspects of communicator credibility. If this contention is correct, it should be empirically demonstrable: i.e., we should be able to demonstrate that individuals who have negative attitudes toward Negroes will be relatively uninfluenced by a Negro communicator of high relevant credibility, while at the same time, they see him as being highly credible.

The present experiment was designed, then, to investigate the relative effectiveness of objectively relevant and irrelevant aspects of communicator credibility. This was done by comparing the extent of opinion change brought about by a given communication as a function of: (a) whether it was attributed to a person whose description and occupational status clearly demonstrated that he was an expert in the area of the communication, or to a person whose description and occupational status implied that he had little or no knowledge in the area of the communication (relevant credibility); (b) whether it was attributed to a Negro or a Caucasian (irrelevant credibility); (c) the attitude of individual members of the audience toward Negroes.

If objectively irrelevant aspects of a communicator's credibility, in fact, do influence his effectiveness, we can make the following predictions:

1. In general, a white communicator will be more effective than a Negro communicator of equal relevant credibility. This prediction is based upon the assumption that more members of an audience will have negative attitudes toward Negroes than toward Caucasians, thus diminishing the credibility of the Negro and reducing his over-all influence.

2. The more negative an individual's attitude toward Negroes is, the less will he be influenced by the Negro communicator regardless of the objectively relevant credibility of the communicator.

METHOD

In general, the procedure involved ascertaining the opinions of Ss concerning arithmetic and then presenting them with a communication extolling the value and importance of arithmetic. For some Ss the communicator had high relevant credibility and high irrelevant credibility; he was introduced as an engineer and was a Caucasian. For some Ss the communicator had high relevant and low irrelevant credibility; he was introduced as an engineer and was a Negro. For a third group of Ss the communicator had low relevant and high irrelevant credibility; he was introduced as a dishwasher and was a Caucasian. For the fourth group of Ss the communicator had low relevant and low irrelevant credibility; he was introduced as a dishwasher and was a Negro. After the communication each S's opinion of arithmetic was measured again. The changes in opinion could then be compared across experimental conditions.

The Ss were 113 white sixth-grade students in two schools within the same city. The experiment was conducted in their classrooms. There were two sixth-grade classes in each school; one classroom was used in each of the four experimental conditions.

The Pre-Communication Measure

In each classroom, the teacher introduced the E_1 to her class as Mr. Aronson from Harvard University who had come to talk to them for a little while. She then left the room. The first session was used to measure each S's attitudes toward arithmetic. E_1 explained to the Ss that he was visiting all of the schools in the Boston area in order to get some idea of the students' feelings about arithmetic:

> I would like to know what your real feelings are about arithmetic. I'd like to know whether you think it is important or worthless—whether you like it or dislike it—whether you like arithmetic so much that you would rather work arithmetic problems than go to a movie, or whether you dislike arithmetic so much that you would rather scrub the kitchen floor than work arithmetic problems. I simply want to find out how pupils in different schools feel about arithmetic. What I want is your frank, honest opinion. I do not want you to tell me how your mother feels about arithmetic, or how your teacher feels about it, or how you think you *should* feel about it. I want your own honest opinion. This is for my own use. Your teacher will not be told what your opinions are.

E_1 then handed each S a rating scale consisting of 36 evaluative statements concerning the usefulness and pleasurableness of arithmetic—e.g., "I enjoy doing arithmetic problems" and "I can get along perfectly well in everyday life without knowing much about arithmetic." Ss were asked to pretend that each of these items was a statement made by a person. They were instructed simply to indicate the extent of their agreement or disagreement with the statement by circling a number on a five-point scale which appeared beneath each statement.

Attitudes Toward Negroes

Four weeks later a different E appeared in each of the four classrooms. He told the students that he was interested in finding out how they felt about different kinds of people. E_2 said that today he was going to ask them questions about colored people and that he would return at a later date and ask them questions about other kinds of people. He then distributed a 19-item questionnaire, which the investigators had constructed at a level appropriate for sixth-grade children. Each item was a statement about Negroes; e.g., "Most colored people are dumb," "Colored people are not lazier than other people," etc. The Ss were asked to pretend that they had heard a person make each of these statements. They were then asked to indicate the extent of their agreement or disagreement with each statement by circling a number on a five-point scale which appeared beneath each statement.

The Communication and the Communicators

Six weeks after obtaining Ss' opinions about arithmetic, E_1 returned to each classroom, accompanied by a communicator, reintroduced himself and said:

> As you may remember, I am interested in arithmetic. During the past few weeks I have been visiting many of the schools in Massachusetts, together with several different people whom I have asked to talk to the students about arithmetic. These people come from all walks of life. Some are doctors, some are janitors, some are policemen, some are lawyers, some are plumbers, some are garbage collectors, some are bankers, some work in factories. Although these people work at very different jobs, they have one thing in common: they all have some ideas about arithmetic and would like to express them to you. Today our guest is Mr. Bill Robinson.

In both of the high relevant credibility conditions, it was important that the communicator's expertness, trustworthiness, and intelligence be presented as unambiguously and as irrefutably as possible. For this reason, not only was he introduced as an engineer, but he was also described as being a graduate of a prestigious university, and as doing well at a responsible and demanding job. E described the communicator in the following manner:

> Mr. Robinson is an *engineer*. He is a recent graduate of the School of Engineering at MIT (Massachusetts Institute of Technology). At present, Mr. Robinson is working for the government on missile and space projects. Mr. Robinson is using his skills as an *engineer* on a project which is concerned with launching a man into space. The government has a lot of confidence in Mr. Robinson and he has been doing an excellent job for them. Today he has come with me because he would like to talk to you about arithmetic.

In both of the low relevant credibility conditions, E said:

> Mr. Robinson is a *dishwasher*. He *washes dishes* at the Olympia restaurant in Boston. He attended public school in Boston but he did not finish high school. He has been employed as a *dishwasher* for about three years. Today, he has come with me because he would like to talk to you about arithmetic.

It was of the utmost importance that the actual communication be identical in all four conditions—identical both in content and in manner of delivery. For this reason, a tape recording of the communication was played in all four conditions. But the design of the experiment required the physical

presence of the communicator in order that he might be readily identified as
either a Negro or a Caucasian. To justify the use of a tape-recorded message in the presence of the would-be speaker, *E* explained to the *S*s:

> Mr. Robinson would like to speak to you about arithmetic, but un-
> fortunately he cannot. He's been making so many speeches during the
> past few days that he has been getting hoarse. Just this morning his
> voice gave out completely. Luckily, yesterday, when his voice started
> to crack, he took the precaution of tape recording one of his speeches.
> We'll play that for you now.

The actual communication was a 6½ minute speech stressing the importance and usefulness of arithmetic in a variety of situations. The vocabulary, syntax, and choice of examples used in the communication were simple
but accurate; thus, the speech did not appear to be inappropriate for either
an engineer or a dishwasher.

Two visual but noncommunicating communicators were used in the
experiment. One was obviously Caucasian, the other was obviously Negro.
They were both 21 years old, and of average height and weight. During the
experiment neither spoke, but each simply smiled shyly at appropriate
moments.

The engineer was dressed conservatively in a grey flannel suit; the dishwasher was dressed humbly but neatly in a white shirt (no tie), sweater, and
khaki trousers. In one school the Negro communicator played the role of
the engineer and the Caucasian played the role of the dishwasher. After
the communication was played, the communicators adjourned to an empty
classroom where they simply exchanged clothes (and roles) before proceeding to the second school.

The Postcommunication Measure

Immediately after the tape recording was played, *E* thanked the communicator, the students applauded, and the communicator left the room. *E*
then announced to the *S*s that he would like to find out how they felt about
arithmetic. He then distributed a questionnaire, identical to the one he had
distributed six weeks earlier, and instructed the students on its use.

In addition, *S*s were asked to rate the communicator's intelligence and
sincerity, respectively, on a seven-point scale. This scale was administered
as a means of determining the effectiveness of the manipulation of objectively
relevant credibility.

Finally, *S*s were asked to recognize the occupation of the communicator
by circling one of four alternatives. Seven of the 113 students in the
original sample were unable to recognize the occupation of the communicator;
for this reason, they were discarded from the sample.

RESULTS AND DISCUSSION

What was the relative effectiveness of the four communicators?
I.e., how much did each communicator change the opinions of his
audience toward arithmetic? Since the precommunication opinions
concerning arithmetic differed across classrooms, an analysis of

covariance was computed. This technique adjusts the postcommunication means for initial differences in opinion. The precommunication means, the postcommunication means, and the adjusted after-means are presented in Table 1. The results indicate that all of the communicators had some effect on the opinions of the audience. The significance of the differences between each pair of adjusted means was computed by t test. The results are summarized in Table 2. The tables indicate that the Negro engineer and the white engineer were equally effective. Moreover, both the Negro engineer and the white engineer were significantly more effective than the Negro dishwasher, while neither was significantly more effective than the white dishwasher. The white dishwasher was substantially more effective than the Negro dishwasher, although the difference fell just short of the 5 per cent level of significance.

Thus, from a cursory examination of these gross data it appears that objectively relevant factors are decisive in determining opinion change. The greatest change occurred when the communicator was

TABLE 1
PRECOMMUNICATION AND POSTCOMMUNICATION OPINIONS
ABOUT ARITHMETIC

	N	Mean of Precommunication Opinion	Mean of Postcommunication Opinion	Adjusted After-Mean
Negro dishwasher	31	18.71	24.48	30.34
Negro engineer	18	29.61	40.61	36.23
White dishwasher	24	30.25	38.96	33.98
White engineer	23	24.17	35.30	36.03

TABLE 2
SIGNIFICANCE LEVELS OF OPINION CHANGE BETWEEN
EXPERIMENTAL CONDITIONS

	Negro dishwasher	White dishwasher	Negro engineer
White engineer	$t = 2.92$ $p^a < .01$	$t = 1.03$ n.s.	$t = .09$ n.s.
Negro engineer	$t = 2.75$ $p < .01$	$t = .99$ n.s.	
White dishwasher	$t = 1.85$ $p < .10$		

a All p values are based upon both tails of the t distribution.

---

introduced as an engineer—whether he was Negro or Caucasian apparently made no difference, if his occupational position placed him in the role of an expert.

Before drawing this conclusion, however, it would be prudent to take a closer look—to examine changes in opinions about arithmetic as a function of individual differences in attitudes toward Negroes. In each of the two Negro-communicator conditions, Ss' scores on the prejudice questionnaire were divided at the median. Those Ss who scored above the median were classified roughly as "prejudiced"; those Ss who scored below the median were classified roughly as "unprejudiced." Changes in opinion concerning arithmetic were computed separately for prejudiced and unprejudiced Ss and an analysis of covariance was computed. Table 3 shows the precommunication mean, the postcommunication mean, and the adjusted after-mean for prejudiced and unprejudiced Ss in the Negro engineer and Negro dishwasher conditions. In each of these conditions, the unprejudiced Ss were influenced to a greater extent than the prejudiced Ss. The significance of the differences was computed by t test. The results are quite striking. The unprejudiced Ss in the Negro engineer condition were influenced to a greater extent than were the prejudiced Ss in the same condition ($t = 2.72$, $p < .02$).[2] Simi-

TABLE 3

PRECOMMUNICATION AND POSTCOMMUNICATION OPINIONS ABOUT ARITHMETIC OF PREJUDICED AND UNPREJUDICED Ss IN THE NEGRO CONDITIONS

	N	Mean of Pre-communication Opinion	Mean of Post-communication Opinion	Adjusted After-Mean	
Negro dishwasher unprejudiced	14[a]	15.36	28.57	35.56	$t = 2.66$
Negro dishwasher prejudiced	14[a]	20.21	19.86	23.96	$p^b < .02$
Negro engineer unprejudiced	9	28.89	46.67	44.41	$t = 2.72$
Negro engineer prejudiced	9	30.33	34.56	31.25	$p^b < .02$

[a] Three of the Ss in the Negro dishwasher condition were absent from school when the prejudice questionnaire was administered.
[b] p values based upon both tails of the t distribution.

[2] All p values are based upon both tails of the t distribution.

larly, in the Negro dishwasher condition, the unprejudiced Ss were more influenced by the communication than were the prejudiced Ss in the same condition ($t = 2.66$, $p < .02$).

Moreover, the unprejudiced Ss in the Negro engineer condition were more influenced by the communication than the Ss in the white engineer condition ($t = 2.32$, $p < .05$).[3] Similarly, the prejudiced Ss in the Negro engineer condition tended to be less influenced by the communication than were the Ss in the white engineer condition; this difference does not reach statistical significance, however ($t = 1.35$, $p < .20$).

A similar trend appears in the Negro dishwasher condition. Here, the prejudiced Ss show a great reluctance to be influenced; they are less influenced by the communication than are the Ss in the white dishwasher condition ($t = 2.74$, $p < .01$). The unprejudiced Ss in the Negro dishwasher condition show a tendency to be more influenced by the communication than the Ss in the white dishwasher condition; however, this difference is not statistically significant ($t = 1.38$, $p < .20$).

These results indicate that objectively irrelevant aspects of the communicator were a major source of variance. This trend did not show up in a gross analysis of the data because the irrelevant sources of communicator effectiveness were operating in different directions for different people. Not only was there a tendency for prejudiced individuals to be undersusceptible to the influence of a Negro communicator, but there was also a tendency for unprejudiced Ss to be oversusceptible to the influence of a Negro communicator.

It is possible to argue that for prejudiced subjects, the fact that a communicator was Negro is not an irrelevant aspect of his credibility. That is, prejudiced individuals probably believe that most Negroes are stupid. Since stupidity in a communicator is objectively relevant, it may be reasonable to assume that the behavior of the prejudiced subjects was reasonable. That is, it may be that they were less influenced by the Negro engineer because they were responding to aspects of the communicator which had great relevance vis-a-vis the communication. However, it is unlikely that prejudiced

[3] In the white engineer condition and in the white dishwasher condition there was virtually no difference in changes of opinion between prejudiced and unprejudiced Ss. Therefore, the scores of prejudiced and unprejudiced Ss were combined for purposes of this comparison and others in the "white" treatment conditions presented below.

subjects perceived the Negro engineer as being stupid. Recall that the Negro engineer was described in an extremely positive manner. He was introduced as an engineer, a graduate of MIT, working for the U.S. government. It was stated, further, that the government had a high degree of confidence in him. It seems unreasonable to assume that sixth-graders would feel that such a person was too stupid to give them advice about simple arithmetic. Furthermore, there is evidence to indicate that the above manipulation was effective. It will be recalled that, following the communication, Ss were asked to rate the intelligence of the speaker. There was virtually no difference between the manner in which the prejudiced and unprejudiced Ss rated the intelligence of the Negro engineer. The mean ratings were 5.70 (prejudiced) and 5.53 (unprejudiced); this difference is in the opposite direction from the Negro stereotype and does not approach statistical significance.

Of course, the fact that the measure of perceived intelligence fails to discriminate the prejudiced Ss from the unprejudiced Ss cannot be accepted as definitive proof. It may reflect nothing more than an insensitive instrument. However, there is evidence that the measure was a sensitive one. For example, there was a clear and significant difference between the over-all rating of the intelligence of the engineers and that of the dishwashers ($p < .01$). The scale also reflected a difference between the prejudiced and unprejudiced Ss on their ratings of the Negro dishwasher; the mean for the prejudiced Ss was 4.38, and for the unprejudiced Ss was 5.46 ($p < .01$).

In addition, Ss were asked to rate the sincerity of the communicator. There were no significant differences in the general ratings of the communicator in the four experimental conditions. Moreover, there were no differences between the ratings made by prejudiced and unprejudiced Ss in any of these conditions. In fact, there was virtually no variance, since almost all of the Ss rated the communicator as extremely sincere. These data are not surprising, since there was nothing in the procedure which could have led S to suspect the communicator of being insincere. The communication was a simple, honest, and straightforward message; the communicators were earnest, guileless young men, who obviously had nothing to gain by influencing the Ss, and who were introduced in a manner that strongly implied that they were sincerely concerned with the welfare of the Ss.

The evidence concerning Ss' ratings of the intelligence and sincerity of the communicators strongly suggests that, in the Negro engineer condition, prejudiced Ss were responding to irrelevant aspects of the communicator's credibility. Their opinion about arithmetic was influenced less than was the opinion of the unprejudiced individuals. At the same time, they considered the Negro engineer to be as intelligent and as sincere as the unprejudiced Ss did.

What about the unprejudiced Ss in the Negro engineer condition? The fact that they were influenced to a greater extent than the Ss in the white engineer condition can be interpreted in at least two ways: (*a*) It may be that these so-called unprejudiced individuals, in fact, *were* prejudiced—prejudiced in favor of Negroes. I.e., the mere fact that a communicator was Negro appears to have rendered him more attractive and more credible than his Caucasian counterpart. (*b*) On the other hand, it may be reasonable to consider a Negro who has managed to attain a high-status position to be especially bright—considering the prejudice that exists against Negroes. Thus, unprejudiced individuals may not be prejudiced in favor of Negroes, but may be aware of the unequal treatment accorded Negroes, and thus may be taking into account the realities of the educational and occupational system, when evaluating the expertness of the communicator. If unprejudiced Ss actually considered a Negro engineer to be more intelligent than a white engineer this would be expected to manifest itself in the ratings Ss made of the intelligence of the communicators. But there is no difference between the rated intelligence of the Negro engineer (made by unprejudiced Ss) and the rating of the intelligence of the white engineer (made by unprejudiced Ss). Moreover, as stated previously, there is no difference between the rated intelligence of the Negro engineer by prejudiced and unprejudiced Ss. Thus, these data tend to favor the first interpretation: that the behavior of the unprejudiced Ss in the Negro engineer condition reflect "crow-Jimism"—prejudice in favor of a Negro communicator. It is reasonable to infer that the so-called unprejudiced Ss (like the prejudiced Ss) were responding to objectively irrelevant aspects of the communicators' credibility; i.e., they were relatively more influenced by a Negro engineer than a white engineer without having perceived the

Negro engineer as being more intelligent or more sincere than the white engineer.

SUMMARY

An experiment was conducted to test the relative importance of objectively relevant and objectively irrelevant aspects of communicator credibility on changes in audience opinion. A speech, extolling the virtues of arithmetic was recited to sixth-grade students by one of four communicators: (a) high relevant and high irrelevant credibility (a white engineer); (b) high relevant and low irrelevant credibility (a Negro engineer); (c) low relevant and high irrelevant credibility (a white dishwasher); (d) low relevant and low irrelevant credibility (a Negro dishwasher).

The results indicated that both relevant and irrelevant aspects of credibility are important determinants of opinion change. There was a strong tendency for the engineers to be more effective than the dishwashers. There was also a strong tendency for those Ss who were prejudiced against Negroes to be underinfluenced by the Negro communicators, and for those Ss who were unprejudiced against Negroes to be overinfluenced by the Negro communicators.

REFERENCES

ARNETT, C. E., DAVIDSON, HELEN H., & LEWIS, H. N. Prestige as a factor in attitude changes. *Sociol. soc. Res.*, 1931, **16**, 49-55.

ASCH, S. E. *Social psychology.* New York: Prentice-Hall, 1952.

HAIMAN, F. S. An experimental study of the effects of Ethos in public speaking. *Speech Monogr.*, 1949, **16**, 190-202.

HOVLAND, C. I., JANIS, I. L., & KELLEY, H. H. *Communication and persuasion.* New Haven: Yale Univer. Press, 1953.

HOVLAND, C. I., & WEISS, W. The influence of source credibility on communication effectiveness. *Publ. Opin. Quart.*, 1951, **15**, 635-650.

KELMAN, H. C., & HOVLAND, C. I. "Reinstatement" of the communicator in delayed measurement of opinion change. *J. abnorm. soc. Psychol.*, 1953, **48**, 327-335.

KULP, D. H. Prestige as measured by single-experience changes and their permanency. *J. educ. res.*, 1934, **27**, 663-672.

PART II

MESSAGE

Is it better to present only one side of a controversial issue, or both sides? If both sides are presented, will the arguments heard first have any advantage over those heard last? Is persuasion in the guise of an emotional communication as effective as rational persuasion? What are the motivational processes set in motion by exposure to a threatening message? Can a communication frighten recipients into changing their personal beliefs?

Unqualified versus
Qualified Messages

Early in 1945, as a result of the Allied military success in Europe, the war with Germany was drawing to a close. American soldiers, cheered by this success, were highly optimistic about a similar early end to the war in the Pacific. However, this apparent "overoptimism" and its adverse effect on morale worried the American military. As a result, a directive was issued to impress upon our troops the magnitude of the task remaining in defeating the Japanese.

This was the problem that confronted Carl Hovland, Arthur A. Lumsdaine, Fred D. Sheffield, and their colleagues in the Research Branch of the War Department's Information and Education Division. Their solution to the problem is described in the paper which follows.

This paper is one in an impressive series of experimental, field, and theoretical studies carried out by psychologists, sociologists, and statisticians under the auspices of the U. S. Army during World War II.[1] Those carefully designed studies reflect one of the earliest and most successful attempts at programmatic research in persuasion and opinion change. Methodology in experimental communications research as we know it today is, to a significant degree, a function of those initial systematic programs of investigation.

We noted earlier that one immediate result of the war research was the formation, under Hovland's direction, of the Yale Communication Research Program. The inchoation of a wealth of principles in behavioral science can be traced to hypotheses conceived during World War II in the creativity of Hovland, Lumsdaine, Sheffield, and many

---

[1] The Hovland, Lumsdaine, and Sheffield paper is reported in *Studies in social psychology in world war II. Vol. III. Experiments on mass communication.* Princeton, N. J.: Princeton Univer. Press, 1949. Other volumes in this series include reports of similar wartime social research: Stouffer, S. A., Suchman, E. A., DeVinney, L. C., Star, S. A., & Williams, R. M., Jr. Vol. I. *The American soldier—Adjustment during army life;* Stouffer, S. A., Lumsdaine, A. A., Lumsdaine, M. H., Williams, R. M., Jr., Smith, M. B., Janis, I. L., Star, S. A., & Cottrell, L. S., Jr. Vol. II. *The American soldier—Combat and its aftermath;* Stouffer, S. A., Guttman, L., Suchman, E. A., Lazarsfeld, P. F., Star, S. A., & Clausen, J. A. Vol. IV. *Measurement and prediction.*

others. Here, the principal question raised by Hovland and his associates is how best to accomplish the task set forth in the Army directive. How could the soldiers be persuaded to take a more "realistic" view of our future progress in the Pacific war? Should a persuasive appeal present "both sides" of the issue, or should the Army's view be the only one represented? What types of soldiers should be influenced more by an unqualified, or one-sided communication, and what types by a qualified, or two-sided, communication? Was the extent of their education a factor? Did some already favor the Army's position and, if so, should this influence the nature of the persuasive appeal? These are the kinds of questions raised by the investigators. Let us see how well they succeeded in arriving at the answers.

Reprinted from Studies in Social Psychology in World War II, Vol. 3, "Experiments on Mass Communication," pp. 201–227, by permission of Princeton University Press.

THE EFFECTS OF PRESENTING "ONE SIDE" VERSUS "BOTH SIDES" IN CHANGING OPINIONS ON A CONTROVERSIAL SUBJECT

By Carl I. Hovland, Arthur A. Lumsdaine, and Fred D. Sheffield

IN DESIGNING Army orientation programs an issue which was frequently debated was this question: When the weight of evidence supports the main thesis being presented, is it more effective to present only the materials supporting the point being made, or is it better to introduce also the arguments of those opposed to the point being made?

The procedure of presenting only the arguments supporting a thesis is often employed on the grounds that when the preponderance of the evidence supports the point being made, the presentation of opposing arguments and misconceptions merely raises doubts in the minds of the audience. On the other hand, the procedure of presenting the arguments for both sides was defended on the grounds of "fairness"—the right of members of the audience to have access to all relevant materials in making up their minds. Furthermore, there is reason to expect that those audience members who are already opposed to the point of view being presented may be distracted by "rehearsing" their own arguments while the topic is being presented and will be antagonized by the omission of the arguments on their side. Thus, presentation of the audience's arguments at the outset possibly would produce better reception of the arguments which it is desired to convey.

The present experiment was set up to provide information on the relative effectiveness of these two types of program content in changing the opinions of individuals initially opposing as compared with those favoring the position advocated in the program. Controlled variation of treatment was introduced by preparing two transcrip-

201

tions with the same orientation message in alternative forms.   In one form arguments were presented on only one side of the issue; in the other both sides were presented.

METHODS OF STUDY

1. THE TWO PROGRAMS USED

At the time the experiment was being planned (early 1945) the war in Europe was drawing to a close and it was reported that Army morale was being adversely affected by overoptimism about an early end to the war in the Pacific.   A directive was issued by the Army to impress upon troops a conception of the magnitude of the job remaining to be done in defeating Japan.   This furnished a controversial topic on which arguments were available on both sides but where the majority of experts in military affairs believed the preponderance of evidence supported one side.   It was therefore chosen as a suitable subject for experimentation.

Radio transcriptions rather than films were used, primarily because of the simplicity with which they could be prepared in alternative forms.   The basic outline of the programs' content was prepared by the Experimental Section.   All materials used were official releases from the Office of War Information and the War Department.   The final writing and production of the programs were carried out by the Armed Forces Radio Service.

The two programs compared in this chapter were in the form of a commentator's analysis of the Pacific War.   The commentator's conclusion was that the job of finishing the war would be tough and that it would take at least two years after VE Day.   A brief description of the two programs follows.

Program I ("one side"): The major topics included in the program which presented *only* the arguments indicating that the war would be long were: distance problems and other logistical difficulties in the Pacific; the resources and stockpiles in the Japanese Empire; the size and quality of the main bulk of the Japanese Army that we had not yet met in battle; and the determination of the Japanese people.   The program ran for about fifteen minutes.

Program II ("both sides"): The other program ran for about nineteen minutes and presented all of these same difficulties in exactly the same way.   The difference of four minutes between this and the "one-sided" program was the time devoted to considering arguments for the other side of the picture—U.S. advantages and Japanese weaknesses such as our naval victories and superiority, our previous progress despite a two-front war, our ability to concentrate all our forces on Japan after VE Day, Japan's shipping losses, Japan's manufacturing inferiority, and the future damage to be expected from our expanding air war.   These additional points were woven into the context of the rest of the program.

Before the preparation of these programs, pretests had been conducted in which men were individually interviewed on questions relating to the length of the war with Japan.   The purpose of this was to discover what arguments were actually used by the soldiers who took the position that the war would soon be over.   At the same time, the phrasing of questions for the final questionnaire to be used in the study was worked out.   This qualitative pretest was followed by a quantitative pretest on 200 men to discover the approximate distribution of men's estimates of probable length of the war and the approximate frequency of the various arguments for and against a short or long war.   The information thus gained was then used as a basis for preparing an outline of the factual material to be used in the program, greatest weight being given to the material relevant to countering the arguments most frequently offered by the men as a basis for expecting an early end to the war in the Pacific after VE Day.

In preparing the programs, the sequence and manner of presenting the various arguments was guided, in so far as possible, by principles thought to be those which would most effectively utilize the arguments on both sides so as to convince the men initially opposed to the orientation message.   The major hypothesis governing the preparation of the presentation giving "both sides" was that those who were opposed would be stimulated by a one-sided argument to rehearse their own position and seek new ways of supporting it.   A further aspect of this hypothesis was that those opposed to the position taken would discount a one-sided presentation as coming from a biased source that had failed to consider the arguments on the other side.   The introduction of the arguments "on the other side" was designed to minimize such tendencies among those opposed. In line with these considerations, the following provisional rules or principles of presentation were formulated.

(1) *All of the main arguments on the other side should be mentioned at the very outset.*   This was designed to have the effect of indicating to the opposed members of the audience from the very beginning that their point of view and supporting arguments would not be

neglected. As a consequence it was expected that they would be less likely to start rehearsing their own arguments to themselves, more likely to credit the presentation as having the authenticity that usually goes with unbiased interpretations, and less likely to have their own emotional motivations aroused against accepting the conclusion of the communication.

(2) *Any appeals to the motives of the opposed audience members should be presented early.* On the assumption that appeals to motives are the most important determiners of opinion change, it seems likely that with opposed audience members the rational arguments would be more influential if the emotional appeal had already been made as far as possible. This timing would be less important with individuals already emotionally predisposed to accept the conclusion —the latter group would be highly receptive to the rational arguments that backed up their position.

(3) *Opposed arguments that cannot be refuted should be presented relatively early.* Such arguments actually tend to weaken the conclusion, but they serve to satisfy the opposition and thus reduce antagonism. By high-lighting them fairly early in the communication, the maximal advantage in reducing aggressive tendencies is obtained, but they should also be expected to be remembered less at the conclusion of the communication.

(4) *An attempt to refute arguments on the other side should be made only when an obviously compelling and strictly factual refutation is available.* Here the expectation is that any attempted refutation will have a tendency to antagonize the opposed members of the audience, and may motivate them to seek new arguments to support their position. Therefore, direct refutation should be considered only when it is based on factual evidence so strong that it will be accepted even by those who are opposed.

(5) *An unrefuted opposed argument should be followed by an uncontroversial positive argument.* The inference here is that a negative argument can be offset by an equally strong or even stronger positive argument. It may even be true that the effect will often be greater if a refutable negative argument is left unrefuted in order not to arouse any antagonistic motivation—in order to avoid getting the opposed listener's "ego" involved—and is instead offset by a positive argument that is accepted as valid by the opposition. The order of negative, then positive, should serve to indicate that the negative point is being considered, but that despite this important point on the negative side, the positive point swings the balance in

the direction of the conclusion endorsed. This sequence should take advantage of the appearance of impartiality and satisfy the opposition as to the correctness and relevance of their own considerations, but still leave the weight of evidence against their position.

(6) *The timing in presenting counter arguments of the opposition should be: positive argument leading, objection raised by an opposed counter argument, and then positive argument offsetting the objection.* One purpose of this sequence is to state the negative argument exactly at the time that it is most likely to be aroused implicitly in the opposition group. They therefore should not be so likely to rehearse the argument in an antagonistic frame of mind, but instead be gratified to hear their own position voiced. At the same time their argument is presented in a context of doubt, and the argument that is favored by both primacy and recency is the positive argument that is used to refute or offset the negative counter argument.

(7) *Any refutations, and those positive arguments which are potentially most antagonizing, should come late in the presentation.* This follows from the expectation that a potentially antagonizing refutation will elicit less antagonism if the opposition has already been changed in a positive direction by the preceding portions of the communications. If they have already been partly "won over" to the position of the communication, they may not be at all antagonized by an idea that would have aroused aggression at the outset.

(8) *Members of the opposition should not be given a choice to identify themselves as such.* This principle is perhaps more difficult to utilize than the others. The basis for the principle is that a person is easier to change if he does not have his "ego" involved in supporting a particular point of view. If he feels that he belongs to a group that is being attacked by the communication, he is more likely to respond with aggressive resistance. Anything that can be done to present the communication as if it represented the views of each member of the audience, or to prevent the listeners from taking sides on the issue, should make those initially opposed more susceptible to change.

Not all of these "rules" could be adhered to strictly in the preparation of the actual scripts. However, an outline of the factual material to be presented was organized in such a way as to follow rather closely the implications of the first five rules, and in general to introduce the negative arguments at those points where, as determined by pretests, they seemed most likely to occur spontaneously to the opposed members of the audience. In these pretests, interviewers had actually presented the case for a long war in a face-to-face situation and had attempted to elicit counter arguments from interviewees who felt that the war would be short. In the final scripts used, refutations of the opposed arguments were in general avoided. Counter arguments rarely took the form of trying to *disprove* or *deny* the truth of an important argument; rather, the truth of the argument was admitted but its force was weakened by immediately bringing in additional relevant facts.

The outline of factual material thus organized was used by the script writers as the basis for preparing the program that used arguments on "both sides" of the question. The script for the "one-side" version was identical with that for "both sides" except for the omission of all facts or arguments supporting a short war, plus a very few wording changes necessary for transitional purposes.

At the time of preparing the scripts, the writer knew the purpose of the experiment and the actual wording of the main question to be used in measuring the effects of the transcriptions.

It should be pointed out that while Program II gave facts on *both sides* of the question, it did not give equal space to both sides, nor did it attempt to compare the case for thinking it would be a long war with the *strongest possible case* for believing it would be an easy victory and a short war. It took exactly the same stand as that taken by Program I—namely, that the war would be difficult and would require at least two years. The difference was that Program II mentioned the opposite arguments (e.g., U.S. advantages). In effect it argued that the job would be difficult, even when our advantages and the Japanese weaknesses were taken into account.

2. CONDUCT OF THE EXPERIMENT

The general plan of the experiment has been discussed in another connection in Chapter 5. The procedure was to give a preliminary "opinion survey" to determine the men's initial opinions about the Pacific War and then to remeasure their opinions at a later time, after the transcriptions had been played to them in the course of their orientation meetings. In this way the *changes* in their opinions from "before" to "after" could be determined. A control group, which heard *no* transcription, was also surveyed as a means of determining any changes in response that might occur during the time interval due to causes other than the transcriptions—such as the impact of war news from the Pacific.

Since the purpose of the study was to analyze differential effects of two kinds of content on individuals with differing initial opinions, it was desirable to obtain for analysis the maximum overall effects possible.   For this reason the effects were measured immediately after the presentation of the programs.   It is, of course, conceivable that the effects might have been even greater after a longer time interval, and further that with the longer time interval the pattern of effects might have been different from the immediate effects observed.

The preliminary survey was administered during the first week of April 1945 to eight Quartermaster training companies.   One week later eight platoons, one chosen at random from each of the eight companies, heard Program I (which presented only one side) during their individual orientation meetings.   Another group of eight platoons, similarly chosen, heard Program II (which presented both arguments).   Immediately after the program the men filled out the second questionnaire, ostensibly for the purpose of letting the people who made the program know what the men thought of it. Included in this second questionnaire, with appropriate transitional questions, were some of the same questions that had been included in the earlier survey, asking the men how they personally sized up the Pacific War.   A third group of eight platoons served as the control with no program.   They filled out a similar questionnaire, during their orientation meeting, which, in addition to asking the same questions on the Pacific War, asked preliminary questions about what they thought of their orientation meetings and what they would like in future orientation meetings.   For the control group, the latter questions—in lieu of the questions about the transcriptions—were represented to the men as the main purpose of the questionnaire.

While 24 platoons were used for this experiment, the units were at only about 70 per cent of full strength at the preliminary survey and at the orientation meetings.   The "shrinkage" was therefore quite large as to number of men present *both* times, and the sample available for "before-after" analysis was consequently small (a total of 625 men, with 214 in each experimental group and the remaining 197 men in the control group).   In view of the rapidly changing picture in the Pacific, however, it was considered inadvisable to repeat the experiment at another camp.

3. ADMINISTRATION

For proper administration of the experiment there were three major requirements: presentation of the transcriptions under realistic conditions, preventing the men in the sample from realizing that the experiment was in progress, and getting honest answers in the questionnaires. For realism in presentation, the transcriptions for the experimental groups were incorporated into the training program and scheduled as part of the weekly orientation hour. This not only insured realistic presentation but also helped to avoid indicating that effects of the transcriptions were being tested.

The preliminary "survey." The preliminary "survey" had been presented as being part of a War Department survey "to find out how a cross section of soldiers felt about various subjects connected with the war," with examples being given of previous Research Branch surveys and how the findings had been used. Questionnaires were administered to all the men in a company at once, the men being assembled in mess halls for the purpose. The questionnaires were administered by "class leaders" selected and trained for the job from among the enlisted personnel working at the camp. In an introductory explanation of the survey the class leader stressed the importance of the survey and the anonymity of the answers. No camp officers were present at these meetings and the men were assured that the surveys went directly to Washington and that no one at the camp would get a chance to see what they had written. The questionnaire used in this preliminary "survey" consisted mainly of check-list questions plus a few questions in which the men were asked to write their own answers. The content of most of the questions was the point system for demobilization and the Army's plans for redeployment. This was a convenient context for the questions that formed the measuring instrument per se which dealt with the difficulty of defeating Japan. The questions about the point system and redeployment were not necessary for the actual experimental measurements but were used to give scope to the "survey" and to prevent a concentration of items dealing with material to be covered by the transcription. This was done partly to help make the survey seem realistic to the men but mainly to avoid "sensitizing" them to questions about the topic of the subsequently presented orientation material through placing too much emphasis on it in the survey.

The second questionnaire. To prevent the men from suspecting that an "experiment" was in progress because of the administration of two questionnaires within a short space of time, the second questionnaire differed from the first one both in its form and its announced purpose. Thus the first questionnaire was given as a general War Department "survey" while the second one was given during the orientation meetings to "find out what men thought of the transcriptions" (or, in the control group, "what they thought of their orientation meetings").

An additional difference in the administration of the two questionnaires, which was also designed to reduce the appearance of similarity, was that while the first had been given by company in mess halls the second was administered by platoon in the men's barracks where the orientation meetings were held.

While the ostensible purpose in giving the men the second questionnaire was to get their opinion of the program, appropriate "tie-in" questions, such as whether or not they thought the commentator too optimistic or too pessimistic, were used to lead to the questions as to how long they thought the war would last and on the other topics concerning the difficulty of the job.

As in studies of opinion changes described in earlier chapters, it was considered necessary in the case of the present study to obtain opinions anonymously, and also to measure the effects of the program without awareness on the part of the men that an experiment was in progress. These precautions were dictated by the type of effect being studied—it was felt that if the men either thought their questionnaires were identified by name or if they knew they were being "tested," some men might give "proper" or otherwise distorted answers rather than answers expressing their true opinions in the matter.

ANALYSIS OF RESULTS

The results to be presented are based on an analysis of the responses of men whose preliminary survey could be matched with the "after" questionnaire given in the orientation meetings. Although all of the questionnaires were anonymous, the "before" and "after" questionnaires of the same individual could be matched on the basis of answers to such personal-history questions as years of schooling, date of birth, etc., with handwriting serving as an additional factor among men whose personal history was similar.

1. *Overall Effects of the Two Programs on the Marginal Distribution of Estimates of the Length of the War*

As previously stated, the main question used to evaluate the effectiveness of the two programs was a question asking men for their estimates of the probable length of the war with Japan after VE Day. The wording of this question was the same in both the "before" and the "after" questionnaire and was as follows:

> What is your guess as to how long it will probably take us to beat Japan after Germany's defeat? (Write your best guess below.)
>
> About _____ from the day of Germany's defeat.

The men's answers to this question tended to be in half-year intervals and were accordingly coded by steps of one-half year each.

A marked overall shift in an upward direction in the distribution of estimates was obtained. The results are shown below with the answers dichotomized into those estimating one-and-one-half years or less versus those estimating more than one-and-one-half years.

TABLE 1

OVERALL EFFECTS OF THE TWO PROGRAMS ON DISTRIBUTION
OF ESTIMATED LENGTH OF WAR

	PERCENTAGE ESTIMATING A WAR OF MORE THAN ONE-AND-ONE-HALF YEARS		
	Experimental groups		
	Program I "One side"	Program II "Both sides"	*Control group*
Before	37%	38%	36%
After	59	59	34
Difference	22%	21%	−2%
Probability	<.01	<.01	

The effectiveness of both programs is revealed by the marked change shown for both experimental groups (with practically no change for the control group). However, no advantage for one program over the other for the audience as a whole is revealed.

While changes in overall frequencies of response, such as those shown above, are often useful in evaluating the effectiveness of a program at achieving its educational objective, they are not usually the most sensitive measure of effects.   In the present case if the orientation objectives were specifically to prepare the men to expect a war of at least one-and-one-half years after VE Day, the above analysis does reveal the increase in the number of men holding this desired point of view.   However, an analysis of this form often conceals other effects important for a more complete description of the changes that occur.   Thus shifts occurring within the region below the point of dichotomy (e.g., from an estimate of six months to an estimate of one year) or within the region above this point (e.g., from two-and-one-half years to three years) are not revealed.   A more sensitive analysis of the overall effects is described in the next section.

2. *Analysis in Terms of Net Proportion Who Change*

Since measurements on the same men were made both before and after the programs it was possible to get each man's individual change in estimating the length of the war.   As already stated, the answers tended to be in terms of half-year units, so the minimum change occurring with a sizable frequency was a change of one-half year.   Accordingly, the results were analyzed in terms of whether a man increased or decreased his estimate—from "before" to "after" —by one-half year or more.   This analysis gets at individual shifts all along the time continuum, irrespective of whether they cross a particular cutting point along the marginal distribution.

Using this analysis procedure it was found that in all groups some men increased their estimates and others decreased their estimates. This is to be expected merely from the knowledge that most opinion questions are not perfectly reliable.   In addition, a certain amount of "turnover" of opinion is expected because of various individual experiences during the interval between the two measurements.

The results showed, however, that in the control group the positive shifts (increased estimates) were about equal in number to the negative shifts, but that in both experimental groups the positive shifts greatly exceeded the negative shifts.   These results are shown in Table 2.

Here the programs are seen to have resulted in a net proportion of *two-fifths* of the men increasing their estimates.   On the basis of the analysis procedure used in Table 1 we could only have been sure that a net of around *one-fifth* was affected.

212   C O N T R O L L E D   V A R I A T I O N   S T U D I E S

TABLE 2

Effects of the Programs in Terms of Net Proportion Changing Their Estimates

| Kind of change | PERCENTAGE WHO CHANGED THEIR ESTIMATE BY ONE-HALF YEAR OR MORE | | |
| | Experimental groups | | |
	Program I "One side"	Program II "Both sides"	Control group
No change	46%	45%	63%
Increased estimate	47	47	18
Decreased estimate	7	8	19
Net change (increase minus decrease)	40	39	−1
Net effect (experimental change minus control change)	41	40	
*Probability**	*<.01*	*<.01*	

* The method for determining the significance level of the "net effect" utilizes the fact that the net *change* for each group is the difference between two mutually exclusive proportions in the same sample—namely, the proportion P_1 who gave an increased estimate and the proportion P_2 who gave a decreased estimate. The net *effect*, is the difference between two such differences—i.e., the difference between the net change for an experimental group and that for the control group. Its standard error is given by the formula:

$$\text{Est. } \sigma_{\text{diff} - \text{diff}} = \sqrt{[P_1 + P_2 - (P_1 - P_2)^2]\left[\frac{1}{N_E} + \frac{1}{N_C}\right]}$$

where P_1 and P_2 are the above stated proportions computed for the experimental and control groups *combined*, and N_E and N_C are the N's for the experimental and control groups. (See Appendix, B, pp. 303-304.)

3. Effects of the Programs on Men Initially Opposing and Initially Favoring the Commentator's Conclusion

The results already reported indicate no greater effectiveness of either program on the audience *as a whole*. However, as mentioned earlier, a critical feature in the theory underlying the experiment was the expectation of adverse effects of the "one-sided" program on men initially opposing the commentator's view that the war would take at least two years after VE Day. In line with the theory, therefore, the results were analyzed separately for men who initially opposed and those who initially favored the stand taken by the programs. The basis for distinguishing these two groups was whether their initial estimate of the length of the war in the "before" questionnaire was, respectively, less than two years, or was two years or more. The measure used in the analysis was the "net effect" described in the previous section for changes of one-half year or more.

82   PART II. MESSAGE

The net effects of the two ways of presenting the orientation material are shown below for these two subgroups of men; those initially estimating a war of less than two years (the "opposed" group) and those initially estimating a war of two or more years (the "favorable" group). Control results are omitted for simplicity since the present concern is with comparing the two programs, both of which had the same control.

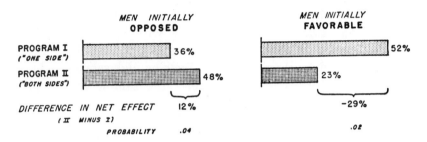

Figure 1.   Differential effects of the two programs on men initially opposing and men initially favoring the commentator's position.
See supplementary Table A, p. 226, for subgroup *N*'s and control results.

The above chart shows that the *net effects* were different for the two ways of presenting the orientation material, depending on the initial stand of the listener. The program giving some of the U.S. advantages in addition to the difficulties was more effective for men initially opposed, that is, for men who, contrary to the programs, expected a war of less than two years. On the other hand, the program giving the one-sided picture was more effective for men initially favoring the stand taken, that is, for the men who agreed with the point of view of the programs that the war would take at least two years. The initial division of opinion was roughly three men opposing to every man favoring the stand taken, but since the differential effect was greater in the latter group the overall net effects on the men as a whole were almost equal for the two programs.[1]

4. Effects on Men with Different Amounts of Education

In line with theoretical considerations and data presented in Chapters 4 and 6, it would be expected that the better educated men would be less affected by a conspicuously one-sided presentation and would conversely be more likely to accept the arguments of a pres-

---

[1] The statistical test used to assess the reliability of the differential effects is exactly analogous to that used in the previous section. In the above case, however, the control is not involved since the experimental subgroups can be directly compared.

entation that appears to take all factors into account in arriving at a conclusion. On the other hand, the consideration of both sides of an issue could weaken the immediate force of the argument for the less well educated insofar as they are less critical and more likely to be impressed by the strength of the one-sided argument without thinking of objections.

When the results were broken down according to educational level, it was found that the program which presented both sides was more effective with better educated men and that the program which presented one side was more effective with less educated men. Figure 2 shows results comparing the effects on men who did not graduate from high school with the effects on high school graduates. This breakdown by education divides the sample into approximately equal halves.

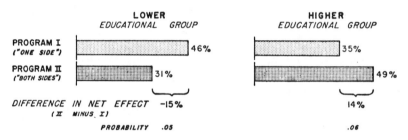

Figure 2. Differential effects of the two programs on men of different educational backgrounds.
See supplementary Table B, p. 226, for detailed computations.

The above results show that the program giving both sides had *less* effect on the nongraduates but *more* effect on the high school graduates.

5. *Effects When Both Education and Initial Estimates Are Considered*

The interesting question arises as to how initial position on the issue presented by the transcription is related to effects among men in each educational group. Definitive results on this point could not be obtained because of the small number of cases involved when the sample is broken into the eight subgroups required for this analysis. The data available are presented, however, to indicate the trends and to suggest a hypothesis deserving further study: that the argument giving both sides is more effective among the better educated regardless of initial position whereas the one-sided presentation is primarily effective with those who are already convinced among the less well educated group (Figure 3).

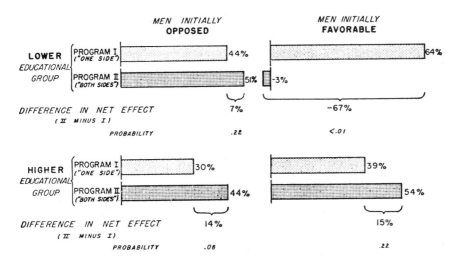

Figure 3.   Differential effects of the two programs on men initially opposing and men initially favoring the commentator's position, shown separately for men with different education.
    See supplementary Table C, p. 227, for detailed computations.

The conclusions suggested by the pattern of results presented thus far may be summarized as follows: Giving the strong points for the "other side" can make a presentation more effective at getting across its message, at least for the better educated men and for those who are already opposed to the stand taken.   This difference in effectiveness, however, may be reversed for the less educated men and, in the extreme case, the material giving both sides may have a negative effect on poorly educated men already convinced of the major position taken by a program.   From these results it would be expected that the total effect of either kind of program on the group as a whole would depend on the group's educational composition and on the initial division of opinion in the group.   Thus, ascertaining this information about the composition of an audience might be of considerable value in choosing the most effective type of presentation.

6. *Men's Evaluation of the Factual Coverage*

One factor that should tend to make a presentation taking into account both sides of an issue more effective than a presentation covering only one side is that the men might believe the former treatment to be more impartial and authoritative.

In the present study, however, the group as a whole did not consider the factual coverage more complete in the program giving U.S. advantages in addition to the difficulties faced. This is illustrated below.[2]

Per cent of men saying that the program did a good job of giving the facts on the Pacific War

Program I ("one side")	61%
Program II ("both sides")	54

Per cent of men saying that the program took all of the important facts into account

Program I ("one side")	48%
Program II ("both sides")	42

It can be seen above that the factual coverage was not considered better in the program giving U.S. advantages as well as the difficulties. The difference obtained was in the opposite direction, although not reliably so. Essentially the same results were obtained for each of the two educational subgroups analyzed.

The explanation of this unexpected result apparently lies in the fact that both programs omitted any mention of Russia as a factor in the Pacific War, and *this omission seemed more glaring in the presentation that committed itself to covering both sides of the question.* This somewhat paradoxical conclusion is well supported by results to be shown shortly and while it was not anticipated it is quite understandable in retrospect.

At the time that the Pacific War was chosen as the orientation subject for the experiment it was recognized that a weakness of this topic was that under existing informational policy no stand could be taken on the help to be expected from Russia. Thus maximum content difference between the two presentations could not be achieved because they *both* had to omit mention of an important argument on the "other side," namely, that Russia might enter the war against the Japanese. It was not anticipated, however, that

---

[2] The N's on which these percentages are based are 214 for Program I and 214 for Program II.

this omission would be more noticeable in the program that otherwise covered both sides.   That this actually happened was indicated by the men's answers to the "write-in" question: "What facts or topics that you think are important in the war with Japan are not mentioned in the program?"   The percentages writing in that aid or possible aid from Russia was not mentioned are shown below.

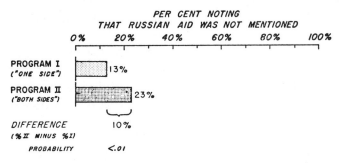

Figure 4.   Frequency with which the omission of the topic of Russian aid was noted by the men.

As shown above, almost twice as many men mentioned the omission of Russia in the program covering "both sides."   The difference was even more pronounced among *groups that would be expected to be especially sensitive to this omission*, such as men who were initially optimistic about the length of the war, men with more education, and men who had indicated in the "before" questionnaire that they expected a great deal of help from Russia in the job against Japan.

7. *Relative Effectiveness of the Two Programs on Men Most Likely to Note the Omission of the Topic of Russian Aid*

In the preceding section it was shown that the program giving "both sides" was *not* considered more adequate than the one-sided program in its factual coverage and that it caused more men to note that Russia was not mentioned.   The question now to be considered is whether this actually detracted from the effectiveness of this program that otherwise took all factors into consideration.   A direct answer to this question cannot be given, but indirect evidence indicates that the omission did detract from this program's effectiveness.

The indirect evidence comes from a separate analysis of the results among men who initially opposed the point of view of the commentator.   These were the men for whom the program giving both sides was more effective, even with the omission of the topic of Russian aid. The question is, would it have been still more effective if this topic could have been included? To get evidence on this question this subgroup of opposed men was further subdivided according to whether or not they were predisposed to note the omission of Russia. The logic of the analysis was that men especially sensitive to the omission (because they were opposed and thought Russia might help) would not accept the commentator's argument, whereas those men who were opposed to his position but did *not* have Russian aid as one of their own important arguments for a short war would show less detrimental effect of the omission. The following question in the "before" questionnaire was used to subdivide the initially opposed men into those anticipating and those not anticipating substantial aid from Russia.

"How much help do you think America will get from other countries when it comes to the job of defeating the Japs?" (Check one)

_____ very little
_____ some, but not a great deal
_____ a great deal   (Which countries? _____)

The breakdown on this question among "opposed" men put about two-fifths of the men in the "sensitive" subgroup, that is, about two-fifths of the "opposed" men said they expected a great deal of help and *wrote in Russia* as one of the countries from which they expected a great deal of help.

When these subgroups of the "opposed" men were compared it was found that the men who counted on a great deal of help from Russia gave a relatively poorer evaluation of the factual coverage in the program giving "both sides" and were relatively less influenced in the direction of increasing their estimates of the probable length of the war.

The results for the men's evaluation of the factual coverage, based on two items, are shown in Figure 5.

The implication of the results in Figure 5 is that the authenticity of the program which presented both sides suffered from the omission of the subject of Russia. Men who counted on Russian aid had a lower evaluation of the factual coverage of this program than of the one-sided program.

The presumption from this indirect evidence is that if the program covering both sides had dealt with the subject of Russia, it might have been considered more complete in its factual coverage, particu-

larly among men who expected Russian aid.   This inference receives corroboration from the fact that in a fairly large-scale pretest
of the two programs, conducted at a time when possible aid from
Russia was a less important news topic, the program covering "both
sides" had been found to be *reliably more accepted* in its factual cov-

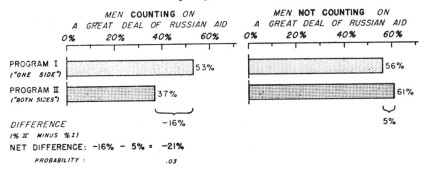

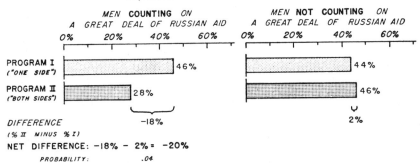

Figure 5.   Differences in evaluation of factual coverage in the two programs, *among men opposed to the commentator's position*, comparing those who did and those who did not count on Russian aid.

For subgroup *N*'s, see supplementary Table D, p. 227.

erage, just the reverse of the results shown on page 216.   This pretest was conducted with a sample of 347 Infantry reinforcements in
March 1945 and practically no difference was obtained between the
two programs in the percentages of men noting the omission of
Russian aid.   In the present study, however, the programs were
played during the second week of April, about a week after the Rus-
sians announced that they would not renew their nonaggression
pact with Japan.

Not only did the omission of the topic of Russia affect men's evaluation of the factual coverage in Program II in the subgroups above, but it may have reduced the effect of the program on the men's estimates of the length of the war.   This is suggested by an analysis of the net effects of the programs on opinions of the men in the same subgroups as those used in Figure 5.   The results of this analysis are shown in Figure 6.

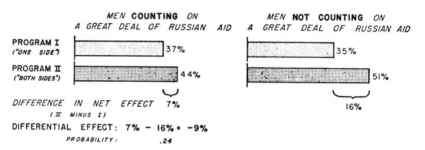

Figure 6.   Differential relative effect of the two programs among men initially opposed but differing as to whether they had counted on a great deal of help from Russia. See supplementary Table D, p. 227, for *N*'s and control group results.

These results are in line with the expectation that among the men for whom the presentation with both sides is most effective (i.e., the men initially opposing the idea of a two-year war) the advantage of the "both-sides" presentation was less among those counting on a great deal of help from Russia than among those not expecting much help.   The differential effect is too small to be reliable with the small number of cases involved in the above subgroups, but they are consonant with the interpretation that the effects of the program giving some of the "other side" would have been even greater on those opposed to the stand taken if *all* of the other side could have been covered.

All of the results dealing with the omission of the topic of Russian aid seem to support one important conclusion, namely, that if a presentation supporting a particular conclusion attempts to take both sides of the issue into account, it must include *all* of the important negative arguments; otherwise the presentation may "boomerang" by failing to live up to the expectation of impartiality and completeness.

Apparently the fact that the commentator in giving "both sides" indicated that he was trying to take *all* factors into consideration in drawing his conclusion prepared the men to expect the inclusion of possible Russian aid as one of the factors to be considered.   Thus the omission in the context of considering all factors stood out more than in the context of the one-sided program where only the difficulties were being considered.   The general conclusion seems to be that a one-sided presentation in which the conclusion is stated in advance and the reasons for this conclusion are then given will be accepted as the argument for a given point of view without much loss of authenticity resulting from failure to cover the other side.   However, if a presentation commits itself to taking everything into account, either by announcing this in advance or by actually covering parts of each side of the issue, it will seem less authentic than a single-sided presentation if any important facts known to the audience are not included in the discussion, and its effectiveness at changing opinions will be reduced among those who are most aware of the point omitted.

8. *Relation of the Results to the Contention That the Initially Opposed Will Be Negatively Affected*

The results of this experiment have an obvious bearing on the frequently made assertion that "propaganda" merely reinforces the opinions already held, i.e., that those initially favoring a point of view tend to be made more favorable, whereas those initially opposed may tend to become even more opposed than at the outset.[3] This would be predicted on the grounds that a person is receptive to arguments having the conclusion he himself has already reached, but that arguments counter to a strongly held opinion serve as the occasion for an individual to rehearse the arguments favoring his side, to think up new arguments to combat the ones presented, to "get his ego involved" in his position, and so forth.

In all of the results shown comparing the net effects of the programs on men "initially opposing" the point of view presented by the commentator, it will be observed that "opposed" men were influenced in the direction of the "message" presented rather than against it.   Thus regardless of educational level or expectation of aid from Russia the "opposed" men were influenced to accept the point of view of the commentator with either program.   This is definitely contrary to the contention that "propaganda" merely reinforces existing beliefs.[4]

[3] Cf. e.g., Murphy, G., L. B. Murphy and T. M. Newcomb, *Experimental Social Psychology* (rev. ed.) New York: Harper, 1937., p. 874f. and 963f.

[4] A word should also be said concerning the interpretations here placed on such expressions as "more opposed."   The frequently stressed distinction between "intensity" of opinion and "content" or "direction" of opinion is relevant to this interpretation. Thus, changes in the direction of "more favorable" or "more opposed" might refer either to changes in the direction of a more extreme position on a content continuum, or to greater intensity of feeling on a given position, or both.   However, the present discussion is limited to the former kind of change because of the absence of adequate measures of intensity.

It might be contended that in the results shown so far the men in the "opposed" group were not sufficiently opposed for the alleged phenomenon to be revealed.   Thus the opposed group contained a sizable proportion who were close to the borderline of two years in their estimate of the length of the war and these could not be said to be very strongly opposed.   But a finer breakdown of initial estimate reveals the same general result.   This is shown below in Table 3 which shows net effects as a function of initial position for less broad categories than those used so far.   The most opposed group possible with the coding used—that is, the group estimating a war of less than six months—is not shown because the number of cases was so small; only about one man in twenty fell in this category. However, even in this tiny group the results come out in the same direction.   The results presented are for both programs combined.

TABLE 3

THE EFFECTS OF RADIO TRANSCRIPTIONS ON OPINIONS ABOUT DURATION OF WAR, FOR THOSE WITH VARIOUS INITIAL OPINIONS

	NET PERCENTAGE CHANGING ESTIMATE BY ONE-HALF YEAR OR MORE AMONG MEN WHOSE INITIAL ESTIMATE WAS:			
	Less than 1 year	*1 year up to 1½ years*	*1½ years up to 2 years*	*2 years or more*
Net change in experimental groups	58%	53%	26%	2%
Net change in the control group	20	6	−12	−34
Net effects	38	47	38	36

It will be seen that the familiar "regression" phenomenon occurs in the control group, that is, because of the imperfect reliability of the question on length of the war the men who initially made long estimates tend to make shorter ones and the men who initially made short estimates tend to make longer ones.[5]   The changes due to regression as indicated by the changes in the control group must be subtracted from the changes in the experimental group to obtain the net effect of the program, shown in the third line of figures in Table 3.

It can be seen from the net effects shown in Table 3 that even with the finer breakdown of initial estimate, all of the subgroups

[5] This regression phenomenon, which may be unfamiliar to some readers, is discussed in Appendix D, p. 329ff.

were influenced in the direction of revising their estimates upward. This was true even of the men with the most extreme opposition—that is, men whose initial estimate was only one year or less.

These results are consistent with the results of analyses of data obtained in other studies reported in this volume. Several analyses were made in connection with the orientation film studies to see how opinion change was related to initial opinion. In all cases it was found that men initially opposed to a particular opinion were nevertheless influenced in the same direction as the men as a whole rather than being driven further in the direction of their original position. An example of such an analysis is adduced here to illustrate the general conclusion.

A scale of five opinion items was used to measure confidence in the "British War Effort" in the before-after study of "The Battle of Britain." This gave six categories of initial response according to whether the individual accepted none of the opinions expressed, one of them, and so on up to accepting *all five*. For the analysis, all men in the film group were sorted into these six categories as determined from their responses on the questionnaire administered *before* the film. The mean scale value for the "after" responses of each of these six subgroups was then determined, and these values compared with similar values for the control group. The mean changes for film and control groups are shown in the tabulation below.

Again we see the phenomenon of regression toward the mean in the control group. Thus men whose initial scale position was 0 re-

TABLE 4

MEAN CHANGE IN SCALE VALUES FOR FILM AND CONTROL SUBGROUPS
GETTING EACH SCALE SCORE BEFORE THE FILM

(SCALE OF 5 OPINION-ITEMS CONCERNING "BRITISH WAR EFFORT")

| | INITIAL SCALE POSITION | | | | | |
	0 (opposing)	1	2	3	4	5 (favoring)
Mean after-minus-before differences for those with each initial position:						
Film group	1.14	0.93	0.35	0.17	−0.10	−0.44
Control group	0.70	0.34	0.15	−0.45	−0.84	−0.91
Film-control difference	.44	.59	.20	.62	.74	.45

gressed *up* to an average of .70 and men whose initial scale position was 5 regressed *down* to an average value of 4.09. But just as in the study of the radio programs *all* groups were affected in the direction of accepting the "message" of the communication, even the most extreme subgroup that had initially been so anti-British that they did not check a single response favorable to the British in the five items making up the British war effort scale.

It may be further argued that the contention that opposed men would be made more opposed applies not to the extremeness of their content position but rather to the intensity with which they hold their opinion or the extent of emotional involvement in supporting their point of view. No answer is available from the present studies on this interpretation of degree of opposition because measurements of intensity of feeling independent of content were not feasible. To the extent, however, that intensity and content are correlated, the present study and all other analyses that were made show negative results regardless of how "opposition" is defined for the type of communication investigated.

This qualification concerning the type of communications investigated is made because it seems theoretically possible that opposition would be fostered with some kinds of "propaganda." This seems especially likely for face-to-face situations in which the communicator and the communicatee become involved in a give-and-take argument. In such a case the individual who constitutes the "audience" himself takes a stand and is likely to have more "ego involvement," actively to seek new arguments in support of his position, and so forth. A similar situation would be the debate form of communication in which there is a protagonist for each side of the issue. If the audience is initially divided in opinion on the issue individual audience members would be expected to identify with the protagonist representing their own initial stand, and a situation similar to the face-to-face argument is created.[6]

9. *Summary of Results*

(1) Presenting the arguments on both sides of an issue was found to be more effective than giving only the arguments supporting the

---

[6] Exposure to debates has been shown to strengthen the initial opinions of those audience members initially expressing an opinion and to reduce the neutral, no-opinion category by shifting some people in one direction and others in the opposite direction. (Cf. Millson, W. A. D., "Problems in Measuring Audience Reaction," *Quart. J. Speech*, 1932, *18*, 621–37.)

point being made, in the case of individuals who were *initially op-posed* to the point of view being presented.

(2) For men who were *already convinced* of the point of view being presented, however, the inclusion of arguments on both sides was less effective, for the group as a whole, than presenting only the arguments favoring the general position being advocated.

(3) Better educated men were more favorably affected by presentation of both sides; less well educated men were more affected by the communication which used only supporting arguments.

(4) The group for which the presentation giving both sides was least effective was the group of poorly educated men who were already convinced of the point of view being advocated.

(5) An important incidental finding was that the absence of one relevant argument against the stand taken by the programs was more noticeable in the presentation using arguments on both sides than in the presentation in which only one side was discussed.   Furthermore, advantage of the program giving both sides among men initially opposed was less for those who regarded the omitted argument as an important one.

(6) Men who were initially very opposed to the point of view being presented—as measured by their deviation in *content* from the position taken by the communication—were nevertheless influenced to alter their opinion in the direction of the "message" rather than being shifted further in the direction of their initial opinion.

SUPPLEMENTARY TABLE A

BREAKDOWN OF CHANGES IN ESTIMATES AMONG MEN INITIALLY FAVORING
AND MEN INITIALLY OPPOSING THE STAND TAKEN

	PER CENT OF MEN					
	PROGRAM I "one side"		*PROGRAM II* "both sides"		*CONTROL* no program	
	initial estimate		*initial estimate*		*initial estimate*	
	Less than 2	2 or more	Less than 2	2 or more	Less than 2	2 or more
No change	45	46	41	56	65	56
Revised estimate upward	50	36	58	16	22	5
Revised estimate downward	5	18	1	27	13	39
Net change (% up minus % down)	45	18	57	−11	9*	−34*
Control net change*	9	−34	9	−34		
Net effect (program net minus control)	36	52	48	23		
Number of cases in each subgroup**	152	45	150	55	140	41

* The net changes in the two subgroups of the *control* represent the familiar "regression" phenomenon due to unreliable test answers. (See p. 329ff., Appendix D.) The greater degree of regression in the subgroups estimating a war of 2 or more years is accounted for by the extent of their deviation from the average estimate of less than 1½ years.

** The numbers of cases given here add to 583 instead of the total of 625 men studied because the analysis could not include the 42 individuals who failed to write legible estimates of the length of the war in either the "before" or the "after" survey. The omission of such individuals applies also to the three following tables.

SUPPLEMENTARY TABLE B

BREAKDOWN OF CHANGES IN ESTIMATES AMONG MEN
WITH DIFFERING EDUCATION

| | PER CENT OF MEN | | | | | |
| EDUCATION: | *Non-graduates* | | | *High school graduates* | | |
PROGRAM:	I ("One side")	II ("Both sides")	Control	I ("One side")	II ("Both sides")	Control
No change	40	45	64	51	45	62
Revised estimate upward	54	44	19	40	50	17
Revised estimate downward	6	11	17	9	5	21
Net change	48	33	2	31	45	−4
Control net change	2	2		−4	−4	
Net effect (program net minus control)	46	31		35	49	
Number of cases in each subgroup*	93	105	104	104	100	77

* See second footnote to Table A.

SUPPLEMENTARY TABLE C

BREAKDOWN OF CHANGES IN ESTIMATES IN THE SUBGROUPS SEPARATED BOTH
ACCORDING TO INITIAL ESTIMATE AND ACCORDING TO EDUCATION

	PER CENT OF MEN							
EDUCATION:	Non-graduates				High school graduates			
INITIAL ESTIMATE:	Less than 2 years		2 or more years		Less than 2 years		2 or more years	
PROGRAM:	I "One side"	II "Both sides"	I "One side"	II "Both sides"	I "One side"	II "Both sides"	I "One side"	II "Both sides"
No change	35	40	52	57	53	41	41	56
Revised estimate upward	59	60	39	3	43	56	32	32
Revised estimate downward	6	—	9	40	4	3	27	12
Net change	53	−60	30	−37	39	53	5	20
Control net change*	−9	9	−34	−34	9	9	−34	−34
Net effect	44	51	64	−3	30	44	39	54
Number of cases in each subgroup**	70	75	23	30	82	75	22	25

* The control net change used above to eliminate the effects of regression is the same as that used in Table A. This procedure assumes that regression was the same at the two educational levels, but it was considered a better estimate than could be obtained from the small separate subgroups of the control. In any case, chief interest is attached to the *differences* between the effects of the two programs; these differences are independent of the estimate of regression used.
** See second footnote to Table A.

SUPPLEMENTARY TABLE D

BREAKDOWN OF CHANGES IN ESTIMATES, AMONG MEN INITIALLY OPPOSED TO
THE STAND TAKEN, FOR THOSE WHO HAD AND THOSE WHO HAD NOT
COUNTED ON A GREAT DEAL OF HELP FROM RUSSIA

| | PER CENT OF MEN | | | | | |
| | Men who had counted on a great deal of help from Russia | | | Men who had not counted on a great deal of help from Russia | | |
	Program I "One side"	Program II "Both sides"	Control	Program I "One side"	Program II "Both sides"	Control
No change	46	48	66	45	34	64
Revised estimate upward	50	52	21	50	63	23
Revised estimate downward	5	0	13	5	2	13
Net change	45	52	8	45	61	10
Control net change	8	8		10	10	
Net effect (program net minus control)	37	44		35	51	
Number of cases in each subgroup	66	71	62	86	79	78

Primary — Recency

An interesting experiment by Chester Insko extends the Hovland, Lumsdaine, and Sheffield findings and yields valuable additional information about the effects of presenting one side versus both sides of an issue. Insko used the prosecution and defense arguments in a summarized law case to provide his experimental communications. By so doing, he reasoned that his subjects would have no prior familiarity with the issues involved. He then sought to determine the normative behavior corresponding to four different combinations of communications and countercommunications. Insko found that when a one-sided communication was followed by a one-sided countercommunication, opinions were no more influenced by the first than by the last communication. (If the communications were equally strong, perhaps the the first communication moved the subjects' opinions a given amount in one direction, while the last communication moved their opinions the same amount in the opposite direction. As a result, their final opinions would have ended up right where they began.) Insko also observed that when a two-sided communication was followed by a two-sided communication, again final opinions did not reflect any greater reaction to the first than to the last two-sided communication. However, when a one-sided was followed by a two-sided communication, subjects responded more to the two-sided communication. When the sequence was reversed, i.e., two-sided followed by one-sided, subjects again were influenced more by the two-sided communication.[1]

What is there about two-sided communications which may make them more potent than one-sided communications? Although we shall pursue this point in greater detail in Part III (pp. 255 ff.), it can be noted here that the two-sided message, *because* it straddles both sides of the question, may inadvertently have the effect of "inoculating"

---

[1] Insko, C. A. One-sided versus two-sided communications and countercommunications. *J. abnorm. soc. Psychol.*, 1962, **65**, 203–206. Even though one might speculate that subjects would be skeptical about a communication in which one side essentially contradicted the other, Wrench has found that people will accept a high degree of internal "contradiction" in a two-sided message before they become incredulous. Wrench, D. F. The perception of two-sided messages. *Human Relat.*, 1964, **17**, 227–233.

recipients against subsequent communication which is counter to their beliefs.[2] The two-sided communication, subjecting the individual as it does to arguments which both support *and* attack his beliefs, may serve to forewarn him of the kind of arguments he subsequently could encounter. Thus, it would have the effect of reinforcing, or bolstering, his original beliefs, thereby leaving him even more resistant to counterpersuasion than he was initially.[3]

An even more intriguing question is one that originally was posed by the social psychologist F. H. Lund more than forty years ago: If both sides of a controversial issue are presented successively, which has the advantage—the side presented first or the side presented last? (When the first side has the greater impact, we call this *primacy*. When the last side is more effective, we call this *recency*.) In an experiment intended to answer this question, Lund presented mimeographed, counterbalanced communications to groups of college students. Each communication argued the pro's and con's of such issues as "whether all men should have equal political rights, whether the protective tariff is a wise policy for the United States, and whether monogamous marriage will continue to be the only socially accepted relation between the sexes." The students completed an opinion questionnaire two days before the communications and again immediately after each communication. Lund observed that when the students received both sides of an issue, the side presented first consistently had an advantage over the side presented last. On the basis of this observation he enunciated the controversial principle we know today as the "law of primacy in persuasion."[4]

Subsequent investigation appeared first to confirm but then to refute the primacy principle. Knower, using communications pro- and antiprohibition, noted that ". . . primacy in the order of reading influenced the amount and possibly the direction of change in attitude which occurred in the group."[5] On the other hand, the possibility that Lund may have overstated his law is suggested by the opposite re-

---

[2]Lumsdaine, A. A., & Janis, I. L. Resistance to counterpropaganda produced by a one-sided versus a two-sided propaganda presentation. *Publ. Opin. quart.*, 1953, **17**, 311–318.

[3]In fact, Sears observes that individuals who have been exposed to only one side of the question often actually seek exposure to the other side. Presumably, a confident decision requires an evaluation of both sides. Sears, D. O. Opinion formation and information preferences in an adversary situation. *J. exp. soc. Psychol.*, 1966, **2**, 130–142.

[4]Lund, F. H. The psychology of belief: A study of its emotional and volitional determinants. *J. abnorm. soc. Psychol.*, 1925, **20**, 174–196.

[5]Knower, F. H. Experimental studies of changes in attitudes: II. A study of the effect of printed argument on changes in attitude. *J. abnorm. soc. Psychol.*, 1936, **30**, 522–532.

sults obtained by Cromwell. Instead of primacy, Cromwell found that recency was the dominating factor.[6]

But it was not until the late 1950's when Hovland and his associates published the now well-known *The Order of Presentation in Persuasion,* that systematic study of the primacy-recency problem began in earnest.[7] In a paper first presented in 1952 at an Eastern Psychological Association meeting, but which attracted wider attention when it was published in *"The Order of Presentation,"* Hovland and Wallace Mandell repeated Lund's experiment. Presenting, as Lund had done, posttest questionnaires after each communication, the investigators were unable to produce any consistent order effects with the Lund communications. When they substituted topics of more current interest, three of four treatment groups yielded recency.[8] These findings, in apparent contradiction to Lund's, led Hovland to conclude that "when two sides of an issue are presented successively by different communicators, the side presented first does not necessarily have the advantage."[9]

In recent years, the primacy-recency problem has become the object of increased attention. Instead of a general "law" of primacy, or recency, we have today an assortment of miscellaneous variables, some of which tend to produce primacy ("primacy-bound variables"), others of which, to produce recency ("recency-bound variables"). Still others produce either order effect, depending on their utilization or temporal placement in a two-sided communication ("free variables").

Nonsalient,[10] controversial topics,[11] interesting subject matter,[12]

---

[6] Cromwell, H. The relative effect on audience attitude of the first versus the second argumentative speech of a series. *Speech Monogr.,* 1950, **17**, 105–122.

[7] Hovland, C. I., Mandell, W., Campbell, E. H., Brock, T. C., Luchins, A. S., Cohen, A. R., McGuire, W. J., Janis, I. L., Feierabend, R. L., & Anderson, N. H. *The order of presentation in persuasion.* New Haven, Conn.: Yale Univer. Press, 1957.

[8] Hovland, C. I., & Mandell, W. Is there a 'law of primacy in persuasion'? In C. I. Hovland (Ed.), *The order of presentation in persuasion.* New Haven, Conn.: Yale Univer. Press, 1957. Pp. 13–22.

[9] Hovland, C. I. *et al. The order of presentation in persuasion.* New Haven, Conn.: Yale Univer. Press, 1957. P. 130.

[10] Rosnow, R. L., & Goldstein, J. H. Familiarity, salience, and the order of presentation of communications. *J. soc. Psychol.,* in press.

[11] Lana, R. E. Controversy of the topic and the order of presentation in persuasive communications. *Psychol. Rep.,* 1963, **12**, 163–170. Lana, R. E., & Rosnow, R. L. Subject awareness and order effects in persuasive communications. *Psychol. Rep.,* 1963, **12**, 523–529.

[12] Lana, R. E. Interest, media, and order effects in persuasive communications. *J. Psychol.,* 1963, **56**, 9–13.

and highly familiar issues[13] tend toward primacy. Salient topics,[14] uninteresting subject matter,[15] and moderately unfamiliar issues[16] tend to yield recency. If arguments for one side are perceived more strongly than arguments for the other, then the side with the stronger arguments has the advantage[17] — "strength" being a free variable. Another free variable is "reinforcement." When incidents that are perceived as rewarding or satisfying are initiated close in time to a persuasive communication, opinions tend to change in the direction of the arguments closer to the rewarding incident. When an incident is dissatisfying, or punishing, opinions tend to change in the direction of the arguments farther in time from it.[18]

Other variables in two-sided communication affect the amount of opinion change. For example, if a message containing information relevant to the satisfaction of a need were presented after the need had been aroused, there would be greater acceptance of the position advocated than if need arousal followed presentation of the message.[19] Also, greater opinion change would result if highly desirable information were presented first, followed by less desirable information, than if the sequence were reversed.[20] So, if we wanted to sell Whiz detergent, first we would make the housewife aware of her "dishpan

[13]Lana, R. E. Familiarity and the order of presentation of persuasive communications. *J. abnorm. soc. Psychol.*, 1961, **62**, 573–577.

[14]Rosnow, R. L., & Goldstein, J. H. Familiarity, salience, and the order of presentation of communications. *J. soc. Psychol.*, in press.

[15]Lana, R. E. Interest, media, and order effects in persuasive communications. *J. Psychol.*, 1963, **56**, 9–13.

[16]Lana, R. E. Familiarity and the order of presentation of persuasive communications. *J. abnorm. soc. Psychol.*, 1961, **62**, 573–577. Rosnow, R. L., & Lana, R. E. Complementary and competing-order effects in persuasive communication. *J. soc. Psychol.*, 1965, **66**, 201–207.

[17]Rosnow, R. L., Holz, R. F., & Levin, J. Differential effects of complementary and competing variables in primacy-recency. *J. soc. Psychol.*, 1966, **69**, 135–147.

[18]Rosnow, R. L., & Russell, G. Spread of effect of reinforcement in persuasive communication. *Psychol. Rep.*, 1963, **12**, 731–735. Rosnow, R. L. A delay-of-reinforcement effect in persuasive communication? *J. soc. Psychol.*, 1965, **67**, 39–43. Rosnow, R. L. 'Conditioning' the direction of opinion change in persuasive communication. *J. soc. Psychol.*, 1966, **69**, 291–303. Corrozi, J. F., & Rosnow, R. L. Consonant and dissonant communications as positive and negative reinforcements in opinion change. *J. Pers. soc. Psychol.*, in press.

[19]Cohen, A. R. Need for cognition and order of communication as determinants of opinion change. In C. I. Hovland *et al.* (Eds.), *The order of presentation in persuasion*. New Haven, Conn.: Yale Univer. Press, 1957. Pp. 79–97.

[20]McGuire, W. J. Order of presentation as a factor in 'conditioning' persuasiveness. In C. I. Hovland *et al.* (Eds.), *The order of presentation in persuasion*. New Haven, Conn.: Yale Univer. Press, 1957. Pp. 98–114.

hands." Then we would show her how Whiz "whizzes away the red-ness and rawness." We would save for last the tidbit that Whiz "costs a little more than other leading brands."

Despite the growing number of empirical findings about the causes of primacy and recency in persuasion (and the research on incremental and decremental factors in two-sided communication),[21] the various attempts to fit those diverse relationships into a theoretical framework have not met with much success.[22] Just as there are different variables capable of producing the same effect, there are different theoretical explanations for those relationships. However, the papers that follow represent two of the most impressive efforts at establishing a parsi-monious framework within which to predict order effects in per-suasion.[23]

The first paper, by Norman H. Anderson, was written while the author was a visiting assistant professor at Yale in 1957–58. His work with Carl Hovland on a mathematical model for predicting primacy-recency effects led to the research that is reported here.[24] The model rests on the assumption that the more opinion change asked for, the more received.[25] Hence, if two successive communications produce

---

[21] A review and classification of most of the variables to date associated with primacy and recency in persuasion is contained in Rosnow, R. L. Whatever happened to the 'law of primacy'? *J. Communication*, 1966, **16**, 10–31.

[22] See reviews by McGuire and Lana. McGuire, W. J. Attitudes and opinions. *Annu. Rev. Psychol.*, 1966, **17**, 487–490. Lana, R. E. Three theoretical interpretations of order effects in persuasive communications. *Psychol. Bull.*, 1964, **61**, 314–320.

[23] Other interesting theoretical schemes have been developed by Schultz using a sensory variation framework, and Asch-Anderson-Barrios-Luchins using *Einstellung*, or "set," theory to predict order effects. McGuire has derived predictions from rein-forcement theory, and Crockett has focused on audience variables in his work relating "cognitive complexity" and primacy-recency. See Schultz, D. P. Primary-recency within a sensory variation framework. *Psychol. Rec.*, 1963, **13**, 129–139. Asch, S. E. Forming impressions of personality. *J. abnorm. soc. Psychol.*, 1946, **41**, 258–290. Anderson, N. H., & Barrios, A. A. Primacy effects in personality impression formation. *J. abnorm. soc. Psychol.*, 1961, **63**, 346–350. Luchins, A. S. Definitiveness of impres-sion and primacy-recency in communications. *J. soc. Psychol.*, 1958, **48**, 275–290. McGuire, W. J. Order of presentation as a factor in 'conditioning' persuasiveness. In C. I. Hovland *et al.* (Eds.), *The order of presentation in persuasion.* New Haven, Conn.: Yale Univer. Press, 1957. Pp. 98–114. Crockett, W. H. Cognitive complexity and im-pression formation. In B. A. Maher (Ed.), *Progress in experimental personality re-search.* Vol. 2. New York: Academic Press, 1965. Pp. 70–81.

[24] Anderson, N. H., & Hovland, C. I. The representation of order effects in communi-cation research. In C. I. Hovland (Ed.), *The order of presentation in persuasion.* New Haven, Conn.: Yale Univer. Press, 1957. Pp. 158–169.

[25] It will be noted later (pp. 405 ff.) that as a result of this assumption, Anderson's model probably applies more to lower than to higher ego-involving topics.

proportionally the same amount of opinion change, the second communication should always have the advantage. This is because the first communication would move opinions a given amount, thereby increasing the attitudinal distance between the recipient and the second communication. If the second communication were proportionally as effective as the first, then, because it demanded more opinion change, it would have the effect of producing greater change.

The second study, by Norman Miller and Donald T. Campbell, is particularly interesting because the model they describe derives from the work carried out by Hermann Ebbinghaus well before the turn of the century. It is fascinating to realize that even though Ebbinghaus' studies were conducted at a time when behavioral science methodology and instrumentation were crude, many of his findings have withstood the test of more than seven decades of scientific inquiry. This work is doubly remarkable when one notes that Ebbinghaus, alone, was both subject and experimenter in his now classic studies on retention—learning, relearning, and measuring his own ability to retain thousands of nonsense syllables. In fact, the empirically derived relationships which he published in 1885 have since been duplicated time and again.[26] The Miller and Campbell paper takes the Ebbinghaus forgetting curves and shows how they can be used to predict primacy and recency effects in persuasion.[27]

---

[26] Finkenbinder, E. O. The curve of forgetting. Amer. J. Psychol., 1913, 24, 8–32. Luh, C. W. The conditions of retention. Psychol. Monogr., 1922, 31 (Whole No. 142).

[27] Most of the Miller-Campbell findings have been replicated by Insko, although one tentative finding is not supported in Insko's results, namely, that the greater the delay in measurement after the second of two successive communications, the increased likelihood of primacy. Insko, C. A. Primacy versus recency in persuasion as a function of the timing of arguments and measures. J. abnorm. soc. Psychol., 1964, 69, 381–391.

Reprinted from Journal of Abnormal and Social Psychology, 1959, Vol. 59, No. 3, pp. 371–381, by permission of Norman H. Anderson and APA.

TEST OF A MODEL FOR OPINION CHANGE[1]

NORMAN H. ANDERSON

EXPERIMENTS in persuasion generally find that the greater is the advocated change in opinion, the greater is the change produced. Such results have been obtained, for instance, by Goldberg (1954), Fisher, Rubinstein & Freeman (1956), Hovland & Pritzker (1957), and Fisher & Lubin (1958). These investigators have also considered the possibility that the observed change is a linear function of (proportional to) the change advocated, and their results give some, not unequivocal, support for this assumption.

These considerations have been formalized and applied to the primacy-recency problem in a recent article (Anderson & Hovland, 1957). Specifically, it was assumed that the opinion before and after the presentation of a communication were linearly related, according to the equation

$$X_1 = X_0 + S(C - X_0) \qquad [1]$$

where

X_0 is the opinion before presentation of the communication

X_1 is the opinion after presentation of the communication

C is the fixed point of the communication

S is a coefficient of proportionality

The quantities, C and S are called the parameters. The fixed point, C, may be considered as the position of the communication on the opinion continuum. Operationally, C is defined as that initial opinion, X_0, which is left unchanged by the presentation of the communication (regardless of the opinion ostensibly advocated by the communication). The coefficient, S, may be thought of as the susceptibility of the person to the communication. It is analogous to the Efficiency Index of Hovland, Lumsdaine, and Sheffield (1949), and to the Conformity score of Fisher, Rubinstein, and Freeman (1956).

[1] This research was conducted during 1956–57 while the author was a Social Science Research Council Postdoctoral Training Fellow. Thanks are due C. I. Hovland for his many helpful ideas, and to Jack Brehm for his critical comments.

From Equation 1, the change in opinion may be written as $S(C - X_0)$, from which it can be seen that the greater is the value of S, the greater is the change in opinion in the direction of the communication. For simplicity, it will be assumed here that the values of S lie between 0 and 1. It may be noted that the change in opinion will be positive if the initial opinion is less than C, negative if the initial opinion is greater than C. In either case, however, the effect of the communication is to move the opinion closer to C.

To apply Equation 1, consider two communications, A and B, which may be given in AB or in BA order. Denote their fixed points by C_A and C_B, and their susceptibility coefficients by S_A and S_B, respectively. By renaming the communications, if necessary, we may assume that $C_B \geq C_A$. This assumption is a matter of convenience, and entails no loss of generality. Its sole consequence is to give a positive rather than a negative sign to a recency effect. For any given initial opinion, denote the final opinion under the AB (BA) presentation order by X_{AB} (X_{BA}). The difference of these two final opinions is defined as the order effect. The algebraic expression for the order effect is

$$X_{AB} - X_{BA} = S_A S_B (C_B - C_A) \qquad [2]$$

Since all three factors on the right side of this equation are non-negative, the order effect will be nonnegative, so that $X_{AB} \geq X_{BA}$. The magnitude of the order effect will increase with increasing S values, and with increasing distance between the two communications. It should be noted that the order effect does not depend on the initial opinion, except indirectly insofar as X_0 is correlated with susceptibility.

Equation 2 is derived by successive applications of Equation 1 as shown in Anderson and Hovland (1957). The reader may find it helpful to work through the following numerical illustration in which we take $C_A = 0$, $C_B = 10$, $S_A = \frac{1}{2}$, $S_B = \frac{1}{5}$, and an initial opinion equal to 5.

371

Considering first the AB presentation order, the opinion after presentation of A will be

$$5 + \tfrac{1}{2}(0 - 5) = 2.5$$

The opinion, X_{AB}, after presentation of both A and B will then be

$$2.5 + \tfrac{1}{5}(10 - 2.5) = 4$$

Similarly, for the BA order, the opinion after presentation of B is

$$5 + \tfrac{1}{5}(10 - 5) = 6$$

Hence X_{BA}, the opinion after presentation of both B and A will be

$$6 + \tfrac{1}{2}(0 - 6) = 3$$

The order effect is thus

$$X_{AB} - X_{BA} = 4 - 3 = 1$$

It will be seen that this is, of course, the value obtained directly from Equation 2 when the given parameter values are substituted in it.

To apply Equation 2 to the primacy-recency problem, we suppose that A and B are communications on opposite sides of an issue. The assumption, $C_B \geqq C_A$, then simply amounts to orienting the opinion scale in such a way that B advocates an algebraically higher opinion than does A. By Equation 2, $X_{AB} \geqq X_{BA}$. Hence the communicator of B will prefer to act second since the final opinion, which will then be X_{AB}, will be greater and so more favorable to his position. Conversely, since $X_{BA} \leqq X_{AB}$, the communicator of A will also prefer to act second since the final opinion will then be X_{BA}, which is nearer to his position than is X_{AB}.[2] Thus, whenever Equation 1 holds, a recency effect will always be obtained.

Equation 2 may be applied as well to the weak-strong problem. In this case, it is supposed that A and B both advocate algebraically higher positions on the opinion scale, but with A weak and B strong, persuasibility-wise. It may be expected that the differences in strength of the two communications will be

[2] This argument involves the implicit assumption, commonly made, that the goal of each communicator is to produce opinions as extreme as possible. More generally, one may desire to produce an opinion of some particular nonextreme value, in which case these considerations may not apply.

reflected in part in differences in their fixed points. Since X_{AB} is the greater of the two possible final opinions, it is seen that the weak-strong presentation order is the more effective.[3] In this case, the order effect would probably be relatively small since the difference between the fixed points, $C_B - C_A$, would not be expected to be as large as in pro-con experiments.

Formally, Equation 1 is identical with the linear operator equation of Bush & Mosteller (1955). It follows, in particular, that if a sequence of communications with the same S and C values were given, a common exponential growth curve for opinion as a function of "trials" would be obtained.

One final deduction from the model became important in the interpretation of the results, although it was not developed beforehand. Suppose one group of Ss is given the AB presentation order, another group is gven the BA presentation order. If each group is then administered the same sequence of further communications, the mean opinions of the two groups will converge toward equality. Because of the successive bifurcation procedure used in the experimental design, this general result implies that an order effect developed at any stage in the present experiment will decay to zero in the trials following. From Equation 1, the decay rate can be shown to be approximately equal to the average S value of the communications involved. For the present data, the S values are such that any order effect should become negligible in a few trials.

Before proceeding to test these predictions, it is well to consider possible objections to the model. The first of these is that the law of opinion change may not be linear in the given opinion scale as is assumed in Equation 1. Fortunately, at least three of the four predictions, excepting only the remark concerning exponential growth curves, are quite insensitive to the exact form of the equation. For instance, if X_0 lies between the two communications, a recency effect will obtain if amount of change is *any* increasing function of the distance between the communication and the S's opinion.

A more serious objection is that there may be systematic changes in susceptibility over

[3] See Footnote 2

successive communications. The exact derivation of the order effect for this may be found in Anderson and Hovland (1957). However, it should be intuitively clear that decreases in S values will decrease the order effect relative to the base-line expression of Equation 2. If this decrease is large enough, the order effect will become negative, i.e., a primacy, or strong-weak effect.

One is thus led to expect that recency and weak-strong effects will be fairly generally obtained. They cannot be guaranteed, of course, without further knowledge about possible changes in susceptibility, but this problem lies beyond the scope of the present model.

The experiment reported here was designed to provide good data, and to test these various aspects of the model. Specifically, it was expected that recency and weak-strong effects would be obtained. More generally, it was hoped that the results would yield information about the adequacy of the linearity assumption of Equation 1, and about changes in susceptibility over successive arguments.

METHOD

The communication materials were taken from the case of Thomas Hoag, who was indicted for making a bigamous marriage to Catherine Secor. The case had been used in a persuasion experiment by Weld and Roff (1938), and their results were of considerable assistance in planning the present experiment. Most of the material given in Wigmore's (1937) summary was used to construct 17 pieces of evidence, here called arguments.[4] They consisted of the indictment, the summarized testimony of 14 witnesses (somewhat reworded, if necessary, to bring all to an approximately equal length of 175 words), and two pieces of court procedure which brought the trial to a close. The testimony of Benjamin Coe, witness for the prosecution, gives the flavor of the trial:

Benjamin Coe testified that he was one of the judges of the court of common pleas in the county of Rockland; that he well knew the prisoner at the bar; that he came to Rockland in the beginning of September, in the year 1800, and there passed by the name of Thomas Hoag; that there was a person with him who passed for his brother, but between those two persons there was no sort of resemblance; that the prisoner worked for witness about a month, dur-

[4] The texts of the arguments, the details of the construction of the sequences of arguments, and the cell means and analysis of variance tables for Exp. 1 have been deposited with the American Documentation Institute. Order Document No. 6036, remitting $2.50 for microfilm or $1.95 for photocopies. Make checks payable to Chief, Photoduplication Service, Library of Congress.

ing which time he ate daily at witness's table, and he, of course, saw him daily; that on the 25th day of December, 1800, witness married the prisoner to one Catherine Secor; that witness is confident of the time, because he recollected that on that very day one of his own children was christened; that during all the time the prisoner remained in Rockland county, witness saw him continually; he was therefore as much satisfied that the prisoner was Thomas Hoag as that he himself was Benjamin Coe.

While not quite as strong as this, the remaining prosecution arguments were equally definite, and the testimony of the defense witnesses appeared to have no less a persuasive effect.

The Ss were Yale undergraduates, who were asked by phone to participate in the experiment. About 90% of those contacted accepted, and of these about 90% came to the experimental session. The procedure was administered to the Ss in groups of 3 to 13 at a time. Nine Ss were eliminated for skipping pages in the booklet, confusing the guilt-innocence orientation of the judgment scale, etc.

At the beginning of the experimental session, a brief account of orienting facts, important dates, and names in the case were listed on the blackboard where they remained throughout the session. General instructions containing the following points were then given: (a) the experiment was on the process of opinion formation; (b) although the evidence from a jury trial was being used, the Ss should not act as jurors, trying to withhold their judgment until all the evidence was in, but instead to give, each time they were asked for a judgment, their current opinion in the light of the evidence up to that point; (c) a description of the rating scale; (d) the case did not turn on some small detail or inconsistency of fact or date; (e) the case was genuine, not a mystery story, so that there was no "right" answer; (f) the case had been used with Cornell law students, and there was no final opinion which had not been defended by some of those students (see Weld & Roff, 1938).

Each S then received a booklet containing the arguments and read a practice argument written in the same style as the case, but unrelated to it and innocuous in content. After answering the Ss' questions, they were told that the remaining arguments were to be read and judgments made in time with E's signals. Conversation, and turning back or forward in the booklet, were disallowed. A general discussion of perhaps five minutes was held upon conclusion of the experiment, after which Ss were thanked for their cooperation and requested not to divulge details of the testimony until the conclusion of the experiment (at a given date).

For about the last two-thirds of the experiment, Ss were also asked to indicate on their booklets whether the time per argument had been too long, just right, or too short. The 247 usable replies were distributed 41%, 53%, and 6%, respectively, in the three categories.

Except as noted for Experiment 2, each page of the booklet contained one argument and a judgment scale. Two minutes were allotted each page, except that the two concluding arguments were given one, and one-half, minutes, respectively, because of their brevity. Judgments were made during the last 10 seconds of the allotted time. The judgment scale contained 11 categories, with abbreviated descriptions of the meaning of each category, ranging from "belief in innocence beyond all reasonable doubt" to "belief in guilt beyond all reasonable doubt." INNOCENCE was written below the leftmost category, GUILT below the rightmost category. The arguments of the 14 witnesses were labelled PROS. or DEF., according as they were unfavorable or favorable to the defendant.

Experiment 1

The experimental variable was the order of arrangement of the prosecution and defense arguments.

Following the indictment, half of the Ss received two prosecution arguments, then two defense arguments (PD order), while the other half received two defense, then two prosecution arguments (DP order). The difference in opinion of these two groups after the last of these four arguments is called the Stage 1 order effect.

Within each of these two groups, half the Ss next received two prosecution followed by two defense, or else two defense followed by two prosecution arguments. The difference in opinion of these two pairs of subgroups after the last of these four arguments gives the Stage 2 order effect, unconfounded with presentation order in Stage 1.

In the same way, each of the above four subgroups was further split on Arguments 9–12, and the four pairs of differences in mean opinion after these four arguments give the Stage 3 order effect.

Following Stage 3, the same four arguments were given in the same order to all Ss. The first two were prosecution arguments, while the last two brought in a revelation of innocence and concluded the experiment.

To safeguard against results accidental to a particular sequence of arguments, a number of different sequences were employed. The arrangement details were somewhat complicated and are only indicated below.[5] A fixed set of six prosecution and six defense arguments was used in Stages 1–3. Within each of the above eight subgroups, six different sequences of particular arguments were used. These sequences were so chosen as to evaluate the order effect at each of three stages as listed above, to completely counterbalance arguments across ordinal position, and also to yield an assessment of the weak-strong vs. strong-weak presentation order. This was accomplished by random formation of three pairs of prosecution and three pairs of defense arguments. Each pair was used in both forward and reverse order so that altogether 12 pairs were so formed, and these pairs constituted the unit in the construction of the sequences. To illustrate the procedure, let P_1, P_2, D_1, and D_2 denote particular prosecution and defense arguments. If one S received $P_1P_2D_1D_2$, in that order, then another S received $D_1D_2P_1P_2$, thus yielding a primacy-recency comparison after the fourth argument. Also, a third S received $P_2P_1D_2D_1$, and a fourth S received $D_2D_1P_2P_1$, yielding a similar comparison. At the same time, these sequences allow an evaluation of the weak-strong effect by testing P_1P_2 against P_2P_1, and D_1D_2 against D_2D_1.

In Stage 1, where there were only two different

presentation order subgroups, there were only 12 distinct sequences. Each of these bifurcated, in harmony with the splitting of these two subgroups, to yield 24 distinct sequences leading through Stage 2. A similar bifurcation gave 48 distinct sequences leading through Stage 3. The order effect comparison at the end of each stage is thus between Ss treated alike prior to that stage.

A random assignment of booklets was made in each batch of Ss, with the restriction that one replication of the $8 \times 6 = 48$ distinct sequences was complete before another was begun. Four replications were run so that $N = 192$.

Experiment 2

The initial argument (indictment) and the last four arguments were the same as in Experiment 1. The intervening 12 arguments were presented either as six prosecution arguments followed by six defense, or else as six defense followed by six prosecution arguments. Six permutations of the defense and of the prosecution arguments were constructed randomly according to a latin square, so that each argument appeared equally often in each position. A randomly chosen two of the defense permutations followed each of two randomly chosen prosecution permutations, and conversely, so that there were 24 different particular sequences of arguments.

In addition to evaluating an order effect after 12 arguments, the experiment compared three judgmental conditions: Condition 1: judgments were made after each argument; Condition 2: judgments were made after the indictment, and the sixth, twelfth, and final arguments; Condition 3: judgments were made after the indictment, and the twelfth, and the final arguments.

For Condition 1, the booklets were similar to those of Exp. 1. For Conditions 2 and 3, the rating scales were cut off the bottom of the sheets containing the arguments, and sheets containing only a judgment scale were interleaved appropriately. Ss in Conditions 2 and 3 were run in separate sessions since the judgment schedule was different. There were 48 Ss in each condition, 24 in PD order, 24 in DP order, so that $N = 144$.

Experiment 2 was begun after completion of the first replication of Experiment 1, at which time it became clear that a sufficient number of Ss would become available. Thereafter the two experiments were run concurrently.

RESULTS

The numbers 0 through 10 were assigned to the judgment scale categories for purposes of analysis, with 0, 5, and 10, in particular, standing for "complete belief in innocence", "neutral", and "complete belief in guilt", respectively.

The main results of Exp. 1 are shown in Figs. 1, 2, and 3, which plot mean opinion as a function of successive judgments, or trials. Successive figures show the mean opinion for the PD (denoted by O) and DP (denoted by X)

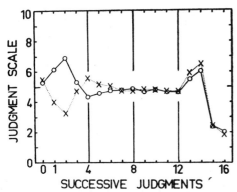

FIG. 1. MEAN OPINION ON SUCCESSIVE JUDGMENTS
FOR THE TWO PRESENTATION ORDERS IN STAGE 1
OF EXP. 1; PD AND DP ORDERS DENOTED BY O
AND X, RESPECTIVELY; LARGER NUMBERS ON
THE VERTICAL SCALE INDICATE GREATER
BELIEF IN GUILT

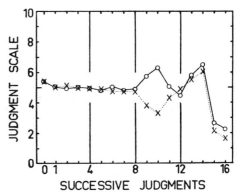

FIG. 3. MEAN OPINION ON SUCCESSIVE JUDGMENTS
FOR THE TWO PRESENTATION ORDERS IN STAGE
3 OF EXP. 1
(Notation as in Fig. 1)

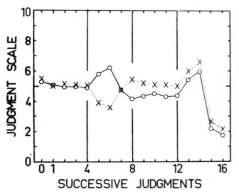

FIG. 2. MEAN OPINION ON SUCCESSIVE JUDGMENTS
FOR THE TWO PRESENTATION ORDERS IN STAGE
2 OF EXP. 1
(Notation as in Fig. 1)

presentation orders within each of the three main stages of the experiment. In Fig. 1 are the results for the two presentation orders in Stage 1. Starting with a slight bias towards guilt, Ss in both conditions show marked changes. The PD Ss increase from an initial value of 5.31 to a value of 6.91 after two prosecution arguments, then decline to 4.36 under the influence of the two following defense arguments. The DP Ss, receiving the opposite order, swing in the reverse direction, and the crossing of the curves at J4 is the graphical equivalent of a recency effect. In the PD order, the defense, coming second, has the advantage

since the final opinion at J4 is more toward innocence. Similarly, the prosecution comes second in the DP order and there has the advantage, since in this case the opinion at J4 is higher, indicating a stronger belief in guilt. The difference of 1.22 in mean opinion for the two presentation orders at J4 gives the magnitude of the Stage 1 recency effect, which is significantly different from zero; see Table 1, Line A.

Following J4, the curves for these same two subgroups of Ss are averaged over their successive bifurcations in Stages 2 and 3. It is seen that the Stage 1 recency effect decays away in a few trials, and thereafter the two subgroups remain sensibly equal except perhaps at J13 and J14.

The Stage 2 results are given in Fig. 2. It will be recalled that there are actually four subgroups in this stage, corresponding to the splitting of each of the two Stage 1 subgroups at J4. Those two subgroups receiving the PD order in Stage 2 have been combined, as have those two subgroups receiving the DP order, and this same combining has been carried out in the preceding and following trials as well. The same pattern of behavior is found here as was obtained in Stage 1, although there is somewhat less yielding to the communications. Again a recency effect is found, of size 1.26, which is again significant. In contrast to Stage 1, this recency effect does not disappear in the succeeding trials, but after some initial decay,

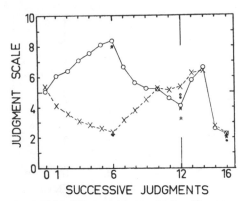

FIG. 4. MEAN OPINION ON SUCCESSIVE JUDGMENTS FOR EXP. 2. CONNECTED CURVES REPRESENT CONDITION 1, WITH PD AND DP PRESENTATION ORDERS DENOTED BY O AND X, RESPECTIVELY. SMALL FILLED CIRCLES REPRESENT CONDITION 2, SMALL UNFILLED CIRCLES REPRESENT CONDITION 3; EARED CIRCLES DENOTE PD ORDER, UNEARED CIRCLES DENOTE DP ORDER

is thereafter maintained without appreciable change till the last judgment.

Figure 3 compares similarly the two presentation orders in Stage 3, each curve being the average of the four subgroups which received the given presentation order in that stage. As before, the averaging was carried out over the prior and subsequent trials as well. Here also the order effect, measured by the mean difference at J12, is a recency effect. However, it is small (0.40) and falls short of significance. Differing in its further course from each of the two previous stages, the Stage 3 recency effect reverses to become a primacy effect in the four trials following. Thus, despite the fact that all Ss were treated alike on these last four trials, the apparent advantage in being second in Stage 3 which appears at J12 is lost at once, and the final gain accrues to that side which was first in Stage 3.

Figure 4 displays the results of Exp. 2. The two order subgroups in Condition 1 first diverge, then converge and cross to yield a recency effect of size 1.21 at J12 which, however, disappears in the subsequent testimony. Condition 2, which is evidently no different from Condition 1 at J6, gives a similar recency effect at J12, and reaches essentially the same final level at J16 as does Condition 1. In Condition 3, the recency effect is again obtained at

J12, and the final levels at J16 (omitted on the graph) are little different from the other four subgroups.

Table 1 gives the relevant quantities from the analyses of variance, and in each case includes all effects that were significant at the .05 level. Although the tests for the order effect itself in each stage are straightforward, the further breakdown of the treatment SS is more complicated and is not given in detail.

From Line A in Table 1, it is seen that the Stage 1 order effect is evidently real. The sequence effect indicates significant differences in the six means formed by pooling the paired PD and DP sequences which used the same particular arguments (e.g., $P_1P_2D_1D_2$ + $D_1D_2P_1P_2$). The nonsignificance of the interaction indicates that the magnitudes of the order effects for these same six pairs of sequences were not greatly different.

The analysis of the later stages is complicated in two ways. First, it would be expected that there will be a correlation between Stage 1 treatment and Stage 2 response, with Ss who received the same arguments in Stage 1 responding more alike in Stage 2 than Ss who received different Stage 1 arguments. For proper significance tests, a split-plot (Snedecor, 1956) analysis, of which the repeated measure-

TABLE 1
SUMMARY OF ANALYSES OF VARIANCE
OF ORDER EFFECTS

Source	df	F	Error ms	Error df
A. Stage 1 (J4)				
Stage 1 order	1	24.58*	2.90	180
Sequences	5	6.54*	2.90	180
Interaction	5	1.65	2.90	180
B. Stage 2 (J8)				
Stage 2 order	1	23.83*	3.20	84
Sequences	5	6.44*	3.30	77
C. Stage 3 (J12)				
Stage 3 order	1	2.85	2.64	72
Stage 2 order	1	3.87	5.51	69
Sequences	5	2.21	5.51	69
D. J13–J16				
Stage 3 order	1	4.29*	38.55	72
Stage 1 order × Stage 3 order	5	3.25*	38.55	72
× Sequences				
Stage 2 order	1	4.93*	53.05	69
E. Exp. 2 (J12)				
Order	1	9.95*	3.92	72
Conditions	2	1.78	3.92	72
Conditions × Order	2	0.96	3.92	72

* $p < .05$.

ments design is a special case, is thus required. Second, there are 24 different sequences of arguments in Stage 2, so the over-all treatment SS has 23 df. Of these, 1 df corresponds to the mean Stage 2 order effect. The remaining 22 df may be further broken down into SS's representing effects of Stage 1 order, sequences, and the interaction of these with Stage 2 order. Although this breakdown involves some confounding between Order in prior stages and Sequences, it increases sensitivity to possible inhomogeneities arising from the particular sequences of arguments used in the experiment.

The Stage 2 order effect is seen in Line B of Table 1 to be significant, as is the main effect of sequences. The near equality of the two error terms implies that the correlation mentioned above is small. Hence, the split-plot analysis on the J12 response in Line C allowed only for a possible correlation between Ss treated alike in Stage 2, by considering as main plots the 24 different sequences administered in Stage 2. No significant effects were found at J12, although Stage 3 order, Stage 2 order, and sequences approach significance. The large difference in the two error terms indicates that Ss treated alike in Stage 2 have a significantly correlated response at J12.

The analysis of Line D, carried out on the total score over the last four trials, shows that the Stage 2 order still has a significant effect, verifying, for these four trials, the observed retention of the Stage 2 recency effect seen in Fig. 2. The significance of Stage 3 order attests to the reality of the hidden primacy effect seen in Fig. 3. The significant interaction warns that these two effects may not be homogeneous over the sequences used, although the significance of 1 out of the 11 interactions evaluated in this analysis may be only a Type I error.

The retention of the Stage 2 order effect and the reversal of the Stage 3 order effect deserve further comment since they become important in the interpretation of the results. Although the Stage 2 recency effect falls slightly short of significance in the analysis at J12, this analysis uses only the data from that one trial. The effect is significant in the test over the last four trials because of the increased reliability of the score, even though the size of the effect is somewhat smaller, and the within-trial error variance is somewhat larger, than at J12. The Stage 3 primacy effect of the last four trials of Fig. 3 is the average of four comparisons, one from each of the paired subgroups in Stage 3. In the given analysis, all four comparisons were primacy effects. Indeed, making these four comparisons separately for each of the last four trials yields 16 comparisons. Of these, 14 are primacy effects, one is a recency effect, and one is zero. It is thus evident that the hidden primacy effect is not the result of one aberrant subgroup. Finally, it should be noted that this primacy effect is significant per se, over and above the J12 recency effect which it had to overcome.

As a check on the possibility that the S population became progressively contaminated by word of mouth report during the course of the experiment, the replication effect was tested in the analyses of Lines B, C, and D of Table 1, but the F was small and nonsignificant in each case.

The analysis for Experiment 2 is given in Line E of Table 1. No significant effects, except for sequences, were found at J6 or J16, so this information is omitted. At J12, the mean order effect is significant, but there were no significant differences between the order effects for the three conditions, or between their overall means.

Estimating the parameters, and testing the linearity assumption present considerable difficulty for a number of reasons. In particular, it should be noted that the procedure of assigning a priori values to the fixed points of the communications (such as $C = 0$ for defense arguments, $C = 10$ for prosecution arguments), which has been used by some workers, would be incorrect from the standpoint of the present model. However, some rough information in these two respects may be gained from inspection of Fig. 5. Here is plotted mean change in opinion as a function of initial opinion for each judgment in Stages 1–3 of Experiment 1, for each of the eight presentation order subgroups. In each panel, the points above the line represent the influence of prosecution arguments, those below the line correspond to defense arguments.

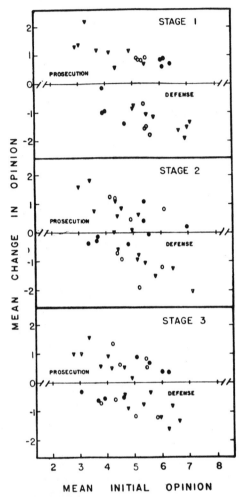

MEAN CHANGE IN OPINION

MEAN INITIAL OPINION

Fig. 5. Mean Change in Opinion as a Function of Mean Initial Opinion for Exp. 1. Circle and Triangle Denote First and Second Halves Within Each Stage, Respectively; Open and Filled Figures Denote First and Second Arguments Within Each Half Stage, Respectively

The points are further classified according as they were in the first or second half of the given stage, and according as they were first or second within a half stage.

Ideally, were Equation 1 true, the six sets of points would lie on a straight line with slope equal to $-S$, and horizontal intercept equal to C. Fitting straight lines by eye

suggest the following observations. The horizontal intercepts are somewhat closer to the center of the scale in Stages 2 and 3 than in Stage 1. Within each of the six sets of points, there appear to be systematic differences between the lines for the first and second half-stages (circle vs. triangle), with the line for the second half-stage showing intercepts closer to the center of the scale. Except for Stage 3, there do not seem to be marked differences between the lines through the points for the first and for the second arguments within a half-stage (open vs. filled symbols). Considered as a whole, no set or subset of points shows marked deviations from linearity.

The remarks of the previous paragraph suggest that the parameters are not constant over trials, and inspection of Figs. 1–3 suggests that there is a decreased over-all responsiveness in Stages 2 and 3 as compared to Stage 1. To test this, each S was assigned three total change scores by adding up his four opinion changes within each stage, giving to each a plus or minus sign according as it was or was not in the direction advocated by the argument. The mean total change scores for Stages 1, 2, and 3 were 4.40, 3.38, and 3.12, respectively. The difference between the first two means was significant, $F(1, 144) = 16.4$, while the F for the comparison of latter two was less than 1.

The interpretation of this decrease in total change scores as indicative of a decreased responsiveness needs justification, since there is involved a comparison of the amounts of change induced in opinions which are systematically different. The interpretation appears warranted here because of the pro–con counterbalancing in each stage, and because there is no marked asymmetry between the prosecution and defense arguments.

Since the three pairs of arguments of each type were given in both forward and reverse order, it is possible to test the relative effectiveness of the weak-strong and strong-weak presentation orders. Each argument was assigned a score equal to the total change which it induced over Stages 1–3. The members of each pair were classed as weak or strong according as this score was the smaller or larger. Members of one pair had identical scores and were omitted from the further analysis. Using next the individual change scores induced by the pairs of arguments acting as a unit, the analysis of the mean over-all difference of weak-strong and strong-weak order yielded a significant $F(1, 720) = 6.71$, with the weak-strong order being the more effective. The actual effect was rather small, about 7% of the total change produced, as would be expected from the model.

DISCUSSION

As suggested by the model, recency effects were obtained at each of the three places at which it was planned to evaluate them. Support was also found for the predicted superiority of the weak-strong presentation order. To this extent, then, the predictive goodness of the model is substantiated.

The principal deviations from the model are seen in the further course of the order effects past the stages where they were formed. Although the decay of the Stage 1 recency effect is in accord with expectation, the maintenance of the Stage 2 recency effect throughout the remainder of the experiment, and the reversal of the Stage 3 recency effect in the subsequent testimony, are definitely contrary to the model.

The following, somewhat speculative, explanation of these discrepancies involves two assumptions one general and one specific. The general assumption states that opinion has two components: a basal component which is relatively little affected by the communications once it is formed, and a superficial component which is quite labile, and which obeys the original model. The two components act together to produce the observed opinion response.

Now at the beginning of the experiment, the basal opinion is presumably vague, or nonexistent, but begins to form as successive arguments accumulate. The special assumption locates the major portion of this basal opinion formation in the last half of Stage 2 and in the first half of Stage 3.

These two assumptions will account for the discrepancies according to the following argument. In Stage 1, there is as yet little basal opinion. Hence the obtained Stage 1 recency effect is created entirely by the superficial component. Since this component obeys

the model, the decay of the Stage 1 recency effect is in accord with the prediction made in the introduction. The opinion at the end of Stage 2 has both superficial and basal components, and both contribute to the recency effect at this stage, the former because it obeys the model, and the latter because it is formed in the second half of the stage. In the succeeding arguments, that portion of the Stage 2 recency effect which is due to the superficial component decays away as seen in Fig. 2. The basal component, however, being resistant to change, is carried along beneath the perambulations of the observed opinion at a fairly constant value thereafter. The formation of the basal component in the first half of Stage 3 would of itself produce a primacy effect in this stage. The observed recency effect presumably arises from the overriding influences of the superficial component. Following Stage 3, the decay of the superficial component reveals the primacy effect caused by the basal component formed in Stage 3.

Although this explanation is *ad hoc*, there is an additional consideration which appears to lend support to the special assumption. On the basis of the linear model, it would be expected that the total change score and the order effect should be small or large together. It has been seen that the total change score is about equal in Stages 2 and 3, and in each smaller than in Stage 1. Yet, the recency effects are about equal in Stages 1 and 2, and in each considerably larger than in Stage 3. This relation of total change score and order effect would, however, seem to be consistent with the special assumption. For, if basal opinion is formed in the second half of Stage 2, it should act to enhance the recency effect relative to the average responsiveness in this stage. Also, if basal opinion formation occurs in the first half of Stage 3, it will act to reduce the recency effect relative to the responsiveness in this stage. This argument should be considered only as suggestive, however, since it cannot be made rigorous without a more precise specification of the way in which the two components jointly produce the observed opinion.

The central question for the model, as originally conceived, was whether the linearity assumption would prove adequate, or whether it would be necessary to use a more complicated function to relate change in opinion to current opinion. The two-component hypothesis suggests a more basic problem, namely, that the structure of opinion may be too complex to be represented by a single number on an opinion scale. It should be noted that the idea of two independent components involves more than a simple increase in the "inertia" of the opinion. It had been realized that the opinion would probably become more resistant to change as its informational base accumulated over successive communications, but such an increased "inertia" could be represented in the model as a change in S values. One possible formulation would be to assume, as above, that Equation 1 holds for the superficial component, and that the basal component, although it comes into being, is largely resistant to change. Such an extended model would require provision for representing the amount of basal component present at any time, as well as the scale value of the opinion to which it corresponded. A rule for specifying how the two components combine to produce the observed response would also be needed. Under such a formulation, the present model would apply to situations in which the basal component either does not arise, or is already fully formed prior to the experiment.

Some comments on limitations and possible flaws in the results and interpretation deserve mention. It is in the first place evident that replication with other stimulus materials is needed. The present results may depend not only on having a situation in which there is essentially no initial opinion, but also on a set to reach a definite yes-no conclusion which might have been present. It is also possible that the results may arise specifically from the particular orders and sequences used. The general nonsignificance of the interactions in Experiment 1 gives some assurance as regards sequence peculiarities, but the nonappearance of a basal component in Experiment 2 suggests that the presentation orders used will be important. It should further be noted that, although the perseveration of the Stage 2 order effect virtually forces a two component assumption, these two components may correspond to two subsets of the S population rather than two opinion components within each S. Finally, even if the hypothesis of two components is basically correct, it may be oversimplified and in need of amplification.

With regard to the primacy-recency problem itself, these data make it amply clear that no general law of primacy or recency can exist, in agreement with Hovland's (1957) conclusion in his survey of the literature. Hovland goes on to suggest that recency effects will tend to be found when there is prior familiarity with the topic, and that primacy effects will tend to be obtained when the material is unfamiliar. The first suggestion would seem to be in accord with the model presented here as well as with the two component hypothesis since, with familiar material, there should be no great decrease in susceptibility and/or little formation of basal opinion consequent to the first communication. However, the second suggestion might well be weakened to state that with unfamiliar material, primacy effects are *possible*, but that the sign and size of the order effect will depend strongly on the particular arrangement of the sequence of communications, as well as on the time at which the opinion is measured. Here, with unfamiliar material, the particular arrangements used apparently acted so as to emphasize the recency effect in Stage 2, and to decrease the recency effect in Stage 3, with a subsequently appearing Stage 3 primacy effect. If the two-component hypothesis is reasonably correct, one would expect that primacy effects would be most easily obtainable at the locus of formation of the basal component.

In view of the above, it might be suggested that the order effect problem is not fundamental, but that order effects should be derived from more general principles. While this is probably true, the usefulness of the order effect paradigm as a tool in isolating such principles should not be overlooked.

Finally, it is worthwhile commenting on the finding in Experiment 2 that frequency of opinion measurement had no significant effect on the observed response, confirming and extending the result of Hovland and Mandell (1957). If this is further substantiated, it will allow a continuous record of the course of opinion formation without restricting the generality of the results.

SUMMARY

Two experiments designed to test a mathematical model for opinion change were presented. In each experiment, subjects read 17 successive arguments summarized from the testimony and procedure of a jury trial.

In Experiment 1, only presentation order was varied. In agreement with predictions from the model, recency and weak-strong effects were obtained at each place at which their evaluation had been planned. In further accord with the model, the recency effect formed in the first stage of the sequence of arguments rapidly decayed in the arguments following. However, the further course of the recency effects formed in the two later stages of the experiment was contrary to prediction. The recency effect from the second stage, after some initial decay, persevered at a fairly constant level through the remainder of the experiment. The recency effect formed in the third stage reversed itself to become a primacy effect in the trials following.

A two-component hypothesis about the structure of opinion was tentatively set forth to explain these discrepancies. According to this hypothesis, the opinion had a superficial component which obeyed the model, and a basal component, formed during the middle arguments of the experiment, which was largely resistant to change once it had come into being.

The order effect paradigm was used again in Experiment 2, which also compared three frequencies of opinion measurement. Recency effects were again obtained, but the frequency with which opinion was measured had no reliable effect.

REFERENCES

ANDERSON, N. H., & HOVLAND, C. I. The representation of order effects in communication research. In C. I. Hovland (Ed.), *The order of presentation in persuasion.* New Haven: Yale Univer. Press, 1957.

BUSH, R. R., & MOSTELLER, F. *Stochastic models for learning.* New York: Wiley, 1955.

FISHER, S., & LUBIN, A. Distance as a determinant of influence in a two-person serial interaction situation. *J. abnorm. soc. Psychol.*, 1958, **56**, 230–238.

FISHER, S., RUBINSTEIN, I., & FREEMAN, R. W. Intertrial effects of immediate self-committal in a continuous social influence situation. *J. abnorm. soc. Psychol.*, 1956, **52**, 200–207.

GOLDBERG, S. C. Three situational determinants of conformity to social norms. *J. abnorm. soc. Psychol.*, 1954, **49**, 325–329.

HOVLAND, C. I. Summary and implications. In C. I. Hovland (Ed.), *The order of presentation in persuasion.* New Haven: Yale Univer. Press, 1957.

HOVLAND, C. I., LUMSDAINE, A. A., & SHEFFIELD, F. D. *Experiments on mass communication.* Princeton: Princeton Univer. Press, 1949.

HOVLAND, C. I., & MANDELL, W. Is there a "law of primacy in persuasion"? In C. I. Hovland (Ed.), *The order of presentation in persuasion.* New Haven: Yale Univer. Press, 1957.

HOVLAND, C. I., & PRITZKER, H. A. Extent of opinion change as a function of amount of change advocated. *J. abnorm. soc. Psych.*, 1957, **54**, 257–261.

SNEDECOR, G. W. *Statistical methods.* (5th ed.) Ames: Iowa State Coll. Press, 1956.

WELD, H. P., & ROFF, M. A study in the formation of opinion based upon legal evidence. *Amer. J. Psychol.*, 1938, **51**, 609–628.

WIGMORE, J. H. *The science of judicial proof.* (3rd ed.) Boston: Little, Brown, 1937.

Reprinted from Journal of Abnormal and Social Psychology, 1959, Vol. 59, No. 1, pp. 1–9, by permission of Norman Miller and APA.

RECENCY AND PRIMACY IN PERSUASION AS A FUNCTION OF THE TIMING OF SPEECHES AND MEASUREMENTS[1]

NORMAN MILLER AND DONALD T. CAMPBELL

I N A recent volume, Hovland, Campbell, Brock, Luchins, Cohen, McGuire, Janis, Feierabend, and Anderson (1957) have summarized and added to the perplexing literature on the conditions under which the first or the second of two opposing arguments have an advantage due to position per se. Their findings seem to have ruled out any completely general principle of primacy in persuasion, but have specified several sets of conditions under which a primacy effect may be expected. In adding to this growing literature, the present paper pays relatively less attention to primacy, although we do find a primacy effect. Instead, attention is called to a pervasive and probably universal psychological principle generating recency effects, a principle about which psychology already knows enough to predict confidently the temporal conditions of presentation and measurement under which recency should appear most strongly. As a complement, the principle also predicts the temporal conditions under which a primacy effect appears most strongly, if indeed one is present.

Our judgments, our responses, our social perceptions, are a function of some net resultant of the past experiences both recent and remote. To the net resultant of the moment not all past experiences contribute equally: the casual experiences of this morning weigh more heavily than the comparably casual experiences of any single morning one year ago, one month ago, or even yesterday, all other things being equal. Were it not so, unlearning and new learning could hardly take place. But the advantage that this morning's experience now has will dissipate rapidly. By next month, its advantage over yesterday's contribution will be scarcely noticeable. The momentary advantage of the very recent may allow trivial

events of this morning to overweigh momentarily more significant learnings of the past, but this momentary advantage will dissipate rapidly, allowing the relative influence of the older learnings to recover spontaneously tomorrow or the next day, if events like this morning's prove to be untypical and do not recur.

These homely truisms are economically summarized in the oldest dependable achievement of the scientific study of learning, the negatively accelerated forgetting curve of Ebbinghaus (1913), and in its implications for the relative strength of competing associations of different ages and strengths. From it, Jost's (1897) second law can be derived—of two associations equally strong at the moment, the older will decay less rapidly. These same considerations also predict spontaneous recovery (Miller & Stevenson, 1936). Hovland, Janis, and Kelly (1953, p. 126), although not making explicit use of the forgetting curve, have provided a parallel analysis of the effect of delays in measurement upon the relative strength of a first and second message:

Yet another important factor to consider is the time interval between the learning of the second communication and the occasion when remembering is required. In experimental results on simple verbal material one would predict recency effects when the time interval is short. But the passage of time would tend to decrease this recency effect and permit the other factors making for primacy to become relatively stronger. Underwood [1948] has shown that for verbal learning the relative superiority of the second list with respect to retention decreases as the time between learning and testing becomes greater. If the same factors operate in social communication one would expect to find that when the issue is raised quite a while after the communication, recency would be less likely to be operative. Striking data are offered on this point in an experiment by Bateman and Remmers [1941].... The results show that immediately after the two communications the attitudes changed in the direction of the second communication. This is the predicted recency effect. Two months later however, the attitudes had changed in the direction of the first communication. Thus primacy effects occurred with time. While the data are consistent with the analysis suggested here, the experiment cannot be

[1] This paper is based upon a Master of Science thesis (1957) done by the first author under the direction of the second. Additional analyses of the data beyond the original report have been supported in part by funds from the Graduate School, Northwestern University.

1

considered as presenting conclusive evidence because it did not include a control group and the order of presentation was not rotated.

The present study examines with better controls this effect of delay in measurement, and in addition considers the still stronger factor of the time interval between the first and second communication.

Figure 1 presents the implications of the Ebbinghaus curve as it applies to the relative weighting of two competing communications presented and measured at varying intervals, assuming no interaction of one with the other. In this diagram, the solid line (Line A) represents the contribution of a communication presented first, its strength decaying as time elapses. The two dashed lines (B and B') represent the contributions of a second opposing communication. In one instance this second communication is presented immediately after the first (Line B), in the other instance, one week after the first (Line B'). Net effects of the two communications in combination are reflected by the vertical distance between Line A and Line B or B' at any given point in time. The numbered vertical slicings in the diagram represent four possible schedulings of a measure of net effect, designated as Conditions 1–4. Five predictions emerge, stated in terms of the relative magnitude of the recency effect, i.e., the dominance of the second communication in the composite under the four conditions: 3 > 4, 3 > 1,

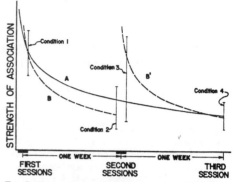

FIG. 2. HYPOTHETICAL FORGETTING CURVES FOR TWO COMPETING COMMUNICATIONS WITH AN ADDED PRIMACY EFFECT; THE PRIMACY EFFECT IS REPRESENTED BY THE HIGHER INITIAL STARTING POINT AND FINAL ASYMPTOTE OF LINE A IN COMPARISON WITH LINES B OR B'

3 > 2, 1 > 2, and 4 > 2. The relative magnitudes of Conditions 1 and 4 cannot be predicted without specific knowledge of the parameters of the curve. The others follow from the simple assumption of similar negatively accelerated decrements for the three curves involved.

Figure 1 has been drawn assuming equal initial strength for the first and the second messages at the time of their delivery. But the ordering of the test conditions as to their *relative* favorableness to the second message is independent of this assumption of initial equality. These general decremental processes occur no matter how strong any given message happens to be. As can be seen from Figure 1, by assuming this initial equality in the strength of the two communications, though the magnitude of the effects varies, *only* recency effects can be generated. However, in persuasion studies there frequently appears an advantage to the first message, a primacy or prior entry effect, strong enough to show up even under conditions of testing such as Condition 1 in which a weak primacy effect would be covered over by a recency effect. Figure 2 has been drawn to indicate some degree of primacy effect, interpreted as an initially higher level for the first message at its onset than for the second message at its highest and, correspondingly, a higher eventual asymptotic level of strength for the first message than for the

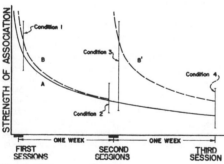

FIG. 1. HYPOTHETICAL FORGETTING CURVES FOR A FIRST AND A SECOND COMPETING PERSUASIVE COMMUNICATION WHEN BOTH ARE PRESENTED DURING A SINGLE SESSION (CURVES A AND B) OR WHEN THE TWO ARE PRESENTED ONE WEEK APART (CURVES A AND B'); THE FOUR CONDITIONS, APPEARING AS VERTICAL SLICINGS, REPRESENT THE TIMING OF MEASUREMENTS

second. Under this assumption, a manifest or net primacy can occur, as in Condition 2. Note that such a primacy effect does *not* occur *instead of* a recency effect but, rather, *in addition* to a recency effect. Thus, attention is drawn to a conceptual distinction between recency effects which are a function of the general rates of decrement with the passage of time, and primacy effects which appear as a function of the higher asymptote eventually resulting from the advantage of prior entry. To predict whether primacy or recency will appear at any single point in time, knowledge of the specific parameters of the curves would of course be essential. But even without specification of parameters, solely upon the basis of assuming similar negatively accelerated decrements, the rank order of the four testing situations in terms of the relative advantage to recency can be specified, and are the same for Fig. 2 as for Fig. 1. However, the absolute magnitudes have been shifted, so that under Condition 2, which is the least advantageous condition for recency in both figures, a strong net primacy effect is predicted in Fig. 2. In general, the more delayed the test period relative to the time gap between the two presentations, the more favorable are conditions for the appearance of a primacy effect.

METHOD

Subjects

A total of 144 Northwestern freshman and sophomore students from introductory psychology and social science courses served as Ss. All Ss were volunteers. Some of the Ss were acquainted with the experimenter, but these were distributed in approximately equal numbers among the groups serving under different experimental conditions.

Communications

A desirable consideration that has not been met in most two-sided communication studies is that the subject matter or theme of the communications be one about which Ss have not already formed opinions or attitudes prior to the experiment. Learning prior to the experiment can eliminate the possibility of controlling or determining the effect of order of learning (Hovland et al., 1953; Lund, 1925). With such the case, primacy of the communication that is experimentally presented first may be a misnomer if the communication is considered in the context of all the communications received by the individual on the particular issue in question. It was therefore considered advantageous to experimentally create attitudes rather than arouse previously learned attitudes. As Weld and Roff (1938),

we used a modified courtroom procedure to introduce experimentally pro and con statements about a topic with which Ss had no prior experience. A transcript of an actual trial involving a suit for damages supposedly incurred as a result of a defective vaporizer was edited for the purposes of the present experiment.[2] Repetitious sections of the testimony were condensed and the names of the principals were changed. The sequence of the proceedings was rearranged so that all material for the plaintiff appeared in one consecutive block, and all material for the defendant appeared in another block. The testimony of witnesses for the plaintiff, the cross-examination by the plaintiff's lawyer of the witnesses for the defense, and the opening and closing speeches of the plaintiff's lawyer, will be called the "Pro" communication, the testimony of witnesses for the defense, etc. the "Con." These two communications were approximately equal, both in length and in the number of points to their arguments. Slight differences in persuasive strength of the two communications were present but are unimportant because of the counterbalanced design employed. The experimental communications were recorded, with different persons reading the parts of the different characters, lawyers, witnesses, etc. Each took approximately 45 minutes to run.

Response Measures

Four response measures were used. A graphic scale with nine described points (e.g., defendant is somewhat more responsible) enabled each S to express the degree to which he thought either the plaintiff or the defendant was responsible for the accident, the midpoint of 5 representing equal responsibility. Higher values indicated plaintiff's responsibility, i.e., persuasion to the "Con" point of view. This scale served as the direct attitude measure. It was accompanied by a scale on which the S estimated how certain he was of his response, with possible values ranging from zero to 100%.

A multiple choice test was constructed to determine the amount of factual information that could be recalled from the two communications. The test contained a total of 28 four-choice items, 14 based on the material from the Pro communication and 14 based on the material from the Con communication.

The one other response measure used was included in an effort to get at differences in acceptance. Ss were requested to list those parts of the two communications that they could not believe or accept. This response measure was preceded by a statement to the effect that no person believes everything he is told even if it is supposedly factual. Then, a list of the names of the persons who testified at the trial (a brief identifying description following each name) was supplied to each S in order to facilitate recall and identification of unacceptable statements. The response measures collectively took approximately 30 minutes.

Procedure

The two spacings of the first and second communication (immediate and one week apart), and, for each, the

---

[2] The authors are indebted to Fred L. Strodtbeck of the University of Chicago for this material.

two spacings of the measurement efforts (immediately after the second and one week after the second) generate the four experimental conditions indicated in Figs. 1 and 2. Replicating these four conditions with the Pro-Con order and the Con-Pro order generates the eight basic experimental groups. Each of these groups contained 18 Ss, all presented the communications and tested together. All groups met in the same classroom at about the same time of day. Ss sat one seat apart from each other, and adjacent Ss had booklets in which the test materials were assembled in different orders. Through these precautions it was hoped to minimize the "neighbor effect" or "social diffusion," well-known reducers of the variability of the test scores of college students. Each group was measured but once in a Posttest Only Design (Campbell, 1957). For Condition 1, the single session took approximately 2½ hrs. with 5-minute breaks following both communications.

To make the findings on the various measures independent of the order in which the students filled them out, the three instruments (attitude and certainty being treated as one) were stapled together in the six possible orders, and three of each of these assemblies employed in each group of 18. Extra Ss were run in each group to allow for the inevitable loss through failure to keep appointments one week apart. Surplus Ss were discarded to leave 3 Ss each in the 48 cells of the total design. Since the order of the response measures turned out to have no effect in any of several analyses (Miller, 1957) it has been omitted in this report.

RESULTS

Attitude. In Table 1 are presented the mean attitude scores for each of the eight groups. Using Table 1 as a reference, two types of comparisons can be designated. The vertical comparisons within each of the two columns are appropriate to testing the predictions about the relative strength of the second message. For this purpose, each column represents an independent experiment of four groups. It is for these comparisons that the Ebbinghaus curve predictions are made. Table 2 and the discussion of it below treat these results. The predictions in Table 2, and the columns of means of Table 1 taken individually, are silent on whether or not for any given condition the manifest effect found is one of primacy or recency. The predictions merely indicate under which condition a primacy effect, if present, should appear most strongly (i.e., Condition 2) and under which a recency effect, if present, should appear most strongly (i.e., Condition 3), etc. For any one mean to be directly interpretable in terms of primacy and recency, one would need proof that the Pro and Con messages were exactly equal in persuasive power and that the assigned midpoint of 5 was the

effective neutral point of judgment in absence of persuasive communications. But if one makes use of the comparison of the Pro-Con and the Con-Pro orders, i.e., makes the horizontal comparisons of Table 1, the presence of manifest net primacy or recency effects can be examined, because the groups being compared have heard identical materials under identical spacings, and differ only in the order with which these have been heard. In Table 1 (and Tables 4 and 7), the higher the scores the more the Con material has been effective. Thus a comparison of the two Condition 2 groups shows that the Con material was weakest when occurring second, strongest when coming first, indicating a primacy effect, significant at the .01 level (using a two-tailed test, since direction was not predicted). Condition 3 shows a recency effect, significant at the .02 level. The results conform to the pattern predicted by Fig. 2, in which a general primacy and recency effect coexist, the recency effect dominating under Condition 3, the condition predicted as most favorable to recency; the primacy effect dominates under Condition 2, predicted as least favorable to recency, and therefore as the place where a primacy effect would appear most strongly, if present. The two effects cancel each other in the two conditions of predicted intermediacy.

While the *t* tests reported in Table 1 and Table 2 provide more specific information, a double classification analysis of variance offers a more general test of the main hypothesis that the temporal spacing of communications and measurements determines the relative effec-

TABLE 1
MEAN ATTITUDE SCORES

Condition	Pro-Con Presentation	Con-Pro Presentation	Diff.	t	p^{**}	Direction
1(X_1X_1O)*	5.94	5.88	.06			
2(X_1X_1—O)	4.50	6.61	−2.11	2.81	.01	Primacy
3(X_1—X_1O)	6.00	4.33	1.67	2.46	.02	Recency
4(X_1—X_1—O)	5.47	5.58	−.11			

* The shorthand characterization of the conditions employs a standardized symbolization of experimental treatments (Campbell, 1957), in which X_1 and X_1 represent the experimental stimuli, O the process of observation and measurement, and spacing from left to right the time dimension.

** Two-tailed, inasmuch as direction of difference not predicted.

tiveness of the communications in the composite. However, with a counterbalanced design, this hypothesis must be stated as an interaction rather than a main effect; the shifts in attitude occurring over conditions with the Pro-Con presentation should be analogous, but reciprocal or in opposite direction to those occurring with the Con-Pro order. In a 2 × 4 analysis of variance of the attitude scores, the F ratio for the interaction between Conditions and Order of Presentation is the only one that obtains significance. With 1 and 3 degrees of freedom, this F ratio of 4.06 is significant beyond the .01 level.

Table 2 presents, separately, for the Pro-Con and Con-Pro orders, the comparisons between conditions in terms of their predicted relative favorableness to recency. The positive signs indicate that the direction of difference was as predicted. (Note that for the Con-Pro groups, greater recency effects are indicated by lower scores.) All differences are in the direction predicted. This score of 10 correct out of 10 predictions looks highly significant by a simple sign test, although since the same values have been re-used, independence of sampling error from comparison to comparison cannot be claimed. Table 2 also presents the t ratios and p values for the predicted comparisons of means and a compound p value (Baker, 1952) for the Pro-Con and the Con-Pro groups treated jointly. The most clearly significant difference occurs for the comparison for which the largest contrast was expected, i.e., between

TABLE 3
MEAN NUMBER OF ITEMS CORRECT ON RECALL

Condition	Pro-Con Presentation		Con-Pro Presentation	
	Pro	Con	Pro	Con
$1(X_1X_2O)$	10.00	9.44	10.72	9.83
$2(X_1X_2{-}O)$	9.28	9.06	8.94	8.33
$3(X_1{-}X_2O)$	7.31	9.69	9.94	6.67
$4(X_1{-}X_2{-}O)$	7.50	8.50	7.78	6.89

Conditions 3 and 2. The other differences approach significance in the predicted directions. All in all, results seem strongly confirmatory of the predictions.

Recall of Information. Table 3 presents the recall data in terms of the mean number of Pro and Con items correctly answered in each condition. To state recall in terms of a net weighting, each S was given a score of Con items right minus Pro items right. The means of these net recall scores are presented in Table 4. The comparisons made in Table 4 parallel those in Table 1. In an analysis of variance of the net recall scores, a significant interaction obtains between Conditions and Order of Presentation. With 1 and 3 degrees of freedom, the F ratio of 21.46 for the interaction is significant well beyond the .001 level. All horizontal comparisons show a net recency effect (conforming more to the model of Fig. 1 than Fig. 2), with the recency effect most highly significant for Condition 3, as expected.

Table 5 is constructed parallel to Table 2. Of the ten predicted differences, nine are confirmed for sign. The three predictions involving Condition 3 are all very highly significant. The comparison between Conditions 1 and 2 fails of significance in either the Pro-Con or Con-Pro order. Considering the small number of items in the test, and their employment as a difference score (which should further increase their random variability), the results seem in general as confirmatory as one could expect. In both columns, two independent replications, the gap between Condition 3 and any other is most dramatically confirmed, as would be expected from Fig. 1.

Nonacceptance. The mean number of Pro and Con arguments recalled as unbelieved under the eight conditions is shown in Table 6. As a net effect score, the number of unaccept-

TABLE 2
COMPARISON OF MEANS FOR ATTITUDE SCORES [a]

Prediction for Conditions	Pro-Con Presentation			Con-Pro Presentation			Combined
	Diff	t	p	Diff.	t	p	p
1 > 2	+1.44	1.79	.04	+.73	1.00	.16	<.05
3 > 1	+.06	.08	.47	+1.55	2.03	.025	<.07
3 > 2	+1.50	2.14	.02	+2.28	3.12	.005	<.001
3 > 4	+.53	.78	.22	+1.25	1.56	.06	<.08
4 > 2	+.97	1.21	.11	+1.03	1.35	.09	<.06
(1, 4)	.47	.59	.56	.30	.38	.70	

[a] The Diff. column values are differences between the group means presented in Table 1, with positive signs applied to indicate differences in the predicted direction as favoring recency, thus reversing the natural subtraction signs for the Con-Pro groups for which favoring recency implies lower scores. No prediction was made for Conditions 1 vs. 4, and two-tailed p values are therefore presented for this comparison, while one-tailed values are used for the others.

TABLE 4
MEAN NET RECALL SCORES

Condition	Pro-Con Presentation	Con-Pro Presentation	Diff.	t	p*	Direction
$1(X_1X_2O)$	−.56	−.89	+.33	.39		
$2(X_1X_2-O)$	−.22	−.61	+.39	.55		
$3(X_1-X_2O)$	2.38	−3.27	+5.65	7.90	.001	Recency
$4(X_1-X_2-O)$	1.00	−.89	+1.89	2.62	.02	Recency

* Two-tailed.

TABLE 5
COMPARISON OF MEAN RECALL DIFFERENCE SCORES

Prediction for Conditions	Pro-Con Presentation			Con-Pro Presentation			Combined
	Diff.[a]	t	p	Diff.	t	p	p
1 > 2	−.34	.39	.64	+.28	.40	.36	> .20
3 > 1	+2.94	3.42	.0004	+2.39	3.21	.001	< .0001
3 > 2	+2.60	3.80	.0001	+2.67	3.54	.0002	< .0001
3 > 4	+1.38	1.76	.04	+2.39	3.52	.0003	< .0001
4 > 2	+1.22	1.54	.065	+.28	.45	.34	< .10
(1, 4)	1.56	1.67	.10	.00	.00	.50	

[a] See the footnote to Table 2.

able Con items was subtracted from the number of unacceptable Pro items. The means of these net scores for each group are presented in Table 7. For this measure, the interaction F ratio for Order × Conditions was insignificant. The Pro-Con vs. Con-Pro differences are predominantly in the primacy direction, although not of clear statistical significance. The most significant difference is in the primacy direction under Condition 2, predicted most favorable to primacy. The only difference in the recency direction is in Condition 3, predicted most favorable to recency. Table 8 presents the differences among the Pro-Con conditions, and among the Con-Pro conditions, arranged in terms of the predictions, although it is not clear that the predictions are appropriate to this measure. For the Pro-Con groups, all differences are trivial, and the predicted direction of difference is found in only two of the five pairs. The Con-Pro groups offer four out of five confirmations, all those that approach significance being in the predicted direction.

In retrospect, it can be seen that our particular measure of nonacceptance is far from

ideal. A more interpretable procedure would have asked for recall of testimony found particularly convincing in addition to testimony disbelieved. With only the recall of unacceptable material, the influence of credibility is mixed with the influence of greater readiness of recall, with opposing effects. For an item to be mentioned as unbelievable it has to be remembered. But mention of second message material as disbelieved is scored as a credibility advantage to the first. If, for the reason of greater recency, second message material is more easily remembered and therefore mentioned more often, the net effect gets scored as a primacy advantage for acceptance and credibility purposes.

Other Analyses. To assist in the interpretation of the processes that would allow a primacy effect for the attitude measure without a primacy effect for recall, correlation coefficients were computed among the three main variables, separately for each of the eight groups. The average of these values are: Attitude and Recall −.10, Attitude and Nonacceptance .43 ($p < .01$), Recall and Nonacceptance −.04. For the last two, the correlations for the individual groups are adequately represented by these averages. However, as a provocative item for contemplation if confirmed in future research, it can be noted that

TABLE 6
MEAN NUMBER OF STATEMENTS FOUND UNACCEPTABLE

Condition	Pro-Con Presentation		Con-Pro Presentation	
	Pro	Con	Pro	Con
$1(X_1X_2O)$	1.28	.56	2.27	.33
$2(X_1X_2-O)$	1.39	.78	2.27	.44
$3(X_1-X_2O)$	1.31	.81	1.39	.95
$4(X_1-X_2-O)$	1.33	.39	1.33	.39

TABLE 7
MEAN NET NONACCEPTANCE SCORES

Conditions	Pro-Con Presentation	Con-Pro Presentation	Diff.	t	p*
$1(X_1X_2O)$	.72	1.94	−1.22	1.66	.10
$2(X_1X_2-O)$	.61	1.83	−1.22	1.91	.06
$3(X_1-X_2O)$	.50	.44	.06	.10	.92
$4(X_1-X_2-O)$	.94	.94	.00	.00	.50

* Two-tailed.

TABLE 8

COMPARISON OF MEAN NET NONACCEPTANCE SCORES[a]

Comparison	Pro-Con Presentation			Con-Pro Presentation			Combined
	Diff.	*t*	*p*	Diff.	*t*	*p*	*p*
1 > 2	+.11	.15	.44	−.11	.17	.57	>.20
3 > 1	−.22	.31	.64	+1.50	2.27	.012	<.05
3 > 2	−.11	.17	.57	+1.39	2.21	.014	<.05
3 > 4	−.44	.98	.84	+.50	.83	.21	>.20
4 > 2	+.33	.64	.26	+.89	1.53	.06	<.10
(1, 4)	.22	.38	.65	1.00	1.63	.10	

[a] See footnote for Table 2.

the correlations between Attitude and Recall seem to show systematic variance from substantial positive correlation under Condition 1 (.49 and .27) to substantial negative correlation under Condition 4 (−.51 and −.40).

As reported more fully elsewhere (Miller, 1957), certainty scores proved unrelated to the experimental conditions. Similarly, certainty of attitude did not correlate with amount of recalled information, nor did the usual curvilinear correlation between certainty and attitude-extremity appear. While the information test was not deliberately designed for the purpose, it was possible to order the wrong alternatives in the degree to which they implied conclusions favorable to the Pro or the Con argument, and to give each *S* a score indicating the preponderant directionality of his errors. This indirect attitude test (Campbell, 1950) correlated but .08 with the direct attitude score and showed no systematic relationship to the experimental conditions.

DISCUSSION

Recency. The clear-cut results for the attitude and recall measures clearly support the application of the Ebbinghaus curves to the field of persuasion. Nor would there seem to be any rival theory that could so economically predict the complex set of results. The ubiquity of the negatively accelerated forgetting curve in learning studies further supports the possibility of a thoroughly general recency principle, with the strength of recency being maximal for a long delay between first and second communication coupled with immediate measurement after the second communication, the strength of recency being minimal when the

two presentations are contiguous and the testing delayed. One study does not make a general principle, and the area of persuasion has been particularly frustrating to such attempts, but the antecedent probabilities plus this clear-cut experimental confirmation give promise. The recognition that a recency effect (such as the Ebbinghaus curves predict) can be a concomitant of, rather than an excluding alternative to, a primacy effect makes the postulation of this general principle not in the least incompatible with any of the previous literature on order effects. Indeed, the only other study containing both a question of order of arguments and measurement at various removes in time confirms some of the predictions of this principle, although that study is by today's standards so lacking in controls as to be uninterpretable (Bateman & Remmers, 1941).

Ebbinghaus' curve is simple and perhaps obvious, yet, as indicated, the simultaneous application of several such curves generates the nonobvious Jost (1897) law number 2, and even spontaneous recovery (Miller & Stevenson, 1936). Considering the length of time that the principle has been with us and its potential fertility, it is surprising that it has been so little used. One of the historical reasons is that with the observations of lack of forgetting during sleep and more rapid forgetting with similar materials during the interposed period, forgetting became something to be explained, and therefore attention was distracted from its use as an explanation. But even accepting an interference theory of forgetting, and even employing a psychological time scale (perhaps average interference rate during waking hours) the negatively accelerated curve has explanatory power and can be accepted at a molar level as a given for social psychology.

One of the most general findings in persuasion studies, involving repeated measurements over a long period of time, is that the change induced by persuasion dissipates with time. Similarly in everyday observations, successful remedial efforts and conversions are often followed by recidivism and backsliding. Usually such phenomena are interpreted as due to the competing effects of other communications occurring subsequent to the persuasive message, but under the aegis of Ebbinghaus' curves, one can interpret this decrement as a literal backsliding, due to the increasingly effective competition of the great bulk of pre-persuasion communications, as time since the persuasive effort increases. On the other hand, when one considers the volumes of communications that Ss have received prior to an experimental session, it becomes far from obvious that a 10-minute speech on a familiar topic could have any appreciable effect. Yet the most general finding in both published studies and in unpublished ones is that almost any speech will have an effect in its intended direction if the effect is measured immediately. If this fact needs explanation, as we think it does, it is found in the Ebbinghaus curves, which predict an extreme recency advantage under this condition. By the same token, the advantage rapidly dissipates. And if the speech is on a familiar topic, then even if no further communications were to be received, by next year the ten-minute speech will indeed be but a drop in the bucket.

Primacy Effects Upon Attitude Measures. Paradoxically enough, the postulation of this general recency principle improves the case for a general primacy principle. The experimental arena employed in primacy-recency studies so far has been most similar to our Condition 1, immediate testing after contiguous presentations. This is a condition that is not optimal to the manifestation of either primacy or recency. In the present study they cancel each other out under this condition. The inconsistent evidence obtained at this point by the half-dozen studies which Hovland et al. (1957) review and report thus could be interpreted, if one wished, as consistent with an always present primacy effect. The strength of this primacy effect would necessarily vary with the experimental conditions particular to each of the different studies and would frequently be masked by the recency effects also present. Testing this assumption would involve, in part, studies with sufficiently long delayed measurements to explore that end of the dimension represented by our Condition 2. It is not the purpose of this paper to argue the case for a general primacy effect but merely to point out that the evidence to date does not rule one out.

Would such a general primacy effect include learning phenomena as well as attitude phenomena? Here, again, test conditions such as Condition 2 are very rare. The trends in the available long delay studies favor primacy (Underwood, 1948), significantly so in one instance (Briggs, 1954). But in these studies, the first list learned was presented for more trials than the second, and none have employed as long a delay as one week. In our own recall data, no slightest hint of a net manifest or phenotypic primacy effect occurs. It seems clear that in the present study the primacy effect in the attitude measure is at very least much stronger than whatever hidden primacy effect might be latent in the recall data. The primacy effect for attitudes is thus not to be explained in terms of a primacy effect upon learning or memory of evidence or argument. Similarly, it cannot be explained in terms of such factors as set, attention, or reinforcement (Hovland et al., 1957), which assume that the second communication is less well listened to, less well assimilated content-wise, or subjected to stronger interference effects and, as a result, less well remembered. Our recall data are contrary to any such assumption. The primacy effect in attitude change seems related in the present instance to acceptance factors, as Hovland anticipated it might be (Hovland et al., 1953, p. 126). In this interpretation, the evidence on nonacceptance, rough though it is, mediates between the attitude and recall data. Coming first gives a statement no greater probability of being remembered, but does give it greater probability of being believed. We have a general tendency to find one side of an argument persuasive, providing we have not heard the other. Hearing it after we have heard the other, we are apt to be more critical and skeptical.

SUMMARY

The order in which opposing arguments were presented (Pro-Con and Con-Pro), the time interval between them (none and one week), and the time of testing (immediately after the second argument or one week after) were varied for eight groups, each tested once. For the attitude measure, a significant recency effect was found under the conditions most favorable to recency as predicted from the application of Ebbinghaus decay curves. A significant primacy effect was found under the conditions predicted to be least favorable to recency. For recall of information, only recency effects were found, these being strongest under conditions predicted to be most favorable.

REFERENCES

BAKER, P. C. Combining tests of significance in cross validation. *Educ. psychol. Measmt.*, 1952, **12**, 300–306.

BATEMAN, R. M., & REMMERS, H. H. A study of the shifting attitude of high school students when subjected to favorable and unfavorable propaganda. *J. soc. Psychol.*, 1941, **13**, 395–406.

BRIGGS, G. E. Acquisition, extinction, and recovery functions in retroactive inhibition. *J. exp. Psychol.*, 1954, **47**, 285–293.

CAMPBELL, D. T. The indirect assessment of social attitudes. *Psychol. Bull.*, 1950, **47**, 15–38.

CAMPBELL, D. T. Factors relevant to the validity of experiments in social settings. *Psychol. Bull.*, 1957, **54**, 297–312.

EBBINGHAUS, H. *Memory.* H. A. ROGER & C. E. BUS-SENIUS (Trans.) New York: Teachers College Columbia Univer., 1913. (Original, *Über das Gedächtnis*, Leipzig, 1885).

HOVLAND, C. I., JANIS, I. L., & KELLY, H. H. *Communi-cation and persuasion.* New Haven: Yale Univer. Press, 1953.

HOVLAND, C. I., MANDELL, W., CAMPBELL, ENID H., BROCK, T., LUCHINS, A. S., COHEN, A. R., Mc-GUIRE, W. J., JANIS, I. L., FEIERABEND, ROSALIND L., & ANDERSON, N. H. *The order of presentation in persuasion.* New Haven: Yale Univer. Press, 1957.

JOST, A. Die Assoziationsfestigkeit in ihrer Abhangig-keit von der Verteilung der Wiederholungen. *Zeitschrift für Psychologie und Physiologie der Sinnesorgane*, 1897, **14**, 436–472.

LUND, F. H. The psychology of belief: IV. The law of primacy in persuasion. *J. abnorm. soc. Psychol.*, 1925, **20**, 183–191.

MILLER, N. E., & STEVENSON, S. S. Agitated behavior of rats during experimental extinction and a curve of spontaneous recovery. *J. comp. Psychol.*, 1936, **21**, 205–231.

MILLER, N. Primacy versus recency: The changing relative effectiveness of two opposing communi-cations with the passage of time. Unpublished master's thesis, Northwestern Univer., 1957.

UNDERWOOD, B. J. Retroactive and proactive inhibition after five and forty-eight hours. *J. exp. Psychol.*, 1948, **38**, 29–38.

WELD, H. P., & ROFF, M. A study in the formation of opinion based upon legal evidence. *Amer. J. Psychol.*, 1938, **51**, 609–628.

Emotional versus Rational Communication

If the reader is from New England or from one of the Middle Atlantic states, he probably remembers a Democratic-sponsored TV commercial designed to capitalize on a Barry Goldwater quote in the 1964 presidential campaign. Goldwater, in a fit of pique, had been quoted as saying, "Sometimes I think this country would be better off if we could just saw off the Eastern seaboard and let it float out to sea." The Democratic spot reminded its Yankee viewers of the Republican Senator's provocative comment. A representation of the continental United States was shown being sawed in half at Mississippi. As the film displayed the Eastern seaboard floating off, the Goldwater comment was heard droning in the background.

Another TV commercial by the Democrats may have had an even grander nettling effect. The reader may recall the compelling film clip which showed a little girl plucking petals from a daisy, while in the background a male voice somberly counted down to zero. As the last petal disappeared, and the count reached zero, an atomic explosion filled the screen. At that point the voice of the President was heard saying, "These are the stakes. To make a world in which all of God's children can live, or go into the dark. We must either love each other, or we must die." With that, the announcer's voice returned, urging the viewers to vote for President Johnson, and intoning, "The stakes are too high for you to stay home."

There was also the controversy stirred up by the Republican film documentary *Choice*. The film, sponsored by a group with the intriguing name "Mothers for a Moral America," was intended to raise the question of moral decay in this country. Even before it could be formally released to the public, it aroused such intense emotional reaction and controversy that it was withdrawn and its scheduled bookings canceled.

Is this the usual reaction to an emotional persuasive appeal? Not at all. Many people defended the 1964 political communications as clever, imaginative propaganda, deftly designed to turn voters from one party to the other. Others vehemently condemned the communications as unfair and unethical. Bernard Rubin, a political scientist at Boston University, comments in his recent book, *Political Television:*

> In 1964, the campaign opened a Pandora's box, and out poured the hit-them-below-the-belt productions that demean democratic standards. In that campaign both major parties appear to have erred seriously. In politics, as in sports, it is not always whether you win or lose that counts; most important is how you play with peoples' emotions and sensibilities and capacities to reason.[1]

In contrast to the "emotional" appeals in the '64 election, at one time or another most of us have been exposed to the "rational" appeals for money, physical checkups, or just plain sympathy, emanating from several of the public-supported charitable organizations. Many of the communications of the American Cancer Society are examples of rational appeals. They assert persuasively, using simple and concise arguments, the "facts that may help you save your life." Some immediate evidence of their impact is the knowledge that few among us cannot name most of cancer's "seven danger signals."

Other persuasive communications may combine the emotional with a rational tack, hoping thereby to accentuate the unique advantages of each.

Which type of appeal is more effective—rational or emotional? A study by George W. Hartmann attempted to answer this question. Although Hartmann's study is a highly engaging one, his results are not conclusive.[2] The study's great value lies in the novel and interesting field situation with which Hartmann chose to explore the problem. It is for this reason that the paper is reprinted here—to provide an imaginative model for future research on this subject.

---

[1] Quoted from Rubin, B. *Political television.* Belmont, Calif.: Wadsworth, 1967. P. 187. By permission of the author and the publisher.

[2] Hartmann's results show the greater efficacy of the emotional over the rational appeal. There is some support for this finding in a later study by Menefee and Granneberg, which attempted to change students' opinions about United States foreign policy. An experiment by Knower, however, shows that sometimes a rational can be more effective than an emotional appeal. Obviously, source and audience factors play an important part in determining which type of communication will be more effective. Other factors may also increase or decrease the potency of one or the other appeal. Sears and Freedman, for example, have found that novel arguments are more persuasive than familiar ones, even when the novelty is implied and not real. Weiss, Rawson, and Pasamanick have shown how argument strength and manifest anxiety can interact to influence persuasibility. These are all factors which could affect the potency of an emotional or rational communication. Menefee, S. C., & Granneberg, A. G. Propaganda and opinions on foreign policy. *J. soc. Psychol.,* 1940, **11**, 393–404.

Knower, F. H. Experimental studies of changes in attitudes: I. A study of the effect of oral argument on changes of attitudes. *J. soc. Psychol.*, 1935, **6,** 315–347. Sears, D. O., and Freedman, J. L. Effects of expected familiarity with arguments upon opinion change and selective exposure. *J. Pers. soc. Psychol.*, 1965, **2,** 420–426. Weiss, R. F., Rawson, H. E., & Pasamanick, B. Argument strength, delay of argument, and anxiety in the 'conditioning' and 'selective learning' of attitudes. *J. abnorm. soc. Psychol.*, 1963, **67,** 157–165.

Reprinted from Journal of Abnormal and Social Psychology, 1936, Vol. 31, pp. 99–114, by permission of APA.

A FIELD EXPERIMENT ON THE COMPARATIVE EFFECTIVENESS OF "EMOTIONAL" AND "RATIONAL" POLITICAL LEAFLETS IN DETERMINING ELECTION RESULTS *

By GEORGE W. HARTMANN[1]

THE EMERGENCE OF POLITICAL PSYCHOLOGY

POLITICAL psychology as a separate branch of scientific inquiry is all but non-existent. As an art or practice, however, it has long ranked among the essentials of statecraft and is now a powerful and flourishing factor in the intricate world of affairs. Dictatorships and democracies make different, but apparently equally extensive, use of it in the process of molding public opinion and shaping attitudes. Like all technologies, political psychology may be employed for a variety of ends—it is a "tool" skill for attaining efficiently the goals established by some sort of systematic or unformulated political philosophy.

By the very nature of the field which gives it its name, political psychology is bound to have close relations with advertising and salesmanship, two regions of modern commercial life in which applied psychology has been conspicuously influential. The practices of publicity, propaganda, and intentional indoctrination are the very life-blood of political activity and other "institutional" behavior—remove them and the human interests supporting even the worthiest of movements lose most of their power to affect the course of group conduct or even to maintain their own coherence. He who lacks control over the required stimuli cannot obtain the desired responses.

Despite the serious need for an organized corpus of knowledge about political psychology—which in this generation of large-scale "conflict" promises to become the most important single division of social psychology—the phrase itself is barely found in current usage. The available information and techniques comprising it

---

[1] Performed while serving as a post-doctoral Fellow of the Advanced School of Education, Teachers College, Columbia University.

are loosely distributed in incoördinated fragments among experienced politicians, reflective journalists, and copy-writers, curious social scientists and an occasional laboratory man whose versatility or heterodoxy have allowed him to be sensitive to a broader range of interests. This is a strange circumstance when one recalls that American political parties, "machines" and individual candidates annually spend unascertained millions either to get or to hold public office with its associated benefits. A substantial fraction of this sum is undoubtedly sheer waste, not only from the standpoint of positive social gain, but even from the point of view of the seekers for power, irrespective of motive. If the direct and indirect expenditures involved in incessant campaigning were correctly totalled, they would probably approach in the aggregate the amount spent on public education in the United States. To enhance the efficiency of the latter process we have developed an army of educational psychologists and allied specialists, but neither the professions nor the universities recognize such an individual as the "political psychologist."

However, if psychologists on the basis of Strong's law can recommend that the small business man spread his modest budget for a little advertising over a number of periodicals rather than concentrating all in one journal, why should they not be able to guide a minority political party in using its limited funds to secure the maximum number of votes?[2] The social utility in both cases may be low, but it is surely no lower in the competitive political field of a democracy than in the competitive business sphere of our economic system. The politician would like to know more exactly the relative vote-getting strength of an equal expenditure of time, money, and effort on newspaper, billboard, radio, personal interview, and speech-making publicity, but the psychologist has given him little or no help in this or related matters.[3] So far as the writer knows, the present study is the first experimental[4] attempt to develop a *rapprochement* between the two fields of endeavor on other than insecure laboratory analogies.

[2] The Psychological Corporation through its national network of regional representatives is ideally organized to do such work.

[3] Perhaps an exception should be made of W. H. Wilke's "An experimental comparison of the speech, the radio and the printed page as propaganda devices". Archives of Psychology, 1934, No. 169.

[4] "Experimental" at least in the sense that deliberate intervention in a pre-election situation was planned. This distinguishes it from the post hoc researches of the type reported by Stuart Rice in his Quantitative Methods in Politics, Knopf, 1928.

WILL "APPEALS TO REASON" OR APPEALS TO THE EMOTIONS WIN MORE VOTES?

Both Gestalt theory and the doctrine of the "total situation" have shown that the capacity of apparently "identical" stimuli to evoke certain desired responses is dependent upon the setting, context, or "manner" in which they occur. Will an appeal, request, or command to vote for a certain party, policy, issue, or individual be more influential when it accompanies or follows a logical exposition of the case or when it appears with or after an emotional approach to the unanalyzed existing loyalties of the voter? The question as phrased implies an extreme dichotomy and opposition between the two types of mental process, whereas it is more likely that the real "contrast" is between two appeals containing various combinations of rationality and emotionality. The contrast here proposed is between a complex fusion of excitement, resentment, vague enthusiasms, strongly aroused fears and hopes, and a calm, orderly, and restrained presentation of either concrete proposals or abstract objectives. It does not take a high degree of psychological sophistication to bet (other things being equal) on the greater strength of the "emotional" attack with any random sample of the American population. However, it is important to remember that this prediction rests exclusively upon theoretical and empirical considerations, and not upon the measured findings of any deliberately devised experiment on the problem of political behavior under complex motivation. It is this kind of confirmation which the investigation here reported seeks to supply.[5]

THE 1935 ELECTION SITUATION IN PENNSYLVANIA

The possibility of a really effective test was provided by the local and state elections held in Pennsylvania on November 6, 1935. At the time, many municipal and county offices were to be filled, as well as two important state-wide judgeships. Because it met certain extraneous considerations, such as ease of access for the experimenter, the use of voting machines, which are generally believed to enhance, if they do not guarantee, the accuracy of the

---

[5] Similar researches could be built around such pairings as the relative effectiveness of constructive vs. destructive political appeals, emphasis upon "ideas" versus personalities, the use of praise and blame, the strength of group vs. self interests, material vs. "spiritual" incentives, and even the specific advantages of placards with and without the portraits of candidates. Our existing knowledge of these matters is exceedingly shaky.

poll, etc., the city of Allentown in Lehigh county was chosen as the scene of operations. For a similar variety of reasons the Socialist party in that community was made the beneficiary of the special appeals whose relative potency was being measured. The local Democratic and Republican parties were so closely matched that any publicity which would have favored one rather than the other would have created an intolerably delicate situation for an experimenter whose motives could hardly have been made clear or acceptable to a suspicious populace.[6] The Socialist party, on the other hand, was admirably suited to this purpose, since it was universally agreed that its candidates were not likely to win in this area; its exaltation of principles and ideals over individual standard bearers made possible more sharply defined contrasts without the danger of wounding personal feelings.

PREPARATION OF THE MOTIVATING STIMULI

The next task was the construction of the contrasting leaflets. This was much harder than anticipated because a search through Socialist propaganda "literature" gave types of printed appeals which were too mixed and "impure" in style, content, and length to meet the prescribed conditions. Consequently, the experimenter wrote the texts for three pairs of emotional and rational leaflets of the desired brevity. These were submitted to thirty rank-and-file adults in Allentown; the pair finally used was the pair overwhelmingly adopted by them as the most "liked". Inspection showed that the rejected leaflets had a more involved sentence structure, heavier vocabulary burden, and lower persuasiveness than those retained. Six competent psychologists agreed that in the pair finally selected, one—the academic "test" involving some reflective judgment—was predominantly "reasonable" in character, and the other—an intimate family letter—mainly "sentimental".

Five thousand copies of each of the two appeals were printed on heavy white paper in identical typography in the form of a four-page (one sheet folded) leaflet, the cover pages bearing the titles, "Try this test on yourself" (= rational) and "Will you answer this letter?" (= emotional), respectively. The two inside pages are reproduced below. The last or back page simply bore a straightforward list of the party candidates with the respective city, county, and state offices opposite their names.

---

[6] The present writer was the 1935 Socialist candidate whose vote appears in the tables below. This union of psychologist and "politician" explains how the present study came into being.

You've heard of intelligence tests, haven't you? Well, we have a little examination right here which we are sure you will enjoy taking, even if you didn't care much for school when you were a youngster. The beauty of this test is that you can score it yourself without any teacher to tell you whether you passed or failed.

This is how it works. First read each one of the seven statements printed below. If you *approve* the idea as it stands, *underline* the word AGREE; if you *disapprove* of the idea, underline the word DISAGREE. Simple, isn't it? All right, then. Get your pencil ready. All set? Go!

1. We would have much cheaper electric light and power if this industry were owned and operated by the various governmental units for the benefit of all the people. AGREE—DISAGREE.

2. No gifted boy or girl should be denied the advantages of higher education just because his parents lack the money to send him to college. AGREE—DISAGREE.

3. The Federal Government should provide to all classes of people opportunity for complete insurance at cost against accident, sickness, premature death and old age. AGREE—DISAGREE.

4. All banks and insurance companies should be run on a non-profit basis like the schools. AGREE—DISAGREE.

5. Higher income taxes on persons with incomes of more than $10,000 a year should be levied immediately. AGREE—DISAGREE.

6. The only way most people will ever be able to live in modern sanitary homes is for the government to build them on a non-profit basis. AGREE—DISAGREE.

7. Many more industries and parts of industries should be owned and managed co-operatively by the producers (all the workers) themselves. AGREE—DISAGREE.

Have you answered them all? Fine. Now go back and count the number of sentences with which you AGREED. Then count the number with which you DISAGREED. *If the number of agreements is larger than the number of disagreements, you are at heart a Socialist*—whether you know it or not!

Now that you have tested yourself and found out how much of a Socialist you really are, *why don't you try voting for the things you actually want?* The Republicans and Democrats don't propose to give these things to you, because a mere look at their records will show that they are opposed to them. Do you get the point?

HELP BUILD THE AGE OF PLENTY!

VOTE: SOCIALIST X

Allentown, Pennsylvania
November 1, 1935

Dear Mother and Father:

We youngsters are not in the habit of giving much thought to serious things. You have often told us so and we admit it.

But while we like to play football and have a good time dancing and cause you a lot of amusement as well as worry with our "puppy loves," we sometimes think long and hard. You ought to know what many of us young folks are quietly saying to ourselves.

Our future as American citizens in 1940 looks dark. We want jobs—and good jobs, too—so that we can help in the useful work of the world. But we know that many of our brightest high-school and college graduates find it absolutely impossible to get any kind of employment. We also know that this condition is not temporary, but that it will last as long as we stick to harmful ways of running business, industry and government.

We want to continue our education, but we haven't the heart to ask you to make that sacrifice. With Dad working only part-time on little pay and Mother trying to make last year's coat and dress look in season, we feel we ought to pitch in and help keep the family's neck above water. But we can't. The world as it is now run has no use for us.

Many of our teachers know what is wrong, although we can see that most of them are afraid to say what they really think. Luckily, the text-books and school magazines keep us in touch with new ideas, and we have learned how to read between the lines of the ordinary newspaper. Please don't be frightened if we tell you what we have decided!

We young people are becoming Socialists. We have to be. We can't be honest with ourselves and be anything else. *The Socialist Party is the only party which is against all wars*—and we have learned from our history courses what awful wars have taken place under both Republicans and Democrats. We refuse to be slaughtered (like Uncles Bob and Charles were in 1918) just to make profits for ammunition manufacturers.

The Socialist Party seeks to create a world in which there will be no poverty. In our science classes we learn how power machinery and other modern inventions make it possible for all of us to have enough of all the goods and services we need. Yet look at our town with its unpainted shacks, suffering parents, half-starved children! We might have everything, but we continue to live on next to nothing.

It is all so unnecessary. You have had to lead a poor workingman's life, because you and most of the workers and farmers of this country have regularly voted for either the Republican or Democratic parties, between which there is no real difference. These old machines are not for us.

The youth of 1935 want to Build a Better America, in which there will be no poverty, no fear of unemployment, no threat of war. We ask you to follow the lead of the Socialist Party this year because that is the most direct way for you to *help hasten the day when Peace and Plenty and lasting Prosperity will be the lot of all men.* Good parents such as you desire these things for us. But we can never have them as long as you are controlled by your old voting habits.

We are profoundly earnest about this. Our generation cannot enjoy the beauty and justice of the *New America* if you block our highest desires. There was a time when you too were young like us. We beg you in the name of those early memories and spring-time hopes to *support the Socialist ticket in the coming elections!*

Your Sons and Daughters

VOTE: | SOCIALIST [X] |

COMPOSITION OF THE TESTING POPULATION

Having settled upon the differential stimuli, the next step was the mapping out of the city into experimental and control areas. The variations in the size of the wards, density of population, assessed real-estate valuation, previous voting habits, and presumptive socio-economic status made the problem of establishing "comparable" groups unexpectedly difficult. While it is not pretended that all the obstacles were overcome, a feasible apportionment consisted in matching wards 2, 9, and 10 (= the emotional) with wards 3, 4, 5, and 7 (= the rational); the remaining twelve wards (there are nineteen in all) were simple "controls". The two experimental regions consequently had the nature of adjacent islands in a large control sea. Table I contains some of the relevant data concerning these three areas which may be used in interpreting the results.

APPLICATION OF THE STIMULUS PATTERNS

The stimulation plan consisted in distributing the two sets of leaflets in their assigned districts so that every family residing therein would be affected. The distributors were interested adults, all party members, who discharged their task by giving the recipient the leaflet with a polite request that it be read when convenient. If no one was at home to receive the leaflet in this manner, it was simply thrust under the door. About one-half of the prospective voters was given the leaflet in person; the other half presumably found it upon returning home. The material was all distributed between Monday and Thursday of the week preceding Election Day. Apart from a few radio talks, which affected the entire city uniformly, no other campaign activity or prose- lytizing was carried on during this season.

RESULTING CHANGES IN THE PROPORTION OF VOTES RECEIVED IN THREE AREAS

The reaction to such stimulation with a specific purpose can be tested only at the ballot-box, *i.e.*, the final measure of belief or conviction is the readiness and willingness to act. Here we need to know not only the present vote, but also the base-line or refer- ence vote of the preceding year. This has to be calculated in terms of percentages because of the fluctuating participation of the elec- torate in successive years. Schematically, a clear-cut check would be provided if in 1934 the Socialist vote in Allentown as a whole were 4 per cent of the total for all parties and if in 1935 it were 5 per cent in the rational wards, 6 per cent in the emotional wards, and 3 per cent in the control wards (assuming statistically reliable differences). This comparison made it necessary to contrast figures for the state-wide "heads of the tickets" which in 1934 were the governor and in 1935 the judge of the Supreme Court. Other offices fluctuate slightly from the figures for the party can- didates for these leading positions. Table I contains the neces- sary data for an appraisal of the effect of the two kinds of propaganda.

ANALYSIS OF THE TABULAR RECORD

The first item to be noted is that the total vote cast increased by 3,594, or 16.69 per cent, from 21,533 in 1934 to 25,127 in 1935. This decided increase in public participation is a fact which com- plicates the remaining calculations. The official Allentown regis- tration list contained 34,424 names—17,236 Democrats, 15,001 Republicans, and 187 Socialists. The Socialists polled about three and one-half times as many ballots as they had registered adherents, while the other two parties received from two-thirds to four-fifths of their overt registration. This is a common American

GEORGE W. HARTMANN

TABLE I

COMPARATIVE INCREASE IN VOTING BEHAVIOR UNDER DIFFERENTIAL STIMULATION

WARD	VOTE FOR GOVERNOR, 1934			VOTE FOR SUPREME COURT JUDGE, 1935			ASSESSED VALUATION PER CAPITA	INHABITANTS PER ACRE
	Democrat	Republican	Socialist	Democrat	Republican	Socialist		
Rational								
3	334	378	4	518	496	14	$1,663.64	32.51
4	402	347	10	374	381	8	2,786.19	44.08
5	283	209	14	320	321	19	3,094.01	40.70
7	484	556	20	575	650	24	1,478.73	41.40
Total	1553	1490	48	1787	1848	65	2,070.12 (Mean)	38.44 (Mean)
Per cent of Party	14.58	14.56	9.62	14.63	15.08	9.95		
Raw increase				234	358	17		
Percentage increase				15.07	24.03	35.42		
Emotional								
2	497	311	30	541	302	33	1,581.26	29.44
9	613	284	16	666	337	29	851.69	43.89
10	1188	623	64	1282	828	103	615.82	38.37
Total	2308	1218	110	2489	1467	165	871.72 (Mean)	37.28 (Mean)
Per cent of Party	21.32	11.90	22.04	20.37	11.97	25.27		
Raw increase				186	249	55		
Percentage increase				8.08	20.44	50.00		

TABLE I—Continued.

WARD Control	VOTE FOR GOVERNOR, 1934			VOTE FOR SUPREME COURT JUDGE, 1935			ASSESSED VALUATION PER CAPITA	INHABITANTS PER ACRE
	Democrat	Republican	Socialist	Democrat	Republican	Socialist		
1	502	408	25	512	422	39	$941.34	11.82
6	591	177	23	782	114	18	624.80	15.97
8	1383	1371	101	1635	1835	110	721.53	24.06
11	1264	2358	28	1430	2648	47	1,202.87	20.23
12	605	419	51	665	606	49	1,089.54	3.36
13	748	1206	19	730	1399	22	1,264.51	18.83
14	577	208	48	626	277	64	704.56	6.35
15	507	436	25	551	472	32	1,021.68	2.01
16	341	186	13	468	268	22	556.76	4.85
17	160	408	1	167	428	2	2,380.04	2.24
18	67	158	—	83	171	1	447.78	10.50
19	200	190	7	291	303	17	773.89	13.42
	6945	7525	341	7940	8943	423	946.19 (Mean)	7.58 (Mean)
Per cent of Party Total	64.30	73.54	68.34	65.00	72.96	64.78	1,088.08 (City Mean)	10.17 (City Mean)
Raw increase				995	1418	82		
Percentage increase				14.33	15.86	24.05		
Party Total	10,801	10,233	499	12,216	12,258	653		
Per cent of all ballots	50.16	47.52	2.32	48.62	48.78	2.60		
Raw increase				1415	2025	154		
Percentage increase				13.10	19.79	30.86		

phenomenon, since economic discretion probably causes many Socialist sympathizers to enroll on the other lists. Even in the nearby city of Reading, which has had Socialist administrators and consequently greater party prestige, the Socialist vote normally trebles its registration.

The second fact to be observed is that the Socialist vote in Allentown as a whole (and even in the control wards where there was no definite "activity") rose proportionately more than did that of the other parties.[7] With about 17 per cent more general participation in 1935 than in 1934, the total Socialist vote increased 30.86 per cent, the Republican 19.79 per cent, and the Democrat 13.10 per cent, indicating a relative loss for the last party despite an absolute gain. The crucial detail for our purpose is that the Socialist vote in the "emotional" wards rose 50 per cent, in the "rational" 35.42 per cent, and in the control 24.05 per cent—all differences large enough to be reliable even though no single adequate measures of this are applicable. This is wholly in harmony with the predicted outcomes and is a gratifying confirmation of the general hypothesis. The relations may be seen more clearly from an inspection of Figure 1.

Although the use of percentages rather than absolute figures may create a faulty emphasis, these diagrams nevertheless portray best the main finding of this study, viz., that specific "revealed" propaganda definitely accelerates a tendency already present. This general "secular" trend, of course, may in turn be due to widespread contributory propaganda of a more diffuse sort.

The efficacy of these two leaflets may be brought out more fully by comparing the actual with the predicted increases of each party's total vote in the various regions under consideration. This has been done in Table II.

If the $\frac{\text{Actual}}{\text{Expected}}$ ratio is 1.00, this means that the two values coincide; if it is less it means that the party involved obtained less than its proportionate share; if more than 1.00, the party affected gained "unduly". Since they are based upon the same raw data, these computations tell essentially the same story con-

---

[7] Does this mean that the larger the total participation in balloting, the greater will be the relative minority vote? Is it not possible that the customary non-voters are more plastic in their political convictions, and that they contain a proportionately larger number of protest and opposition voters who usually refrain from exercising the franchise because of a sense of futility? In this case, only severe social crises will bring them out. Cf. the extraordinarily high rate of suffrage utilization in Germany from 1918 to 1933.

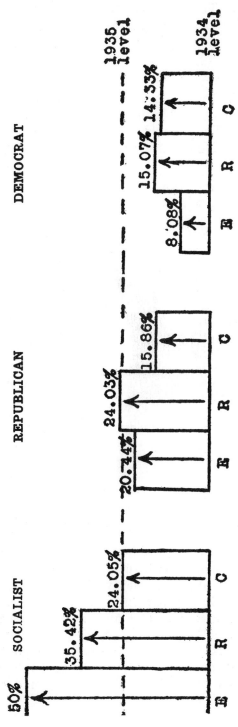

FIGURE I.—Rough schema indicating differential gains in voting preference under various types of stimulation. Although all parties received more votes in 1935 than in 1934, the Socialists gained relatively more in the areas where "emotional," (E) and "rational," (R) appeals were used; (C) stands for "control" district.

veyed by Figure 1. The increase in the Socialist vote in the "rational" and "emotional" areas was about two or three times, respectively, its probable gain if these stimuli had been omitted.

SOME NECESSARY PRECAUTIONS AND CORRECTIONS

In order to correct for the inevitable exaggerative effect which such phrases as "per cent of gain" evidently produce, Table III has been prepared. This should effectively dispel the spurious impression of a "landslide" suggested by some types of comparison.

TABLE II
HOW THE THREE PARTIES FARED IN THREE DIFFERENTLY TREATED AREAS

Party	District	1934 Vote	1935 Vote	Expected Increase	Actual Increase	A-E	A/E
Socialist	Rational	48	65	8	17	9	2.13
	Emotional	110	165	18	55	37	3.06
	Control	341	423	57	82	25	1.44
	Entire City	499	653	83	154	71	1.86
Democrat	Rational	1553	1787	259	234	—25	.94
	Emotional	2303	2489	384	186	—198	.48
	Control	6945	7940	1159	995	—164	.86
	Entire City	10801	12216	1803	1415	—388	.78
Republican	Rational	1490	1848	249	358	109	1.44
	Emotional	1218	1467	203	249	46	1.23
	Control	7525	8943	1256	1418	138	1.13
	Entire City	10233	12258	1708	2025	317	1.17

Note: The "Expected Increase" column is obtained by multiplying the 1934 vote by the coefficient of increase in public participation, viz., 16.69.

TABLE III
PER CENT WHICH SOCIALIST VOTE IS OF TOTAL FOR ALL PARTIES IN DIFFERENT SECTIONS OF ALLENTOWN

	1934	1935
Control wards.	2.30	2.44
Rational wards.	1.55	1.76
Emotional wards.	3.03	4.00
Entire City.	2.32	2.60

If we select the most favorable showing—that made in the "emotional" district—we see that the effect of the leaflet has been to make one voter out of every twenty-five support the Socialist ticket where before only one person in thirty-three had done so. Had no leaflets been distributed at all, the entire Socialist vote presumably would have been 619 (*i.e.*, 499 plus 499 x 24.05, the control rate of increase); if the superior emotional leaflet had been spread evenly throughout the town, the probable total would have been 749 (*i.e.*, 499 plus 499 x .50); actually, under the mixed conditions obtaining where most of the community was the "control", the total was 653.

Because of the selective treatment which these leaflets received, they may be presumed to be above the average of their kind. Nevertheless, even these relatively good broadsides have an "efficiency" of but one-half of 1 per cent, since it took 10,000 leaflets to produce 72 additional votes in the emotional and rational wards combined. Moreover, about half of these added votes were "in the bag" anyhow because of the general situation. It may be estimated that one person in 200 who would not otherwise have voted Socialist was impelled to do so by virtue of the motivation directly traceable to these leaflets. Since it took an absolute commercial minimum of one cent per leaflet for printing and delivery, it will be seen that even this cheap form of legitimate political propaganda costs about three dollars for each additional party voter it secures.[8] To be sure, this stimulation probably has some deferred propaganda value in the sense that cumulative increments at some later date may be made to function more readily because of the "summation of stimuli" involved.

CONFIRMATORY POST-ELECTION INTERVIEWS

About two weeks after Election Day, personal interviews were arranged with 45 householders (22 men and 23 women) chosen at random from different streets in the rational and emotional districts. It seemed desirable to supplement the objective record of the polls with some qualitative clues as to the way in which the personalities of the voters had been affected by these appeals. Four simple questions were asked of each interviewee with the results shown in Table IV.

Incomplete as this evidence is, it shows plainly the greater impressive and retentive effect of the sentimental appeal. It is axiomatic that a piece of "printed salesmanship" must be attended to and remembered before the message it contains can achieve the end desired by the purveyor. This the emotional leaflet did much more decisively than the rational one, even though both produced more pure "good will" than immediately significant action. As soon as reasonable certainty was attained on these points, the interviews were discontinued, since additional cases did not promise to yield any new information.

---

[8] Cf. the expenditure estimate given in the third paragraph of this article. Congressional and legislative limitations on campaign expenditures are notoriously ineffective because of the many exemptions provided, the failure to include "voluntary" services, etc. The full cost per major party vote is many times that of the minority vote.

SOME WEAKNESSES AND OBJECTIONS

Although this study bears the formal pattern of the familiar parallel-group experiment, it rests upon an exceedingly imperfect matching of the contrasted populations. The mean density of population in the emotional and rational wards was purposely kept practically identical, but the latter region has more than twice the per capita real-estate valuation of the former (tax exempt property is excluded in these calculations). In matching for one

TABLE IV

RESPONSES OBTAINED IN FOLLOW-UP INTERVIEWS FOR DETERMINING THE IMPRESSIVE-NESS OF TWO TYPES OF CAMPAIGN LITERATURE

Question (given orally)	Reply
1. Do you remember receiving any Socialist literature recently?	29 out of 45 answered "Yes"
2. What was its nature?	8 out of 12 in the emotional wards said, "An open letter"; only 7 out of 33 in the rational wards knew it was a pamphlet or folder, and only one said it contained "questions"
3. Did the literature you read influence you to vote for any Socialist candidates?	Four said it made them "split" their votes for the first time; no effect on others
4. What did you think of the Socialist literature you saw?	24 said they were "not interested"; 6 said it contained "good principles"; 4 said "very good"; 2 said they would never read any Socialist material; 1 said it was "too deep, he couldn't understand it"; 8 others expressed some degree of favor

factor, we have unmatched for another. Are not the preëxisting attitudes of prospective Socialist voters strongly affected by their economic status?

The answer, of course, is a qualified "Yes", but this does not mean that there is an inverse relation between receptivity to the Socialist appeal and financial well-being. Observation indicates that the correlation is zero or slightly positive. Both the well-to-do and the poor may be persuaded to vote Socialist, although they may respond differentially to a specific approach.[9] The control group occupies the same financial level as the "emotional" popula-

---

[9] It may be necessary to remind the reader that the Socialist vote does not come primarily from the "disinherited" or underprivileged. A glance at the returns from poverty-stricken areas, both urban and rural, shows this plainly. Socialist sympathizers in the universities are proportionately greater than among the general public; American labor unions are still strongly non-Socialist, if not anti-Socialist; and Dr. George Gallup of the American Institute of Public Opinion found that 82 per cent of the people now on relief voted Democratic in 1932.

tion, but because of the absence of stimulation no comparable voting increase occurred. To be sure, the rational group did not gain as much as the emotional one, but this was not due to its superior economic position—these people were simply bombarded with an inferior instrument.[10] Absolute assurance that this interpretation is correct can be obtained only by reversing the appeals in another community.

Admittedly, pure experimental conditions are hard to maintain in a study of this sort, but it is an unscientific counsel of despair to refrain from using to best advantage whatever approximations thereto one can achieve. Election results are not the outcomes of single stimulation—they resemble more a complex resultant of intricate forces. Thus, energetic Socialist propaganda would undoubtedly call forth more effort from the other parties, but that would probably occur only where they sensed a genuine threat to their position, which was not the case in this city.

CONCLUSIONS

There seems to be no escape from the decision that the emotional political appeal is a better vote-getting instrument than the rational approach, at least in the sense in which these terms describe the essential difference between the two leaflets reproduced above. The sentimental open letter integrates itself easily with such strong permanent central attitudes as parental affection and the desire for a "better life". It employs a familiar literary form, is concrete in imagery, "breathes sincerity", and is not obviously or even basically untrue. It is interesting because it digs deeply into the inner personality and links Socialism with some vital needs.

The "intelligence test", on the other hand, is straightforward, matter of fact, and unexpectedly manoeuvres the reader into an acknowledgment that he is more of a Socialist than he realizes.[11] Save for a faint inferiority feeling which this form may create, these features are positive advantages, although they evidently do not outweigh the factors of strength in the other leaflet. Thus

---

[10] As a matter of fact, the per capita valuation per resident is a misleading index to the apparent wealth of the rational group. These wards are in the downtown business section where rented apartments above the ground floors are the commonest type of housing. The buildings are largely owned by persons living in the control wards.

[11] The seven propositions which appear in this appeal are items favored by a definite majority of sample Pennsylvania populations. Hence, the high probability of obtaining a preponderance of "Agrees" from a new random selection. Otherwise, they would have been to risky to use. With many individuals, of course, these statements definitely prejudice the case "against" rather than "for".

GEORGE W. HARTMANN

the ancient educational maxims of the Herbartians are vindicated anew in the field of political psychology! Those ideas will be most readily assimilated by the voter which fit in with his present "apperceptive mass", which are joined with some prepotent wants, which meet him on his own level and lead him on from where he is.

From a certain point of view, this investigation may be considered a research in "political pedagogy". Thorndike has repeatedly insisted that "education is a process of changing human beings for the better", and much of current educational technique consists in discovering and applying ways for making these modifications more efficiently. Political propaganda for good or ill does more to influence people's knowledge and attitudes in the field of the social sciences than all the formal educational apparatus of our time. Since so many desirable social changes are not made because the public refuses to admit that they would constitute an improvement, it is important for educational statesmanship to know what *means* of persuasion will increase the probability of realizing these *ends*. The present problem is just one aspect of this larger issue.

SUMMARY

During the election campaign of 1935, the city of Allentown, Pennsylvania, was divided for experimental purposes into three types of wards: 1, an "emotional" area in which all the resident adults received leaflets written in vigorous advertising style urging support of the Socialist ticket; 2, a "rational" region, in which a more academic type of persuasion was used; and 3, a control district where nothing was distributed. The increase in the minority party vote was greatest in the emotional wards, next largest in the rational wards, and lowest in the control wards. These facts may constitute a significant beginning for an experimentally grounded political psychology and pedagogy.

Efficacy of Threat: The Fear Appeal

Up to this point we have only alluded to the motivational processes involved in opinion change. The study in Part I by Zimbardo, Weisenberg, *et al.* showed how psychological justification in the face of cognitive dissonance could effect opinion change. What are some other conditions which might motivate, or rouse, a person to change his opinions on a controversial issue?

Motivation connotes movement. A person pursues some goals and avoids others. Those he pursues and those he avoids are the product of a long history of experiences with rewards and punishments, satisfactions and dissatisfactions, incentives and deterrents. If, for example, an individual were confronted by Hartmann's emotional communication, designed to persuade him to vote Socialist, he would react to the appeal in accord with the satisfactions or dissatisfactions that would be forthcoming were he to comply, or were he not to comply.

Hovland, Janis, and Kelley depict the chain of responses evoked during exposure to an emotional communication as follows: [1]

$$C \longrightarrow E$$
$$(C+E) \longrightarrow R$$

This paradigm makes the assumption that two separate habits are acquired when an emotional communication succeeds in effecting behavioral compliance. First, content cues (C) in the communication arouse a heightened state of emotional tension (E). (Hartmann's communication accomplished this by threatening the voters with an increased likelihood of war and economic depression.) Second, the emotional tension is reduced by a reassuring recommendation (R) embedded in the communication. (In Hartmann's appeal, the reassuring recommendation was the advice to vote Socialist so as to reduce the likelihood of war and depression.) Hovland-Janis-Kelley think that this sequence of responses $(C \longrightarrow E \longrightarrow R)$ may "become a habitual chain, such that whenever a topic or subject matter similar

---

[1] Hovland, C. I., Janis, I. L., & Kelley, H. H. *Communication and persuasion.* New Haven, Conn.: Yale Univer. Press, 1953.

to that of the original communication comes to the focus of attention, the person will again experience emotional tension and will tend to think of the reassuring recommendation."[2]

We referred in the preceding section to the "rational" appeals emanating from the American Cancer Society. These appeals also fit the Hovland-Janis-Kelley paradigm. Consider the slogan, "Facts That May Help You Save Your Life." The content cue "save your life," has the effect of arousing emotion. The resulting tension is reduced by the reassuring recommendations in the communication that tell *how* "You can help protect yourself." The recommendations are simple and straightforward: (1) "A yearly physical examination is the best defense against cancer." (2) "For women, the simple and painless 'Pap' test is an annual 'must'." (3) "If you don't smoke cigarettes, *don't start*, if you do smoke, *stop*." (4) "Every adult should have a 'procto' exam as part of his annual checkup." (5) "Women should learn to examine their breasts monthly."[3]

Thus, the rational Cancer Society appeal initially has the effect of arousing minimal emotional tension, then reducing that tension by providing the recipient with a few short and simple rules to "save his life." Hartmann's emotional political communication followed a similar sequence. It began, "Our future as American citizens in 1940 looks dark" (E). It ended, "The youth of 1935 want to Build a Better America, in which there will be no poverty, no fear of unemployment, no threat of war. We ask you to follow the lead of the Socialist Party this year because that is the most direct way ... to ... Peace and Plenty and lasting Prosperity. . ." (R).

What would have been the effect of arousing greater tension? Had the threat of loss of life, or of poverty-unemployment-war, been over-emphasized, would a reassuring recommendation have been any more reinforcing? Would compliance have been greater? Or, would compliance have decreased as threat increased?

Most of the present-day research on the efficacy of threat in persuasion grows out of an experiment by Irving L. Janis and Seymour Feshbach.[4] The Janis and Feshback study used three different in-

---

[2] In the absence of a reassuring recommendation, with no provision made for alleviating the subject's discomfort, this would have the deleterious effect of leaving the hapless recipient in a heightened state of tension. Besides the obvious prediction that the persuasive appeal would probably fail, there is also a possibility that the subject might displace his negative affect onto the communicator.

[3] *Cancer and you.* Pamphlet 40MM–9/65–No. 2099. Amer. Cancer Soc., Massachusetts Division.

[4] Janis, I. L., & Feshbach, S. Effects of fear-arousing communications. *J. abnorm. soc. Psychol.*, 1953, **48**, 78–92.

tensities of fear appeal in a communication on dental hygiene. Results indicated that though all three forms were equally effective in teaching their factual content, the greatest conformity was to the position advocated in the "minimal" threat communication. The "moderate" threat communication was somewhat less effective. The "strong" fear appeal was the least effective for producing conformity to the recommended actions.

Janis and Feshbach took these results as support for the general hypothesis that communications which elicit a great deal of fear or anxiety tend to provoke a defensive reaction which then interferes with acceptance of the message. Hence, the greater the threat, the less opinion change in the direction advocated. This is a principle which, in the last decade, has often been cited without qualification. Only recently has it been asserted that the Janis-Feshbach finding may not be an unqualified generalization of what can happen when a person is confronted by a fear appeal.[5] The relationship "minimal threat-maximum compliance" is not always true.

Consider a more recent experiment on fear arousal by Fredric Powell.[6] Powell used civil defense communications to establish two levels of anxiety—"high" vs. "mild." Reasoning that people would be less likely to invoke defensive behavior when a threat was directed at a loved one than when it was directed at themselves, Powell concluded that a message which contains a strong fear appeal directed at a loved one should produce greater opinion change in the direction advocated than a message containing a mild fear appeal. His results provide strong support for this conclusion, thus yielding a relationship between threat and compliance diametrically opposite to that of Janis and Feshbach.

Similarly, when messages are attributed to a highly credible source, high fear produces more opinion change than mild fear.[7] And when the source of fear is independent of the content of the

[5]Leventhal, H. Fear communications in the acceptance of preventive health practices. *Bull. N.Y. Acad. Med.*, 1965, **41**, 1144–1168. Smith, M. B. Three textbooks: A special review. *J. exp. soc. Psychol.*, 1966, **2**, 114. McGuire, W. J. Attitudes and opinions. *Annu. Rev. Psychol.*, 1966, **17**, 484.

[6]Powell, F. A. The effects of anxiety-arousing messages when related to personal, familial, and impersonal referents. *Speech Monogr.*, 1965, **32**, 102–106.

[7]Hewgill, M. A., & Miller, G. R. Source credibility and response to fear-arousing communications. *Speech Monogr.*, 1965, **32**, 95–101. See also Miller, G. R. Studies on the use of fear appeals: A summary and analysis. *Central States Speech J.*, 1963, **14**, 117–124.

communication, high fear again results in greater attitudinal compliance than low.[8]

There are many other relevant studies. Some support the Janis-Feshbach minimal threat-maximum compliance relationship.[9] Others suggest a direct positive relationship between threat and compliance.[10, 11]

William J. McGuire, in a penetrating and insightful analysis of the threat-compliance problem has shown the relevance of an impressive mathematical model which he has developed to predict susceptibility to social influence.[12] McGuire's model is constructed primarily about two factors — reception and yielding. He argues that analyzing either factor, but not both, leads to the usual oversimplification about the relationship between influencibility and fear arousal.

If, for example, one only thinks about the role of *yielding* (to persuasion) as a mediator, one probably would predict a direct positive relationship. The more anxious a person is as a result of his having

---

[8] Simonson, N. R., & Lundy, R. M. The effectiveness of persuasive communication presented under conditions of irrelevant fear. *J. Communication*, 1966, **16**, 32–37.

[9] Haefner, D. P. Some effects of guilt-arousing and fear-arousing persuasive communications on opinion change. Unpublished doctoral dissertation, Univer. of Rochester, 1956. Nunnally, J., & Bobren, H. Variables governing the willingness to receive communications on mental health. *J. Pers.*, 1959, **27**, 38–46. Janis, I. L., & Terwilliger, R. F. An experimental study of psychological resistances to fear-arousing communications. *J. abnorm. soc. Psychol.*, 1962, **65**, 403–410. Kegeles, S. S. Some motives for seeking preventative dental care. *J. Amer. Dental Ass.*, 1963, **67**, 110–118. DeWolfe, A. S., & Governale, C. N. Fear and attitude change. *J. abnorm. soc. Psychol.*, 1964, **69**, 119–123.

[10] Berkowitz, L., & Cottingham, D. R. The interest value and relevance of fear-arousing communications. *J. abnorm. soc. Psychol.*, 1960, **60**, 37–43. Leventhal, H., & Niles, P. A field experiment on fear-arousal with data on the validity of questionnaire measures. *J. Pers.*, 1964, **32**, 459–479. Niles, P. The relationship of susceptibility and anxiety to acceptance of fear-arousing communications. Unpublished doctoral dissertation, Yale Univer., 1964. Insko, C. A., Arkoff, A., & Insko, V. M. Effects of high and low fear-arousing communication upon opinions toward smoking. *J. exp. soc. Psychol.*, 1965, **1**, 256–266. Leventhal, H., Singer, R., & Jones, S. Effects of fear and specificity of recommendation upon attitudes and behavior. *J. Pers. soc. Psychol.*, 1965, **2**, 20–29.

[11] Chu has found that although the advantage of strong arousal in a communication is more pronounced when the recommended solution is perceived as highly efficacious, effects achieved under mild arousal (though initially lower) are more resistant to counterpropaganda. Chu, G. C. Fear arousal, efficacy, and imminency. Mimeographed rep., Inst. for Communication Res., Stanford Univer., 1964.

[12] McGuire, W. J. Effectiveness of fear appeals in advertising. Research proposal submitted to the Amer. Advertising Found., 1963. McGuire, W. J. Personality and susceptibility to social influence. In E. F. Borgatta & W. W. Lambert (Eds.), *Handbook of personality theory and research*. Chicago: Rand-McNally, in press.

been threatened by a fear appeal, the more insecure he will be and the greater will be his lack of self-confidence, etc. Hence, the more anxiety, the more prone he will be to yield to persuasion. If, on the other hand, one considers only *receptivity,* one probably would predict a negative relationship. The more anxious a person is, the more he will tend to be withdrawn and preoccupied with his own problems. Distracted by his personal worries, he will not be highly receptive to persuasion. Thus, McGuire hypothesizes a nonmonotonic function for the threat (fear)-compliance relationship.[13] He predicts a negative relationship between anxiety and the reception mediator in the relatively high ranges of anxiety, while for low levels of initial concern he predicts that increased fear arousal enhances opinion change.[14]

The nonmonotonic relationship is an appealing one because of its applicability to a wide range of diverse human behavior. Lemming-like conformity is frowned upon in our culture, as is nonconformity. The extreme right wing is anathema, as is the extreme left. To be "too bright" is to be cursed, as is to be "dull." Youth is desired to infancy or old age. For most people, too much food, or too little, is dissatisfying. And on and on.

In the papers that follow we can trace the brief history of research on fear arousal in persuasion, starting with the monotonic relationship and ending with the nonmonotonic. The first paper is the classic Janis-Feshbach study. It has been the primary stimulus for most of the work in this area, and it still is often cited uncritically as evidence for a negative relationship between fear arousal and compliance. The second paper, by Howard Leventhal, reviews the author's own extensive research on this subject and introduces evidence for a more complex relationship between fear arousal and compliance.

---

[13] The nonmonotonic relationship is predicted for other variables as well. This point is amplified in Part III, pp. 201 ff.

[14] McGuire also predicts interactions with chronic level of anxiety, with concern over the issue, and with message complexity. He suggests that raising any of these three factors should have the effect of lowering the level of fear arousal that would be optimal for opinion change. McGuire, W. J. Attitudes and opinions. *Annu. Rev. Psychol.,* 1966, **17,** 484.

Reprinted from Journal of Abnormal and Social Psychology, 1953, Vol. 48, No. 1, pp. 78–92, by permission of Irving L. Janis and APA.

EFFECTS OF FEAR-AROUSING COMMUNICATIONS

IRVING L. JANIS AND SEYMOUR FESHBACH

I⊤ is generally recognized that when beliefs and attitudes are modified, learning processes are involved in which motivational factors play a primary role. Symbols in mass communications can be manipulated in a variety of ways so as to arouse socially acquired motives such as need for achievement, group conformity, power-seeking, and the more emotion-laden drives arising from aggression, sympathy, guilt, and anxiety.

The present experiment was designed to study the effects of one particular type of motive-incentive variable in persuasive communications, namely, the arousal of fear or anxiety by depicting potential dangers to which the audience might be exposed.[1] Fear appeals of this sort are frequently used to influence attitudes and behavior. For example, medical authorities sometimes try to persuade people to visit cancer detection clinics by pointing to the dangerous consequences of failing to detect the early symptoms of cancer; various political groups play up the threat of war or totalitarianism in an attempt to motivate adherence to their political program. Our interest in such attempts is primarily that of determining the conditions under which the arousal of fear is effective or ineffective in eliciting changes in beliefs, practices, and attitudes.

Implicit in the use of fear appeals is the assumption that when emotional tension is aroused, the audience will become more highly motivated to accept the reassuring beliefs or recommendations advocated by the communicator. But the tendency to accept reassuring ideas about ways and means of warding off anticipated danger may not always be the dominant reaction to a fear-arousing communication. Under certain conditions, other types of defensive reactions may occur which could give rise to highly undesirable effects from the standpoint of the communicator.

Clinical studies based on patients' reactions to psychiatric treatment call attention to three main types of emotional interference which can prevent a person from being influenced by verbal communications which deal with anxiety-arousing topics.

1. When a communication touches off intense feelings of anxiety, communicatees will sometimes fail to pay attention to what is being said. Inattentiveness may be a motivated effort to avoid thoughts which evoke incipient feelings of anxiety. This defensive tendency may be manifested by overt attempts to change the subject of conversation to a less disturbing topic. When such attempts fail and anxiety mounts to a very high level, attention disturbances may become much more severe, e.g., "inability to concentrate," "distractibility," or other symptoms of the cognitive disorganization temporarily produced by high emotional tension (4).

2. When exposed to an anxiety-arousing communication, communicatees will occasionally react to the unpleasant ("punishing") experience by becoming aggressive toward the communicator. If the communicator is perceived as being responsible for producing painful feelings, aggression is likely to take the form of rejecting his statements.

3. If a communication succeeds in arousing intense anxiety and if the communicatee's emotional tension is not readily reduced either by the reassurances contained in the communication or by self-delivered reassurances, the residual emotional tension may motivate defensive avoidances, i.e., attempts to ward off subsequent exposures to the

[1] This study was conducted at Yale University as part of a coordinated program of research on attitude and opinion change, financed by a grant from the Rockefeller Foundation. The attitude change research project is under the general direction of Professor Carl I. Hovland, to whom the authors wish to express their appreciation for many valuable suggestions concerning the design of the experiment. Special thanks are due to Dr. Isador Hirschfeld of New York City and Dr. Bert G. Anderson of the Yale Medical School for their helpful advice in connection with the preparation of the illustrated talks on dental hygiene. The authors also wish to thank Dr. S. Willard Price, Superintendent of Schools at Greenwich, Connecticut, and Mr. Andrew Bella, Principal of the Greenwich High School for their generous cooperation.

78

anxiety-arousing content. The experience of being temporarily unable to terminate the disturbing affective state elicited by a discussion of a potential threat can give rise to a powerful incentive to avoid thinking or hearing about it again; this may ultimately result in failing to recall what the communicator said, losing interest in the topic, denying or minimizing the importance of the threat.

The above reaction tendencies, while formulated in general terms, take account of three specific types of behavior observed during psychoanalytic or psychotherapeutic sessions (1, 2, 3). The first two refer to immediate reactions that often occur when a therapist gives an interpretation which brings anxiety-laden thoughts or motives into the patient's focus of awareness: (a) attention disturbances, blocking of associations, mishearing, evasiveness, and similar forms of "resistance"; and (b) argumentativeness, defiance, contempt, and other manifestations of reactive hostility directed toward the therapist. The third refers to certain types of subsequent "resistance," displayed during the later course of treatment, as a carry-over effect of the therapist's disturbing comments or interpretations.

Although the three types of defensive behavior have been observed primarily in clinical studies of psychoneurotic patients (whose anxiety reactions are generally linked with unconscious conflicts), it seems probable that similar reactions may occur among normal persons during or after exposure to communications which make them acutely aware of severe threats of external danger. Nevertheless, it remains an open question whether such sources of emotional interference play any significant role in determining the net effectiveness of fear-arousing material in mass communications, especially when the communications are presented in an impersonal social setting where emotional responses of the audience are likely to be greatly attenuated.

The present experiment was designed to investigate the consequences of using fear appeals in persuasive communications that are presented in an impersonal group situation. One of the main purposes was to explore the potentially adverse effects which might result from defensive reactions of the

sort previously noted in the more restricted situation of psychotherapy.

METHOD

The experiment was designed so as to provide measures of the effects of three different intensities of "fear appeal" in a standard communication on dental hygiene, presented to high school students. The influence of the fear-arousing material was investigated by means of a series of questionnaires which provided data on emotional reactions to the communication and on changes in dental hygiene beliefs, practices, and attitudes.

The Three Forms of Communication

A 15-minute illustrated lecture was prepared in three different forms, all of which contained the same essential information about causes of tooth decay and the same series of recommendations concerning oral hygiene practices. The three (recorded) lectures were of approximately equal length and were delivered in a standard manner by the same speaker. Each recording was supplemented by about 20 slides, which were shown on the screen in a prearranged sequence, to illustrate various points made by the speaker.

The three forms of the illustrated talk differed only with respect to the amount of fear-arousing material presented. Form 1 contained a strong fear appeal, emphasizing the painful consequences of tooth decay, diseased gums, and other dangers that can result from improper dental hygiene. Form 2 presented a moderate appeal in which the dangers were described in a milder and more factual manner. Form 3 presented a minimal appeal which rarely alluded to the consequences of tooth neglect. In Form 3, most of the fear-arousing material was replaced by relatively neutral information dealing with the growth and functions of the teeth. In all other respects, however, Form 3 was identical with Forms 1 and 2.

The fear appeals were designed to represent typical characteristics of mass communications which attempt to stimulate emotional reactions in order to motivate the audience to conform to a set of recommendations. The main technique was that of calling attention to the potential dangers that can ensue from nonconformity. For example, the Strong appeal contained such statements as the following:

> If you ever develop an infection of this kind from improper care of your teeth, it will be an extremely serious matter because these infections are really dangerous. They can spread to your eyes, or your heart, or your joints and cause secondary infections which may lead to diseases such as arthritic paralysis, kidney damage, or total blindness.

One of the main characteristics of the Strong appeal was the use of personalized threat-references explicitly directed to the audience, i.e., statements to the effect that "this can happen to you." The Moderate appeal, on the other hand, described the dangerous consequences of improper oral hygiene in a more factual way, using impersonal language.

In the Minimal appeal, the limited discussion of unfavorable consequences also used a purely factual style.

The major differences in content are summarized in Table 1, which is based on a systematic content analysis of the three recorded lectures. The data in this table show how often each type of "threat" was mentioned. It is apparent that the main difference between the Strong appeal and the Moderate appeal was not so much in the total frequency of threat references as in the variety and types of threats that were emphasized. The Minimal appeal, however, differed markedly from the other two in that it contained relatively few threat references, almost all of which were restricted to "cavities" or "tooth decay."

TABLE 1

CONTENT ANALYSIS OF THE THREE FORMS OF THE COMMUNICATION: REFERENCES TO CONSEQUENCES OF IMPROPER CARE OF THE TEETH

TYPE OF REFERENCE	FORM 1 (STRONG APPEAL)	FORM 2 (MODERATE APPEAL)	FORM 3 (MINIMAL APPEAL)
Pain from toothaches	11	1	0
Cancer, paralysis, blindness or other secondary diseases	6	0	0
Having teeth pulled, cavities drilled, or other painful dental work	9	1	0
Having cavities filled or having to go to the dentist	0	5	1
Mouth infections: sore, swollen, inflamed gums	18	16	2
Ugly or discolored teeth	4	2	0
"Decayed" teeth	14	12	6
"Cavities"	9	12	9
Total references to unfavorable consequences	71	49	18

One of the reasons for selecting dental hygiene as a suitable topic for investigating the influence of fear appeals was precisely because discussions of this topic readily lend themselves to quantitative and qualitative variations of the sort shown in Table 1. Moreover, because of the nature of the potential dangers that are referred to, one could reasonably expect the audience to be fairly responsive to such variations in content—the teeth and gums probably represent an important component in the average person's body image and, according to psychoanalytic observations, the threat of damage to the teeth and gums can sometimes evoke deep-seated anxieties concerning body integrity. In any case, by playing up the threat of pain, disease, and body damage, the material introduced in Form 1 is probably representative of the more extreme forms of fear appeals currently to be found in persuasive communications presented via the press, radio, television, and other mass media.

The fear appeals did not rely exclusively upon verbal material to convey the threatening consequences of nonconformity. In Form 1, the slides used to illustrate the lecture included a series of eleven highly realistic photographs which vividly portrayed tooth decay and mouth infections. Form 2, the Moderate appeal, included nine photographs which were milder examples of oral pathology than those used in Form 1. In Form 3, however, no realistic photographs of this kind were presented: X-ray pictures, diagrams of cavities, and photographs of completely healthy teeth were substituted for the photographs of oral pathology.

Subjects

The entire freshman class of a large Connecticut high school was divided into four groups on a random basis. Each of the three forms of the communication was given to a separate experimental group; the fourth group was used as a control group and was exposed to a similar communication on a completely different topic (the structure and functioning of the human eye). Altogether there were 200 students in the experiment, with 50 in each group.

The four groups were well equated with respect to age, sex, educational level, and IQ. The mean age for each group was approximately 15 years and there were roughly equal numbers of boys and girls in each group. The mean and standard deviation of IQ scores, as measured by the Otis group test, were almost identical in all four groups.

Administration of the Questionnaires

The first questionnaire, given one week before the communication, was represented to the students as a general health survey of high school students. The key questions dealing with dental hygiene were interspersed among questions dealing with many other aspects of health and hygiene.

One week later the illustrated talks were given as part of the school's hygiene program. Immediately after the end of the communication, the students in each group were asked to fill out a short questionnaire designed to provide data on immediate effects of the communication, such as the amount of information acquired, attitudes toward the communication, and emotional reactions. A follow-up questionnaire was given one week later in order to ascertain the carry-over effects of the different forms of the communication.

RESULTS

Affective Reactions

Evidence that the three forms of the illustrated talk differed with respect to the amount of emotional tension evoked during the communication is presented in Table 2. Immediately after exposure to the communication, the students were asked three questions concerning the feelings they had just

TABLE 2

FEELINGS OF WORRY OR CONCERN EVOKED DURING THE COMMUNICATION

QUESTIONNAIRE RESPONSES	STRONG GROUP ($N=50$)	MODERATE GROUP ($N=50$)	MINIMAL GROUP ($N=50$)
Felt worried—a "few times" or "many times"—about own mouth condition	74%	60%	48%
Felt "somewhat" or "very" worried about improper care of own teeth	66%	36%	34%
Thought about condition of own teeth "most of the time"	42%	34%	22%

experienced "while the illustrated talk was being given." Their responses indicate that the fear stimuli were successful in arousing affective reactions. On each of the three questionnaire items shown in the table, the difference between the Strong group and the Minimal group is reliable at beyond the .05 confidence level.[2] The Moderate group consistently falls in an intermediate position but does not, in most instances, differ significantly from the other two groups.

Further evidence of the effectiveness of the fear-arousing material was obtained from responses to the following two questions, each of which had a checklist of five answer categories ranging from "Very worried" to "Not at all worried":

1. When you think about the possibility

[2] All probability values reported in this paper are based on one tail of the theoretical distribution, since the results were used to test specific hypotheses which predict the direction of the differences.

that you might develop diseased gums, how concerned or worried do you feel about it?

2. When you think about the possibility that you might developed decayed teeth, how concerned or worried do you feel about it? Since these questions made no reference to the illustrated talk, it was feasible to include them in the pre- and postcommunication questionnaires given to all four groups.

Systematic comparisons were made in terms of the percentage in each group who reported relatively high disturbance (i.e., "somewhat" or "very worried") in response to both questions. The results, presented in Table 3, show a marked increase in affective disturbance among each of the three experimental groups, as compared with the control group. Paralleling the results in Table 2, the greatest increase is found in the Strong group. The difference between the Moderate and the Minimal groups, however, is insignificant.

TABLE 3

PERCENTAGE OF EACH GROUP WHO REPORTED FEELING SOMEWHAT OR VERY WORRIED ABOUT DECAYED TEETH AND DISEASED GUMS

	STRONG GROUP ($N=50$)	MODERATE GROUP ($N=50$)	MINIMAL GROUP ($N=50$)	CONTROL GROUP ($N=50$)
One week before the communication	34	24	22	30
Immediately after the communication	76	50	46	38
Change	+42%	+26%	+24%	+8%

GROUP	RELIABILITY OF DIFFERENCE *	
	CR	p
Strong vs. Control	3.06	<.01
Strong vs. Minimal	1.59	.06
Strong vs. Moderate	1.37	.09
Moderate vs. Control	1.54	.06
Moderate vs. Minimal	0.17	.43
Minimal vs. Control	1.43	.08

* The statistical test used was the critical ratio for reliability of differences in amount of change between two independent samples, as described by Hovland, Lumsdaine, and Sheffield (5, p. 321).

In order to obtain an over-all estimate of the relative degree of emotional arousal evoked by the three forms of the communication, a total score was computed for each individual in each experimental group, based on answers to all five questions: two points credit was given to each response specified in Tables 2 and 3 as indicative of high disturbance; one point credit was given to intermediate responses on the checklist; zero credit was given for the last two response categories in each check list, which uniformly designated a relative absence of worry or concern. Hence individual scores ranged from zero to ten. The mean scores for the Strong, Moderate and Minimal groups were 7.8, 6.6, and 5.9 respectively. The Strong group differs reliably at the one per cent confidence level from each of the other two groups ($t=2.3$ and 3.6). The difference between the Moderate and Minimal groups approaches reliability at the .08 confidence level ($t=1.4$).

In general, the foregoing evidence indicates that after exposure to the communications, the Strong group felt more worried about the condition of their teeth than did the other two groups; the Moderate group, in turn, tended to feel more worried than the Minimal group.

Information Acquired

Immediately after exposure to the illustrated talk, each experimental group was given an information test consisting of 23 separate items. The test was based on the factual assertions common to all three forms of the communication, including topics such as the anatomical structure of the teeth, the causes of cavities and of gum disease, the "correct" technique of toothbrushing, and the type of toothbrush recommended by dental authorities. No significant differences were found among the three experimental groups with respect to information test scores. Comparisons with the Control group show that the three forms of the dental hygiene communication were equally effective in teaching the factual material.

Attitude Toward the Communication

The questionnaire given immediately after exposure to the illustrated talk included a series of seven items concerning the students'

appraisals of the communication. From the results shown in Table 4, it is apparent that the Strong group responded more favorably than the other two groups.[3]

These findings imply that interest in the communication and acceptance of its educational value were heightened by the Strong appeal. But this conclusion applies only to relatively impersonal, objective ratings of the communication. Additional evidence presented in Table 5, based on questions which elicited evaluations of a more subjective character, reveals a markedly different attitude toward the communication among those exposed to the Strong appeal.

One of the additional questions was the following: "Was there anything in the illustrated talk on dental hygiene that you disliked?" Unfavorable ("dislike") answers were given by a reliably higher percentage of students in the Strong group than in the Moderate or Minimal groups (first row of Table 5). A tabulation was also made of the total number of students in each group who gave complaints in their answers to either of two open-end questions which asked for criticisms of the illustrated talk. The results on complaints about the unpleasant character of the slides are shown in row two of Table 5; the difference between the Strong group and each of the other two groups is reliable at the .01 confidence level. Similarly, a reliably higher percentage of the Strong group complained about insufficient material on ways and means of preventing tooth and gum disease (row three of Table 5).[4] The latter type of criticism often was accompanied by the suggestion that some of the disturbing material should be eliminated, as is illustrated by the following comments from two

---

[3] The Strong group differs significantly ($p<.05$) from the Minimal group on five of the seven items and from the Moderate group on three items; the Moderate group does *not* differ reliably from the Minimal group on any of the items.

[4] In row three of Table 5, the difference between the Strong and Moderate groups is reliable at the .01 confidence level, and the difference between the Strong and Minimal groups is significant at the .08 level. Other types of criticisms, in addition to those shown in Table 5, were also tabulated. Most of these involved minor aspects of the presentation (e.g., "a movie would have been better than slides") and were given by approximately equal percentages of the three groups. The vast majority of students in the Moderate and Minimal groups expressed approval of the illustrated talk or stated that they had no criticisms.

TABLE 4

PERCENTAGE OF EACH GROUP WHO EXPRESSED STRONGLY FAVORABLE APPRAISALS OF THE COMMUNICATION

APPRAISAL RESPONSE	STRONG GROUP (N=50)	MODERATE GROUP (N=50)	MINIMAL GROUP (N=50)
The illustrated talk does a very good teaching job.	62	50	40
Most or all of it was interesting.	80	68	64
It was very easy to pay attention to what the speaker was saying.	74	36	50
My mind practically never wandered.	58	46	42
The slides do a very good job.	52	20	22
The speaker's voice was very good.	66	56	58
The illustrated talk definitely should be given to all Connecticut high schools.	74	58	70

students in the Strong group: "Leave out the slides that show the rottiness of the teeth and have more in about how to brush your teeth"; "I don't think you should have shown so many gory pictures without showing more to prevent it." Comments of this sort, together with the data presented in Table 5, provide additional evidence of residual emotional tension. They imply that the Strong appeal created a need for reassurance which persisted after the communication was over, despite the fact that the communication contained a large number of reassuring recommendations.

The apparent inconsistency between the results in Tables 4 and 5 suggests that the Strong appeal evoked a more mixed or ambivalent attitude toward the communication than did the Moderate or Minimal appeals. Some of the comments, particularly about the slides, help to illuminate the differentiation between the individual's *objective* evaluation of the communication and his *subjective* response to it. The following illustrative excerpts from the Strong group were selected from the answers given to the open-end question which asked for criticisms and suggestions:

I did not care for the "gory" illustrations of decayed teeth and diseased mouths but I really think that it did make me feel sure that I did not want this to happen to me.

Some of the pictures went to the extremes but they probably had an effect on most of the people who wouldn't want their teeth to look like that.

I think it is good because it scares people when they see the awful things that can happen.

Such comments not only attest to the motivational impact of the Strong appeal, but also suggest one of the ways in which the discrepancy between subjective and objective evaluations may have been reconciled. In such cases, the ambivalence seems to have been resolved by adopting an attitude to the effect that "this is disagreeable medicine, but it is good for us."

Conformity to Dental Hygiene Recommendations

The immediate effects of the illustrated talks described above show the type of affective reactions evoked by the fear-arousing material but provide little information bearing directly on attitude changes. The questionnaire administered one week later, however, was designed to measure some of the major carry-over effects of fear appeals, particularly

TABLE 5

PERCENTAGE OF EACH GROUP WHO EXPRESSED COMPLAINTS ABOUT THE COMMUNICATION

TYPE OF COMPLAINT	STRONG GROUP (N=50)	MODERATE GROUP (N=50)	MINIMAL GROUP (N=50)
Disliked something in the illustrated talk.	28	8	2
The slides were too unpleasant ("horrible," "gory," "disgusting," etc.).	34	2	0
There was not enough material on prevention.	20	2	8

with respect to changes in dental hygiene practices, beliefs, and preferences. The results provide an empirical basis for estimating the degree to which such communications succeed in modifying attitudes.

Personal practices were investigated by asking the students to describe the way they were currently brushing their teeth: the type of stroke used, the amount of surface area cleansed, the amount of force applied, the length of time spent on brushing the teeth, and the time of day that the teeth were brushed. The same five questions were asked one week before the communication

four groups had very low scores and the group differences were insignificant. By comparing the score that each individual attained one week after the communication with that attained two weeks earlier, it was possible to determine for each group the percentage who changed in the direction of increased or decreased conformity.

The results, shown in Table 6, reveal that the greatest amount of conformity was produced by the communication which contained the least amount of fear-arousing material. The Strong group showed reliably less change than the Minimal group; in fact,

TABLE 6

EFFECT OF THE ILLUSTRATED TALK ON CONFORMITY TO DENTAL HYGIENE RECOMMENDATIONS

TYPE OF CHANGE	STRONG GROUP (N=50)	MODERATE GROUP (N=50)	MINIMAL GROUP (N=50)	CONTROL GROUP (N=50)
Increased conformity	28%	44%	50%	22%
Decreased conformity	20%	22%	14%	22%
No change	52%	34%	36%	56%
Net change in conformity	+8%	+22%	+36%	0%

GROUP	RELIABILITY OF DIFFERENCE CR	p
Control vs. Minimal	2.54	<.01
Control vs. Moderate	1.50	.07
Control vs. Strong	0.59	.28
Strong vs. Moderate	0.95	.17
Strong vs. Minimal	1.96	.03
Moderate vs. Minimal	0.93	.18

and again one week after. These questions covered practices about which the following specific recommendations were made in all three forms of the illustrated talk: (a) the teeth should be brushed with an up-and-down (vertical) stroke; (b) the inner surface of the teeth should be brushed as well as the outer surface; (c) the teeth should be brushed gently, using only a slight amount of force; (d) in order to cleanse the teeth adequately, one should spend about three minutes on each brushing; (e) in the morning, the teeth should be brushed after breakfast (rather than before).

Each student was given a score, ranging from zero to five, which represented the number of recommended practices on which he conformed. Before exposure to the communication, the majority of students in all

the Strong group failed to differ significantly from the Control group, whereas the Minimal group showed a highly reliable increase in conformity as compared with the Control group. The Moderate group falls in an intermediate position, but does not differ reliably from the Strong or Minimal groups. Although there is some ambiguity with respect to the relative effectiveness of the Moderate appeal, the data in Table 6 show a fairly consistent trend which suggests that as the amount of fear-arousing material is increased, conformity tends to decrease. In contrast to the marked increase in conformity produced by the Minimal appeal and the fairly sizable increase produced by the Moderate appeal, the Strong appeal failed to achieve any significant effect whatsoever.

One cannot be certain, of course, that the

findings represent changes in overt behavioral conformity, since the observations are based on the Ss' own verbal reports. What remains problematical, however, is whether the verbal responses reflect *only* "lip-service" to the recommendations or whether they also reflect internalized attitudes that were actually carried out in action. The results, nevertheless, demonstrate that the Strong appeal was markedly less effective than the Minimal appeal, at least with respect to eliciting verbal conformity.

Further evidence in support of the same conclusion comes from responses pertinent to a different type of dental hygiene behavior which had also been recommended in the illustrated talk.[5] The students were asked to give the approximate date on which they had last gone to a dentist. The percentage in each group whose answers indicated that they had gone to the dentist during the week following exposure to the illustrated talk were as follows: 10 per cent of the Strong group, 14 per cent of the Moderate group, 18 per cent of the Minimal group, and 4 per cent of the Control group. The percentage difference between the Minimal group and the Control group was found to be statistically reliable at the .04 confidence level; none of the other comparisons yielded reliable differences. Although not conclusive evidence, these findings are in line with those in Table 6: the Minimal appeal again appears to have been superior with respect to eliciting conformity to a recommended practice.

Beliefs Concerning the "Proper" Type of Toothbrush

The illustrated talk presented an extensive discussion of the "proper" type of toothbrush recommended by dental authorities. Four main characteristics were emphasized: (*a*) the bristles should be of medium hardness, (*b*) the brush should have three rows of bristles, (*c*) the handle should be completely straight, and (*d*) the brushing surface should be completely straight. Personal beliefs concerning the desirability of these four charac-

teristics were measured by four questions which were included in the precommunication questionnaire as well as in the questionnaire given one week after the communication. The main finding was that all three experimental groups, as compared with the Control group, showed a significant change in the direction of accepting the conclusions presented in the communication. Among the three experimental groups, there were no significant differences with respect to net changes. Nevertheless, as will be seen in the next section, the fear-arousing material appears to have had a considerable effect on the degree to which the students adhered to such beliefs in the face of counteracting propaganda.

Resistance to Counteracting Propaganda

In addition to describing the four essential characteristics of the "proper" toothbrush, the illustrated talk contained numerous comments and illustrations to explain the need for avoiding the "wrong" kind of toothbrush. Much of the material on cavities and other unpleasant consequences of tooth neglect was presented in this context. *The importance of using the proper kind of toothbrush* was the theme that was most heavily emphasized throughout the entire communication.

The key questionnaire item, designed to determine initial attitudes before exposure to the communication, was the following:

Please read the following statement carefully and decide whether you believe it is true or false.

It does not matter what kind of toothbrush a person uses. *Any sort of toothbrush* that is sold in a drugstore will keep your teeth clean and healthy— if you use it regularly.

Do you think that this statement is true or false? (Check one.)

One week after exposure to the communications, the question was asked again, in essentially the same form, with the same checklist of five answer categories (ranging from "Feel certain that it is true" to "Feel certain that it is false"). But in the postcommunication questionnaire, the question was preceded by the following propaganda material which contradicted the dominant theme of the illustrated talk:

A well-known dentist recently made the following statement:

---

[5] In all three forms of the illustrated talk, an explicit recommendation was made concerning the desirability of obtaining advice from a dentist about one's own toothbrushing technique. In addition, several references were made to the importance of going to a dentist for prompt treatment of cavities, before the decay spreads to the inner layers of the tooth.

Some dentists, including a number of so-called "experts" on dental hygiene, claim it is important to use a special type of toothbrush in order to clean the teeth properly. But from my own experience, I believe that there is no sound basis for that idea. My honest opinion, as a dentist, is that it does not matter what special kind of toothbrush a person uses. Any sort of toothbrush that is sold in a drugstore will keep your teeth clean and healthy—if you use it regularly.

That this propaganda exposure had a pronounced effect is revealed by the attitude changes shown by the Control group. A statistically reliable change in the direction

definite answer emerges from the results in Table 7, which shows the percentage of each group who changed in the direction of agreement or disagreement with the counterpropaganda statement.

Before exposure to the illustrated talk, the group differences were negligible: approximately 50 per cent of the students in each of the four groups agreed with the statement that "it does not matter what kind of toothbrush a person uses." But two weeks later (immediately after exposure to the counter-

TABLE 7

EFFECT OF THE ILLUSTRATED TALK ON REACTIONS TO SUBSEQUENT COUNTERPROPAGANDA: NET PERCENTAGE OF EACH GROUP WHO CHANGED IN THE DIRECTION OF AGREEING WITH THE STATEMENT THAT "IT DOES NOT MATTER WHAT KIND OF TOOTHBRUSH A PERSON USES"

TYPE OF CHANGE	STRONG GROUP (N=50)	MODERATE GROUP (N=50)	MINIMAL GROUP (N=50)	CONTROL GROUP (N=50)
More agreement	30	28	14	44
Less agreement	38	42	54	24
No change	32	30	32	32
Net change	−8	−14	−40	+20
Net effect of exposure to the illustrated talk	−28	−34	−60	

GROUP	RELIABILITY OF THE DIFFERENCES IN NET CHANGE CR	p
Control vs. Minimal	3.66	<.001
Control vs. Moderate	2.05	.02
Control vs. Strong	1.71	.05
Strong vs. Moderate	0.36	.36
Strong vs. Minimal	2.03	.02
Moderate vs. Minimal	1.66	.05

of more agreement with the counterpropaganda was found in the Control group.[6]

How effective were the three forms of the illustrated talk in preventing students from accepting the propaganda to which they were exposed one week later? Did the fear appeals augment or diminish the students' resistance to the counteracting propaganda? A fairly

[6] In the Control group, the percentage who disagreed with the statement dropped from 54 to 34. This change proved to be significant at below the .02 confidence level, according to the formula described by Hovland, Lumsdaine, and Sheffield (5, p. 319). The Control group did not show any significant change on other questions dealing with dental hygiene beliefs, preferences or practices, all of which were presented in the final questionnaire before the propaganda material was introduced. Consequently, it seems fairly safe to conclude that the propaganda exposure was responsible for the significant change displayed by the Control group.

propaganda) there were marked and statistically reliable differences which indicate that although all three forms of the illustrated talk had some influence, the Minimal appeal was most effective in producing resistance to the counterpropaganda. Thus, the results suggest that under conditions where people will be exposed to competing communications dealing with the same issues, the use of a strong fear appeal will tend to be less effective than a minimal appeal in producing stable and persistent attitude changes.

Some clues to mediating processes were detected in the students' responses to an open-end question which asked them to "give the reason" for their answers to the key attitude item on which the results in Table 7 are based. A systematic analysis was made of the write-in answers given by those students who had disagreed with the counterpropaganda. In their refutations, some of the students made use of material that had been presented one week earlier, either by referring to the illustrated talk as an authoritative source or by citing one of the main arguments presented in the illustrated talk. From the results presented in the first two rows of Table 8, it is apparent that such refutations were given more frequently by the Minimal group than by the other experimental groups. The comparatively low frequency of such answers in the Strong and Moderate groups was not compensated for by an increase in any other type of specific reasons, as indicated by the results in the last row of the table.[7]

were inclined to avoid recalling the content of the fear-arousing communication.

DISCUSSION

The results in the preceding sections indicate that the Minimal appeal was the most effective form of the communication in that it elicited (a) more resistance to subsequent counterpropaganda and (b) a higher incidence of verbal adherence, and perhaps a greater degree of behavioral conformity, to a set of recommended practices. The absence of any significant differences on other indicators of preferences and beliefs implies that the Moderate and Strong appeals had no unique positive effects that would compensate for the observed detrimental effects.

TABLE 8

TYPES OF REFUTATION GIVEN BY STUDENTS WHO DISAGREED WITH THE COUNTERPROPAGANDA

TYPE OF REFUTATION	STRONG GROUP (N=30)	MODERATE GROUP (N=29)	MINIMAL GROUP (N=39)	CONTROL GROUP (N=18)
Explicit reference to the illustrated talk as an authoritative source for the opposite conclusion	7%	14%	18%	0%
One or more arguments cited that had been presented in the illustrated talk	43%	38%	59%	28%
One or more arguments cited that contradicted the content of the illustrated talk	0%	0%	0%	22%
No answer or no specific reason given	50%	52%	36%	50%

Although the group differences are not uniformly reliable, they reveal a consistent trend which suggests an "avoidance" tendency among the students who had been exposed to the fear appeals. Apparently, even those who resisted the counterpropaganda

[7] On the first type of reason (reference to the illustrated talk), the only difference large enough to approach statistical reliability was that between the Minimal group and the Control group (p=.08). On the second type of reason (arguments cited from the illustrated talk), the difference between the Minimal group and the Control group was found to be highly reliable (p=.03) while the difference between the Minimal and Moderate groups approached statistical reliability (p=.08). The Control group differed reliably from each of the experimental groups (at beyond the .10 confidence level) with respect to giving arguments which contradicted those contained in the illustrated talk (row three of the table). None of the other percentage differences in Table 8 were large enough to be significant at the .10 confidence level. (In some columns, the percentages add up to more than 100 per cent because a few students gave more than one type of refutation.)

Thus, the findings consistently indicate that inclusion of the fear-arousing material not only failed to increase the effectiveness of the communication, but actually interfered with its over-all success.

The outcome of the present experiment by no means precludes the possibility that, under certain conditions, fear appeals may prove to be highly successful. For instance, the Strong appeal was found to be maximally effective in arousing interest and in eliciting a high degree of emotional tension. The evocation of such reactions might augment the effectiveness of mass communications which are designed to instigate prompt audience action, such as donating money or volunteering to perform a group task. But if the communication is intended to create more sustained preferences or attitudes, the achievement of positive effects probably depends upon a number of different factors. Our experimental results suggest that in the latter case, a relatively low degree of fear arousal is likely to be the optimal level, that an appeal which is too strong will tend to evoke some form of interference which reduces the effectiveness of the communication. The findings definitely contradict the assumption that as the dosage of fear-arousing stimuli (in a mass communication) is increased, the audience will become more highly motivated to accept the reassuring recommendations contained in the communication. Beneficial motivating effects probably occur when a relatively slight amount of fear-arousing material is inserted; but for communications of the sort used in the present experiment, the optimal dosage appears to be far below the level of the strongest fear appeals that a communicator could use if he chose to do so.

Before examining the implications of the findings in more detail, it is necessary to take account of the problems of generalizing from the findings of the present study. The present experiment shows the effects of only one type of communication, presented in an educational setting to a student audience. Until replications are carried out—using other media, topics, and fear-eliciting stimuli, in a variety of communication settings, with different audiences, etc.—one cannot be certain that the conclusions hold true for other situations. The results from a single experiment are obviously not sufficient for drawing broad generalizations concerning the entire range of fear-arousing communications which are currently being brought to the focus of public attention. Nor can unreplicated results be relied upon for extracting dependable rubrics that could be applied by educators, editors, public relations experts, propagandists, or other communication specialists who face the practical problems of selecting appropriate appeals for motivating mass audiences.

Nevertheless, the present experiment helps to elucidate the potentially unfavorable effects that may result from mass communications which play up ominous threats, alarming contingencies, or signs of impending danger. For instance, the findings tend to bear out some of the points raised concerning the need for careful pretesting and for other cautions when warnings about the dangers of atomic bombing are presented in civilian defense communications that are intended to prepare the public for coping with wartime emergencies (6). Moreover, despite our inability to specify the range of communications to which our conclusions would apply, we can derive tentative inferences that may have important theoretical implications with respect to the dynamics of "normal" fear reactions.

We turn now to a central question posed by the experimental findings: Why is it that the fear-arousing stimuli resulted in less adherence to recommended practices and less resistance to counterpropaganda? Although our experiment cannot give a definitive answer, it provides some suggestive leads concerning potential sources of emotional interference.

In the introduction, we have described three forms of "resistance" frequently observed in psychotherapy that might also occur among normal personalities exposed to mass communications which evoke strong fear or anxiety: (a) inattentiveness during the communication session, (b) rejection of the communicator's statements motivated by reactive aggression, and (c) subsequent defensive avoidance motivated by residual emotional tension. We shall discuss briefly the pertinent findings from the present experiment with a view to making a preliminary assessment of the importance of each of the three types of interfering reactions.

1. Our results provide no evidence that a strong fear appeal produces inattentiveness or any form of distraction that would interfere with learning efficiency during the communication session. The three forms of the communication were found to be equally effective in teaching the factual material on dental hygiene, as measured by a comprehensive information test given immediately after exposure to the communication. Beliefs concerning the desirable characteristics of the "proper" type of toothbrush were also acquired equally well. One might even surmise (from the results in Table 4) that the Strong appeal may have had a beneficial effect on attention, because a significantly higher percentage of the Strong group reported that (a) it was very easy to pay attention to what the speaker was saying and (b) they experienced very little "mind-wandering."

The absence of any observable reduction of

learning efficiency is consistent with numerous clinical observations which imply that normal personalities can ordinarily tolerate unpleasant information concerning potential threats to the self without manifesting any marked impairment of "ego" functions. Our findings definitely suggest that the use of fear-arousing material of the sort presented in the illustrated talks would rarely give rise to any interference with the audience's ability to learn the content of the communication.

It is necessary to bear in mind, however, that in the present experiment the communication was given to a "captive" classroom audience. When people are at home listening to the radio, or in any situation where they feel free to choose whether or not to terminate the communication exposure, the use of strong emotional appeals might often have drastic effects on sustained attention. Consequently, the tentative generalization concerning the low probability of inattentiveness would be expected to apply primarily to those fear-arousing communications which are presented under conditions where social norms or situational constraints prevent the audience from directing attention elsewhere.

Even with a "captive" audience, it is quite possible that under certain extreme conditions a strong fear appeal might interfere with learning efficiency. For instance, the same sort of temporary cognitive impairment that is sometimes observed when verbal stimuli happen to touch off unconscious personal conflicts or emotional "complexes" might also occur when a mass communication elicits sharp awareness of unexpected danger, particularly when the audience immediately perceives the threat to be imminent and inescapable. Hence, the inferences from our experimental findings probably should be restricted to fear appeals which deal with remote threats or with relatively familiar dangers that are perceived to be avoidable.

2. The fact that the Strong group expressed the greatest amount of subjective dislike of the illustrated talk and made the most complaints about its content could be construed as suggesting a potentially aggressive attitude. But if the aggressive reactions aroused by the use of the Strong fear appeal were intense enough to motivate rejection of the conclusions, one would not expect to find this group giving the most favorable appraisals of the interest value of the illustrated talk, of the quality of its presentation, and of its over-all educational success. Thus, although the possibility of suppressed aggression cannot be precluded, it seems unlikely that this factor was a major source of emotional interference. In drawing this tentative conclusion, however, we do not intend to minimize the importance of aggression as a potential source of interference. In the present experiment, the communication was administered as an official part of the school's hygiene program and contained recommendations that were obviously intended to be beneficial to the audience. Under markedly different conditions, where the auspices and intent of communication are perceived to be less benign, the audience would probably be less disposed to suppress or control aggressive reactions. The low level of verbalized aggression observed in the present study, however, suggests that in the absence of cues which arouse the audience's suspicions, some factor other than reactive hostility may be a much more important source of interference.

3. Subsequent defensive avoidance arising from residual emotional tension seems to be the most likely explanation of the outcome of the present study. We have seen, from the data on immediate affective reactions, that the disturbing feelings which had been aroused during the illustrated talk tended to persist after the communication had ended, despite the reassuring recommendations which had been presented. The analysis of complaints made by the three experimental groups (Table 5) provides additional evidence that the need for reassurance persisted primarily among the students who had been exposed to the Strong appeal. Such findings support the following hypothesis: *When a mass communication is designed to influence an audience to adopt specific ways and means of averting a threat, the use of a strong fear appeal, as against a milder one, increases the likelihood that the audience will be left in a state of emotional tension which is not fully relieved by rehearsing the reassuring recommendations contained in the communication.* This hypothesis is compatible with the general assumption that when a person is exposed to signs of "threat," the greater the intensity

of the fear reaction evoked, the greater the likelihood that his emotional tension will persist after the external stimulus has terminated.

Whether or not the above hypothesis is correct, the fact remains that "unreduced" emotional tension was manifested immediately after the communication predominantly by the group exposed to the Strong appeal. Our findings on subsequent reactions provide some suggestive evidence concerning the consequences of experiencing this type of residual tension. In general, the evidence appears to be consistent with the following hypothesis: *When fear is strongly aroused but is not fully relieved by the reassurances contained in a mass communication, the audience will become motivated to ignore or to minimize the importance of the threat.* This hypothesis could be regarded as a special case of the following general proposition which pertains to the effects of human exposure to any fear-producing stimulus: other things being equal, the more persistent the fear reaction, the greater will be the (acquired) motivation to avoid subsequent exposures to internal and external cues which were present at the time the fear reaction was aroused. This proposition is based on the postulate that fear is a stimulus-producing response which has the functional properties of a drive (2, 7).[8]

[8] In the sphere of human communication, the key theoretical assumption could be formulated as follows: If rehearsal of the reassuring statements contained in a communication fails to alleviate the emotional tension elicited by the use of a fear appeal, the audience will be motivated to continue trying out other (symbolic or overt) responses until one occurs which succeeds in reducing fear to a tolerable level. Thus, a strong fear appeal which is intended to motivate the audience to take account of a realistic threat of danger could have the paradoxical effect of motivating the audience to ignore the threat or to adopt "magical," "wishful" or other types of reassuring beliefs that are antithetical to the communicator's intentions. Moreover, according to the same theoretical assumption, when a communication produces a high degree of persistent fear, the audience will be motivated to engage in overt escape activities, some of which may prove to be incompatible with the protective actions recommended by the communicator. Unintended effects of this kind can be regarded as spontaneous "defensive" reactions which are motivated by residual emotional tension. In the present experiment, it would be expected that, in addition to the tendency to avoid thinking about the threat, other defensive reactions would also occur. For example, following exposure to the Strong appeal, some of the students may have succeeded in alleviating their residual emotional tension through spontaneous interpersonal communication with fellow students.

In the context of the present experiment, one would predict that the group displaying the greatest degree of residual fear would be most strongly motivated to ward off those internal symbolic cues—such as anticipations of the threatening consequences of improper dental hygiene—which were salient during and immediately after the communication. This prediction seems to be fairly well borne out by the evidence on carry-over effects, particularly by the finding that the greatest degree of resistance to the subsequent counterpropaganda was shown by the group which had been least motivated by fear. The use of the Strong appeal, as against the Minimal one, evidently resulted in less rejection of a subsequent communication which discounted and contradicted what was said in the original communication. In effect, the second communication asserted that one could ignore the alleged consequences of using the wrong type of toothbrush, and, in that sense, minimized the dangers which previously had been heavily emphasized by the fear-arousing communication.

The results obtained from the students' reports on their dental hygiene practices could be interpreted as supporting another prediction from the same hypothesis. It would be expected that those students who changed their practices, after having heard and seen one of the three forms of the illustrated talk, were motivated to do so because they recalled some of the verbal material which had been given in support of the recommendations, most of which referred to the unfavorable consequences of continuing to do the "wrong" thing. In theoretical terms, one might say that their conformity to the recommendations was mediated by symbolic responses which had been learned during communication. The mediating responses (anticipations, thoughts, or images) acquired from any one of the three forms of the illustrated talk would frequently have, as their content, some reference to unpleasant consequences for the self, and consequently would cue off a resolution or an overt action that would be accompanied by anticipated success in warding off the threat. But defensive avoidance of the mediating responses would reduce the amount of conformity to whatever protective action is recommended by the fear-arousing communication. Hence the prediction would be that when rehearsal of statements concerning potential danger is accompanied by strong emotional tension during and after the communication, the audience will become motivated to avoid recalling those statements on later occasions when appropriate action could ordinarily be carried out. An inhibiting motivation of this kind acquired from the illustrated talk would tend to prevent the students from adopting the recommended changes in their toothbrushing habits because they would fail to think about the unpleasant consequences of improper dental hygiene at times when they subsequently perform the act of brushing their teeth.

Much more direct evidence in support of the "defensive avoidance" hypothesis comes from the analysis of spontaneous write-in answers in which the students explained why they disagreed with the counterpropaganda (Table 8). Those who had been exposed to the least amount of fear-arousing material were the ones who were most likely to refer to the illustrated talk as an authoritative source and to make use of its arguments. The relative absence of such references in the spontaneous answers given by those who had been exposed to the Moderate and Strong appeals implies a tendency to avoid recalling the content of the fear-arousing communication.

Although the various pieces of evidence discussed above seem to fit together, they cannot be regarded as a conclusive demonstration of the defensive avoidance hypothesis. What our findings clearly show is that a strong fear appeal can be markedly less effective than a minimal appeal, at least under the limited conditions represented in our experiment. Exactly which conditions and which mediating mechanisms are responsible for this outcome will remain problematical until further investigations are carried out. Nevertheless, so far as the present findings go, they consistently support the conclusion that the use of a strong fear appeal will tend to reduce the over-all success of a persuasive communication, if it evokes a high degree of emotional tension without adequately satisfying the need for reassurance.

SUMMARY AND CONCLUSIONS

The experiment was designed to investigate the effects of persuasive communications which attempt to motivate people to conform with a set of recommendations by stimulating fear reactions. An illustrated lecture on dental hygiene was prepared in three different forms, representing three different intensities of fear appeal: the Strong appeal emphasized and graphically illustrated the threat of pain, disease, and body damage; the Moderate appeal described the same dangers in a milder and more factual manner; the Minimal appeal rarely referred to the unpleasant consequences of improper dental hygiene. Although differing in the amount of fear-arousing material presented, the three forms of the communication contained the same essential information and the same set of recommendations.

Equivalent groups of high school students were exposed to the three different forms of the communication as part of the school's hygiene program. In addition, the experiment included an equated control group which was not exposed to the dental hygiene communication but was given a similar communication on an irrelevant topic. Altogether there were 200 students in the experiment, with 50 in each group. A questionnaire containing a series of items on dental hygiene beliefs, practices, and attitudes was administered to all four groups one week before the communications were presented. In order to observe the changes produced by the illustrated talk, postcommunication questionnaires were given immediately after exposure and again one week later.

1. The fear appeals were successful in arousing affective reactions. Immediately after the communication, the group exposed to the Strong appeal reported feeling more worried about the condition of their teeth than did the other groups. The Moderate appeal, in turn, evoked a higher incidence of "worry" reactions than did the Minimal appeal.

2. The three forms of the illustrated talk were equally effective with respect to (a) teaching the factual content of the communication, as assessed by an information test, and (b) modifying beliefs concerning four specific characteristics of the "proper"

type of toothbrush. The evidence indicates that the emotional reactions aroused by the Strong appeal did not produce inattentiveness or reduce learning efficiency.

3. As compared with the other two forms of the communication, the Strong appeal evoked a more mixed or ambivalent attitude toward the communication. The students exposed to the Strong appeal were more likely than the others to give favorable appraisals concerning the interest value and the quality of the presentation. Nevertheless, they showed the greatest amount of subjective dislike of the communication and made more complaints about the content.

4. From an analysis of the changes in each individual's reports about his current toothbrushing practices, it was found that the greatest amount of conformity to the communicator's recommendations was produced by the Minimal appeal. The Strong appeal failed to produce any significant change in dental hygiene practices, whereas the Minimal appeal resulted in a reliable increase in conformity, as compared with the Control group. Similar findings also emerged from an analysis of responses which indicated whether the students had gone to a dentist during the week following exposure to the illustrated talk, reflecting conformity to another recommendation made by the communicator. The evidence strongly suggests that as the amount of fear-arousing material is increased, conformity to recommended (protective) actions tends to decrease.

5. One week after the illustrated talk had been presented, exposure to counterpropaganda (which contradicted the main theme of the original communication) produced a greater effect on attitudes in the Control group than in the three experimental groups. The Minimal appeal, however, proved to be the most effective form of the illustrated talk with respect to producing resistance to the counterpropaganda. The results tend to support the conclusion that under conditions where people are exposed to competing communications dealing with the same issues, the use of a strong fear appeal is less successful than a minimal appeal in producing stable and persistent attitude changes.

6. The main conclusion which emerges from the entire set of findings is that the over-all effectiveness of a persuasive communication will tend to be reduced by the use of a strong fear appeal, if it evokes a high degree of emotional tension without adequately satisfying the need for reassurance. The evidence from the present experiment appears to be consistent with the following two explanatory hypotheses:

a. When a mass communication is designed to influence an audience to adopt specific ways and means of averting a threat, the use of a strong fear appeal, as against a milder one, increases the likelihood that the audience will be left in a state of emotional tension which is not fully relieved by rehearsing the reassuring recommendations contained in the communication.

b. When fear is strongly aroused but is not fully relieved by the reassurances contained in a mass communication, the audience will become motivated to ignore or to minimize the importance of the threat.

REFERENCES

1. ALEXANDER, F., & FRENCH, T. M. *Psychoanalytic therapy*. New York: Ronald, 1946.
2. DOLLARD, J., & MILLER, N. E. *Personality and psychotherapy*. New York: McGraw-Hill, 1950.
3. FENICHEL, O. *Problems of psychoanalytic technique*. New York: Psychoanalytic Quarterly, 1941.
4. HANFMANN, EUGENIA. Psychological approaches to the study of anxiety. In P. H. Hoch and J. Zubin (Eds.), *Anxiety*. New York: Grune & Stratton, 1950. Pp. 51–69.
5. HOVLAND, C. I., LUMSDAINE, A. A., & SHEFFIELD, F. D. *Experiments on mass communication*. Princeton: Princeton Univer. Press, 1949.
6. JANIS, I. L. *Air war and emotional stress*. New York: McGraw-Hill, 1951.
7. MOWRER, O. H. *Learning theory and personality dynamics: Selected papers*. New York: Ronald, 1950.

Reprinted from Bulletin of the New York Academy of Medicine, 1965, Ser. 2, Vol. 41, No. 11, pp. 1144–1168, by permission of Howard Leventhal and The New York Academy of Medicine.

FEAR COMMUNICATIONS IN THE ACCEPTANCE OF PREVENTIVE HEALTH PRACTICES*

HOWARD LEVENTHAL

THE primary goal of modern psychology is the description and explanation of behavior. In the area of social and personality psychology, this reduces to the description of behaviors, situational conditions, and biological characteristics related to concepts such as temperament, traits, attitudes, groups structure, and the like. On the other hand, the primary goal of most physicians and health educators is the prevention and cure of damages to the human body and its functions. To the extent that the process of preventing or curing requires one to influence peoples' actions by getting them to, use seat belts, to stop smoking, or to take medical examinations, there is a common ground for these disciplines.

But while there is mutual interest, there are also differences in emphasis. The health educator evaluates behavior, i.e. he is concerned with whether a particular action is good or bad for the health of the actor. He is also concerned with influencing behavior so as to increase beneficial actions and eliminate harmful ones, but he may be relatively unconcerned as to the exact process by which a particular factor brings about behavior change, as his primary concern is likely to be maximizing the conditions favoring "positive" changes.

On the other hand, the purpose of the experimental psychologist is not to evaluate behavior as "good" or "bad," "normal" or abnormal," but to describe it in relation to its determining conditions. The boldness of this undertaking is readily apparent as the factors that can influence behavior are so numerous. At the outset then, the psychologist must

*Based on a paper presented at a combined meeting of the Section on Occupational Medicine, The New York Academy of Medicine, with The New York State Society of Industrial Medicine, Inc., January 27, 1965. This investigation was supported in part by Public Health Service Research Grants MH 06719-01 from the National Institute of Mental Health and CH 00077-02 from the Division of Community Health Services, Bethesda, Md.

make a decision as to which of many possible controlling conditions merit study. We must choose to study some of the determinants of behavior while ignoring others, for we cannot examine everything simultaneously. This choice will depend upon a number of conditions, the primary one being the psychologist's interest in particular phenomena and particular theories. The conditions and phenomena of interest to me and my co-workers are those that affect a person's acceptance of health information; acceptance meaning that the recipient can not only repeat what he has been told, but shows that the information has changed his attitudes and his behavior (Hovland, Janis, and Kelly, 1953).

It should be clear that there are factors influencing health behavior that do not involve the acceptance of health information. For example, an authority may require an individual to take a chest x ray or an inoculation when he applies for a job or a passport. The goal for this type of health action is not to secure protection against disease, but to obtain a permit from a controlling power. An individual may also behave so as to conform to the actions of those about him. Again, however, the response reflects action toward a group goal rather than toward a health goal. Since orders, where they can be given, and conformity pressures, where groups exist, may well have more powerful effects upon behavior than the best presentation of information, they may appear very attractive routes for influence to the health educator. For the purpose of studying the acceptance of persuasive communications, they are, for the moment, less relevant to our interests. A psychologist interested in acceptance would probably point out that obedience and conformity can change behavior while failing to change inner attitudes. In this case the induced behavior will disappear when the force of the authority or group is removed. As examples he could mention the driver who slows down only when a policeman is in sight or when his wife or parents are in the car. Thus the motivation to obey or conform is often insufficient to sustain consistent responses toward health and safety goals. On the other hand, acceptance or change in internal beliefs should lead to a sustained and general awareness of the conditions where appropriate and healthful responses can be made. This does not imply that obedience and conformity cannot lead to internalization. Under certain conditions they do (Brehm and Cohen, 1962; Festinger, 1957).

The question we have put to ourselves, therefore, is: "How can information be presented to maximize change in attitudes and behavior?" One assumption that has been made is that some form of arousal, activation, or drive *is necessary* for change in attitude and action. For example, if we wish to teach an animal to press a lever, we could reduce his food intake, which will make him alert and eager to respond, and then provide food when he presses the lever. Lever pressing could also be established by using a noxious stimulus, such as an electric shock, to motivate the animal. The pain of the shock will give rise to an intense emotional reaction that functions as a drive to avoid the threat situation. The emotional response would occur whenever cues paired with the shock are present. If the instrumental response of pressing the lever allows the animal to escape the shock, i.e., the response is *rewarded*, he will soon press the lever whenever danger cues are present (Miller, 1948; 1951).

While it is clear that human beings are more complex than rats, it it also clear that there may be similarities between the factors controlling acceptance in humans and those in other animal forms. It is reasonable to ask, therefore, how we might apply these ideas to changing health behavior. Suppose our goal is to induce someone to brush his teeth for three minutes after every meal, using an appropriate toothbrush and an up-and-down motion. We have defined the responses, brushing up and down, and the cues, after meals, for brushing. Simply presenting this information to a person would probably have little effect upon his behavior, as we have not aroused any drive or motivation to reward the behavior. As may be seen from the animal paradigm, there are at least two ways in which we can introduce drive and reward. First, we could arouse approach or positive drives about the value of clean teeth. This could be done by emphasizing the social and sexual advantages of healthy teeth. On the other hand, we could use an aversive drive by arousing fear regarding the dangers of dental neglect and make toothbrushing seem instrumental for the avoidance of danger. The first is clearly the more pleasant approach. However, in many cases, e.g. disasters and fatal illnesses, there are few positive drives that one can summon to reinforce preparatory or protective action. In fact, it may, at times, be difficult if not impossible to avoid the arousal of a fear drive when communicating about these issues. Because of their strength and ubiquity in severe health crises, we decided to undertake a detailed investigation of the effects of negative drives upon the acceptance of health recommendations. We did this without assuming that one *ought* to use negative rather than positive drives, or that negative drives are *superior* to positive drives in producing acceptance.

While it is immediately "obvious" that fear is unpleasant, it is less clear how fear affects a person's willingness to undertake a recommended course of action. Common sense gives us contradictory information; it tells us of the person who did not get a check-up "because he was afraid" to see his doctor, and then it tells us about the person who finally went "because he was afraid." Our everyday knowledge provides numerous examples of such inconsistencies, and our goal as investigators is the careful description of conditions and the careful recording of the incidence of behavior, so that we can determine the conditions under which fear will facilitate or will interfere with the acceptance of recommendations.

EARLY FINDINGS

Attracted by just such questions, Janis and Feshbach (1953) performed one of the early and well-known experiments in this area. They compared the effectiveness of fear-arousing and non-fear-arousing communications in generating acceptance of dental hygiene recommendations. In their experiment a common set of recommendations about the care of teeth was presented to each of three groups of high school students. One of the groups (High fear) also received information including slides of bleeding gums and rotted teeth, which provided a vivid account of the dangers of improper dental care. Another group received a similar though far less vivid communication (Mild fear), and a third group (Low fear) received a very mild communication substituting impersonal language and slides giving diagrams of teeth for the vivid language and illustrations used in the high-fear condition. The students had reported their attitudes and actions regarding dental hygiene practices on a questionnaire collected one week prior to the experiment. Immediately after the communication, questions were asked pertaining to the feelings aroused by the message. Finally, the questions on attitude and behavior were repeated one week after the communication. As may be seen from Table I, these authors found that the highest fear level was associated with the lowest degree of acceptance of the recommendations.

While the superiority of the low-fear message fits one form of

TABLE I—COMPARISON OF THREE EXPERIMENTAL CONDITIONS*

Variables	Communication		
	High fear	Mild fear	Low fear
Subjects reporting worry about decayed teeth and diseased gums	76%	50%	46%
Subjects reporting interest	80%	68%	64%
Net percentage of subjects showing favorable change in practices two weeks later	8% (N = 50)	22% (N = 50)	36% (N = 50)

*Used by Janis and Feshbach, 1953.

To economize on space, significant levels from the statistical tests have been omitted. The results discussed reach acceptable levels of significance (p .05) except where indicated otherwise.

common sense, the results are somewhat puzzling as they do not agree with the previous example of avoidance learning in rats. Rats learned to press a lever not only to avoid shock, but to escape from any cues that had been associated with shock. Janis and Feshbach suggest (1953) that their subjects also made strenuous efforts to escape from the fear-producing message and that they did so by *denying* the relevance of the message to themselves. Under those conditions, where the communicator's recommendation cannot be immediately executed, an unrelieved state of tension will persist, motivating defensive avoidance. Supporting data for the defensive avoidance hypothesis are presented in a second study showing that subjects exposed to a fearful communication on smoking and lung cancer were more critical of the communication than were Ss exposed to a less fearful message (Janis and Terwilliger, 1963). However, this study fails to present evidence that criticalness is associated with resistance to stopping smoking.

In their discussion Janis and Feshbach (1953) state that under certain conditions, e.g., where action can be taken immediately, a fear-arousing communication could be more effective than a bland appeal. However, various secondary sources have ignored such qualifications and report the simple conclusion that fear-arousing communications produce less attitude change than nonfearful messages (Berelson and Steiner, 1964; Krech, Crutchfield, and Ballachey, 1962; Health Education Monographs, Supplement No. 1, 1963). Given the misstatement of the findings, the present investigator decided to undertake an experiment to determine if fear would enhance acceptance of an immediately available action and interfere with acceptance of a long-range decision (Leventhal and Niles, 1964).

Two responses were recommended to our subjects, that they take an x ray immediately after the communication and that they embark upon a long-range program of stopping smoking. The experiment was conducted at the New York Health Exposition (held at the New York Coliseum in August 1961), and the participants included any visitor to the fair who was interested in seeing a motion picture. Each group was assigned to one of three conditions: High fear, Mild fear, and a control condition. The control group read a pamphlet giving statistical data on the relationship of smoking to lung cancer. These people were also given the recommendations to stop smoking and to take a chest x ray at the mobile unit located within the exposition hall. Thus a direct record of x-ray behavior was available. People in the Mild- and High-fear conditions read the booklets, were given identical recommendations, and were also exposed to portions of a film on smoking and cancer. The portion of the film shown in the Mild-fear condition told the story of the diagnosis, hospitalization, and preparation for surgery of a young man suffering from lung cancer. The High-fear group was exposed to the same information and to an additional 10-minute sequence, with the camera focused directly on the patient's chest, showing the highlights of the surgical procedure. The entire film was in full color and the vivid surgical scenes were obviously disturbing to a large portion of the audience.

After viewing the film (High or Mild fear), reading the pamphlet, and receiving the two recommendations, everyone completed a questionnaire asking for reports on the amount of fear experienced, and intentions to take x rays and stop smoking. While the communications were highly successful in arousing fear, as may be seen in Table II, the subjects in the control group expressed stronger intentions to give up smoking than the subjects exposed to the Mild- or High-fear stimulus. While this could suggest that fear produced resistance to change, it is important to note that the subjects in the High-fear condition were just as willing to give up smoking as those in the Mild-fear condition despite the fact that the former reported much greater fear.

For intentions to take x rays, there were absolutely no significant differences between the groups. A count of people taking x rays (based

TABLE 11—RESPONSE TO FEAR-AROUSING COMMUNICATIONS†

		Condition	
Variables	High fear	Medium fear	Low fear
Reported fear	4.25	3.24	1.59
	(175)	(204)	(34)
Intentions to			
a) stop smoking (smokers only)	2.4	2.2	3.2
	(62)	(58)	(13)
b) take x rays (eligible Ss only)	2.55	2.28	2.14
	(68)	(89)	(14)
Correlations between (smokers only)			
a) fear and intentions to stop smoking	.40**	.47**	
	(61)	(57)	
b) fear and intentions to take x rays (eligible Ss only)	.42*	.34	
	(24)	(22)	
c) intentions to stop smoking and intentions to take x rays	.46*	.55*	
	(24)	(20)	

Note: scores are for smokers and nonsmokers, unless otherwise specified.
*$p < .05$
**$p < .01$
†Leventhal and Niles, 1964.

only on those who had not had an x ray in the last six months) also showed no differences between the fear conditions. The greater proportion of x rays taken in the experimental groups in comparison to the control condition was also not significant However, a greater proportion of x rays were taken by people exposed to the films than by people not viewing any of the experimental programs (25 per cent; see Leventhal and Niles, 1964, p. 473).

The negligible differences between the experimental groups could suggest that the different levels of fear have no effect upon attitudes and behavior. On the other hand, it is possible that fear does effect attitudes and performance, but that the effects vary so widely from person to person that *group* differences are unobtainable (Lazarus and Ericksen, 1952). An examination of the data revealed that within each treatment condition, people varied both in reported fear and intentions. Therefore, correlations were computed between these measures in each condition. It seemed possible that the arousal of fear could have elicited two reactions to smoking and taking x rays: 1) if you quit smoking, you don't need an x ray, or 2) if **you take an x** ray, you don't need to quit smoking. If so, we might expect negative correlations between these intentions in the High-fear condition. This negative relationship would have also eliminated any possible treatment differences between High and Mild fear. The results (in Table II) show that people who wanted to take x rays also wanted to stop smoking, and that people who reported the greatest amount of fear reported the strongest intentions to take x rays and to stop smoking. These relationships were the same in *both* High- and Mild-fear conditions, disconfirming the notion of an inverse relationship. Moreover, the level of reported fear and desire to quit smoking was higher among x-ray takers than among nontakers.

In summary, the analyses suggested a positive relationship between the intensity of fear reported after a communication, and the desire to take either of the two preventive measures. However, the relationship is an imperfect one, and it is clear that not all people showed increased acceptance when they were made increasingly fearful. That we did not find any over-all superiority for the High-fear groups suggests that a sizable portion of the subjects, though frightened, were less willing to accept the recommendations.

As a final note, we should point out that the study also provided evidence on the validity of questionnaire measures. People who stated that they had a very strong desire to take an x ray were far more likely to do so (75 per cent) than those who said they had a moderate desire (42 per cent) or no desire (5 per cent). Experiments to be reported later suggest that under certain conditions intentions and actions are less clearly related. In the present case the relationship would appear to depend upon the availability of action immediately after the communication. Whether the availability of action is the crucial factor is, at this moment, less important than the fact that few people appear to be motivated to please the experimenter by stating they will take an action when they really do not intend to do so.

Neurotic Anxiety Versus Realistic Fear

It seems clear from the smoking and lung-cancer experiment that fear motivated some people to act but not others. If we could specify the personality factors responsible for these differences, they might suggest environmental conditions that could be used to overcome the resistances. One possible way of approaching this problem would be to elaborate upon a distinction made by Freud (1927) and other writers (Goldstein, 1939; May, 1950; Janis, 1958; Janis and Leventhal, in press; Janis and Leventhal, in press) between realistic fear and neurotic anxiety. In neurotic anxiety, inner conflicts and past fantasies are projected upon the current environment, and the individual alleviates his tension by recourse to various defense mechanisms, such as repression, denial, reaction formation, aggression, and the like. These reactions reduce fear by eliminating *thoughts* about danger although this has no effect upon the danger. On the other hand, the following six characteristics would seem to apply to the individual and his situation for reflective or reality-based fear: 1) the appearance of the fear response depends upon the onset of external stimuli; 2) the intensity of the fear response is proportional to the magnitude of the danger; 3) the individual is alert or vigilant for environmental cues signaling changes in the behavior of the threat agent; 4) active efforts are made to seek information or reassurance against the danger; 5) changes are introduced (and expected to be made by others) in order to minimize or avoid impact with the danger; and 6) upon completion of protective action, or upon receipt of authoritative information signaling the removal of the danger, there is a reduction in the fear response.

When a fear reaction does not exhibit these characteristics, either because of persisting personality characteristics of the subject, or because a particular feature of the environment prevents one or another of these things from taking place, we can expect neurotic and defensive behavior, e.g., panic, chronic anxiety, or other maladaptive responses such as denial, repression, or anger. For example, in the previously discussed experiment by Janis and Feshbach (1954) the authors subsequently divided their subjects on the basis of their scores on a test of neurotic anxiety and found that only the predispositionally anxious students were resistant to the High-fear message and highly accepting of the Mild-threat message. Nonanxious students were equally accepting of both messages. In another study on dental hygiene, Goldstein (1958) has reported a similar effect where subjects classified as *copers* (those who make active efforts to recognize and deal with impulses and dangers) were equally accepting of recommendations under High and Low fear, while those classified as *avoiders* (those who deny dangers) resisted the fear-provoking message. Thus if a person lacks the personality traits to cope with or recognize the outer event determining fear, or is in a situation that prevents him from reacting with realistic fear, we should predict resistance to protective recommendations.

EVIDENCE OF SOURCES OF RESISTANCE TO FEAR COMMUNICATIONS

A series of experiments has been completed that provide considerable empirical evidence on the conditions for neurotic anxiety versus action-oriented or realistic fear. In a second experiment on smoking and lung cancer, a graduate student working in our research unit demonstrated the significance of prior beliefs in vulnerability to disease upon the acceptance of recommendations (Niles, 1964). Prior research had indicated that subjects who believe they are vulnerable to disease threats are very likely to take preventive health actions when given relatively mild warnings (Hochbaum, 1958; Leventhal *et al.*, 1960; Kegeles, 1963). Niles reasoned that if a person is so sensitized that mild warnings arouse considerable fear, then strong danger signals will arouse a disproportionately intense amount of fear, i.e. a kind of neurotic anxiety reaction, which would inhibit acceptance. Thus subjects high in beliefs of personal vulnerability should be increasingly persuaded as fear increases from very low to mild levels and then decreasingly persuaded as fear becomes more intense. On the other hand, people low in vulnerability beliefs may be nonresponsive to moderate increases in fear but become increasingly accepting under intense arousal.

Identical recommendations about x rays and smoking were delivered to three treatment groups, High, Mild, and Low fear. Prior to the communications the subjects, Yale students (all smokers), were given both the anxiety scale used by Janis and Feshbach (1954) and a seven-question attitude scale on susceptibility to illness. On the postcommunication questionnaires, subjects high in vulnerability beliefs stated the strongest desires to take x rays and to stop smoking in the Mild-fear condition. Low-vulnerability belief subjects indicated strongest desires to act under the High-fear stimulus. Despite the resistance to change for high-vulnerability subjects with High fear, the increased accptance for low-vulnerability subjects was so great that the over-all effectiveness of the High-fear communication exceeded that for either the Mild- or Low-fear message.

The vulnerable subjects in the High-fear condition reported less confidence in x rays and surgery as cures for cancer, e.g. they said they would get lung cancer even if they stopped smoking. Thus, their resistance to the High-fear message did not seem to stem from denial of vulnerability, but from a strengthening of vulnerability feelings that led to beliefs in the ineffectiveness of protective action. These results also suggest that our failure to find an over-all superiority of High fear in the New York Exposition study (Leventhal and Niles, 1964) occurred because the sample included more people who regarded themselves as susceptible to disease.

Because the Niles (1964) study used students and omitted a behavioral measure, a third experiment was undertaken (Leventhal and Watts). Leventhal and Watts developed a brief version of the vulnerability-beliefs scale that was suitable for a nonstudent population. Subjects rating themselves as vulnerable to disease were expected to feel the threat to be more relevant and to report more fear when exposed to the communications than Ss who did not rate themselves as vulnerable. Because the threat is more relevant to smokers than nonsmokers, it was expected that smokers would report more fear than nonsmokers. However, it was also hypothesized that heavy smokers, the group most directly in danger, would show relatively strong resistances to admitting fear if they believed themselves to be invulnerable. Thus feelings of invulnerability will inoculate a person against fear, and these beliefs are likely to be especially strong if one is highly committed to behaviors that are alleged to lead to danger.

The three smoking groups, light smokers, heavy smokers, and nonsmokers, were divided into those who believed they were vulnerable to disease and those who believed they were not; a total of six subgroups. These measures were obtained immediately before exposure to a smoking communication. The experiment was conducted at the New York State Fair, and the films comprising the communications were shown in a theatre located in a pavilion called the Hall of Health. A free mobile x-ray unit was at one of the pavilion entrances, and both were at the center of the fair ground. Three experimental treatments, High, Mild, and Low fear, were used.

The amount of *fear* reported by subjects followed predictions closely (Fig. 1). Most striking was the fact that light smokers with high vulnerability beliefs reported considerable fear even when exposed to the Low-fear film that contained only statistics and charts on the

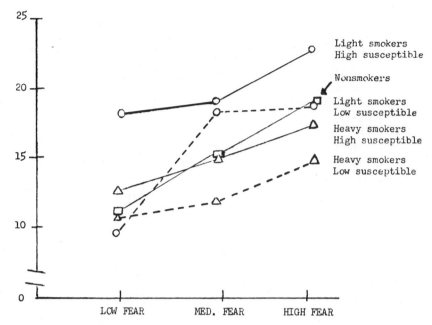

Fig. 1. Emotional response to fear-arousing films on smoking and lung cancer. (Leventhal and Watts)

relationship of smoking to cancer. On the other hand, heavy smokers who had previously rated themselves as invulnerable to disease reported the least fear in each of the three conditions.

The questionnaire measures of intention were disappointing. As in the first study by Levanthal and Niles (1964), there were no statistically significant effects between the fear treatments or between the vulnerability and smoking groupings for acceptance of either the recommendation to stop smoking or to take x rays (Table III). Once again, however, there were positive correlations between fear and acceptance within the conditions. An examination of the frequency of x-ray taking for *eligible smokers* showed a highly significant decrease in x rays going from the *Low- to the High-fear* condition! Fear had apparently produced resistance to x-ray taking. However, many people in the High-fear condition indicated they would prefer to go to their doctors for an x ray rather than take one at the mobile unit. This would be plausible if they thought something could really be amiss with themselves. Therefore a follow-up questionnaire was mailed to the

Table III—REACTIONS OF HEALTH EDUCATION VISITORS TO
FEAR COMMUNICATIONS ON SMOKING**

Reactions of Smokers	Communication High fear	Medium fear	Low fear
1) Strength of negative emotion (fear, nausea, etc.)	18.2 (61)	16.2 (47)	12.1 (71)
2) Intention to			
a) stop smoking	3.7 (55)	3.7 (45)	3.4 (61)
b) take x ray	5.5 (60)	5.1 (51)	5.1 (71)
3) Took x ray at exposition	6% (17)	44% (16)	53% (19)
4) Stopped or decreased smoking	73% (23)	57% (30)	57% (29)
5) Correlations between			
a) fear and intentions to decrease smoking	.40*	—.08	.11
b) fear and intentions to take x rays	.37*	.32*	.28*
c) belief in effectiveness of stopping smoking and intentions to decrease smoking	—.03	.05	.30*
d) belief in effectiveness of x rays and intentions to take an x ray	.09	.34*	.51*
e) fear and belief in effectiveness of stopping smoking	.25*	.26	.18
f) fear and belief in effectiveness of taking x rays	.15	.28*	.06

*$p < .05$
**Leventhal and Watts.

participants five months later to check on the subsequent taking of x rays and, at the same time, to determine how many people cut down or stopped smoking.

Because only 45 per cent of the subjects returned their questionnaires, the data may be biased and must be interpreted with caution. However, two factors suggest that the returns were representative of the original sample: 1) the proportion of returns was not significantly different for each of the three conditions, and 2) people who had taken x rays at the fair stated this on the questionnaire. Few new x rays were reported, and the greatest number of x rays remained in the Low-fear condition. However, for smoking, the proportions attempting to stop were the same across the fear groups, but significantly more subjects in the High-fear condition **reported** *success* in stopping.

The above results are opposed to the hypothesis initially stated by Leventhal and Niles (1964), that fear will enhance immediately available actions, e.g. x-ray taking, and interfere with long-range actions, e.g. stopping smoking. Yet if we realize that the threat is not only death through lung cancer, but death through surgery, the result of decreased x-ray taking for smokers makes good sense (the rate of x-ray taking for nonsmokers was equivalent across the fear conditions).* An x ray as a necessary precursor to surgery leads *to* threat as well as away from threat. Stopping smoking, though it may entail deprivation, is not a step toward threat. Thus where escape was possible (for smoking) the subjects showed realistic fear, and where they were "trapped" (x rays) they showed neurotic or unrealistic fear.

Since plausibility is an insufficient criterion for accepting a hypothesis, evidence for this new assumption was sought by computing correlations between the responses given by subjects within each condition. In the Low-fear condition, desire to conform to protective recommendations was correlated with beliefs in their effectiveness. As the communication became more fearful, desire to act was increasingly correlated with fear, and the correlations between desires to take x rays and beliefs in effectiveness became zero. Thus, with a threatening recommendation, fear rather than beliefs in the effectiveness of the recommendation appeared to be the primary motive for acceptance. This result confirms Niles' (1964) earlier conclusion that the arousal of fear increases acceptance unless the recommended actions appear inadequate to protect oneself from danger. In the Niles' study the recommendations were seen to be inadequate only among students high in vulnerability beliefs. For smokers in the present population (older, from less well-to-do homes, probably less accustomed to seeing themselves as able to fend off environmental threats than Niles' [1964] Yale subjects) the fear communication produced an over-all decrease in acceptance regardless of the subjects' vulnerability beliefs. Since beliefs in the effectiveness of stopping smoking remain correlated with fear it would appear that effectiveness beliefs for smoking were somewhat less shaken by the fear message. Moreover, as quitting smoking probably occurred later in time than the x-ray taking, the fear could have dissipated, permitting confidence in the action to return to normal. Whatever the process,

*In the Leventhal and Niles (1964) study, the results reported for x-ray taking combine smokers and nonsmokers. There were relatively few smokers in that sample who were eligible for x rays, and their behavior did not differ from that of the nonsmoking group.

HOWARD LEVENTHAL

the threat message induced realistic fear and action with regard to smoking.

A number of parallels exists between the reactions described in the previous experiments and responses observed during times of extreme danger. For example, as with heavy smokers who believe themselves invulnerable to disease, people adapted so rapidly and thoroughly to the threat of aerial bombardment during World War II that they ceased to follow authoritative warnings of danger. Few people left cities such as London during even the most severe phases of the blitz (Glover, 1942; Schmideberg, 1942). The same types of reactions have been observed in response to natural disasters such as the Kansas City flood and threats of mine cave-ins (Logan, Killian, and Marrs, 1952). As discussed in detail by Janis (1958) and Janis and Leventhal (in press), invlunerability defenses develop under conditions where warnings are repeated without the approach of danger. But when a powerful warning occurs (e.g. similar to High-fear communications), it may break through invulnerability beliefs, arouse fear, and motivate protective behavior. Severe breaks in invulnerability defenses are vividly illustrated by near-miss experiences in disasters, e.g., where people are helpless against the threat, trapped in wreckage, thrown by blast, but uninjured. Such experiences often produce chronic sensitivity to threat analogous to the hypervigilant behavior seen in people with high beliefs in vulnerability. High levels of fear are readily stimulated in these people and the fear does not lead to a meaningful pattern of escape behavior.

FEAR AND HIGH-EFFECTIVENESS RECOMMENDATIONS

Unlike cancer or heart disease, many danger situations pose less risk to the organism or offer far greater possibility for controlling the threat agent. For example, preventives or cures are now available for a number of otherwise fatal infectious diseases. In a recent study on acceptance of warning communications, Leventhal, Singer, and Jones (1965) made use of an issue high in threat and high in preventibility. For their high-threat communication the authors used a booklet that presented a case history of a patient who died from tetanus. Color photographs illustrated various aspects of treatment, e.g., tracheotomy wounds, drainage tubes, etc., and the language of the booklet was vivid and frightening. For a Low-fear message the booklets gave the same

TABLE IV—REACTIONS TO TETANUS COMMUNICATIONS*

	Communication		
	A. *High fear*	*Low fear*	*No fear*
Response measure	Specific and nonspecific recommendation	Specific and nonspecific recommendation	Specific recommendation only
Reported fear	9.2 (30)	4.5 (29)	3.0 (29)
Belief in the importance of shots	11.6 (30)	10.2 (29)	8.8 (29)
Strong intentions to get shots	60% (30)	31% (29)	18% (29)

	B. *High and Low fear*	*High and Low fear*	*No fear*	*No fear*
	Specific recommendation	Nonspecific recommendation	Specific recommendation	No recommendation
Took shots	28% (29)	3% (30)	0% (30)	0% (60)

*Leventhal, Singer, and Jones, 1965.

information about the disease but substituted innocuous black and white photographs for the color pictures, and used bland instead of emotional language. A recommendation was made to *all* subjects (college students) to get a free tetanus shot at the University Health Service. Half the students in each fear group also received a map of the campus with the Student Health Service clearly circled. Detailed suggestions were also given for planning a trip to the Health Service. For example, explicit mention was made of several class changes, routes to the library, etc., that would bring the student near the Health Service. Two control groups were also included. One received only the detailed instructions on how to get a tetanus shot. The other was a randomly drawn sample unexposed to any messages and whose shot-taking behavior was also recorded. Thus, there were four experimental groups, High fear with and without specific instructions and Low-fear with and without instructions, and the two controls.

On the questionnaire given immediately after the communication, subjects exposed to the High-fear booklets (specific and nonspecific) reported significantly greater tension, fear, and nausea, more favorable attitudes toward inoculation, and stronger intentions to take shots than subjects exposed to the Low-fear booklet (Table IV). The control group exposed only to specific recommendations reported considerably less favorable attitudes toward shots and less desire for inoculation than either the High- or Low-fear groups. When a count was made of subjects getting shots, it was found that students who received the specific recommendations along with either fear communication were significantly more likely to get tetanus inoculations than those not receiving the instructions (specific and fear, 28 per cent; nonspecific and fear, 3 per cent). But while specific instructions were necessary for behavior, the High-fear group receiving specific instructions showed no greater proportion of shot takers than the comparable Low-fear group. Neither information alone nor fear alone was sufficient for behavior. It should be emphasized that all of the students were seniors and all knew the location of the Health Service.

It may be seen that while some level of fear was necessary for behavior, the highest level of fear was successful in creating further increases in attitude change but not in behavior. However, this failure of the attitude change to carry over to action may be more apparent than real. The increased verbal acceptance for High fear relative to Low fear was measured *immediately after* exposure. All shot-taking behaviors occurred three days to three weeks later. As time passes both fear about contracting tetanus and favorable attitudes or intentions toward getting shots should return to their pre-exposure level. Thus, an equal proportion of shots might be expected in both High- and Low-fear groups when the behavior is measured after a delay.

To verify that both attitudes and fear decay over time, Leventhal and Niles (1965) measured attitudes at four points in time (immediately, 1 to 2 hours, 1 day, and 1 week) after exposure of 1 to 4 different durations (8, 16, 24, or 32 minutes) of fearful motion pictures of automotive accidents. Concern about accidents, and the desire to drive safely were significantly stronger for people exposed to the longer films. However, the increased effectiveness of long exposures was noticeable only for groups measured very near to the time of exposure. For people whose attitudes were recorded a day or week afterward, the differences were largely absent.

While the automotive **accident** study (Leventhal and Niles, 1965) verifies the hypothesis that both changes in attitude and feelings of fear dissipate with time, it does not account for the fact that fear *combined* with specific recommendations produced a lasting change. In the auto study, attitudes and behaviors of people exposed to any of the four durations returned, in time, to the positions held by subjects who were *unexposed* to messages on driving. Although a delayed attitude measure is lacking in the tetanus study (Leventhal, Singer, and Jones, 1965), the subjects given *specific* information in the High- and Low-fear groups took many more shots than those in the *No*-fear controls (28 per cent versus 0 per cent). Thus, combining some amount of fear with specific recommendations caused a "permanent" change for a significant proportion of subjects but the level of fear (High or Low) did not differentially affect this change. However, it must be remembered that a tetanus shot is a single act (or two- to three-visit affair at most), while safe driving is a day-by-day affair. In the accident study, driving practices may have changed temporarily and then gradually reverted to their earlier state. There is no way of detecting reversion to early practices for shot taking. In addition, there are likely to be many more factors sustaining present driving practices and thereby resisting change than there are factors in favor of not taking tetanus shots.

Three conclusions seem warranted from the two studies. First, when the actions recommended are clearly effective, attitude and behavior change is more likely to take place than if doubts exist about response effectiveness. Second, the effects of fear communications are subject to dissipation over time, though the loss of effectiveness is less likely when specific recommendations are given and/or when the behavior recommended is a simple one-shot measure.* Third, when specific instructions for action accompany a fear message, it is doubtful whether there is any long-range gain in acceptance once fear is raised above some "adequate" threshold.

REPLICATIONS AND EXTENSION OF FINDINGS TO DENTAL HYGIENE

The only health topic where the research reviewed in this paper exclusively supports the hypothesis that High fear generates less acceptance than Low fear is dental hygiene. Since it is possible that

---

*In a just-completed study on smoking, it appears that specific instructions are the critical factor in maintaining and *increasing* behavior change.

the original result obtained by Janis and Feshbach (1953) is more readily replicated with this issue, Leventhal and Singer (1965) undertook a new study comparing the effectiveness of fear-arousing and nonfear-arousing communications for the acceptance of dental hygiene practices. An effort was also made in this experiment to assess the importance of the reduction of the fear drive for the acceptance of specific reassurances (see also Miller, 1963). To manipulate the association of recommendations with fear arousal and fear reductions, Leventhal and Singer used several groups to vary the order of presentation of the fear and recommendation stimuli (see also Aronfreed, 1964; Cohen, 1957; Moltz and Thistlethwaite, 1955). It was predicted that presenting the recommendations *after* the fear stimuli would result in pairing the recommendations with the greatest reduction of fear, and lead to the greatest acceptance. On the other hand, recommendations given prior to the fear communications (where there is no fear to be reduced) are less likely to be recalled and used to reassure oneself (Cohen, 1957). A third group was used with recommendations intermixed with the fear material. This replicated the Janis and Feshbach order and was predicted to be less effective than the fear followed by recommendations, yet more effective than recommendations followed by fear. A fourth group, where fear stimuli were given without reassuring recommendations provided the condition for unrealistic fear and the very lowest acceptance. (Four groups such as these were run for both the High- and Low-fear messages.) Two control groups, one exposed only to recommendations, the other to neither fear or recommendations, were also used.

The tape-recorded communications and slides were presented to small groups of people attending the New York State Fair. The data, consisting entirely of questionnaire responses given immediately after the communication, showed that the groups exposed to the High-fear communications were more fearful, more accepting of the recommendations (intending to carry out the recommended practices) and more convinced of the effectiveness of the recommendations than were Ss given the less fearful messages (Table V). To see if increased acceptance depends upon fear reduction, the fear measures and the acceptance scores were compared for the different orders among the High-fear groups. As predicted, the position of the recommendations did affect level of fear, with the level of reported fear among the High-fear

TABLE V—REACTIONS TO DENTAL HYGIENE COMMUNICATIONS BY
HEALTH EXPOSITION VISITORS* AND BY HIGH SCHOOL STUDENTS**

Variables	Fear only	High fear Rec.-Fear	Mixed	Fear-Rec.	Low fear	Rec. only	Base
A) Exposition visitors							
1) Fear arousal (1-35)	21.03	19.79	17.12	15.47	10.51	11.10	10.47
2) Intentions (acceptance)	27.87	29.11	28.24	30.03	26.15	27.68	25.24
3) Effectiveness	34.31	35.55	35.12	35.47	32.51	34.06	33.87
n	35	41	35	32	36	30	35
B) High school students (college-prep course)							
1) Fear (1-7)			3.72	3.17	1.35	1.42	
2) Intentions			28.97	28.39	28.26	28.16	
3) Effectiveness			35.49	34.46	35.13	30.77	
4) Toothbrush taking			88%	80%	79%	61%	
n			41	35	38	23	
C) High school students (general course)							
1) Fear (1-7)			4.29	3.90	2.01	2.12	
2) Intentions			29.15	29.65	27.12	25.77	
3) Effectiveness			37.89	35.90	35.76	31.79	
4) Toothbrush taking			84%	84%	81%	70%	
n			38	25	27	20	

*Leventhal and Singer.
**Singer, 1965.

treatments increasing as follows: 1) recommendations after fear arousal, 2) recommendations and fear arousal intermixed, 3) recommendations prior to fear arousal, and 4) fear arousal without reassuring recommendations. However, there were no significant differences between these groups in their intentions to follow the recommendations.

It is possible that the superiority of the fear-recommendation sequence in generating attitude change will appear only after some lapse of time, i.e. over time the acceptance induced by fear will dissipate in those High-fear conditions where all of the fear has not been reduced by the recommendations. Since all measures were obtained immediately after the communication in the Leventhal and Singer study, Singer

(1965) conducted a second study to investigate the persistence of the effects. The study was conducted in two high schools that drew their students from highly similar ethnic and social backgrounds. All of the ninth-grade classes in each school were assigned to one of the four conditions, High fear followed by recommendations, High or Low fear intermixed with recommendations, or a control group receiving only the recommendations. Groups using intermixed recommendations were designed to follow the procedure of the Janis and Feshbach (1953) study. The effects upon acceptance of differences in fear reduction was to be tested by a delayed (two weeks) comparison of High-fear-intermixed with High fear followed by recommendations.

Because he was working with high school students, Singer was able to obtain measures of anxiety, dental attitudes, and reports of current dental hygiene practices two weeks prior to the communication. Immediately after the communication, measures were taken of fear and of intentions to carry out the recommendations. The measure of attitudes and a second report on dental hygiene practices were obtained two weeks later. In one of the schools the students were given the opportunity to obtain a free toothbrush at any time during a three-day period following the communication. The same opportunity was given in the other school but two weeks later in time, when the second measure was made of dental practices.

The results replicated the findings of the Leventhal and Singer study in showing that intentions to engage in proper dental hygiene practices, as measured immediately after the film, are strongest in the High-fear group, next in the Low-fear group, and weakest in the recommendations-only control. The results were weaker but basically the same for the behavioral response of getting toothbrushes during the three days following the communication. However, 80 per cent of the students obtained toothbrushes, and it is clear that the action was much simpler and less threatening than x-ray taking, stopping smoking, or taking tetanus inoculations. Two weeks after the communication there were essentially *no* differences between the groups. Thus, the Janis and Feshbach (1953) finding of the superiority of Low to High fear was *not* repeated for the reported practices measure.* The absence of a differential effect for the fear treatments on the delayed measures of attitude and behavior parallels our earlier findings

---

*Janis and Feshbach (1953) found no differences between groups for their attitude measures.

from the automotive (Leventhal and Niles, 1965) and tetanus (Leventhal, Singer, and Jones, 1965) experiments.† In fact, as the rate of toothbrush taking was almost as high two weeks after the communication (78 per cent) as it was immediately afterwards (80 per cent), one might conclude that, as in the tetanus study, there was retention of the communciations effects over the delay period. However, it seems more reasonable to assume that many of the factors that maintained a high level of motivation for free toothbrushes had little to do with the communications.

Singer's data also revealed effects highly suggestive of social class differences. The immediate increase in intentions that was caused by fear was much stronger for students registered in the *noncollege* preparatory program. Those in the college preparatory program were equally accepting under Low and High levels of fear. It is worth noting that the basic findings of both the Leventhal and Singer (1965) and the Singer (1965) studies have been independently replicated by Haefner (1964) at the University of Michigan. Haefner reports High fear to be more effective than Low fear in motivating subjects to obtain a dental hygiene booklet but finds no differences between his fear groups in later reports of adherence to recommended dental practices. His fear effects are also stronger among students in lower socioeconomic groupings.

The dental studies both reinforce and add to our earlier discussion by suggesting that: 1) the added strength given to a recommended attitude or related behavior by a fear-arousing communication, in comparison to a non-fear arousing communication, is greatest at the time of the communication and decreases thereafter; 2) fear strengthens acceptance when beliefs in the adequacy of recommended actions are either undisturbed or strengthened by the fearful communication; 3) while a minimal level of fear arousal seems to be necessary for acceptance, increases in fear to higher levels seem unlikely to facilitate acceptance, especially for subjects from upper socioeconomic groups.

It should also be noted that we have recorded long-term behavioral influences in only two instances, success in stopping smoking (Leventhal and Niles, 1964) and receiving tetanus inoculations (Leventhal, Singer, and Jones, 1965). In the tetanus study, specific recommenda-

---

†It is possible that a delayed difference would have resulted if a high-fear-only group had been run. However, the automotive results (Leventhal and Niles, 1965) suggest that this may not be true.

tions produced more tetanus shots regardless of the fear level, as long as some fear-arousing material was presented along with the recommendations. Because of the questions that can be raised regarding the loss of subjects in the smoking study, one must conclude that the evidence is still unclear as to whether the maintenance of influence over time depends upon the specific nature of the tetanus recommendations (i.e. suggestions on when and how to carry them out) or upon the fact that the recommended response can be performed on a single occasion versus one requiring repetitive action.

At present, our evidence for changes in more complex responses, such as driving habits and dental care, is restricted to changes in verbal intention and attitudes. However, these acts might have shown change if the reports of behaviors (direct observation was not used) were taken on the day(s) immediately after the communication. It should be pointed out that difficulty in sustaining change is not unique to attitude studies using communications. The difficulty is also reported by investigators using intensive group methods in smoking clinics (Ross, 1965). It may be that success in producing change is closely related to the "magnitude" of the change that is required, i.e. whether we are simply *inhibiting* an old reaction or requiring the acquisition of a new and complex habit, and to the degree to which the investigator can maximize transfer by creating realistic conditions for practice.

At the outset, I took special pains to justify focusing on a particular problem. Now the strengths and weaknesses of focusing are apparent. While we know a fair amount about a small problem, we are plagued by unanswered questions. For example, we have not compared acceptance produced by fear-arousing messages with that produced by messages arousing other affects, such as joy, shame, disgust, and other emotions. Such comparisons are difficult to make as it is difficult to vary the emotions provoked by different messages while holding communication content constant. Thus, it is conceivable that any form of arousal is adequate to generate acceptance and that the results are not specific to fear. Moreover, it is not clear that emotion is directly responsible for the effects that have been recorded. It is possible that the "fear message" is effective by virtue of presenting a more adequate picture of the threat. If so, one could presumably generate acceptance by using this manipulation under conditions where the fear itself was minimized.

Clearly many questions remain to be answered regarding the relationship of "emotion" to measures of acceptance. In addition, the manifest difficulty in maintaining the changes that have been produced suggests the need to investigate the relationship of emotion-provoking communications to various factors that are known to maintain action, e.g., public commitment (Lewin, 1943), or group norms (Festinger et al., 1960). However, knowing what we now do about fear and acceptance, we are ready to extend our efforts in answering these questions and in providing ways of constructing effective techniques for influencing health actions.

BIBLIOGRAPHY

Aronfreed, J. Origin of self-criticism, Psychol. Rev. 71:193, 1964.

Berelson, B. and Steiner, G. A. Human Behavior. New York, Harcourt Brace, 1964.

Brehm, J. W. and Cohen, A. R. Explorations in Cognitive Dissonance. New York, Wiley, 1962.

Cohen, A. R. Need for cognition and order of communication as determinants of opinion change. In: Hovland, C., ed., Order of Presentation. New Haven, Yale Univ. Press, 1957.

Festinger, L. A Theory of Cognitive Dissonance. Evanston, Row Peterson, 1957.

Festinger, L. et al. The operation of group standards. In: Cartwright, D. and Zander, A. F., eds. Group Dynamics, Research and Theory, 2nd. ed., Evanston, Row Peterson, 1960, p. 241.

Freud, S. Inhibitions, Symptoms and Anxiety. J. Strachey ed., London, Hogarth Press and Institute Psycho-Analysis, 1961.

Glover, E. Notes on the psychological effects of war conditions on the civil population: Part 3, the blitz, Int. J. Psychoanal. 23: 17, 1942.

Goldstein, K. The Organism, a Holistic Approach to Biology, New York, Amer. Book, 1939.

Goldstein, M. Relationship between coping and avoiding behavior and response to fear arousing propaganda, J. Abnorm. Soc. Psychol. 58:247, 1959.

Haefner, D. Use of fear arousal in dental health education. Paper read at the 92nd Annual Meeting of the American Public Health Association, Dental Health Section, October 7, 1964.

Hochbaum, G. M. Public participation in medical screening programs: a socio-psychological study. Washington, D.C., Public Health Service Publication No. 572, Govt. Printing Office, 1958.

Hovland, C. I., Janis, I. L. and Kelley, H. H. Communication and Persuasion. New Haven, Yale Univ. Press, 1953.

Janis, I. L. Psychological Stress. New York, Wiley, 1958.

Janis, I. L. and Feshbach, S. Effects of fear-arousing communications, J. Abnorm. Soc. Psychol. 48:78, 1953.

Janis, I. L. and Feshbach, S. Personality differences associated with responsiveness to fear-arousing communications, J. Personality, 23:154, 1954.

Janis, I. L. and Leventhal, H. Human reactions to stress. In: Borgatta, E. and Lambert, W., eds., Handbook of Personality Theory and Research. Boston. Rand McNally. In press.

Janis, I. L. and Leventhal, H. Psychological aspects of physical illness and hospital care. In: Wollman, B. ed., Handbook of Clinical Psychology. New York, McGraw-Hill. In press.

Janis, I. L. and Terwilliger, R. An experimental study of psychological resistances to fear-arousing communication, J. Abnorm. Soc. Psychol. 65:403, 1962.

Kegeles, S. S. Some motives for seeking preventive dental care, J. Amer. Dent. Ass. 67:110, 1963.

Krech, D., Crutchfield, R. S. and Ballachey, E. L. *Individual in Society*. New York, McGraw-Hill, 1962.

Lazarus, R. S. and Ericksen, C. W. Psychological stress and personality correlates: effects of failure stress upon performance, *J. Exp. Psychol. 43*:100, 1952.

Leventhal, H. *et al.* The impact of the 1957 epidemic of influenza upon the general population in two cities. Washington, D.C., U.S. Dept. Health, Educ. Welfare, 1960.

Leventhal, H. and Niles, P. A field experiment on fear arousal with data on the validity of questionnaire measures, *J. Personality, 32*:459, 1964.

Leventhal, H. and Niles, P. Persistence of influence for varying durations of exposure to threat stimuli, *Psychol. Rep. 16*: 223, 1965.

Leventhal, H., Singer, R. P. and Jones, S. H. The effects of fear and specificity of recommendation, *J. Pers. Soc. Psychol. 2*:20, 1965.

Leventhal, H. and Singer, R. P. Order of affect arousal and recommendations as determinants of attitude change, mimeo copy, 1965.

Leventhal, H. and Watts, J. Sources of resistance to fear-arousing communication, *J. Personality*. In press.

Lewin, K. Psychological ecology. In: Cartwright, D., ed., *Field Theory in Social Science*. New York, Harper, 1951.

Logan, L., Killian, L. M. and Marrs, W. A study of the effect of castastrophe on social disorganization. Chevy Chase, Md.

Operations Research Office, 1952.

May, R. *The Meaning of Anxiety*. New York, Ronald Press, 1950.

Miller, N. E. Fear as an acquirable drive, *J. Exp. Psychol. 38*:89, 1948.

Miller, N. E. Learnable drives and rewards. In: Stevens, S. S., ed., *Handbook of Experimental Psychology*. New York, Wiley, 1951, p. 435.

Miller, N. E. Some reflections on the law of effect produce a new alternative to drive reduction. In: Jones, M. R., ed., *Nebraska Symposium on Motivation*. Lincoln, Univ. Nebraska Press, 1963, 65-112.

Moltz, H. and Thistlethwaite, D. Attitude modification and anxiety reduction, *J. Abnorm. Soc. Psychol. 50*:231, 1955.

Niles, P. The relationship of susceptibility and anxiety to acceptance of fear-arousing communications. Unpublished doctoral dissertation, Yale Univ., 1964.

Ross, C. Roswell Park Smoking Clinic. Paper read at the Connecticut Conference on Smoking Behavior, January 1965.

Schmideberg, M. Some observations on individual reactions to air raids, *Int. J. Psychoanal. 23*:146, 1942.

Singer, R. P. The effects of fear-arousing communications on attitude change and behavior. Unpublished doctoral dissertation, Univ. Conn., 1965.

Young, M., DiCicco, L., Paul, A. and Skiff, A. Methods and materials in health education (communication). Section 3 in: Review of research related to health education practice, *Health Educ. Monog., suppl. No. 1*, 1963.

PART III

RECIPIENTS

Having observed what the effects in persuasion are of source- and message-related variables, now let us add another component to the communication model and find out what audience-related variables can influence the potency of a communication. We shall begin by considering the characteristics of recipients which affect their susceptibility to a persuasive appeal. What are the factors of persuasibility, inherent in the individual, which enhance his susceptibility to influence? Then we shall consider how persuasibility can be augmented by inducing external stimuli which modify the psychological environment. Next, methods of inducing resistance to persuasion are reviewed. Finally, we discuss the role of active versus passive participation in persuasion, and the effect of intentional and overheard communication.

Inherent Factors

Some people are extremely gullible. They tend to accept un-
reservedly almost anything authoritative they read, see, or hear. They
adopt one opinion, then its very antithesis. Like the branches of a
willow in the wind, they seem to sway first one way, then the other.
Others, though more reserved in their reaction to persuasion, tend to
be highly susceptible to special appeals. Emotional communications
affect some people more than others. Some are more susceptible to
the subtle coercion of a fear appeal, and others to rational but seldom
to emotional propaganda. Still others seem to be impervious to all intentional efforts at persuasion. They often appear to go out of their way
not to react, and even when they do grudgingly respond it may be in
just the opposite direction recommended.[1] Most of us, of course, fall
somewhere in the middle of the persuasibility continuum.

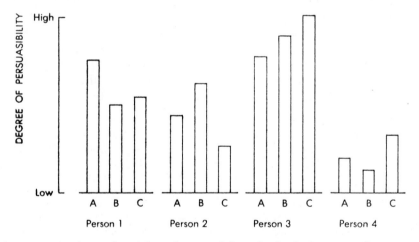

FIG. 1. Topic-free and topic-bound persuasibility of individuals. A, B, and C represent different communication topics.[2]

---

[1]This latter reaction has been termed the "boomerang effect." There are several possible reasons why the boomerang might occur. Opinion might change in a direction
opposite the one intended by the communicator because: (1) the communicator's arguments were poorly written, or (2) the communication induced aggression and unallevi-

Figure 1 differentiates among four individuals in the type and the approximate intensity of their persuasibility. Each person was exposed to three communications on three different topics. We shall assume that communication "A" was a fear appeal on dental hygiene, "B" an emotional appeal telling them to vote Socialist, and "C" a rational appeal from the American Cancer Society.

Following a system of nomenclature devised by Janis and Hovland,[3] the reaction of Person 3 can be characterized as *communication-free*. He was easily persuaded whatever the communication. He responded more than anyone else to all three appeals. Person 4 was more susceptible to the rational communication than Person 2, who in other respects was more persuasible than Person 4. Of these four subjects, Person 3 is the most persuasible, and Person 4 the least.

Sometimes persuasibility is not communication-free but, instead, bound to some special characteristic of the message. Some people are predisposed to a particular topic *(topic-bound)*, others to a particular kind of appeal *(appeal-bound)*, or argument *(argument-bound)*, or style *(style-bound)*. These types of persuasibility can best be characterized as *communication-bound*.[4]

Consider, for example, the findings in a study by Walter Weiss and Bernard Fine on one of the personality correlates of topic-bound persuasibility. Using the standard before-after design, they compared the opinions of recipients and nonrecipients of a report urging strict and harsh punishment as the most effective way to cope with the problem of juvenile delinquency. The groups were subdivided on the basis of their responses to items from two projective tests admin-

---

ated emotional arousal, or (3) the communication made salient the subject's own counterbeliefs and counternorms, e.g., Catholics exposed to a communication advocating birth control by artificial means. See Hovland, C. I., Janis, I. L., & Kelley, H. H. *Communication and persuasion.* New Haven, Conn.: Yale Univer. Press, 1953. Pp. 36, 63, 142, 164, 286. Cohen, A. R. A dissonance analysis of the boomerang effect. *J. Pers.,* 1962, **30,** 75–88. Greenberg, B. S. On relating attitude change and information gain. *J. Communication,* 1964, **14,** 157–171. Von Cranach, M., Irle, M., & Vetter, H. Zur analyse des bumerang-effektes. *Psychol. Forsch.,* 1965, **28,** 535–561.

[2]Reprinted from Secord, P. F., & Backman, C. W. *Social psychology.* New York: McGraw-Hill, 1964. P. 168. By permission of C. W. Backman and the publisher.

[3]Janis, I. L., & Hovland, C. I. An overview of persuasibility research. In I. L. Janis & C. I. Hovland (Eds.), *Personality and persuasibility.* New Haven, Conn.: Yale Univer. Press, 1959. Pp. 1–26.

[4]Janis and Hovland, *ibid.,* also propose three additional classes of predispositional factors: *communicator-bound, media-bound,* and *situation-bound.*

istered prior to the delinquency report. The results showed clearly that those whose own personalities could be characterized as hostile and extrapunitive were the ones most persuaded by the report. Subjects lowest in hostility and extrapunitiveness were the least persuaded by the (punitively oriented) report.[5]

In contrast to Janis and Hovland's conception of communication-free persuasibility as a general trait of susceptibility to influence, Kelman and Cohler maintain instead "that the relationship between personality variables and change in response to social influence [always] depends on the *type of influence situation* to which the person is exposed and the *type of change* that we are observing." One example from the implied myriad of personality variables is "need for cognitive clarity." High-need individuals who react to incongruity by seeking clarification would be likely to show the greatest amount of positive opinion change. These "clarifiers" would react to the ambiguity by seeking clarification, exposing themselves to new information, and by trying to make sense of the ambiguity. High-need individuals who tend to deal with incongruity by seeking simplification would be likely to show the greatest resistance to change, perhaps even a boomerang effect. These "simplifiers" would achieve cognitive clarity by simplifying their psychological environment. They would avoid new information, or misperceive it, or deny its implications.[6]

A simpler, dichotomous typology has been proposed by Michael Goldstein. Where a fear appeal is the stimulus, there are "copers," people who cope with a threatening stimulus directly by problem-solving, and "avoiders," people who try to bypass, or avoid, the threat. Copers, Goldstein finds, tend to recall disturbing material best, while avoiders are better at recalling neutral material. As a result, when high and low fear appeals are directed at these two per-

[5]Weiss, W., & Fine, B. J. Opinion change as a function of some intrapersonal attributes of the communicatees. *J. abnorm. soc. Psychol.*, 1955, **51**, 246–253. These results were supported in a follow-up study where aggressiveness was experimentally induced. In the later experiment, subjects failed a difficult problem-solving task and then were insulted for their failure. Consistent with results in the earlier study, the aggressively aroused subjects were the ones most influenced by a punitively oriented communication. The results can be interpreted as displacement of aggression following frustration. Weiss, W., & Fine, B. J. The effect of induced aggressiveness on opinion change. *J. abnorm. soc. Psychol.*, 1956, **52**, 109–114.

[6]Kelman, H. C., & Cohler, J. Personality factors in reaction to persuasion. *Science*, in press.

sonality types, the copers tend to be influenced more by the high fear appeals and the avoiders more by the low.[7]

What other factors, inherent in the individual's personality, are related to persuasibility? The literature on this subject, though extensive, is not always conclusive, nor is it necessarily consistent. For instance, it is as plausible to assert that the factor of intelligence is positively correlated with persuasibility as it is to assert a negative correlation, or even no correlation. On the one hand, the more intelligent a person, the better able he is to comprehend the issues. The less intelligent person, because of his limited comprehension, is less susceptible to persuasion on complex issues. On the other hand, the more intelligent a person, the greater is his critical ability, and the less he is influenced by persuasion. There is literature in support of the null,[8] the positive,[9] and the negative[10] relationship.

The relationship obtained between sex and persuasibility is more

---

[7]Goldstein, M. J. The relationship between coping and avoiding behavior and response to fear-arousing propaganda. *J. abnorm. soc. Psychol.*, 1959, **58**, 247–252.

[8]In a recent experiment in which Harold Skinner varied the medium of presentation, no relationship was found between intelligence and persuasibility. Murphy, Murphy, and Newcomb, in their survey of the social-psychology literature prior to 1937, also find zero or near-zero correlations between intelligence and persuasibility. Skinner, H. R. Individual differences in susceptibility to persuasive messages communicated via print, tape recordings, and motion pictures. Unpublished doctoral dissertation, Indiana Univer. School of Educ., 1963. Murphy, G., Murphy, L. B., & Newcomb, T. M. *Experimental social psychology.* New York: Harper & Row, 1937. P. 930.

[9]Hyman and Sheatsley contend that uninformed people are harder to reach whatever the level or nature of the message. In support of this contention is Swanson's finding of a positive relation between intelligence and information receptivity. Hyman, H. H., & Sheatsley, P. B. Some reasons why information campaigns fail. *Publ. Opin. quart.*, 1947, **11**, 412–423. Swanson, C. E. Predicting who learns factual information from the mass media. In H. Guetzkow (Ed.), *Groups, leadership and men: research in human relations*. Pittsburgh, Pa.: Carnegie Press, 1951.

[10]Wegrocki finds a negative correlation between IQ and opinion change when the communications used as stimuli contain specious arguments. Carment, Miles, and Cervin have observed that the more intelligent and extraverted subjects are, the more persuasive they are but the less persuasible. Another study by Carment and his associates Schwartz and Miles concludes that there is a complex interaction between persuasibility, intelligence, and emotional responsiveness. Wegrocki, H. J. The effect of prestige suggestibility on emotional attitude. *J. soc. Psychol.*, 1935, **5**, 384–394. Carment, D. W., Miles, C. G., & Cervin, V. B. Persuasiveness and persuasibility as related to intelligence and extraversion. *Brit. J. soc. clin. Psychol.*, 1965, **4**, 1–7. Carment, D. W., Schwartz, F. S., & Miles, C. G. Persuasiveness and persuasibility as related to intelligence and emotional responsiveness. *Psychol. Rep.*, 1963, **12**, 767–772.

straightforward. Females, on the average, tend to be more susceptible to persuasive communication than males.[11]

Numerous other inherent factors have been reported to be correlated with persuasibility: cognitive need,[12] ego-defensiveness,[13] authoritarianism,[14] self-esteem,[15] aggressiveness,[16] need for social approval,[17] dogmatism,[18] etc.

[11] Janis, I. L., & Field, P. B. Sex differences and personality factors related to persuasibility. In I. L. Janis & C. I. Hovland (Eds.), *Personality and persuasibility*. New Haven, Conn.: Yale Univer. Press, 1959. Pp. 55–68. King, B. T. Relationships between susceptibility to opinion change and childrearing practices. In I. L. Janis & C. I. Hovland (Eds.), *Personality and persuasibility*. New Haven, Conn.: Yale Univer. Press, 1959. Pp. 207–221. Whittaker, J. O. Sex differences and susceptibility to interpersonal persuasion. *J. soc. Psychol.*, 1965, 66, 91–94. Whittaker, J. O. Consistency of individual differences in persuasibility. *J. Communication*, 1965, 15, 28–34. Although the inverse relationship has not been observed, the null has been obtained: Abelson, R. P., & Lesser, G. S. The measurement of persuasibility in children. In I. L. Janis & C. I. Hovland (Eds.), *Personality and persuasibility*. New Haven, Conn.: Yale Univer. Press, 1959. Pp. 141–166. Abelson, R. P., & Lesser, G. S. A developmental theory of persuasibility. In I. L. Janis & C. I. Hovland (Eds.), *Personality and persuasibility*. New Haven, Conn.: Yale Univer. Press, 1959. Pp. 167–186. Skinner, H. R. Individual differences in susceptibility to persuasive messages communicated via print, tape recordings, and motion pictures. Unpublished doctoral dissertation, Indiana Univ. School of Educ., 1963. Scheidel, T. M. Sex and persuasibility. *Speech Monogr.*, 1963, 30, 353–358.

[12] Cohen, A. R. Need for cognition and order of communication as determinants of opinion change. In C. I. Hovland (Ed.), *The order of presentation in persuasion*. New Haven, Conn.: Yale Univer. Press, 1957. Pp. 79–97. Baron, R. M. Cognitive basis of attitude change as a function of motivational, stylistic, and stimulus factors. *J. Pers. soc. Psychol.*, 1965, 2, 219–230.

[13] Sarnoff, I., & Katz, D. The motivational bases of attitude change. *J. abnorm. soc. Psychol.*, 1954, 49, 115–124. Katz, D., Sarnoff, I., & McClintock, C. Ego-defense and attitude change. *Human Relat.*, 1956, 9, 27–45. Katz, D., McClintock, C., & Sarnoff, I. The measurement of ego-defense as related to attitude change. *J. Pers.*, 1957, 25, 465–474. Sarnoff, I. Psychoanalytic theory and social attitudes. *Publ. Opin. quart.*, 1960, 24, 251–279.

[14] Berkowitz, L., & Lundy, R. M. Personality characteristics related to susceptibility to influence by peers or authority figures. *J. Pers.*, 1957, 25, 306–316. Linton, H., & Graham, E. Personality correlates of persuasibility. In I. L. Janis & C. I. Hovland (Eds.), *Personality and persuasibility*. New Haven, Conn.: Yale Univer. Press, 1959, Pp. 69–101.

[15] Leventhal, H., & Perloe, S. I. A relationship between self-esteem and persuasibility. *J. abnorm. soc. Psychol.*, 1962, 64, 385–388. Dabbs, J. M. Self-esteem, communicator characteristics, and attitude change. *J. abnorm. soc. Psychol.*, 1964, 69, 173–181. Silverman, I. Differential effects of ego threat upon persuasibility for high and low self-esteem subjects. *J. abnorm. soc. Psychol.*, 1964, 69, 567–572. Crowne, D. P., & Conn, L. K. The hypnotic enhancement of self-esteem and persuasibility. Paper read at Midwest. Psychol. Ass., St. Louis, 1964. Stern, G. S., Lana, R. E., & Paul-

There is also a wealth of research and information from areas outside persuasion which may be relevant to the personality-persuasibility problem. There is the enormous and growing body of literature on conformity,[19] the work on influencibility in affiliation,[20] and the research on factors of suggestibility in hypnosis.[21] It is an understatement to say that these diverse findings on influencibility have existed as a vast, loose array of empirical data without much underlying theoretical structure. Because much of the research was designed expressly for the purpose of testing *ad hoc* hypotheses of only incidental theoretical significance, it is often only happenstance that discloses any commonality at all in this miscellany.

Recently, an impressive effort has been made by the social psychologist William J. McGuire to tie together these loose threads from persuasion, suggestion, and conformity in a single, parsimonious theory

---

ing, F. J. Fear arousal and order of presentation of persuasive communications. *Psychol. Rep.*, 1965, **16**, 789–795.

[16] Roland, A. Persuasibility in young children as a function of aggressive motivation and aggression conflict. *J. abnorm. soc. Psychol.*, 1963, **66**, 454–461.

[17] Crowne, D. P., & Marlowe, D. *The approval motive.* New York: Wiley, 1964. Chapt. 8. Buckhout, R. Need for social approval and attitude change. *J. Psychol.*, 1965, **60**, 123–128. Buckhout, R. Need for social approval and dyadic verbal behavior. *Psychol. Rep.*, 1965, **16**, 1013–1016.

[18] Miller, N. Involvement and dogmatism as inhibitors of attitude change. *J. exp. soc. Psychol.*, 1965, **1**, 121–132.

[19] Sherif, M. A study of some social factors in perception. *Arch. Psychol.*, 1935, **27**, No. 187. Asch, S. E. Opinions and social pressure. *Sci. Amer.*, 1955, **192**, 31--35. Crutchfield, R. S. Conformity and character. *Amer. Psychologist*, 1955, **10**, 191–198. Asch, S. E. Studies of independence and conformity: I. A minority of one against a unanimous majority. *Psychol. Monogr.*, 1956, **70**, No. 9 (Whole No. 416). Hollander, E. P. Conformity, status, and idiosyncrasy credit. *Psychol. Rev.*, 1958, **65**, 117–127. Luchins, A. S., & Luchins, E. H. On conformity with judgments of a majority or an authority. *J. soc. Psychol.*, 1961, **53**, 303–316. Milgram, S. Nationality and conformity. *Sci. Amer.*, 1961, **205**, 45–52. Gerard, H. B. Conformity and commitment to the group. *J. abnorm. soc. Psychol.*, 1964, **68**, 209–211. Allen, V. L. Situational factors in conformity. In L. Berkowitz (Ed.), *Advances in experimental social psychology.* Vol. 2. New York: Academic Press, 1965. Pp. 133–175. Milgram, S. Liberating effects of group pressure. *J. Pers. soc. Psychol.*, 1965, **1**, 127–134.

[20] Schachter, S. *The psychology of affiliation.* Stanford, Calif.: Stanford Univer Press, 1959.

[21] Weitzenhoffer, A. M. *Hypnotism: An objective study in suggestibility.* New York: Wiley, 1953. Orne, M. T. The nature of hypnosis: Artifact and essence. *J. abnorm. soc. Psychol.*, 1959, **58**, 277–299. Barber, T. X. Hypnotizability, suggestibility, and personality: V. A critical review of research findings. *Psychol. Rep.*, 1964, **14**, 299–320. Moore, R. K. Susceptibility to hypnosis and susceptibility to social influence. *J. abnorm. soc. Psychol.*, 1964, **68**, 282–294.

of social influence.[22] We noted earlier (pp. 150 f.) how McGuire's formulation would resolve with a curvilinear nonmonotonic function the controversial finding of a positive versus a negative relationship between fear arousal and opinion change. Although it is beyond the scope of this book to dwell on this important new theoretical formulation in any great detail, McGuire's theory is so relevant at this point in our discussion that at least a brief overview of it is in order. In our zealous attachment to brevity, what follows may give the impression that his theory of social influence is imprecise and ambiguous. In fact, it is neither.

Underlying the theory are six general principles: (1) Mediation, (2) Combination, (3) Situational-Weighting, (4) Confounding, (5) Interaction, and (6) Compensation. The first two principles lay the foundation for McGuire's prediction of a nonmonotonic relationship between behavior and personality. On the basis of these two principles, McGuire is able to derive an elaborate mathematical model for predicting compliance to social influence. In contrast to Kelman and Cohler who reject the idea of a general trait of susceptibility to social influence,[23] McGuire accepts the assumption of a weak general factor of susceptibility, but with group and specific factors as well. The last four principles in McGuire's formulation qualify the preliminary derivations, taking into account, as do Kelman and Cohler, the effects of confounding and interacting variables related to influencibility.

The first principle—Mediation—states that opinion change is the residual outcome of a series of behavioral steps. In place of the simple, familiar Stimulus-Response (S-R) explanation of opinion change,[24] McGuire substitutes a more complex mediation-type hypothesis.[25] McGuire hypothesizes a five-step process in behavior leading to opinion change. The first three steps encompass the traditional learn-

---

[22] McGuire, W. J. Personality and susceptibility to social influence. In E. F. Borgatta & W. W. Lambert (Eds.), *Handbook of personality theory and research.* Chicago: Rand-McNally, in press.

[23] Kelman, H. C., & Cohler, J. Personality factors in reaction to persuasion. *Science,* in press.

[24] S-R implies that opinion change is the simple direct response to a persuasive communication.

[25] cf. Osgood, C. E. *Method and theory in experimental psychology.* New York: Oxford Univer. Press, 1953. Pp. 392–412. Jakobovits, L. A. Mediation theory and the 'single-stage' S-R model: Different? *Psychol. Rev.,* 1966, **73,** 376–381.

ing model of opinion change[26]: *(a)* the individual must attend to the communication, *(b)* he must understand it, and *(c)* he must yield to what he understood. To these three steps, McGuire adds *(d)* the individual must retain what he has accepted, and *(e)* he must act in accord with what he accepted.

Were one to emphasize only the first two steps, attention and comprehension (described collectively as *reception*), and to ignore the third step of *yielding*, one would have an oversimplified and distorted conception of the persuasion process. We noted earlier how a concern only with receptivity would lead one to predict a negative relationship between fear arousal and opinion change. (The more anxious the person is, the more he is preoccupied with his own worries, and the less likely he is to attend to, or comprehend, extraneous stimuli.) Concern only with the yielding machanism would lead instead to a positive relationship. (The more anxious the person is, the more he will be threatened by a fear appeal, and the more prone he will be to yield to it.) It is McGuire's contention that we too often overemphasize the third step in this chain (yielding) and overlook the first two steps (reception).

The Combinatory Principle asserts, simply, that the individual will change insofar as he effectively receives the message and yields to the point received. The relationship between personality and influencibility is defined by Principle 2 in terms of the relationship of the personality variable to receptivity and yielding, and also the relationship of these two steps to influencibility. Although both receptivity and yielding are positively related to influencibility, it is McGuire's contention that when any given personality variable is introduced, the net relationship can be more complex and even nonmonotonic. Consider again the factor of intelligence. It can be argued that the more intelligent the person, the better will be his ability to attend to and comprehend a persuasive communication. But it also can be argued that the more intelligent he is, the greater is his critical ability. The first assertion implies a positive relationship between intelligence and receptivity; the second, a negative relationship between intelligence and yielding. If one combines these factors, the result is a kind of platykurtic, upside-down, U-shaped curve to describe the

---

[26] Hovland, C. I., Janis, I. L., & Kelley, H. H. *Communication and persuasion.* New Haven, Conn.: Yale Univer. Press, 1953. Schramm, W. *The process and effects of mass communication.* Urbana, Ill.: Univer. of Illinois Press, 1955. Pp. 3–13. Hartman, F. R. A behavioristic approach to communication: A selective review of learning theory and a derivation of postulates. *Audio-Visual Communication Rev.*, 1963, **11**, 155–190.

probability of compliance to social influence at different levels of intelligence. The greatest compliance is predicted for around the middle of the intelligence continuum. People who are high in intelligence, though better able to attend and comprehend, are less prone to yield. People who are low in intelligence, though more prone to yield, are less able to attend and comprehend. For those in the middle, an optimum relationship between receptivity-yielding and attitude change is obtained.

A similar nonmonotonic relationship can be posited if one substitutes the factor of self-esteem for intelligence. The higher a person's self-esteem, the greater is his self-confidence, and the less likely it is that he will yield to persuasion. But since self-esteem is probably positively related to intelligence, the greater his self-esteem, the better able he will be to attend to and comprehend the message. The lower his self-esteem, the greater his social withdrawal, and the less receptive he will be to persuasion. If one thinks of the net effect of these variables, one has again a nonmonotonic relationship.

The third principle, Situational Weighting, makes the point that the relationship between influencibility and any given characteristic of personality may vary from situation to situation. Sometimes, as in hypnosis, influencibility depends more on whether or not an individual yields to the stimulus than whether he attends to and comprehends it. Almost everyone has the capacity to receive hypnotic instruction. But not everyone is equally prone to yield. Some situations are at the opposite extreme. They put a heavy strain on receptivity and little on yielding. As a general principle, it can be stated that if situations are very hard or very easy in the strain they exert on the receptivity mechanism, then personality variables will tend to affect influencibility through yielding. In situations of intermediate strain, influencibility is more a function of both receptivity and yielding.

The Confounded-Variable Principle asserts that because some personality factors are highly related to others, when one considers the effect of a given factor on influencibility one must also consider its relation to other factors and the relationships of these other factors to receptivity and yielding. For example, the factor of depression would probably correlate negatively with self-esteem, but positively with social withdrawal tendencies.

The fifth principle, Interaction, takes into account interactions between and among components in the communication model. Specific source and message variables may interact with influencibility factors. The reader will learn in Part IV how different channels of communication can affect receptivity. Yielding can be influenced by source credibility. The number of possible combinations is infinite.

Finally, the Compensation Principle states that there is an optimum level of influencibility—a kind of "golden-mean"—in order for there to be adequate adaptation to the environment. Thus, influencibility is maintained within an optimum range by means of a dynamic equilibrium between opposed personality forces.

Because McGuire's theory is new, there has been only a limited opportunity to test derivations from it. One of the studies that follows, by Donald F. Cox and Raymond A. Bauer, was reported several years before McGuire's publication of the theory of social influence, yet in these findings there is strong support for the nonmonotonic relationship which is the very essence of McGuire's theory. The study preceding Cox and Bauer is by Irving Janis and Peter B. Field. This study is one of the best known and most often cited in support of the hypothesis of a general factor of persuasibility. The third study is by Harry F. Gollob and James E. Dittes. Its findings, too, are relevant to the McGuire formulation. The relationship between self-esteem and persuasibility is shown empirically to be a complex interaction of esteem with several message variables and with the factors of learning and acceptance.

Reprinted from Sociometry, 1956, Vol. 19, No. 4, pp. 241–259, by permission of Irving L. Janis and the publisher.

A Behavioral Assessment of Persuasibility: Consistency of Individual Differences[1]

Irving L. Janis and Peter B. Field

A number of recent investigations (1, 3, 4, 5, 6) have been concerned with individual differences in responsiveness to persuasive communications and have raised the possibility that there may be a general factor of susceptibility to persuasion, or "persuasibility." The latter term does not refer to attitudes predisposing the individual to accept or reject communications which favor a *particular type of conclusion*, but rather to those attitudes or personality factors leading to low or high resistance to a *wide variety of persuasive communications on many diverse topics*. The existence of one or more general factors of susceptibility to persuasion would imply that some individuals tend to be indiscriminately influenced by the many persuasive communications to which every modern urban community is continually exposed, while other individuals tend to be generally unresponsive to such communications.

Previous studies bearing on general persuasibility have been limited in scope and in generality because of their use of a small number of communications, relatively homogeneous in argumentation and in type of persuasive appeal. An initial study by Janis (5) used three communications which dealt with different topics, but which were relatively homogeneous in that they all advanced predictions of future events and used logical argumentation rather than other possible persuasive appeals (e.g., fear-arousing appeals or prestigeful endorsements). A second study by the same author (6) used five communications which were heterogeneous in content, but all of them were again limited to predominantly logical argu-

[1] The present research study was conducted in connection with an undergraduate research stipend which was awarded by the Social Science Research Council to the junior author in the summer of 1954. The study was carried out under the auspices of the Yale Communication Research Program, which is supported by a grant from the Rockefeller Foundation and which is under the general direction of Professor Carl I. Hovland, to whom the authors are indebted for valuable suggestions and criticisms. Special thanks are also due Dr. Robert P. Abelson for advice on problems of statistical analysis and for valuable suggestions concerning the formulation of the factor analysis findings. The authors also wish to express their thanks to John Forsythe, Lawrence Hilford, and Joyce Montgomery, who assisted the authors in administering the tests; and to Eileen Beier, who carried out the factor analysis computations. The data for this study were obtained from the Milford High School in Milford, Connecticut, and the authors are deeply grateful to Mr. Herbert R. French, principal of the high school, and to the social science faculty for their helpful cooperation.

mentation. Both studies were conducted with male college students and the results supported the conclusion that there are consistent individual differences in persuasibility which are related to personality factors such as feelings of personal inadequacy.

One of the main questions which the present investigation was designed to answer is the following: Are individual differences in susceptibility to persuasion consistent enough to warrant the assumption that there is a more or less general factor of persuasibility? To help answer this question we have developed a test for assessing a person's susceptibility to persuasion, modeled after the behavioral measures of persuasibility used in Janis's earlier studies (5, 6). The method consists of three steps: first, the subjects are given an initial attitude test; next they are exposed to a series of persuasive communications; then, they are given a postcommunication attitude test to determine the degree to which their attitudes change in the direction of the communicators' conclusions.

The new test of general persuasibility to be described in the present paper differs from the ones used in the earlier studies in the following important respects: the series of communications used is much larger and represents a much wider variety of topics and of persuasive appeals. By administering the new test to a large sample of subjects, it was possible to examine the consistency of opinion changes in response to the various different communications. If specific topic-bound predispositions are the only major factors which determine individual differences in responsiveness to persuasive communications, correlations close to zero should be found among the resulting opinion changes. A different prediction follows from the hypothesis that there is a general factor (or set of factors) underlying individual differences in susceptibility to persuasion. According to this hypothesis, the resulting opinion changes will be positively intercorrelated: those persons who are most strongly influenced by any one of the persuasive communications should show a tendency to be most strongly influenced by each of the others, irrespective of the particular subject matter.

The present report will be devoted to describing and discussing the evidence pertaining to test reliability and the consistency of individual differences in persuasibility. A later report will deal with additional evidence bearing on potential *sources* of consistent individual differences—sex differences, I.Q. differences, and various motivational factors that predispose a person to high or low susceptibility to persuasive communications.

METHODS AND PROCEDURES

The Persuasibility Test

The new test of persuasibility consists of three different components: (*a*) the "Before" questionnaire designed to measure initial opinion on 15 different items; (b) Booklet I, a mimeographed booklet containing five persuasive communications on five different topics, each of which is followed by three pertinent questions identical with three of the questions included in the Before questionnaire; and (c) Booklet II, a second series of five persuasive communications on exactly the same topics as the first series but taking diametrically opposite positions to those taken in the first series. After each communication in Booklet II the subjects are given the same opinion questions which they had answered earlier in the Before questionnaire and in Booklet II. Thus, at three different times the subjects are asked to express their opinions on the pertinent issues discussed in the persuasive communications: the first time, before any communication is presented; a second time, after reading the initial set of communications (Booklet I); and a third time, after reading an opposing set of communications (Booklet II).

The persuasibility scores obtained from the test are based on a total of 30 questions (3 questions for each of 10 communications). The method of scoring will be described below.

In Booklet I, the articles present various types of arguments and persuasive appeals in support of the following main conclusions:

1. The U. S. Civil Defense organization should be greatly expanded to include 25,000,000 men and women.

2. An effective cure for cancer can be achieved within one or two years if an all-out research effort is made; about 50 per cent of all medical research specialists should concentrate on this task.

3. General Von Hindenburg, president of the German Republic after the First World War, was a democratic leader and a great statesman.

4. Radio stations should (and soon will) cut down on the amount of classical music they dish out because it is dull stuff, strictly for the long-haired highbrows and stuffed shirts.

5. Jack O'Keefe, a corny comedian who is trying to break into TV, is not worth watching and his TV show will be a complete flop.

In Booklet II, the same type of argumentation and persuasive appeals are used to support the opposite conclusions; e.g., the civil defense organization should be cut down to about 2000 well-trained people so that our main defense effort can be concentrated on using our air power; a cure for cancer cannot be expected for at least 30 years and it would be a mistake to take scientists away from other, more promising tasks to work on this one; and so on.

In addition to the wide range of topics covered in each booklet, there is also a wide variety of special persuasive appeals. An attempt was made to include representative examples of major types of persuasive appeals currently found in mass communications, ranging from the logical argumentation employed in the communications about cancer research to the hy-

TABLE 1

Subject Matter and Special Appeals Used in the Persuasibility Test Communications

Topic	Communicator's position		Special appeal used in pro and anti communications
	Booklet I	Booklet II	
1. Public participation in Civil Defense effort	Pro	Anti	Fear-arousing threat statements (e.g., danger of unpreparedness, destructiveness of atomic warfare)
2. Expansion of cancer research	Pro	Anti	Logical arguments and specialized information (citing expert scientific opinion)
3. General Von Hindenburg	Pro	Anti	Stereotyped characterizations (overidealized hero or exaggerated villain)
4. Classical music	Anti	Pro	Social incentives (predictions that the given preference will be a means of attaining social approval)
5. A new television comedian	Anti	Pro	Hedonic incentives (predictions that the given choice will lead to enjoyment or nonenjoyment.)

perbolic, stereotyped journalism in the comments about the television comedian. Table 1 summarizes the topics and the main types of appeal used in the ten communications.

In selecting the communication topics, care was taken to avoid such possible confounding dimensions as a consistent "liberal" or "intellectual" position, or a consistent tendency to believe the good or the bad about people. Moreover, it was for the specific purpose of avoiding correlations with specific ideological predispositions that we included the subjects' opinion changes in response to communications presenting both the pro- and anti- position on each issue in arriving at the over-all persuasibility score. A person agreeing with both the pro- and anti-communication on a given issue would be likely to do so not because of some specific preference for one side of the issue, but rather because of a general tendency to accept the communications regardless of the initial attractiveness of their conclusions. Thus, the inclusion of opposing communications in the persuasibility test should help ensure that positive correlations among opinion changes will not be attributable to some tendency to accept either all pro- or all anti- communications, or to accept a given set of ideologically related opinions, but will reflect a more general persuasibility tendency.

We attempted also to vary the degree of structuring with respect to the subjects' previously formed opinions and amount of prior knowledge. The communications range from those on which the subjects could be expected to hold definite initial opinions (e.g., preference for classical music) to those on which they could have no previous opinions (e.g., the unknown television comedian). One of our initial assumptions, which is tested in the present study, was that if a general factor of susceptibility to persuasion is present, consistent individual differences should be found on all topics but should show up most strongly on the *unstructured* topics, i.e., those for which initial opinions are not based on familiarity with the nature of the issue or on prior information about the pros and cons. For instance, with high-school students one would expect that opinion changes on the Von Hindenburg and the unknown comedian communications would be the most sensitive indicators of any general persuasibility tendency.

Every one of the ten communications, whether pro or con, took a sufficiently extreme position to ensure that practically none of the subjects would initially agree with the position advocated by the communication. It should be noted that any question or communication which yielded complete acceptance or complete rejection would not have been satisfactory for our purposes, because it could not be used to study individual differences in susceptibility to persuasion. The communications and questions were repeatedly revised on the basis of successive individual and group pretests so that (a) the communications would be intelligible and interesting to high-school students, and (b) the questions could differentiate subjects who were influenced by the communications from those who were not.[2] From a preliminary analysis of the changes in opinion produced by the communications in a sample of 100 cases, it was found that on all 30 post-communication questions a significant degree of change occurred.

Procedures for Investigating Consistency

The persuasibility test was administered to approximately 185 high-school juniors in their history classes. The Before test questionnaire and Booklet I, including the second questionnaire, were administered successively in the same session; Booklet II, including the third questionnaire, was administered a week later. For each class, the regular teacher intro-

---

[2] The three questions included for each communication were to some extent redundant, but not completely so because they covered somewhat different aspects or implications of the main conclusion. For example, after exposure to the first communication in Booklet I and in Booklet II, the following questions were asked:

a. During the past year there have been several million men and women serving as volunteers in the United States Civil Defense Program. During the coming year, how many people do you think the United States *should* have as volunteers in civil defense work?

b. Do you think the United States ought to spend more money or less money than it spends at present on civil defense?

c. If it ever happens that American cities are attacked by atomic bombs, how much help do you think a large civil defense organization would be with respect to saving lives?

Copies of the entire questionnaire and of the ten communications used in the Persuasibility Test are available upon request from the authors.

duced the experimenter as a member of a university research organization "which is conducting studies in this and other high schools throughout the state." The experimenter administered the Before test and then gave a standardized introduction, explaining the material in Booklet I.

The subjects were informed that the articles were written by reporters presenting their opinions on controversial, newsworthy topics. Each communication and both booklets were headed with the title "Opinions in the News" and with a by-line designed to impress upon the reader the fact that the communications had been written by reporters. The students were told that the experimenter wanted to know whether they agreed or disagreed with the articles, and they were instructed to express their own personal opinions on the questions following each article. They were also assured that their answers would be kept strictly confidential and would not be seen by the teacher or by anyone else at the school. In order to avoid implicit or explicit pressure for opinion change, the following instructions were given orally by the experimenter, immediately after the subjects had finished filling out the first (pre-communication) questionnaire:

Now I am going to ask you to read some articles on the topics that I have just asked you about. I would like you to answer some more questions about your opinions after you have read these articles.

I am giving you the articles to show you what some other people are thinking about these matters. You are perfectly free to agree or disagree with these articles, of course. After you have read each article you will be asked whether you agree or disagree with it. Remember, I want to know what you think, so give me your own personal opinion.

The articles that you're going to read have been taken from a professional news service. This news service brings together articles about opinions in the news today.

There are many different opinions about these different subjects. The reporters who wrote the articles you're going to read have put down their own points of view. There are other people, of course, who think differently about these topics. For instance, my own personal views do *not* happen to agree with certain of these articles, although there are some other articles with which I am inclined to agree.

Now if I showed these articles to a lot of people in [name of city]—including for instance all the teachers in this high school—I would get a good deal of disagreement. The average person would probably agree with some of the articles and disagree with others. These articles are on matters of opinion, you see, and some people have one opinion while others have a different opinion about each topic. So feel free to decide *for yourself* whether you agree or disagree with each of these articles.

Please read these articles the same way you would read an article in a magazine or a newspaper, and then answer the questions about your own opinion.

Similar instructions were used when Booklet II was administered, one week after Booklet I.[3] Three weeks later a personality questionnaire was

---

[3] The introduction for Booklet II included the following:

I have come here today to ask you to read some more news service articles of the same kind you read before. You remember that last week you read some articles in

administered by the high-school teachers to the same students. Included
in this questionnaire were items asking the subject to rate himself on his
general susceptibility to influence by mass communications (newspaper
articles, radio and television programs) and his tendency to conform with
the opinions of his friends.

Scoring of the Persuasibility Test

A persuasibility score was assigned to each individual to represent his
opinion changes in response to the communications in the two booklets.
This score was the sum of the number of questions on which the subject
changed from his Before test position in the direction advocated by any
given communication. (About 3 per cent of the cases failed to answer
2 or more questions out of the 30 and were eliminated from the sample;
persuasibility scores for cases with one or two "no answer" responses were
prorated.) Changes in the negative direction (i.e., in the direction opposite
to that advocated in the communication) rarely occurred and did not
exceed 10 per cent on any item; they were counted the same as no change,
or zero. There was no differentiation in this method of scoring with respect
to magnitude of change: a change of one unit received a score of 1 just as
would a change of many units. The main reason for adopting this procedure is that there is no simple way to equate the *magnitude* of change on
one question with that on another, especially since about half the ques-

---

which newspaper reporters expressed their opinions about topics in the news today.
As you were told last week, there are many different opinions on these topics. Today
you will read some articles by some other reporters who take a different point of
view on these matters.

The Opinion News Service gives a chance for many different viewpoints to be
expressed, and so they often put out articles by writers who take opposite points of
view on the same topics. I am going to ask you to read these new articles and then
answer the same questions as before, after you've read the other side of the story and
after you've had a chance to see what some of the different opinions are on these
topics.

Let me remind you that you are perfectly free to agree or disagree with these
articles, and you will be asked whether or not you do agree with each article after
you have read it.

As I mentioned last week, if I showed any of these articles to people here J would
probably find a good deal of disagreement. Some people would agree and others would
disagree with each one. As for myself, I agree with some of the articles and disagree
with some others.

Remember, you should decide *for yourself* whether you agree or disagree with
each of these articles. Please read the articles in the same way you would read an
article in a magazine or newspaper, and then answer the questions about your
opinions.

And remember, all your answers will be kept strictly private in our study and
none of your teachers will see any of your answers.

tions required the subjects to express their opinions as quantitative estimates, while the other half required the students to place a check mark opposite one of the verbal answer categories presented in a standard check-list.

Since only the direction of the change was counted, the scores on the persuasibility test vary from zero to 30, representing the number of items on which the subject changed his opinion in the direction of a conclusion advocated by one of the communications he had just read. The response to each question in Booklet I was examined in relation to the response given to the same question on the Before test. For each item on which the subject changed in the direction of the communication, he was given a score of 1; for each item on which he showed no change, or a negative change, he was given a score of zero.

The scoring of the opinion changes following Booklet II was somewhat more complicated. A simple scoring of change in the direction of the second communication on a given topic might involve a serious methodological error. On the basis of prior studies of the stability of opinion changes produced by persuasive communications (4), it is expected that as a result of forgetting and other processes opinions would tend to regress (from their level immediately following Booklet I toward their original level) during the week's time which intervened between Booklet I and Booklet II. Thus if the identical questions had been asked a week later, even without any intervening opposing communications, a change away from the position expressed immediately after exposure to Booklet I would probably have occurred. Such a change could give rise to spurious change scores that do not reflect accurately the individual differences in responsiveness to the persuasive communications in Booklet II. In order to minimize this source of error, the criterion of change after Booklet II was defined as a shift from the answer given on the Before test. If the individual had shown a positive change following the Booklet I communication, then, following the Booklet II communication he had to change all the way back to his original position, or beyond, to be scored as a change in the direction of the latter communication. Consider, for example, an individual who changes twice on the following opinion question: "What is your own opinion as to how much time the average radio station should devote to classical music each week?" Let us say that he changes from 30 hours to 15 hours after reading the anti communication in Booklet I, but then changes to 25 hours on the same question after reading the pro communication in Booklet II. The change following Booklet I would be scored as 1 but the change following Booklet II would be scored as zero because the individual failed to return to his initial opinion. This individual would have to change back to 30 hours or more to receive a positive score on the given question in Booklet II.

Split-half Reliability

The reliability of the persuasibility test was investigated in a subsample of approximately 100 cases, constituting about two thirds of the total sample to which the test was administered. The subsample was a stratified random sample, including approximately equal numbers of male and female subjects. The split-half reliability was determined by giving each subject one persuasibility score on the 15 odd items and another persuasibility score on the 15 even items. Just as with the total scores based on all 30 items, the subtest scores represent the number of items on which the individual showed an opinion change (from the precommunication test to the postcommunication test) in the direction advocated by one or another of the communications. The raw reliability coefficient was found to be .69; the estimated value of the reliability coefficient is .81, when corrected by the Spearman-Brown formula. This finding indicates that the persuasibility scores are sufficiently reliable for making group comparisons.

Item Analysis

The internal consistency of the persuasibility test was studied in the same subsample of approximately 100 cases. Table 2 gives the results of an item analysis. It shows the results of plotting the changes on every item against the sum of the positive changes (or the "total persuasibility score"). The dichotomization of the total score was at the median. The dichotomization of item scores was between a change in the direction of the communication and no change or negative change.

Additional evidence of internal consistency is presented in Table 3, which shows tetrachoric correlations for each persuasibility subscore (on each communication of the persuasibility test) plotted against every other subscore on the test. Since there were three opinion questions for each communication, the scores for each communication ranged from zero (no positive change on any of the three questions) to 3 (positive change on all three questions). Dichotomizations were made so as to yield a split as close as possible to the median; the best split was found to be between scores of zero or 1 *vs.* 2 or 3.

Both the item analysis (Table 2) and the table of tetrachoric correlations (Table 3) clearly show a strong positive relationship among changes on the various topics comprising the persuasibility test. In Table 3, 39 out of 45 correlations are positive. Only 6 are negative, all very small and nonsignificant. The item analysis in Table 2 shows that 23 out of 30 questions are positively related to the total score at the .10 confidence level (two tail) or better; 11 out of 30 are significant at the .01 confidence level. Only 3 of the

TABLE 2

Item Analysis of the Persuasibility Test: Chi Square for Score on each Item vs. Sum of Persuasibility Scores for Booklets I and II

Topic	Item	Chi square (1 d.f.)	Confidence level (two tails)
I			
	1	7.28	< .01
1. Pro civil defense	2	5.84	.02
	3	5.92	.02
	4	1.64	.20
2. Pro cancer research	5	2.64	.11
	6	0.37	> .40
	7	8.40	< .01
3. Pro Von Hindenburg	8	5.73	.02
	9	12.35	< .01
	10	3.36	.08
4. Anti classical music	11	2.51	.12
	12	5.91	.02
	13	15.98	< .01
5. Anti TV comedian	14	37.35	< .01
	15	25.10	< .01
II			
	16	4.19	.05
1. Anti civil defense	17	6.08	.02
	18	5.77	.02
	19	9.28	< .01
2. Anti cancer research	20	3.22	.08
	21	7.88	< .01
	22	12.76	< .01
3. Anti Von Hindenburg	23	21.62	< .01
	24	5.79	.02
	25	2.48	.13
4. Pro classical music	26	00.01	> .40
	27	5.81	.02
	28	4.50	.04
5. Pro TV comedian	29	11.72	< .01
	30	0.81	> .35

NOTE: N = approximately 100, with an occasional decrement of from one to four cases because of omission of "no answer" responses.

30 items are very weakly correlated (above the .20 confidence level) but each of these was retained in the test because the very same question in the other booklet yields a significant relationship with the total score. No items correlated negatively with the total score.

The results indicate that for our sample of high-school students, the persuasibility test has a relatively high degree of internal consistency. The

TABLE 3

Tetrachoric Correlations among Persuasibility Subscores from Each Communication in the Persuasibility Test

	I-1	I-2	I-3	I-4	I-5	II-1	II-2	II-3	II-4	II-5
I-1 Pro civil defense	—	−.06	.50	.25	.22	.38	.05	.34	.21	.33
I-2 Pro cancer research		—	−.05	.10	.07	−.12	.14	−.12	.17	.16
I-3 Pro Von Hindenburg			—	.25	.31	.28	.05	.47	.25	−.07
I-4 Anti classical music				—	.44	.09	.05	.15	.23	.13
I-5 Anti television comedian					—	.50	.30	.52	.22	.27
II-1 Anti civil defense						—	.29	.49	−.08	.02
II-2 Anti cancer research							—	.30	.15	.27
II-3 Anti Von Hindenburg								—	.02	.27
II-4 Pro classical music									—	.33
II-5 Pro television comedian										—

NOTE: N = approximately 100, with an occasional decrement of from one to four cases because of omission of "no answer" responses.

findings support the general hypothesis that there are consistent individual differences in the opinion changes elicited by a series of diverse communications.

Factor Analysis

A centroid factor analysis was computed from the array of tetrachoric correlations shown in Table 3. The results are shown in Table 4. The proportion of the communality which enters into the first centroid factor is .60; this supports the assumption that the persuasibility test scores are determined to some degree by a single general factor. Three factors were found necessary, however, to account satisfactorily for the entire set of intercorrelations. These three factors were rotated obliquely and a clear simple structure emerged. On two of the rotated factors, denoted A and B, pro and anti communications on the same topic had similar loadings: either both were high positive or both were close to zero. This result, whereby pro and anti communications on the same issue cling together in the factor space, is in accord with the assumption that individual differences in opinion change are partially determined by factors other than the predisposition to develop a pro or anti attitude on the issue. The analysis indicates that there is a tendency for individuals to change either *both* ways on a given topic, or *neither* way. Factors A and B constitute two correlated clusters each showing this tendency. On factor A, both pro and anti communications on the following topics have high positive loadings (.35 or above): cancer research, classical music, and the new television comedian. Other loadings are negligible. On factor B, the four highest positive loadings occur on the following: the pro and anti communications on Von Hindenburg and civil defense.

As a preliminary interpretation of the difference between factors A and B, it is plausible to suppose that the factor A topics have directly favorable or unfavorable implications for the individual, while factor B topics are on more remote, impersonal political issues. A more extensive factor analysis using a much larger number of topics would be needed to test this possibility. In any case, factors A and B correlate .42 with each other, and thus may be construed as variations on a single theme, whatever their individual

TABLE 4

Factor Analysis Results for Persuasibility Subscores: Centroid Factor Matrix, Rotated Oblique Factor Matrix, and Pearsonian Correlations between Factor Axes. (Based on Data in Table 3)

Centroid factor matrix (unrotated)

	I	II	III	Communality (h^2)
I-1 Pro civil defense	.58	.31	.24	.49
I-2 Pro cancer research	.10	−.41	.04	.18
I-3 Pro Von Hindenburg	.53	.41	.38	.59
I-4 Anti classical music	.45	−.19	.26	.31
I-5 Anti television comedian	.71	−.03	−.17	.53
II-1 Anti civil defense	.50	.39	−.32	.50
II-2 Anti cancer research	.40	−.15	−.35	.30
II-3 Anti Von Hindenburg	.63	.30	−.29	.57
II-4 Pro classical music	.39	−.32	.28	.33
II-5 Pro television comedian	.43	−.29	−.06	.27

Rotated oblique factor matrix

	A	B	C
I-1 Pro civil defense	.05	.56	.47
I-2 Pro cancer research	.40	−.31	−.10
I-3 Pro Von Hindenburg	−.06	.62	.62
I-4 Anti classical music	.40	.06	.26
I-5 Anti television comedian	.41	.33	.00
II-1 Anti civil defense	−.06	.59	−.02
II-2 Anti cancer research	.34	.07	−.28
II-3 Anti Von Hindenburg	.09	.57	.01
II-4 Pro classical music	.48	−.08	.21
II-5 Pro television comedian	.48	−.04	−.07

Correlations between factor axes

	A	B	C
A	—	.42	.00
B	.42	—	−.42
C	.00	−.42	—

interpretations. That theme is a general persuasibility factor which can be visualized as lying between factors A and B.

Factor C, which accounts for the least variance of the three factors, has high loadings on only two communications: pro civil defense and pro Von Hindenburg. The anti versions of these communications have negligible loadings, as do all other communications. Factor C is thus a more specific, content-bound factor than either A or B. Factor C correlates .00 with factor A and $-.42$ with factor B. No explanation is offered for factor C.

Self-ratings

The personality inventory, a 130-item questionnaire which was administered three weeks after the final part of the persuasibility test, included the following three questions for the purpose of obtaining the subjects' own self-ratings on susceptibility to *influence by mass communications*:

1. Do you usually agree or disagree with the articles that you read in newspapers and magazines?

(__Agree with practically *everything* I read; __Agree with *most* of the things I read; __Agree with *about half* and *disagree* with half; __Disagree with *most* things I read; __Disagree with practically *everything* I read.)

2. Nowadays when the American people listen to the radio or look at television, they see or hear a great deal of advertising, publicity, and information that attempts to influence their opinions and attitudes. As compared with the average person of your own age, how much are your own ideas likely to be influenced by the things you hear or see on the radio or television?

(__Much *more influenced* than the average person; __Somewhat *more influenced*; __Slightly *more influenced*; __About the *same*; __Slightly *less influenced*; __Somewhat *less influenced*; __Much *less influenced*.)

3. Consider all the magazine articles and newspaper columns presenting a specific point of view which you may have read during the past year. About how many of them may have influenced your opinions?

(__Practically none of them; __Very few; __Some; __A fairly large number; __Most of them; __Practically all of them.)

The answer to each question was given a score ranging from zero, or not influenced, to 5, highly influenced (the extreme categories in question 2 being combined). The S's total score for the entire cluster was obtained by adding together the score values for his answers to the three questions.

The same scoring procedure was used with another cluster dealing with susceptibility to *influence by friends*. The following eight questions were included in this cluster, each of which was accompanied by a self-rating check-list of five categories:

1. How often do you change your opinion if you discover that most other people you know do *not* share your point of view?

2. When one of your friends wants to convince you of his point of view, does he usually have a hard time or an easy time?

3. As compared with the average person of your own age, how much are you usually influenced by the ideas expressed by your friends?

4. As compared with the average person of your age, how strongly do you usually hang on to your own opinions or beliefs at times when your friends are trying to get you to change your mind?

5. How easy is it for your friends to get you to do what they want?

6. When other people criticize your ideas or object to your opinion, how often do you end up feeling that they are right and you are wrong?

7. How often do you become uneasy when the opinions of one of your friends is different from your own on some important topic?

8. How often do your feel sure you know what is right or wrong about the ideas expressed by the people you know?

Table 5 shows correlations between total persuasibility scores (sum of the positive opinion changes shown on the 30 questions in Booklets I and II) and each of the two clusters of self-ratings on susceptibility to influence. These correlations are based on a total sample of 86 males and 96 females who answered all the pertinent questions.

The correlation between the persuasibility test scores and self-ratings on susceptibility to influence by mass communications is significant at the .02 level for males, but the correlation is close to zero for females. The difference between the correlation for males and for females is not significant (p = .18, determined by Fisher's z-transformation formula). The fact that the persuasibility test scores of the female subjects bear no relationship to their self-ratings indicates that the two procedures are not measuring the same thing. In the case of the male subjects, however, there is some degree of overlap since the persuasibility test scores enable one to predict better than chance what a subject will say about his responsiveness to mass communications in general. The second relationship studied (persuasibility and susceptibility to influence by friends) shows no strong relationship for either males or females, although the trend is in the expected (positive) direction.

TABLE 5

Correlations (Pearsonian r) between Persuasibility Test Scores and Self-ratings on Susceptibility to Social Influence

Persuasibility test scores correlated with:	Females (N = 96)	Males (N = 86)
1. Self-ratings on responsiveness to persuasive mass communications	.06 (p > .25)	.26 (p = .02)
2. Self-ratings on responsiveness to the influence of friends	.11 (p > .25)	.10 (p > .25)

NOTE: P values are for two tails.

Consistency of Individual Differences

The null hypothesis tested in the present study is that changes in opinion resulting from persuasive communications are wholly topic-bound and are always highly specific to the subject matter of each particular communication. According to this hypothesis, the opinion changes produced by any two communications arguing unrelated cases on unrelated issues would generally be unrelated, and opinion changes following two opposing communications would be negatively related. In the light of the data presented in Table 3 and the factor analysis results in Table 4, the null hypothesis is inadequate. We found a strong relationship between change in opinion on unrelated topics (e.g., between pro civil defense and pro television comedian) and also a strong positive relationship between changes in opinion following opposing communications on the same topic (e.g., between pro civil defense and anti civil defense). The latter type of relationship was found in the case of every one of the five topics, and in four of the five instances the positive correlation is large enough to be regarded as statistically significant. The hypothesis that opinion change is exclusively determined by topic-bound predispositions fails to explain the positive relationships among opinion changes on diverse and opposing communications.

The factor analysis yielded two common persuasibility factors which were positively correlated. This finding suggests that persuasibility may be determined by a general factor combined with one or more group factors that are less limited in scope than the highly specific factors underlying susceptibility to influence on particular topics.

Some further implications concerning the nature of the general persuasibility variable can be gleaned from an examination of the individual differences in opinion changes produced by different communications. It will be recalled that we gave a rationale for predicting that opinion changes in response to the Von Hindenburg and television comedian communications would be the most sensitive indicators of general persuasibility. Our hypothesis was that specific content predispositions are apt to become less important as determinants of change, in comparison with any general persuasibility factor, when the persuasive communications touch upon unfamiliar topics or issues about which the individual has not yet developed any strong (precommunication) interests and motivations. Since Von Hindenburg is virtually an unknown figure to present-day American high-school students, and since the television comedian is in reality fictitious, it was predicted that these two topics would have highest loadings on any general factor of persuasibility. The results of the factor analysis and inspection of the table of tetrachorics largely substantiate this prediction.

In column one of the Centroid Factor Matrix in Table 4 it will be noted that the first communication on the television comedian had the highest loading on the first (unrotated) centroid factor, and the second communication on Von Hindenburg had the next highest loading. The other communications on Von Hindenburg and the comedian also showed high loadings on this factor. Moreover, among the ten communications included in the persuasibility test, the three highest communalities (h^2 in the Centroid Factor Matrix) are those for the two communications on Von Hindenburg and the first communication on the TV comedian. The reliability and internal consistency of the persuasibility test could probably be improved by using more communications on unstructured attitudes of this sort in place of the ones that had the lowest factor loadings.

There is only one communication with a very small loading on the first (unrotated) centroid factor, viz., the first communication on cancer research. This communication is unique in that the opinion changes it elicited turned out to have only a very small, nonsignificant correlation with the opinion changes evoked by each of the other nine communications (cf. Table 3). Individual differences were noted in response to this communication—it was by no means overwhelmingly accepted—but the individual differences were not strongly related to those observed on the other nine communications. Perhaps the explanation lies in the scientific nature of the subject matter. Scientific reports, even when given in popularized form, may be perceived by many laymen as unquestionably authoritative and therefore as noncontroversial. This type of communication might therefore fail to be a persuasive communication comparable to the others in the test; acceptance of this particular communication may be related more closely to other attitude or ideological variables (e.g., attitude toward science). The lack of relationship to the rest of the persuasibility test was not apparent, however, in the second communication on cancer research. The explanation of this may be that the second communication on cancer, taking a diametrically opposite position to the first communication, made the subjects aware for the first time that the issues pertaining to research on a cure for cancer are genuinely in the realm of controversy. In the second booklet, then, this topic may have lost the distinguishing qualities of a scientific communication, and the determinants of individual differences in reaction to this communication may then have become much more similar to those for other controversial topics. In any case, the reliability and the internal consistency of the persuasibility test would be improved if this topic were eliminated.

Relationship of the Persuasibility Test to Self-ratings

The correlations between self-ratings on susceptibility to influence and the behavioral measures obtained from our persuasibility test give some pertinent information concerning the equivalence or nonequivalence of the two types of measures. A significant correlation was found between persuasibility test scores and self-ratings on influence by mass communications for the male sample. This finding increases slightly the plausibility of the assumption that both types of measures are tapping a common persuasibility tendency. Nevertheless, one cannot overlook the fact that in Table 5 there is only one significant correlation, which is not a very large one, while the other three are too small to approach statistical significance. From these results it is apparent that the persuasibility test is measuring something quite different from what is measured by the self-ratings on susceptibility to influence.[4] The findings in Table 5 suggest that it will not be an easy task to discover a test of simple self-rating questions to replace the more cumbersome and time-consuming procedure of assessing persuasibility by obtaining a behavioral measure of opinion changes induced by actual exposure to a series of persuasive communications.

If we were to assume that the self-rating scores concerning the influence of friends have some degree of face validity, it would follow that persuasibility, as measured by our behavioral test, is not equivalent to general amenability to social influence. This possibility raises the complex problem of the generality vs. specificity of various forms of suggestion and social influence. [Cf. Allport (2)]. It remains for future research to determine whether susceptibility to influence by formal communications of the type presented in our test is predictive of responsiveness to any of the various forms of social pressure or suggestion which occur in direct interpersonal interaction.

Generality of the Findings

The generality of our present findings is limited by the fact that the experimental communications were delivered to high-school students in a classroom setting. From the outset, we were aware of the possibility that their opinion changes might sometimes represent merely a superficial conformity with a point of view attributed to the school authorities or to a prestigeful experimenter. We attempted to minimize this possibility by emphasizing the fact that none of the teachers would see the subjects' answers and by including an explicit statement by the experimenter to the effect that he personally was inclined to agree with some of the communications and not with others. In order to obtain a mental set comparable to

---

[4] Perhaps the main reason for the low correlations is that the self-rating scores have low reliability. It should be noted, however, that the self-rating score on influence by mass communications, based on only three items, yielded the one significant correlation whereas an approximately zero relationship was found for the self-rating score concerning the influence of friends, which was a more reliable measure, based on eight items.

that occurring in everyday experience with persuasive communications, the subjects were instructed to read the articles as they would articles in a magazine or newspaper. Nevertheless, in spite of all these precautions, generalization beyond the classroom setting may not be justified. It is conceivable that opinion changes occurring in response to the persuasive communications received at home via TV, radio, or other media do not correspond closely to the opinion changes measured by a persuasibility test administered in a classroom setting. Investigations of opinion outside the classroom are needed to determine how far the present findings can be generalized. Obviously, replications with samples of other populations are also needed before one can determine whether or not the persuasibility findings that emerge from our study of high-school students hold true for the entire population of modern urban society.

SUMMARY AND CONCLUSIONS

A new behavioral test of persuasibility was devised, which involves measuring the opinion changes evoked when subjects are exposed to a series of ten persuasive communications, varying widely in topic and type of persuasive appeal. The persuasibility test was administered to a sample of 185 high-school students. Changes following the communications were examined to determine whether or not there is any general tendency for opinion changes on unrelated topics to be associated. The persuasibility test scores were also examined in relation to self-ratings on susceptibility to social influence, obtained from a personality inventory.

The results support the following conclusions:

1. The persuasibility test is sufficiently reliable and has sufficient internal consistency to be useful for research on group differences. The corrected split-half reliability was .81. An item analysis showed that all 30 items in the test were positively related to the total score, with 23 of the items being significantly related at or beyond the 10 per cent (two-tail) confidence level.

2. Opinion changes following one persuasive communication tend to be positively related to opinion changes on other communications dealing with unrelated topics. A factor analysis was computed, based on tetrachoric correlations among the subtest scores for the ten communications in the persuasibility test. The results support the hypothesis that there is a general factor in persuasibility; they clearly indicate that the predisposition to change one's opinions is not wholly specific to the topic or subject matter of the persuasive communications to which one is exposed. There appear to be fairly consistent individual differences in persuasibility such that those persons who are most readily influenced by persuasive communications advocating a given set of attitudes or opinions are also most likely to

be influenced in the reverse direction by communications which take an opposing stand on the same issues.

3. For the male subsample, self ratings on susceptibility to influence by mass communications showed a slight but significant relationship to scores on the persuasibility test. The parallel correlation for the female subsample was nonsignificant. In general, self-ratings on susceptibility to social influence do not appear to be measuring the same thing that is measured by the persuasibility scores obtained from our behavioral test of opinion changes following actual exposures to a series of persuasive communications.

REFERENCES

1. Abelson, R., and G. Lesser, "Correlates of Persuasibility in Children," in preparation.
2. Allport, G. W., "The Historical Background of Modern Social Psychology," in Gardner Lindzey (ed.), *Handbook of Social Psychology*, Cambridge, Massachusetts: Addison-Wesley, 1954.
3. Ferguson, L. W., "An Analysis of the Generality of Suggestibility to Group Opinion," *Character and Personality*, 1944, 12, 237–244.
4. Hovland, C. I., I. L. Janis, and H. H. Kelley, *Communication and Persuasion*, New Haven, Connecticut: Yale University Press, 1953.
5. Janis, I. L., "Personality Correlates of Susceptibility to Persuasion," *Journal of Personality*, 1954, 22, 504–518.
6. Janis, I. L., "Anxiety Indices Related to Susceptibility to Persuasion," *Journal of Abnormal and Social Psychology*, 1955, 51, 663–667.
7. Janis, I. L., and S. Feshbach, "Personality Differences Associated with Responsiveness to Fear-arousing Communications," *Journal of Personality*, 1954, 23, 154–166.

Reprinted from Public Opinion Quarterly, 1964, Vol. 28, pp. 453–466, by permission of Donald F. Cox and the publisher.

SELF-CONFIDENCE AND PERSUASIBILITY IN WOMEN

BY DONALD F. COX AND RAYMOND A. BAUER

A WELL-ESTABLISHED finding in the literature on personality and persuasibility is that males low in self-esteem, or *generalized* self-confidence, are on the whole more readily persuaded than males high in self-confidence.[1] Generally, this finding has not held for females.[2] One of the purposes of this paper will be to test the hypothesis that, at least in some situations, there is a relationship between generalized self-confidence (a personality variable) and persuasibility in women.

Another well-established finding is that people low in *specific* self-confidence with regard to a particular influence situation (i.e. confi-

---

[1] See S. E. Asch, "Effects of Group Pressure upon the Modification and Distortion of Judgments," in E. E. Maccoby, T. M. Newcomb, and E. L. Hartley, eds., *Readings in Social Psychology*, New York, Holt, 1958, pp. 174-182; L. Berkowitz and R. M. Lundy, "Personality Characteristics Related to Susceptibility to Influence by Peers or Authority Figures," *Journal of Personality*, Vol. 25, 1957, pp. 306-316; I. L. Janis, "Personality Correlates of Susceptibility to Persuasion," *Journal of Personality*, Vol. 22, 1954, pp. 504-518; I. L. Janis, "Anxiety Indices Related to Susceptibility to Persuasion," *Journal of Abnormal and Social Psychology*, Vol. 51, 1955, pp. 663-667; I. L. Janis and D. Rife, "Persuasibility and Emotional Disorder," in C. I. Hovland and I. L. Janis, eds., *Personality and Persuasibility*, New Haven, Yale University Press, 1959, pp. 121-137; G. S. Lesser and R. P. Abelson, "Personality Correlates of Persuasibility in Children," in Hovland and Janis, *op. cit.*, pp. 187-206; H. Linton, "Rorschach Correlates of Response to Suggestions," *Journal of Abnormal and Social Psychology*, Vol. 49, 1954, pp. 75-83; H. Linton and E. Graham, "Personality Correlates of Persuasibility," in C. I. Hovland and I. L. Janis, *op. cit.*, pp. 69-101; A. L. Messer, E. D. Hinkley, and C. I. Mosier, "Suggestibility and Neurotic Symptoms in Normal Subjects," *Journal of General Psychology*, Vol. 19, 1938, pp. 391-399; H. A. Witkin *et al.*, *Personality through Perception*, New York, Harper, 1954.

[2] For example, see I. L. Janis and P. B. Field, "Sex Differences and Personality Factors Related to Persuasibility," in Hovland and Janis, *op. cit.*, pp. 55-68. An exception appears in the work of A. H. Maslow, "Dominance, Personality and Social Behavior in Women," *Journal of Social Psychology*, Vol. 10, 1939, pp. 3-39, who reported that "prestige suggestibility has a fairly high negative correlation with dominance feeling." Dominance feeling, which includes high self-confidence, was assessed by personal interviews. The sample included 130 college women. However, no quantitative data were reported.

dence in performing a specific task or in solving a specific problem) are more readily persuaded in that influence situation than are people high in specific self-confidence.[3] This finding apparently holds for both males and females.

Although research in both these traditions has found an inverse linear relationship between self-confidence and persuasibility,[4] the behavioral explanations that have been advanced in each case are vastly different. In the case of general self-confidence, the explanation is based on a desire to solve problems of social relations or ego defense. That is, those low in self-esteem comply with the suggestions of others in order to avoid social disapproval,[5] or, as in an alternate explanation that has been advanced, to utilize preferred ego-defense mechanisms that vary according to the level of self-esteem.[6] With specific self-confidence, it might be argued that subjects are motivated by a desire to make a correct judgment, i.e. to solve the problem presented by the task. The argument is that those low in specific self-confidence accept help in order to deal better with the problem, and hence are more persuasible. Those high in specific self-confidence know they can handle the problem properly, do not accept help, and are less persuasible.

As long as the two research traditions are considered separately, the explanations that have been advanced to explain the relationship between two types of self-confidence and persuasibility cause no theoretical difficulty. But what happens when the two types of self-confidence are studied simultaneously, in relation to the same influence situation? What happens, for instance, when people high in specific self-confidence but low in general self-confidence are given an opportunity to alter a previously made judgment in a problem-solving situation? Do they change their judgment in the direction advocated by the communicator in the hope of avoiding social disapproval or solving ego-defense problems? Or do they tend to stick to their original judgment because they feel confident that the judgment was correct and they

[3] Examples of research in this tradition include: S. E. Asch, "Studies of Independence and Conformity: I. A Minority of One against a Unanimous Majority," *Psychological Monographs*, Vol. 70, 1956; G. M. Hochbaum, "The Relation between Group Members' Self-Confidence and Their Reactions to Group Pressures to Uniformity," *American Sociological Review*, Vol. 19, 1954, pp. 678-687; P. London and H. Lim, "Yielding Reason to Social Pressure: Task Complexity and Expectations in Conformity," *Journal of Personality*, Spring, 1964, pp. 75-89; J. F. Coleman, R. R. Blake, and J. S. Mouton, "Task Difficulty and Conformity Pressures," *Journal of Abnormal and Social Psychology*, Vol. 57, 1958, pp. 120-122.

[4] We shall use the term "persuasibility" to mean just that—regardless of whether the subject is persuasible in only one situation or in a set of situations.

[5] I. L. Janis, "Anxiety Indices Related to Susceptibility to Persuasion," *Journal of Abnormal and Social Psychology*, Vol. 51, 1955, pp. 663-667.

[6] A. R. Cohen, "Some Implications of Self-esteem for Social Influence," in Hovland and Janis, *op. cit.*, pp. 102-120.

want to solve the problem presented by the task? As far as we know, the two types of self-confidence have never been studied together.

Our intention is to attempt to join the two research traditions by examining the relationship of both specific and generalized self-confidence to persuasibility among one set of subjects in one particular influence situation. A major purpose of this examination will be to test the hypothesis that, in certain specifiable situations, the desire to perform properly in the task is a more reasonable explanation of the self-confidence–persuasibility relationship than is the desire to avoid social disapproval or to indulge in one's favorite defense mechanism.

The empirical basis of this paper is a study of the relationship between self-confidence (both specific and generalized) and persuasibility in lower- and middle-class women.

METHOD

Subjects. A total of 297 lower- and middle-class housewives were divided into three groups, composed of members of the "Ladies' Sodality" of three Roman Catholic churches in the Boston area. Most subjects were between thirty-five and fifty years of age, had completed high school, had family incomes of $400 to $800 monthly, and were married. All were Catholic.[7] A donation of $2 per subject was made to the Sodality to which the subject belonged, as a means of securing the cooperation of the group.

Procedure. Before being informed of the nature of the primary task, subjects were asked to indicate how good they generally were at judging people, colors, fashions, fabrics, and nylon stockings. Subjects were then asked to evaluate "two brands" of nylon stockings and to indicate how confident they were about their evaluation. The stockings were in fact identical, except for the identifying letters R and N. After making the evaluations on eighteen attributes, subjects heard a tape-recorded "salesgirl's" opinion that Brand R stockings were better on six attributes—feel, weight, texture, fit, weave, and versatility. Subjects then re-evaluated the nylons; evaluated the salesgirl; indicated how confident they were about their evaluations of the salesgirl; answered some questions on stocking-buying habits and attitudes; completed three personality tests (one of which was a measure of self-confidence); and, finally, provided information on their age, education, marital status, and income. The same procedure was followed with each group, providing three replications of the experiment.[8]

[7] A comparison of the results of Catholic with twenty-two non-Catholic subjects (used in the pretest) on other variables in the larger study revealed no patterned differences.

[8] In the analyses to follow, the results for each group were pooled to provide larger cell sizes.

MEASURES

Change in evaluation. For each of the six attributes mentioned by the salesgirl, a comparison was made of each subject's before and after evaluations of the nylons. One point was given for a change of one point on the nine-point rating scale (for example, a change on a particular attribute from "neither brand better" to one brand "slightly better" was worth one point). If the change on an attribute was in the direction advocated by the salesgirl, the score for that attribute was given a positive sign; if in the opposite direction, a negative sign. Each subject therefore had six change scores (one for each attribute mentioned by the salesgirl). These six scores were then summed algebraically to provide an index of change in evaluation—an index that measures both the amount and the direction of the change. Inclusion of magnitude as well as net direction does not affect the conclusions but vastly complicates the presentation of data. This analysis, therefore, will be based only on *direction* of change.

Generalized self-confidence. The measure of generalized self-confidence consisted of nine items from the twenty-three-item Janis and Field measure of feelings of inadequacy.[9] Because of the time required for the entire procedure, it was not possible to use the full twenty-three items. For reasons that will be discussed below, it was necessary to administer the self-confidence test about ten minutes after the subjects had re-rated the stockings. This sequence was used by Janis and Rife,[10] using the same twenty-three-item Janis and Field measure of self-confidence, in studying the relationship of self-confidence and persuasibility, with no apparent undesirable effects.

A preferred procedure, used in some but not all experiments, is to obtain personality measurements under circumstances removed as far as possible from the actual experiment. This was physically impossible in our situation. Furthermore, our expectation, which proved to be warranted, that the personality items might cause problems of rapport prompted us to administer these items after the experiment with the stockings. (In two of the three groups, the subjects were told that the two parts of the procedure—the stocking experiment and the personality data—were two separate, unrelated marketing studies.) In all groups, a series of questions requiring about ten minutes to answer, which included two other personality tests of cognitive needs and styles, intervened between the stocking-judgment questions and the self-confidence test.

It is possible that ratings of generalized self-confidence might have

[9] *Op. cit.,* pp. 300-301.
[10] *Op. cit.*

been contaminated by the subjects' experience in the preceding experiment. However, the fact that this measure correlated with prior measures of ability to judge people, colors, fabrics, fashion, and nylon stockings indicates that it tapped some generalized aspect of personality rather than a momentary reaction to success or failure in the experiment. More to the point, some of the patterns of data that emerged were too complex to be explained in terms of contamination resulting from administering the personality test after the experiment.

Specific self-confidence (degree of confidence in a judgment). Subjects could be divided into three groups according to whether they were (1) more confident in judging the nylons than in judging the salesgirl, (2) less confident in judging the nylons than in judging the salesgirl, or (3) equally confident in both judgments. There is a special reason for using this particular system of categorization. An integral feature of the major work of which this is a part[11] is the concept of preferred *cues.* In the major study it was predicted that, given more than one cue, a cue rated with a relatively high degree of confidence would be more likely to be used than another cue rated with less confidence, even if the second cue was considered more important. Both with respect to these particular data and to the data of the broader study, analyses have been made incorporating both relative confidence and evaluation of cues. Including evaluation (*how* competent was the salesgirl?) strengthens all the conclusions we present here. However, for the sake of simplicity, we will confine ourselves to employing relative level of confidence (which cue did the subject have more confidence in rating?), since it operates with sufficient power independently of the actual evaluation given to the cue, and the presentation of data, naturally, is vastly simplified.

FINDINGS

Generalized self-confidence and persuasibility in women. With the possible exception of Maslow's study,[12] no relationship has been found between such "personality" variables as self-esteem or self-confidence and persuasibility among female experimental subjects. They have generally been found to be more persuasible than male subjects, but this greater persuasibility exhibited itself independently of the personality dimension of self-confidence. As an interpretation of this lack of relationship, Janis and Hovland suggest that "the culture seems to demand of girls greater acquiescence in relation to prestigeful sources

---

[11] D. F. Cox, "Information and Uncertainty: Their Effects on Consumers' Product Evaluations," Boston, Harvard University, Graduate School of Business Administration, 1962, unpublished doctoral dissertation.

[12] *Op. cit.*

of information . . . , with the result that girls on the whole are more susceptible to influence regardless of their personality traits."[13] In other words, the cultural pressures for compliance are so great that level of general self-confidence is either inoperative or becomes smothered.

Two conditions may affect the generality of this explanation: (1) the population of subjects studied and (2) the nature of the issue or problem involved. In previous studies of female subjects, the populations have been high school or college girls, who may represent a relatively small range of self-confidence levels compared with women from the general population. In connection with the problem involved, it seems likely that in some situations women might be more concerned with the substance of the issue than with "conforming." In fact, Janis and Hovland anticipate such a possibility by pointing out that certain responses are "content bound."[14]

We anticipated that, if there was a relationship between generalized self-confidence and following the salesgirl's suggestion, it would take the form of the simple negative correlation between self-confidence and persuasibility that had been found with male subjects. To our surprise, we found the relationship to be curvilinear, and quite pronounced (see Table 1). These data depart from previous findings, therefore, on two dimensions: (1) the establishment of a relationship between self-confidence and persuasibility in women, and (2) the establishment of a curvilinear relationship where all previous relationships had been roughly linear. (Correspondence with Janis established the fact that he and Field actually plotted their data, and that their "zero" correlation among female subjects did not result from suppressed curvilinearity.)

As Table 1 reveals, among subjects high in self-confidence, 45 per

TABLE 1

CHANGE IN EVALUATION IN RELATION TO FEELINGS OF
GENERALIZED SELF-CONFIDENCE
(in per cent)

Degree of Generalized Self-confidence	Change in Evaluation				(Base)
	Positive	None	Negative	Total	
High	45	42	13	100	(121)
Medium	62	27	11	100	(74)
Low	37	34	29	100	(102)

$$\chi^2 = 16.8 \quad p < .01$$

[13] I. L. Janis and C. I. Hovland, "Summary and Implications for Future Research," in Hovland and Janis, op. cit., p. 240.
[14] Ibid.

cent changed in the direction advocated by the salesgirl, among subjects of medium self-confidence 62 per cent changed, and among subjects low in self-confidence only 37 per cent changed.[15] The relationship is significant beyond the .01 level. Furthermore, the curvilinear pattern was replicated in each of the three experimental groups.

A possible and plausible explanation of the behavior of the low self-confidence group is that they are reacting in a defensive manner. These are people whose ego defenses are so brittle that they cannot stand the strain of contradictions or even implied criticism by another person. They lash back in an effort to maintain a precariously protected ego. Fortunately, a test of this explanation is available. If the defensive-reaction hypothesis is valid, then very low self-confidence subjects should not only be less likely to exhibit positive change, they should also be more likely than any other group to change in the direction opposite to that advocated by the salesgirl. Table 1 shows this to be the case. Only 13 per cent of the high and 11 per cent of the medium self-confidence groups changed in the negative direction, but more than double those proportions, 29 per cent, of the low self-confidence group showed negative change. When the high and medium group data are pooled, the difference between the proportion of negative changes among high-medium subjects and the proportion among lows is significant beyond the .003 level (two-tailed test).

A way of looking at these data that makes them less neatly curvilinear is to consider *total change*, i.e. change in either direction. Viewed thus, the data indicate that there was almost as much total change in the low self-esteem group (66 per cent) as in the medium group (73 per cent). This view assumes that a systematic move counter to the suggested direction is also "persuasion," though possibly of a perverse form.

Thus, a variant of the relationship between self-confidence and persuasibility holds for our lower- and middle-class housewives. The curvilinear relationship may be due to the types of subjects used in this study; for example, we may have had a substantial group of subjects who were markedly less self-confident than those used in other experiments. If this is not the explanation of the curvilinear relationship,

---

[15] It will be noted in Table 1 that the high, medium, and low groups are not of exactly equal size. The groups were split at the natural inflection points indicated by the data. We recognize that splitting the groups in this fashion can be controversial. Obviously, the pattern would hold in a slightly attenuated fashion if we took "top third," "middle third," and "lower third." But there is no conceivable theoretical or empirical argument to support the notion that the inflection points should occur at any particular point on this particular scale. Further work with this or another scale might establish some proper "break points," but, in the meantime, we defend our division on the simple ground that it gives a more accurate description of what happened with these particular data.

then we still do not know why other investigations failed to find a relationship of any sort among female subjects.

Preferred defense mechanisms vs. desire to be correct. Cohen proposes differences in preferred defensive mechanisms as an explanation of differential persuasibility.[16] According to Cohen's scheme, situational factors should affect the relative persuasibility of people with different levels of self-esteem. For example, he hypothesizes that threatening appeals are more likely to be rejected by people high in self-esteem, while appeals that enhance the individual's self-picture are more likely to be accepted by them than by the lows. Leventhal and Perloe present data that can be interpreted as supporting Cohen's hypothesis.[17]

Since the salesgirl definitely favored Brand R, her message should have been self-enhancing to subjects who initially favored Brand R.[18] According to Cohen, the subjects high in self-confidence should be especially persuasible in this situation because of their propensity for ego-enhancing defense mechanisms. Because of the curvilinear pattern of our data, it is not clear *exactly* what prediction Cohen's hypothesis would lead to; in general, however, the highs who favored Brand R should be more persuasible than the mediums or lows. In any event, the *pattern* should be different among the group who initially preferred Brand R than among those initially preferring Brand N. Table 2 shows that the pattern is identical in both the "ego-enhancing" and the more threatening situation, though the absolute level of influence is greater across the board in the ego-enhancing condition. In both conditions, subjects with medium self-confidence were considerably more persuasible and those with low self-confidence exhibited the greatest negative reaction.

Although ego enhancement and "threat" do not produce the pattern of differential ego defense that Cohen predicted, these factors do not seem to be trivial on an across-the-board basis. Note that those subjects who initially favored Brand R had the least possibility to shift in the direction advocated by the salesgirl, since their own judgment of the variables was already on the average in closer agreement with her judgment than was the average judgment of all other subjects. Yet, at each level of self-confidence, at least 20 per cent more subjects were persuaded among those who initially preferred Brand R. The salesgirl's statement apparently was ego-enhancing to those who initially preferred Brand R. Hence, it is all the more interesting that these data do

[16] *Op. cit.*

[17] H. Leventhal and S. I. Perloe, "A Relationship between Self-esteem and Persuasibility," *Journal of Abnormal and Social Psychology*, Vol. 64, 1962, pp. 385-388.

[18] On the other hand, subjects who preferred R only slightly might have felt that the salesgirl was too pro-R, in which case the message would be less self-enhancing and more threatening.

TABLE 2

CHANGE IN EVALUATION AS A FUNCTION OF GENERALIZED
SELF-CONFIDENCE AND INITIAL BRAND PREFERENCE
(*in per cent*)

Degree of Generalized Self-confidence	Change in Evaluation				(Base)
	Positive	None	Negative	Total	
Initially preferred Brand R:					
High	59	31	10	100	(39)
Medium	77	12	11	100	(26)
Low	59	11	30	100	(27)
Initially preferred Brand N or neither:					
High	39	48	13	100	(82)
Medium	54	36	10	100	(48)
Low	30	42	28	100	(75)

not exhibit the *difference in pattern* between the two situations that is implied by Cohen's specific notion of differential ego defenses among persons of varying levels of self-confidence. However, the *general* notion of different patterns of ego defense at varying levels of self-confidence is bolstered by the counter-suggestibility of the low self-confidence group under *both* conditions.

Social approval vs. desire to be correct. Janis places emphasis on desire for social approval as a factor that makes persons of lesser self-esteem more persuasible.[19] Even considering the curvilinear nature of our data, Janis's hypothesis could still be made consistent with the analysis to this point. It would be reasonable to interpret the counter-suggestibility as a reaction formation to an extreme desire for social approval. However, the hypothesis that subjects are motivated to avoid social disapproval is couched only in terms of the subjects' relationship to the source of influence. Our analysis considers also the subjects' relationship to the object being judged, i.e. specific self-confidence.

Perhaps the study that bears most clearly on the issue of specific self-confidence and persuasibility is that of Hochbaum, in which he argues that "a person's dependence on social referents is inversely related to his confidence in his competence to judge the issue in question."[20] In support of this argument, Hochbaum demonstrates that when male and female college students were told that they were good at performing a particular type of judgment (predicting the behavior of a person described in a case history), they were less likely to change their judgment to conform to a group judgment.

This general notion that people are likely to accept help when they

[19] *Op. cit.*
[20] *Op. cit.*, p. 679.

need it could be extended across a wide range of psychological findings reaching back over many decades. (Such findings range from conclusions that may be drawn from the classical experimental work of Asch to the recent conclusion of London and Lim that the "influence of one's peers over his decisions in a group problem solving situation increases directly as the problem becomes more complex.")[21] But it does not tell us what to expect when specific and general self-confidence are considered simultaneously.

Deutsch and Gerard come closest to dealing with this issue in a paper in which they distinguish between "normative social influence" (an influence to conform with the positive expectation of another) and "informational social influence" (an influence to accept information obtained from another as obtained from reality). Their data led them to conclude that groups can exert normative or informational social influence on individuals, and that informational influence ("in the sense that the judgments of others are taken to be a more or less trustworthy source of information about the objective realities with which [the subject is confronted]") can occur even if the subject is not normatively influenced.[22]

It is our intention to carry this line of reasoning further and, in effect, through the mechanism of self-confidence measurement, specify those situations in which informational influence is most likely to occur. Our hypothesis is that in those situations in which people are confronted with a task of reasonable importance to them, and for which there is presumably a "correct" answer,[23] they are more likely to be motivated by a desire to achieve such a correct answer than by a desire for social approval or ego defense. This position is not necessarily "competitive" with that of either Janis or Cohen. Our faith in the existence and importance of ego defense and desire for social approval as motives is high. Rather than deprecate these motives in any sense, we shall end by arguing that they are better understood and their operation better predicted if we are *simultaneously* aware of subjects' perceived confidence in handling the specific task.

As will be recalled, subjects not only were categorized on the basis of general self-confidence but also were divided into three groups according to the degree of confidence they had in their *initial* judgments of the nylons relative to the degree of confidence they had in their

21 *Op. cit.*, p. 83.

22 M. Deutsch and H. Gerard, "A Study of Normative and Informational Social Influences upon Individual Judgment," *Journal of Abnormal and Social Psychology*, Vol. 51, 1955, pp. 629-636.

23 By a correct answer, we mean the solution to a problem that has only one answer, or a situation in which subjects assume that a correct answer could be supplied by a competent judge.

judgments of the salesgirl. The "social approval" explanation would have nothing to say about differential persuasibility under these conditions. Our prediction was that subjects relatively more confident in judging nylons than in judging the salesgirl would, in their effort to make a correct judgment, tend to follow their own inclinations. Among this group, therefore, level of generalized self-confidence should be less of a factor. Or, to put it somewhat differently, when *specific* self-confidence is relatively high, generalized self-confidence will play a reduced role.

We see in Table 3 that this prediction is borne out more cleanly than one might have hoped. Among subjects relatively more confident in their ability to judge nylons, general self-confidence plays practically no role.[24] Changes in the direction of adopting the salesgirl's views are 35 per cent among the high self-confidence group, 37 per cent among the medium, and 33 per cent among the low. True, those low in self-confidence in this group continue to show a greater rate of counter-persuasibility. But, in general, the pattern for this group is extremely flat compared with the other two groups.[25]

Among subjects who were less confident about judging nylons or who evaluated the two cues with equal confidence, level of general self-confidence was definitely related to persuasibility. In both groups medium self-confidence subjects were most likely to change their evaluations; subjects high or low in self-confidence were least likely to change. Furthermore, the degree of change is regularly greater among those subjects who were less confident in evaluating stockings than among those who were equally confident in evaluating the stockings and the salesgirl. As a matter of fact, of those thirty-five subjects who were less confident in judging the stockings and had medium self-confidence, 86 per cent changed in the direction advocated by the salesgirl.

These data do not constitute a negation of Janis's hypothesis. Unquestionably the desire for social approval is overriding in some situa-

24 The distinction between *specific* and *general* self-confidence is made with the realization that it is theoretically possible to make and measure further gradations in self-confidence level, e.g. intermediate self-confidence or an even more general level of self-confidence than that used in this study. We used the most specific and the most general measures available to us. An intermediate measure was also used: "How good a judge of nylons (in general) are you?" vs. "How good a judge of salesgirls (in general) are you?" This measure was less useful than either the general self-confidence measure or the specific measure in predicting probability of change in the direction advocated.

25 For the benefit of those who are curious about what is contributed by adding the *evaluation* of the salesgirl to the relative degree of confidence in rating her, the following can be reported: for those subjects who are more confident in rating the stockings *and* have a low opinion of the salesgirl's ability, the *net* change is approximately zero.

TABLE 3

CHANGE IN EVALUATION AS A FUNCTION OF GENERALIZED SELF-CONFIDENCE
AND RELATIVE DEGREE OF CONFIDENCE IN EVALUATING CUES
(*in per cent*)

Degree of Generalized Self-confidence	Change in Evaluation				
	Positive	None	Negative	Total	(Base)
Subjects *more* confident in evaluating the stockings:					
High	35	49	16	100	(37)
Medium	37	48	15	100	(27)
Low	33	41	26	100	(42)
Subjects equally confident in evaluating the stockings and the salesgirl:*					
High	30	63	7	100	(27)
Medium	50	42	8	100	(12)
Low	16	58	26	100	(19)
Subjects *less* confident in evaluating the stockings:†					
High	60	28	12	100	(57)
Medium	86	6	8	100	(35)
Low	51	17	32	100	(41)

* It will be noted that the "equally confident" group falls out of line in that *as a whole* this group shows less change than the "more confident" group. It appears that this group is contaminated by a subgroup of subjects who were not "playing the game" but used the same scale point for all ratings. This accounts for their being equally confident *and* unchanged. This dilution by apparently spuriously homogeneous data depresses the apparent rate of change in this group. $\chi^2 = 6.2$ $p < .05$.
† $\chi^2 = 17.7$ $p < .01$.

tions. The discussion by Janis and Hovland certainly lays adequate theoretical ground for such variation. However, in this instance, the hypothesis that our subjects were seeking a "correct" judgment fits the data better than either of the theories of persuasibility that have heretofore been put forth to explain the role of self-confidence.

DISCUSSION

Contrary to most previous findings, our data strongly support the notion of a relationship between self-confidence and persuasibility in women *under some conditions*. The requisite condition may be that women be genuinely involved in the task at hand. The generality of this needs testing.

Furthermore, the results suggest that the linear relationship previously found among male subjects requires modification. The results of the present study, showing that under some conditions, at least, women very low in self-confidence become counter-persuasible, were significant beyond the .01 level. Furthermore, the curvilinear pattern was replicated in each of three experimental groups. It is, therefore, doubtful that these results are accidental.

The existence of a curvilinear relationship even under special circumstances calls into question the implied condescension found in most discussions of persuasibility. A reasonable interpretation of our data is that the subjects, confronted with a difficult task, generally went about handling it in a reasonable way. The task, incidentally, was not too far removed from real-life situations. The fact that the two stockings were identical was a matter of experimental convenience: it kept the design clean. Choices between nearly similar, or even among dissimilar, objects varying on a number of dimensions can be just about as difficult as the choice between Brand N and Brand R. Hence, it is scarcely unreasonable that persons lacking confidence in their own judgment should make use of available "expert testimony." As a matter of fact, it might well be argued that the counter-suggestible low self-confidence subjects were the ones who were psychologically victimized, but they were victimized not so much by the salesgirl as by their own defensiveness. Although it is true that the experimental situation involved factual deception, the bulk of the subjects apparently took it on face value, and it is in this context that we say they acted reasonably. We should not make the error of assuming that, because the experimental deception was successful, the subjects were dupes.

In the most general fashion, we believe that the introduction of the problem-solving orientation in relationship to personality factors is the crucial differentiating factor in our experiment. The range of human tasks that may be engaged in at any one time can be grouped into three convenient categories: (1) solution of an immediate external problem, (2) management of social relations, (3) ego defense. The solution of immediate problems is not a task foreign to psychology, but in studies of persuasibility it has seldom been related to the other two tasks. A previous study has already suggested quite strongly that the amount of risk involved in handling the immediate task affects the subjects' handling of interpersonal relations. Specifically, physicians faced with more risky decisions are less likely to comply with the wishes of drug company salesmen.[26]

While the trio of "tasks" referred to above would be generally recognized, they have been treated as competitive explanations in various areas of the social sciences. The solution of immediate problems is the type of "rational" activity favored by proponents of "economic man." Psychologists and sociologists, on the other hand, have favored social adjustment and ego defense as preferred explanatory principles. This,

[26] R. A. Bauer, "Risk Handling in Drug Adoption: The Role of Company Preference," *Public Opinion Quarterly*, Vol. 25, 1961, pp. 546-559.

we believe, has taken place largely because it has fallen to the social scientist to explain behavior that appeared to be "irrational" when considered from the point of view of the traditional "rationalist." The deliberate inclusion of the problem-solving aspect in the study of persuasion promises to throw additional light on the problems of social relations and ego defense.

Reprinted from Journal of Personality and Social Psychology, 1965, Vol. 2, No. 2, pp. 195–201, by permission of Harry F. Gollob and APA.

EFFECTS OF MANIPULATED SELF-ESTEEM ON PERSUASIBILITY DEPENDING ON THREAT AND COMPLEXITY OF COMMUNICATION [1]

HARRY F. GOLLOB   AND   JAMES E. DITTES

Self-esteem, manipulated by inducing success or failure on an ego-involving task, had the following predicted effects on persuasibility: (a) Lowered self-esteem increased persuasibility when the advocated opinion was not threatening and the communicator's position was clearly stated. (b) Lowered self-esteem decreased persuasibility when acceptance of the advocated opinion would generally result in substantially increased threat to Ss. (c) Lowered self-esteem decreased persuasibility when the communication was complex and contained misleading, closure-inducing phrases. In the first 2 cases, self-esteem affected acceptance components; and in the last case, it affected learning components of persuasibility.

The purpose of this experiment was to investigate some possible relationships between self-esteem and persuasibility. It was expected that these relationships would vary with different characteristics of a communication.

The hypothesis is widespread that self-esteem is inversely related to various forms of conformity behavior, including persuasibility. Evidence for the inverse relation between self-esteem and persuasibility has been reported by Janis (1953b, 1954, 1955), Janis and Field (1959), Janis and Rife (1959), and, for children, Lesser and Abelson (1959). However, it seems probable that different types of communication would interact with self-esteem and produce different effects on persuasibility. We reasoned that the findings of increased persuasibility with lower self-esteem probably depended on quite specific characteristics of the communication. By varying crucial aspects of the communication, we predicted varying relationships between self-esteem and persuasibility.

[1] This experiment was supported by Grant M-3857 to James E. Dittes from the National Institute of Mental Health, United States Public Health Service. Part of the results were presented to the 1963 American Psychological Association convention.

The authors wish to thank Howard Leventhal, George Wolf, Philip K. Oltman, and Alan Feirstein for their helpful comments on this paper, and Sally Kasparek and Karen White for assistance in conducting the experimental sessions.

Simple Hypothesis

When the advocated opinion is nonthreatening and clearly and unambiguously stated, there is an inverse relationship between self-esteem and persuasibility. This hypothesis, without any limiting conditions being imposed on the content and form of the communications, is the one which has been tested in the research cited above. It may be derived from the following considerations: Subjects feeling low in self-esteem think more unfavorably of themselves and their opinions, and therefore, in attempting to enhance their self-esteem are more likely to accept the opinions of others. In addition, it is assumed that being in agreement with others has, for most people in our culture, an acquired reward value, and that reassurance resulting from agreeing with others enhances self-esteem.

Fear Hypothesis

In cases where acceptance of a clearly and simply stated opinion would cause a substantial threat to the self, there is a direct positive relationship between self-esteem and persuasibility. It is assumed, except perhaps in some cases of pathological depression, that people with threatened self-esteem do what they can to compensate for or minimize their feelings of inferiority, that is, they try to raise their level of self-esteem. They are likely to defend against accepting any opinion that would make them feel still more insecure and threatened.

Complexity Hypothesis

There is a direct positive relation between self-esteem and persuasibility when the communication is complex, and especially when it contains the kind of complexity which results from the presence of misleading, closure-inducing phrases. The simple and fear hypotheses concern the effect of self-esteem on the *acceptance* of the communicator's opinion, and assume negligible effects on learning the content of the communicator's position. These hypotheses assume that people understand the communication but do or do not accept its opinion, according to the conditions specified in the hypotheses. The complexity hypothesis, however, concerns the effect of threatened self-esteem on the *learning* of the communicator's position. If people do not learn the position, they cannot be "persuaded" by it. The distinction between acceptance and learning, as distinct components of persuasibility, has also been made by Janis (1953a).

Several studies have shown that anxiety facilitates performance on simple tasks and interferes with performance on complex tasks (Child, 1954). The complexity hypothesis applies these findings regarding task complexity and anxiety to the relation of self-esteem and persuasibility. For present purposes it is assumed that threatened self-esteem functions as anxiety.

Taylor and Spence (1952) present the theory that when complex tasks evoke many competing response tendencies, high anxiety may lead to poorer performance by increasing the probability that conflicting or erroneous responses will occur. Child (1954) has pointed out that high anxiety may result in more task-irrelevant responses, which interfere especially with performance on complex tasks.

In studying the effects of threatened self-esteem on closure, Dittes (1959, 1961) has specified circumstances under which conditions of threat lead to increased probability that competing erroneous responses will occur. He has proposed that the act of closure commonly acquires a reward value as a means of enhancing self-esteem and that damage to self-esteem increases the strength of the tend-

ency to achieve closure as one means of restoring or enhancing self-esteem.

Applied to persuasibility, Dittes' theory states that the reading of a communication without obtaining closure (i.e., a feeling of having understood the communication) is threatening to self-esteem, and that subjects with already lowered or threatened self-esteem are particularly motivated to avoid this further threat and therefore impose closure readily. When a communication is simple, such a tendency to form rapid closure should facilitate performance; but when a communication is complex, and particularly when it contains misleading, closure-inducing phrases, such an effort toward rapid closure is likely to result in misunderstanding the communication.

The theoretical positions of Taylor and Spence, Child, and Dittes all lead to the hypothesis that if a communication is complex, and especially if it also contains misleading, closure-inducing cues, subjects with threatened self-esteem will not learn the content of the communication as well as subjects with enhanced self-esteem.

Interactions between Hypotheses

The effects postulated by all the hypotheses of this study are presumably operating with all communications. It is assumed that they can interact with each other and, depending on the relative strength of the various processes which are activated, result in a net relationship between self-esteem and persuasibility which, theoretically, can range anywhere between a correlation of -1.00 and $+1.00$. Thus, in testing the fear hypothesis, we selected a threatening opinion which we felt would activate processes which would *override* the effects postulated by the simple hypothesis. In a similar manner, again in order to override the effects hypothesized by the simple hypothesis, we emphasized the complexity and misleading, closure-inducing features of the portion of the communication used to test the complexity hypothesis.

Relation between Manipulated and Predispositional Self-Esteem

Previous studies of the relation between self-esteem and persuasibility have been concerned with predispositional self-esteem, as measured by subjects' self-report on questionnaires. In this study we have experimentally manipulated self-esteem by varying failure or success on an ego-involving task. It was, however, a secondary purpose of the study to compare the effects on persuasibility of predispositional and manipulated self-esteem. Although we recognize that there are probably several important differences in manipulated and predispositional self-esteem, we expected that the hypotheses advanced above would hold for both manipulated, situationally affected levels of self-esteem, and predispositional levels of self-esteem. In presenting our hypotheses we have cited studies which supported analogous hypotheses using self-report measures of predispositional self-esteem or predispositional anxiety.

Cohen (1959), though, has proposed that people high in predispositional self-esteem tend to use avoidance defenses which lead them to reject threatening communications and accept optimistic ones; while people low in self-esteem tend to use sensitizing defenses which lead them to reject optimistic communications and accept threatening ones. Thus, Cohen's hypotheses concerning predispositional self-esteem are contrary to the predictions of our simple and fear hypotheses. Cohen's hypotheses have been partially supported by Goldstein (1959) and Leventhal and Perloe (1962). Dabbs (1962), though, found that the optimism-pessimism of communications produced no effect. He did find that the effect of predispositional self-esteem on persuasibility depended on whether the communicator was portrayed as a "coper" or "noncoper."

METHOD

Subjects were made to experience either success or failure on an ego-involving task. They then gave their opinion on three questions (pretest), read the communication, and then again, in the light of what they had just read, stated their opinion on the same three questions (posttest). Then, in order to measure possible differences in learning factors, the subjects were given an information test which asked for the communicator's opinion on these same three questions. At the end of the experimental session subjects completed a questionnaire which included questions intended to check on the effectiveness of the experimental manipulations.

Two self-report measures of predispositional self-esteem were administered to subjects at the beginning of the experimental session. The questionnaires were presented to subjects as unrelated to the later procedures and were completed in a room separate from the one in which the experimental procedures were conducted. The questionnaires were the 23-item measure of "feelings of inadequacy" which Janis and Field (1959) found was positively related to persuasibility in male high-school students, and the 12-item scale previously found by Dittes (1959, 1961) to interact with the effects of manipulated self-esteem on closure.

Subjects

The experimental materials were completed by 165 Yale freshmen who were recruited from their dormitories and paid for participating in the experiment. To minimize any effects of interpersonal interaction and anticipated opinion of others, all work was anonymous. After a brief general introduction, subjects began work on the tasks, which were all self-administered. The various experimental materials were presented as a series of unrelated tasks. Each subject took a folder of experimental materials as he entered the room. The folders containing the experimental manipulations had been shuffled in advance.

Success-Failure Manipulation

Subjects took Items 1–10 and Items 31–40 of the Space Relations Test published by the Psychological Corporation. This test is difficult enough to prevent subjects from having much subjective certainty about the quality of their performance and it is therefore open to manipulation of reported performance results, and thus of success or failure. The test is also abstract enough to allow it to be represented as measuring almost anything; this provided opportunity for making it an ego-involving task. A special answer sheet was devised, so that answers were recorded, by carbon, onto a keyed sheet so as to permit self-scoring after the seal was broken. Anonymity was emphasized by repeated written instructions during the procedures that subjects should not write their names on the materials and that the experimenter's interest was only in group averages and not individual results.

In order to make it an ego-involving task, the written instructions described the Space Relations Test as one measuring

skills of abstraction . . . of central importance in almost all occupations . . . highly related to personal effectiveness and professional success.

Fictitious keys and norms were used to affect the subjects' feelings of having performed well or poorly on the Space Relations Test. For subjects assigned to the success condition ($N = 79$), a special answer key was devised, to maximize the number of apparently correct responses. A fictitious set of norms was provided so that all success subjects would find their scores ranging among the high percentiles of Yale freshmen. For subjects in the failure condition (N

= 86) a false key was provided indicating that many of the common responses were incorrect. A set of norms was also devised in such a way as to make the scores of all failure subjects range in the lower percentiles as compared with other Yale freshmen. To guarantee that subjects would inspect the norms carefully, a form was provided on which they were required to record their own score and percentile.

A final questionnaire was intended to check on the effectiveness of the experimental manipulations. On four items on this questionnaire, success subjects reported that their results were above average, higher than they had expected, pleasing, and esteem enhancing, while subjects in the failure condition reported that their results were below average, lower than they expected, disturbing, and not esteem enhancing. The differences between the success and failure subjects on these four items were all significant at well beyond the .001 level of probability.

Communication and Measures of Opinion Change

The communication was about 1,200 words long and was entitled, "How Much Should We Spend on Cancer Research?" The stated source of the article was either a low prestige, poorly qualified author (Mr. Lewis—sophomore student at Andover High School) or a high prestige, well-qualified author (Dr. Lewis—Executive Director of the American Association for Medical Research).[2] Different segments of the communication were constructed to test the different hypotheses. The threatening portion occupied the first segment, and the complex, closure-inducing portion occupied the final segment. The point which was neither threatening nor complex was introduced in the middle of the communication. For reasons to be given later, two counterbalanced forms of the final segment were used.

Simple hypothesis. Both forms of the communication clearly expressed the belief that a diffuse research program is now the best strategy for using research facilities in doing research on cancer. Opinion was measured, on a 6-point scale, by asking subjects:

Consider the following two strategies for using research facilities in doing research on cancer: (1) a massive, concentrated crash program, focusing on a few clear problems, vs. (2) a widespread, diffuse program of many people working in many different places and in many different ways. Which do you think is *now* the best strategy?

This item was intended to provide a measure of opinion change in which impulsive closure would play a negligible role and in which affective reac

---

[2] The manipulation of qualifications and prestige of communicator did not show any statistically significant effects on any of the measures of opinion change used in this report. The main effects and first- and second-order interactions with the failure-success conditions and with Forms A and B of the communication were all nonsignificant.

---

tions to the content of the question would be relatively slight.

Fear hypothesis. The first two paragraphs clearly stated and elaborated the opinion, "At present the whole cancer problem seems almost hopeless." The communication included statements such as:

When your chances of getting a disease are as high as one in four, you might as well admit that it COULD happen to you! . . . your chances of escaping cancer are not better than just that—four to one. . . . What is more, cancer is becoming a bigger problem every year. . . . You can't be vaccinated against cancer. . . . You can't even rely on the latest wonder drug in your doctor's black bag to pull you through once you have it.

In order to measure opinion change on this issue, subjects gave one of six responses ranging from "Agree very much" to "Disagree very much" to the following statement: "At present the whole cancer problem seems almost hopeless."

This item was intended to provide a measure of opinion change where any effects of impulsive closure would be negligible and where it would be probable that subjects would feel threatened by the content of the item, and the relevant portion of the communication.

Complexity hypothesis. The complexity hypothesis states that subjects with lowered self-esteem, when given a complex communication, will be more likely to misread the communication and not learn the communicator's intended opinion, and hence not be influenced by it.

To test the complexity hypothesis, we constructed a portion of the communication as follows: The communication presented a complex argument in favor of one opinion—on the relative costliness of a crash program versus a diffuse program of cancer research. It also provided—by means of underlining, quotations marks, and otherwise making selected phrases prominent—certain closure-inducing cues which could lead the subject to a conclusion the opposite of that actually expressed in the total communication.

In this way we ensured that at least one competing erroneous response would be very high on the response hierarchy, and also made it easy for a subject, particularly if he felt threatened and was seeking closure, to jump to a quick, but incorrect, conclusion as to the communicator's opinion. Through this technique we were able to study an extreme case of the common situation in which a rapid, impulsive, closure-producing reading of a complex communication leads to a misunderstanding of the communicator's actual opinion.

Two counterbalanced forms of the communication were used to test the complexity hypothesis. One form actually argued that a diffuse research program is more expensive than a concentrated program; but the complex closure-inducing portions of the communication made it easy for subjects, if they were so inclined, to come to the conclusion that the author was arguing in favor of the opposite position, that is that a crash research program is more expensive than a diffuse research program. The second form argued in the opposite direction.

Counterbalanced forms were used in order to control for the possibility of an effect of the success-failure manipulation on subjects' preferences for spending more or less money on cancer research. Opinion change results showed no significant interaction between the two forms of communication and the success-failure manipulation ($t = -.51$).

The item used in testing the complexity hypothesis was: "Which type of strategy in cancer research do you think is more expensive, a massive concentrated crash program, or a widespread diffuse program?" Subjects gave one of four responses ranging from "The crash program is much more expensive" to "The diffuse program is much more expensive." To aid comparison with other scales, these four responses are expanded to a 6-point scale.

The information test for this item provides a measure of whether or not subjects correctly learned the communicator's position on the issue. Subjects were asked to indicate on a similar 4-point scale whether the author regarded the diffuse or crash program as more expensive. Subjects whose responses were consistent with the misleading closure-inducing phrases, rather than with the communicator's actual opinion, were regarded as having misunderstood or misread the communication.

RESULTS AND DISCUSSION

The proportion of subjects changing in the direction advocated by the communication was used as a measuse of opinion change. The mean change on each item showed the same pattern of results as the proportion of subjects changing positively.[8]

Simple Hypothesis

An inverse relationship between manipulated self-esteem and persuasibility was observed when the advocated opinion was not threatening and the communicator's position was clearly stated. As shown in Row 1 of

[8] The investigators wish to thank Robert P. Abelson for suggesting use of the arc-sine transformation (Walker & Lev, 1953, p. 424) in analyzing the data.

Straightforward applications of the arc-sine transformation were used to test for interactions of the failure and success conditions with other variables. This test, unlike most other tests for analyzing interactions among proportions, does not require the assumption that no main effects exist in order to test for the significance of interaction terms.

For the benefit of those readers who distrust statistical transformations of this type, chi-square tests of the main effects for all the hypotheses of this study gave p values of approximately the same magnitude as those obtained using the arc-sine transformation.

TABLE 1

PROPORTION OF SUBJECTS CHANGING IN DIRECTION ADVOCATED BY COMMUNICATION

Hypothesis	Opinion question	Experimental conditions		t
		Failure	Success	
1. Simple	Diffuse versus crash program as best strategy	.50	.34	2.08*
2. Fear	Cancer problem seems hopeless	.31	.48	−2.22*
3. Complexity	Diffuse versus crash program as most expensive	.26	.43	−2.34*

* $p < .02$, one-tailed test.

Table 1, failure subjects showed significantly more opinion change than success subjects ($p < .02$).

The fact that the difference between the mean information scores of the two groups was so small (Row 1 of Table 2) permits us to conclude that the experimental manipulation probably had its effect on *acceptance* of the communicator's position rather than on *learning* his position on the issue.

There were no differences in initial opinion between the failure and success groups that could account for the observed differences in opinion changes. Similarly, with the opinions used to test the fear and complexity hypotheses, initial positions were virtually identical; all t's were $< .60$.

Fear Hypothesis

A direct positive relationship between manipulated self-esteem and persuasibility was observed when acceptance of the advocated opinion would generally result in substantially

TABLE 2

MEAN INFORMATION SCORE: LEARNING OF COMMUNICATOR'S POSITION

Hypothesis	Opinion question	Experimental conditions		t
		Failure	Success	
1. Simple	Diffuse versus crash program as best strategy	5.0	4.8	.79
2. Fear	Cancer problem seems hopeless	4.9	4.8	.55
3. Complexity	Diffuse versus crash program as most expensive	4.1	5.2	−3.12*

* $p < .001$, one-tailed test.

increased threat to subjects. Row 2 of Table 1 shows that, as compared with success subjects, the subjects in the failure condition showed significantly less acceptance of the threatening opinion, "At present the whole cancer problem seems almost hopeless" ($p < .02$). Since there is no significant difference between the groups on the information test for this item (Row 2 of Table 2), it is again concluded that the experimental manipulation probably affected the *acceptance* component of opinion change, rather than *learning* components.

Complexity Hypothesis

A direct positive relationship between manipulated self-esteem and persuasibility was observed in the case where the communication presented a complex argument in favor of an opinion and contained misleading, closure-inducing phrases. As shown in Row 3 of Table 1, success subjects showed significantly more opinion change than failure subjects ($p < .01$).

Difference in learning, not acceptance. On this item, it was predicted that the experimental manipulation of self-esteem would affect opinion change via *learning* components of persuasibility. Row 3 of Table 2 shows that the information score on this item, unlike that of the other items, was significantly higher for success subjects than for failure subjects ($p < .001$). Thus, on the complexity item, the finding of more opinion change by success subjects (Row 3 of Table 1) can be adequately explained by the fact that significantly more of the success subjects had correctly learned the communicator's actual opinion.

Results with Predispositional Self-Esteem

Our results provided little illumination concerning comparisons between the effects on persuasibility of manipulated and predispositional self-esteem. Neither of the two measures of self-esteem was significantly related to any of the opinion measures, nor was any interaction between predispositional self-esteem and the success-failure conditions significant. We are not clear about the reasons for failure to replicate previous findings ob-

tained using these measures of self-esteem; perhaps the intrusion of the experimental manipulation swamped any overall effects of predispositional self-esteem.

A Final "Complexity" Hypothesis

The results of this experiment, and other recent work, emphasize that the relation between self-esteem and persuasibility is quite complex. Our results or others' indicate that increased self-esteem may enhance or decrease persuasibility, or have no effect, depending on how it interacts with such variables as the following: the characteristics of the communication, the characteristics of the communicator, and whether self-esteem is conceived as predispositional or situationally manipulated. Finally, our results emphasize that self-esteem may affect persuasibility through differential *learning* of the communication as well as through the more commonly considered process of the *acceptance* of the communication.

REFERENCES

CHILD, I. L. Personality. *Annual Review of Psychology*, 1954, **5**, 149–170.
COHEN, A. R. Some implications of self esteem for social influence. In C. I. Hovland & I. L. Janis (Eds.), *Personality and persuasibility*. New Haven: Yale Univer. Press, 1959. Pp. 102–120.
DABBS, J. M., JR. Self-esteem, coping, and influence. Unpublished doctoral dissertation, Yale University, 1962.
DITTES, J. E. Effect of changes in self-esteem upon impulsiveness and deliberation in making judgments. *Journal of Abnormal and Social Psychology*, 1959, **58**, 348–356.
DITTES, J. E. Impulsive closure as reaction to failure-induced threat. *Journal of Abnormal and Social Psychology*, 1961, **63**, 562–569.
GOLDSTEIN, M. J. The relationship between coping and avoiding behavior and response to fear-arousing propaganda. *Journal of Abnormal and Social Psychology*, 1959, **58**, 247–252.
JANIS, I. L. Fear-arousing appeals. In C. I. Hovland, I. L. Janis, & H. H. Kelley, *Communication and persuasion*. New Haven: Yale Univer. Press, 1953. Pp. 56–98. (a)
JANIS, I. L. Personality and susceptibility to persuasion. In C. I. Hovland, I. L. Janis, & H. H. Kelley, *Communication and persuasion*. New Haven: Yale Univer. Press, 1953. Pp. 174–214. (b)
JANIS, I. L. Personality correlates of susceptibility to persuasion. *Journal of Personality*, 1954, **22**, 505–518.

JANIS, I. L. Anxiety indices related to susceptibility to persuasion. *Journal of Abnormal and Social Psychology,* 1955, **51,** 663–667.

JANIS, I. L., & FIELD, P. B. Sex differences and personality factors related to persuasibility. In C. I. Hovland & I. L. Janis (Eds.), *Personality and persuasibility.* New Haven: Yale Univer. Press, 1959. Pp. 55–68.

JANIS, I. L., & RIFE, E. Persuasibility and emotional disorder. In C. I. Hovland & I. L. Janis (Eds.), *Personality and persuasibility.* New Haven: Yale Univer. Press, 1959. Pp. 121–137.

LESSER, G. S., & ABELSON, R. P. Personality correlates of persuasibility in children. In C. I. Hovland & I. L. Janis (Eds.), *Personality and*

persuasibility. New Haven: Yale Univer. Press, 1959. Pp. 187–206.

LEVENTHAL, H., & PERLOE, S. I. A relationship between self-esteem and persuasibility. *Journal of Abnormal and Social Psychology,* 1962, **64,** 385–388.

TAYLOR, J. A., & SPENCE, K. W. The relationship of anxiety level to performance in serial learning. *Journal of Experimental Psychology,* 1952, **44,** 61–64.

WALKER, HELEN M., & LEV, J. *Statistical inference.* New York: Holt, 1953.

Induced Factors:
Heightening Persuasibility via
Sensory Deprivation

It has long been recognized that changes in the individual's psychological environment often tend to be reflected in his behavior. From the experiment by Gollob and Dittes we learned that when someone succeeds or fails in an ego-involving task, this can affect his self-esteem and, as a result, his suceptibility to social influence.[1]

A more dramatic illustration of the effect on behavior of altering the individual's psychological environment were the hallucinations suffered by Robert Manry during his solitary 78-day journey across the Atlantic, in 1965, in the 13½ foot sloop *Tinkerbelle.*

> I imagined that people were with me, and I heard voices coming from the wake calling for help. One time I even found myself looking down over the stern to see who was there.[2]

And, another time—

> I thought I was in the Place of the Sea Mountains controlled by a man named MacGregor. I sailed in circles. I met a little gremlin character, and he said, "The trouble is that you have been sailing clockwise. You have to sail counterclockwise to get out." I did, and finally I came to this place where the seas were in giant steps that led me out of the Place of the Sea Mountains.[3]

Manry's hallucinations were due in part to his having been deprived of normal perceptual and sensory stimulation, the similar effect of which has been observed in patients undergoing long-term hospital confinement,[4] and in people deprived of sleep for extended periods of time.[5]

---

[1]Gollob, H. F., & Dittes, J. E. Effects of manipulated self-esteem on persuasibility depending on threat and complexity of communication. *J. Pers. soc. Psychol.*, 1965, **2**, 195–201.

[2]Aboard 'Tinkerbelle' on her run to glory. *Life*, September 17, 1965, p. 31. Quoted by permission of the publisher.

[3]*Ibid.*, p. 34. Quoted by permission of the publisher.

[4]Leiderman, P. H., Mendelson, J. H., Wexler, D., & Solomon, P. Sensory deprivation: Clinical aspects. *Arch. intern. Med.*, 1958, **101**, 389–396.

[5]Williams, H. L., Morris, G. O., & Lubin, A. Illusions, hallucinations, and sleep loss. In L. J. West (Ed.), *Hallucinations.* New York: Grune & Stratton, 1962.

When, in 1959, the New York disc jockey, Peter Tripp, voluntarily went without sleep for over a week, the hallucinations he suffered became terrifying, amost psychotic episodes.

> . . . A doctor walked into the . . . booth in a tweed suit that Tripp saw as a suit of furry worms. A nurse appeared to drip saliva. A scientist's tie kept jumping. . . . Around 120 hours, he opened a bureau drawer in the hotel and rushed out calling for help. It seemed to be spurting flames. Tripp thought the blaze had been set deliberately to test him. . . . By about 150 hours he became disoriented, not realizing where he was, and wondering who he was. He developed a habit of glancing oddly at the large clock on the wall of the booth. As the doctors later found, the clock bore the features of an actor he knew, made up like Dracula for a television show. He began to wonder whether he was Peter Tripp or the actor whose face he saw on the clock. . . . On the final morning of the final day, a famous neurologist arrived to examine him. The doctor carried an umbrella, although it was a bright day, and had a somewhat archaic manner of dress. To Tripp he must have appeared funereal. He always insisted that patients undress and lie down on the examining table. Tripp complied, but as he gazed up at the doctor he came to the morbid conclusion that the man was actually an undertaker, there for the purpose of burying him alive. With this gruesome insight, Tripp leapt for the door with several doctors in pursuit. Nightmare hallucination had merged with reality, and the only explanation seemed to be that the doctors had formed a sadistic conspiracy in which he was the victim.[6]

Hallucinatory behavior has also been observed under laboratory conditions in which volunteer subjects have been placed in isolation and deprived of normal perceptual and sensory stimulation,[7] though, more important, it also has been found that deprivation has the effect of heightening susceptibility to influence.[8] After extended sensory or

---

[6]Quoted from Luce, G. G., & Segal, J. *Sleep.* New York: Coward-McCann, 1966. Pp. 91, 92, 93. By permission of J. Segal and the publisher.

[7]Heron, W. Cognitive and physiological effects of perceptual isolation. In P. Solomon, P. E. Kubzansky, P. H. Leiderman, J. H. Mendelson, R. Trumbull, & D. Wexler (Eds.), *Sensory deprivation.* Cambridge, Mass.: Harvard Univer. Press, 1961. Pp. 6–33. Zubek, J. P., Pushkar, D., Sansom, W., & Gowing, J. Perceptual changes after prolonged sensory isolation. *Canad. J. Psychol.*, 1961, **15**, 83–100.

[8]Bexton, W. H. Some effects of perceptual limitation in human subjects. Unpublished doctoral dissertation, McGill Univer., 1953. Gibby, R. G., & Adams, H. B. Receptiveness of psychiatric patients to verbal communication. *Arch. gen. Psychiat.*, 1961, **5**, 366–370. Suedfeld, P. Attitude manipulation in restricted environments: I. Conceptual structure and response to propaganda. *J. abnorm. soc. Psychol.*, 1964, **68**, 242–247. Suedfeld, P., & Vernon, J. A. Attitude manipulation in restricted environments: II. Conceptual structure and the internalization of propaganda received as a reward for compliance. *J. Pers. soc. Psychol.*, 1966, **3**, 586–589.

perceptual deprivation, the subject, in his eager quest for novel stimulation, is highly receptive to all kinds of information.[9]

In his compelling book, *Inside the Black Room*, Jack Vernon notes that although the United States has never used and presumably never would use techniques of brainwashing based on heightening persuasibility through sensory deprivation, the fundamental idea is entirely plausible from a theoretical point of view.

> . . . Assume that we wish to instill a particular belief in a person. Assume, for example, that we wished to convert this individual to Islam, a belief we knew to be repulsive to him, but one about which he knew very little. Let us further assume that he holds very strongly to a Protestant belief about which he also understands very little. To "convert" him, the best procedure would be: First, place him in S.D. [sensory deprivation] for four days in order to get him receptive to novelty—any novelty. At the end of four days introduce two switches without any instruction into the cubicle. If he operated Switch A, he would hear a thirty-second speech favoring his brand of Protestantism. If he operated Switch B, he would hear a thirty-second speech favoring Islam. The main difference between the two switches is that Switch A always produces the *same* speech, whereas Switch B always produces a *different* one and always by a different voice. In this manner the monotony of S.D. would become associated with the monotony of the repetitious speech on Protestantism, and the desire for novelty would lead to the selection of Switch B. Now arrange the switches so that he can operate them less often, and our battle is practically won. We have caused this individual, *by his own choice*, to listen to our propaganda. If we can get him to listen, we can get him to believe by making our propaganda clever enough. . . . If our hypothetical prisoner had insisted upon a repetition of Switch A, this too could work in our favor, for repetition can weaken meaning. We have all experienced what happens to a word when we repeat it over and over. Its sound becomes strange to us, as though it were a new word. We still know the definition of the word, but it has changed, its meaning has weakened. . . . Once we have him listening to our propaganda, we should then reward any evidences of conversion. For example, we might occasionally ask questions about Islam. This should be done over an intercommunication system so as not to interrupt S.D. visually. If he gives the proper answers to our questions, he should be rewarded, perhaps by a little light. Later, if his answers get better, we might introduce a novel food item to replace a highly repetitious diet, and still later we might reward his answers by social contacts.[10]

The study that follows, by Peter Suedfeld and Jack Vernon, while

---

[9]Hebb, D. O. Drives and the C.N.S. *Psychol. Rev.*, 1955, **62**, 243–254. Jones, A., Wilkinson, H. J., & Braden, I. Information deprivation as a motivational variable. *J. exp. Psychol.*, 1961, **62**, 126–137. Schultz, D. P. *Sensory restriction: Effects on behavior.* New York: Academic Press, 1965.

[10]Quoted from Vernon, J. A. *Inside the black room.* New York: Clarkson N. Potter, 1963. Pp. 28–31. By permission of the author and the publisher.

not as dramatic as Vernon's prescription above, does, however, take into account two inherent personality factors which can interact with an experimental condition of sensory deprivation and thereby affect the individual's susceptibility to persuasion.

Reprinted from Journal of Personality and Social Psychology, 1966, Vol. 3, No. 5, pp. 586–589, by permission of Peter Suedfeld and APA.

ATTITUDE MANIPULATION IN RESTRICTED ENVIRONMENTS:

II. CONCEPTUAL STRUCTURE AND THE INTERNALIZATION OF PROPAGANDA RECEIVED AS A REWARD FOR COMPLIANCE [1]

PETER SUEDFELD   AND   JACK VERNON

Conceptually complex (abstract) and simple (concrete) Ss underwent 24 hr. of sensory deprivation (SD) or nonconfined control (NC) treatment. Towards the end of this period, each S had to evaluate the meaning of each of 7 passages which presented 2-sided information about Turkey. If S responded so as to show that the passage was pro-Turk, he was rewarded by the presentation of the next passage; otherwise, the questions were repeated. This was a test of compliance; internalization was measured by changes on an attitude scale presented several weeks before, and again immediately after, the experimental session. Abstract SD Ss showed a greater degree of compliance than abstract controls and concrete SD Ss; there was no difference between the 2 concrete groups. Concrete Ss evidenced more attitude change (internalization) than abstracts; in SD, abstract Ss were less and concretes more persuasible than in NC (where the 2 groups were about equal). The results were interpreted in terms of conceptual structure theory.

Several studies have investigated the effects of sensory deprivation (SD) upon susceptibility to persuasive messages (see Suedfeld, 1963). In the most recent of these (Suedfeld, 1964a), it was suggested that the heightened persuasibility of SD subjects may be the result of the suboptimal availability of information which characterizes the deprivation situation and which leads to the increased importance of the information presented in the message itself. As a corollary of this explanation, individual differences in persuasibility were hypothesized. Using the theoretical approach of Schroder, Driver, and Streufert (in press), it was predicted that abstract persons (individuals who are able to make complex integrations of information) would be less responsive to propaganda than would concrete subjects (whose conceptual structure is less complex and flexible). The results showed that SD subjects did change their attitudes more than nonconfined controls (NC) after hearing a taped propaganda passage, and further that concrete subjects evidenced more change than abstracts.

The current study is concerned with the extension of this problem. Vernon (1963) has described a method for producing attitude change in sensorially deprived subjects. Among other

[1] This research, carried out at Princeton University, was financed by Grant G-27162 from the National Science Foundation.

things, this method involves reinforcing the subject who shows the desired attitude change by "a little light . . . a novel food item . . . social contacts [pp. 30–31]." While this technique would probably be quite effective in producing change, another type of reinforcement may be more subtle and more powerful.

In an excellent series of papers, Jones and his associates (Jones, 1964a, 1964b; Jones & McGill, 1963; Jones, Wilkinson, & Braden, 1961) have demonstrated that SD subjects are motivated to obtain informational stimuli. If we consider the propaganda material as information, we could then reinforce subjects who evidence compliance by giving them a new propaganda message. Thus, we would have a spiral process in which each piece of propaganda would present another opportunity for compliance, with the next piece of propaganda as the reward.

The question arises whether behavioral compliance would lead to actual attitude change—internalization, as described by Kelman (1961). Obviously, it would be quite easy to respond to propaganda in the "desired" way for the sake of the reinforcer; this would not necessarily involve actual attitude change.

A related question is that of personality differences. Again referring to the theory of Schroder et al. (in press) we would say that abstract individuals—whose need for information is relatively high and who find SD more unpleasant than do concretes (Suedfeld, 1964b)—would consequently show a higher degree of compliance in order to obtain information; being capable of more complex conceptual functioning, however, they would not feel the need to change their actual attitudes towards the subject matter. We thus predicted that among abstract subjects the SD condition will result in greater compliance but less internalization than the NC treatment; in the concrete group, SD subjects should evidence more compliance *and* more internalization than NCs.

METHOD

Subjects and Procedure

A group of 248 male undergraduates of Rutgers University volunteered to undergo 24 hours of SD. From this group, we chose subjects whose opinions about Turkey and the Turks were neutral (see Suedfeld, 1964a). Fourteen abstract and 14 concrete subjects, all of whom met the neutrality criterion, were then selected by use of the Sentence Completion Test (Schroder & Streufert, 1962). Half of each group was randomly assigned to the SD (darkness, silence, and restricted mobility) and half to the NC (nonconfined control) treatment (for complete description of these two treatments, see Suedfeld, 1964a).

Propaganda Material

The material was the same as had been used in the previous study (Suedfeld, 1964a), which had been derived from passages originally devised by Murphy and Hampton (1962). In the current experiment, however, the combined pro- and anti-Turk passage was broken down into seven brief statements. Each of these consisted of a pro-Turkish item followed by a negative item related to the same aspect of Turkish life (e.g., "Turkish justice is swift and impartial, as seen when . . . . On the other hand, the police force and the courts are sometimes over-hasty and harsh; for example . . . . "). After each two-sided statement, three evaluative items of the Turk attitude scale were presented on the tape, and the subject responded by pressing a button from one to three times. The passages were presented during a 1-hour period beginning 23 hours after the start of the experimental session.

Instructions to Subjects

Before beginning the experimental session, each subject was instructed as follows:

We are interested in what happens to cognitive efficiency under unusual conditions. You have probably taken tests where you were supposed to answer questions about a passage which you had just read; we will ask you to do something similar. Sometime during the session, you will

hear some passages; at the end of each one, you will be asked some questions about it. If you get the majority of the answers *right,* there will be a short pause; then you will hear a new passage, will be asked questions about what it said, and so on. If you get the majority of the answers *wrong,* there'll be a longer pause; then the questions, but not the passage itself, will be repeated. This will go on until you do get the answers right, at which time we'll go on to the next passage. Remember, we're not interested in your own opinion about the topic—just tell us what the passage said.

These instructions were repeated and explained until all subjects understood the scheme; subjects were also taught how to indicate their answers.

After these instructions had been given, all subjects were told that the "comprehension test" would be administered approximately 23 hours after the beginning of the experiment. SD subjects were then confined and were left undisturbed until, 23 hours later, they were alerted by a buzzer and the propaganda tape began. Control subjects were conditionally dismissed (see Suedfeld, 1964a) and heard the passages begin as soon as they were put into the SD chamber for that purpose 23 hours afterwards. At no time during the experimental session did the experimenter know whether a given subject was abstract or concrete.

Pro-Turkish responses were arbitrarily treated as "correct." Figure 1 shows the process graphically. (These time sequences were used for all subjects.) Technically, there was no limit on the number of "errors" (negative evaluations) possible; in actuality, the number ranged from 0 to 10, with higher numbers indicating less compliance.

At the end of the session, all subjects were presented with the Turk attitude scale used in the earlier study; they were told that we wanted to know their own personal opinions about the Turks, since it was possible that their performance on the passage tests might be related to their attitudes. As before, the maximum degree of internalization of the propaganda was indicated by a change of plus 12 points (change in the opposite direction would be minus 12 points at most).

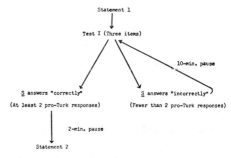

FIG. 1. Presentation of propaganda material.

TABLE 1
MEAN NUMBER OF "INCORRECT" RESPONSES

Conceptual structure	SD	NC
Concrete	3.71	3.57
Abstract	1.00	4.29

RESULTS

As a measure of the degree of compliance, we counted the number of "incorrect" (i.e., anti-Turk) responses given as evaluations of the two-sided propaganda messages (see Table 1). Because the distribution of scores was not normal, nonparametric methods were used to evaluate the data. When we applied Wilson's (1956) analysis of variance, significance was on the borderline for both the treatments effect ($\chi^2 = 3.59$, $p = .059$) and the interaction effect ($\chi^2 = 3.60$, $p = .057$). SD subjects in general were more compliant than NCs; furthermore, abstract SD subjects were significantly more compliant than concrete subjects in the same condition (corrected for ties, $U = 5.5$, $p < .01$, one-tailed). NC-SD differences were not significant for concrete subjects, but were significant in the abstract group (corrected for ties, $U = 9.5$, $p = .036$, one-tailed).

Table 2 shows mean attitude change from the initial to the postexperimental test. Analysis of variance of these data indicates that concrete subjects changed significantly more than abstracts ($F = 4.659$, $p < .05$) and that there was a significant interaction effect ($F = 5.897$, $p < .05$); while SD resulted in more change than NC for concrete subjects, the opposite was the case for the abstract group.

DISCUSSION

In this experiment, noncompliance was measured by the number of "incorrect" (anti-Turk) responses the subject made in evaluating the passages. As expected, abstract subjects who had undergone SD showed a higher degree of compliance than did abstract controls; within the SD treatment, abstract individuals complied to a higher degree than concretes. Both of these findings are in accord with theoretical predic-

TABLE 2
MEAN ATTITUDE CHANGE

Conceptual structure	SD	NC
Concrete	5.86	2.14
Abstract	1.00	2.43

tions: being highly information oriented, abstract subjects are stressed by low-information environments and thus would be expected to strive harder for an informational reward than either concretes in the same environment or than abstract individuals who are in a relatively information-rich situation. It is possible, of course, that the difference between the two SD groups resulted from differential ability to recognize the correct response—but this reasoning fails to explain the difference between the confined and the nonconfined abstract groups.

The fact that concrete subjects complied no more in the SD than in the NC treatment was not in accordance with predictions. Two possible explanations present themselves. One is that concrete individuals are so low in information motivation that environments as severely suboptimal as SD do not raise information need to an appreciable degree; this hypothesis is contradicted by a finding that in a relatively mildly suboptimal game situation concrete subjects do increase their information-search activity (Suedfeld & Streufert, 1964). The second interpretation is based upon previous findings that relatively extreme environmental pressures are needed to produce compliance in concrete subjects (Allen, 1962; Janicki, 1960). It may be that the pressure provided by the SD situation is insufficient to overcome their strong resistance to change, which may be a dissonance-avoiding technique. In this view, compliance may be seen as a relatively complex response in which the subject takes an "as-if" attitude and acts contrary to his own beliefs (thus arousing dissonance) in order to obtain a reward. Subsequent internalization, by the same token, is a simple (or at least simplifying), dissonance-reducing behavior.

The attitude change (internalization) data are generally as hypothesized. As in the earlier study (Suedfeld, 1964a), there was no difference between the abstract and the concrete subjects in the NC condition. After SD, however, the abstract and the concrete groups diverged. Greater attitude change on the part of concrete SD subjects had been predicted as a result of behavioral simplification. Abstract SD subjects evidenced relatively little attitude change; this datum may be explained by positing that the SD situation caused less behavioral simplification in abstract than in concrete subjects.

REFERENCES

ALLEN, L. H. The effects of instructional variation and stress on the perception of aniseikonic distortion. Unpublished senior thesis, Princeton University, 1962.

589

JANICKI, W. P. The effects of variation in conceptual structure on dyadic interaction. Unpublished doctoral dissertation, Princeton University, 1960.

JONES, A. Drive and incentive variables associated with the statistical properties of sequences of stimuli. *Journal of Experimental Psychology*, 1964, **67**, 423–431. (a)

JONES, A. How to feed the stimulus hunger: Problems in the quantification of an incentive. Paper read at American Psychological Association, Los Angeles, 1964. (b)

JONES, A., & McGILL, D. Auditory information satiation in humans. Paper read at Eastern Psychological Association, New York City, 1963.

JONES, A., WILKINSON, H. J., & BRADEN, I. Information deprivation as a motivational variable. *Journal of Experimental Psychology*, 1961, **62**, 126–137.

KELMAN, H. C. Processes of opinion change. *Public Opinion Quarterly*, 1961, **25**, 57–78.

MURPHY, D. B., & HAMPTON, G. L. A technique for studying attitude change. In, *Collected papers related to the study of the effects of sensory deprivation and social isolation.* (Task Pioneer VI—Endorse) Alexandria, Va.: Human Resources Research Office, 1962.

SCHRODER, H. M., DRIVER, M. J., & STREUFERT, S. *Personality structure, information processing, and social organization.* New York: Holt, Rinehart, & Winston, in press.

SCHRODER, H. M., & STREUFERT, S. The measurement of four systems varying in level of abstractness (sentence completion method). *Off. Naval Res. tech. Rep.*, 1962, No. 11.

SUEDFELD, P. Conceptual and environmental complexity as factors in attitude change. *Off. Naval Res. tech. Rep.*, 1963, No. 14.

SUEDFELD, P. Attitude manipulation in restricted environments: I. Conceptual structure and response to propaganda. *Journal of Abnormal and Social Psychology*, 1964, **68**, 242–247. (a)

SUEDFELD, P. Conceptual structure and subjective stress in sensory deprivation. *Perceptual & Motor Skills*, 1964, **19**, 896–898. (b)

SUEDFELD, P., & STREUFERT, S. Information search as a function of conceptual and environmental complexity. Unpublished manuscript, University of Illinois, 1964.

VERNON, J. *Inside the black room.* New York: Potter, 1963.

WILSON, K. V. A distribution-free test of analysis of variance hypotheses. *Psychological Bulletin*, 1956, **53**, 96–101.

Induced Factors:
Inoculation against Persuasion

The technique of sensory deprivation provides a fascinating means of reducing resistance to persuasion. But what of the other side of the coin—increasing resistance? Would an individual who had been "saturated" by sensory or perceptual stimuli become less susceptible to propaganda? After having endured a dozen TV commercials, does their cumulative effect reduce the impact of the thirteenth? One can only conjecture on this point. Several other techniques, however, are available for achieving substantially the same effect, that of increasing resistance.

One of the first experimental investigations of the problem of inducing resistance to persuasion was conducted in the spring of 1949 by Arthur Lumsdaine and Irving Janis. The experiment grew out of the earlier study by Hovland, Lumsdaine, and Sheffield (pp. 71–97) dealing with the comparative effects of one-sided versus two-sided communication.[1] Lumsdaine and Janis recognized possible implications in the Hovland *et al.* design which, if empirical support could be obtained, would extend vastly the generality of the earlier findings. Where the original study had probed only the immediate effects of the two forms of persuasive communication, Lumsdaine and Janis now set out to determine what the delayed effects might be—particularly in the face of recipients' exposure to subsequent counterpropaganda. Would initial exposure to a one-sided or two-sided propaganda presentation leave the recipient more resistant to counterpersuasion? To answer this question, four different classes of high school students were exposed initially to either one-sided or two-sided radio transcriptions which took the position that it would be at least five years before Russia could produce atomic bombs in quantity.[2] A week later,

---

[1]Hovland, C. I., Lumsdaine, A. A., & Sheffield, F. D. The effects of presenting 'one side' versus 'both sides' in changing opinions on a controversial subject. In *Studies in social psychology in world war II.* Vol. 3. *Experiments on mass communication.* Princeton, N.J.: Princeton Univer. Press, 1949. Pp. 201–227.

[2]The study was conducted several months before President Truman announced Russia's first successful atomic explosion.

two of the groups (one having received the one-sided presentation, and the other the two-sided) were presented with a lengthy counterappeal which argued that Russia had probably already developed the atomic bomb and that within two years she would be producing it in great quantities. For the two groups which were not exposed to the counterpropaganda, the one-sided and two-sided appeals were found to be about equally effective in modifying opinions. But for the groups subsequently exposed to the counterappeal, the initial two-sided communication was found to have the greater sustained effect.[3] Why did the two-sided communication induce greater resistance to the contradictory point of view advocated in the counterappeal? Lumsdaine and Janis account for this finding on the basis of the "inoculation" effect of the two-sided communication.

> . . . if the initial communication is . . . a two-sided one it will already have taken into account both the positive and negative arguments and still have reached the positive conclusion. When the listener is then subsequently exposed to the presentation of opposing arguments in the counterpropaganda, he is less likely to be influenced by them. He is not only familiar with the opposing point of view, but has been led to the positive conclusion in a context in which the negative arguments were in evidence. In effect, he has been given an advance basis for ignoring or discounting the opposing communication and, thus "inoculated," he will tend to retain the positive conclusion.[4]

In the more than a decade and a half since Lumsdaine and Janis carried out their now classic study on resistance to persuasion, numerous other pertinent findings have come to light. The paper that follows, by William J. McGuire, reviews the mass of theoretical and empirical findings which have accumulated and describes several other techinques whereby resistance may be heightened. In addition, it summarizes McGuire's own impressive program of research on this problem, for which he shared the 1963 Socio-Psychological Prize of the American Association for the Advancement of Science.[5]

---

[3]Lumsdaine, A. A., & Janis, I. L. Resistance to 'counterpropaganda' produced by one-sided and two-sided 'propaganda' presentations. *Publ. Opin. quart.*, 1953, **17**, 311–318.

[4]*Ibid.*, p. 318. Quoted by permission of the publisher.

[5]McGuire was corecipient of the 1963 prize with Dr. Morris Rosenberg. Dr. Rosenberg's award winning paper was entitled "Society and the Adolescent Self-Image."

Reprinted from Advances in Experimental Social Psychology, 1964, Vol. 1, pp. 191–229, by permission of William J. McGuire and Academic Press.

INDUCING RESISTANCE TO PERSUASION

Some Contemporary Approaches[1]

BY WILLIAM J. McGUIRE

[1] The research by the author which is reported in this chapter was greatly facilitated by two successive grants from the National Science Foundation, Division of Social Sciences. He wishes to acknowledge the aid itself and the enlightened manner in which it was administered by the Foundation.

191

I. Introduction

Several years ago I thought of doing research on ways of inducing resistance to persuasion, under the impression that while much experimental work was being done on factors that increased persuasive effectiveness, little was being done on ways of producing resistance to persuasion. As I considered the problem further, however, I realized that there are many people investigating resistance to persuasion, only they—like M. Jourdain speaking prose—haven't always been aware of it. The first part of this chapter briefly sketches a dozen or so approaches to producing resistance to persuasion currently under active study; the balance of the chapter presents a more detailed résumé of my own work in the area. The disproportionate coverage of my own work does not (necessarily) mean I believe it merits this much space relative to the others, but simply that it is my own, and hence what I know best and can most competently describe.

Before we review the theories and findings regarding inducing resistance to persuasion, it would be useful to make explicit several points regarding our conceptualization of the process, since this conceptualization has determined the range of coverage. The scope of this inquiry is the uncovering of pretreatments which, when applied to the person, make him less susceptible to persuasive messages than he is found to be without these pretreatments. Hence, studying resistance to persuasion is not simply the inverse of studying persuasion itself. Suppose, for example, persuasive messages are known to be more effective if they are presented with their conclusions explicitly drawn, rather than left to be drawn by the recipient. This fact would not imply that resistance to persuasion—in the sense used here—could be enhanced by presenting messages whose conclusions are left to the recipient to draw. Rather, our interest is in pretreatments which would lessen the effectiveness of any given persuasive message (with or without its conclusion explicitly drawn).

A second preliminary point concerns the "healthiness" of resistance to persuasion. In our society we are inclined to accept the romantic notion that the autonomous man is admirable, while the man easily swayed by argument is weak and deplorable. Such a view suggests that we should look for resistance-conferring treatment among healthy processes. However, a consideration of the close psychological relation between susceptibility to persuasion and ability to learn, a closeness that makes it difficult to distinguish (at least on the basis of the psychological processes involved) between propaganda and education, shows that this resistance is not always "healthy." Anyone can be made impervious to the most skillful propaganda if we reduce him to catatonic schizophrenia and anyone can, with a bare bodkin, be made forever free from influence. The best of both worlds would be to discover pretreatments that would make the person receptive to the true and resistant to the false. But since the distinction between truth and falsity is not strictly germane to the psychological processes under discussion, such a consideration will be ignored here. Hence, as ways of inducing resistance to persuasion some possibly "unhealthy" pretreatments—like enhancing the person's tendency to use perceptual distortion in the defense of his preconceptions—are included.

A final preliminary point deals with the generality of the induced resistance to persuasion. The most general type would involve making the person resistant to the change toward any side of all issues, regardless of the variables (source, channel, message, etc.) involved. The technique involving enhancing self-esteem comes the nearest to such a panacea against persuasion, and even this procedure tends to have limitations. A more specific type of conferred resistance is restricted to a certain type of issue, or to only one of the two sides of an issue. For example, inducing aggressiveness tends to make the person less susceptible to benevolent appeals but, if anything, more vulnerable to malevolent ones.

Other resistance-inducing techniques tend to be specific to certain sources, for example, pairing that source in advance with unpopular stands on other issues. Another form of specificity involves conferring resistance to any argument on either side from any source but restricted to a given issue. An example of a technique which does this is sensitizing the person in advance of the persuasive attack to how closely his belief on the given issue is tied with his beliefs on other issues. This chapter concentrates on techniques that are general to the extent that the resistance they induce is not specific to certain sources or to just one side of the issue. At least on a given issue, these treatments make the subject more resistant to any kind of a persuasive attempt.

The next section briefly reviews four general approaches to the problem of inducing resistance to persuasion, and mentions a number of variations on each approach. The limited space available permits little more than a statement of the main points involved, along with a few illustrative experiments. The succeeding sections of the chapter will describe my own experiments on this problem in somewhat greater detail.

II. Some Contemporary Approaches to the Problem

A. The Behavioral Commitment Approach

The "behavioral commitment" approaches to inducing resistance to persuasion all involve the believer's taking some more or less irrevocable step on the basis of his belief, thereby committing himself to it. Insofar as commitment makes changing the belief dangerous, costly, awkward, or at least harmful to self-esteem, it strengthens the believer's tendency to resist social influence attempts aimed at this belief. The approaches that fall under this rubric can be grouped into several classes differing among themselves with respect to the nature of the committing behavior or the way of eliciting it. Below are four subclasses, listed in order of increasing externality of the commitment.

1. Private Decision

The most tenuous kind of commitment to the belief is created simply by having the person come to a private decision that he does indeed hold the belief. Edith Bennett (1955) found a significant tendency for subjects who are asked to come to a private (or at least anonymous) decision to persist longer in their intention than those not so requested. Such enhanced persistence may readily be interpreted as an increased resistance to the contrary pressures occurring in the interim. Lewin (1951, 1958) felt that decision-making, even of this anonymous sort, would have a "freezing" effect which could result in the belief's being maintained more firmly in the face of subsequent events. However, it appears that such private decision-making fails to confer any resistance under some conditions. Studies on the primacy-recency effect have generally yielded negative results (Hovland and Mandell, 1957; N. H. Anderson, 1959). Likewise, studies comparing the before-after vs. the after-only designs have failed to show any such freezing effects of the prior decision (Lana, 1959; Hicks and Spaner, 1962).

2. Public Announcement of One's Belief

It has also been suggested (e.g., Lewin, 1958) that public identification of one's belief should constitute a firmer commitment than that established by private decision-making. To the extent this is so, more resistance to subsequent persuasive attempts should follow a public rather than private statement of one's beliefs. Confirmatory evidence has been reported by a number of experimenters (Deutsch and Gerard, 1955; Hovland et al., 1957; Cohen et al., 1959). On the other hand, Bennett (1955) found private decision-making to be at least as effective as publicly identified decisions. Fisher and associates (1956) found that the public decisions did confer resistance to peer conformity pressures on the specific point decided upon, but that accommodations of a basic sort were made so that subsequently the person tended to anticipate and submit in advance to the expected, disparate judgment of the group.

3. Active Participation on the Basis of the Belief

Still more committing, it would seem, than simply stating one's belief is to take some further action on the basis of this belief. A typical action of this type which has been widely studied is the overt defense of one's belief by writing an essay or delivering a speech in support of it. McGuire's studies on the efficacy of active participation reported later in this chapter are examples. Another somewhat relevant set of experiments are the studies dealing with "overt compliance" (Kelman, 1953; King and Janis, 1956; Festinger, 1957; Cohen et al., 1958). These latter studies suggest some conditions under which such compliance has the greatest committing effect (e.g., when elicited with the least pressure; when many alternatives were available).

The use of belief-defensive essays as the form of active participation is somewhat unfortunate for it leaves a theoretical ambiguity: Is the increased resistance resulting from such behavior due simply to acting overtly on the basis of the belief, or is it due to the self-indoctrination and rehearsal of one's defenses involved in this particular type of activity? Fortunately, there have been a number of "forced compliance" studies in which the active participation did take other forms, forms that did not involve this rehearsal of one's defenses (Brehm, 1960; Smith, 1961; Raven and Fishbein, 1961). These studies yield the same implications as did the rehearsal ones just considered.

4. External Commitment

The final type of commitment, and by far the most tenuous of those considered here, is that called "external commitment." Rosenbaum (see Rosenbaum and Franc, 1960; Rosenbaum and Zimmerman, 1959) has shown that if the person is committed to a belief "externally," by being told someone else thinks the person holds that belief, the person does indeed show an increased adherence to the belief. It seems rather surprising that so mild a commitment could have a detectable effect; and yet, when confronted by the data, the phenomenon seems provocative rather than inexplicable.

B. ANCHORING THE BELIEF TO OTHER COGNITIONS

A second family of approaches to inducing resistance to persuasion can be classified as "anchoring the belief to other cognitions." They have in common the notion of somehow linking the belief in question to other cognitions, or at least sensitizing the believer to the fact that such links exist. This procedure makes it more difficult for the person to change his belief because such a change would require his changing all the linked beliefs correspondingly. Otherwise, he would have to endure the discomfort of cognitive inconsistency. It will be recognized that this analysis accepts the basic assumption of the many current balance theories. Three such anchoring approaches, which differ regarding the type of cognitions to which a given belief is to be linked, are considered below.

1. Linking to Accepted Values

A number of theorists have suggested that a belief is held firmly to the extent that it is perceived as instrumental to the attainment of positively valenced goals, and/or as facilitating avoidance of negatively valenced goals (Carlson, 1956; Rosenberg, 1956; Zajonc, 1960). According to this approach, any pretreatment that would strengthen the believer's perception that his opinion did have such linkage to valenced goals (or, alternatively, made him increase the valence of the goals involved in the perceived instrumentality relationship) would enhance his adherence to the belief, making him more resistant to subsequently received pressures to change.

2. Linking to Other Beliefs

A very popular area in this anchoring category of studies involves the linkage of the given beliefs to other beliefs in the person's cognitive system. The various balance theories are all relevant to this point. The general idea is that sensitizing the person to the fact that the given belief is logically related to many beliefs which he holds will make him adhere to it more strongly. Changing it will introduce a whole series of imbalances into his cognitive system, and these imbalances cause psychological discomfort. Much of the work so far has been confined to showing that this reasoning is indeed correct (Abelson and Rosenberg, 1958; Harary, 1959). However, some studies have actually manipulated these belief linkages (see Rosenberg and Hovland, 1960). McGuire's "Socratic effect" studies are also pertinent. They suggest that merely asking the person to rehearse the related beliefs which he already possesses makes more salient these linkages to the given belief, and thereby confers enhanced resistance to subsequent attacks—at least to the extent that such attacks will introduce inconsistencies into his belief system (McGuire, 1960a,b).

3. Linking to Valenced Sources and Reference Groups

A final class of anchoring effects considered here involves tying the given belief to positively valenced sources of one kind or another. The general assumption is that if the believer is made to see that his opinion is shared by others whom he values highly, the opinion will be more resistant to subsequent attacks. Many experiments have demonstrated the importance of this "source" variable in persuasion. Even anonymous individuals and groups have been shown to confer such resistance when the believer is made to recognize that they share his belief (Schachter and Hall, 1952; Bennett, 1955). The effect has also been demonstrated for positively valenced reference groups (Kelley and Volkhart, 1952; Kelley and Woodruff, 1956; Dittes and Kelley, 1956; Charters and Newcomb, 1958; Newcomb, 1961). Still other experimenters have demonstrated that tying the belief to highly regarded, specific individuals establishes the belief more firmly (Tannenbaum, 1956; Kelman and Hovland, 1953).

Each anchoring approach can be utilized to confer resistance in two ways. The believer can be provided with new information which connects the given belief with the other cognitions he already holds. Alternatively, work can be done within his already existing cognitive system by making more salient to him the linkages that already exist. For example, he might be questioned so as to call his attention to these linkages (as in the "Socratic effect" study cited above) or the social setting might be manipulated (as in the "salience of reference groups" studies cited above).

C. Inducing Resistant Cognitive States

It has been proposed that certain personality, motivational, or ideological states are correlated with resistance to social influence pressures. Hence, any treatment that induces such states in the believer should enhance his resistance to persuasion. One difficulty in applying this approach is that, despite very extensive work on the problem, few states have been discovered which are generally effective in predisposing the person to resist persuasion. Let us now examine a rather heterogeneous set of such variables.

1. Inducing Anxiety about the Issue

A good deal of research has been done on the use of fear-arousing appeals in persuasion usually with the notion that when we attach anxiety to a given issue, the person is subsequently inclined to avoid the topic. He should therefore avoid exposure to subsequent messages (including those attacking his position) on the issue and, consequently, should be less influenced by them. Nunnally and Bobren (1959) found that people do say they are less willing to receive further information on the topic after reading an anxiety-arousing message on it. On the other hand, Janis and Feshbach (1953) found that the greater the prior anxiety arousal, the *less* the resistance to a subsequent attack on the issue. Indeed, other studies (e.g., Berkowitz and Cottingham, 1960) have suggested that the effects of fear appeals are more complex than indicated by the original formulation.

2. Inducing Aggressiveness

We might also think that the person who has been made hostile to others would be more resistant to influence attempts. Contrary to such an expectation, Weiss and Fine (1956) have shown that the actual result of inducing aggressiveness is quite different: this treatment does increase the person's resistance to benevolent arguments but makes him *more* susceptible to misanthropic arguments. Nevertheless, since several studies do indicate that chronic hostility is associated (at least in males) with resistance to persuasion, this proposition apparently deserves further study (Lesser and Abelson, 1959; Linton and Graham, 1959; Janis and Rife, 1959; Janis and Field, 1959).

3. Raising Self-Esteem

Perhaps the most successful demonstrations of induced resistance to persuasion via personality restructuring are those in which the person's self-esteem is manipulated. A number of investigators have demonstrated that a prior success experience enhances the believer's resistance to subsequent social influence attempts (Kelman, 1950; Mausner, 1954; Samelson, 1957). Resistance is increased, even when the task on which the individual succeeds is quite different from the task employed in the influence attempt.

4. Ideological Preconditioning

The suggestion by some students of the "brainwashing" process that "ideological preconditioning" can induce resistance to influence attempts is also relevant here. This method involves giving the individual certain cognitive content that will increase his ideological autonomy. Among the contents that have been suggested are: pervasive ideologies, such as well-worked-out sets of religious beliefs that allow the person to counter the subsequent indoctrinator's ideology with his own; the belief that he has supporters as well as others dependent on his resisting (e.g., by inculcating ésprit-de-corps); the consciousness that he has secret resources of which the indoctrinator is unaware, etc. (U.S. Senate, 1956). Little if any experimental work has been done to test these notions. Such support as they have received comes from anecdotal reports. The success with which Westerners have resisted indoctrination attempts by the Chinese is greater for clergymen than for businessmen; for those who identify with their parents than for those who reject them; for Marines than for Army personnel, etc.

This technique of inducing cognitive states which produce resistance to persuasion calls for further study. There is a double problem involved here: identifying states that do indeed enhance resistance, and discovering ways of creating these states. The approach seems promising if pursued creatively, but to date confirmatory evidence is scant.

D. Prior Training in Resisting Persuasive Attempts

A final approach to conferring resistance to persuasion considered here involves giving the person some specific training that would enhance his ability to adhere to his belief when subsequently confronted with influence attempts. We shall mention briefly a number of such educational procedures that have been suggested and evaluated.

The most generic method involves general education. It has often been claimed that with better education the individual becomes more resistant to persuasion. However, empirical research does not consistently support such a proposition. Weitzenhoffer's (1953) review of the suggestibility literature shows there is no simple, negative relationship between intelligence and resistance to suggestion. There is some evidence that the more intelligent are more resistant to conformity pressures from peers (Crutchfield, 1955; Stukát, 1958); but they also seem to be, if anything, more susceptible to the mass-media kind of persuasion attempts (Hovland et al., 1949; Janis and Rife, 1959). Hence, it is by no means clear that any general-education manipulation (i.e., such as would increase scores on IQ tests) would have the effect of increasing resistance to persuasion.

Training more specifically tailored to reduce susceptibility to persuasion might be more successful. One type of such training has an aura of unhealthiness: namely, training that will enhance the selective avoidance or perceptual distortion of information that is at variance with one's beliefs. For selective avoidance to be effective, the believer must learn to recognize that the attacking message will be dissonant with his beliefs. Training to perceive the indexing characteristics of the message (Tannenbaum, 1955) would be an approach to this end. Perceptual distortion has also been shown to facilitate resistance to persuasion (Kendall and Wolf, 1949; Cooper and Dinerman, 1951; Kelley, 1957; Cantril, 1958). As with other defense mechanisms, facility in the use of such perceptual distortion can probably be acquired, although the training procedure would no doubt require considerable time and ingenuity. The effectiveness of this particular "clinical" approach remains in the realm of conjecture.

A presumably "healthier" type of specific pretraining involves enhancing the person's critical capacities so that he will be better able to recognize and discount persuasive attempts. A number of studies have shown that training in the critical evaluation of propaganda can increase the person's resistance to such material when he subsequently encounters these communications (Biddle, 1932; Collier, 1944; Allport and Lepkin, 1945; Citron and Harding, 1950). Also effective in this regard is providing the person with special instruction which urges him to be critical just before the attack on his beliefs. (Das *et al.,* 1955; Luchins, 1957). In these cases, the conferred resistance tends to be small. The work by McGuire stemming from inoculation theory, which is considered in the subsequent sections of this chapter, probes more deeply into the immunizing effectiveness of such prior training and warnings.

III. The Inoculation Approach

A. USE OF CULTURAL TRUISMS

McGuire's series of experiments on inducing resistance to persuasion stems from a biological analogy, whence the term "inoculation theory." In the biological situation, the person is typically made resistant to some attacking virus by pre-exposure to a weakened dose of the virus. This mild dose stimulates his defenses so that he will be better able to overcome any massive viral attack to which he is later exposed, but is not so strong that this pre-exposure will itself cause the disease. Alternatively, biological resistance can be augmented by supportive therapy such as adequate rest, good diet, and vitamin supplements. Inoculation is likely to be superior to supportive therapy to the extent that the person has previously been brought up in a germ-free environment. It is a seeming paradox that individuals raised aseptically tend to appear vigorously healthy (even without supportive therapy) but are highly vulnerable when suddenly exposed to massive doses of the disease virus.

Since the experimenter wished to make heuristic use of the inoculation analogy in deriving hypotheses about producing resistance to persuasion, he chose to deal as far as possible with beliefs that had been maintained in a "germ-free" ideological environment, that is, beliefs that the person has seldom, if ever, heard attacked. Nearly all beliefs should be of this sort, according to the selective-avoidance postulate, which implies that a person avoids dissonant information wherever possible. While this has been widely accepted (Festinger, 1957; Klapper, 1949, 1960), the empirical evidence for it is not clear-cut (Steiner, 1962). Hence, to be more certain that the beliefs used in these experiments met the conditions of inoculation theory, "cultural truisms" were used as the beliefs to be made resistant to persuasive attacks. "Cultural truisms" are beliefs that are so widely shared within the person's social milieu that he would not have heard them attacked, and indeed, would doubt that an attack were possible. Beliefs maintained in so monolithic an ideological environment would approximate, as regards inoculation theory, the health status of an organism raised in a germ-free environment.

After much pretesting (which showed that cultural truisms were rarer in our college samples than had been expected), one area was finally found that abounded in almost unanimously accepted propositions, namely, health beliefs. Upwards of 75% of the student samples checked "15" on a 15-point scale to indicate their agreement with propositions like: "It's a good idea to brush your teeth after every meal if at all possible"; "Mental illness is not contagious"; "The effects of penicillin have been, almost without exception, of great benefit to mankind"; "Everyone should get a yearly chest X-ray to detect any signs of TB at an early stage." These truisms (which, as shown below, proved quite vulnerable when exposed to massive attacks without any prior "immunizing" treatment) were used, in the experiments described below, as the beliefs to be made resistant to persuasion by procedures derived by analogy from biological inoculation.

B. Basic Assumptions and Relevant Variables

1. Underlying Assumptions

McGuire's version of the inoculation theory assumes that pretreatments designed to make truisms resistant to subsequent persuasive attacks will be effective to the extent that they overcome two basic difficulties: one, the believer is unpracticed in defending his belief; and two, he is unmotivated to undertake the necessary practice. He is unpracticed because he has never been called upon to defend the truism. He is unmotivated to start practicing because he regards the belief as unassailable.

It follows that any prior treatment designed to improve the believer's defenses must motivate him to develop a defense of a truism whose validity he regards as obvious. Motivation can be supplied by making him aware of the vulnerability of the truism. That is, to be effective the prior defense of a truism presumably should be threatening rather than reassuring about the belief. An obvious way of threatening him is by pre-exposure to weakened forms of the attacking arguments.

It also follows that supplying motivation alone is inadequate for an effective defense. Because of the believer's lack of prior practice, he may not be able to bolster his belief sufficiently unless he is given careful guidance in developing defensive material; or, if he is required to develop such material on his own initiative, he must at least be given considerable time to do so.

From this background of assumptions, we derive a number of predictions about the relative immunizing effectiveness of various kinds of prior defenses. The three basic variables which are involved in most of these predictions are described first. The derivation of the specific predictions involving them is taken up in the later sections of this chapter which present the separate experiments.

2. The Defensive Variables

The first of these three variables is the amount of threat contained in the defenses. Two basic types of defenses were used which differed in amount of threat: "supportive" and "refutational." The supportive defense was nonthreatening; it consisted of giving the believer various arguments in support of the truism. The refutational defense was more threatening; instead of positively supporting the truism, it mentioned several arguments attacking the belief, and then proceeded to refute these attacking arguments. The experimenter reasoned that this pre-exposure would be threatening enough to be defense-stimulating, but not so strong as to overwhelm the truism.

These refutational defenses, considered in relation to the subsequent attacks, were one of two types. Either they mentioned and refuted the very arguments against the truism that were to be used in the subsequent attacks, or they mentioned and refuted arguments different from the ones to be used in the attacks. This refutational-same vs. refutational-different defensive variation is useful in determining whether any increased resistance to persuasion derives from the generalized motivational effect of the threatening mention of the arguments against the truism (as required by inoculation theory), or whether it stems from the useful defensive material provided directly by the refutations.

A second defensive variable that was manipulated in many of the experimenter's inoculation studies was the amount of unguided, active participation in the defense required of the believer. Two levels of this variable were generally used: a relatively passive condition, in which the believer read a defensive essay that had been prepared for him, and an active condition, in which the believer wrote such an essay. This variable was relevant to both of the assumed difficulties in immunizing cultural truisms: the believer's lack of practice and his lack of motivation.

A third variable manipulated in several of the experiments was the interval between the defense and attack. This time period ranged from a few minutes to a maximum of one week. Here the primary concern was the interaction between time and the other variables. The theoretical relevance of these three variables will be discussed later, along with the description of the experiments that tested the predictions in which they were involved.

A number of additional variables were manipulated to clarify certain theoretical ambiguities in one or another of the studies described below, but they are described later in the chapter with the experiment where they were employed.

IV. General Experimental Procedure

The basic procedures were quite similar from experiment to experiment in the series reported below. Hence, for economy of exposition the general methodological paradigm will be described at the outset. Then, in describing each individual experiment, its method will need to be described only in so far as it departs in important ways from this general paradigm.

The experiments involved two sessions, the first devoted to the defenses; the second, to the strong attacks and to measuring the resultant belief levels. The interval between the two sessions varied from a few minutes to 7 days. The subjects were usually college students enrolled in introductory psychology courses at large state universities who were fulfilling a course requirement that they participate in a certain number of hours of psychological experiments. The present studies were usually represented to them as studies of verbal skills. The issues being defended and attacked were the health truisms described above.

A. First (Defensive) Session

The subjects were told the experimenter was studying the relation between reading and writing skills in the two-session experiments. In the first 50-minute session the subject actually participated in several defensive conditions, e.g., he might receive an active-refutational, passive-refutational, active-supportive, and passive-supportive defense, each defense dealing with a different truism.

An active refutational defense consisted of a sheet of paper on which was listed a truism—e.g., "Everyone should brush his teeth after every meal if at all possible." Then would come a one-sentence argument against this truism—e.g., "Too frequent brushing tends to damage the gums and expose the vulnerable parts of the teeth to decay"—and the instructions to use the white space below to write a paragraph refuting this argument against the truism. Halfway down the page came another argument against the truism and instructions to refute it in the space following. The passive-refutational defense stated the truism and the two arguments against it in an introductory paragraph; then followed two further paragraphs, each refuting one of these arguments. The active and passive supportive defenses were analogous to the refutational in format, except that instead of arguments against the truism, they cited two arguments supporting it, and then (in the active condition) asked the subject to write paragraphs defending these supportive arguments, or (in the passive condition) presented two such defensive paragraphs for him to read. In the passive defenses, to substantiate the subterfuge that we were studying reading skills, the subject was asked to pick out and underline the crucial clause in each paragraph.

In some of the experiments, the subject filled out an opinionnaire on the truisms after completing these defenses, so we could measure the direct strengthening effects of the defenses prior to the attacks. More typically, no opinionnaire was administered until the end of the second session, and the direct strengthening effect was determined by including defense-only, no-attack conditions in the design.

B. Second (Attacking) Session

Immediately after (or 2 or 7 days after this defensive session) followed a 50-minute second session devoted to attacks on the truisms and administration of an opinionnaire to determine final belief levels on the truisms. The attacks all had the form of a three-paragraph essay (similar in format to the passive defenses). The first paragraph stated the truism, remarked that some informed people were beginning to question its validity, and mentioned two attacking arguments. Each of the next two paragraphs developed in detail one of these attacking arguments. For those conditions in which a refutational defense had been given, half were followed by an attack using the same arguments against the truism as had been refuted in the prior defense (constituting it a "refutational-same" defense); the other half were followed by attacks using quite different arguments against the truism from those that had been refuted in the defense (constituting a "refutational-different" defense). The designs typically had each subject furnish control data on a "defense-only" and a "neither-defense-nor-attack" truism. The specific truisms were, of course, rotated around the conditions from subject to subject.

After reading (and underlining the crucial clause in) the attacking messages, the subject filled out some personality tests (introduced to substantiate the claim that the experiment was investigating personality correlates of verbal skills). He then filled out the opinionnaire on the truisms, purportedly to determine if the subject's feelings about the topics had any effect on his ability to utilize his verbal skills in the reading and writing "tests." The opinionnaire consisted of four statements dealing with each truism. The subject was called upon to check off his agreement with the statement on a scale from one to 15. The direction of the statement was varied, so that sometimes 15 represented complete acceptance of the truism, and sometimes complete rejection. However, in the results reported below, to make reading easier, the appropriate responses are reversed so that the 15 score always represents complete acceptance of the truism and a one score, complete rejection of it.

After completing the opinionnaire, the subject replied to standardized questions probing his actual perception of the experiment. Finally, the true purpose of the experiment was revealed to him, and the various deceits used and the reasons for employing them were explained. Approximately 3 months later a follow-up letter was sent to him, reminding him that the argumentative material he had dealt with had been selected solely for experimental purposes and that the arguments were not necessarily true. More detailed information on the materials, designs, etc., are given in the original published reports of the experiments cited in the paragraphs that follow.

V. Supportive vs. Refutational Defenses

A series of experiments were carried out to test the hypothesis that defenses of truisms are effective to the extent that they contain threatening mention of arguments against the truism. These studies, in which the experimenter manipulated the extent to which the defenses mentioned arguments supporting the truism vs. arguments attacking the truism, are described in the present section. The first study showed that defenses which present arguments supporting the truism are less effective in conferring resistance to subsequent strong attack than are refutational-same defenses (which ignore arguments positively supporting the truism but do mention and refute the same arguments against the belief as are to be used in the subsequent attack). The second experiment demonstrated that a refutational defense is almost as effective when it refutes arguments against the truism which are different from those to be used in the later attack as when it refutes the very same arguments used in the attack.

A third study illustrated that, when combined with the threatening refutational defense, the supportive defense gains an efficacy that it lacks when used alone. In the fourth study, it was demonstrated that an extrinsic threat (forewarning of the impending attack) prior to the defenses, enhances their immunizing effectiveness, especially that of the otherwise not-threatening supportive defense. Conversely, a fifth study showed that a prior reassurance (feedback that one's peers also agree with the truism) decreases the effectiveness of the defenses. A sixth study revealed that the immunizing efficacy of the refutational defense derives at least as much from the threatening prior mention of the attacking arguments as from the reassuring earlier refutations of the attacking arguments which had been mentioned. Each of these studies is described in more detail, together with additional findings of interest, in the paragraphs below.

A. Supportive vs. Refutational-Same Study

1. Experimental Conditions

In a first experiment (McGuire and Papageorgis, 1961), each of 130 students read a defensive essay on one truism and wrote a defensive essay on another in a regular meeting of his freshman English course. Two days later, he read messages attacking these two truisms and also a third, non-defended truism. On a fourth truism he received neither defense nor attack (the four specific truisms being rotated around the four conditions from student to student). He then filled out an opinionnaire measuring his beliefs on all four truisms.

For 66 of the students, each defensive essay was supportive, mentioning four arguments supporting the truism and then presenting a paragraph substantiating each argument (in the reading, passive condition), or then asking the student to write a substantiating paragraph for each argument (in the writing, active condition). For the other 64 students, each defensive essay was refutational, ignoring supportive arguments and mentioning four arguments against the truism and then presenting a paragraph refuting each (in the passive condition), or then calling upon the student to write a refuting paragraph against each argument (in the active condition). The passive-condition subjects were allowed 5 minutes to read each of the 1000-word essays; the active-condition subjects were allowed 10 minutes to write each essay. The attacks 2 days later consisted of 1000-word essays to be read, each mentioning four arguments against the belief and then presenting a paragraph substantiating each argument.

2. Immunizing Effectiveness

As Table I shows, the more threatening, refutational defense was clearly superior to the supportive defense in conferring resistance to the subsequent attacks. The attacks, when not preceded by a defense, reduced adherence to the truisms from 12.62 to 6.64 on the 15-point scale. When the refutational defense preceded the attacks, the mean belief score was reduced only to 10.33, which is significantly ($p < .001$) higher than in the attack-only condition. The supportive defenses were much less successful in inducing resistance. In the supportive defense conditions, the mean belief score after the attacks was 7.39, which is not only significantly ($p < .001$) lower than in the refutational-defense treatment, but is not even significantly higher than the no-defense, attack-only condition ($p = .16$). Hence the supportive defense is not only much less effective

TABLE I

MEAN BELIEF LEVELS AFTER ATTACKS[a] PRECEDED BY REFUTATIONAL–SAME VS SUPPORTIVE DEFENSES[b,c]

Type of participation	Refutational defense then attack	Supportive defense then attack	Refute minus support
Passive reading	11.51 (35)[d]	7.47 (32)	+4.04
Reading and underlining	11.13 (31)	7.63 (32)	+3.50
Writing from outline	9.19 (31)	7.94 (32)	+1.25
Writing without guidance	9.46 (35)	6.53 (32)	+2.93
Weighted mean	10.33 (132)	7.39 (128)	+2.94

[a] Control levels: neither attack nor defense = 12.62 (N = 130); attack only (with no prior defense) = 6.64 (N = 130).

[b] 15.00 indicates complete adherence to the truism; 1.00 indicates complete disagreement.

[c] Data from McGuire and Papageorgis (1961).

[d] Numbers in parentheses give the number of cases on which cell means were based.

than the refutational in conferring resistance, but has not clearly been shown to be effective at all.

3. Direct Strengthening Effect

In this experiment, the subjects completed the opinionnaire not only at the end of the second session, but also at the end of the first session. Comparing each subject's two responses provides a measure of the direct strengthening effects of the various defenses (as opposed to their conferred resistance to the later attacks). In terms of this criterion, the supportive defenses apparently were superior to the refutational. Immediately after the supportive defenses, the mean belief score was 14.34; immediately after the refutational, it was 13.91 (p = .10 for the difference). Furthermore, while the refutational defense was superior to the supportive one in all four participation conditions as regards resistance conferral (see Table I), the supportive defense was superior in producing a direct strengthening effect. This type of reversal was found repeatedly in the present series of experiments: the defenses which left the beliefs seemingly strongest tended to be the defenses which conferred the least resistance to subsequent attacks. This reversal, called the "paper tiger" phenomenon, shows the peril of assuming the immunizing effectiveness of a defense to be a direct function of its apparent strengthening effect, and is in accord with the inoculation theory.

B. REFUTATIONAL-SAME VS. -DIFFERENT

1. Hypotheses

A later experiment by Papageorgis and McGuire (1961) compared the resistance-conferring efficacy of the refutational defense when the later attacks used arguments which differed from those mentioned and refuted in the defense, with their efficacy when the later attacks used the same arguments used in the defense. If, as implied by the inoculation theory, the refutational defense derives immunizing efficacy from the motivation-stimulating threatening mention of arguments against the truism, then its effectiveness should be general and manifested even against attacks using novel arguments. On the other hand, if the refutational defense gains its effectiveness solely from the refutation rather than the mention of the arguments, the resistance it confers should be more specific to attacks by the same arguments that had been refuted.

2. Procedure

The study designed to distinguish between these two explanations employed only refutational defenses, since the hypotheses did not concern the supportive defenses. Also, only passive (reading) defenses were employed, since the relevance of the active defenses (even of the refutational type) to the predictions is less clear; the amount of refutational material received was more under the subject's control than the experimenter's in the active condition. Alternative forms of the passive refutational defense were made up for each truism. Each form employed a different pair of arguments against the truism, the defensive message first mentioning and then refuting this pair in a 600-word essay. Correspondingly, there were two forms of the message attacking each truism, each form mentioning and then corroborating one of these pairs of attacking arguments. A crossover design was used so that each given pair of arguments refuted in a defense was followed by an attack using the same arguments for half the subjects, and by one using the different pair of arguments for the other half. A total of 73 summer school students served in the two sessions, defensive and attacking, which were separated by a one-week interval.

3. Results

Once again the attacks proved very damaging to the truisms when they were not preceded by a defense. In the attack-only condition, the mean belief level went down to 5.73 on the 15-point scale as compared to a mean of 13.23 in the neither-defense-nor-attack control condition, a drop significant at well above the .001 level. The refutational defenses did confer appreciable resistance to the attack: When the attack had been preceded by the refutational-same defense, the mean belief level was 9.25; after one preceded by the refutational-different defense, it was 8.70. Each of these means in the defense-and-attack conditions is significantly higher than the 5.73 mean in the attack-only condition, and they are not significantly different from one another. These outcomes tend to conform to inoculation theory, since the refutational defense confers resistance even to novel attacks. Indeed, the resistance to novel attacks that was produced is not significantly less than the resistance to attacks by the very same arguments that were refuted.

In a further attempt to identify the mechanisms underlying the resistance-conferral by the refutational defense, two additional variables were measured at the end of the second (attacking) session. One of these was a semantic-differential-type scale designed to measure the perceived quality and credibility of the arguments used in the attack. The attacks were seen as significantly ($p < .05$) less credible when preceded by a refutational defense (whether the defense was refutational-same or refutational-different) than when not preceded by any defense. A second post-attack test called upon the person to write down as many arguments as he could in support of the truism. The inoculation theory prediction was that the motivational stimulation from the threatening refutational defense would result in the believer's accumulating more supportive material for the truism during the week following the attack. However, although there was a slight tendency for the subjects who had received the refutational defense to think up more supportive arguments than those who had received no defense, the difference was not significant ($.20 > p > .10$).

C. COMBINATIONAL EFFECTS

1. Hypotheses and Method

A third experiment (McGuire, 1961b), like the second, used passive (reading) defenses only and compared the immunizing efficacy of combinations of supportive and refutational defenses with that of single defenses. In keeping with inoculation theory, the experimenter attributed the ineffectiveness of the supportive defense [found in McGuire and Papageorgis (1961) described above] to the believer's lack of motivation to assimilate its arguments; the supporting statements seemed to belabor the obvious. The refutational defense did supply some motivation by its threatening mention of arguments against the truism, but did not, in the case of the refutational-different defense, supply any specifically useful material to the unpracticed subject for acting on this induced motivation to bolster the truism. Hence, it was predicted that the supportive and refutational defenses used together would confer more resistance than the sum of their individual effects. It was further predicted that this "whole greater than the sum of its parts" effect would be more pronounced when the supportive defense was added to refutational-different than when added to refutational-same defenses.

One hundred sixty-two students enrolled in introductory college courses were used to test these predictions. They received supportive-only, refutational-only, or supportive-plus-refutational defenses on different truisms. In the cases of refutational defenses, half were refutational-same, and half, refutational-different. The attacking session followed immediately after the defensive.

2. Results

Both of the combination predictions were confirmed. When used alone, neither the refutational-different nor the supportive defenses conferred significant resistance to the immediate attacks. When used in combination, they produced considerable ($p < .01$) resistance. Also confirmed was the prediction that the combination with the supportive defense would be especially effective for the refutational-different defense; there was a significant interaction ($p < .01$) in the predicted direction between the refutational-only vs. refutational-plus-supportive variable and the -same vs. -different variable. The refutational-different defense profited more from the addition of the supportive defense as regards producing resistance to an immediate post-defense attack. These and other findings of the study under discussion are described more fully elsewhere (McGuire, 1961b).

D. ADDED THREATS AND REASSURANCES

1. Theory

According to the inoculation theory, prior defenses lose effectiveness in making truisms resistant to persuasion because the believer is over-confident and therefore unmotivated to assimilate the defenses adequately. This motivational deficit is particularly pronounced in the case of the supportive defense, while the refutational defense does contain an intrinsic threat—mention of attacking arguments—which arouses some motivation. If this theoretical analysis is correct, it follows that any extrinsic threat to the truism (e.g., a forewarning that it will be attacked), presented to the believer before the defense material, should increase his motivation to assimilate the material and hence enhance its immunizing effectiveness.

This extrinsic threat should be especially beneficial to the supportive defense which is particularly needful of such additional motivation. Conversely, a predefense reassurance that the truisms were indeed beyond controversy (e.g., by feedback that everyone in the believer's group agreed with them) should actually decrease the effectiveness of the defenses by further depressing the already inadequate motivation to assimilate these defenses. To test these derivations, two experiments were carried out, one manipulating extrinsic threats, the other, extrinsic reassurance.

2. Extrinsic Threat Manipulation

In the first of these two studies (McGuire and Papageorgis, 1962), each of the 96 subjects received supportive, refutational-same, and refutational-different defenses of three truisms and no defense of a fourth belief. All the defenses were of the passive (reading) type. Then the subjects were given four attacking messages, one aimed at each of the truisms. Finally, their opinions regarding each truism were measured.

For half the subjects the experiment was introduced in the usual way, as a verbal skills test dealing with health topics, and no mention was made of the fact that the truisms would be attacked in the later reading passages. The 48 subjects so instructed constituted the "no-forewarning" condition. The other 48 subjects, those in the "forewarning" condition, received a quite different rationale for the experiment. They were told the experimenter was measuring how persuasible they were by asking them to read attacks on four health truisms which they took for granted. Before they read the attacks, they also were informed, they would be allowed to read defenses of some of those beliefs.

3. Results

The forewarning of attack did indeed enhance the immunizing effectiveness of the defenses, as shown in Table II. It can be calculated from the scores in Table II that after the defenses and attacks in the forewarning condition, the mean belief level was 11.67, and in the no-forewarning condition it was only .10.93, a difference significant above the .05 level. Also as predicted, this enhancement due to the threatening forewarning is greater for the supportive than the refutational defense, the interaction being significant at the .05 level.

There are several possible explanations for these results, however. For example, the higher means in the forewarning conditions after defenses and attacks might not be due to the hypothesized enhancement of the defenses caused by the increased motivation which the threat produced, but rather could stem from a direct reduction in the impact of the attack due to its identification as such by the forewarning. The means in the

212 WILLIAM J. MCGUIRE

TABLE II
Final Belief Levels with and without Forewarning before the Defenses[a,b]

Foreknowledge of attack prior to defense	Attack-only (no prior defense)	Defense and attack conditions			Neither defense nor attack
		Supportive defense	Refut.-same defense	Refut.-diff. defense	
Yes	9.95	12.09	11.79	11.12	12.52
	(24)[c]	(48)	(48)	(48)	(24)
No	10.23	10.11	11.68	10.98	13.20
	(24)	(48)	(48)	(48)	(24)
Combined	10.09	11.10	11.73	11.05	12.86
	(48)	(96)	(96)	(96)	(48)

[a] 15.00 indicates complete adherence to the truism.
[b] Data from McGuire and Papageorgis (1962).
[c] Numbers in parentheses give the number of cases on which cell means were based.

attack-only control conditions shown in Table II rule out this alternative interpretation; when not preceded by a defense the attacks are at least as effective in the forewarning as in the non-forewarning condition. Further evidence along these lines is presented in the original publication.

4. Extrinsic Reassurance Manipulation

In the second of these two studies (Anderson, 1962), each of 96 subjects received a pattern of defenses and attacks similar to that in the forewarning study described above. However, in this study, instead of a threatening forewarning manipulation, there was a reassuring feedback prior to the defenses. At the beginning of the group-administered defensive session, all the subjects were asked to give their opinions on a series of health truisms, including the four crucial ones. By a subterfuge, 48 subjects were then given feedback which indicated that the other subjects had almost unanimously agreed that the four crucial beliefs were true beyond a doubt. These "high reassurance" subjects received no feedback on the "filler" truisms. The other 48 subjects (who constituted the "low reassurance" condition) received no feedback regarding the crucial truisms, although they did receive reassuring feedback regarding four filler truisms.

5. Results

The outcome of this study is shown in Table III. The final belief levels in the three defense-and-attack conditions combined was 10.63 in the reassurance condition and 11.53 in the no-reassurance condition, a difference significant at the .01 level. Hence, as predicted on the basis of

TABLE III

FINAL BELIEF LEVELS WITH AND WITHOUT REASSURING FEEDBACK
BEFORE THE DEFENSES[a,b]

Reassuring feedback of group agreement	Attack-only (no prior defense)	Defense and attack conditions			Neither defense nor attack
		Supportive defense	Refut.-same defense	Refut.-diff. defense	
Yes	10.20	9.58	11.52	10.80	12.40
	(24)[c]	(48)	(48)	(48)	(24)
No	10.74	11.06	12.12	11.41	12.68
	(24)	(48)	(48)	(48)	(24)
Combined	10.47	10.32	11.82	11.10	12.54
	(48)	(96)	(96)	(96)	(48)

[a] 15.00 indicates complete adherence to the truism.
[b] Data from Anderson (1962).
[c] Numbers in parentheses give the number of cases on which cell means were based.

inoculation theory, reassurance prior to the defenses actually lessens their immunizing effectiveness. That the effect is produced via the defenses (rather than through any direct effect of the reassurance manipulation upon the attacks) is shown by the fact that the difference between the high and low reassurance groups in the attack-only conditions is trivial.

The predicted interaction of reassurance and type of defense was not found in this study. It can be seen in Table III that the reassurance reduced the effectiveness of the supportive defense more than that of the refutational defenses. However, this trend is significantly only at the .20 level.

E. INDEPENDENT MANIPULATION OF THREAT AND REASSURANCE

1. Theory and Method

Yet another investigation sought to determine whether the immunizing efficacy of the refutational defense derives, as predicted from inoculation theory, from their threatening components. A final experiment (McGuire, 1963a) in this series utilized independent manipulation of the two components of the refutational defenses: namely, the threatening component (mention in the first paragraph of some arguments attacking the truism); and the reassuring component (refutations of these attacking arguments in the later paragraphs). To isolate the separate effects of these two components, they were manipulated orthogonally in the present experiment. Specifically, half of the refutational defenses were "high threat," mentioning four arguments attacking the truisms; and half were "low threat," mentioning two such arguments. Each of these types was further dichotomized so that half were "high reassurance" defenses, in which two of the mentioned attacking arguments were refuted; and half were "low reassurance" defenses, which refuted none of the mentioned arguments. The design is sketched in Table IVA.

TABLE IVA
NUMBER OF COUNTERARGUMENTS PRESENTED IN THE VARIOUS
REFUTATIONAL DEFENSE CONDITIONS

| Reassurance | Threat | |
	High threat	Low threat
High reassurance	4 mentioned 2 refuted	2 mentioned 2 refuted
Low reassurance	4 mentioned 0 refuted	2 mentioned 0 refuted

A total of 288 subjects served in this study, participating in a defensive and an attacking session separated by 2 days. All the defenses were of the "passive" type, requiring of the subject only that he read the prepared refutational-defense messages.

2. Results

The outcome, shown in Table IVB, indicates that both the threatening and the reassuring components of the refutational defenses contributed to

TABLE IVB
FINAL BELIEF LEVELS AFTER ATTACKS PRECEDED BY DEFENSES
INVOLVING VARYING NUMBERS OF COUNTERARGUMENTS[a,b]

| Reassurance | Threat | | |
	High	Low	Overall
High	11.07 (96)[c]	10.54 (144)	10.75 (240)
Low	10.97 (96)	9.75 (144)	10.23 (240)
Overall	11.02 (192)	10.14 (288)	10.49 (480)

[a] 15.00 indicates complete adherence to the truism.

[b] Data from McGuire (1963a).

[c] Numbers in parentheses give the number of cases on which cell means were based.

their resistance to attack. As regards reassurance, the superiority of high reassurance over low is significant at the .05 level ($F = 4.85$); in the case of the threat variable, the superiority of high threat over low is significant at the .01 level ($F = 13.52$).

These results confirm the inoculation theory prediction that the more threatening defense will be more effective in making truisms resistant to subsequent attacks. The theory did not rule out the possibility that other components of the refutational defense also would contribute to resistance to persuasion, any more than Boyle's law implies the invalidity of Charles's law. Hence, the finding that reassurance promotes resistance is not necessarily in conflict with inoculation theory. The experimenter's conjecture is that if the reassurance comes before the threat, the believer's confidence in the truisms is increased and his tendency not to heed the defenses is augmented. If, on the other hand, the reassurance comes after the threat has already stimulated the believer's motivation to assimilate the defense, then it will heighten resistance to attack. Further study should clarify this point.

VI. Effects of Active Participation in the Defense

A. THEORY

A second series of hypotheses derived from the inoculation notion dealt with the effects of requiring the believer to participate actively, without guidance, in the prior defense of the truisms. Our initial analysis of the resistance of cultural truisms to attack assumed that because these truisms had been maintained in an ideologically "germ-free" environment, there would be two deficits making it difficult to utilize prior defense to make them resistant to persuasion. First, there would be a practice deficit: since the believer would seldom if ever have been called upon to defend the truism, he would not find it easy to do so unless he was carefully guided in the defense. Second, there would be a motivational deficit: because the believer would be too confident of to the validity of these supposedly obvious and unassailable truisms, he would be little motivated to assimilate defensive material that was presented to him.

It follows that this "active participation in the defense" variable is relevant in opposite ways to both the practice and the motivational deficits of the truisms. With regard to the deficit in prior practice, the active (writing) defensive condition is more disadvantageous than the passive (reading) condition, since it imposes more demands upon the believer to summon up bolstering material from his inadequate cognitive repertory. He will tend to perform the writing task poorly and, consequently, the active defensive session tends to be unproductive and wasted. In contrast, the passive defense makes relatively little demand on the believer's prior preparation; he has only to read the presented defensive material. Hence, his lack of practice is no great handicap. In the case of the motivational deficit, on the other hand, the active condition is at less of a disadvantage than the passive, since the very poorness of the believer's performance at the essay-writing task should bring home to him how inadequately based is his confidence in the truism. This should motivate him to correct this state of affairs.

Since the theoretical analysis indicates that the two processes touched off by this active-passive manipulation have opposite effects on the dependent variable (conferred resistance), the experimenter might seem to be left in a sorry state for making predictions. Such is not the case, however. Predictions can be made regarding interaction effects between this activity variable and other variables which tend to intensify the advantages or disadvantages of active participation with respect to conferring resistance.

B. Effects of Requiring Participation

1. Theory and Method

The first experiment designed to test the effect on conferred resistance of manipulating the amount of unguided, active participation in the defense varied this participation over four levels. The highest degree of unguided participation was called "unguided writing." It consisted of giving the subjects a sheet of paper headed by a statement of the truism and telling him that he had 20 minutes to write an essay defending the truism. Subjects were assigned either to a supportive-defense condition by being told that their essays should be restricted to presenting arguments positively supporting the truism, or to a refutational-defense condition by being told that their essays should mention and then refute possible arguments against the truism. They were told that their essays would be scored for argumentative skill and relevance, but were given no further guidance.

A slightly less demanding condition, called "guided writing" was the same as above, except that the sheets headed by the truisms also listed arguments that could be used in writing the essay. The people in the supportive-defense condition were given one-sentence synopses of each of four arguments supporting the truisms. Those in the refutational defense conditions were given four pairs of sentences, each pair consisting of a statement of an argument attacking the truism, and a statement suggesting a refutaton of that argument.

Still less demanding was the "reading and underlining condition." Here each subject received a mimeographed, defensive essay about 1000 words long to read. In the supportive condition the first paragraph mentioned four arguments supporting the truism, and then followed four paragraphs, each developing more fully one of the supporting arguments. In the refutational condition the first paragraph mentioned four arguments attacking the beliefs, and then followed four paragraphs, each refuting one of these attacking arguments. The subjects in this reading condition were instructed that they would have 5 minutes to read and to underline in each paragraph the shortest clause that contained the gist of the whole paragraph. They were told they would be scored on the basis of their accuracy at this task and their ability to answer a later series of reading comprehension questions.

The least demanding participation condition, called "passive reading," was the same as the reading and underlining condition, except that the underlining task was omitted so that the subject had simply to read the paragraph passively during the 5 minutes and prepare for the later reading comprehension questions.

In this experiment (McGuire and Papageorgis, 1961), each of the 130 subjects served in two defensive conditions in the first session: a writing defense on one truism and a reading defense on another. All the refutational defenses were of the refutational-same type. In the second session 2 days later, each received attacks on the two defended truisms and also an attack on a third, undefended truism (to yield an attack-only control score), and no attack on still a fourth truism (to yield a neither-defense-nor-attack control score). The four specific truisms were rotated around these four conditions from subject to subject. Beliefs were measured at the ends of both the first and second sessions.

While there are, as described above, both beneficial and detrimental effects to be expected from requiring active participation in the defense, it is possible under the experimental conditions obtaining here to make a main order prediction: the detrimental effects are likely to be dominant so that the active-participation requirement will probably have the net effect of interfering with the immunizing effectiveness of the defense. The reason is that the relative disadvantage of the active conditions (their being too demanding for the unpracticed subject) is likely to be fully operative, while their relative advantage (supplying motivation to take part seriously in the defense) is somewhat obviated by the moderate degree of such motivation established by the present conditions, even in the passive group. As the previously described series of experiments showed, the refutational defense, even in the passive condition, contains a motivation-stimulating threat to the belief. In addition, the reading-comprehension instructions also motivate these college student subjects to address themselves seriously to assimilating these defensive essays, even though the essays seem to belabor the obvious.

The above reasoning enables the experimenter to make predictions regarding both main effects and interactions in this study. Forced-compliance studies (Kelman, 1953; King and Janis, 1956; Brehm and Cohen, 1962) usually find that active participation in the defense of a belief opposing one's own views generally augments the amount of internalized attitude change. However, in the present case of defending already accepted truisms, the opposite is predicted: namely, the greater the active participation requirement, the less the conferred resistance to subsequent attacks.

The above considerations also give rise to the interaction prediction: the superiority of the passive over the active defense will be more pronounced with the refutational defense than with the supportive. As pointed out in the analysis of the experimental conditions, whatever advantage the active condition might offer—its motivation-inducing threat—is lost in the case of the refutational defense because here even the passive condition offers two sources of motivation to assimilate the defense: the mention of the threatening, attacking arguments which are to be refuted, and the achievement motivation to do well, produced by the announcement of the reading comprehension test.

2. Main Effect Results

The outcome of this experiment has already been presented in Table I, which shows the final belief scores in the eight defense-and-attack conditions (i.e., four levels of active participation for the supportive and for the refutational defenses) and in the attack-only and neither-defense-nor-attack control conditions. As Table I shows, the main effect prediction is confirmed; over the four levels of increasing participation there is a steady decline in immunizing effectiveness. With regard to the main manipulation of this variable, reading vs. writing, the superiority of the former is significant at the .001 level. (Also noteworthy is the finding of the same consistent trend over the four conditions in the direct strengthening effects of the defense, as shown by the mean belief levels at the end of the first session. The superiority of reading over writing in this regard reached the .05 level of significance, despite the low ceiling restraining any further increase in the pre-attack means.) This immunizing superiority of reading over writing is especially striking considering that the time allowed for the writing defense (20 minutes) was four times that allowed for the reading.

3. Interaction Result

The interaction prediction is also confirmed by the results. While the reading defense was superior to the writing for both supportive and refutational defenses, reading was only slightly superior to writing for the sup-

portive defense (7.56 vs. 7.23) but considerably superior for the refutational defense (11.33 vs. 9.33). This interaction was significant at the
.05 level. Several subsequent studies (McGuire, 1963a,c) confirmed both
the main and the interaction effects reported here. However, they showed
in addition that the sizable superiority of reading over writing for the refutational-same defense, which was demonstrated in this study, does not hold
also for the refutational-different defense. Indeed, the superiority of reading over writing tends to be even less for the refutational-different defense
than for the supportive defense. The next section discusses this lack of
superiority with the refutational-different defense which can be derived from
the inoculation theory.

C. Active and Passive Combinational Effects

1. Theory

In the case of refutational defenses, the inoculation theory has implications regarding the advisability of using double defenses, active plus
passive (i.e., having the subject both read and write a refutational essay
defending the truism), as compared with using just one of these. The implications follow from the same assumptions that were used to derive the
previous predictions. The refutational-same defense presumably owes its
efficacy to two factors. The first is its mild, motivating threat to the truism,
due to its mentioning arguments attacking the truism and from demonstrat-
ing to the believer (especially in the active defense condition) how poorly
prepared he is to defend the truism. The second immunizing source is the
refutational material which is useful in resisting subsequent attacks that
employ the same attacking arguments that had been refuted. This refutational material, however, is less useful against attacks employing novel
arguments. Hence, the refutational-same defense derives its efficacy from
both components, the threatening mention and the reassuring refutation of
attacking arguments. But the refutational-different derives its efficacy
mainly from the first component. From this now-familiar analysis, two
interaction predictions follow.

The first prediction deals solely with the single defenses and involves
an interaction between the active vs. passive variable and the refutational-
same vs. -different variable. As discussed above, the active defense more
effectively supplies the threatening motivational component and the passive
better supplies the reassuring refutational content. Stringing together these
various assumptions into a polysyllogism, we can derive the conclusion
that for refutational-same defenses, the passive defense will be superior
to the active, but for refutational-different defenses, the active will be
superior to the passive.

The second prediction, dealing with an interaction between the single vs. double variable and the refutational-same vs. -different variable, is reached through reasoning very similar to the above. The attacking arguments are refuted less well in the single defense and, hence, the single defense supplies the motivation-inducing threatening component more effectively, while the double (active plus passive) defense more effectively supplies the reassuring refutational content. By again stringing together a polysyllogism of assumptions, we derive the following prediction: For refutational-same defenses, the double defense will be superior to the single, but for the refutational-different defense the single will be superior to the double.

2. Method

To test these two hypotheses within a single design, we used six refutational defense conditions: active-only, passive-only and active-plus-passive, each of these three being further dichotomized into refutational-same and refutational-different. (No supportive defenses were used in this study.) The second session, in which the usual attacking essays were presented, came 2 days later. There were also attack-only and neither-defense-nor-attack control conditions. A total of 168 college students served in both sessions, each furnishing data for four different conditions. Further details regarding the method can be found in McGuire (1961a).

When the double defenses (active plus passive) were used, the order in which they came was counterbalanced, so that half the subjects first wrote a refutational essay and then read an already prepared one; the other half read such an essay before they wrote their own. In the results reported below, both orders are combined, since the effect of order turned out to be trivial. It should be at least mentioned here, however, that this null effect of order is embarrassing to inoculation theory; on the basis of the same assumptions used throughout these studies, this theory yields a number of predictions regarding order effects. Yet in neither of the two studies designed to test order-effect predictions (McGuire, 1961a,b) were these predictions confirmed. The two studies cited discuss these embarrassing results more fully.

3. Results

The prediction regarding the single-defense condition was confirmed, at least in a weak, interaction reformulation. As seen in Table V, the passive defense is superior to the active for the refutational-same defense, but the reverse is true for the refutational-different defense. Considering the refutational-same and -different conditions separately, the superiority of the passive over active for the refutational-same defense is significant at the .08 level (two-tails), which tends to corroborate the result of the McGuire and Papageorgis (1961) study reported in the previous section; while the predicted reversal for the refutational-different defense, the superiority of the active over the passive, attains the .13 level of significance. Combining these two reverse trends, the predicted interaction is significant at the .02 level.

TABLE V

FINAL BELIEF LEVELS AFTER COMBINATIONS OF ACTIVE AND PASSIVE
REFUTATIONAL DEFENSES AND ATTACKS[a,b]

Type of attack	Participation in defense			
	Active only	Passive only	Active, then passive	Passive, then active
None	12.94 (48)[c]	12.75 (48)	12.57 (24)	13.37 (24)
Same counterarguments	10.66 (48)	11.47 (48)	12.15 (48)	12.18 (48)
Different counterarguments	11.42 (48)	10.62 (48)	10.92 (48)	10.71 (48)

[a] Control levels: neither-defense-nor-attack = 12.78 ($N = 96$); attack-only = 8.60 ($N = 48$).

[b] 15.00 indicates complete adherence to the truism.

[c] Numbers in parentheses give the number of cases on which cell means were based.

The second prediction regarding the single vs. double defense is also confirmed in its interaction formulation by the present study, as seen in Table V. For the refutational-same condition, the double defense is sizably superior to the single, the final means being 12.17 and 11.02, respectively, a difference significant at the .01 level. For the refutational-different defense, the double is only slightly superior to the single, the means being 10.82 and 11.06, respectively. This predicted interaction effect is significant at the .01 level.

VII. Persistence of the Induced Resistance

A. THEORY

1. Underlying Assumptions

The theoretical discussions in this chapter have continually assumed that the immunizing efficacy of the prior defenses derives from two mechanisms: from a threatening realization of the vulnerability of the belief, which, in the case of cultural truisms, supplies the much needed motivation to assimilate bolstering material; and from the actual presentation of such material. In the case of the active (essay-writing) defenses, the second mechanism is largely inoperative since little information is presented and the unpracticed believer is unable to summon up much defensive material from his own cognitive repertory. For the passive (essay-reading) defenses, however, the situation is more complex. The efficacy of the supportive defense derives primarily from the first mechanism; of the refutational-different, from the second; and of the refutational-same, from both.

Making additional assumptions about the different temporal trends of the two underlying mechanisms, this line of reasoning yields predictions about the persistence of the resistance conferred by the various kinds of defenses. The first of these assumed resistance-conferring mechanisms, the motivation-stimulating threat, may show a nonmonotonic time trend for the following reasons. Once the threat has motivated the previously overconfident believer to accumulate belief-bolstering material, he will still need time before he can act effectively on this motivation, since material relevant to these uncontroverted truisms is rather scarce in the ordinary, ideological environment. Hence, the believer will continue to accumulate additional material for a considerable time after being exposed to the threatening defense, resulting in a delayed-action effect as far as resistance to later attacks is concerned. On the other hand, as time passes and the threat recedes, the induced motivation to accumulate material will itself tend to decay. The result of these two tendencies is a nonmonotonic time trend (first rising, then falling) for induced resistance deriving from this first mechanism. Note that this time trend is the same as that for the typical biological inoculation; there too, a few days or weeks must pass after exposure to the weakened inoculation dose before the resistance builds up to its full strength, after which it tends to decay gradually. The parallel is not surprising since the analogy between the mechanisms in the two situations was our theoretical point of departure.

The second resistance-conferring mechanism, the actual communicating of belief-bolstering material in the defense, should show a much simpler relationship to time. Since the resistance conferred by this mechanism is a direct function of the retention of the bolstering material, we would expect its decay to follow the ordinary forgetting curve.

2. Prediction Regarding Actively Conferred Resistance

Since we hypothesize different persistence curves for the resistance conferred by the two underlying mechanisms, we can make distinctive predictions regarding the time trends of the resistance conferred by each type of defense, depending on the extent that each of the two mechanisms is assumed to be involved in that defense. The prediction is much the same for all types of active (essay-writing) defenses, whether supportive, refutational-same or -different. None of these variations presents appreciable amounts of useful belief-bolstering material in the active condition, and thus the second mechanism is inoperative from the start and does not contribute to the time trend. Such resistance as is conferred derives from the first (motivation-stimulating threat) mechanism, and hence the net time trend should be nonmonotonic. Most interesting, all three types of defense should show a delayed-action effect in the active condition, producing actually more resistance to attacks coming some time after the defense than to immediate attacks.

3. Predictions Regarding Passively Conferred Resistance

In the passive (essay-reading) condition, the predictions depend on the type of defense. What resistance is conferred by reading the supportive essay stems from the second mechanism (retention of the direct bolstering material it contains), so a simple decay function is predicted; the resistance conferred by the passive, supportive defense should decline progressively as the interval between the defense and attack increases. Since, as we have already seen, the passive refutational-different defense derives its efficacy almost entirely from the second (motivating-threat mechanism), we would expect its time trend to show the same nonmonotonic trend as would all three types of active defense. Since the efficacy of the passive refutational-same defense depends on both mechanisms we predict its time trend to be a composite of those of the two: namely, little decline at first, while the "forgetting" trend of the second mechanism is being largely offset by the delayed-action trend of the first mechanism, after which there is a much faster fall-off as both underlying trends are downward. Two studies that were designed to test these various time trend predictions are described in the sections following.

4. Selection of the Time Parameters

To test hypotheses about time trend differentials, especially when the functions are nonmonotonic or decay to a common asymtote (e.g., to zero in this case), it is necessary to set the time parameters at theoretically-strategic points in order that the predicted effects can be demonstrated. Selecting these strategic points presents a formidable methodological difficulty when, as in the present case, the theory is not well formed enough quantitatively to specify the exact time parameters. In anticipation of this problem, in the earlier studies reported above, the interval between defense and attack was deliberately set at different points from experiment to experiment. An examination (McGuire, 1962) of how these different settings appeared to affect the outcomes suggested that the critical persistence predictions could be tested by varying the intervals between defense and attack over the range of a few minutes to one week. Hence, in the studies reported below, these settings were selected as the range over which time was to vary.

B. Persistence of Passively Conferred Resistance

1. Method

The experiment designed to test the predictions about the differential decay rates of the resistance conferred by the three types of defense (supportive, refutational-same and refutational-different) under the passive (reading) conditions involved a mixed design in which each of the 160 subjects served in four conditions. Each subject received the defense of one truism several days before the attack (for 80 subjects, it was 2 days before; and for the other 80, 7 days before), and all received another defense a few minutes before the attack, so that the design included three different intervals between defense and attack. Equal numbers of subjects received supportive, refutational-same, and refutational-different defenses at all three intervals. Further details of the design, analyses, and other aspects of the procedure can be found in an earlier publication (McGuire, 1962).

2. Results

The persistence of the resistance conferred by the three types of passive defense is shown by the final belief scores contained in Table VI. As predicted, such small resistance as the supportive defense confers against immediate attacks has decayed ($p < .05$) almost completely within 2 days. At both the 2- and the 7-day intervals, the level to which the attack reduced the belief is approximately the same after a supportive defense as in the no-defense, attack-only condition.

For the refutational-same defense, however, the conferred resistance, as predicted, decays at a much slower rate. It is particularly in the early stages (again, as predicted) that the resistance produced by the refutational-same defense is more persistent. The interaction between the time (immediate vs. 2-day) variable and the supportive vs. refutational-same type of defense variable is significant at the .01 level. It can be seen that the direction of this interaction effect is in the opposite direction from that which would tend to result from a simple regression artifact.

The predicted nonmonotonic effect in the refutational-different condition is also confirmed. Resistance to attacks 2 days later is actually greater than to immediate attacks. This predicted delayed-action effect is significant at the .05 level. The predicted greater persistence during the first 2

TABLE VI

MEAN BELIEF LEVELS AFTER DEFENSES AND ATTACKS[a] SEPARATED BY
VARIOUS TIME INTERVALS, SHOWING THE PERSISTENCE OF THE
RESISTANCE TO PERSUASION CONFERRED BY THREE TYPES OF
PRIOR, PASSIVE BELIEF DEFENSES[b,c]

Interval between defense and attack	Defense-and-attack conditions		
	Supportive defense	Refutational-same defense	Refutational-different defense
Immediate	9.71	11.36	10.41
	(80)[d]	(80)	(80)
2 Days	8.51	11.08	11.45
	(40)	(40)	(40)
7 Days	8.82	9.49	9.68
	(40)	(40)	(40)

[a] Control levels: neither defense nor attack = 11.74 (N = 80); attack-only = 8.49 (N = 80).

[b] 15.00 indicates complete adherence to the truism.

[c] Data from McGuire (1962).

[d] Numbers in parentheses give the numbers of cases on which cell means were based.

days of the resistance conferred by the refutational-different over that conferred by the refutational-same defense is significant at the .05 level.

C. PERSISTENCE OF ACTIVELY CONFERRED RESISTANCE

1. Method

In a final experiment designed to test the relative persistence of actively and passively conferred resistance, the experimenter adopted the questionable economy of dropping out the 2-day interval condition. Each of the 72 subjects received an active and a passive defense (of two different truisms) one week prior to the attacks, and an active and passive defense of a third and fourth truism immediately prior to the attacks. The specific truisms were rotated around the defensive conditions from subject to subject. Then all four truisms were subjected to the usual attacks and the final belief levels were measured. Twenty-four of the subjects received supportive defenses, another 24, refutational-same, and a third 24, refutational-different defenses.

2. Results

The primary interest in this study was in the active conditions and the comparison between the active and passive. Thus, the 2-day condition, which is a crucial interval for some of the passive-defense effects that were demonstrated in the previous experiment, was omitted in this study. Even under these conditions, however, the distinctive effect in the passive condition was still apparent (see Table VII): the resistance conferred by the passive refutational-different defense showed significantly less of a decline over the week than that produced by the other two types of passive defenses, supportive and refutational-same. In fact, the slight increase in resistance conferred by the passive, refutational-different defense (not significant) suggests a delayed action effect even after one week, although, as the previous experiment showed (see Table VI) this effect is more apparent at the shorter, 2-day interval. For the active condition it

TABLE VII

Mean Belief Levels after Defenses and Attacks Separated by
Various Time Intervals, Showing the Persistence of
Actively and Passively Conferred Resistance[a,b]

Type of defensive material	Active defense		Passive defensive		All 4 combined
	Immediate attack	Attack one week later	Immediate attack	Attack one week later	
Supportive	8.30 (24)[c]	9.89 (24)	9.72 (24)	9.47 (24)	9.34 (24)
Refutational-same	9.61 (24)	10.13 (24)	12.12 (24)	10.42 (24)	10.57 (96)
Refutational-different	9.77 (24)	9.98 (24)	9.61 (24)	9.99 (24)	9.84 (96)
All 3 Combined	9.22 (72)	10.00 (72)	10.48 (72)	9.96 (72)	9.91 (288)

[a] 15.00 indicates complete adherence to the truism.
[b] Data from McGuire (1963b).
[c] Numbers in parentheses give the number of cases on which cell means were based.

was predicted that all three types of defense (supportive, refutational-same, and refutational-different) would show delayed action effects and, as seen in Table VII, just this was found. The greater resistance to attacks one week later than to immediate attacks for the three active types combined is significant at the .05 level. The design (as described above) used four different truisms for each of the three types of active defenses, and in nine of the twelve resulting comparisons there was the predicted delayed-action effect as regards conferred resistance.

The greater persistence of the actively-conferred resistance as compared to that produced by the passive defenses can be seen by inspecting the Table VII means. The belief level in the active condition has generally increased over the week, while it has weakened in the passive groups. This predicted interaction between time and activity is significant at the .01 level. Furthermore this interaction effect derives, as predicted, almost entirely from the supportive and the refutational-same types of defenses. As required by the theory, the resistance stemming from refutational-different defense is about equally persistent whether conferred actively or passively.

VIII. General Conclusion

The strategy used in this research program involved starting with relatively few assumptions and deriving from them a wide range of predictions. These were tested under a standardized set of conditions in experiments designed to be highly sensitive. The accumulating knowledge derived from the successive experiments clarified some of the parameters left undefined in the theory and thus allowed the experimenter to test progressively more elegant and complex derivations from the theory as he proceeded.

Space has not allowed a discussion of all the predictions and findings in this program. The positive was slightly accentuated by the experimenter's passing off with brief mention and references the failure to confirm the predicted order effects. Also omitted were results regarding cross-issue generalizations, effects of forewarnings, and effects of various kinds of prior commitments which were included in some of the studies reported. These findings were not described here because they were only peripherally related to inoculation theory.

The reader will note that all the studies reported here dealt with conferring resistance on a special type of belief, cultural truisms. The same inoculation theory which yielded these largely confirmed predictions regarding immunizing cultural truisms against persuasion might yield different hypotheses regarding the effects of the same defensive variables on making controverted beliefs resistant to persuasion. Hence, generalization from the above studies to the latter type of belief is not warranted. Further experiments will have to determine if inoculation theory will predict the immunizing efficacy of various types of defenses in the case of controversial beliefs as successfully as it has for truisms.

REFERENCES

Abelson, R. P., and Rosenberg, M. J. (1958). *Behav. Sci.* **3**, 1–13.
Allport, F., and Lepkin, M. (1945). *J. Abnorm. Soc. Psychol.* **40**, 3–36.
Anderson, L. R. (1962). M A. Thesis. University of Illinois, Urbana, Illinois.
Anderson, N. H. (1959). *J. Abnorm. Soc. Psychol.* **59**, 371–381.
Bennett, E. B. (1955). *Human Relat.* **8**, 251–273.
Berkowitz, L., and Cottingham, D. R. (1960). *J. Abnorm. Soc. Psychol.* **60**, 37–43.
Biddle, W. W. (1932). *Teach. Coll. Contrib Educ. No.* **531.**
Brehm, J. W. (1960). *In* "Attitude Organization and Change" (C. I. Hovland and M. J. Rosenberg, eds.), pp. 164–197. Yale Univ. Press, New Haven, Connecticut.

Brehm, J. W., and Cohen, A. R. (1962). "Explorations in Cognitive Dissonance." Wiley, New York.

Cantril, H. (1958). *In* "Readings in Social Psychology" (E. Maccoby, T. M. Newcomb, and E. Hartley, eds.), 3rd ed., pp. 291–300, Holt, New York.

Carlson, E. R. (1956). *J. Abnorm. Soc. Psychol.* **52,** 256–61.

Charters, W. W., and Newcomb, T. M. (1958). *In* "Readings in Social Psychology" (E. Maccoby, T. M. Newcomb, and E. Hartley, eds.), 3rd ed., pp. 276–281. Holt, New York.

Citron, A. F., and Harding, J. (1950). *J. Abnorm. Soc. Psychol.* **45,** 310–328.

Cohen, A. R., Brehm, J. W., and Fleming, W. H. (1958). *J. Abnorm. Soc. Psychol.* **56,** 276–278.

Cohen, A. R., Brehm, J. W., and Latané, B. (1959). *J. Pers.* **27,** 63–73.

Collier, R. M. (1944). *J. Social Psychol.* **20,** 3–17.

Cooper, E., and Dinerman, H. (1951). *Public Opin. Quart.* **15,** 243–264.

Crutchfield, R. S. (1955). *Am. Psychol.* **10,** 191–198.

Das, J. P., Rath, R., and Das, R. S. (1955). *J. Abnorm. Soc. Psychol.* **51,** 624–628.

Deutsch, M., and Gerard, H. (1955). *J. Abnorm. Soc. Psychol.* **51,** 629–636.

Dittes, J. E., and Kelley, H. H. (1956). *J. Abnorm Soc. Psychol* **53,** 100–107.

Festinger, L. (1957. "A Theory of Cognitive Dissonance." Row, Peterson, Evanston, Illinois.

Fisher, S., Rubenstein, I., and Freeman, R. W. (1956). *J. Abnorm. Soc. Psychol.* **52,** 200–207.

Harary, F. (1959). *Behav. Sci.* **4,** 316–323.

Hicks, J. M., and Spaner, F. E. (1962). *J. Abnorm. Soc. Psychol.* **65,** 112–120.

Hovland, C. I., and Mandell, W. (1957). *J. Abnorm. Soc. Psychol.* **47,** 581–588.

Hovland, C. I., Lumsdaine, A. A., and Sheffield, F. (1949). "Experiments on Mass Communication." Princeton Univ. Press, Princeton, New Jersey.

Hovland, C. I., Campbell, E., and Brock, T. (1957). *In* "Order of Presentation in Persuasion" (C. I. Hovland, ed.), pp. 23–32. Yale Univ. Press, New Haven, Connecticut.

Janis, I. L., and Feshbach, S. (1953). *J. Abnorm. Soc. Psychol.* **48,** 78–92.

Janis, I. L., and Field, P. B. (1959). *In* "Personality and Persuasibility" (I. L. Janis and C. I. Hovland, eds.), pp. 55–68. Yale Univ. Press, New Haven, Connecticut.

Janis, I. L., and Rife, D. (1959). *In* "Personality and Persuasibility" (I. L. Janis and C. I. Hovland, eds.), pp. 121–140. Yale Univ. Press, New Haven, Connecticut.

Kelley, H. H. (1957). *In* "Emerging Problems in Social Psychology" (M. Sherif and M. O. Wilson, eds.), pp. 229–248. Univ. of Oklahoma, Norman, Oklahoma.

Kelley, H. H., and Volkhart, E. H. (1952). *Am. Sociol. Rev.* **17,** 453–465.

Kelley, H. H., and Woodruff, C. L. (1956). *J. Abnorm. Soc. Psychol.* **52,** 67–74.

Kelman, H. C. (1950). *J. Abnorm. Soc. Psychol.* **45,** 267–285.

Kelman, H. C. (1953). *Human Relat.* **6,** 185–214.

Kelman, H., and Hovland, C. I. (1953). *J. Abnorm. Soc. Psychol.* **48,** 327–335.

Kendall, P., and Wolf, K. M. (1949). *In* "Communications Research, 1948–1949" (P. F. Lazarsfeld and F. N. Stanton, eds.), pp. 152–179. Harpers, New York.

King, B. T., and Janis, I. L. (1956). *Human Relat.* **9,** 177–186.

Klapper, J. T. (Aug., 1949) "Effects of the Mass Media." Bureau of Applied Social Research, Columbia Univ. (mimeo), New York.

Klapper, J. T. (1960). "Effects of Mass Communication," Free Press, Glencoe, Illinois.

Lana, R. E. (1959). *Psychol. Bull.* **56,** 293–300.

Lewin, K. (1951). *In* "Field Theory in Social Science" (D. Cartwright, ed.). Harper, New York.

Lewin, K. (1958). *In* "Readings in Social Psychology" (E. Maccoby, T. Newcomb, and E. Hartley, eds.), 3rd ed., pp. 197–211. Holt, New York.

Lesser, G. S., and Abelson, R. P. (1959). *In* "Personality and Persuasibility" (I. L. Janis, and C. I. Hovland, eds.), pp. 187–206. Yale Univ. Press, New Haven, Connecticut.

Linton, H., and Graham, E. (1959). *In* "Personality and Persuasibility" (I. L. Janis and C. I. Hovland, eds.), pp. 69–101. Yale Univ. Press, New Haven, Connecticut.

Luchins, A. S. (1957). *In* "The Order of Presentation in Persuasion" (C. I. Hovland. ed.), pp. 33–61. Yale Univ. Press, New Haven, Connecticut.

McGuire, W. J. (1960a). *J. Abnorm. Soc. Psychol.* **60,** 345–353.

McGuire, W. J. (1960b). *J. Abnorm. Soc. Psychol.* **60,** 354–358.

McGuire, W. J. (1961a). *J. Abnorm. Soc. Psychol.* **63,** 326–332.

McGuire, W. J. (1961b). *Sociometry* **24,** 184–197.

McGuire, W. J. (1962). *J. Abnorm. Soc. Psychol.* **64,** 241–248.

McGuire, W. J. (1963a). Threat and reassurance as factors in conferring resistance to persuasion. (In preparation.)

McGuire, W. J. (1963b). Comparative persistence of actively and passively conferred resistance to persuasion. Unpublished manuscript.

McGuire, W. J. (1963c). Cross-issue generalization of conferred resistance to persuasion. Unpublished manuscript.

McGuire, W. J., and Papageorgis, D. (1961). *J. Abnorm. Soc. Psychol.* **62,** 327–337.

McGuire, W. J., and Papageorgis, D. (1962). *Public Opin. Quart.* **26,** 24–34.

Mausner, B. (1954). *J. Abnorm. Soc. Psychol.* **49,** 65–68.

Newcomb, T. M. (1961). "The Acquaintance Process." Holt, New York.

Nunnally, J., and Bobren, H. (1959). *J. Pers.* **27,** 38–46.

Papageorgis, D., and McGuire, W. J. (1961). *J. Abnorm. Soc. Psychol.* **62,** 475–481.

Raven, B. H., and Fishbein, M. (1961). *J. Abnorm. Soc. Psychol.* **63,** 411–416.

Rosenbaum, M. E., and Franc, D. E. (1960). *J Abnorm. Soc. Psychol* **61,** 15–20.

Rosenbaum, M. E., and Zimmerman, I. M. (1959). *Public Opin. Quart.* **23,** 247–254.

Rosenberg, M. J. (1956). *J. Abnorm. Soc. Psychol.* **53,** 367–372.

Rosenberg, M. J., and Hovland, C. I., eds. (1960). "Attitude Organization and Change." Yale Univ. Press, New Haven, Connecticut.

Samelson, F. (1957). *J. Abnorm. Soc. Psychol.* **55,** 181–187.

Schachter, S., and Hall, R. (1952). *Human Relat.* **5,** 397–406.

Smith, E. E. (1961). *Public Opin. Quart.* **25,** 626–639.

Steiner, I. D. (1962). *J. Abnorm. Soc. Psychol.* **65,** 266–267.

Stukát, K. G. (1958). *Acta Psychol. Gothoburgensia* **2.**

Tannenbaum, P. H. (1955). *Public Opin. Quart.* **19,** 292–302.

Tannenbaum, P. H. (1956). *Public Opin. Quart.* **20,** 413–425.

U.S. Senate, Committee on Government Operations. (1956). "The Interrogation, Indoctrination and Exploitation of American Military and Civilian Prisoners." U.S. Government Printing Office, Washington, D.C.

Weiss, W., and Fine, B. J. (1956). *J. Abnorm. Soc. Psychol.* **52,** 109–114.

Weitzenhoffer, A. M. (1953). "Hypnotism." Wiley, New York.

Zajonc, R. (1960). *J. Abnorm. Soc. Psychol.* **61,** 159–167.

Self-Persuasion and
the Cognitive Dissonance Controversy

Cognition has been described by Arthur Cohen as "the image or map of the world held by the individual . . ."[1] Cognition refers to the individual's knowledge, opinions, and/or beliefs about himself and about all aspects of his psychological and physical environment. In a preceding section, Suedfeld and Vernon demonstrated how altering individuals' sensory and perceptual environment can influence their susceptibility to persuasion. Now we shall consider the effect on persuasibility of modifying their cognitions.

Man is both voluntarily and involuntarily bombarded by a continuous stream of information. Some of that information is consistent with his existing beliefs, and, as a result, he may be highly receptive to it. When, however, one considers the magnitude of man's complexity, particularly in light of his numerous and varied public and private commitments, his various beliefs, his learned and unlearned reactions, one is immediately struck by how exceedingly high the odds must be that much of this informational input will be discrepant with his existing opinions. However psychologically uncomfortable discrepant information may be, it simply cannot be altogether avoided.

There is conclusive evidence to indicate the self-preservative nature of public opinion. Man's rationalizations about himself seem most imaginative when, in his attempt to cope with discrepant information, he tries tenaciously to cling to his existing beliefs.[2] This should not imply that he seeks information only in support of his existing beliefs while attempting to avoid all dissonant information, although consonant material is at least easier for him to learn.[3] At one

---

[1] Cohen, A. R. *Attitude change and social influence.* New York: Basic Books, 1964. Pp. 62–63.

[2] Cooper, E., & Jahoda, M. The evasion of propaganda: How prejudiced people respond to anti-prejudice propaganda. *J. Psychol.* 1947, **23**, 15–25. Kelley, H. H. Resistance to change and the effects of persuasive communications. In M. Sherif & M. O. Wilson (Eds.), *Emerging problems in social psychology.* Norman, Okla.: Univer. of Oklahoma Book Exchange, 1957.

[3] Havron, M. D., & Cofer, C. N. On the learning of material congruent and incongruent with attitudes. *J. soc. psychol.* 1957, **46**, 91–98.

time it was thought that if an individual's confidence in a belief were shaken by exposure to propaganda, he would tend naturally to be more receptive to consonant than to dissonant information.[4] Since Ivan Steiner[5] and, more recently, Jonathan Freedman and David Sears[6] reexamined that assumption, we now know that only sometimes do people prefer supportive[7] or avoid dissonant communication.[8] Other times, they may actively seek out information which is discrepant with their existing beliefs.[9, 10]

The student of social psychology learns early of the great number of theories in behavioral science which proceed from some variation of the premise that man strives for *cognitive consistency.* Sumner speaks of the "strain toward consistency"[11]; Lund, of the "need for consistency"[12]; Newcomb, of the "strain toward symmetry."[13] From

[4]Brodbeck, M. The role of small groups in mediating the effects of propaganda. *J. abnorm. soc. Psychol.* 1956, **52**, 166–170.

[5]Steiner, I. D. Receptivity to supportive versus nonsupportive communications. *J. abnorm. soc. Psychol.* 1962, **65**, 266–267.

[6]Freedman, J. L., & Sears, D. O. Selective exposure. In L. Berkowitz (Ed.), *Advances in experimental social psychology.* Vol. 2. New York: Academic Press, 1965. Pp. 57–97.

[7]Ehrlich, D., Guttmann, I., Schonbach, P., & Mills, J. Post-decision exposure to relevant information. *J. abnorm. soc. Psychol.*, 1957, **54**, 98–102. Mills, J., Aronson, E., & Robinson, H. Selectivity in exposure to information. *J. abnorm. soc. Psychol.*, 1959, **59**, 250–253. Adams, J. S. Reduction of cognitive dissonance by seeking consonant information. *J. abnorm. soc. Psychol.*, 1961, **62**, 74–78. Rosen, S. Post-decision affinity for incompatible information. *J. abnorm. soc. Psychol.*, 1961, **63**, 188–190. Freedman, J. L., & Sears, D. O. Voters' preferences among types of information. *Amer. Psychologist*, 1963, **18**, 375. Diab, L. N. Studies in social attitudes: II. Selectivity in mass communication media as a function of attitude-medium discrepancy. *J. soc. Psychol.*, 1965, **67**, 297–302.

[8]Mills, J. Avoidance of dissonant information. *J. Pers. soc. Psychol.*, 1965, **2**, 589–593.

[9]Feather, N. T. Cigarette smoking and lung cancer: A study of cognitive dissonance. *Australian J. Psychol.*, 1962, **14**, 55–64. Freedman, J. L. Preference for dissonant information. *J. Pers. soc. Psychol.*, 1965, **2**, 287–289.

[10]A number of factors are responsible for determining what type of information individuals will seek. Freedman has found that utility is a significant variable. Brock finds that information receptivity depends on the recipient's degree of commitment to exposure. Berkowitz has observed that strongly dissonant people, particularly men, prefer consonant input discrepant with their beliefs. Freedman, J. L. Confidence, utility, and selective exposure: A partial replication. *J. Pers. soc. Psychol.*, 1965, **2**, 778–780. Brock, T. C. Commitment to exposure as a determinant of information receptivity. *J. Pers. soc. Psychol.*, 1965, **2**, 10–19. Berkowitz, L. Cognitive dissonance and communication preferences. *Human Relat.*, 1965, **18**, 361–372.

[11]Sumner, W. G. *Folkways.* Boston: Ginn, 1907.

[12]Lund, F. H. The psychology of belief. *J. abnorm. soc. Psychol.*, 1925, **20**, 63–81, 174–196.

[13]Newcomb, T. M. An approach to the study of communicative acts. *Psychol. Rev.*, 1953, **60**, 393–404.

Steiner and from Freedman and Sears we know that the individual's pursuit of consistency may sometimes encompass devious detours. We know also, from common sense, that the pursuit of consistency should not imply that the ultimate state of the cognitive system is one in which no new message input is possible. Obviously, other processes are in interaction and wield their influence as well. We know, for example, that people are attracted to novel stimuli,[14] and presumably, therefore, to novel communication.[15] Other variables wield a similar influence, with the result that the cognitive repertoire continues to grow and to increase in complexity with the addition of each new element. The *cognitive consistency* hypothesis simply implies that there is a tendency to maintain, or to return to, a state of cognitive balance, and that this tendency toward equilibrium determines not only the kind of persuasive communication to which the individual may be receptive but also the nature of the communication he emits.

Although the consistency hypothesis is fundamental in numerous theoretical formulations, including those of Feather,[16] Heider,[17] Newcomb,[18] Osgood and Tannenbaum,[19] Hovland, McGuire, Abelson, and Brehm,[20] of all the consistency-type formulations it is Leon

---

[14] Fiske, D. W., & Maddi, S. R. *Functions of varied experience*. Homewood, Ill.: Dorsey Press, 1961.

[15] Schultz, D. P. Primacy-recency within a sensory variation framework. *Psychol. Rec.*, 1963, 13, 129–139. Schultz, D. P. Spontaneous alternation behavior in humans: Implications for psychological research. *Psychol. Bull.*, 1964, 62, 394–400.

[16] Feather, N. T. A structural balance model of communication. *Psychol. Rev.*, 1964, 71, 291–313.

[17] Heider, F. Attitudes and cognitive organization. *J. Psychol.*, 1946, 21, 107–112. Cartwright, D., & Harary, F. Structural balance: A generalization of Heider's theory. *Psychol. Rev.*, 1956, 63, 277–293. Heider, F. *The psychology of interpersonal relations*. New York: Wiley, 1958.

[18] Newcomb, T. M. An approach to the study of communicative acts. *Psychol. Rev.*, 1953, 60, 393–404. Newcomb, T. M., Turner, R. H., & Converse, P. E. *Social psychology*. New York: Holt, Rinehart, & Winston, 1964.

[19] Osgood, C. E., & Tannenbaum, P. H. The principle of congruity in the prediction of attitude change. *Psychol. Rev.*, 1955, 62, 42–55. Tannenbaum, P. H., & Norris, E. L. Effects of combining congruity principle strategies for the reduction of persuasion. *Sociometry*, 1965, 28, 145–157. Tannenbaum, P. H., Macauley, J. R., & Norris, E. L. Principle of congruity and reduction of persuasion. *J. Pers. soc. Psychol.*, 1966, 3, 233–238. Tannenbaum, P. H., & Gengel, R. W. Generalization of attitude change through congruity principle relationships. *J. Pers. soc. Psychol.*, 1966, 3, 299–304. Tannenbaum, P. H. Mediated generalization of attitude change via the principle of congruity. *J. Pers. soc. Psychol.*, 1966, 3, 493–499.

[20] Rosenberg, M. J., Hovland, C. I., McGuire, W. J., Abelson, R. P., & Brehm, J. W. *Attitude organization and change*. New Haven, Conn.: Yale Univer. Press, 1960.

Festinger's *theory of cognitive dissonance*[21] which has been the object of greatest interest and controversy.

Festinger's theory has been reviewed by Asch,[22] Borden,[23] Brown,[24] Cohen,[25] McGuire,[26] Osgood,[27] Weick,[28] and Zajonc.[29] The imaginative research which it has stimulated has been critically evaluated by Chapanis and Chapanis,[30] Jordan,[31] Mowrer,[32] vigorously defended by Brehm,[33] Silverman,[34] Zimbardo,[35] and numerous others.

The fundamental idea in the theory of cognitive dissonance is that "if a person knows various things that are not psychologically consistent with one another, he will, in a variety of ways, try to make them more consistent."[36] The concept of *cognitive dissonance* refers to the psychological state of affairs that exists once an individual

[21] Festinger, L. A *theory of cognitive dissonance.* Stanford, Calif.: Stanford Univer. Press, 1957. Festinger, L. Cognitive dissonance. *Sci. Amer.,* 1962, **207,** 93–102. Lawrence, D. H. & Festinger, L. *Deterrents and reinforcement.* Stanford, Calif.: Stanford Univer. Press, 1962. Brehm, J. W., & Cohen, A. R. *Explorations in cognitive dissonance.* New York: Wiley, 1962. Festinger, L. *Conflict, decision, and dissonance.* Stanford, Calif.: Stanford Univer. Press, 1964.

[22] Asch, S. E. Review of L. Festinger: A theory of cognitive dissonance. *Contemp. psychol.,* 1958, **3,** 194–195.

[23] Borden, G. A. Cognitive dissonance: A theory of persuasion. *The Pennsylvania Speech Annu.,* 1965, **22,** 43–50.

[24] Brown, R. W. Models of attitude change. In *New directions in psychology.* New York: Holt, Rinehart, & Winston, 1962. Pp. 3–85.

[25] Cohen, A. R. *Attitude change and social influence.* New York: Basic Books, 1964.

[26] McGuire, W. J. Attitudes and opinions. *Annu. Rev. Psychol.,* 1966, **17,** 475–514.

[27] Osgood, C. E. Cognitive dynamics in the conduct of human affairs. *Publ. Opin. quart.,* 1960, **24,** 341–365.

[28] Weick, K. E. When prophecy pales: The fate of dissonance theory. *Psychol. Rep.,* 1965, **16,** 1261–1275.

[29] Zajonc, R. B. The concepts of balance, congruity, and dissonance. *Publ. Opin. quart.,* 1960, **24,** 280–296.

[30] Chapanis, N. P., & Chapanis, A. Cognitive dissonance: Five years later. *Psychol. Bull.,* 1964, **61,** 1–22.

[31] Jordan, N. The mythology of the non-obvious – Autism or fact? *Contemp. Psychol., 1964,* 9, 140–142. Jordan, N. Reply to Zimbardo's note. *Contemp. Psychol.,* 1964, 9, 333.

[32] Mowrer, O. H. Cognitive dissonance or counterconditioning? A reappraisal of certain behavioral paradoxes. *Psychol. Rec.,* 1963, **13,** 197–211.

[33] Brehm, J. W. Comment on "Counter-norm attitudes induced by consonant versus dissonant conditions of role-playing." *J. exp. Res. Pers.,* 1965, **1,** 61–64.

[34] Silverman, I. In defense of dissonance theory: Reply to Chapanis and Chapanis. *Psychol. Bull.,* 1964, **62,** 205–209.

[35] Zimbardo, P. G. A reply to Jordan's attack on dissonance theory. *Contemp. Psychol.,* 1964, **9,** 332–333.

[36] Festinger, L. Cognitive dissonance. *Sci. Amer.,* 1962, **207,** 93.

has made and is committed to a decision. Because commitment to one particular alternative implies the dissolution of any previous commitments to obverse alternatives, the individual, having chosen among the alternatives, is immediately struck with the psychological discomfort which comes from accepting one not totally perfect alternative and rejecting others. The discomfort has the effect of motivating him to try to reduce his cognitive dissonance and thus to alleviate his discomfort. The greater the dissonance, the more intense is his motivation to alleviate his discomfort by achieving consonance. He can accomplish this in several different ways. *He may alter his behavior:* Someone decides to go on a picnic, but once he starts out, it begins to rain. So he turns around and goes back home. *He may alter his cognitive environment:* If he is psychotic, he may tell himself that it really is not raining at all. And, drenched to the skin, sandwiches soaked and soggy, and soda popped, he goes his way, oblivious to the elements. *He may add new cognitive elements:* He calls the weather operator, who tells him that this is only a brief April shower, and on the basis of this new information he proceeds as he originally planned.

In Part I (pp. 29–51), Zimbardo, Weisenberg, Firestone, and Levy presented empirical support for a relationship derived from cognitive dissonance theory that a negative communicator is sometimes more influential than one who is perceived positively. The reader will encounter cognitive dissonance theory again in Part V (pp. 407 ff.) in the Sherif-Hovland versus Festinger controversy about the relationship between involvement and opinion change. Here, we would simply point out that Festinger's theory has stimulated an enormous volume of experimental research[37] and, concomitantly, a heated and fascinating controversy about its validity. Morton Deutsch and Robert Krauss comment, "Undoubtedly Festinger would rather be stimulating than right."[38] Asserting that this is an entirely reasonable attitude, they add,

> In the present state of development of social psychology, no one is ever "right" for very long. The life span of any theory is short. By its very provocativeness and bold generalization, Festinger's work stimulates the research which will create new ideas, some of which constitute a more systematic development of ideas that he first brought to life.[39]

---

[37] Brehm, J. W., & Cohen, A. R. *Explorations in cognitive dissonance.* New York: Wiley, 1962.

[38] Deutsch, M., & Krauss, R. M. *Theories in social psychology.* New York: Basic Books, 1965. P. 76.

[39] *Ibid.*, quoted by permission of M. Deutsch and the publisher.

In the remainder of this section, we shall trace briefly one of the controversies precipitated by cognitive dissonance theory, and, at the same time, try to establish what the effect would be on a communicator's private beliefs of bribing him to communicate something which he believed to be false.

Probably the best known experiments on self-persuasion are those on which Irving L. Janis and Bert King collaborated. In their first experiment, they tested the hypothesis that people who are required to verbalize communication aloud to others tend to be more influenced by its content than passive participants. We shall discuss in greater detail in the following section the comparative effects of active versus passive participation, but it is important here to note that the results of Janis and King's study supported their hypothesis. *Saying is believing!*[40]

Janis and King's second experiment probed the significance of two factors emerging from the first: (1) the role of improvisation in self-persuasion (Does opinion change in the communicator result because he has been stimulated to think of new arguments?), (2) satisfaction with one's performance (Or, do opinions change as a result of the reinforcement derived from doing something which is satisfying?). To answer these questions, the investigators had three groups of college students defend the position that they would soon be drafted into the Army and required to serve a year longer than current draftees. A group of passive controls read a prepared argument to themselves. A second group read the same argument aloud, and a third group was made to improvise their own arguments after they had read the prepared communication. A higher degree of satisfaction was evoked in the second than in the third group, but the only group in which significant opinion change was produced was the third—the active-improvisation group.[41]

An intriguing application of the principle of self-persuasion through active participation preceded the Janis-King experiments by a couple of decades. Jacob Moreno used staged role-playing, or "psychodrama," as a technique for psychotherapy.[42] And even before the in-

---

[40]Janis, I. L., & King, B. T. The influence of role-playing on opinion-change. *J. abnorm. soc. Psychol.*, 1954, 49, 211–218.

[41]King, B. T., & Janis, I. L. Comparison of the effectiveness of improvised versus non-improvised role playing in producing opinion change. *Human Relat.*, 1956, 9, 177–186.

[42]Moreno, J. L. *Who shall survive?* Washington, D. C.: Nerv. & Ment. Dis. Monogr., No. 58, 1934.

ception of Moreno's imaginative utilization of this technique, de Coulmier at the Charenton Asylum in France, between the years 1797 and 1811, is attributed with having used active participation in staged drama as a means of psychotherapy for modifying behavior. [43]

Festinger's position on self-persuasion is different from that of Janis and King, though also taking into account the factor of incentive. The question Festinger raises is how much incentive it would require to bribe someone to actually change his *private* beliefs:

> Consider, for example, a situation where a man came up to you and said that he would give you a million dollars if you publicly stated that you liked reading comic books. Let us assume, for the sake of the example, that you believe him and that you do not like reading comic books. Very likely you would publicly announce your preference for comic books, pocket the million dollars, and be quite content. There is some slight dissonance, to be sure. You said that you liked comic books and you really do not. But there are some very important elements that are consonant with having uttered this public statement, namely, the knowledge of the money now in your pocket. Relative to this, the dissonance is negligible. Essentially the same situation would ensue if a person threatened to shoot you unless you publicly declared you liked comic books. As the promised reward, or threatened punishment, becomes smaller in importance the dissonance resulting from compliance increases. The maximum possible dissonance would be created if the reward, or punishment, was just barely enough to elicit the desired overt behavior or expression. [44]

If the incentive for saying that he liked comic books were great, then the subject would be able to comply without actually having to change his private beliefs about comic books. He could justify his overt behavior with the rationalization that he said what he did because of the money. But if the incentive were small and the subject said that he liked comic books, he would not be able to justify his overt behavior with the bribe. Because the psychological discomfort resulting from the cognitive dissonance he would experience would be great, he would be motivated to change his opinion about comic books, thereby bringing his private beliefs into line with his public behavior.

Thus, from cognitive dissonance theory, we have a paradoxical negative relationship between magnitude of incentive, or reinforce-

---

[43] Program note. In *Playbill* (for "The Persecution and Assassination of Marat as Performed by the Inmates of the Asylum of Charenton under the Direction of the Marquis de Sade"). Vol. 3, No. 4, April, 1966.

[44] Quoted from Festinger, L. *A theory of cognitive dissonance.* Stanford, Calif.: Stanford Univer. Press, 1957. P. 91. By permission of the author and the publisher.

ment, and opinion change. The greater the bribe, the less the cognitive dissonance, and the less the amount of opinion change. The smaller the bribe (up to a point), the greater the cognitive dissonance, and the greater the opinion change. So, according to Festinger, if you want to change someone's opinions, you should pay him just enough to motivate him to tell others just the opposite of what he really believes, but not enough to permit him to justify his public behavior by rationalizing that he did it for money.

A clever experiment by Leon Festinger and J. M. Carlsmith tested this proposition. Subjects who took part in a boring and monotonous task were pressured to tell waiting subjects that the task was interesting. Festinger refers to this type of active participation in self-persuasion as "forced compliance." Subjects who were paid $1.00 for their prevarication experienced more opinion change about the task than subjects paid $20.00.[45] *The smaller the bribe, the greater was the opinion change.*

Milton Rosenberg questions the generality of this finding. Contending that the dissonance hypothesis is more appropriate for predicting the effects of simple and limited counterattitudinal acts than for complex counterattitudinal advocacy, he writes,

> . . . it may be argued that the subjects in both the high and low reward conditions did not actually engage in complex counter-attitudinal improvisation. Instead their performances, probably as guided by the instructions they received from the experimenter, were mainly limited to asserting that the "experiment" in which they had just participated was "interesting," "a lot of fun," etc. In voicing such assertions, they do not appear to have provided any argumentative support for them; that is, they seem not to have attempted to show what aspects of the experiment were "interesting" and why or how they were "fun." In general, the subjects appear to have made no attempt to show how such characterizations of the experimental situation that they were describing could be meaningfully drawn. Thus, beyond asserting their false positive judgments of the dull experimental task, and reasserting those judgments in the face of the doubts of the confederate disguised as the next subject, the true subjects do not seem to have developed any arguments and cognitive elaborations that could have worked to produce significant inconsistency between their negative feelings toward the dull task and new, improvised precepts relating that task in positive ways to some important preferences and values.
>
> It is questionable, then, whether the Festinger and Carlsmith experiment ought to be viewed as involving any true counter-attitudinal advocacy at all. In a very real sense, little more than simple public commitment to a counter-

---

[45] Festinger, L., & Carlsmith, J. M. Cognitive consequences of forced compliance. *J. abnorm. soc. Psychol.*, 1959, **58**, 203–210.

attitudinal position may have been involved. If this be granted, it then follows that even if these data are taken as valid . . . they do not confirm the dissonance prediction that counter-attitudinal advocacy, as such, will lead to attitude change in inverse proportion to the payment offered or received for such advocacy. Instead, a more parsimonious conclusion would be that these data confirm the applicability of the dissonance prediction to a quite different situation: that in which attitude change follows upon the execution of simple, rather undifferentiated, and overt acts or assertions of a counter-attitudinal nature.[46]

Chapanis and Chapanis also take issue with the Festinger-Carlsmith findings, but on different grounds. The Chapanises argue that $20.00 is an implausible reward for simply telling somebody else that a boring task was pleasant. They contend that Festinger and Carlsmith were not really comparing a small versus a large incentive, but rather a reward which is plausible against one which is implausible. Viewed in this perspective, they conclude that it is not at all surprising that the plausible bribe effected the greater change.[47]

In defense of cognitive dissonance theory, and in response to the Chapanis and Chapanis criticism, Irwin Silverman cites an experiment by Jack Brehm and Arthur R. Cohen and a doctoral dissertation by Stanley Lependorf, the results of which support the dissonance hypothesis using even smaller gradations of reward than did Festinger and Carlsmith.[48] Brehm and Cohen used $.50, $1.00, $5.00, or $10.00 as a reinforcement for subjects who wrote essays defending a dissonant position.[49] Lependorf obtained less opinion change in a $.50 incentive condition than in a $.05 condition.[50]

And, if one can assume that "verbal justification" is, like money, but another kind of incentive, then studies by Brock and Blackwood,[51]

[46] Quoted from Rosenberg, M. J. Some limits of dissonance: Toward a differentiated view of counter-attitudinal performance. In S. Feldman (Ed.), *Cognitive Consistency.* New York: Academic Press, 1966. Pp. 147–148. By permission of the author and the publisher.

[47] Chapanis, N. P., & Chapanis, A. Cognitive dissonance: Five years later. *Psychol. Bull.*, 1964, **61**, 5–7.

[48] Silverman, I. In defense of dissonance theory: Reply to Chapanis and Chapanis. *Psychol. Bull.*, 1964, **62**, 206.

[49] Brehm, J. W., & Cohen, A. R. *Explorations in cognitive dissonance.* New York: Wiley, 1962. Pp. 73–78.

[50] Lependorf, S. The effects of incentive value and expectancy on dissonance resulting from attitude-discrepant behavior and disconfirmation of expectancy. Unpublished doctoral dissertation, State Univer. of New York at Buffalo, 1964.

[51] Brock, T. C., & Blackwood, J. E. Dissonance reduction, social comparison, and modification of others' opinions. *J. abnorm. soc. Psychol.*, 1962, **65**, 319–324.

Cohen, Brehm, and Fleming,[52] and Rabbie, Brehm, and Cohen[53] can also be cited in support of the cognitive dissonance hypothesis. In all three studies, the subjects were given either high or low verbal justification for writing an essay advocating a position counter to their own beliefs. The low justification groups consistently became more positive toward the initially dissonant attitude than did the high justification groups.

However, Barry Collins replicated the Rabbie-Brehm-Cohen study, even to the extent of using the same subject population (Yale undergraduates), and failed to find significant differences between high and low incentives.[54] Janis and Gilmore, too, using high versus low incentives ($1.00 vs. $20.00) failed to find support for the negative relationship predicted by cognitive dissonance theory.[55] Some of their observations seem consistent with the Chapanises' criticism:

> For those paid $1, most subjects asserted in the final interview that the pay was felt to be satisfactory and ample. The comments of those paid $20, however, indicated that this payment was perceived as being so extremely large that it was a highly ambiguous stimulus. Most subjects who received $20 reported feeling puzzled because they could not understand why such a huge overpayment was being made. Every one of these subjects asserted that it was in excess of what he regarded as appropriate for the work involved. Seventeen of the 18 expressed clear-cut surprise (for example, "This I cannot comprehend . . . it was too much; $5 would be quite sufficient . . . I was rather shocked.") A few subjects reported that despite their puzzlement they responded to the large reward as a strong positive incentive, but a larger number reported having reacted in the opposite way, regarding the unbelievable large payment as a source of vague suspicions, guilt, or conflict (for example, "I feel like a bastard for going against my cause; but for $20, what the hell.")[56]

Janis and Gilmore, however, are taken to task by Brehm:

> There is no doubt that Ss [subjects] can be offered $20 in such a way as to be puzzling, but neither is there doubt that the same reward can be made to seem reasonable. An incentive which arouses suspicion entails processes other than consonant cognition, and would provide a poor way to contrive a

[52]Cohen, A. R., Brehm, J. W., & Fleming, W. H. Attitude change and justification for compliance. *J. abnorm. soc. Psychol.*, 1958, **56**, 276–278.

[53]Rabbie, J. M., Brehm, J. W., & Cohen, A. R. Verbalization and reactions to cognitive dissonance. *J. Pers.*, 1959, **27**, 407–417.

[54]Cited in Collins, B. E., & Helmreich, R. Studies in forced compliance. II: Mechanisms of attitude change. Mimeod paper, Yale Univer., 1965.

[55]Janis, I. L., & Gilmore, J. B. The influence of incentive conditions on the success of role playing in modifying attitudes. *J. Pers. soc. Psychol.*, 1965, **1**, 17–27.

[56]*Ibid.*, p. 21. Quoted by permission of I. L. Janis and the Amer. Psychol. Ass.

"low dissonance" condition. Since Festinger and Carlsmith were trying to establish a low dissonance condition by offering $20, we may assume that they tried to make the amount seem reasonable. Specifically, they informed all experimental Ss that the money was not only for performing the immediate task but also to be on call in case their services should be needed again. The effect of "being on call" would be to make the $20 seem relatively reasonable and $1 rather little. Personal communications from both Festinger and Carlsmith have indicated that there was little or no suspiciousness on the part of Ss about the $20. While the possibility that suspicion was aroused cannot be completely ruled out, there is good reason to believe that this factor does not account for the results.[57]

What is so fascinating about the dissonance controversy, and what in itself seems to provide serendipitously a kind of "real life" corroboration of the consistency hypothesis, is that findings by supporters of dissonance theory seem consistently to confirm it, while findings by its opponents seem consistently to refute it. If Deutsch and Krauss are correct in their assertion that Festinger would rather be "stimulating than right,"[58] then it is obvious from the preceding dialogue that Festinger has achieved his aim.

A statement by Donald Campbell and Julian Stanley, although written in another context, seems highly relevant at this point in our discussion:

> When one finds, for example, that competent observers advocate strongly divergent points of view, it seems likely on a priori grounds that both have observed something valid about the natural situation, and that both represent a part of the truth. The stronger the controversy, the more likely this is.[59]

The papers that follow permit the reader to contrast the controversial Festinger-Carlsmith study with a more recent investigation by Rosenberg and, finally, with a third study by Carlsmith, Collins, and Helmreich which presents a plausible reconciliation of the diametrically opposite findings in the former two studies.

In the study by Leon Festinger and J. M. Carlsmith there is support for the relationship from cognitive dissonance theory that the greater

---

[57] Quoted from Brehm, J. W. Comment on "counter-norm attitudes induced by consonant versus dissonant conditions of role-playing." *J. exp. Res. Pers.*, 1965, 1, 62. By permission of the author and Academic Press.

[58] Deutsch, M., & Krauss, R. M., *loc. cit.*

[59] Quoted from Campbell, D. T., & Stanley, J. C. Experimental and quasi-experimental designs for research in teaching. In N. L. Gage (Ed.), *Handbook of research on teaching.* Chicago: Rand-McNally, 1963. P. 173. By permission of D. T. Campbell and the publisher.

the incentive to participate in a counterattitudinal act, the less is the magnitude of opinion change.

As a partial explanation for those findings, Milton Rosenberg elaborates on the relevance of his own *evaluation apprehension* hypothesis, or anxiety on the part of subjects that they be positively, or at least not negatively, evaluated by the experimenter and a modification of their behavior accordingly. Rosenberg's findings, though contrary to cognitive dissonance theory, are consistent with the traditional reinforcement position that the greater the reinforcement the greater will be the magnitude of opinion change.

The third paper reports a cleverly conceived study by J. M. Carlsmith, Barry E. Collins, and Robert K. Helmreich which replicates both the negative relationship proposed by dissonance theory and the positive relationship proposed by reinforcement.

Reprinted from Journal of Abnormal and Social Psychology, 1959, Vol. 58, pp. 203–210, by permission ot Leon Festinger and APA.

COGNITIVE CONSEQUENCES OF FORCED COMPLIANCE

LEON FESTINGER AND JAMES M. CARLSMITH[1]

WHAT happens to a person's private opinion if he is forced to do or say something contrary to that opinion? Only recently has there been any experimental work related to this question. Two studies reported by Janis and King (1954; 1956) clearly showed that, at least under some conditions, the private opinion changes so as to bring it into closer correspondence with the overt behavior the person was forced to perform. Specifically, they showed that if a person is forced to improvise a speech supporting a point of view with which he disagrees, his private opinion moves toward the position advocated in the speech. The observed opinion change is greater than for persons who only hear the speech or for persons who read a prepared speech with emphasis solely on elocution and manner of delivery. The authors of these two studies explain their results mainly in terms of mental rehearsal and thinking up new arguments. In this way, they propose, the person who is forced to improvise a speech convinces himself. They present some evidence, which is not altogether conclusive, in support of this explanation. We will have more to say concerning this explanation in discussing the results of our experiment.

Kelman (1953) tried to pursue the matter further. He reasoned that if the person is induced to make an overt statement contrary to his private opinion by the offer of some reward, then the greater the reward offered, the greater should be the subsequent opinion change. His data, however, did not support this idea. He found, rather, that a large reward produced less subsequent opinion change than did a smaller reward. Actually, this finding by Kelman is consistent with the theory we will outline below but, for a number of reasons, is

[1] The experiment reported here was done as part of a program of research supported by a grant from the National Science Foundation to the senior author. We wish to thank Leonard Hommel, Judson Mills, and Robert Terwilliger for their help in designing and carrying out the experiment. We would also like to acknowledge the help of Ruth Smith and Marilyn M. Miller.

not conclusive. One of the major weaknesses of the data is that not all subjects in the experiment made an overt statement contrary to their private opinion in order to obtain the offered reward. What is more, as one might expect, the percentage of subjects who complied increased as the size of the offered reward increased. Thus, with self-selection of who did and who did not make the required overt statement and with varying percentages of subjects in the different conditions who did make the required statement, no interpretation of the data can be unequivocal.

Recently, Festinger (1957) proposed a theory concerning cognitive dissonance from which come a number of derivations about opinion change following forced compliance. Since these derivations are stated in detail by Festinger (1957, Ch. 4), we will here give only a brief outline of the reasoning.

Let us consider a person who privately holds opinion "X" but has, as a result of pressure brought to bear on him, publicly stated that he believes "not X."

1. This person has two cognitions which, psychologically, do not fit together: one of these is the knowledge that he believes "X," the other the knowledge that he has publicly stated that he believes "not X." If no factors other than his private opinion are considered, it would follow, at least in our culture, that if he believes "X" he would publicly state "X." Hence, his cognition of his private belief is dissonant with his cognition concerning his actual public statement.

2. Similarly, the knowledge that he has said "not X" is consonant with (does fit together with) those cognitive elements corresponding to the reasons, pressures, promises of rewards and/or threats of punishment which induced him to say "not X."

3. In evaluating the total magnitude of dissonance, one must take account of both dissonances and consonances. Let us think of the sum of all the dissonances involving some particular cognition as "D" and the sum of all the consonances as "C." Then we might

think of the total magnitude of dissonance as being a function of "D" divided by "D" plus "C."

Let us then see what can be said about the total magnitude of dissonance in a person created by the knowledge that he said "not X" and really believes "X." With everything else held constant, this total magnitude of dissonance would decrease as the number and importance of the pressures which induced him to say "not X" increased.

Thus, if the overt behavior was brought about by, say, offers of reward or threats of punishment, the magnitude of dissonance is maximal if these promised rewards or threatened punishments were just barely sufficient to induce the person to say "not X." From this point on, as the promised rewards or threatened punishment become larger, the magnitude of dissonance becomes smaller.

4. One way in which the dissonance can be reduced is for the person to change his private opinion so as to bring it into correspondence with what he has said. One would consequently expect to observe such opinion change after a person has been forced or induced to say something contrary to his private opinion. Furthermore, since the pressure to reduce dissonance will be a function of the magnitude of the dissonance, the observed opinion change should be greatest when the pressure used to elicit the overt behavior is just sufficient to do it.

The present experiment was designed to test this derivation under controlled, laboratory conditions. In the experiment we varied the amount of reward used to force persons to make a statement contrary to their private views. The prediction [from 3 and 4 above] is that the larger the reward given to the subject, the smaller will be the subsequent opinion change.

PROCEDURE

Seventy-one male students in the introductory psychology course at Stanford University were used in the experiment. In this course, students are required to spend a certain number of hours as subjects (Ss) in experiments. They choose among the available experiments by signing their names on a sheet posted on the bulletin board which states the nature of the experiment. The present experiment was listed as a two-hour experiment dealing with "Measures of Performance."

During the first week of the course, when the requirement of serving in experiments was announced and explained to the students, the instructor also told them about a study that the psychology department was conducting. He explained that, since they were required to serve in experiments, the department was conducting a study to evaluate these experiments in order to be able to improve them in the future. They were told that a sample of students would be interviewed after having served as Ss. They were urged to cooperate in these interviews by being completely frank and honest. The importance of this announcement will become clear shortly. It enabled us to measure the opinions of our Ss in a context not directly connected with our experiment and in which we could reasonably expect frank and honest expressions of opinion.

When the S arrived for the experiment on "Measures of Performance" he had to wait for a few minutes in the secretary's office. The experimenter (E) then came in, introduced himself to the S and, together, they walked into the laboratory room where the E said:

This experiment usually takes a little over an hour but, of course, we had to schedule it for two hours. Since we have that extra time, the introductory psychology people asked if they could interview some of our subjects. [Offhand and conversationally.] Did they announce that in class? I gather that they're interviewing some people who have been in experiments. I don't know much about it. Anyhow, they may want to interview you when you're through here.

With no further introduction or explanation the S was shown the first task, which involved putting 12 spools onto a tray, emptying the tray, refilling it with spools, and so on. He was told to use one hand and to work at his own speed. He did this for one-half hour. The E then removed the tray and spools and placed in front of the S a board containing 48 square pegs. His task was to turn each peg a quarter turn clockwise, then another quarter turn, and so on. He was told again to use one hand and to work at his own speed. The S worked at this task for another half hour.

While the S was working on these tasks, the E sat, with a stop watch in his hand, busily making notations on a sheet of paper. He did so in order to make it convincing that this was what the E was interested in and that these tasks, and how the S worked on them, was the total experiment. From our point of view the experiment had hardly started. The hour which the S spent working on the repetitive, monotonous tasks was intended to provide, for each S uniformly, an experience about which he would have a somewhat negative opinion.

After the half hour on the second task was over, the E conspicuously set the stop watch back to zero, put it away, pushed his chair back, lit a cigarette, and said:

O.K. Well, that's all we have in the experiment itself. I'd like to explain what this has been all about so you'll have some idea of why you were doing this. [E pauses.] Well, the way the experiment is set up is this. There are actually two groups in the experiment. In one, the group you were in, we bring the subject in and give him essentially no introduction to the experiment. That is, all we tell him is what he needs to know in order to do the tasks, and he has no idea of what the experiment is all about, or what it's going to be like, or anything like that. But in the other group, we have a student that we've hired that works for us regularly, and what I do is take him into the next room where the subject is waiting—the same room you were waiting in before—and I introduce him as if he had just finished being a subject in the experiment. That is, I say: "This is so-and-so, who's just finished the experiment, and I've asked him to tell you a little of what it's about before you start." The fellow who works for us then, in conversation with the next subject, makes these points: [The E then produced a sheet headed "For Group B" which had written on it: It was very enjoyable, I had a lot of fun, I enjoyed myself, it was very interesting, it was intriguing, it was exciting. The E showed this to the S and then proceeded with his false explanation of the purpose of the experiment.] Now, of course, we have this student do this, because if the experimenter does it, it doesn't look as realistic, and what we're interested in doing is comparing how these two groups do on the experiment—the one with this previous expectation about the experiment, and the other, like yourself, with essentially none.

Up to this point the procedure was identical for Ss in all conditions. From this point on they diverged somewhat. Three conditions were run, Control, One Dollar, and Twenty Dollars, as follows:

Control Condition

The E continued:

Is that fairly clear? [Pause.] Look, that fellow [looks at watch] I was telling you about from the introductory psychology class said he would get here a couple of minutes from now. Would you mind waiting to see if he wants to talk to you? Fine. Why don't we go into

the other room to wait? [The E left the S in the secretary's office for four minutes. He then returned and said:] O.K. Let's check and see if he does want to talk to you.

One and Twenty Dollar Conditions

The E continued:

Is that fairly clear how it is set up and what we're trying to do? [Pause.] Now, I also have a sort of strange thing to ask you. The thing is this. [Long pause, some confusion and uncertainty in the following, with a degree of embarrassment on the part of the E. The manner of the E contrasted strongly with the preceding unhesitant and assured false explanation of the experiment. The point was to make it seem to the S that this was the first time the E had done this and that he felt unsure of himself.] The fellow who normally does this for us couldn't do it today—he just phoned in, and something or other came up for him—so we've been looking around for someone that we could hire to do it for us. You see, we've got another subject waiting [looks at watch] who is supposed to be in that other condition. Now Professor ———, who is in charge of this experiment, suggested that perhaps we could take a chance on your doing it for us. I'll tell you what we had in mind: the thing is, if you could do it for us now, then of course you would know how to do it, and if something like this should ever come up again, that is, the regular fellow couldn't make it, and we had a subject scheduled, it would be very reassuring to us to know that we had somebody else we could call on who knew how to do it. So, if you would be willing to do this for us, we'd like to hire you to do it now and then be on call in the future, if something like this should ever happen again. We can pay you a dollar (twenty dollars) for doing this for us, that is, for doing it now and then being on call. Do you think you could do that for us?

If the S hesitated, the E said things like, "It will only take a few minutes," "The regular person is pretty reliable; this is the first time he has missed," or "If we needed you we could phone you a day or two in advance; if you couldn't make it, of course, we wouldn't expect you to come." After the S agreed to do it, the E gave him the previously mentioned sheet of paper headed "For Group B" and asked him to read it through again. The E then paid the S one dollar (twenty dollars), made out a hand-written receipt form, and asked the S to sign it. He then said:

O.K., the way we'll do it is this. As I said, the next subject should be here by now. I think the next one is a girl. I'll take you into the next room and introduce you to her, saying that you've just finished the experiment and that we've asked you to tell her a little about it. And what we want you to do is just sit down and get into a conversation with her and try to get across the points on that sheet of paper. I'll leave you alone and come back after a couple of minutes. O.K.?

The E then took the S into the secretary's office where he had previously waited and where the next S was waiting. (The secretary had left the office.) He introduced the girl and the S to one another saying that the S had just finished the experiment and would tell her something about it. He then left saying he would return in a couple of minutes. The girl, an undergraduate hired for this role, said little until the S made some positive remarks about the experiment and then said that she was surprised because a friend of hers had taken the experiment the week before and had told her that it was boring and that she ought to try to get out of it. Most Ss responded by saying something like "Oh, no, it's really very interesting. I'm sure you'll enjoy it." The girl, after this listened quietly, accepting and agreeing to everything the S told her. The discussion between the S and the girl was recorded on a hidden tape recorder.

After two minutes the E returned, asked the girl to go into the experimental room, thanked the S for talking to the girl, wrote down his phone number to continue the fiction that we might call on him again in the future and then said: "Look, could we check and see if that fellow from introductory psychology wants to talk to you?"

From this point on, the procedure for all three conditions was once more identical. As the E and the S started to walk to the office where the interviewer was, the E said: "Thanks very much for working on those tasks for us. I hope you did enjoy it. Most of our subjects tell us afterward that they found it quite interesting. You get a chance to see how you react to the tasks and so forth." This short persuasive communication was made in all conditions in exactly the same way. The reason for doing it, theoretically, was to make it easier for anyone who wanted to persuade himself that the tasks had been, indeed, enjoyable.

When they arrived at the interviewer's office, the E asked the interviewer whether or not he wanted to talk to the S. The interviewer said yes, the E shook hands with the S, said good-bye, and left. The interviewer, of course, was always kept in complete ignorance of which condition the S was in. The interview consisted of four questions, on each of which the S was first encouraged to talk about the matter and was then asked to rate his opinion or reaction on an 11-point scale. The questions are as follows:

1. Were the tasks interesting and enjoyable? In what way? In what way were they not? Would you rate how you feel about them on a scale from −5 to +5 where −5 means they were extremely dull and boring, +5 means they were extremely interesting and enjoyable, and zero means they were neutral, neither interesting nor uninteresting.

2. Did the experiment give you an opportunity to learn about your own ability to perform these tasks? In what way? In what way not? Would you rate how you feel about this on a scale from 0 to 10 where 0 means you learned nothing and 10 means you learned a great deal.

3. From what you know about the experiment and the tasks involved in it, would you say the experiment was measuring anything important? That is, do you think the results may have scientific value? In what way? In what way not? Would you rate your opinion on this matter on a scale from 0 to 10 where 0 means the results have no scientific value or importance and 10 means they have a great deal of value and importance.

4. Would you have any desire to participate in another similar experiment? Why? Why not? Would you rate your desire to participate in a similar experiment again on a scale from −5 to +5, where −5 means you would definitely dislike to participate, +5 means you would definitely like to participate, and 0 means you have no particular feeling about it one way or the other.

As may be seen, the questions varied in how directly relevant they were to what the S had told the girl. This point will be discussed further in connection with the results.

At the close of the interview the S was asked what he thought the experiment was about and, following this, was asked directly whether or not he was suspicious of anything and, if so, what he was suspicious of. When the interview was over, the interviewer brought the S back to the experimental room where the E was waiting together with the girl who had posed as the waiting S. (In the control condition, of course, the girl was not there.) The true purpose of the experiment was then explained to the S in detail, and the reasons for each of the various steps in the experiment were explained carefully in relation to the true purpose. All experimental Ss in both One Dollar and Twenty Dollar conditions were asked, after this explanation, to return the money they had been given. All *S*s, without exception, were quite willing to return the money.

The data from 11 of the 71 *S*s in the experiment had to be discarded for the following reasons:

1. Five *S*s (three in the One Dollar and two in the Twenty Dollar condition) indicated in the interview that they were suspicious about having been paid to tell the girl the experiment was fun and suspected that that was the real purpose of the experiment.
2. Two *S*s (both in the One Dollar condition) told the girl that they had been hired, that the experiment was really boring but they were supposed to say it was fun.
3. Three *S*s (one in the One Dollar and two in the Twenty Dollar condition) refused to take the money and refused to be hired.
4. One *S* (in the One Dollar condition), immediately after having talked to the girl, demanded her phone number saying he would call her and explain things, and also told the *E* he wanted to wait until she was finished so he could tell her about it.

These 11 *S*s were, of course, run through the total experiment anyhow and the experiment was explained to them afterwards. Their data, however, are not included in the analysis.

Summary of Design

There remain, for analysis, 20 *S*s in each of the three conditions. Let us review these briefly: 1. *Control condition*. These *S*s were treated identically in all respects to the *S*s in the experimental conditions, except that they were never asked to, and never did, tell the waiting girl that the experimental tasks were enjoyable and lots of fun. 2. *One Dollar condition*. These *S*s were hired for one dollar to tell a waiting *S* that tasks, which were really rather dull and boring, were interesting, enjoyable, and lots of fun. 3. *Twenty Dollar condition*. These *S*s were hired for twenty dollars to do the same thing.

RESULTS

The major results of the experiment are summarized in Table 1 which lists, separately for each of the three experimental conditions, the average rating which the *S*s gave at the end of each question on the interview. We will discuss each of the questions on the interview separately, because they were intended to measure different things. One other point before we proceed to examine the data. In all the comparisons, the Control condition should be

TABLE 1
Average Ratings on Interview Questions for Each Condition

Question on Interview	Experimental Condition		
	Control (*N* = 20)	One Dollar (*N* = 20)	Twenty Dollars (*N* = 20)
How enjoyable tasks were (rated from −5 to +5)	−.45	+1.35	−.05
How much they learned (rated from 0 to 10)	3.08	2.80	3.15
Scientific importance (rated from 0 to 10)	5.60	6.45	5.18
Participate in similar exp. (rated from −5 to +5)	−.62	+1.20	−.25

regarded as a baseline from which to evaluate the results in the other two conditions. The Control condition gives us, essentially, the reactions of *S*s to the tasks and their opinions about the experiment as falsely explained to them, without the experimental introduction of dissonance. The data from the other conditions may be viewed, in a sense, as changes from this baseline.

How Enjoyable the Tasks Were

The average ratings on this question, presented in the first row of figures in Table 1, are the results most important to the experiment. These results are the ones most directly relevant to the specific dissonance which was experimentally created. It will be recalled that the tasks were purposely arranged to be rather boring and monotonous. And, indeed, in the Control condition the average rating was −.45, somewhat on the negative side of the neutral point.

In the other two conditions, however, the *S*s told someone that these tasks were interesting and enjoyable. The resulting dissonance could, of course, most directly be reduced by persuading themselves that the tasks were, indeed, interesting and enjoyable. In the One Dollar condition, since the magnitude of dissonance was high, the pressure to reduce this dissonance would also be high. In this condition, the average rating was +1.35, considerably on the positive side and significantly different from the Control condition at the .02 level[2] (*t* = 2.48).

[2] All statistical tests referred to in this paper are two-tailed.

In the Twenty Dollar condition, where less dissonance was created experimentally because of the greater importance of the consonant relations, there is correspondingly less evidence of dissonance reduction. The average rating in this condition is only $-.05$, slightly and not significantly higher than the Control condition. The difference between the One Dollar and Twenty Dollar conditions is significant at the .03 level ($t = 2.22$). In short, when an S was induced, by offer of reward, to say something contrary to his private opinion, this private opinion tended to change so as to correspond more closely with what he had said. The greater the reward offered (beyond what was necessary to elicit the behavior) the smaller was the effect.

Desire to Participate in a Similar Experiment

The results from this question are shown in the last row of Table 1. This question is less directly related to the dissonance that was experimentally created for the Ss. Certainly, the more interesting and enjoyable they felt the tasks were, the greater would be their desire to participate in a similar experiment. But other factors would enter also. Hence, one would expect the results on this question to be very similar to the results on "how enjoyable the tasks were" but weaker. Actually, the result, as may be seen in the table, are in exactly the same direction, and the magnitude of the mean differences is fully as large as on the first question. The variability is greater, however, and the differences do not yield high levels of statistical significance. The difference between the One Dollar condition ($+1.20$) and the Control condition ($-.62$) is significant at the .08 level ($t = 1.78$). The difference between the One Dollar condition and the Twenty Dollar condition ($-.25$) reaches only the .15 level of significance ($t = 1.46$).

The Scientific Importance of the Experiment

This question was included because there was a chance that differences might emerge. There are, after all, other ways in which the experimentally created dissonance could be reduced. For example, one way would be for the S to magnify for himself the value of the reward he obtained. This, however, was un-

likely in this experiment because money was used for the reward and it is undoubtedly difficult to convince oneself that one dollar is more than it really is. There is another possible way, however. The Ss were given a very good reason, in addition to being paid, for saying what they did to the waiting girl. The Ss were told it was necessary for the experiment. The dissonance could, consequently, be reduced by magnifying the importance of this cognition. The more scientifically important they considered the experiment to be, the less was the total magnitude of dissonance. It is possible, then, that the results on this question, shown in the third row of figures in Table 1, might reflect dissonance reduction.

The results are weakly in line with what one would expect if the dissonance were somewhat reduced in this manner. The One Dollar condition is higher than the other two. The difference between the One and Twenty Dollar conditions reaches the .08 level of significance on a two-tailed test ($t = 1.79$). The difference between the One Dollar and Control conditions is not impressive at all ($t = 1.21$). The result that the Twenty Dollar condition is actually lower than the Control condition is undoubtedly a matter of chance ($t = 0.58$).

How Much They Learned From the Experiment

The results on this question are shown in the second row of figures in Table 1. The question was included because, as far as we could see, it had nothing to do with the dissonance that was experimentally created and could not be used for dissonance reduction. One would then expect no differences at all among the three conditions. We felt it was important to show that the effect was not a completely general one but was specific to the content of the dissonance which was created. As can be readily seen in Table 1, there are only negligible differences among conditions. The highest t value for any of these differences is only 0.48.

DISCUSSION OF A POSSIBLE ALTERNATIVE EXPLANATION

We mentioned in the introduction that Janis and King (1954; 1956) in explaining their findings, proposed an explanation in terms of the self-convincing effect of mental rehearsal and thinking up new arguments by the person who had to improvise a speech. Kelman (1953), in the previously mentioned study, in attempting to explain the unexpected finding that the persons who complied in the moderate reward condition changed their opinion more than in the high reward condition, also proposed the same kind of explanation. If the results of our experiment are to be taken as strong corroboration of the theory of cognitive dissonance, this possible alternative explanation must be dealt with.

Specifically, as applied to our results, this alternative explanation would maintain that perhaps, for some reason, the Ss in the One Dollar condition worked harder at telling the waiting girl that the tasks were fun and enjoyable. That is, in the One Dollar condition they may have rehearsed it more mentally, thought up more ways of saying it, may have said it more convincingly, and so on. Why this might have been the case is, of course, not immediately apparent. One might expect that, in the Twenty Dollar condition, having been paid more, they would try to do a better job of it than in the One Dollar condition. But nevertheless, the possibility exists that the Ss in the One Dollar condition may have improvised more.

Because of the desirability of investigating this possible alternative explanation, we recorded on a tape recorder the conversation between each S and the girl. These recordings were transcribed and then rated, by two independent raters, on five dimensions. The ratings were, of course done in ignorance of which condition each S was in. The reliabilities of these ratings, that is, the correlations between the two independent raters, ranged from .61 to .88, with an average reliability of .71. The five ratings were:

1. The content of what the S said *before* the girl made the remark that her friend told her it was boring. The stronger the S's positive statements about the tasks, and the more ways in which he said they were interesting and enjoyable, the higher the rating.

2. The content of what the S said *after* the girl made the above-mentioned remark. This was rated in the same way as for the content before the remark.

3. A similar rating of the over-all content of what the S said.

4. A rating of how persuasive and convincing the S was in what he said and the way in which he said it.

5. A rating of the amount of time in the discussion that the S spent discussing the tasks as opposed to going off into irrelevant things.

The mean ratings for the One Dollar and Twenty Dollar conditions, averaging the ratings of the two independent raters, are presented in Table 2. It is clear from examing the table that, in all cases, the Twenty Dollar condition is slightly higher. The differences are small, however, and only on the rating of "amount of time" does the difference between the two conditions even approach significance. We are certainly justified in concluding that the Ss in the One Dollar condition did not improvise more nor act more convincingly. Hence, the alternative explanation discussed above cannot account for the findings.

SUMMARY

Recently, Festinger (1957) has proposed a theory concerning cognitive dissonance. Two derivations from this theory are tested here. These are:

1. If a person is induced to do or say something which is contrary to his private opinion, there will be a tendency for him to change his opinion so as to bring it into correspondence with what he has done or said.

2. The larger the pressure used to elicit the

TABLE 2

AVERAGE RATINGS OF DISCUSSION BETWEEN SUBJECT AND GIRL

Dimension Rated	Condition		
	One Dollar	Twenty Dollars	Value of *t*
Content before remark by girl (rated from 0 to 5)	2.26	2.62	1.08
Content after remark by girl (rated from 0 to 5)	1.63	1.75	0.11
Over-all content (rated from 0 to 5)	1.89	2.19	1.08
Persuasiveness and conviction (rated from 0 to 10)	4.79	5.50	0.99
Time spent on topic (rated from 0 to 10)	6.74	8.19	1.80

overt behavior (beyond the minimum needed to elicit it) the weaker will be the above-mentioned tendency.

A laboratory experiment was designed to test these derivations. Subjects were subjected to a boring experience and then paid to tell someone that the experience had been interesting and enjoyable. The amount of money paid the subject was varied. The private opinions of the subjects concerning the experiences were then determined.

The results strongly corroborate the theory that was tested.

REFERENCES

Festinger, L. *A theory of cognitive dissonance.* Evanston, Ill: Row Peterson, 1957.

Janis, I. L., & King, B. T. The influence of role-playing on opinion change. *J. abnorm. soc. Psychol.*, 1954, **49**, 211–218.

Kelman, H. Attitude change as a function of response restriction. *Hum. Relat.*, 1953, **6**, 185–214.

King, B. T., & Janis, I. L. Comparison of the effectiveness of improvised versus non-improvised role-playing in producing opinion changes. *Hum. Relat.*, 1956, **9**, 177–186.

Reprinted from Journal of Personality and Social Psychology, 1965, Vol. 1, No. 1, pp. 28–42, by permission of Milton J. Rosenberg and APA.

WHEN DISSONANCE FAILS:

ON ELIMINATING EVALUATION APPREHENSION FROM ATTITUDE MEASUREMENT [1]

MILTON J. ROSENBERG

Some propositions concerning evaluation apprehension and affect arousal as systematic, data-biasing contaminants are presented. The earlier finding, in support of dissonance theory, that the degree of reward for counterattitudinal advocacy has an inverse effect upon consequent attitude change is attributed to the operation of these contaminants. An altered replication of 1 major study on counterattitudinal advocacy is reported. By reducing the likelihood that the posited contaminants will be activated it is found that when S writes an essay opposite to his own attitude this changes his attitude in direct proportion to the amount of payment received. Additional data show a generalization of this effect to a related attitude. These data are interpreted as supporting a consistency theory analysis of this type of attitude change and as calling the dissonance-theory interpretation into question.

Certain studies that have been important in advancing the dissonance-theory explanation of attitude-change phenomena seem to be open to a particular kind of reinterpretation. After an explanatory discussion of some general considerations from which this reinterpretation derives we shall turn to an experiment that attempts to put it to a critical test.

Theorists from Thomas and Znaniecki (1918) to Lewin (1935) have contended that the person's "definition of the situation" is the ground from which behavior emerges and takes its direction. But psychologists have tended to miss the relevance of this nearly banal proposition as it might apply to the understanding of psychological research itself. For most human subjects psychological experiments are ambiguous situations, sometimes exhilarating, sometimes provocative of curiosity or anxiety; and all these forms of arousal are likely to set them searching for the possibly veiled meanings of the experimental situation. Just how the subject *does*

define the situation, and thus how he is likely to behave in it, may often be affected by those differences in treatment manipulations or in instructions that distinguish one experimental condition from another. When such intercell differences in definition of the situation are not intended they may contaminate the design and lead to false confirmation, or for that matter to false disconfirmation, of hypotheses. Two separate ways in which this may happen will be explicated here.

Evaluation Apprehension as a Research Contaminant

It is proposed that the typical human subject approaches the typical psychological experiment with a preliminary expectation that the psychologist may undertake to evaluate his (the subject's) emotional adequacy, his mental health or lack of it. Members of the general public, including students in introductory psychology courses, have usually learned (despite our occasional efforts to persuade them otherwise) to attribute special abilities along these lines to those whose work is perceived as involving psychological interests and skills.[2] Even when the

[1] This study was carried out while the author was a member of the Psychology Department at Ohio State University. It was supported by Contract 495 (24) with the Group Psychology Branch of the Office of Naval Research. The author is indebted to Frederick Weizmann for his assistance in executing the experiment and to David Glass and Irving Janis who raised a number of useful questions.

[2] As used in this paper the term "psychologist" is merely a convenient categorical simplification. It denotes anyone who "runs" subjects through an experimental or interview procedure and is perceived as being at least somewhat skilled at, and

28

subject is convinced that his adjustment is not being directly studied he is likely to think that the experimenter is nevertheless bound to be sensitive to any behavior that bespeaks poor adjustment or immaturity.

In experiments the subject's initial suspicion that he may be exposing himself to evaluation will usually be confirmed or disconfirmed (as he perceives it) in the early stages of his encounter with the experimenter. Whenever it *is* confirmed, or to the extent that it is, the typical subject will be likely to experience *evaluation apprehension;* that is, an active, anxiety-toned concern that he win a positive evaluation from the experimenter, or at least that he provide no grounds for a negative one. Personality variables will have some bearing upon the extent to which this pattern of apprehension develops. But equally important are various aspects of the experimental design such as the experimenter's explanatory "pitch," the types of measures used, and the experimental manipulations themselves.

Such factors may operate with equal potency across all cells of an experiment; but we shall focus upon the more troublesome situation in which treatment differences between experimental groups make for differential arousal and confirmation of evaluation apprehension. The particular difficulty with this state of affairs is that subjects in groups experiencing comparatively high levels of evaluation apprehension will be more prone than subjects in other groups to interpret the experimenter's instructions, explanations, and measures for what they may convey about the kinds of responses that will be considered healthy or unhealthy, mature or immature. In other words, they will develop *hypotheses* about how to win positive evaluation or to avoid negative evaluation. And usually the subjects in such an experimental group are enough alike in their perceptual reactions to the situation so that there will be considerable similarity in the hypotheses at which they separately arrive. This similarity may, in

professionally interested in, figuring people out. For example, this is certainly the case when undergraduate subjects participate in a study conducted by an advanced psychology major or graduate student.

turn, operate to systematically influence experimental responding in ways that foster false confirmation of the experimenter's predictions.

Let us consider one example of a situation in which some well-known findings might be accounted for in these terms. It seems quite conceivable that in certain dissonance experiments the use of surprisingly large monetary rewards for eliciting counterattitudinal arguments may seem quite strange to the subject, may suggest that he is being treated disingenuously. This in turn is likely to confirm initial expectations that evaluation is somehow being undertaken. As a result the typical subject, once exposed to this manipulation, may be aroused to a comparatively high level of evaluation apprehension; and, guided by the figural fact that an excessive reward has been offered, he may be led to hypothesize that the experimental situation is one in which his autonomy, his honesty, his resoluteness in resisting a special kind of bribe, are being tested. Thus, given the patterning of their initial expectations and the routinized cultural meanings of some of the main features of the experimental situation, most low-dissonance subjects may come to reason somewhat as follows: "they probably want to see whether getting paid so much will affect my own attitude, whether it will influence me, whether I am the kind of person whose views can be changed by buying him off."

The subject who has formulated such a subjective hypothesis about the real purpose of the experimental situation will be prone to resist giving evidence of attitude change; for to do so would, as he perceives it, convey something unattractive about himself, would lead to his being negatively evaluated by the experimenter. On the other hand, a similar hypothesis would be less likely to occur to the subject who is offered a smaller monetary reward and thus he would be less likely to resist giving evidence of attitude change.

Affect toward the Experimenter as a Research Contaminant

Yet another and even simpler type of possible systematic bias should be noted. This involves the unsuspected affective consequences of designs which call for the experimenter to behave differently toward persons in different conditions of an experiment. Under certain circumstances such differences may generate further differences in how subjects feel toward the experimenter or toward his experiment; and these intercell affective differences too may have the final consequence of influencing experimental responses in ways which make for false confirmation of hypotheses. Thus, turning again to dissonance studies in which subjects are offered large rewards for the writing of counterattitudinal essays, this manipulation, instead of creating low dissonance, may establish comparatively high arousal of the suspicion that one is being deceived; and this in turn may generate anger. A possible consequence is that the low-dissonance subject, provoked to hostility by the suspected duplicity, may find emotional release in refusing to show the response (attitude change) that he perceives the experimenter to be after.

Contaminant Control by Altered Replication

One way of checking upon the presence of these types of contamination is to ask the subject how he interpreted the purpose and meaning of the experiment. This will often be possible but it may sometimes involve one major hazard: such interviewing in itself can be open to the very kinds of contamination it seeks to disclose. Another approach is to conduct an altered replication of the original experiment, one in which we redesign those of its aspects that are presumed to have fostered the contaminating processes. Not only does such an approach enable application of the law of parsimony in interpreting the relation of data to theoretical claims, it also facilitates further study of the social psychology of the psychological experiment.[3] In pursuit of these goals much

[3] For a programmatic statement that defines some outstanding prospects and problems in this area see the useful article by Riecken (1962). In his comments on the subject's desire to "put his best foot forward" Riecken is speaking of something rather like the concept of "evaluation apprehension" that has been developed here and more briefly treated earlier (Rosenberg, 1961, 1963). However, for Riecken this is basically a source of "unintended

of this paper will report and discuss an altered replication of one important study that has been presented as confirming the prediction that counterattitudinal advocacy will generate greater attitude change when undertaken for a small reward than when undertaken for a large one. First it will be necessary to consider the background, design, and results of the original study upon which the present altered replication is based.

From the dissonance point of view counterattitudinal behavior, or even the commitment to undertake it, will lead to attitude change in inverse proportion to the strength and number of cognitions that could be used to justify such behavior (Brehm, 1960). Of the many conceivable types of counterattitudinal performance the one that has been most frequently studied both by dissonance theorists and others has been advocacy, in oral or written form, of an attitude position opposite to the subject's actual private attitude (Carlson, 1956; Culbertson, 1957; Janis & King, 1954; Kelman, 1953; Scott, 1957, 1959).

In most of the relevant dissonance studies the justification variable has been operationalized in one of three ways: subjects are given high or low choice in deciding whether to undertake counterattitudinal advocacy (for example, Cohen & Latané in Brehm & Cohen, 1962); they are told that their performances will be of great or little value for interested other parties (for example, Cohen, Brehm, & Fleming, 1958); or they are given or promised large or small monetary, or

variance" in data and the possibility that it will exert systematic influence making for false validations of hypotheses is not directly examined. Orne (1962) and Rosenthal (1963) have suggested other types of systematic bias. The former has argued that subjects are often motivated to help the experimenter "prove his hypothesis" while the latter has presented evidence that the experimenter's hypotheses or expectations are often indirectly communicated in ways that shape the subject's experimental responding. These views are not in conflict with, nor are they particularly close to, the interpretations offered here. More directly related are the studies on "social desirability" by Edwards (1957) and Crowne and Marlowe (1960). However, these investigators have been basically concerned with sources of invalidity in psychological testing rather than with systematic bias in experiments.

other, rewards (for example, Festinger & Carlsmith, 1959).

The study upon which the present paper is focused was conducted by Cohen and is one of the many recently reported by Brehm and Cohen (1962). Its general design was similar to earlier dissonance studies except that it used four levels of monetary reward, instead of the usual two. The prediction was that with this graded range of monetary rewards the resulting attitude change would be monotonically and inversely related to the size of the reward.

The subjects were Yale undergraduates. The issue concerned the actions of the New Haven police in a campus riot that had occurred a few weeks earlier. The experimenter, appearing at randomly chosen dormitory rooms, introduced himself as a "member of an Institute of Human Relations research team," ascertained by verbal inquiry that the subject disapproved of the actions of the police and asked him to write an essay in support of the actions of the police.[4] The request for the counterattitudinal essay was explained in this way:

> It has been shown that one of the best ways to get relevant arguments, on both sides of an issue, is to ask people to write essays favoring only one side. . . . What we really need now are some essays favoring the police side. I understand that you have very different views on the matter, but as you can see it's very interesting to know what kinds of arguments people bring up in their essays if they have different opinions about it.

---

[4] It is not clear from the research report whether the experimenter actually referred to himself as a psychologist. But belonging to an "Institute of Human Relations research team" would have been sufficient to establish that he was some sort of psychologist or advanced psychological trainee who would be reporting back to a more senior colleague. This was because the "Institute of Human Relations" was the name of the building that housed the Yale psychology department; no other department that gave undergraduate courses was located there and the research organization for which it was named had long since ceased to exist. The experimenter also described himself as a "fellow student." This may have worked to further heighten the arousal of evaluation apprehension, since the Yale undergraduate culture places great emphasis upon the competitive show of maturity, sophistication, and "all around balance." It would probably be particularly important to the subject that the evaluation of him formed by a psychologically trained "fellow student" be a positive one.

The reward manipulation was then introduced by telling the subject that he would receive a particular sum for "writing the essay against your own position." Eight subjects were offered $.50, 6 were offered $1, 10 others were offered $5, 6 others were offered $10. The subject wrote his essay on a blank sheet headed "Why the New Haven Police Actions Were Justified." He was then told:

> Now that you have looked at some of the reasons for the actions of the New Haven police, we would like to get some of your reactions to the issue: *you may possibly want to look at the situation in the light of this.* So, would you please fill out this questionnaire.

The questionnaire on which the subject was invited to indicate approval of the New Haven police, if so inclined, began with this query: "Considering the circumstances, how justified do you think the New Haven police actions were in the recent riot?" An a priori 31-point scale was used with labels at every fifth point and ranging from "completely justified" to "not at all justified." Additional questionnaire items were used to check that the subject correctly perceived the amount of payment that he had been promised and that he had understood that he was to write a strong essay opposite to his own attitude. A control group was given the attitude questionnaire but received neither the manipulation nor the other measures.

It was found that the $5 and $10 groups did not differ significantly from the control group in expressed attitude toward the New Haven police. However, the subjects in the $.50 group were less negative toward the New Haven police than the $1 subjects ($p < .05$) who in turn were less negative than the $10 subjects ($p < .05$); and both the $.50 and $1 groups differed significantly from the control group.

Thus in the main the data appeared to confirm the original prediction. However, the point of view outlined above would suggest that in this study, as in others of similar design, the low-dissonance (high-reward) subjects would be more likely to suspect that the experimenter had some unrevealed purpose. The gross discrepancy between spending a few minutes writing an essay and the large sum offered, the fact that this large sum had not yet been delivered by the time the subject was handed the attitude questionnaire, the fact that he was virtually invited to show that he had become more positive toward the New Haven police: all these could have served to engender suspicion and thus to arouse evaluation apprehension and negative affect toward the experimenter. Either or both of these motivating states could probably be most efficiently reduced by the subject refusing to show anything but fairly strong disapproval of the New Haven police; for the subject who had come to believe that his autonomy in the face of a monetary lure was being assessed, remaining "antipolice" would demonstrate that he *had* autonomy; for the subject who perceived an indirect and disingenuous attempt to change his attitude and felt some reactive anger, holding fast to his original attitude could appear to be a relevant way of frustrating the experimenter.[5] Furthermore, with each *step* of increase in reward we could expect an increase in the proportion of subjects who had been brought to a motivating level of evaluation apprehension or affect arousal.

[5] Some other reasons (see Footnote 4 for the first) why the experimenter calling himself a "fellow student" might have increased the potency of these biasing processes are worth noting here. Given the fact that the antipolice attitude was highly normative among Yale undergraduates at this time many subjects would have been likely to assume that the experimenter was also antipolice. Thus among the high-reward subjects who made this attribution to the experimenter any tendency to inhibit showing themselves capable of being "bought off" would be further strengthened by the expectation that the experimenter would personally disapprove of the subject's new attitude. On the other hand if the experimenter was perceived, as he might have been by some subjects, to actually be propolice, the fact that he was a "fellow student" would lead to his being seen as violating an important group standard; and this, particularly for high-reward subjects who might interpret the experimenter as trying to "buy them off" for the propolice side, would have engendered even more anger toward the experimenter than would otherwise be the case. In turn this would have increased the likelihood that the high-reward subject would resist showing any change in the propolice direction. Thus both the evaluation apprehension and affect arousal patterns of contamination might well have been intensified by the experimenter being perceived as a fellow student.

How can such an interpretation be tested? If it is correct it points to the importance of the fact that the experimenter conducts both the dissonance arousal and the attitude measurement. Evaluation apprehension and negative affect, if they exist, have been focused upon the experimenter; and it would be either to avoid his negative evaluation or to frustrate him, or both, that the high-reward subject would hold back (from the experimenter and possibly even from himself) any evidence of having been influenced by the essay he has just completed.

The most effective way then to eliminate the influence of the biasing factors would be to separate the dissonance arousal phase of the experiment from the attitude measurement phase. The experiment should be organized so that it appears to the subject to be two separate, unrelated studies, conducted by investigators who have little or no relationship with each other and who are pursuing different research interests. In such a situation the evaluation apprehension and negative affect that are focused upon the dissonance-arousing experimenter would probably be lessened and, more important, they would not govern the subject's responses to the attitude-measuring experimenter and to the information that he seeks from the subject.

This was the main change introduced into the original design.[6] A second change was that the reward manipulation involved not only telling the subject that he would be paid a certain amount, but also the actual delivery of that amount to him immediately after he completed the essay. It was assumed that this change too would work to reduce the likelihood that the high-reward subjects would develop suspicions concerning the

[6] The author is aware of only one dissonance study in which some attempt was made to separate counterattitudinal advocacy from subsequent attitude measurement; this is the experiment by Festinger and Carlsmith (1959). However, the degree of separation may well have been insufficient. That experiment did not involve, as did the present one, disguising the two phases as two different studies conducted in two different departments. Furthermore the dependent variable was not change in a previously stable social attitude but rather a momentary rating of how much the subject liked or disliked an experiment just completed.

experimenter's possible duplicity and unrevealed purposes.

Adherence to the dissonance view would suggest that under these altered conditions the results would still show an inverse relationship between magnitude of reward and extent of attitude change. Indeed the significance of the dissonance-confirming relationship might be expected to increase; for now with each subject having actually received a monetary reward the cognitions concerning reasons for undertaking the counterattitudinal performance would be less variable within experimental groups than could have been the case in the original experiment.

However, the consistency theory developed by the present author (Rosenberg, 1956, 1960) suggests the opposite prediction. It holds that the most usual basis for attitude change is the establishment of new beliefs about the attitude object, beliefs that are inconsistent with the original affective orientation toward that object. In this view the significance of a reward received for writing a counterattitudinal essay (that is, for improvising or rehearsing inconsistency-generating cognitions) would be different from that claimed in dissonance theory: such a reward would, in proportion to its magnitude, be likely to have a positive effect both upon the development and the stabilization of the new cognitions. From this it would be predicted that with the removal of the biasing factors the degree of attitude change obtained after the subjects have written counterattitudinal essays will vary directly, rather than inversely, with the amount of reward. Thus the altered design outlined here may afford something approximating a critical test between this approach and the dissonance approach as regards their applicability to predicting the attitude-change effects of counterattitudinal advocacy.

METHOD

Attitude Issue and Subjects

To replicate as closely as possible, except for the major changes that distinguish the present study from its model, the author sought an issue comparable to "the actions of the New Haven police." Late in 1961 the Ohio State University football team, having won the Big Ten championship,

received an invitation to the Rose Bowl. Concerned with the extent to which its reputation as the "football capital of the world" weakened OSU's academic reputation and performance, the faculty council of the University voted to reject the invitation and thereby engendered, both in the student body and the surrounding community, a sense of incredulous outrage. This, through the promptings of local news media, was rapidly turned toward active protest. The immediate result was a riot in which a large crowd of undergraduates (estimates varied between one to three thousand) stormed through University buildings shouting pro-Rose-Bowl and antifaculty slogans. The more longlasting result was the stabilization among the undergraduates of an attitude of disapproval toward any limitation upon Rose Bowl participation. This attitude remained salient during the following year and even in the face of the fact that during that year the faculty council, by a close vote, reversed its original decision. In general interested students felt that future faculty interference with participation in bowl games continued to be a real possibility.

With a pilot questionnaire administered early in 1963 it was confirmed that opposition to a Rose Bowl ban remained a consensual position among the undergraduate body; more than 94% of the sample indicated strong disapproval toward any restoration of the ban in the future. Upon completion of this pilot study a new group of male subjects was recruited from sections of introductory psychology for participation in the present study. In all 51 subjects were finally used. Ten were randomly assigned to each of three experimental conditions and 21 to a control condition.

Dissonance Arousal

As each experimental subject arrived at the author's office he found him busily engaged either in writing or in a conversation with another "student." The experimenter then told the subject:

I'm sorry but I'm running late on my schedule today and I'll have to keep you waiting for about 15 or 20 minutes. Is that all right?

Most subjects simply said it was though a few expressed concern about getting to their next class on time. All of the latter, when assured that the work the experimenter wanted them to do would take no more than 20 minutes, accepted the situation with equanimity. The experimenter then said:

Oh, I've just thought of something; while you are waiting you could participate in another little experiment that some graduate student in education is doing.

The experimenter explained that he had had a call the previous day from the "graduate student" who needed volunteers in a hurry for

some sort of study he's doing—I don't know what it's about exactly except that it has to do with attitudes and that's why he called me, because my research is in a similar area as you'll see later. [The experimenter went on to say] Of course he can't give you any credit [the usual research credit point used to keep up experimental participation rates in introductory psychology courses] but I gather they have some research funds and that they are paying people instead. So if you care to go down there you can.

All but three subjects indicated that they did want to participate in the other study. (The three who did not were eliminated from the experiment.) With some show of effort and uncertainty the experimenter then recalled the name of the education graduate student and the room, actually located in the education department, where he could be found.

Upon reporting to the "education graduate student" the subject received an explanation modeled word-for-word upon that used in the earlier experiment reported by Brehm and Cohen. Also, as in that experiment, it was determined by verbal inquiry that the subject held an attitude position opposite to the one he was to argue for in the essay. Subjects were randomly assigned to one of three reward conditions ($.50, $1, $5), and the amount that each subject was to receive was made clear to him before he undertook to write an essay on why the OSU football team should not be allowed to participate in the Rose Bowl. After the subject had completed the essay he was *paid* the amount that he had been promised, then thanked for his participation and dismissed. He then returned to the experimenter's office and, under the guise of participating in another study, his attitudes toward the Rose Bowl ban and toward various other issues were ascertained.

Attitude Measurement

This phase of the study began by the experimenter telling the subject that the study for which his participation had originally been solicited was a continuing survey on student attitudes "that I run every semester as a sort of Gallup poll to keep a check on opinion patterns on different University issues." (The experimenter, of course, did not know at this point which of the three magnitudes of reward the subject had received for writing the essay.) The subject then filled out an attitude questionnaire dealing with eight different issues. One of these read, "How would you feel if it were decided that from now on the OSU football team would not be allowed to participate in the Rose Bowl?" Following the procedure in the earlier study the subject responded on a 31-point graphic scale, marked at every fifth point by these labels: I think this decision would be not justified at all; very little justified; little justified; slightly justified; rather justified (instead of "quite justified" as in the earlier study); very justified; completely justified.

The same scale form was used with the other seven issues. One of these dealt with the area of varsity athletics and read, "How would you feel if it were decided that the University would no longer give any athletic scholarships?" This issue was included to provide another and more indirect test of the attitude-change consequences of writing the anti-Rose-Bowl essay under varying conditions of reward. The other six issues dealt with nonathletic matters such as dormitory regulations, University admission policies, library rules, etc.

When the subject had completed this questionnaire he was asked what he thought the experiment was really about. His responses during a period of subsequent inquiry were transcribed and these were to be analyzed for the extent to which they reflected any suspicion that the two experiments were actually related to one another. The subject then filled out a follow-up questionnaire. The first item asked, "while you were filling out the opinion questionnaire did it occur to you that there might be some connection between this experiment and the one you worked on in the education department?" After he had answered this item the subject was told that in fact there had been "a connection between the two experiments" and that it would all be explained after he completed the questionnaire. The subject then proceeded to answer the other questions which asked how strong an essay he had agreed to write, how strong an essay he did write, how free he had felt in his decision to write the essay, how getting paid for the essay had made him feel, etc. Each of the questions was answered by choosing one of a number of alternative positions.

The experimenter then told the subject about the nature (but not the purpose) of the deception that had been used and proceeded to engage him in an interview designed to elicit further evidence of any doubts or suspicions that the subject might have felt during the experiment. The experimenter then explained the actual purpose of the experiment, commenting both upon its basic hypothesis and its design, and then answered all of the subject's questions. Before the subject was thanked and dismissed he was urged not to speak of the experiment to any fellow students during the remainder of the academic semester. All subjects promised to comply with this request.

In distinction to the experimental subjects each of the control subjects, upon reporting for his appointment, was merely told that the experimenter was conducting "a sort of Gallup poll on University issues" and then filled out the attitude questionnaire.

RESULTS

In all 62 subjects were originally run through the experiment. Eleven were discarded from the final analysis because on one basis or another they failed to meet necessary conditions that had been specified in advance. Six subjects (two originally assigned to the control condition and four to the experimental conditions) were rejected because post-experimental questioning revealed that they were members of varsity athletic teams. It had been decided that persons in this category would not be used since their pro-Rose-Bowl attitudes could be assumed to be considerably stronger, more firmly anchored, than those of other students. Two other subjects, originally assigned to experimental groups, were discarded from the analysis because they evidenced virtually complete and spontaneous insight into the deception that had been employed. One other subject was discarded because he reported, on the postexperimental questionnaire, that he had been asked to write a "weak" rather than a "strong" essay. Two additional experimental subjects were discarded because they impressed both the experimenter and his assistant as showing psychotic tendencies. However, when the analysis reported below is repeated with the last three rejected subjects *included* the findings are in no wise altered.

Except for the manipulated independent variable other factors that might influence attitudinal response appear to have remained constant across experimental groups. Thus on the postexperimental questionnaire the subjects in the three experimental groups do not differ in their perceptions as to how strong an essay they were asked to write or actually did write; nor do they differ in their self-reports on how free they felt to refuse. From the postexperimental interview data it appears that though a few subjects were surprised to find the Rose Bowl situation featured in the "two different experiments," the groups were equally lacking in insight both as regards the deception that was used and as regards the real purpose of the experiment.[7]

[7] It has been already suggested that in interviews, as in experiments, subjects' responses may often be influenced by their private interpretations of the situation. Thus the postexperimental data collected in this study cannot necessarily be taken at simple face value. But there is at least one important consideration (probably relevant whenever the credibility of an experimental deception is being assessed) that suggests that the subjects were not holding back evidence of having discerned the true design of the experiment or of having doubted the explanations that were given them. Experienced experimenters

It will be remembered that the measurement phase of the present study consisted of a questionnaire concerned with eight different University issues. On the six issues concerning matters unrelated to athletic policy, and thus not subjected to manipulation through the essay-writing procedure, statistical analysis reveals no overall differences and no differences between any specific groups taken two at a time.

On the main matter of experimental interest, whether attitude change on the Rose Bowl and athletic-scholarship issues varies directly or inversely with the magnitude of monetary reward, the data reviewed below reveal that the former is the case; that is, the prediction drawn from a consistency-theory interpretation appears to be confirmed and the opposite prediction based upon dissonance theory appears thereby to be disconfirmed.

Scoring the 31-point attitude scale from 1.0 (for the banning of Rose Bowl participation would be "not justified at all") through 1.2, 1.4 . . . to 6.8, 7.0 (banning Rose Bowl par-

will probably agree that college student subjects usually desire to represent themselves as sophisticated and as not easily misled. Thus when the post-experimental interview situation is a permissive one the subjects are likely to disclose, rather than withhold, promptings toward insight. *Yet none of the present subjects revealed any such insights when, after completion of the experiment, they were asked "what do you think the experiment was really about?"* Later on when *told* by the experimenter that the "two experiments" were really one or still later when the full explanation was given, only a few subjects (two or three per group) claimed to have had suspicions suggestive of what had now been revealed. However, in their attitudinal responses on the two athletic issues these subjects do not differ from others in their groups (that is, they are not clustered in the low, middle, or high portions of the within-group attitude score rankings). Thus it seems likely that most of these particular subjects were exaggerating, and some perhaps were even imagining, their earlier doubts and in so doing were seeking positive evaluation from the experimenter after they had been shown capable of being "taken in." As intended, then, the procedures of the present experiment seem to have achieved their basic purpose which was to avoid, or at least to minimize, the kind of suspicion and disturbing confusion that tends to activate such biasing processes as affect arousal and evaluation apprehension.

TABLE 1

GROUP MEANS AND DIFFERENCES BETWEEN GROUPS
ON ATTITUDE TOWARD THE ROSE BOWL BAN

Group	M	Group differences[a]			
		$.50	$1	$.50 and $1	$5
Control	1.45	$z = 1.97$, $p < .03$	$z = 1.80$, $p < .04$	$z = 2.31$, $p < .015$	$z = 3.93$, $p < .0001$
$.50	2.24		$z = .11$		$z = 1.77$, $p < .04$
$1	2.32				$z = 1.81$, $p < .04$
$.50 and $1	2.28				$z = 2.11$, $p < .02$
$5	3.24				

Note.—Overall difference between groups as assessed by Kruskal-Wallis test: $H = 17.89$, $p < .001$.
[a] Tested by Mann-Whitney z, one-tailed.

ticipation would be "completely justified") we find the following mean scores: 1.45 for the control group, 2.24 for the $.50 reward group, 2.32 for the $1 reward group, and 3.24 for the $5 reward group. The attitude score ranges are 1–3 for the control group, 1–4 for the $.50 group, 1–5 for the $1 group, and 2–6 for the $5 group.

The significance of the reward variable in its influence upon attitude toward a Rose Bowl ban was assessed by computing the Kruskal-Wallis one-way analysis of variance from the ranked scores of all groups. H, which is distributed as chi square, equals 17.89 and has a chance probability of less than .001 (see Table 1). In addition to this overall confirmation of the original prediction it is desirable to test the significance of differences between the specific groups.

Analysis by the Mann-Whitney rank sum test (computing z; see Mosteller & Bush, 1954) reveals that there is no significant difference between the $.50 and $1 groups. Accordingly in some of the additional analyses these two groups were combined. As Table 1 indicates the combined $.50–$1 group is significantly more favorable toward banning Rose Bowl participation than is the control group ($p < .015$) and significantly less favorable than the $5 group ($p < .02$). When the $.50 and $1 groups are analyzed separately each is found to be significantly different

from both the control and $5 conditions (see Table 1). As would be expected the difference between the control and $5 groups is of very large significance ($p < .0001$).

Thus the only deviation from the original prediction in this set of findings is the absence of a significant difference between the $.50 and $1 groups. Since these groups do differ as predicted from both the control and $5 groups, respectively, it might be conjectured that the $.50 difference between them does not generate a large enough *subjective* difference in the magnitude of payment. However, the alternative possibility that even this small magnitude of difference in reward does have some subtler influence upon attitude is suggested by the additional data regarding the issue of abandoning the policy of giving athletic scholarships.

This issue was used as a second test of the basic hypothesis. The expectation was that attitude change on the Rose Bowl issue should tend to *generalize* toward a similar issue, one that suggests another way of deemphasizing the role of varsity sports in university life. It would of course be expected that the group differences would be of lesser magnitude on this issue than on the Rose Bowl issue since the latter served as the actual topic for the counterattitudinal essay.

Analysis of the subjects' responses on the athletic-scholarship issue reveals again a pattern of findings that supports the original hypothesis. Responding on a 31-point scale from 1.0 to 7.0 (with higher scores indicating greater approval for "abandoning athletic scholarships") the groups yield the following mean scores: 2.28 for the control group, 2.26 for the $.50 group, 3.04 for the $1 group, and 3.88 for the $5 group. The score ranges are 1–7 for the control group, 1–4.8 for the $.50 group, 1–6 for the $1 group, and 1.2–7 for the $5 group.

Application of the Kruskal-Wallis test indicates a significant main effect ($H = 14.50$, $p < .005$); thus the extent to which the writing of the essay affects an attitude *related* to the topic of the essay is shown to be a positive monotonic function of the amount of reward.

Analysis of the differences between the specific groups as reported in Table 2 clarifies certain interesting details. While the mean attitude scores of the control and $.50 groups are virtually identical there is a slight and insignificant trend ($p < .20$) toward a greater concentration of extreme negative scores in the control group. The difference between the control and $1 groups comes closer to an acceptable probability level ($p < .10$) reflecting the greater differences in means (control = 2.28, $1 = 3.04$) reported above.

As predicted, the control and $.50 groups do show significantly less approval of abandoning athletic scholarships than does the $5 group; $p < .01$ in both cases. When the control and $.50 groups are combined the difference from the $5 group has a probability of less than .005 as compared to less than .08 when the difference between the combined group and the $1 group is assessed. The $1 group clearly stands in an intermediate position. While its mean attitude score reflects greater endorsement of the antiathletic scholarship view than does the $.50 group and less endorsement than the $5 group, neither of these differences ($p < .15$ and $p < .12$, respectively) reaches significance.

Thus in comparison to the $.50 group the $1 group is less clearly differentiated from the $5 group and more clearly differentiated from the control group. From this it is apparent that the difference in size of reward between the $.50 and $1 groups does have some in-

TABLE 2

GROUP MEANS AND DIFFERENCES BETWEEN GROUPS ON ATTITUDE TOWARD ENDING ATHLETIC SCHOLARSHIPS

Group	M	Group differences[a]		
		$.50	$1	$5
Control	2.28	$z = .95$, $p < .20$	$z = 1.33$, $p < .10$	$z = 2.45$, $p < .01$
$.50	2.26		$z = 1.09$, $p < .15$	$z = 2.36$, $p < .01$
Control and $.50	2.27		$z = 1.44$, $p < .08$	$z = 2.67$, $p < .005$
$1	3.04			$z = 1.24$, $p < .12$
$5	3.88			

Note.—Overall difference between groups as assessed by Kruskal-Wallis test: $H = 14.50$, $p < .005$
[a] Tested by Mann-Whitney z, one-tailed.

fluence upon the extent to which the writing of the essay affected the subjects' attitudes on a related issue; and that influence too is consistent with the prediction that attitude change following counterattitudinal performance will be a *positive* function of the degree of reward received for such performance.

A question of considerable interest is why the difference between the $.50 and $1 groups shows up more clearly on a related issue rather than on the issue with which the essay was directly concerned. One possible interpretation emerges when we recall that the $.50 group does differ significantly from the control group on the Rose Bowl issue but does not show such a difference on the athletic-scholarship issue. With this small amount of reward there may be a minimal likelihood that the induced attitude change will generalize to a similar issue; with the somewhat larger reward of $1 a somewhat stronger tendency toward generalization may be operative.

On the basis of the findings that have so far been presented, the following conclusion seems warranted: when the design of the original study reported by Brehm and Cohen is altered so as to eliminate aspects that were likely to have generated evaluation apprehension and unsuspected affect arousal, the prediction that guided the present study is confirmed and the original dissonance prediction is disconfirmed.

DISCUSSION

This paper has combined two purposes: to present some propositions about how subjects' perceptions of experimental situations may affect their experimental performances; and, on this basis, to report an experimental reexamination of the dissonance-theory interpretation of attitude change due to counterattitudinal advocacy.

As regards the first purpose, the confirmation of the predictions in the present study lends support to the original propositions about evaluation apprehension and affect arousal; for it was in part on the basis of those propositions that the experimental predictions were formulated. However, more direct investigation of these contaminating processes is possible and desirable. For example, in two recent studies the author has, by intention rather than by inadvertence, supplied cues to the subjects about types of responding that might connote maturity and immaturity. In one of these studies some subjects were led to believe that mature persons like strangers more than immature people do while other subjects were led to believe the opposite. In a second study some subjects were led to believe that mature people perform well on dull arithmetic tasks while others were led to believe that immature people do better at such tasks. The results of these studies, to be reported elsewhere, strongly demonstrate the power of evaluation apprehension in controlling experimental responding.

However, it is necessary that we go beyond such demonstration studies if these contaminating processes are to be better understood and thus more effectively controlled. A number of questions remain to be investigated. Do such personality variables as passivity, low self-esteem, and the need for social approval predict to the likelihood that evaluation apprehension will be aroused in the experimental situation? Does evaluation apprehension, once aroused, interact with experimenter bias (see Rosenthal, 1963) in a way that guides the subject in his hypothesizing about the kinds of responding that will win approval? Will exposure to psychological perspectives, as in the introductory courses from which so many subjects are drawn, tend to heighten the likelihood of experiencing evaluation apprehension in the experimental situation? Is there a minority of subjects who seek *negative* evaluation for masochistic purposes or as a way of asking for help, and will this affect their experimental responding? Can the presence of evaluation apprehension be uncovered by postexperimental inquiry? Comparable questions about the arousal of aggressive and other contaminating affective states could just as readily be formulated. Indeed it would seem desirable in further studies to attempt an operational separation of the two types of contamination that have been stressed in this paper.

In general the recently developed interest in investigating the experimenter-subject interaction as a source of bias in psychological research is a long needed innovation. The work of Orne (1962), Riecken (1962), Rosenthal (1963) and others has provided a most useful beginning. To the list of research contaminating processes that they have investigated, might well be added those that have been discussed here.

As regards the second major focus of this paper, do the present findings call the validity of dissonance theory into question? Recently there have been reported many challenging studies testing that theory's pertinence not only to attitude change but also to perceptual and motivational processes and even to learning phenomena.[8] Thus the present study, taken alone, cannot be interpreted as challenging the general theory as such. However, it does seem to indicate that, at least in its account of the attitude-change consequences of counterattitudinal advocacy, dissonance theory has been overextended.

[8] For example, and despite the fact that the author has found it possible to reinterpret one of the experiments reported by them, the work of Brehm and Cohen (1962) does seem to establish the relevance of the dissonance approach to the study of certain aspects of motivation and does so with considerable inventiveness and concern for methodological issues. Similarly the work of Lawrence and Festinger (1962) has opened a very interesting new line of inquiry on some problems in the psychology of learning.

In the author's view the kind of counter-attitudinal performance that best fits the dissonance paradigm is a simple overt act that directly violates one's private attitude (for example, eating or agreeing to eat a disliked food; expressing approval of a disliked proposal or candidate; merely *committing* oneself to develop counterattitudinal arguments; etc.). But when a person actually *does* elaborate a set of arguments opposite to his own attitude the dissonance he experiences is probably of much wider scope than dissonance analysis would have it; it encompasses considerably more than merely realizing that he has argued against his own position. The broader pattern of inconsistency that he encounters is that between the content and apparent plausibility, on the one hand, of the new arguments that he has developed and, on the other hand, his original affective judgment of the attitude object.

Thus the subject who opposes the Rose Bowl ban and then argues in favor of it may come up with some good arguments (for example, "If we ban going to the Rose Bowl we will improve our reputation as a serious University . . . we will draw better students," etc.). In so doing he may become convinced of the validity of those arguments. This will produce intraattitudinal inconsistency; that is, the newly established beliefs relating the Rose Bowl ban to positive ends and values will be inconsistent with the original negative affect toward the ban.

As was suggested earlier, the author's theoretical model (Rosenberg, 1956, 1960) takes this sort of inconsistency to be a basic condition for the occurrence of attitude change. It will be useful to show how this alternative model may be applied to interpreting the process of counterattitudinal advocacy. From this standpoint attitudes normally are stable, affective-cognitive structures and feature considerable internal consistency. It is assumed that the production of *inconsistency* through change in either the affective or cognitive component (the latter being more usual and likely) will, if it transcends the individual's tolerance limits, motivate further symbolic activity. This may lead either to the restoration of the original attitude or, if this line of defense is not available, to its reorganization in the opposite direction.

For the sequence that begins with cognitive alterations what is required is that the new cognitions be sufficiently internalized and difficult to reverse; then the most likely outcome will be for the affective disposition toward the attitude object to move in the direction consistent with the newly established cognitions. Thus attitude change in its conventional sense will have occurred.

In this context a basic question is: what will render the new, inconsistency-generating cognitions sufficiently internalized and difficult to reverse? Many variables could have this influence; but in the present study the necessary suggestion would be that the most important is the amount of reward expected and received for *developing* such cognitions. Putting this another way it may be hypothesized that the demonstrated influence of the magnitude of payment upon ultimate attitude change is mediated through its effects upon the cognitive processes that are activated during the essay-writing task.

Broadly speaking, two separate kinds of mediation are easily conceivable: the *expectation* of payment for counterattitudinal advocacy may operate as an incentive and thus affect the quality of the arguments advanced in support of the new cognitions; the *receipt* of payment may operate as a reinforcement that further fosters the internalization of the counterattitudinal cognitions; and of course the scope of these two processes would be expected to vary as a function of the actual amount of payment.

A subsidiary analysis of the essays themselves tends to support and clarify this view. One unequivocal finding is that the $.50 and $1 groups differ in the actual number of words per essay, the latter group writing the longer ones ($p < .05$).[9] However, the $1 and $5 groups do not show any such difference. Considering that the $.50 and $1 groups do not differ on the Rose Bowl issue while the

[9] All probability estimates reported in this discussion are based on a one-tailed interpretation of the Mann-Whitney statistic; in each case it was possible to make a unidirectional prediction about the attitude-change effects of the mediational variable under study.

$1 and $5 groups do, sheer verbal productivity does not seem to mediate the main effect. Furthermore, separate analyses within each of the three experimental groups reveal absolutely no relationship between essay length and the postessay attitude toward the Rose Bowl ban.

But do the essays vary in quality, in the actual *persuasiveness* with which they are written; and if so does this relate to the postessay attitude score? Two judges, working without knowledge of the different reward conditions and using a 5-point scale, rated all the essays for their basic persuasiveness. As part of their instructions they were asked to ignore the length of essays "because a long one may often be less persuasive than a short one." The interjudge reliability of these ratings proved quite adequate: for 80% of the essays the two ratings were either identical or within 1 point of each other.

Six of the 20 subjects in the combined $.50 and $1 group had persuasiveness scores that were lower (1 and 1.5, based on the pooled ratings of the two judges) than any that occurred in the $5 group. Four of these 6 subjects also had extreme negative attitudes. A comparable finding is obtained when we split the $.50–$1 group into approximately equal low persuasiveness and high persuasiveness halves. Those who wrote comparatively unpersuasive essays show significantly more attitudinal negativism toward the Rose Bowl ban than those who wrote comparatively persuasive essays ($p < .03$). When the same sort of analysis is separately performed with the $.50 and $1 groups, respectively, similar findings are obtained with borderline significance ($p < .10$ in both, instances). On the other hand within the high-reward group a division of the subjects into those who got the five lowest (though not as low as the comparable subjects in the low-reward group) and the five highest persuasiveness ratings does not yield any corresponding difference in attitudes toward the Rose Bowl ban.

An exactly similar finding is obtained when we use as the estimate of persuasiveness not the judges' ratings but the subjects' own postexperimental judgments of "how strong" their essays actually were. In the combined low-reward group those below the median in

their self-ratings are less favorable to the Rose Bowl ban than those above the median ($p < .05$). Again no such effect is discovered in the high-reward group.

From these findings it may be concluded that one mediating source of the overall difference between the low- and high-reward groups is that some of the subjects in the former group were insufficiently motivated by the small reward that had been promised them: in consequence they wrote insufficiently developed essays, essays that were essentially unpersuasive to themselves. Thus it would seem appropriate to conclude that the overall positive relationship between reward and attitude change reflects the operation of an incentive or effort variable.

However, our analysis need not stop at this point. While some low-reward subjects wrote essays that are rated as extremely low on persuasiveness others did not. Thus it is possible to match the low- and high-reward groups on this factor and by so doing we can test for the presence of some other process that may also play a role in mediating the overall relationship between reward and attitude change. This was done by simply excluding from the analysis those low-reward subjects who got extremely low ratings (1 and 1.5) on the 5-point persuasiveness scale. With persuasiveness thus equalized (actually the mean persuasiveness score is then slightly *higher* for the remaining low-reward subjects than for the high-reward subjects) the high-reward group *still* shows significantly greater acceptance of the Rose Bowl ban ($p < .05$) and also of the proposal that athletic scholarships be abandoned ($p < .05$). These last findings do thus seem to confirm the expectation that, in addition to the incentive effect of variations in promised reward, there is yet another factor that contributes to the positive relationship between reward and attitude change. It would seem reasonable to interpret this other factor as based not upon the *promise* of reward but rather upon its *receipt;* thus our original conjecture that a reinforcement dynamic may be operative seems, on these grounds, to be rendered more plausible.

The use here of the term reinforcement should not, of course, be taken as referring solely to the kinds of relationships emphasized in conventional models of instrumental learning. In the present study the $5 payment, once received, could have increased the habit strength of the improvised counter-attitudinal cognitions by directly increasing their attractiveness and credibility. Similarly, working for an expected large reward could have made the essay-writing a more ego-involving task and thus could have sensitized the subject to pay closer attention to the persuasive worth of his own arguments or to find greater merit in them. Furthermore, the amount of payment may also have affected the very clarity with which the new counterattitudinal arguments were remembered after the essay writing session.

In this discussion we have attempted to state, and also to present some additional data in support of, a consistency theory view of how counterattitudinal advocacy produces attitude change. That view can be summarized in the following set of propositions: the counterattitudinal improvisation establishes new cognitions that are inconsistent with the original attitudinal affect; the extent to which the affective judgment of the object will move toward the content of these new cognitions will depend upon the degree of affective-cognitive inconsistency they generate; this in turn will depend upon the strength and stability of the new cognitions; the strength and stability of the new cogninations are influenced, among other things, by the degree of reward received for their improvisation—and this is probably due both to the promised reward operating as an incentive and the received reward as a reinforcement; in consequence when counterattitudinal advocacy is investigated in a way that circumvents certain biasing factors it will be found, as in the present study, that it produces attitude change in proportion to the magnitude of the reward for such advocacy.

Turning again to dissonance theory and shifting from its approach to one type of attitude change to its approach toward attitude change *generally*, the author would venture the judgment that dissonance research in this area has been complicated by certain difficult methodological and interpretive issues. Thus, as Chapanis and Chapanis (1964) have noted, it is common to many of these studies that they do not investigate the subject's personal reactions to the dissonance-arousing situation, that the magnitudes of attitude change are often quite small and that often a rather large number of subjects is, for one or another theory-based reason, eliminated from analysis. To this must be added the present demonstration that, in experiments on counterattitudinal advocacy, certain data-biasing processes may be invoked to account for reported findings. Indeed, since dissonance studies on other types of attitude change also place some, but not other, subjects in highly puzzling and unexpected situations it should be recognized that in these studies as well biased contamination may often affect the results obtained. In the light of all these points it would seem desirable to undertake an empirical reexamination of some of the major studies that have been offered as confirming the dissonance analysis of attitude change. In the opinion of the present author the consequence of such reexamination would not be the disconfirmation of the dissonance view of attitude processes but the discovery that its generality is of somewhat smaller scope than its advocates have estimated and that certain kinds of attitude change are better predicted and accounted for by other theories.

REFERENCES

BREHM, J. W. A dissonance analysis of attitude-discrepant behavior. In M. J. Rosenberg, C. I. Hovland, W. J. McGuire, R. P. Abelson, & J. W. Brehm, *Attitude organization and change.* New Haven: Yale Univer. Press, 1960. Pp. 164–197.

BREHM, J. W., & COHEN, A. R. *Explorations in cognitive dissonance.* New York: Wiley, 1962.

CARLSON, E. R. Attitude change and attitude structure. *Journal of Abnormal and Social Psychology,* 1956, **52,** 256–261.

CHAPANIS, NATALIA P., & CHAPANIS, A. C. Cognitive dissonance: Five years later. *Psychological Bulletin,* 1964, **61,** 1–22.

COHEN, A. R., BREHM, J. W., & FLEMING, W. H. Attitude change and justification for compliance. *Journal of Abnormal and Social Psychology,* 1958, **56,** 276–278.

CROWNE, D. P., & MARLOWE, D. A new scale of social desirability independent of psychopathology. *Journal of Consulting Psychology,* 1960, **24,** 349–354.

CULBERTSON, F. M. Modification of an emotionally held attitude through role playing. *Journal of Abnormal and Social Psychology,* 1957, **54**, 230–233.

EDWARDS, A. L. *The social desirability variable in personality assessment and research.* New York: Dryden Press, 1957.

FESTINGER, L., & CARLSMITH, J. M. Cognitive consequences of forced compliance. *Journal of Abnormal and Social Psychology,* 1959, **58**, 203–210.

JANIS, I. L., & KING, B. T. The influence of role playing on opinion change. *Journal of Abnormal and Social Psychology,* 1954, **49**, 211–218.

KELMAN, H. C. Attitude change as a function of response restriction. *Human Relations,* 1953, **6**, 185–214.

LAWRENCE, D. H., & FESTINGER, L. *Deterrents and reinforcement: The psychology of insufficient reward.* Stanford: Stanford Univer. Press, 1962.

LEWIN, K. *Dynamic theory of personality.* New York: McGraw-Hill, 1935.

MOSTELLER, F., & BUSH, R. R. Selected quantitative techniques. In G. Lindzey (Ed.), *Handbook of social psychology.* Vol. 1. *Theory and method.* Cambridge, Mass.: Addison-Wesley, 1954. Pp. 289–334.

ORNE, M. T. On the social psychology of the psychological experiment: With particular reference to demand characteristics and their implications. *American Psychologist,* 1962, **17**, 776–783.

RIECKEN, H. W. A program for research on experiments in social psychology. In N. F. Washburne

(Ed.), *Decisions, values and groups.* Vol. 2. New York: Pergamon Press, 1962. Pp. 25–41.

ROSENBERG, M. J. Cognitive structure and attitudinal affect. *Journal of Abnormal and Social Psychology,* 1956, **53**, 367–372.

ROSENBERG, M. J. An analysis of affective-cognitive consistency. In M. J. Rosenberg, C. I. Hovland, W. J. McGuire, R. P. Abelson, & J. W. Brehm, *Attitude organization and change.* New Haven: Yale Univer. Press, 1960. Pp. 15–64.

ROSENBERG, M. J. A research program on consistency and change in social attitudes. Columbus: Ohio State University, 1961. (Mimeo)

ROSENBERG, M. J. Simulated man and the humanistic criticism. In S. S. Tomkins & S. J. Messick (Eds.), *Computer simulation of personality.* New York: Wiley, 1963. Pp. 113–124.

ROSENTHAL, R. On the social psychology of the psychological experiment: The experimenter's hypothesis as unintended determinant of experimental results. *American Scientist,* 1963, **51**, 268–283.

SCOTT, W. A. Attitude change through reward of verbal behavior. *Journal of Abnormal and Social Psychology,* 1957, **55**, 72–75.

SCOTT, W. A. Attitude change by response reinforcement: Replication and extension. *Sociometry,* 1959, **22**, 328–335.

THOMAS, W. I., & ZNANIECKI, F. *The Polish peasant in Europe and America.* Boston: Badger, 1918. 5 vols.

Reprinted from Journal of Personality and Social Psychology, 1966, Vol. 4, No. 1, pp. 1–13, by permission of Barry E. Collins and APA.

STUDIES IN FORCED COMPLIANCE:

I. THE EFFECT OF PRESSURE FOR COMPLIANCE ON ATTITUDE CHANGE PRODUCED BY FACE-TO-FACE ROLE PLAYING AND ANONYMOUS ESSAY WRITING [1]

J. MERRILL CARLSMITH, BARRY E. COLLINS, AND ROBERT L. HELMREICH

$\frac{1}{3}$ of the experimental Ss (male high school students) were enticed to tell the next S (a female accomplice) that the experimental task was interesting, exciting, fun, and enjoyable (when, in fact, it was quite dull). The other $\frac{1}{3}$ of the experimental Ss wrote an anonymous essay to the same effect. Experimental Ss were paid an additional $.50, $1.50, or $5 for this counterattitudinal response. Control Ss merely worked on the experimental task and completed the posttest. The data from the face-to-face condition replicates the original Festinger and Carlsmith experiment; small amounts of money were most effective in convincing Ss that the task was really fun and interesting. Data from the essay condition, however, indicated just the opposite. Large amounts of money produce the most attitude change.

An encouragingly large body of literature has appeared in recent years which suggests that inducing a person to adopt a counterattitudinal position causes him to change his attitude in the direction of the position adopted. Unfortunately, there is a growing disagreement concerning the relationship between the size of the incentive which is used to induce the person to adopt a counterattitudinal position and the amount of attitude change. The empirical question is straightforward: Does increasing the amount of incentive offered to a person to engage in counterattitudinal role playing *increase* or *decrease* the amount of attitude change which results from that role playing? Theoretically, there are two opposing predictions which correspond to each of the opposite empirical results.

Dissonance-Theory Prediction

Dissonance theory (Festinger, 1957) predicts that the greater the inducement offered

to the subject to adopt a position with which he does not agree, the less the resultant attitude change. The reasoning behind this prediction is spelled out in some detail by Festinger (Ch. 4) and by Festinger and Carlsmith (1959, pp. 203–204). Briefly, the argument goes as follows: The two cognitions "I believe X" and "I am publicly stating that I believe not X" are dissonant. However, all pressures, threats, and rewards which induce one to state that he believes "not X" are consonant with the cognition "I am publicly stating that I believe not X." Consequently, the greater the pressures, threats, or rewards, the more consonant cognitions the individual holds, and the lower the magnitude of the dissonance. Since one primary means of dissonance reduction in this situation is to change one's attitude in the direction "not X," it follows that the larger the reward for stating "not X," the *less* the resultant attitude change in that direction should be.

Incentive or Reinforcement Theory Prediction

On the other hand, various forms of "incentive theory" (Janis & Gilmore, 1965), "consistency theory" (Rosenberg, 1965), or "reinforcement theory" argue that the greater the incentives for the counterattitudinal role playing, the greater should be the resultant attitude change. Thus, advocates of this position state:

[1] This research was supported by funds from National Science Foundation Grant NSF GS 492 to Yale University. The data were collected while J. Merrill Carlsmith was supported by funds from the Office of Naval Research, Contract 4269 (00). Thanks are extended to Juliet Vogel and Katherine Flynn who gave invaluable assistance during data collection.

1

... the significance of a reward received for writing a counterattitudinal essay ... would be different from that claimed in dissonance theory: such a reward would, in proportion to its magnitude, be likely to have a positive effect both upon the development and the stabilization of the new cognitions. From this it would be predicted that with the removal of the biasing factors the degree of attitude change obtained after the subjects have written counterattitudinal essays will vary directly, rather than inversely, with the amount of reward [Rosenberg, 1965, p. 33].

... two separate kinds of mediation are ... conceivable: the *expectation* of payment for counterattitudinal advocacy may operate as an incentive and thus affect the quality of the arguments advanced in support of new cognitions; the *receipt* of payment may operate as a reinforcement that further fosters the internalization of the counterattitudinal cognitions ... [Rosenberg, 1965, p. 39].

[Janis and Gilmore, 1965, make a similar argument:] According to this "incentive" theory, when a person accepts the task of improvising arguments in favor of a point of view at variance with his own personal convictions, he becomes temporarily motivated to think up all the good positive arguments he can, and at the same time suppresses thoughts about the negative arguments which are supposedly irrelevant to the assigned task. This "biased scanning" increases the salience of the positive arguments and therefore increases the chances of acceptance of the new attitude position [pp. 17–18].

Empirical Controversy

Let us briefly review some of the experiments which have dealt with this question. The first such experiment was conducted by Kelman (1953), who asked seventh-grade students to write essays favoring one or another kind of comic book. Different subjects were offered different amounts of incentive to adopt the opposite position of the one they actually held. He found that, among subjects who complied with the request, there was more attitude change among those who were offered a low incentive than among those who were offered a high incentive. Although such a finding is in line with the prediction made by dissonance theory, the fact that many fewer subjects complied with the request in the low-incentive group than in the high-incentive group leaves open the possibility that self-selection may have affected the results. Also, since incentives were offered for compliance and for noncompliance, it is not always

easy to identify the "high-incentive" conditions.

In order to check on this possibility, Festinger and Carlsmith (1959) carried out an experiment where the subject was offered varying amounts of money to publicly adopt a counterattitudinal position. Specifically, the subjects were requested to tell a waiting girl (actually a confederate) that an experiment that they had just participated in was interesting and exciting. (In fact, the experiment had been dull and boring.) Subjects were told that the experimenter's assistant, who usually performed this role, had, unexpectedly, failed to show up, and subjects were offered either $1 or $20 to perform this task, and to be on call for a possible similar task in the future. Festinger and Carlsmith found that subjects who had been paid only $1 changed their attitudes more in the direction of the position they had publicly advocated than did $20 subjects.

Although this finding provides good support for the dissonance-theory prediction, several criticisms have been directed toward the experiment. Most of these criticisms argue that the $20 inducement was inordinately large, and would produce guilt, suspicion, or some other reaction which would interfere with the attitude change. To counter this criticism, Cohen (Brehm & Cohen, 1962) carried out a similar experiment using smaller amounts of money. In this experiment, subjects were approached in their rooms by a fellow student who asked them to write an essay in favor of the actions of the New Haven police. (Most students privately disagreed with this position.) Subjects were offered either $.50, $1, $5, or $10 for writing such an essay. After writing the essays the subjects' attitudes toward the police actions were assessed. Cohen's results fit closely with the dissonance-theory predictions; there was decreasing attitude change with increasing amounts of incentive for performing the counterattitudinal behavior. Taken together, the Festinger and Carlsmith and Cohen experiments support the empirical generality of the negative relationship between incentive and attitude change predicted by dissonance theory.

Several more recent experiments, however,

have cast some doubt on the generality of the dissonance-theory interpretation of these results. In the first of these experiments (Janis & Gilmore, 1965) subjects were asked to write an essay which argued that all college students should be required to take an extra year of mathematics and of physics. In an attempt to show that the results obtained by Festinger and Carlsmith were due to the use of an "extraordinarily large reward of $20 [which] might have unintentionally generated some degree of suspicion or wariness," they repeated the use of $1 and $20 as rewards. They also added a variation in the sponsor of the project. In one case, the sponsor was described as a new publishing company, in the other as a research organization on the behalf of a number of universities. Unfortunately, they made two major changes in the offering of money, which prevents a direct comparison with the Festinger and Carlsmith experiment. Rather than offering subjects the money as payment *and* as a retainer for possible future work, they made no mention of any possible future work. In addition, whereas in the Festinger and Carlsmith study the money was offered for performing a task for which a sudden, unexpected, and pressing need had arisen, Janis and Gilmore offered this money for a task which was being done by several people, and which many other people might have done just as well. These two factors may have contributed to the fact that Janis and Gilmore report that their subjects perceived the money as a surprising and inappropriate payment.

Janis and Gilmore found that—with their technique of presentation—variations in monetary reward produced no differences in attitude change. Whether this failure to replicate is due to these changed techniques of presentation or due to suspicion and negative feelings is an empirical question.

The one finding that Janis and Gilmore do report is an interaction between role playing and sponsorship conditions. In the role-playing conditions, the public welfare sponsorship produced significantly more attitude change than did the commercial sponsorship; in the control conditions, there was no significant difference. Unfortunately, the role-playing subjects differed from the control subjects not only by virtue of the fact that they wrote an essay against their position, but also because they were given a few "general questions," for example, "Considering the type of career you are likely to be in, how might a background in physics and math enable you to function more adequately?" Such questions might well serve as a persuasive communication, and the difference between the sponsorship conditions would then be attributable to prestige or "demand" effects of the more positive sponsor.

The finding from Janis and Gilmore which is of major interest for our purposes here is the failure to find an effect of incentive on attitude change where the large incentive was designed especially to arouse suspicion. In a more recent experiment, Elms and Janis (1965) were able to detect some effects of incentive under similar circumstances—effects which tended to go in the opposite direction from that predicted by dissonance theory. Varying amount of incentive, nature of sponsorship, and presence or absence of role playing in a $3 \times 2 \times 2$ factorial, Elms and Janis asked subjects to write an anonymous essay advocating that qualified United States students should be sent to study in Russia for 4 years. The alleged sponsor of the research program was a private firm hired by the Soviet Embassy in one condition (negative sponsorship), while in the other condition the firm had been hired by the United States State Department (positive sponsorship). Subjects were paid either $.50, $1.50, or $5 to write an essay counter to their position. Only 1 of the 10 experimental groups showed significant attitude change. This was the group paid $10 under favorable sponsorship conditions. This group showed more attitude change than those subjects paid $.50. (However, the relationship is not linear. These $.50 subjects showed more—although not significantly—change than those subjects paid $1.50.) Under unfavorable sponsorship conditions, there were no significant effects. The $.50-$10 comparison for favorable sponsorship is the opposite of that predicted by dissonance theory, and is interpreted by Elms and Janis as being in support of "incentive theory."

Stronger evidence for increasing attitude change with increasing incentive is reported by Rosenberg (1965). His study, which is similar to Cohen's (Brehm & Cohen, 1962) study, asked subjects to write essays advocating that the Ohio State football team be banned from playing in the Rose Bowl (a strongly counterattitudinal position). Rosenberg changed Cohen's procedure by separating the "compliance inducer" from the posttester. The person who asked the subject to write the essay was not the same person as the experimenter who gathered the information on the subject's attitudes following the manipulation. In addition to a control condition, in which subjects wrote no counterattitudinal essay, there were three levels of reward for writing the essay—$.50, $1, and $5. The results of the experiment were exactly the opposite of Cohen's—the group paid $5 changed their attitudes much more than did the groups paid $.50 or $1, who in turn changed more than the control condition.

Unfortunately, the interpretation of these results must remain equivocal. As Nuttin (1964) points out:

Rosenberg's study is, like most replications, not a "duplicate" of Cohen's study, but a very complex chain of interactions which are functionally more or less equivalent or similar to the ones Cohen investigated. Not only the attitude object itself but also the social status of the E and the experimental situation as a whole were quite different in both studies . . . . Notwithstanding this, Rosenberg interprets his discrepant findings as due to *his* definition of the difference between the two experiments [pp. 4ff. for other critical discussion of Rosenberg's study].

The most recent study of this problem is a large experiment by Nuttin (1964), for which only preliminary results are available. Nuttin ran 20 experimental conditions in which he essentially attempted to replicate both studies, adding what he felt had been missing control groups in Rosenberg's study. The most clearcut results he reports are on his replication of the Rosenberg study, where he finds exactly the opposite of what Rosenberg found. Thus, even when some degree of "perceptual separation" is maintained, Nuttin finds identical results to those of Cohen—the larger the incentive, the less the attitude change. However, Nuttin was unable to replicate the Festinger and Carlsmith results.

Since most of the criticisms which are applied to one individual study do not apply to the others, the meaning of all studies, in concert, is not clear. At the very least, these data suggest that the original formulation of the attitude-change process by Festinger and Carlsmith was incomplete. At the most, they suggest that the dissonance results were due to trivial artifacts. Because of the many differences in procedure among these various studies, it would be worthwhile to study differences in procedure which might have produced different results.

There are, of course, many differences, but let us turn our attention to just one. Contrast the Festinger and Carlsmith experiment with, say, that of Elms and Janis. In the study by Festinger and Carlsmith, the subject is asked to make a public statement (at least in front of one other person) which conflicts with his private belief. Furthermore, the person to whom he is making this statement is *unaware* that this is in fact in conflict with the private belief. Such a situation is certainly one in which dissonance would be aroused.

Consider on the other hand the position of the subject in the Elms and Janis experiment. He is being asked to write an essay in favor of a position which he does not agree with. He is assured that his essay wil be kept anonymous—no one will ever know that he wrote it except the experimenter. And the experimenter —the only person to read the essay—knows full well that the essay does *not* express the subject's private opinion. The experimenter, in essence, is asking him whether he has the intellectual ability to see some arguments on the opposite side of the issue from that which he holds. It can be argued that writing such an essay will create no dissonance. Stated in an extreme form, the question is whether the cognition "I am, for good *reasons*, listing some arguments in favor of the position 'not-X' is dissonant with the cognition 'I believe X.'" It is plausible that, especially among college students, the cognition that one is listing such arguments is not at all dissonant with the cognition that one believes the opposite. Rather, the ability intellectually to adopt such a position is the hallmark of the open-minded and intellectual.

The argument in the paragraph above is

not altogether different from the emphasis which Brehm and Cohen (1962) have placed on the role of commitment in the arousal of dissonance. A person who is merely writing arguments in favor of a position, but who has not committed himself to that position, would not experience dissonance *about the fact that he was writing arguments.* This is not to say that there may not be dissonance of some other kind, or that there may not be other nondissonance processes operating to produce attitude change as a result of writing these arguments. For example, insofar as the arguments he produces are good ones, there is dissonance aroused between the cognition— "This good argument in favor of not X exists" and the cognition "I believe X." This dissonance-theory process sounds quite similar to the incentive-theory process which Janis and Gilmore posit to explain attitude change produced by role playing. The point to be made here is that writing an anonymous essay may not produce dissonance *of the particular kind* studied by Festinger and Carlsmith, and that the predictions from dissonance theory about incentive effects may not be relevant in such situations.

In order to test this post hoc explanation, we attempted to design an experiment which would demonstrate that the results reported by Festinger and Carlsmith could be repeated under appropriate conditions, whereas the opposite kind of results might be expected under different conditions.

One further difference between experiments which have obtained results consistent with the dissonance-theory predictions and those experiments which have not has been the theoretical predilection of the experimenters. With the exception of the work of Nuttin, the results in line with dissonance-theory predictions have been obtained by experimenters who were to some extent identified with dissonance theory and who might be expected to "hope for" results consistent with dissonance theory. The converse has been true of experimenters who have obtained results inconsistent with dissonance theory. In light of the increasing interest in subtle effects of so-called "experimenter bias" (Rosenthal, 1963) we carried out the present experiment using two experimenters of different theo-

retical backgrounds. One of the experimenters (JMC) was presumably identified with a dissonance-theory approach; the other (BEC) was somewhat identified with a more behavioristic or reinforcement theory approach.

The basic design of the experiment to be reported here is a $2 \times 2 \times 4$ factorial. Subjects were asked to adopt a counterattitudinal position in two very different ways. Half of the subjects were asked to lie to a confederate in a face-to-face confrontation. They were asked to tell a confederate that a decidedly dull task was, in fact, interesting—a manipulation essentially identical to that of Festinger and Carlsmith. The other half of the subjects were asked to write an anonymous essay in favor of the same position—an essay which would ostensibly be used to help the experimenter prepare another description which would then be presented to future subjects. Half of the subjects were run by each experimenter. Finally, experimental subjects were paid one of three different amounts of money for performing the task, while a control group was paid no additional money and performed no counterattitudinal responses.

METHOD

Subjects

An advertisement was placed in the local paper offering to pay high school age students (14–18) $2.50 for 2 hours of participation in a psychological experiment. When males called the listed number, they were given appointments for the experiment. Females were put on a "waiting list."

Two hundred and two male subjects participated in the experiment. A total of 11 subjects were eliminated from the reported results. Four subjects (2 pairs of brothers) were discarded because, in the judgment of the experimenter administering the posttest, they did not comprehend the meaning of the 11-point rating scale. Typically they expressed strong approval or disapproval and then chose a number on the opposite end of the scale. The posttester did not know which condition the subject was in, and, therefore, could not bias the results by selective elimination. Four more subjects (2 $.50 role play, 1 $1.50 role play, and 1 $.50 essay) were discarded because they did not follow through on the assigned role play or essay. Typically they admitted the task was dull and stated that they had been asked to say it was interesting. Only 1 subject showed any detectable sign of suspicion, and he was eliminated before he took the posttest. One subject accidentally saw the confederate in conversation with one of the experimenters. Finally, 1 subject, when he heard from the confederate that her friend "told her it was kind of dull," called in the experimenter and suggested that the accomplice be assigned to a control group since she knew the task was dull.

The subjects were extremely heterogeneous. They ranged from those who could barely master the complexities of an 11-point scale or could produce only 20 or 25 words of essay in 10 minutes to numerous prep-school students and children from professional families. The sample included a substantial number of Negroes.

Setting and Personnel

The study was conducted in six rooms of the Yale Psycho-Educational Clinic over a 3-week period. The five personnel conducting the experiment were the two principal investigators (BEC and JMC, who alternated as "project director" and "posttester"), a graduate assistant who served as experimenter (RLH), a receptionist, and a female high school age accomplice.

Overview of Design

The basic procedure was similar to that used by Festinger and Carlsmith (1959). Experimental subjects were asked either to write an essay or to tell a second, presumably naïve, subject that the experimental task was fun, interesting, exciting, and enjoyable. The subjects knew from their own experience with the task that it was dull and uninteresting. Subjects were paid an *additional* $5, $1.50, or $.50 to role play or write the essay. Control subjects were paid no additional money and were not asked to role play or write an essay. One-half of the subjects were run with BEC as project director and JMC as posttester, and the other half were run with the roles reversed. Attitudes toward the experimental task were then measured in a posttest-only design. The accomplice rated the several dimensions of the role-play performance, and the transcripts of the role plays and the essays were rated on a number of variables by three judges.

Procedure

All subjects. On arriving at the building, each subject was greeted by the receptionist who verified his age and high school status and conducted him to an experimental room furnished with desk, chairs, and writing materials. After the subject had waited alone for several minutes, the experimenter entered the room, introduced himself as Mr. Helmreich, and announced that he was ready to start the experiment. The experimenter then explained that the experiment itself would only take a little over an hour and that since subjects were being paid for 2 hours' participation, arrangements had been made for every subject to take part in a record survey being conducted in the building by a "man from some consumer research outfit in New York." At this point, the subject was presented with the experimental task— 20 5-page booklets of random numbers. Each booklet had a cover sheet which instructed the

subject to strike out each occurrence of two of the digits (e.g., 2s and 6s) contained in the booklet. The subject was told that he should work at a comfortable rate, correct mistakes, and continue working until stopped by the experimenter. The experimenter then explained that he would describe the purpose of the study when he stopped the subject on completion of the task. The subject was then left alone to work for an hour. The supply of booklets left with the subject was many times the number which could be completed in an hour. The task itself was designd to be so dull and repetitious that the subject would leave with a generally negative feeling.

At the end of an hour, the experimenter re-entered the room and told the subject that he could stop as the experiment was completed. The experimenter then seated himself next to the subject and said he would explain the purpose of the study. The experimenter described the project as a large-scale study designed to investigate how a person's prior expectation of the nature of a task might affect the amount and accuracy of work performed. The subject was told that the project was investigating the best ways to describe routine tasks so that people would be motivated to work hard and accurately. Each subject was told that he was in a control condition and, therefore, had been given no expectation about how pleasant the task would be. He was told that his group would serve as the standard comparison for other groups which were given positive expectations.

At this point the explanations began to differ according to the experimental condition to which the subject was assigned. Four different procedures were used: role-play control, role-play experimental, essay control, and essay experimental.

Role-play control subjects. Subjects in this condition were told that subjects in the other condition were introduced by the experimenter to a high school boy named Anderson who, presumably, had just finished the experimental task. In fact, continued the experimenter, the boy was paid by the experimenter to say the task was fun, interesting, exciting, and enjoyable. The experimenter remarked that after the paid assistant had been with a subject in the other condition 2 minutes, telling the subject how the experiment was fun, interesting, etc., the experimenter would return to the room, excuse the assistant, and start the subject on the same random-number task. The experimenter pointed out that a high school age assistant was necessary in order to make the description of the task plausible.

At this point, the experimenter asked if the subject had any questions concerning the purpose of the study. After dealing with any questions, the experimenter stated that the project director (BEC or JMC) would like to thank him. The experimenter then left the room and returned with the project director, who then gave the termination speech.

Role-play experimental subjects. In this condition, as the experimenter was finishing the same description given to role-play control subjects and asking for questions, the project director knocked on the door, entered the room, excused himself, and asked the experimenter if he knew where Anderson was. After the experimenter replied that he had not seen him, the director remarked that a subject was waiting in a condition where he was supposed to be told that the task was fun and interesting. He then asked the experimenter if he knew how to get in touch with Anderson and received a negative reply. After a pause, the director asked the experimenter if the subject with him was finished. The experimenter replied that the subject had completed the task and that he was explaining the purpose of the study. The director then remarked that perhaps the subject could help them; that, as the experimenter had no doubt explained, Anderson had been hired to tell some of the waiting subjects that the task was fun, interesting, exciting, and enjoyable. The subject was told that he could help the director out of a jam by describing the task in those terms to a girl who was waiting to start the experiment. The director said that since he was in a bind, he could pay $.50 ($1.50, $5) for doing this job. After the subject agreed (every subject agreed to undertake the task), the experimenter was sent to obtain the proper amount of money and a receipt form. While the experimenter was gone, the director rehearsed the points (fun, interesting, exciting, enjoyable) that the subject was to make to the waiting confederate. After the experimenter returned, the subject took his money, signed a receipt, and was conducted by the director to another room where the female confederate was waiting, ostensibly to start the experiment.

The director told the confederate that the subject had just finished the experiment and that he would tell her something about it. He then left, saying he would be back in a couple of minutes. The girl said little until the subject made some positive remarks about the task, then remarked that a friend of hers had taken the test and had not said much about it except that it was rather dull. Most subjects attempted to counter this evaluation, and the accomplice listened quietly accepting everything the subject said about the task. The interaction between the subject and the accomplice was recorded on a concealed tape recorder.

After 2 minutes, the director returned to the room, told the accomplice that the experimenter would be in to get her started on the experiment, and led the subject from the room. The director then gave the termination speech common to all subjects.

Essay control subjects. Procedures in this condition were the same as in the role-play control condition except that subjects were told that subjects in the other condition read a short essay describing the task positively. The experimenter stated that after reading the essay, subjects in this other group were given the same random-number task. After answering any questions concerning the purpose of the study, the experimenter brought in and introduced the project director who gave the termination speech.

Essay experimental subjects. In this condition, subjects were treated in the same manner as essay

controls until the project director was introduced. At this point the director seated himself beside the subject, stated that he had a problem and that the subject might be able to help. He remarked that, as the experimenter described, some subjects in other conditions read an essay describing the task as fun, interesting, exciting, and enjoyable. But he further commented that the experimenters were unhappy with this essay. The director felt that the essays were unsatisfactory because they did not sound like they had been written by high school students and that they did not have the perspective of someone who had taken the experiment. The experimenters had decided to write a new description of the task and felt that the best way to proceed would be to ask a few of the subjects to write positive descriptions of the task. He emphasized that no other subjects would read these essays because he would merely use them as sources of phrases and ideas for an essay which he, the director, would write. He then added that since they were "in a bind" he could pay the subject $.50 ($1.50, $5) to write a 5- or 10-minute description of the task. After the subject agreed to do so (all subjects agreed to write the essay), the experimenter was sent to obtain the proper amount of money and a receipt form. While the experimenter was gone, the director rehearsed with the subject the points he should make in the essay—that the task was fun, interesting, exciting, and enjoyable. After the experimenter returned, the subject took his money, signed a receipt, and followed the director to another office where he was given paper and pen and told to write for 5 or 10 minutes. He was to press a buzzer which would notify the director when he was finished. The subject was then left alone, and an electric timer was started in the adjoining office. The subject stopped the timer when he pressed the buzzer to signify that he had finished the essay. If the subject had not completed the essay by the end of 15 minutes, the director appeared in the room and told him that he had been working about 15 minutes and should finish up in the next couple of minutes. If still working, subjects were told to stop at the end of 17 minutes (1,000 seconds). After collecting the essay, the director gave the termination speech.

Termination speech. (Identical for all subjects.) While walking away from the experimental room, the director remarked that, as the experimenter had mentioned, a man from Consumer Research Associates had asked if he could have the subjects rate some records since the experiment did not last the full 2 hours. He stated that he did not know much about what the survey was about, but he would show the subjects where to go. As in the Festinger and Carlsmith (1959) study, the experimenter then stated, "I certainly hope you enjoyed the experiment. Most of our subjects tell us they did." He then directed the subject to the posttest room, thanked him, and made a strong request for secrecy about the experiment. It was clear to the subject that the experiment was over at this point.

Posttest. The subject then arrived at a comfortably

appointed office labeled Consumer Research Associates on the door. As the subject entered the office, he was greeted by the posttester (BEC or JMC) who introduced himself as Ted Johnson of Consumer Research Associates. Johnson then ushered the subject into the office and seated him before a desk. Next to the desk was a portable record player equipped with stereo earphones. The desk itself was littered with papers bearing Consumer Research Associates' letterhead and titled "Teen Age Market Survey—Connecticut." Johnson introduced the posttest by saying that his company was interested in the type of music teen-agers listened to and 'the types of music they liked for specific activities. He added that this was important because teen-agers bought 68% of the records sold in this country.

The subject was then asked to listen to a "practice" record for 30 seconds. Johnson then asked the subject to rate the practice record on several questions. He explained the use of an 11-point scale running from −5 to +5 using a graphic illustration of the scale. The subject rated the record as to how much he liked it generally, how much he would like to listen to it on a date, how much he would like to dance to it, and how much he would like to study by it—each rating on the 11-point scale. After the practice record, Johnson announced that they were ready to start the survey. As he started to hand the earphones to the subject he stated:

> Oh. There is one thing I forgot. As you might imagine, the kind of mood you are in and the kind of experiences you have just had might influence the ratings you give in a situation like this. [The preceding spoken slowly to give the subject opportunity to agree.] If you had a splitting headache, you would not like much of anything we played through those earphones. [Subjects usually laughed—the volume was moderately high.] So I do want to ask you a question or two about that sort of thing. I don't know much about what they are doing up there, but would you say the test they had you working on was sort of pleasant or unpleasant? [slight pause] As a matter of fact, why don't we put it in terms of the same scale we used for the records? A minus 5 would be very unpleasant and a plus 5 would be very pleasant.

Since the subject had already used the rating scale for the practice record, the other five questions were covered quickly, and the subject immediately began to listen to the first "survey record." The word "test" was used in each question to make sure that the subjects were reacting to the experimental task only, and not the total experiment.

The six questions asked in the posttest were:

1. How pleasant did you find the test?
2. Was it an interesting test?
3. Did you learn anything from the test?
4. Would you recommend the test to a friend?
5. Would you describe the test as fun?
6. What is your general overall mood at the present time?

In each case a +5 represented a highly positive reaction and a −5 a strongly negative reaction. All subjects seemed convinced about the genuineness of the posttest; several hesitated to discuss the test because the project director had cautioned them to secrecy.

RESULTS

There are 15 subjects in each of the four control groups, and 11 subjects in all but one of the 12 experimental groups. There are only 10 subjects in the $.50, BEC, essay cell. The results can be discussed in three broad categories: the six questions in the posttest, measures evaluating the quality of the role-play performance and of the essays, and experimenter effects.

Posttest Variables

The mean response for each of the six questions in the posttest is shown in Table 1. Consider first the questions dealing with words the subject actually used while role playing or essay writing—"How interesting

TABLE 1

MEANS FOR POSTTEST VARIABLES COLLAPSED OVER EXPERIMENTERS

	Control	$.50	$1.50	$5
Interesting				
RP	−1.43	1.23	−0.86	−1.18
E	−1.00	−0.86	1.32	2.41
Fun				
RP	−1.43	0.76	−0.81	−1.10
E	−1.28	−0.80	1.62	1.55
Fun plus interesting				
RP	−2.71	1.81	−1.62	−2.19
E	−2.14	−1.80	3.24	3.95
Pleasant				
RP	0.77	1.18	0.82	1.55
E	0.93	0.86	2.14	2.55
Learn anything				
RP	−0.37	−0.50	−2.00	−0.32
E	−2.27	−0.10	−0.41	−0.64
Recommend				
RP	2.53	2.50	1.59	2.27
E	2.33	2.38	2.50	3.56
Mood				
RP	1.83	2.18	2.27	3.41
E	2.83	2.19	3.32	3.36

Note.—Scores from single questions range from −5 (extremely negative toward the task) to +5 (extremely positive). Fun plus interesting can range from −10 to +10. RP = role play; E = essay.

TABLE 2

A PRIORI HYPOTHESES FOR POSTTEST VARIABLES PLUS MAIN EFFECT FOR ROLE PLAY-ESSAY

	Interest- ing	Fun	Fun plus interesting	Pleasant	Learn anything	Recom- mend	General mood
Role play, rank-order linear trend	8.1**	5.4*	7.1*	<1	<1	<1	<1
Essay, rank-order linear trend	18.1***	13.6***	19.3***	8.5***	1.6	1.6	2.0
Role play versus essay (from Table 3)	5.0*	4.0*	5.7*	2.7	<1	1.0	2.9
Percentage of between-cell variance contributed by 3 hypotheses	73	73	74	63	23	23	20

Note.—Unweighted mean solution. Error term from Experimenter $\times$ Role Play-Essay $\times$ Money analysis (Table 3).
* $p < .05$.
** $p < .01$.
*** $p < .005$.

would you say the test was?" and "How much fun would you say the test was?" Table 1 shows that both essay and role-play control subjects found that the test, or random-number task, was uninteresting ($M = -1.2$) and not much fun ($M = -1.4$).

Our major hypotheses concerned the differential effects of pressure for compliance in the role-playing and essay-writing situations. Specifically, it was anticipated that subjects who engaged in a face-to-face confrontation (role play) would show a *negative* relationship between money offered for the role playing and attitude change. Thus subjects offered $.50 to role play should show maximal change, followed by subjects offered $1.50, and then those offered $5; the control subjects should, of course, be lowest.

Subjects who had written counterattitudinal essays, on the other hand, should show exactly the opposite trend. In this case, those subjects paid $5 should be most positive to-

ward the task, followed in order by subjects paid $1.50, subjects paid $.50, and control subjects. In other words, the hypothesis anticipates a *positive* relationship between attitude change and money for subjects who wrote essays.

Figures 1 and 2 reveal two facts. First, it can be seen that subjects who adopted a counterattitudinal position, whether this was done by publicly announcing the position or by privately writing an essay adopting the position, changed their attitudes to bring them into line with the counterattitudinal position. That is, they felt that the experiment had been relatively more fun and interesting than did control subjects.

Moreover, both hypotheses are strongly confirmed. The amount of money offered to adopt this counterattitudinal position had sharply different effects for role players and essay writers. When a subject is asked to publicly adopt a position which he does not pri-

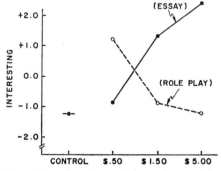

FIG. 1. Responses to posttest question on interesting. (The value drawn for the control group represents the average on all control groups.)

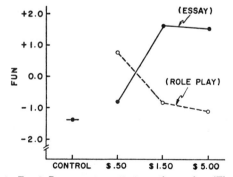

FIG. 2. Responses to posttest question on fun. (The value drawn for the control group represents the average of all control groups.)

vately believe in a face-to-face confrontation, he changes his attitude less if he is paid large amounts of money to adopt this position. Thus subjects paid $5 thought that the experiment was much less interesting and fun than did subjects paid $.50. An analysis of variance showed that the test for linear trend in the role-playing conditions was significant at the .05 level or better (see Table 2).

When a subject is asked to write a private essay which disagrees with his beliefs, however, the effect is exactly the opposite. The more the subject is paid to write this essay, the more his attitude changes in the direction of the position he is adopting. Thus, subjects paid $5 thought the experiment was more fun and interesting than did subjects paid $.50. Again an analysis of variance shows a significant linear trend in the hypothesized direction (see Table 2).

In general, essay subjects evidenced more attitude change. This finding should be interpreted with some caution, however. A glance at Figures 1 and 2 suggests that, if the study had used only $.50 incentives, it would have been the role-play subjects who evidenced the most attitude change.

As can be seen from the last line in Table 2, the two a priori hypotheses and the role play-essay main effect account for most of the between-cell variance for fun and interesting. The fact that these 3 degrees of freedom (out of a total of 15) account for so much of the variance indicates the unimportance of experimenter main effects and higher order interactions.

As Festinger and Carlsmith found, this ef-fect seems to be quite specific to the particular words used in adopting the counteratti-tudinal position. When subjects were asked how pleasant the experiment had been, or how much they had learned from it, or whether they would recommend it to a friend, there were no effects in the role-playing conditions, and only one significant effect in the essay-writing condition (see Tables 1 and 2). Only the questions asking the subjects how interesting and how much fun the experiment had been seem to show the effects of role playing which are predicted.

Subjects were also asked to rate their general mood, and on this question an interesting trend appears. Although the effect of incentive is not significant for either essay-writing or role-playing subjects taken individually, the trend is identical in both cases, so that there is a significant main effect of money. As inspection of Table 1 shows, the more subjects were paid, the better the mood they were in at the end of the experiment, irrespective of whether they were paid to write essays or to engage in face-to-face role playing. Such an effect may seem hardly surprising for the subjects who wrote essays. Essay subjects said that they were in a better mood after they had been paid $5; they also said that the experiment had been more fun and more interesting.

However, subjects who had engaged in face-to-face role playing and were paid $5 said that they were in a better mood, but thought that the experiment had been *less* fun and *less* interesting than subjects paid $.50. Thus, the results for essay-writing sub-

TABLE 3

Experimenter, Role Play-Essay, and Money Standard Analyses (2 × 2 × 4 Analysis of Variance)

Source	df	Interesting	Fun	Fun plus interesting	Pleasant	Learn anything	Recommend	Mood
Role play versus essay	1	5.05*	3.98*	5.73*	2.69	<1	1.02	2.90
Money	3	3.05*	2.90*	3.42*	2.60	<1	<1	3.17*
Interaction	3	7.04**	4.74**	7.15**	1.28	1.60	<1	<1
MS_e		9.91	9.75	31.64	5.14	15.67	10.05	4.22
df error		175	167[a]	167[a]	175	175	175	175

Note.—Since none of the experimenter main effects and none of the experimenter interactions reached the .05 level (only 1 of 28 reached the .10 level), they have been omitted from the table. The unweighted mean solution was used.
[a] The fun measure was not included in the posttest until 8 subjects (all in different cells) had been run. Consequently the N for fun and for fun plus interesting is only 183.
* p < .05.
** p < .01.

jects might be interpreted as a simple generalization: they had been paid more money, were consequently in a better mood, and consequently rated the experiment as more fun and more interesting. Such a possible effect is, of course, impossible for the role-playing subjects. The more they were paid, the better the mood they were in, but the less they thought the experiment was fun and interesting. Such a finding is especially interesting in view of the interpretation of the results of Festinger and Carlsmith offered by several writers (e.g., Elms & Janis, 1965) which focuses on the hypothesis that subjects paid $20 failed to show attitude change because they felt anxious or guilty. Insofar as this question about mood can tap some of these presumed feelings, we find that contrary to this hypothesis, the more subjects are paid for performing a task like this, the better they feel.

Role-Play and Essay Performance

Evidence on the subjects' actual performances was gathered when all three authors independently rated the essays and transcripts of the role plays. Transcriptions of role-play performance were rated on the following six scales:

1. Persuasiveness and emphasis before the accomplice remarks that she has heard the task is dull.
2. Persuasiveness and emphasis after remark.
3. Overall positiveness.
4. Overall persuasiveness and conviction.
5. Percent of time spent on assigned topic.
6. Dissociation of self from content of message.

Ratings by the acomplice are also available on role-play subjects for the first four scales and for:

5. Apparent conflict.
6. Signs of discomfort.

Essays were rated on the following four scales:

1. Emphasis used in making points.
2. The extent to which the subject went beyond the statements given and created reasons in support of his general theme.
3. Overall quality and persuasiveness.
4. Apparent effort (with an attempt to control for ability).

It was anticipated that, if any differences were found at all, high incentives should improve the quality of both role-play and essay performance. (Control groups were, of course, omitted from all analyses, and separate analyses were performed for essay and role-play measures.) The interjudge reliabilities were typically in the 70s and 80s, and the various performance measures were highly correlated among themselves. None of these ratings of role-play transcripts showed even a .10 trend in any analysis of variance. Similarly, evaluations of the content of the essays show no glimmer of a difference among treatment groups. Also, there is no evidence that any of the measures of role-play or essay performance were correlated with posttest attitudes. According to the ratings made by the accomplice, role-play subjects showed highest conflict when they were paid only $.50 (the $F = 5.58, p < .01$, for the 2×3 Experimenter $\times$ Money analysis of variance). But this is the only "quality of performance" accomplice rating which shows any sign of a money effect.

Experimenter Effects

The results from the two experimenters are remarkably similar. The Fs for experimenter main effects and experimenter interactions are, in general, smaller than might be expected by chance. There are two variables, however, which produced significant experimenter effects: the accomplice's ratings of conflict (necessarily for role-play subjects only since it is an accomplice rating) and the "number of words used once" measure. According to the accomplice's ratings of conflict, subjects run by BEC indicated more conflict than those run by JMC ($p < .05$). Since the role play occurred before the subject met the post-tester, we can safely assume the effect was created in the experimental manipulations and not in the posttest. Posttest attitudes show no parallel trend.

Subjects were told to use four words: interesting, exciting, enjoyable, and fun. Each role play and essay was scored for the number of these words which were used at least once. Both role-play ($p < .05$) and essay ($p < .01$) subjects run by BEC used more words than subjects run by JMC in both conditions. This effect is easily understood in terms of the heavier emphasis placed on the four words by BEC. In contrast to JMC, he asked the subjects to repeat the words back to him after he had stated them to the subjects. For the *role-play subjects only*, subjects run by JMC tended to use more words in high-incentive conditions, while BEC's subjects show no such trend (interaction $p < .05$). The attitude data show no patterns similar to any of those revealed by the number of words measure.

Discussion

As can be seen in Figures 1 and 2, the major hypotheses from the study have been dramatically confirmed. There is one set of circumstances where increasing pressure for compliance leads to smaller amounts of attitude change. A subject who was enticed to make a patently false statement before a peer who believed the subject was sincere showed less attitude change with increased pressure for compliance. Figures 1 and 2 clearly indicate that the comparison between the $.50 group and the $1.50 group is the more crucial for role-play subjects. The highly significant difference between these two relatively small rewards represents a very strong replication of the original Festinger and Carlsmith study. These results, taken in conjunction with those of Cohen (Brehm & Cohen, 1962), make it highly unlikely that the original Festinger and Carlsmith result is an artifact of the unusual magnitude of the $20 reward.

It is equally clear, however, that there is another set of circumstances in which increasing pressure for compliance produces more attitude change. A subject who wrote an anonymous essay (to be read only by the experimenter) showed more attitude change with increasing pressure for compliance. This dramatic interaction is quite consistent with the theory outlined in the introduction.

The results for the experimenter manipulation are also encouraging. The two experimenters produced remarkably similar effects. It is clearly the case that the differing theoretical orientations of the experimenters—and their somewhat different expectations about the outcomes—had no effect whatsoever on attitude change.

What remains unspecified, however, is the

crucial difference between the role-play and essay-writing conditions. The following list describes just a few of the many components in the complex manipulation used in this study: The essays were written while the role plays were oral; the role-play sessions lasted for a maximum of 2 minutes while the essay sessions lasted for a maximum of 17 minutes; as a result of the differing justifications used to entice compliance, role-play subjects performed under somewhat more "hectic" or "crisis" circumstances than essay subjects; finally, if looked at from the subjects' perspective, the social consequences or implications of the compliant act differed greatly between the two conditions. In the essay condition, the only reader of the essays would be the experimenter, who understood why the essay had been written. In the role-play condition, however, the audience—the experimental accomplice—presumably believed that the subject was sincere when he said that the task was fun, interesting, exciting, and enjoyable. It seems quite clear that the latter condition is more dissonance producing.

What is unclear from dissonance theory, however, is why the essay condition should show an *increasing* amount of attitude change with increased incentive. If there is no dissonance at all produced in the essay condition, then the different incentives should have no effect on attitude change—there should, in fact, be no attitude change. If the amount of effort is greater for high-incentive subjects, then dissonance theory can predict a positive relationship between the amount of incentive and attitude change. *If* subjects in the high-incentive conditions exerted more effort, then this greater effort should lead to greater dissonance in the high-incentive conditions, and, consequently, greater attitude change. A long and careful examination of both essays and role-play performance, however, unearthed no evidence whatsoever that the high-incentive essays were in any way superior. The fact that the finished product in the high-incentive condition is not better, of course, does not imply that the students did not try harder. Subjects were given four words to repeat, and there was little else that they could do other than repeat the four words and include them in complete sentences. It is possible that an increased effort in the high-incentive condition would not be reflected in higher quality essays.

It is probably necessary to turn somewhere other than dissonance theory for an explanation of the positive relationship between pressure for compliance and attitude change. One very plausible explanation of our results for the essay-writing subjects is a simple generalization phenomenon. We know that the more subjects were paid the better the mood they were in. It would not be surprising if this good mood generalized to the task they had been doing, so that they would report that the task had been more fun and interesting. This explanation would assume that in the role-playing conditions, this tendency to generalize was overcome by the dissonance produced.

Alternatively, it is possible that the theoretical orientation proposed by Hovland (Hovland, Lumsdaine, & Sheffield, 1949) and Janis (Janis & Gilmore, 1965) is needed in order to explain the attitude change in the essay condition. But, as we understand them, these theories also must predict that the performance in the high-incentive condition will be superior in some way to the performance in low-pressure conditions. Nor do they make clear why the opposite effect should be found in the role-play conditions.

One final point should be made about the sensitivity of the incentive manipulation. A quick glance at Figures 1 and 2 indicates that the results would have appeared quite different had the $.50 group been omitted. There would have been no incentive effects for either essay or role-play subjects, and there would have remained only the main effect indicating that essay subjects showed more attitude change than role-play subjects.

Finally, it should be noted that our results for the role-playing subjects are consistent with several other experiments using different techniques for varying pressure for compliance. Studies on the use of strong or weak threats to induce counterattitudinal behavior (Aronson & Carlsmith, 1963; Freedman, 1965; Turner & Wright, 1965) have con-

sistently shown more attitude change when weaker pressures are applied for compliance. Another kind of evidence comes from experiments by Freedman (1963) in which he shows more attitude change when little justification is provided for the counterattitudinal behavior than when high justification is provided.

REFERENCES

ARONSON, E., & CARLSMITH, J. M. Effect of the severity of threat on the devaluation of forbidden behavior. *Journal of Abnormal and Social Psychology*, 1963, 66, 584–588.

BREHM, J. W., & COHEN, A. R. *Explorations in cognitive dissonance.* New York: Wiley, 1962.

ELMS, A., & JANIS, I. Counter-norm attitudes induced by consonant versus dissonant conditions of role-playing. *Journal of Experimental Research in Personality*, 1965, 1, 50–60.

FESTINGER, L. *A theory of cognitive dissonance.* Stanford: Stanford University Press, 1957.

FESTINGER, L., & CARLSMITH, J. M. Cognitive consequences of forced compliance. *Journal of Abnormal and Social Psychology*, 1959, 58, 203–210.

FREEDMAN, J. L. Attitudinal effects of inadequate justification. *Journal of Personality*, 1963, 31, 371–385.

FREEDMAN, J. L. Long-term behavior effects of cognitive dissonance. *Journal of Experimental Social Psychology*, 1965, 1, 145–155.

HOVLAND, C. I., LUMSDAINE, A. A., & SHEFFIELD, F. D. *Experiments on mass communication.* Princeton: Princeton University Press, 1949.

JANIS, I. L., & GILMORE, J. B. The influence of incentive conditions on the success of role playing in modifying attitudes. *Journal of Personality and Social Psychology*, 1965, 1, 17–27.

KELMAN, H. C. Attitude change as a function of response restriction. *Human Relations*, 1953, 6, 185–214.

NUTTIN, J. M., JR. Dissonant evidence about dissonance theory. Paper read at Second Conference of Experimental Social Psychologists in Europe, Frascati, Italy, 1964.

ROSENBERG, M. J. When dissonance fails: On eliminating evaluation apprehension from attitude measurement. *Journal of Personality and Social Psychology*, 1965, 1, 28–42.

ROSENTHAL, R. On the social psychology of the psychological experiment: The experimenter's hypothesis as unintended determinant of experimental results. *American Scientist*, 1963, 51, 268–283.

TURNER, E. A., & WRIGHT, J. C. Effects of severity of threat and perceived availability on the attractiveness of objects. *Journal of Personality and Social Psychology*, 1965, 2, 128–132.

Active versus Passive Participation

There are several reasons why a person who actively participates in persuasion should be more susceptible to influence than a passive participant.

Cognitive dissonance theorists would attribute the effect to the greater amount of energy expended by the active participant.[1] The information that the effort which he exerted is great would be dissonant with the fact that, nevertheless, he continued to participate. One way for him to achieve consonance would be by his altering his private beliefs about the activity. If, in his own mind, he increased the attractiveness of the activity, then he would have justified his having expended so much energy. "Effort," though absent in the original formulation of the theory, is now purported to be a major factor in producing cognitive dissonance.[2]

Some interesting empirical evidence has recently been presented by Zimbardo in support of the cognitive dissonance interpretation. Zimbardo manipulated the degree of effort in a self-persuasion experiment utilizing the technique of delayed auditory feedback. In a high effort condition, subjects read aloud a persuasive communication while, at the same time, hearing themselves 1/4 of a second later. Anyone who has ever experienced this effect realizes the amount of effort it takes to continue in a given verbal task despite the distraction of the auditory feedback. "Talk shows" on the radio and TV use a version of this technique. To permit them to be able to censor any questionable conversation which may occur, they tape the dialogue and introduce a few seconds' delay before presenting it over the air. The caller must turn off his own radio or TV while he converses with

---

[1] Lawrence, D. H., & Festinger, L. *Deterrents and reinforcement.* Stanford, Calif.: Stanford Univer. Press, 1962.

[2] Cohen, A. R. Communication discrepancy and attitude change: A dissonance theory approach. *J. Pers.*, 1959, **27**, 386–396. Cohen, A. R. Attitudinal consequences of induced discrepancies between cognitions and behavior. *Publ. Opin. quart.*, 1960, **24**, 297–318. Festinger, L., & Aronson, E. The arousal and reduction of dissonance in social contexts. In D. Cartwright & A. Zander (Eds.), *Group dynamics.* (2nd ed.) New York: Row, Peterson, 1960. Pp. 214–231. Aronson, E. The effect of effort on the attractiveness of rewarded and unrewarded stimuli. *J. abnorm. soc. Psychol.*, 1961, **63**, 375–380.

the interviewer, or else he will be distracted by the delayed sound of his own voice. In his experiment, Zimbardo contrasted the high effort group with a low effort group that received delayed feedback of less than 1/100 of a second. Cognitive dissonance theory would predict greater dissonance for the high than for the low effort group and, consequently, greater opinion change for the high. This is precisely what Zimbardo found. Opinion change increased as the amount of effort required to deliver the persuasive (counternorm) communication was increased.[3]

We referred in the preceding section to the series of experiments on self-persuasion by Janis and King.[4] For effort, they would substitute the factor of "improvisation" to explain the differential effectiveness of active over passive participation. Improvisation forces the individual to consider new supporting arguments, and in this way he persuades himself to change his beliefs. Thus, if we wanted to get people to reenlist in the Armed Forces, one possibility would be to send them out to recruit others. In having to improvise arguments to persuade others to enlist, the servicemen might end up persuading themselves to reenlist.

A third interpretation takes a learning theory tack.[5] According to this approach active participation is more effective than passive participation because of the increased likelihood of the subject's attention to and comprehension of the stimuli. When a person is the passive recipient of a persuasive appeal, he may not fully attend to the arguments presented. His mind may wander. He might think about other things: the communicator's attractiveness, his intent, counterarguments, etc. By so doing, he might miss the premise of the arguments, or he might fail to hear some main point which clarified the issues. An active participant, particularly one who was forced to improvise his own arguments, would at least listen to himself. And, having had to improvise his own arguments, it seems all the more reasonable to expect that he would understand them.

Since John Mann, in 1956, noted the scarcity of experimental re-

---

[3]Zimbardo, P. G. The effect of effort and improvization on self-persuasion produced by role-playing. *J. exp. soc. Psychol.*, 1965, **1**, 103–120.

[4]Janis, I. L., & King, B. T. The influence of role-playing on opinion-change. *J. abnorm. soc. Psychol.*, 1954, **49**, 211–218. King, B. T., & Janis, I. L. Comparison of the effectiveness of improvised versus non-improvised role playing in producing opinion change. *Human Relat.*, 1956, **9**, 177–186.

[5]Rosnow, R. L. "Conditioning" the direction of opinion change in persuasion. *J. soc. Psychol.*, 1966, **69**, 300.

search on this subject,[6] there has been a growing literature on the efficacy of active participation and improvisation, particularly role-playing, as a procedure for modifying behavior.[7] Even before Mann's paper, there was a hint of the greater effectiveness of active participation in the experimental research of Kurt Lewin and his associates on group decision making.[8] In one of the most widely quoted studies in that series, the investigators demonstrated the influence on behavioral compliance of active participation in a discussion leading to a decision about the subjects' future behavior. The study was conducted during the Second World War as one solution to the problem of shortages of some of the more popular foods. In order to get housewives to increase their consumption of less popular foods such as beef hearts, sweetbreads, and kidneys, the investigators compared two procedures. In a passive procedure, housewives heard a lecturer talk about the dietary value and economy of the less popular meats and how to prepare them appetizingly. An active procedure consisted of imparting the same information, but in a group discussion in which the housewives participated. At the end of the discussion, the housewives were asked to indicate whether they intended to serve the less popular meats. It was found in a follow-up study that only 3 per cent of the housewives in the lecture groups actually used the meats,

[6]Mann, J. H. Experimental evaluations of role playing. *Psychol. Bull.*, 1956, **53**, 227–234.

[7]Carlson, E. R. Attitude change through modification of attitude structure. *J. abnorm. soc. Psychol.*, 1956, **52**, 256–261. Lieberman, S. The effects of changes in roles on the attitudes of role occupants. *Human Relat.*, 1956, **9**, 385–402. Culbertson, F. M. Modification of an emotionally held attitude through role playing. *J. abnorm. soc. Psychol.*, 1957, **54**, 230–233. Stanley, J. C., & Klausmeier, H. J. Opinion constancy after formal role playing. *J. soc. Psychol.*, 1957, **46**, 11–18. Mann, J. H., & Borgatta, E. F. Personality and behavior correlates of changes produced by role playing experience. *Psychol. Rep.*, 1959, **5**, Monogr. Suppl. 4, 505–526. Harvey, O. J., & Beverly, G. Some personality correlates of concept change through role playing. *J. abnorm. soc. Psychol.*, 1961, **63**, 125–130. Jansen, M. J., & Stolurow, L. M. An experimental study of role playing. *Psychol. Monogr.*, 1962, **76** (Whole No. 550). Elms, A. C. Influence of fantasy ability on attitude change through role playing. *J. Pers. soc. Psychol.*, 1966, **4**, 36–43. Crawford, T. J., & Gergen, K. J. Task concept, self-esteem, and attitude change through role playing. Paper read at East. Psychol. Ass. Convention, New York, 1966. Watts, W. A. Relative persistence of opinion change induced by active compared to passive participation. *J. Pers. soc. Psychol.*, 1967, **5**, 4–15.

[8]Lewin, K. Group decision and social change. In G. E. Swanson, T. M. Newcomb, & E. L. Hartley (Eds.), *Readings in social psychology.* (2nd ed.) New York: Holt, Rinehart, & Winston, 1952.

while almost one third of the housewives in the discussion group complied.

More recently, Arthur Salman, incorporating the Crowne-Marlowe construct "need for social approval,"[9] compared high versus low need approval subjects at different levels of participation in persuasion. In general, the opinions of those subjects with a high need for social approval tended to shift in the direction advocated to a greater extent than low need approval subjects. More important here, however, Salman found in the high need subjects a relationship between the magnitude of their compliance and the degree of their participation. Actively participating "communicators" (who were required to improvise and to present an impromptu argument) experienced greater positive opinion change than passive "receivers" (whose assigned task was to evaluate the communicator's leadership ability) who, in turn, experienced greater opinion change than passive "observers" (who performed the same task as the receivers but who, in addition, were physically separated from the other subjects by a one-way-vision mirror).[10]

Holzberg and Gewirtz also provide evidence of the greater effectiveness of active participation as a procedure for modifying beliefs. A group of college student volunteers for the mental health Companion Program at Connecticut Valley Hospital were compared with a control group of students who volunteered for other social service activities. Results of a before-after opinion study of the two groups indicated that only the mental health volunteers experienced a significant positive shift in their beliefs about mental illness.[11]

The greater effectiveness of active participation is also implied in the audiovisual literature where it has been pointed out that learning via films is enhanced when an audience actively participates in the learning process by taking notes, asking themselves questions about the material, etc.[12] And, presumably one of the great virtues of pro-

---

[9]Crowne, D. P., & Marlowe, D. *The approval motive.* New York: Wiley, 1964.

[10]Salman, A. R. The need for approval, improvisation, and attitude change. Unpublished master's thesis, Ohio State Univer., 1962.

[11]Holzberg, J. D., & Gewirtz, H. A method of altering attitudes toward mental illness. *Psychiat. quart. Suppl.,* 1963, 37, 56–61.

[12]Michael, D. N., & Maccoby, N. Factors influencing verbal learning from films under varying conditions of audience participation. *J. exp. Psychol.,* 1953, **46,** 411–418. Maccoby, E. E., & Wilson, W. C. Identification and observational learning from films. *J. abnorm. soc. Psychol.,* 1957, **55,** 76–87. Brown, J. W., Lewis, R. B., & Harcleroad, F. F. *A-V instruction: Materials and methods.* New York: McGraw-Hill, 1959.

grammed instruction is that it gets the student to *actively* take part in the learning process.

The participation-compliance relationship is not, however, an unqualified one. In fact, at the other end of the continuum, extremely passive participation may be more effective than moderately active participation. We saw earlier in this section (pp. 272 f.) how a passive reading of a communication may actually strengthen existing beliefs against subsequent countercommunication more than would actively writing a defensive essay from a provided outline.[13] Also, the simple positive relationship does not take into account the possibility of a confounding interaction with existing beliefs. McGinnies, Donelson, and Haaf find that although active participation can influence moderate and neutral attitudes, it may have little effect on extreme beliefs.[14]

Even though their results are somewhat confounded by the factor of awareness, an experiment by Walster and Festinger implies the effectiveness of extremely passive participation as a technique for modifying behavior. College students who toured an observation room in which they were able to watch through a one-way-vision mirror and "overhear" a group discussion on the relationship between smoking and cancer shifted their opinions more in the direction of the overheard discussion than other students who were told that the discussants knew they were listening. A second study found that the differences between the overheard and the regular conditions tended to be greatest when the issue was an involving one and least when it was not involving.[15]

These are interesting findings, for they raise the possibility that not only can extremely active participation be significantly effective in modifying behavior, but that when the degree of participation is at the other end of the activity continuum, i.e., when the recipient passively overhears someone else's conversation, a significant effect can also be achieved.

Viewed in the context of learning theory, it is possible to reconcile

---

[13] McGuire, W. J., & Papageorgis, D. The relative efficacy of various types of prior belief-defense in producing immunity against persuasion. *J. abnorm. soc. Psychol.*, 1961, **62**, 327–337.

[14] McGinnies, E., Donelson, E., & Haaf, R. Level of initial attitude, active rehearsal, and instructional set as factors in attitude change. *J. abnorm. soc. Psychol.*, 1964, **69**, 437–440.

[15] Walster, E., & Festinger, L. The effectiveness of "overheard" persuasive communication. *J. abnorm. soc. Psychol.*, 1962, **65**, 395–402.

these findings by positing a nonmonotonic relationship between magnitude of opinion change and level of participation. If we consider just the receptivity variables, attention and comprehension, an asymptotic function can be hypothesized for both extremely high and extremely low levels of activity. At one end of the activity continuum, impromptu role-playing heightens receptivity because the subject is forced to listen to (and, presumably, comprehend) his own arguments. At the other end of the continuum, where the subject is the passive recipient of information which he "inadvertently" happens to overhear, on commonsense grounds it can be hypothesized that receptivity again is heightened. This effect would be expected to increase further were the subject made to believe that the "overheard" information was *purposely* communicated out of earshot. There is a certain aura of intrigue about overhearing something not intended to be made public. The effect would be to increase the individual's curiosity and interest and, concomitantly, his receptivity.

Taken together, the results of the two studies that follow imply the possibility of such a nonmonotonic relationship. The first study is by Timothy C. Brock and Lee Alan Becker. The Brock and Becker experiment is an interesting systematic replication of the Walster and Festinger finding regarding the potency of overheard information. The second study is by Irving L. Janis and Leon Mann. Its results imply the asymptote hypothesized for the active participation end of the continuum.

Reprinted from Journal of Personality and Social Psychology, 1965, Vol. 2, pp. 654–660, by permission of Timothy C. Brock and APA.

INEFFECTIVENESS OF "OVERHEARD" COUNTERPROPAGANDA[1]

TIMOTHY C. BROCK   AND   LEE ALAN BECKER

90 college women heard an E take a rigged phone call in which he advocated an event which was either neutral, unacceptable, or acceptable to the listeners. For ⅓ the listeners, E took the call in their presence and, for the others, he ran around to his office saying "I can't talk about that here." Dependent variable consisted of opinions on compulsory ROTC, increasing, and decreasing tuition. Data corroborated Walster and Festinger: overheard communications were especially effective for involved listeners when the advocated position was acceptable. However, overhearing was not more effective for the unacceptable propaganda. Results were ordered to a model in which information receptivity and communicator credibility combine multiplicatively to determine propaganda effectiveness.

Walster and Festinger (1962) have clarified the conditions under which a *regular* communicator is less effective than an *overheard* communicator, that is, a speaker perceived to be unaware of his listeners:

when the position advocated by the persuasive communication is one which the involved subjects would like to accept, overheard communications are more effective for involved subjects and not particularly more effective for subjects not directly involved in the issue [p. 400].

Communications advocating positions which the listeners would *not* like to accept, were not employed, but Walster and Festinger suspected that

if the communication urges the listeners in a direction in which they do not want to move, quite different results might be obtained [p. 401].

In the present version of the Walster-Festinger experiment, conditions were included in which the communicator advocated a position contrary to that held by the listeners. Empirical knowledge about the potency of overheard counterpropaganda will facilitate theoretical understanding of the effectiveness of overheard communications.

METHOD

An after-only design with appropriate controls was employed. Subjects participated in a

[1] Supported by Grant GS-343 to the first writer from the National Science Foundation. We thank Elaine Walster for her comments. The assistance of James Berns is gratefully acknowledged. The senior author was at Iowa State University during the data collection.

"fingertip-sight" experiment during which one of the experimenters received a rigged phone call. The first independent variable was the experimenter's contribution to the "phone conversation" in which he strongly advocated a course of action which was either unacceptable, acceptable, or a matter of indifference to the listening subjects. The second independent variable was the listening condition. For half the subjects, the experimenter took the call in the same room and, for the other half, he "ran around" to his office after saying "I can't talk about that here." In both conditions the conversation was perfectly audible to the subjects. The dependent variable consisted of opinion scores on three issues: compulsory ROTC, increasing tuition, and reducing tuition.

Subjects

The subjects were 90 experimentally naive underclass women who paid a quarterly fee of $99.

Procedure

Fingertip-sight experiment. The subjects were run in groups of five by two experimenters. The subjects began by reading the following instructions.

There are two parts in today's project. Part one is an experiment on tactual color perception. Part two is a survey of student opinion. Please follow the instructions attentively and quietly. It has recently been discovered by psychologists in the United States and Russia that some persons can discern the color of an unseen object by touching that object. We are testing for the ability to judge color by touch at Iowa State.

After you have finished reading these instructions, the procedure will be as follows. You will place black goggles over your eyes so that you cannot see anything; three colored squares of paper, covered with thin glass, will be placed in front of you; two of the squares will be of the same color and the third will be of a different color. You judge which color is different from the other two by touching and feeling the squares. Place one color square aside from the other two to indicate your decision and then place your hands in your lap. When everyone has finished a set of colors a new set will be presented. The experimenter will say "Ready Start" each time you are to begin touching a new set of three colored squares. A report on tactual color perception research will be mailed to you. No talking is permitted once the experiment has begun.

After the subjects had indicated their goggles were securely placed, the experiment began. A trial was completed when all five subjects indicated that they had made their decision about the odd color by placing their hands in their laps. The average time per trial was about 2.5 minutes. There were eight trials in the entire experiment. After the eighth trial the subjects were told to remove their goggles and fill out an opinionnaire. On the last page of the opinionnaire they signed a "voluntary agreement" to refrain from discussing the experiment for 2 weeks. Since the entire experiment was run in 1 day, contamination was precluded. A mimeographed report on fingertip sighting (Plumb, 1964) was mailed to each subject.[2]

Manipulation of overheard versus regular listening conditions. A phone was on view to all subjects when they entered the experimental room; it was placed on a sill extended into an adjoining office. The sill is about 3.5 feet above the floor and the opening above it is about 14×14 inches. A square panel on hinges closes the opening. This arrangement is common in many so-called "temporary" buildings constructed on campuses and elsewhere during World War II; it enables the occupants of both rooms to share the same phone.

At the end of the second trial, the first experimenter, the speaker, electrically signaled an accomplice in another part of the building. The accomplice immediately dialed the number of the phone in the experimental room. The speaker answered and said he was "busy," "cannot talk to anyone right now" and quickly replaced the receiver after saying "I'll call you back," "I'm sorry I have to hang up." At the end of the fourth trial the speaker signaled his accomplice and again the phone rang. The speaker insisted that he "cannot talk now," "I'm all tied up right now" but his ostensible caller was adamant and the speaker was "forced" to engage in a conversation. (There were three standardized conversations as described in a later section.) The speaker read his part of the conversation from a script while holding his thumb over the earphone

of the receiver. The accomplice played a tape recording of the script into the telephone. When the speaker lifted his thumb, for "pause" in the script, the subjects heard the metallic "squawking" of the voice of the ostensible caller. The words and phrases from the other end were mainly incomprehensible to the subjects but those that did come through were, because of the tape recording, germane to the speaker's message. During the second phone conversation the speaker made two "unsuccessful" attempts to break it off. In sum, the impression of an authentic phone conversation was conveyed. The effect was well established in extensive pilot research.

At the beginning of the seventh trial, the speaker elicited a third phone call from the accomplice and terminated it quickly and irritatedly. The first and third phone calls contributed to the overall impression of an experimenter harassed by unwanted interruptions.

In the *regular* condition, the speaker, upon "failing" to dismiss his caller, simply took the call in the experimental room. In the *overheard* condition, the speaker said "I'm sorry I can't talk about that in here. I'm going to run around to my office. Please hold on." As the speaker rushed out, the second experimenter said "Should we wait?" and the speaker called from the corridor "Go ahead, I'll be right back." The second experimenter insured that the speaker's conversation was completely audible to all the subjects by adjusting the aforementioned panel covering the opening between the experimental room and the adjoining office.

Three communication treatments. There were three persuasive messages. The first, compulsory ROTC, advocated a resumption of the ROTC obligation for all physically fit male students. The second, reduce tuition, presented reasons for reducing the quarterly fee from $99 to $33. The third, triple tuition, presented reasons for increasing the quarterly fee from $99 to $297. It was assumed that coeds were less involved in the ROTC issue than they were in the amount of tuition they paid. It was further assumed that reducing tuition is an acceptable course of action for virtually all students while tripling tuition is an unacceptable event for all students. Hence, the three messages made it possible to compare regular versus overheard treatments for involving and uninvolving messages and for messages advocating acceptable and unacceptable events.

Each of the three scripts, including interpolated pauses, required about 2 minutes to read. To begin the speaker said the "faculty board" had met "more than a dozen times this year" and its "conclusions throughout have always been unanimous on this problem." In the compulsory ROTC treatment the speaker forcefully presented the "faculty's" arguments for resumption of obligatory ROTC. Principal themes were: voluntary system had failed; advantages of being an officer; services get 85% of officers from ROTC; West Point, Annapolis cannot do job alone; new freshmen don't know the score and should be required to give ROTC and the university a "full chance."

---

[2] A detailed description of procedures and results in the fingertip-sight experiment is available from the second writer.

In the reduce tuition treatment, the speaker forcefully presented the reasons behind the "faculty's recommendation" to "cut the quarterly registration fee by two thirds—to around $33 per quarter for *all* students." Principal themes were: "grim fact" of students in good standing dropping out because of financial difficulties; popular misconception that working during college is valuable; in space-race America cannot afford not to educate a single talented person; high tuition inimical to land-grant ideals; faculty disgusted that wealth rather than ability determines acquisition of an education; fees can never be reduced too much.

In the triple tuition treatment, the speaker forcefully presented the reasons behind the "faculty's recommendation" that the "quarterly registration fee should be tripled . . . right, tripled . . . to just less than $300 per quarter for *all* students." Principal themes were: "grim fact" of 15% loss of graduate faculty owing to inadequate salary; young enthusiastic professors leave first, old drones are left to drone on; attenuation of excellence limits graduates' choices in job market; "well-known fact" that the average salary of our graduates is only $5,000 compared with $7,000 for graduates of east and west coast universities; university had to turn away one million dollars in federal research grants for lack of appropriate facilities; "temporary" buildings are "eyesores," library, a "jungle"; faculty and students disgusted with third-rate status; investment in education can never be too great.

Dependent Variable

Three items, keyed to the three treatments, were included in an opinionnaire containing many items dealing with current campus issues. For the compulsory ROTC treatment the key item was "As regards making participation in ROTC compulsory at ISU for physically qualified male students, I am . . . ." For the reduce tuition treatment, the key item was "As regards reducing the quarterly registration fee at ISU, from $99 to $33 per quarter, I am . . . ." For the triple tuition treatment, the key item was "As regards increasing the quarterly registration fee

at ISU, from $99 to $297 per quarter, I am . . . ." Answers were indicated along a 75-point scale, each fifteenth point identified by labels running from strongly in favor (75.0) to strongly opposed (0.0). Many of the dummy items in the opinionnaire were very specific, for example, one concerned the amount of time that should be devoted to movies in the introductory psychology course and another dealt with the exact amount of traffic penalties below which no report should be made in the student newspaper.

All subjects answered the same opinionnaire except that the key item for a communication treatment appeared before the items which were keyed to the other two treatments. To illustrate, the order of appearance of key items in the triple tuition treatment was increase tuition item, compulsory ROTC item, and reduce tuition item. This order in the opinionnaire was reversed in the reduce tuition treatment.

Summary of Design

Ninety subjects were randomly assigned to 18 groups of five. These groups were randomly assigned to six treatments resulting from the two listening conditions, overheard and regular, and the three communication treatments, compulsory ROTC, reduce tuition, and triple tuition. The dependent variable consisted of measures of opinions about requiring ROTC, reducing tuition, and increasing tuition. There were 14 instead of 15 subjects in three of the six treatments because 3 subjects did not keep their appointments.

RESULTS

Corroboration of Walster and Festinger's Findings

Walster and Festinger (1962) found that overheard persuasive communications were not more effective than regular communications when the issue was not personally in-

TABLE 1

MEAN OPINION SCORES ON TUITION AND ROTC ISSUES

| | Opinion issues | | | | | | |
| | Increase tuition | | | Require ROTC | | Reduce tuition | |
Communication treatment	N	M	SD	M	SD	M	SD
Regular, compulsory ROTC	15	5.47	5.69	43.00	16.25	30.67	19.77
Overheard, compulsory ROTC	15	5.93	6.82	37.87	20.30	25.60	17.02
Regular, reduce tuition	15	4.93	5.48	22.27	16.21	50.33	27.65
Overheard, reduce tuition	14	5.93	8.77	21.79	12.79	67.71	19.92
Regular, triple tuition	14	14.57	13.61	27.07	21.40	29.36	24.64
Overheard, triple tuition	14	16.43	16.29	28.07	19.53	25.50	25.37

Note.—The higher the score, the more favorable the opinion.

volving for the listeners. When the event advocated by the communication was both involving and acceptable to the listeners, the overheard communication was more effective than the regular communication. The present results, shown in Table 1, corroborated the Walster-Festinger findings.

Favorableness toward compulsory ROTC was generally greater in the compulsory ROTC treatment than in the control treatments, reduce tuition and triple tuition. Of the eight possible comparisons between the mean opinion scores in the compulsory ROTC treatments and the mean scores in the other treatments, six were statistically significant at the .05 level, or better, by t tests[3] and the other two comparisons were in the same direction. Although the compulsory ROTC treatment was shown to be effective, there was no evidence that, within that treatment, overheard was more powerful than regular.

The reduce tuition communication was also effective. Favorableness toward reducing tuition was generally greater in the reduce tuition treatments than in the control treatments, compulsory ROTC and triple tuition. Mean opinion scores under reduce tuition were statistically larger: all comparisons yielded t-test p values of .05 or less. Within reduce tuition, the mean opinion score for the overheard treatment was more favorable than for the regular treatment: $t = 1.93$, $p < .06$.

Ineffectiveness of Overheard Counterpropaganda

The triple tuition communication was generally effective: favorableness toward increasing tuition was greater in the triple tuition treatments than in the control treatments, compulsory ROTC and reduce tuition. Of the eight possible comparisons between the mean scores under triple tuition and those in the other treatments, five were statistically significant by t test at the .05 level and the other three, at the .06 level. The mean score for the overheard treatment was slightly greater than that for the regular treatment, but this effect must be attributed to chance

[3] All t tests were two-tailed. Where variances were heterogeneous an approximation by Edwards (1950, p. 168) was employed.

for the t did not even approach reliability. In sum, the triple tuition treatment was effective, but there was no evidence that the overheard treatment was more powerful than the regular treatment.

Correlations between Opinion Scores

Correlations between scores on the three key items were computed for each of the six treatment combinations. Correlations involving the compulsory ROTC item hovered close to zero in all treatments. The relationship between favoring an increase and favoring a reduction in tuition was reliably inverse in each of the treatment combinations. The r's ranged from $-.45$ to $-.50$.

Since favoring an increase and favoring a reduction in tuition are opposed responses, one may ask why scores on the increase tuition item were not lower under reduce tuition than under compulsory ROTC. Similarly, those subjects who heard the triple tuition communication should have been different in their responses to the reduce tuition item than those who heard the compulsory ROTC communication. Both of these apparent inconsistencies were attributed to the strong opposition to increasing tuition. Scores on the increase tuition item were at one extreme and this ceiling effect may account for the failure of the reduce tuition treatment to have *measurable* influence on opposition to tuition increase.

DISCUSSION

The two main findings were a reproduction of the Walster-Festinger (1962) results and a failure to show an advantage for overheard counterpropaganda. Walster and Festinger found that overheard communications were more effective for involved listeners when the communications urged the listeners toward a position they would like to accept. The present overheard treatment was more effective than the regular treatment for the involving, and acceptable, position (reduce tuition) but not for the uninvolving recommendation (compulsory ROTC). It is worth emphasizing that the present study replicated Walster and Festinger even though many aspects of the two methodologies were radically dissimilar. The most noteworthy differences pertained to the speaker's identification of the listeners prior to the treatment and his withdrawal from the presence of his listeners in the overheard treatment. In the Walster-Festinger studies the speaker did not interact at all with his listeners and the choice of overheard or regular was perceived as up to the experimenter, not the speaker.

Within the same context in which the Walster-Festinger results were replicated, additional findings suggested that communications advocating unacceptable events are not more powerful when they are overheard. The overheard effect can now be placed in sharper perspective and gains in theoretical understanding are possible.

Walster and Festinger considered three factors which might make overheard communications more effective. The overheard speaker aroused less defensiveness than the regular speaker; listeners were especially influenced by communications they were not supposed to hear; and ulterior motives were imputed to a greater extent to the regular than to the overheard speaker. Each of these factors, by itself, is insufficient to explain either the Walster-Festinger data or the present results.

The listener's defenses are likely to be instigated to the extent he perceives a direct attempt to influence. However, it surely seemed improbable that the speaker, who had tried to dismiss his caller, and who was trying to break off a phone conversation, was, at the same time, engaged in a direct attempt to influence the subjects. The speaker appeared to be no more prepared for the unwanted interruption than were his listeners. In both the regular and overheard treatments the subjects were occupied judging colors and therefore *both* treatments were, to some degree, overheard and not construable as a direct attempt to influence. Furthermore, the term "defenses," as Walster and Festinger noted, is inapplicable when an acceptable position is advocated by the communication, as in the reduce tuition treatment.

The second factor, hearing things one is not supposed to hear, does not explain the lack of effect for the uninvolving issue, nor can it adequately account for the lack of effect when the persuasive communication was involving but counter to the listener's position. The third possibility, differential imputation of ulterior motives, hardly fits the behavior of the present speaker who was at pains to cut off the communication. There is the further question, noted by Walster and Festinger, as to why involved listeners would impute ulterior motives to a speaker recommending a desirable event.

A satisfactory account must explain why overheard persuasive communications are not more powerful when the issue is uninvolving and when an unacceptable position is advocated. As part of a recent theory of persuasion (Brock, 1964) two factors are identified which relate multiplicatively in determining the effectiveness of propaganda: communicator credibility and receptivity (eagerness to expose oneself to information). As receptivity approaches zero, differences in credibility, however great, have decreasing influence on propaganda effectiveness. This simple model clarifies the first experiment reported by Walster and Festinger in which the effectiveness of the overheard speaker was limited to the involved listeners, namely, the smokers. Both smokers and nonsmokers rated the overheard speaker as more honest, more sincere, and therefore more credible, than the regular speaker. However, differences in speakers' credibility did not affect listeners' opinions unless the listeners were involved in the communication issue, smoking and lung cancer. Three recent studies (Brock, 1965; Feather, 1962, 1963) have clearly shown that involved persons, smokers, are more receptive to information about smoking and cancer than nonsmokers. Walster and Festinger's smokers were undoubtedly more receptive to the communications than the nonsmokers. Hence, the theorized multiplicative effect of receptivity and credibility explains why overheard communications are more powerful for involved but not for uninvolved recipients. The explanation depends in part on the assumption, supported by data from the first Walster-Festinger experiment, that overheard communicators are considered more trustworthy than regular communicators.

The credibility × receptivity formulation integrates Walster and Festinger's data, the present replications of their conditions, as well as earlier data on source credibility.[4] In the present study some additional concept is necessary to explain why the combination of high receptivity and high credibility did not increase opinion change under the overheard counterpropaganda treatment.

The believableness of the overheard speaker was undoubtedly augmented by the present technique in which he withdrew from the presence of his listeners. The listeners may well have regarded the speaker's subsequent words as the unvarnished truth, free of inhibition and distortion. Under these circumstances, learning that the faculty board had recommended tripling the tuition probably mobilized more defensiveness than in the regular treatment. For there is a tendency in informal social communication to withhold bad news from the appropriate recipients. When the bad news is really true, the likelihood that it will be withheld or not communicated in a straightforward fashion is increased. Hence, if a communicator has attempted to conceal some adverse information, the truth of the information may appear especially compelling. If, in the triple tuition treatment, the overheard speaker mobilized more defensiveness and fear than the regular speaker, that arousal of concern and resistance could have countervailed any favorable

[4] The theorized combination of receptivity and credibility may resolve a long-standing discrepancy appearing in the classical studies of source credibility by Hovland and his associates. Walster and Festinger (1962, p. 395) and Hovland, Janis, and Kelley (1953, p. 35) have noted that in two studies (Hovland & Weiss, 1951; Kelman & Hovland, 1953) large differences in source credibility reliably influenced opinions while in a third (Hovland & Mandell, 1952), the effect of source credibility was quite weak. Reexamination of the three studies disclosed that the opinion issues of the first study (antihistamines, atomic submarines, steel shortage) and of the second study (treatment of delinquents) were timely and interesting for their audience. In contrast, the issue of the third study (Hovland & Mandell, 1952) was complicated and abstruse. The opinion issue concerned currency devaluation and the authors recommended that subsequent replications employ less complex issues, "particularly ones with a higher degree of ego-involvements [p. 587]." The inferred low degree of receptivity in the Hovland and Mandell study explains why the large manipulated difference in communicator trustworthiness had only a weak effect on opinions.

effects of high receptivity and heightened credibility.

Subsequent research requires direct tests of the emergent hypothesis: adverse information elicits belief and discomfort to the extent it appears the communicator has expended effort to conceal or distort the information. The relationship of the communicator to the recipient, whether friendly, neutral, or antagonistic, would, of course, interact with the effort-to-conceal variable. The psychology of secrets is still unexplored terrain.

A final question concerns the general significance of the effectiveness of overheard persuasive communications. Professional propagandists, opinion leaders, educators, parents, etc., are mainly concerned with urging their listeners in a direction the listeners would *not* like to move, at least initially. Informal social communication is directed toward perceived deviates (Festinger, 1950). On the other hand, there exists a welter of inducements which can make a person adopt a more extreme position in his current values and opinions. The present results suggested that the power of overheard propaganda is restricted to moving persons in a direction they want to go anyway. The present analysis has attempted to place the "overheard" effect in a theoretical perspective in which communicator credibility, together with other factors, predicts propaganda effectiveness. The overheard versus regular variation may be added to the list of factors which affect communicator credibility.

REFERENCES

BROCK, T. C. Notes toward a theory of persuasion. Unpublished manuscript, Iowa State University, 1964.

BROCK, T. C. Commitment to exposure as a determinant of information receptivity. *Journal of Personality and Social Psychology*, 1965, 2, 10–19.

EDWARDS, A. L. *Experimental design in psychological research*. New York: Rinehart, 1950.

FEATHER, N. T. Cigarette smoking and lung cancer: A study of cognitive dissonance. *Australian Journal of Psychology*, 1962, 14, 55–64.

FEATHER, N. T. Cognitive dissonance, sensitivity, and evaluation. *Journal of Abnormal and Social Psychology*, 1963, 66, 157–163.

FESTINGER, L. Informal social communication. *Psychological Review*, 1950, 57, 271–282.

HOVLAND, C. I., JANIS, I. L., & KELLEY, H. H. *Communication and persuasion.* New Haven: Yale Univer. Press, 1953.

HOVLAND, C. I., & MANDELL, W. An experimental comparison of conclusion-drawing by the communicator and by the audience. *Journal of Abnormal and Social Psychology,* 1952, **47**, 581–588.

HOVLAND, C. I., & WEISS, W. The influence of source credibility on communication effectiveness. *Public Opinion Quarterly,* 1951, **15**, 635–650.

KELMAN, H. C., & HOVLAND, C. I. "Reinstatement" of the communicator in delayed measurement of opinion change. *Journal of Abnormal and Social Psychology,* 1953, **48**, 327–335.

PLUMB, R. K. Woman who tells colors by touch mystifies psychologists. *New York Times,* January 8, 1964, 23.

WALSTER, ELAINE, & FESTINGER, L. The effectiveness of "overheard" persuasive communications. *Journal of Abnormal and Social Psychology,* 1962, **65**, 395–402.

Reprinted from Journal of Experimental Research in Personality, 1965, Vol. 1, pp. 84–90, by permission of Irving L. Janis and Academic Press.

Effectiveness of Emotional Role-Playing in Modifying Smoking Habits and Attitudes[1]

IRVING L. JANIS AND LEON MANN

This experiment was designed to investigate the effectiveness of "emotional" role-playing in modifying smoking habits and attitudes toward cigarette smoking. Fourteen women were asked to play the role of a lung cancer patient who receives bad news from a physician. This role-playing group showed markedly greater changes in attitudes than an equivalent group of 12 control Ss, each of whom received identical information by listening to a tape recording of a role-play session. The high level of fear and vigilance aroused by the realistic quality of the experimental situation appears to be a factor responsible for the increased anti-smoking attitudes and the changes reported in smoking habits two weeks later.

The persistence of undesirable habits such as heavy smoking and overeating, despite the desire of many people to modify their overindulgences, poses a major challenge for research on attitude change. The problem of smoking has attained prominence because of the incongruity between the average smoker's continuance of the habit and his knowledge that it might cause lung cancer. In general it appears that rational appeals, making use of cogent scientific evidence, have little sustained effect, if any, on the cigarette smoker. Even when influenced by persuasive messages that vividly convey the threatening consequences of the smoking habit, most smokers are affected only temporarily and usually return to the habit within a few days, bolstering their original attitude by minimizing, distorting, or denying the content of the message. It is a well-known fact that the cancer scare promoted by repeated publicity campaigns in the mass media during the past decade has had little residual effect on the American population and the consumption of cigarettes has continued to increase (Toch, Allen, and Lazer, 1961; Cannell and MacDonald, 1956; Greenberg, 1964).

A number of individual cases have been observed, nevertheless, in which dramatic conversions took place as a result of direct personal encounters with the threat, as in the case of physicians, cancer scientists, and the relatives of cancer victims (Snegireff and Lombard, 1959; Lawton and Goldman, 1961). It seems probable that when people stop smoking after direct encounters with cancer victims, it is partly because of an empathic reaction involving the realization that, if it can happen to others, it can happen to themselves. A marked change in attitude and behavior is likely to occur if a smoker can no longer relegate the feared consequences to the category of remote or irrelevant dangers.

The present study was devised to investigate the possibility that the technique of role-playing, which has been found to be effective in facilitating attitude change, might be used in a way that would provide an empathic "contact" experience similar

[1] The experimental sessions were conducted during the summer of 1963, approximately 5 months before the release of the Surgeon General's report on *Smoking and Health*. The analysis of the data for this research was partly financed by a grant to Irving L. Janis, principal investigator, from the National Institute of Mental Health (MH08564-02) for research on factors influencing deprivation tolerance. This study was also partly financed by a grant from the Rockefeller Foundation for the Yale Studies in Attitude and Communication.

84

to the type of direct contact that occasionally leads to a spectacular conversion. Several experiments (e.g., Culbertson, 1957; Janis and King, 1954, 1956; Kelman, 1953) have shown that when a person verbalizes a belief or judgment to others he becomes more inclined to accept it himself. The role-playing procedure in these experiments requires the person to take the part of a rational advocate of a position contrary to his personal opinions, so that he is induced to scan the opposing viewpoint and to improvise new arguments. Thus the person finds himself examining belief systems that were formerly sealed off, as he conscientiously executes the task of examining the other side of the issue. It is quite possible, however, for a person to carry out a cognitive role-playing assignment in a defensive way with a minimum of emotional involvement and with covert denial of the relevance of what he is saying to his personal outlook. This type of defensiveness might explain why modest success was attained in Horn's (1960) study, which was a unique attempt to use a role-playing technique for the purpose of trying to influence smoking habits. In Horn's experiment, high school students took the role of providing information to their parents on the dangers of smoking and this led to only a small decrease in the number of students who would have otherwise commenced smoking.

When rational appeals fail, some degree of success in modifying deep-seated habits may nevertheless be achieved by vivid emotional appeals that personalize the threat, as in the case of audiences exposed to dramatic "scare" films depicting the suffering and mutilation of cancer victims (Janis, in press). It seems plausible, therefore, to expect that some comparable degree of success in breaking through the defensive facade might be attained by using an "emotional" type of role-playing, which induces the person to become empathically involved in a life-like situation. "Emotional" role-playing in this case consists of a standardized psychodramatic procedure in which the E induces the S to give an improvised emotional performance by asking him to act out a fictitious calamity as though it were really happening, using props and other staging devices to enhance the illusion of reality. One of the unique features of this type of role-playing procedure is that the E enters directly into dramatic dialogues with the S, following a standardized script that he has memorized, and thus is able to focus the S's attention on the emotionally arousing features of the distressing episode that is being enacted.

In the present study, the form of emotional role-playing we devised requires the S to play the role of a medical patient who has just completed a series of intensive medical examinations and has asked the physician to tell the truth about the diagnosis. Enacting the role of the physician, the E informs the "patient" that the diagnosis is cancer of the lung, that a lung operation will have to be undergone as soon as possible, and that cigarette smoking must be given up immediately. The role-playing setting and the E's script were designed to facilitate the arousal of fantasies and personalized images of being victimized by lung cancer, with the expectation that when the threat cannot be readily denied or ignored the person may begin for the first time to experience some genuinely fearful anticipations that "it *could* happen to me."

In the literature on psychodrama, there are a few anecdotal accounts of the clinical use of similar role-playing procedures which appear to have been helpful in the treatment of delinquents and other types of "problem" cases (e.g., Moreno, 1957; Corsini, 1958); but so far as we know, the present study represents the first systematic attempt to investigate the effectiveness of emotional role-playing in modifying attitudes and habits.

METHOD

Subjects

The Ss were 26 women, 18–23 years of age, all of whom volunteered to participate in a research study under the auspices of their local State College. None of them knew that the purpose had anything to do with changing their smoking habits. They were screened by telephone to make sure they were moderate or heavy smokers (i.e.,

were consuming at least 15 cigarettes per day).
The rationale given for asking about their smoking habits was simply that the study involved
playing a role that required the person to be a
smoker.

Subjects were randomly assigned to one of two
conditions: 14 were placed in the experimental
group (role-players) and 12 in the control group
(non-role-playing "judges," exposed to the same
instructions and information).

Experimental Procedures

The young women in both the experimental
and control groups were told at the beginning of
the session that role-playing is sometimes used as
a research technique to create life-like situations
when it is difficult to make direct observations of
real-life behavior, such as the emotional reactions
of patients in a doctor's office. The E then explained that the purpose of the research was to
study two important problems concerning the
human side of medical practice, namely how
patients react to bad news and how they feel
about a doctor's advice to quit an enjoyable habit
like smoking.

On the pretext that E would best understand
S's performance of the role of a patient if he knew
her personal opinions on relevant topics, a premeasure of attitudes toward smoking was administered. The questionnaire contained 15 items
which assessed S's beliefs about smoking and
cancer, her feelings of concern about being a
smoker, and her intention to modify or continue
the habit.

The procedures up to this point were identical
for both experimental and control Ss, but after
the initial questionnaire only those assigned to the
experimental condition were given the emotional
role-playing instructions. Each S in the latter
group was asked to imagine that E was a doctor
who was treating her for a "bad cough that was
not getting any better." She was to make believe
that this was her third visit to his office, and that
she had come this time to be informed of the
results of X-rays and other medical tests. The E
gave a brief sketch of five different scenes and S
was asked to act out each one as realistically as
possible:

Scene 1. Soliloquy in waiting room: The S is
asked to give her thoughts out loud, expressing
worry while awaiting the doctor's diagnosis and
feeling conflicted about whether or not to smoke
a cigarette.

*Scene 2. Conversation with the physician as he
gives the diagnosis:* In acting out the standard
(memorized) script of the physician's role, E

begins by informing the patient that he will tell
her the whole truth, since this is what she had
requested last time. He goes on to say that a
definite diagnosis can now be made on the basis
of the X-ray and sputum tests and that, unfortunately, it is bad news. Pointing to an actual chest
X-ray obtained from the Pathology laboratory,
he explains that there is a small malignant mass
in the patient's right lung; an operation therefore is needed as soon as possible. He encourages
the S to ask questions. In the course of this conversation, E again refers to S's former request for
all the facts and then informs her of the fact that
there is only a moderate chance for a successful
outcome from surgery for this condition.

*Scene 3. Soliloquy while physician phones for a
hospital bed:* The S is again asked to express
aloud her thoughts and feelings about the bad
news while E is telephoning in a distant part of
the room.

*Scene 4. Conversation with the physician con-
cerning arrangements for hospitalization:* Continuing to act on the basis of the standard script, E
gives detailed information about reporting to the
hospital the following morning and asks several
questions about the patient's family and personal
circumstances. He informs her that she should
expect to be in the hospital at least six weeks
because surgery of the chest takes a long time to
heal.

*Scene 5. Conversation with the physician about
the causes of lung cancer.* The E raises some questions about the patient's smoking history and asks
her if she is aware of the connection between
smoking and cancer. Then E discusses with the
patient the urgent need to stop smoking immediately and encourages her to speak freely about
the difficulties she expects to encounter in trying
to give up the habit at this time, now that she
knows it is essential.

Control Group

In this group Ss were given no opportunity to
role play, but were exposed to the very same
information as the experimental group. This was
done by asking each S to listen to an authentic
tape recording of a role-playing session.

When the initial questionnaire about smoking
was administered, these Ss were told that, since
people's judgments are sometimes influenced by
their personal habits and opinions, E wanted to
find out how they felt about the various issues
raised in the five scenes that were about to be
heard. The control Ss were told that the recording
was to be judged in terms of the quality of the
role-player's performance and the intensity of
her emotional involvement in the role. The par-

ticular tape that was played for this purpose was of 25 minutes' duration (the average amount of time for the role-playing activity) and was selected because of its exceptionally dramatic and emotional quality.

After hearing the tape, the control Ss were given a questionnaire containing some items requesting them to evaluate the role-player's performance and other items asking them to report their own reactions to the recording.

Follow-Up Interview

At the end of the session, Ss in both groups were again given the questionnaire containing items about attitudes toward smoking. Each S was told that the main purpose was to ask some additional questions about her reactions to the procedure she had just gone through, but that some of the questions would be the same as those asked earlier, all of which should be answered, "according to how you think and feel right now."

As each S was leaving, E mentioned that he would phone her when the results of the experiment became available in order to provide a summary report. Nothing whatsoever was said about a follow-up interview. Then, two weeks after the session, E telephoned S and reported briefly about various types of comments the Ss had made about different types of role-playing procedures that had been tried out, without suggesting that any changes in personal smoking

habits had occurred or were to be expected. As an after-thought, E inquired whether S had thought about the experiment and—if modification in amount of smoking was not spontaneously mentioned—he asked whether her own smoking behavior had changed in any way during the past two weeks.

RESULTS AND DISCUSSION

Immediate Attitude Changes

Both groups were initially similar in attitudes toward smoking, the differences on all items in the initial questionnaire being very slight and nonsignificant. After playing the role of a cancer victim, however, the Ss in the experimental group showed marked changes in attitude as compared with the control group. The findings for the first four items in Table 1 indicate that the role players showed a significantly greater increase in anti-smoking attitudes than the controls on all four of the indicators used to assess the immediate effects of the experimental treatment: (a) personal belief that smoking leads to lung cancer $(p < .01)$, (b) expectation that "much harm can come to me from my smoking" $(p < .01)$, (c) willingness to try to give up smoking $(p < .01)$, and (d) expressed in-

TABLE 1

COMPARISONS BETWEEN EXPERIMENTAL (ROLE-PLAYING) GROUP AND CONTROL GROUP ON ATTITUDE CHANGE AND HABIT CHANGE

Items	Group[a]	Mean score before role play	Mean score after role play	Net change	t test
1. Belief that smoking causes lung cancer	Experimental	4.50	5.86	1.36	2.78**
	Control	4.17	4.17	0	
2. Fear of personal harm from smoking	Experimental	4.36	6.00	1.64	2.93**
	Control	4.25	4.33	0.08	
3. Willingness to attempt modification of smoking	Experimental	2.57	4.50	1.93	2.73**
	Control	2.42	3.00	0.58	
4. Intention to quit smoking	Experimental	2.79	5.08	2.29	2.05*
	Control	2.50	3.58	1.08	
5. Number of cigarettes smoked daily	Experimental	24.1	13.6[b]	−10.5	1.84*
	Control	21.7	16.9[b]	−4.8	

[a] $N = 14$ in experimental group, $N = 12$ in control group.

[b] This measure was obtained two weeks after the session, whereas the other four measures were obtained immediately after the role playing performance (or control condition).

* $p < .05$.

** $p < .01$.

tention to stop smoking immediately ($p <$ .05).[2]

Changes in Smoking Habits Reported Two Weeks Later

One of the major aims of the study was to investigate whether emotional role-playing can produce a conversion-like experience that would lead to a marked and persistent change in actual smoking habits. The results for the fifth item in Table 1 show that initially, before being exposed to the experimental treatments, there was a negligible difference in the amount of daily cigarette consumption reported by the two groups ($p > .40$). In the follow-up interview conducted two weeks after each experimental session, the role-players reported an average decrease of 10.5 in their daily cigarette consumption, whereas the controls reported an average decrease of only 4.8; this difference is statistically significant at beyond the 5% confidence level. The comparatively large drop found for the role-playing group is not attributable to a few extreme cases: The majority of the role-players (10 of the 14 women) reported a sizeable decrease, whereas the majority of the controls (7 of the 12 women) reported no change at all.

Although one must be somewhat skeptical about Ss' verbal reports about their current cigarette consumption, the findings supplement the attitude data in indicating that emotional role-playing was *differentially* more effective in producing manifestations of change than the control condition, which passively exposed the Ss to the same informational inputs and "demand" characteristics. That the Ss' verbal reports about the drop in their cigarette consumption were probably quite genuine is strongly suggested by additional comments they made about the difficulties they were having in avoiding the temptation to resume smoking, and the special efforts

they were making to implement their decision to cut down on smoking. (E.g., "I made a pact with friends to put 30¢ in the bank for every day I don't smoke.")

Fear as the Mediating Source of Motivational Changes

The arousal of fear appears to have been a mediating factor in producing the observed changes in attitudes and reported behavior. This interpretation is strongly suggested by some additional evidence obtained during the role-playing and control sessions. In response to two additional items on the immediate post-treatment questionnaire, the role-players reported much more fear about their health than the controls ($t = 2.37$, $p < .05$) and also expressed much more worry about lung cancer ($t = 2.81$, $p < .01$).

The E's observational notes also indicate that the role players displayed considerable affect arousal during their performance, including tremors, trembling, and flushing. These manifestations of fear impressed us as being far beyond the call of duty, even for whole-hearted adherents of the Stanislavski method of acting. The E's observational notes on the control group, on the other hand, indicated that these Ss showed considerable interest while listening to the dramatic tape recording, but with signs of only a very mild degree of emotional arousal as compared with the role-players, several of whom continued to show signs of being severely shaken long after the performance was over. Spontaneous comments made by almost every role-player at the end of the session indicated awareness of fear arousal: e.g., "You scared me to death"; "I was really getting scared"; "That just shook me up—it does scare me —it does!"

Further evidence of the plausibility of attributing the major motivational impact of the role-playing procedure to fear arousal is provided by correlational data indicating a positive association between reported level of fear about health (regardless of experimental condition) and subsequent reported modification of smoking habits ($\chi^2 = 4.53$, $df = 1$, $p < .05$).

---

[2] All probability values are for a one-tailed test of significance, since the direction of the differences was predicted by the hypothesis that emotional role-playing is more effective in modifying attitudes and habits than passive exposure to the same information.

For many Ss, the intense emotional experience that occurred while playing the role of the cancer victim appears to have functioned as a "last straw" which impelled them to transform their "good intentions" into action. One role-player put it this way: "This is the oomph I needed for giving up"; while another asserted, "I heard so much about the dangers of smoking, and then one more thing and that was it."

The passively exposed control group, in contrast, expressed more disbelief and affective detachment. On the post-treatment questionnaire, for example, the controls were much more likely than the role-players to agree with the following assertions: (a) that a causal relation between smoking and cancer has *not* been proven ($t = 2.19$, $p < .05$); (b) that the seriousness of lung cancer has been exaggerated ($t = 2.05$, $p < .05$); (c) that smoking is "just another one of those risks" ($t = 2.26$, $p < .05$); (d) that individual susceptibility rather than smoking is the important factor in lung cancer ($t = 3.66$, $p < .01$); and (e) that continuing to smoke does *not* imply any "lack of control and will power" ($t = 1.71$, $p < .10$). Along with their efforts to minimize the relevance of the well-publicized scientific evidence concerning the link between smoking and cancer, the control Ss were more likely to react negatively toward those who convey the unpleasant information, as indicated by their relatively strong endorsement of the statement "I feel very annoyed when people warn me about the dangers of smoking" ($t = 2.68$, $p < .01$).

In the follow-up interviews, there were also some indications that the emotional role-playing procedure had activated, over the two-week interval, an increase in vigilance as well as a heightened need for reassurance, in line with theoretical expectations concerning the nature of reflective fear (Janis, 1962). Specifically, three types of fear-related changes were spontaneously mentioned by the role-players while talking with E on the telephone:

1. Increased awareness of the literature on smoking and lung cancer: e.g., "After I saw you so many articles popped out at me"; "I'm more aware of the symptoms and I think about it . . .; and [I would like to get a] book on the warning signs of cancer."

2. Active attempts to obtain reassurance: e.g., "I got scared—I'm glad I did—I went to a doctor for a check-up"; and "I'm planning to go and get an X-ray."

3. Continued realization of personal vulnerability: e.g., "If I'd kept smoking I'm sure something would have happened to me, with my luck"; "Driving home afterwards I got scared—[I thought] what if it would be me—how would I actually react to getting lung cancer?"; "I've really thought about it—especially because Grandmother had cancer—there is a weak spot in the family."

The comments indicating awareness of personal vulnerability, made spontaneously by a few role-players during their follow-up interview, were very similar in content to those that had been made by many role-players immediately after their performance. For example, one girl reported, "I felt after a while I wasn't acting, it was really true"; another commented, "It makes it sound so near"; a third said, "I started to think, this could be me—really!"

Although the role-playing activity as a whole had an impressive emotional quality, certain parts of the psychodramatic sequence seemed to be particularly salient to the Ss as concrete representations of the threat. In response to the question, "Which part made the greatest impression on you?" several role-players mentioned the immediate threat of hospitalization, and a few spontaneously mentioned that the coughing symptoms described in the script were applicable to themselves. (E.g., "I really do have that cough and it's bad in the morning"; and "I felt I was in the part because I do cough.")

This phenomenon of becoming deeply impressed by specific disturbing details from enacting the fictional role of a cancer victim suggests that the procedure may entail more than merely a novel or dramatic way of eliciting attention to the relevant information. During the performance unpleasant outcomes such as pain, physical incapacity, hospitalization and death seem to acquire in fantasy a personal reality that is usually resisted when people are told about these same threatening outcomes in the usual types of warning communications.[3]

Thus, the qualitative observations supplement the quantitative data on attitude change in suggesting that the techniques of emotional role-playing may prove to be an exceptionally successful means for arousing potentially adaptive fear reactions, breaking through the defensive facade that normally prevents many people from taking account of their personal vulnerability to objective sources of danger. As yet we do not know how persistent the effects of emotional role-playing will prove to be, but this question is now being investigated by a follow-up study on the Ss in this experi-

[3] The finding that the controls modified their attitudes and smoking habits to some extent indicates that listening to the information and dramatic presentation in the tape recording of a role-playing session may also have been quite effective with Ss of the type used in this experiment, even though it produced less change than the role-playing procedure. Pilot studies carried out with other types of Ss suggest that young college women may be especially receptive to anti-smoking communications. It is quite possible, therefore, that the results obtained from the role-playing may be partly dependent on the predispositions of the sample used in the investigation. For example, in an older sample, with more deeply ingrained habits and greater inhibitions about acting in a make-believe situation, less involvement and accordingly less change would be expected. Replications of the present study with different types of persons are obviously essential before any firm conclusions can be drawn as to how successful the emotional role-playing technique would be in smoking clinics or in any large-scale program to modify the smoking habits of various sectors of the population.

ment, which will provide information about their smoking habits over a two-year period.

REFERENCES

CANNELL, C., AND MacDONALD, J. The impact of health news on attitudes and behavior. *Journalism Quarterly*, 1956, 33, 315–323.

CORSINI, R. Psychodrama with a psychopath. *Group Psychotherapy*, 1958, 11, 33–39.

CULBERTSON, F. Modification of an emotionally held attitude through role-playing. *Journal of Abnormal and Social Psychology*, 1957, 54, 230–233.

GREENBERG, D. S. Tobacco: After publicity surge, Surgeon General's Report seems to have little enduring effect. (News and Comment). *Science*, 1964, 145, 1021–1022.

HORN, D. Modifying smoking habits in high school students. *Children*. 1960, 7, 63–65.

JANIS, I. Psychological effects of warnings. In D. Chapman and G. Baker (Eds.), *Man and society in disaster*. New York: Basic Books, 1962.

JANIS, I. *The contours of fear: Psychological studies of war, disaster, illness, and experimental stress*. New York: Wiley (in press).

JANIS, I., AND KING, B. The influence of role-playing on opinion-change. *Journal of Abnormal and Social Psychology*, 1954, 49, 211–218.

KELMAN, H. Attitude change as a function of response restriction. *Human Relations*, 1953, 6, 185–214.

KING, B., AND JANIS, I. Comparison of the effectiveness of improvised vs. non-improvised role-playing in producing opinion changes. *Human Relations*, 1956, 9, 177–186.

LAWTON, M., AND GOLDMAN, A. Cigarette smoking and attitude toward the etiology of lung cancer. *Journal of Social Psychology*, 1961, 54, 235–248.

MORENO, J. The psychodrama. In J. E. Fairchild (Ed.), *Personal problems and psychological frontiers*. New York: Sheridan House, 1957.

SNEGIREFF, K., AND LOMBARD, O. Smoking habits of Massachusetts physicians. *New England Journal of Medicine*, 1959, 261, 603.

TOCH, H., ALLEN, T., AND LAZER, W. Effects of cancer scares: the residue of the news impact. *Journalism Quarterly*, 1961, 38, 25–34.

PART IV

CHANNEL

Like the Sirens of Greek mythology whose enchanting songs bewitched all men who heard them and which lured passing seamen to their doom, some channels of communication have a mystique of prestige and power about them which entices some communicators to ignore all relevant factors save this one, and which has doomed in advance many an information and propaganda campaign. Robinson has maintained this point in arguing that there is a certain seductive quality about some channels of communication. Advertisers, journalists, and public relations people often are guilty of equating the *act* of communicating in the mass media to the desired effect of actually imparting information or influencing the public.[1]

It should be self-evident, however, that merely using a potentially powerful channel of communication to transmit information does not necessarily guarantee that the information will have a significant impact. Noelle-Neumann observed that even though Radio Stuttgart for two years explained the meaning of the word *Bundestag* every time it was mentioned in a news broadcast, surveys provided no evidence that the information had, in fact, been learned.[2] And in the United States during the height of the McCarthy era, a period when Americans were fed heaping daily doses of relevant information by all of the mass media, nearly a third of the people polled in a national opinion survey were unable to name any Senator or Congressman who played a leading role in the investigation of Communism.[3]

Obviously, for some purposes, one channel of communication might better be used than another. If, for example, we want to prevail upon someone to register to vote, a face-to-face confrontation should be eminently more effective than sending him a leaflet by third-class mail, or bombarding him with a stream of TV and radio commercials designed to impress upon him his rights and obligations as a citizen. What could be more effective than simply pulling into his driveway and offering to take him to City Hall to register and then immediately back home? If, instead, our task were to convince a group of people that Michelangelo was the world's greatest artist and sculptor, more effective and practical than *viva voce* communication would be a filmed tour of the artist's compelling works in the Sistine and Medici

[1] Robinson, E. J. *Communication and public relations*. Columbus, Ohio: Chas. E. Merrill Books, 1966.

[2] Noelle-Neumann, E. Mass communication media and public opinion. *Journ. Quart.* 1959, **36**, 401–409.

[3] Stouffer, S. A. *Communism, conformity, and civil liberties*. New York: Doubleday, 1955.

Chapels and photographs of some of his magnificent sculpture, *Bacchus, David, Moses,* and the *Pieta.* But if our job were to persuade Viet Cong to defect, an obviously more practical solution than producing a propaganda film would be to print leaflets which could be dropped from planes, or to prepare transcribed propaganda appeals which could be piped to the enemy via helicopter-based loud speakers.

The important question, of course, is when to use which channel of communication. It would be helpful in our discussion if we were to begin by categorizing the diverse channels that are available to the communicator. They can be divided roughly into three general classes: the *Mass Media, Specialized Channels,* and *Face-to-Face Confrontation.*

The first class—*Mass Media*—is purposely intended to have a global, diffuse kind of appeal, and, as a result, it comprises the least personal of all the channels of communication. Although their immediate effects may be less dramatic than those of a face-to-face confrontation, it is thought that the mass media have a cumulative impact which lends them more to the production of delayed, or long-range, effects. Wilbur Schramm, discussing those effects, writes,

> . . . [they] are like drops of calcareous water falling from the roof of a cave upon an ancient stalagmite. Sometimes an especially big drop leaves an especially large deposit, in such a position that it can be seen and actually appears to change the shape of the stalagmite. Usually the residue of each new drop simply merges with the older deposits, and the structure grows, almost imperceptibly, in the direction of the source of supply.[4]

The mass media, as a rule, utilize only two of the sense modalities— vision and audition. Most newspapers, some books and magazines, silent movies, the comics, editorial cartoons—all of these are illustrations of mass media which require only the sense of vision. Radio is a medium requiring the sense of audition. Motion pictures and television utilize both senses.

More personal than the mass media are the various *Specialized Channels* of communication. This class can be subdivided on the basis of the purpose or content of the communication—*technical* versus *nontechnical.* Company newspapers and magazines, information kits, teaching machines, some film strips, motion pictures, telephone calls, and closed circuit TV programs are specialized channels of technical

---

[4]Quoted from Schramm, W. The effects of mass communications: A Review. *Journ. Quart.* 1949, **26**, 397. By permission of the author and the Assoc. for Educ. in Journ.

communication. Personal letters, some newspapers, books, and other phone calls are specialized channels of nontechnical communication. As in the case of the mass media, these specialized channels also require the sense modalities of sight and sound. But because they are intended to have a more limited audience appeal, it is sometimes practical for specialized channels to invoke other senses as well. Braille requires the sense of touch. To be fully appreciated, a perfumed love letter requires both vision and olfaction. If the letter is accompanied by a box of cookies, then a third sense — gustation — will also come into play. Other specialized channels include displays, exhibits, information racks, bulletin boards, tape and LP records, stickers, magazine inserts, and posters.

The third general class — *Face-to-Face Confrontation* — varies along a *public* versus *private* dimension. The crucial factor which distinguishes this from the preceding two classes is an assumption of proximity between the communicator and the communicatee — an actual face-to-face confrontation. Lectures are examples of public face-to-face confrontations. Ordinary conversation is an illustration of private face-to-face confrontation. As with the specialized channels, face-to-face confrontation could invoke any or all of the senses.

Although there have been numerous experimental attempts to cross-compare one channel of communication with another,[5] the generalizability of such results, at best, is dubious. Ideally, what one would like to have is a rank-ordering of the various channels on the basis of their potency as catalysts for facilitating or inhibiting the impact of communication. Unfortunately, there is an illusory nature to this request. As Hovland, Lumsdaine, and Sheffield first pointed out,[6] and as Lumsdaine has since amplified,[7] there is an inherent weakness

---

[5] Cherrington, B. M., & Miller, L. W. Changes in attitude as the result of a lecture and of reading similar materials. *J. soc. Psychol.* 1933, **4**, 479–484. Wilke, W. H. An experimental comparison of the speech, the radio, and the printed page as propaganda devices. *Arch. Psychol.*, 1934, No. 169. Carver, M. E. Listening versus reading. In H. Cantril & G. W. Allport (Eds.), *The Psychology of radio.* New York: Harper & Row, 1935. Heron, W. T., & Ziebarth, E. W. A preliminary experimental comparison of radio and classroom lectures. *Speech Monographs*, 1946, **13**, 54–57. Lana, R. E. Interest, media, and order effects in persuasive communications. *J. Psychol.*, 1963, **56**, 9–13. McGinnies, E. A cross-cultural comparison of printed communication versus spoken communication in persuasion. *J. Psychol.*, 1965, **60**, 1–8.

[6] Hovland, C. I., Lumsdaine, A. A., & Sheffield, F. D. *Experiments on mass communication.* Princeton, N. J.: Princeton Univer. Press, 1949. Pp. 120–121, 257–259.

[7] Lumsdaine, A. A. Instruments and media of instruction. In N. L. Gage (Ed.), *Handbook of research on teaching.* Chicago: Rand-McNally, 1963. Pp. 596–600.

in the idea that one entire channel of communication can be compared with another, as, for example, radio with television, or newspapers with television.

To emphasize this point, Hovland, Lumsdaine, and Sheffield distinguish between such cross-comparison-type studies and what has become the traditional type of attitude experiment (e.g., one-sided vs. two-sided communication, pp. 71 *ff.*):

> The advantage of the latter studies is that instead of comparing alternative existing products they compare presentations specifically designed to exemplify alternative *procedures.* In doing this, an attempt is made to control all factors except the ones under investigation. Consequently, any differences or lack of difference in effectiveness may be clearly interpreted as evidence of the importance of the factor that differentiates the two procedures. With this method of study, particularly if the experimental variable is related to theory, there is afforded a more secure basis for generalizing to other products using the same procedures than can be gained from comparison between available existing alternatives that differ with respect to a number of factors in addition to the one presumably differentiating them. [8]

The trouble with the former type of studies, they suggest, is that when questions are raised such as "How does a film-strip compare with a sound-scored motion picture?" or "Isn't a film always superior to a lecture?"

> . . . the questions inherently involve many serious problems concerning the generalizability of specific comparisons of two existing products (no matter how well the comparisons may be conducted in respect to sampling and experimental control). For example, the question, "Which is the better teaching medium, a film or a lecture?" immediately raises further questions such as: "*What* film?" "Who will be giving the lectures—an expert or a novice?" "For what kind of audiences?" "For what kinds of subject matter?" [9]

Although this point is fairly banal, the answer to the question "Which channel?" can only come after the communicator carefully considers the problem at hand, his desired aims, and the resources available to him. In the end, a subjective kind of optimum "efficiency index" will guide his decision. The communicator will decide how he can achieve the greatest impact within the bounds of his available resources.

If, for reasons of efficiency, he decides that his channel of communication must be one of the mass media, which particular medium he

---

[8] Quoted from Hovland, C. I., Lumsdaine, A. A., & Sheffield, F. D. *Experiments on mass communication.* Princeton, N. J.: Princeton Univer. Press, 1949. Pp. 258–259. By permission of Princeton Univer. Press.

[9] *Ibid.*, p. 120. Quoted by permission of Princeton Univer. Press.

finally selects will, if he is a good decision-maker, depend on which medium maximizes the probability that his message will be (a) attended to, (b) understood, (c) accepted, (d) retained, and (e) best able to influence affect, cognition, and/or action-type behavior.

Since exposure to the mass media is usually voluntary, in order to elicit *attention* the communicator will want to consider factors which would increase the likelihood of an initial contact. If his target audience consists primarily of children, he will want to know to which medium children already are most attracted. Who, for instance, reads the funnies?[10] Does TV attract all strata of children—the intelligent and the dull, the emotionally stable as well as the insecure, all age groups, etc.?[11] When children watch television or go to the movies, are they more often accompanied by their peers or by their parents?[12] With regard to *comprehension* and *retention*, he will want to know whether feedback is a significant enough variable influencing understanding so that a programmed format, which assures immediate feedback, would be the optimum means for presenting information via a mass medium.[13] If print is to be used, he will consider the relationship between type face and comprehension.[14] As for *yielding*, he will want to know whether people have greater trust and confidence in information emanating from one medium over another. Do people believe that television is any more trustworthy than the newspapers, or radio more reliable than television, etc.?[15] (As others before him also

---

[10] Heisler, F. A comparison of comic book and non-comic book readers of the elementary school. *J. Educ. Res.*, 1947, **40**, 458–464. Robinson, E. J., & White, D. M. Who reads the funnies—and why? In D. M. White & R. H. Abel (Eds.), *The funnies: An american idiom*. New York: Free Press, 1963. Pp. 179–189.

[11] Himmelweit, H. T., Oppenheim, A. N., & Vince, P. *Television and the child*. New York: Oxford Univer. Press, 1958.

[12] Friedson, E. The relation of the social situation of contact to the media in mass communication. *Publ. Opin. quart.*, 1953, **17**, 230–238.

[13] Lumsdaine, A. A. Instruments and media of instruction. In N. L. Gage (Ed.), *Handbook of research on teaching*. Chicago: Rand-McNally, 1963. Pp. 596–600. Lumsdaine, A. A., & May, M. A. Mass communication and educational media. *Annu. Rev. Psychol.*, 1965, **16**, 475–534.

[14] Fox, J. G. A comparison of gothic elite and standard elite typefaces. *Ergonomics*, 1963, **6**, 193–198. Tinker, M. A. *Legibility of print*. Ames, Iowa: Iowa State Univer. Press, 1963.

[15] Westley, B. H., & Severin, W. J. Some correlates of media credibility. *Journ. quart.*, 1964, **41**, 325–335. Carter, R. F., & Greenberg, B. S. Newspapers or television: Which do you believe? *Journ. quart.*, 1965, **42**, 29–34. Roper, E., & associates. *The public's view of television and other media 1959–1964*. New York: Television Information Office, 1965.

have pointed out, Weiss has noted that the mass media tend to confer a sense of legitimacy on people and events. He suggests that some of the civil rights demonstrations in the South might have been construed as only of local significance had it not been for the attention given to them by radio, television, and the press.[16]) If the communicator is interested only in inducing *affect,* he will consider relevant findings concerning the efficacy of the media in arousing mood states such as anxiety or tension,[17] hostility,[18] etc. If *cognition* is his aim, he will want to consider again the prestige suggestibility notion implied by Weiss above, and such other relevant factors related to information gain and learning as are discussed in Part V.[19] He will ask whether individuals' beliefs predispose them to certain types of information[20] and/or whether information gain alters individuals' belief structure.[21] If the communicator is interested in effecting *action-type behavior* he will have to decide whether it is necessary to supplement the mass media with a secondary channel of communication[22] to assure that audience commitment or social involvement has occurred (pp. 487 ff.).

---

[16]Weiss, W. Effects of the mass media of communication. In G. Lindzey & E. Aronson (Eds.), *Handbook of social psychology.* (2nd ed.) Reading, Mass.: Addison-Wesley, in press.

[17]Lazarus, R. S., Speisman, J. C., Mordkoff, A. M., & Davison, L. A. A laboratory study of psychological stress produced by a motion picture film. *Psychol. Monogr.*, 1962, **76**, (Whole No. 553). Foulkes, D., & Rechtschaffen, A. Presleep determination of dream content: Effects of two films. *Percept. mot. Skills*, 1964, **19**, 983–1005, Monogr. Suppl. 5–V19. Goldstein, M. J., Jones, R. B., Clemens, T. L., Flagg, G. W., & Alexander, F. G. Coping style as a factor in psychophysiological response to a tension-arousing film. *J. Pers. soc. Psychol.*, 1965, **1**, 290–302.

[18]Berkowitz, L., Corwin, R., & Heironimus, M. Film violence and subsequent aggressive tendencies. *Publ. Opin. quart.*, 1963, **27**, 217–229. Eron, L. D. Relationship of TV viewing habits and aggressive behavior in children. *J. Abnorm. soc. Psychol.*, 1963, **67**, 193–196.

[19]Watts and McGuire, pp. 419 ff.

[20]"Selective exposure," Part III, pp. 297 f.; also, "magnitude of impact," Part V, pp. 399 ff.

[21]Greenberg, B. S. On relating attitude change and information gain. *J. Communication*, 1964, **14**, 157–171.

[22]As, for example, a group discussion following a film: *cf.* Mitnick, L., & McGinnies, E. Influencing ethnocentrism in small discussion groups through a film communication. *J. Abnorm. soc. Psychol.*, 1958, **56**, 82–90. McGinnies, E., Lana, R. E., & Smith, C. The effects of sound films on opinions about mental illness in community discussion groups. *J. Appl. Psychol.*, 1958, **42**, 40–46. McGinnies, E., & Altman, I. Discussion as a function of attitudes and content of a persuasive communication. *J. Appl. Psychol.*, 1959, **43**, 53–59.

There is, in summary, an abundant literature on the effects of the mass media to which the communicator may have need to refer. Probably the most concise and comprehensive review of these diverse findings is the recent chapter by Walter Weiss in the Lindzey-Aronson revised *Handbook of Social Psychology*.[23] For other works in this area the interested reader has but to look for such names as Berelson and Janowitz, Dexter and White, Hovland, Katz, Klapper, Lazarsfeld, Merton, Schramm, and Steiner.[24]

A communicator might, however, decide to use a somewhat different strategy. It is generally agreed that face-to-face confrontation, because of its inherent flexibility, is the most effective means of persuasion. What if, instead of using a mass medium to inform the populace, the communicator decided instead only to confront the opinion leaders or influentials in the community and to concentrate his persuasive powers on them? This is a technique which has sometimes been used in public relations practice. It has been suggested by Lazarsfeld, Berelson, and Gaudet,[25] and elaborated upon by Katz and Lazarsfeld,[26] that even information in the mass media only indirectly affects the general population. Ideas flow from the mass media to local opinion leaders, and from them to the rank and file — a "two-step flow" process.[27] Would it be feasible, therefore, to have attractive, highly credible communicators confront the opinion leaders

---

[23] Weiss, W. Effects of the mass media of communication. In G. Lindzey & E. Aronson (Eds.), *Handbook of social psychology*. (2nd ed.) Reading, Mass.: Addison-Wesley, in press.

[24] Berelson, B., & Janowitz, M. (Eds.) *Reader in public opinion and communication* (2nd ed.) New York: Free Press, 1966. Dexter, L. A., & White, D. M. *People, society, and mass communications.* New York: Free Press, 1964. Hovland, C. I. Effects of the mass media of communication. In G. Lindzey (Ed.), *Handbook of social psychology. Vol. 2. Special fields and applications.* Reading, Mass.: Addison-Wesley, 1954. Pp. 1062–1103. Katz, E. The two-step flow of communication: An up-to-date report on an hypothesis. *Publ. Opin. quart.*, 1957, **21,** 61–78. Klapper, J. *The effects of mass communication.* New York: Free Press, 1960. Lazarsfeld, P. *Radio and the printed page.* New York: Duell, Sloan & Pearce, 1940. Merton, R. K. *Mass persuasion.* New York: Harper & Row, 1946. Schramm, W. *The process and effects of mass communication.* Urbana, Ill.: Univer. of Illinois Press, 1954. Steiner, G. A. *The people look at television.* New York: Knopf, 1963.

[25] Lazarsfeld, P. F., Berelson, B., & Gaudet, H. *The people's choice.* New York: Duell, Sloan, & Pearce, 1944.

[26] Katz, E., & Lazarsfeld, P. F. *Personal influence: The part played by people in the flow of mass communications.* New York: Free Press, 1955.

[27] *Ibid.,* and Lazarsfeld, P. F., Berelson, B., & Gaudet, H. *The people's choice.* New York: Duell, Sloan, & Pearce, 1944.

of a community, persuade them of the merits of a target issue, and then sit back and let "nature" (in the form of two-step flow) take its course?

Obviously this is an oversimplification. First, there is no guarantee that the communicators would be successful in persuading, or in even identifying, the opinion leaders. Second, even if there were some initial success, there is no certainty that there would be a diffusion of these ideas to the populace.[28] Still, the idea is an intriguing one when we realize how much more effective than the mass media face-to-face confrontation could be for at least influencing the influentials. Weiss summarizes the advantages as follows:

> The particular effectiveness that informal communications may have lies in the personal relationship binding the participants and in the face-to-face quality of the interaction. . . . The communication process can be timed for propitious occasions and repeated, if necessary; attention is assured and mis-comprehension can be minimized; appeals can be developed to fit the salient motivations and characteristics of the recipient; objections can be countered and arguments elaborated or strengthened; regard for the communicator deriving from the personal relationship will lend weight to his words; the benefits of social conformity and maintaining a satisfactory personal relation-ship may act as incentives to acceptance of the communication. In many instances, the process is initiated by a desire for information or advice; under such circumstances, the initiator is motivated to be influenced and is likely to be influenced.[29]

Although many of the characteristics of the face-to-face confrontation which make it so advantageous as a channel of communication may not be inherently obtainable in the mass media, it is possible to modify the media along these lines to enhance their effectiveness. Many of the specialized channels of communication noted earlier — closed circuit TV, teaching machines, etc. — are hybrids which capitalize on one or more characteristics endemic to face-to-face con-frontation or to the mass media.

The two studies that follow — the first by Edward Levonian, the second by Leon Festinger and Nathan Maccoby[30] — show how one

---

[28] Review by Weiss, W. Effects of the mass media of communication. In G. Lindzey and E. Aronson (Eds.), *Handbook of social psychology.* (2nd ed.) Reading, Mass.: Addison-Wesley, in press, for a critique and an up-to-date account of the two-step flow hypothesis.

[29] Quoted from W. Weiss, *ibid.*, by permission of the author and the publisher.

[30] Rosenblatt successfully replicated the Festinger-Maccoby finding using a slightly different procedure which involved the utilization of slides, instead of film, as the channel of communication. Freedman and Sears, using talks on the subject of teenage driving and thus (possibly the weaker technique) verbal instruction to achieve dis-

medium, film, has been utilized in a novel and imaginative fashion to increase its effectiveness as a channel of persuasion.

---

traction, were only minimally successful in replicating Festinger and Maccoby. It would seem, therefore, that the channel of communication plays a significant role in producing this phenomenon, inasmuch as the channel may facilitate or inhibit use of an adequate distraction procedure. See Rosenblatt, P. C. Persuasion as a function of varying amounts of distraction. *Psychon. Sci.,* 1966, **5,** 85–86. Freedman, J. L., & Sears, D. O. Warning, distraction, and resistance to influence. *J. Pers. soc. Psychol.,* 1965, **1,** 262–266.

Reprinted from AV Communication Review, 1963, Vol. 11, No. 4, pp. 104–113, by permission of Edward Levonian and the publisher.

Opinion Change as Mediated by an Audience-Tailored Film

EDWARD LEVONIAN

Muuch PAST RESEARCH involving mass media communication has been conceptualized within the framework of a model which considers communication as a one-way process, from communicator to communicatee, with the latter considered as reacting to the message of the former. To a greater or lesser extent, this orientation has pervaded much of the thinking on the communication process in education, advertising, and other fields involving social communication.

An alternative, or perhaps complementary, model conceives of communication effectiveness as a function of the intentions and psychological characteristics of both communicator and communicatee (1, 3). This model assumes that a message will be more effective if the message is prepared according to the perceptual-motivational structure of the communicatee.

The extent to which the first model has been tacitly assumed in much past research is revealed by the fact that of 15 studies which have investigated opinion change as mediated by one or more motion picture films (2, 4, 5, 7, 8, 9, 10, 14, 15, 16, 17, 18, 19, 20, 21), none utilized a film prepared on the basis of psychological measures of the audience. The films used in these studies were developed primarily on the basis of the intent of the communicator, and on his perception of—but not his measurement of—the psychological characteristics of the intended audience. Four of these studies found no significant change in opinion, while another four revealed significant changes in opinion in a direction opposite to that intended by the communicator.

The current study was undertaken within the framework of the second model. The purpose was to determine the change in opinion mediated by a film developed on the basis of one psychological measure of the intended audience. The basis for the development of the film was the prefilm opinion of a sample of the intended audience. Previous articles have described the measurement of this prefilm opinion (12) and the utilization of this prefilm opinion in the development of the film (11). The present article reports the change in opinion mediated by this audience-tailored film.

[104]

METHOD

Subjects

The subjects were regular-session UCLA students enrolled in two education classes, one public health class, one business administration class, and two psychology classes. The study involved three groups: E_0, E_1, and C. Since it was administratively impossible to assign students randomly within each class to these three groups, the education classes were assigned as units to the E_0 group, the public health and business administration classes to the E_1 group, and the psychology classes to the C group. Three subjects were eliminated because they appeared in more than one group. Further, because of a restriction imposed by a computer program to be used, a few subjects were removed randomly from the larger groups. Thereafter E_0 contained 216 subjects, E_1 contained 108 subjects, and C contained 216 subjects.

Procedure

A questionnaire was administered to all three groups. A week later the film was shown to the E_0 and E_1 groups in class. The questionnaire was readministered immediately after the film for the E_0 group (0 weeks after the film), and one week later for the E_1 group (1 week after the film). The test-retest interval for the C group was one week, and this group, of course, did not see the film.

Each subject was given the option of identifying himself with his real name or a fictitious name. Some identification was necessary in order to match prefilm and postfilm questionnaires. However, the subjects were not told at the first administration that the questionnaire would be readministered. Whether he chose to use his real name or to remain anonymous, each subject was assured that his responses would be kept confidential and that they would have no bearing on his course grade.

Film

The development of the film has been reported previously (11), and only a brief review will be given here. The film was developed on the basis of a factor analysis of the responses to 69 items presented in the form of a film questionnaire (12). These responses were obtained from 252 regular-session UCLA classes in education and psychology. None of these 252 students are included in the study now being reported. The factor analysis identified the opinion dimensions, and these determined the number of sequences which would appear in the film. The order and length of these sequences were determined by the extent to which the measured opinions diverged from the orientation to be taken by the film.

Questionnaire

The questionnaire, given in Table 1, consisted of 36 items. Of these, 29 were opinion items, and 7 (items 12, 17, 22, 27, 29, 34, and 35) were information items. The items were written with the intent of measuring opinions and information with respect to material presented in the film.

It can be seen from Table 1 that each item was trichotomous, with the middle category designated as uncertain. Each item was dichotomized by combining the middle category with the extreme category with the fewer

TABLE 1—The Questionnaire

(with desired responses and initial response percentages indicated)

1. The more important nation a century from now will be (a) England (13%), (b) uncertain (40%), (c) India (47%).

2. Progress in India doesn't appreciably affect the United States. (a) agree (7%), (b) uncertain (5%), (c) disagree (88%)

3. Mechanized farming is a practical way of increasing India's agricultural yield. (a) agree (79%), (b) uncertain (12%), (c) disagree (9%)

4. In contrast to India, America is more concerned about material progress. (a) agree (56%), (b) uncertain (12%), (c) disagree (32%)

5. India's illiterates should be allowed to vote. (a) agree (21%), (b) uncertain (23%), (c) disagree (56%)

6. India's progress would be more rapid if her religion were more similar to ours. (a) agree (25%), (b) uncertain (18%), (c) disagree (57%)

7. Industrialization of agrarian India is unlikely. (a) agree (14%), (b) uncertain (29%), (c) disagree (57%)

8. India's advancement is democracy's gain. (a) agree (63%), (b) uncertain (30%), (c) disagree (7%)

9. India's principal problem is overpopulation. (a) agree (58%), (b) uncertain (16%), (c) disagree (26%)

10. The United States should increase its aid to India. (a) agree (41%), (b) uncertain (34%), (c) disagree (25%)

11. In poverty-stricken countries progress is necessarily slower if the democratic process is employed. (a) agree (35%), (b) uncertain (20%), (c) disagree (45%)

12. Gandhi had very little formal education. (a) yes (12%), (b) uncertain (48%), (c) no (40%)

13. Would you approve of marriage between a close relative of yours and a student from India studying here? (a) yes (46%), (b) uncertain (26%), (c) no (28%)

14. India, like America, should have a permanent seat in the Security Council. (a) agree (47%), (b) uncertain (27%), (c) disagree (26%)

15. Though India may be progressing, the change is almost imperceptible. (a) agree (15%), (b) uncertain (25%), (c) disagree (60%)

16. Contacts between India and the United States benefit India more than the United States. (a) agree (38%), (b) uncertain (20%), (c) disagree (42%)

17. Has a scholar from India ever won a Nobel Prize? (a) yes (13%), (b) uncertain (74%), (c) no (13%)

18. India's concept of the holy cow is better accounted for in terms of (a) religion (81%), (b) uncertain (7%), (c) economics (12%).

19. Is "spiritualistic East" vs. "materialistic West" a valid distinction? (a) yes (24%), (b) uncertain (16%), (c) no (60%)

20. We should refuse to send any more aid to India until she stops voting against us in the UN. (a) agree (10%), (b) uncertain (20%), (c) disagree (70%)

21. Illiterate people should never be given the responsibility of governing themselves. (a) agree (32%), (b) uncertain (20%), (c) disagree (48%)

22. Since independence from Britain, India has been encouraging the concept of untouchability. (a) agree (10%), (b) uncertain (35%), (c) disagree (55%)

23. Tradition-steeped Hinduism tends to inhibit progress in India. (a) agree (60%), (b) uncertain (24%), (c) disagree (16%)

24. Democratic methods, in contrast to totalitarian, are less effective in under-developed countries. (a) agree (43%), (b) uncertain (19%), (c) disagree (38%)

25. Which is more representative of India: (a) a Hindu farmer (68%), (b) uncertain (12%), (c) the Taj Mahal (20%)?

26. Even though famines create misery, they are the only effective curb to overpopulation in India. (a) agree (16%), (b) uncertain (10%), (c) disagree (74%)

27. India's form of government is (a) democratic (33%), (b) uncertain (47%), (c) totalitarian (20%).

28. Do you think the standard of living in India can reach that of the United States? (a) yes (30%), (b) uncertain (20%), (c) no (50%)

29. India's rate of industrialization is considerably lower than ours. (a) yes (71%), (b) uncertain (16%), (c) no (13%)

30. As many people from India as from France should be allowed to immigrate to the United States. (a) agree (53%), (b) uncertain (22%), (c) disagree (25%)

31. India's neutrality is based upon her desire to get aid from both Russia and the United States. (a) agree (39%), (b) uncertain (30%), (c) disagree (31%)

32. India's concept of the Holy Ganges is better accounted for in terms of (a) economic necessity (13%), (b) uncertain (53%), (c) religious ignorance (34%).

33. India's progress has slowed down since her independence from Britain. (a) agree (8%), (b) uncertain (37%), (c) disagree (55%)

34. The U.S. population increases about 2% a year; in India the rate is significantly higher. (a) yes (63%), (b) uncertain (28%), (c) no (9%)

35. Caste distinctions are encouraged by the government of India. (a) agree (15%), (b) uncertain (33%), (c) disagree (52%)

36. India's underdevelopment is better accounted for in terms of (a) historical circumstances (47%), (b) uncertain (21%), (c) the caste system (32%).

cases. The number in parenthesis after each category represents the percentage of subjects who selected that category during the first administration of the questionnaire. The underlined categories coincide with the orientation taken by the film. A response to one of these categories was defined, for purpose of this study, as a desired response.

Analysis[1]

Responses to the questionnaire yielded four measures: (a) prefilm opinion, (b) prefilm information, (c) change in opinion, and (d) change in information. The first and third measures involved the 29 opinion items. The first measure represents the number of desired responses given by the subject. The third measure represents the ratio of (a) the number of desired responses given after the film minus the number of desired responses given before the film to (b) the total change possible in the direction of change, with this ratio expressed as a percent. For example, if the subject gave 20 desired responses before the film and 18 desired responses after the film, his change in opinion score would be —2 ÷ 20, or —10 percent. However, if the subject gave 20 out of 29 desired responses before the film and 22 desired responses after the film, his change in opinion score would be +2 ÷ 9, or +22.2 percent. The intent was to make change in opinion independent of prefilm opinion in order to circumvent ceiling effects. This method of scoring follows the "effectiveness index" suggested by Hovland, Lumsdaine, and Sheffield (7). The second and fourth

measures were determined similarly, but involved the seven information items.

With respect to these four measures, differences between groups, sex, and identification were tested for significance, with all tests in this study being referred to .01 level.

This study followed the 15 cited studies in measuring change in opinion by change in verbal response. However, this conventional method of measuring change in opinion has the limitation of confounding change in opinion with change in the measuring instrument. The readministered questionnaire is probably perceived differently from the same questionnaire initially administered, especially for subjects exposed to an experience (such as a film) relative to the questionnaire. Change in verbal response probably reflects not only a change in opinion but also the altered meaning of the readministered questionnaire.

RESULTS

Table 2 shows the intergroup differences with respect to the four measures. Whereas E_o and C do not differ significantly with respect to prefilm opinion or information, they do differ significantly with respect to change in opinion and information. The same is true for E_1 and C. Table 2 indicates also that the E_o group showed a significantly larger change in opinion and information than did the E_1 group. This agrees with the general finding that a film (or other communication material) mediates the largest over-all change in opinion and information immediately after the film has been shown. Changes

---

[1] Analysis of the data utilized the equipment and services of the UCLA Computing Facility.

TABLE 2—Group Differences with Respect to the Four Measures

Measure	E_0		E_1		C		E_0 vs. C	E_1 vs. C	E_0 vs. E_1
	Mean	SD	Mean	SD	Mean	SD	t	t	t
1. Prefilm Opinion	15.62	4.33	14.20	4.21	15.13	4.36	1.17	1.85	2.80*
2. Prefilm Information	2.62	1.54	2.44	1.57	2.62	1.57	.00	.92	.97
3. Change in Opinion	51.39	28.09	32.88	26.21	− 2.13	17.22	23.85*	12.60*	5.82*
4. Change in Information	82.98	24.37	72.59	29.71	−11.07	38.25	30.50*	21.60*	3.14*

* Significant at the .01 level

measured by some items, however, may be greater at a later time especially for items which measure broad attitudes with respect to material not covered specifically in the film (7).

The tremendous changes in opinion and information for both experimental groups, particularly E_0, is substantiated by the change in the proportion of desired responses to each dichotomized item. In comparison to the C group, the E_0 group changed significantly in the desired direction for each of the 36 items, except Items 10, 13, 14, 16, and 30. In comparison to the C group, the E_1 group changed significantly in the desired direction for each of the 36 items, except Items 10, 11, 13, 14, 16, 28, 30, and 36. The greatest changes tended to be with respect to those items dealing with material specifically covered in the film, a result which agrees with most previous studies.

Changes in opinion and information are indicated also by the responses of individual subjects. In each experimental group most subjects changed in the desired direction. In the E_0 group of 216 subjects, only 11 had negative scores for change in opinion, and only one had a negative score for change in information. In the E_1 group of 108 subjects, only eight had negative scores for change in opinion and only two subjects had negative scores for change in information. However, in the C group of 216 subjects, 126 had negative scores for change in opinion and 123 had negative scores for change in information, with zero changes proportionately counted as negative or positive.

Table 3 shows the sex differences with respect to the four measures. These results indicate that males tended to score higher on prefilm information, while females tended to show a greater change in opinion. A week later, however, the sex difference with respect to change in opinion was not significant. These results suggest that any extrapolation into the future from the immediate effect of the film should take sex into account. Further, the importance of sex with respect to change in opinion raises a question about the generalizability of results from those film studies utilizing one sex only. Of the 15 studies noted earlier, four employed males only and one employed females only.

Table 4 shows the differences between students who used their real name and students who chose to remain anonymous. No significant identification differences emerged with respect to the four measures, a result previously obtained with respect to personality measures (13). These results would seem to indicate that the identifiable response may be quite as free of dissimulation as the anonymous response, at least with regard to opinion or personality.

TABLE 3—Sex Differences with Respect to the Four Measures

Measure	E_0				
	Female	N=144	Male	N=72	Female vs. Male
	Mean	SD	Mean	SD	t
1. Prefilm Opinion	15.47	4.11	15.92	4.77	.67
2. Prefilm Information	2.42	1.52	3.01	1.51	2.40
3. Change in Opinion	57.18	23.10	39.82	33.32	7.95*
4. Change in Information	84.90	22.23	79.14	27.94	1.51

Measure	E_1				
	Female	N=39	Male	N=69	Female vs. Male
	Mean	SD	Mean	SD	t
1. Prefilm Opinion	14.23	4.42	14.19	4.12	.05
2. Prefilm Information	2.33	1.42	2.51	1.65	.78
3. Change in Opinion	38.28	26.12	29.83	25.95	1.60
4. Change in Information	67.97	34.35	75.20	26.65	1.12

Measure	C				
	Female	N=106	Male	N=110	Female vs. Male
	Mean	SD	Mean	SD	t
1. Prefilm Opinion	15.10	3.95	15.15	4.74	.68
2. Prefilm Information	2.08	1.37	3.14	1.59	5.22*
3. Change in Opinion	− 1.89	17.23	− 2.35	17.28	.20
4. Change in Information	−13.97	41.39	− 8.28	35.14	1.08

* Significant at the .01 level

The C group was administered the questionnaire twice to allow not only a control measure of change in opinion and information but also a measure of questionnaire reliability. This one-week stability reliability was .87.

DISCUSSION

The current study was similar to many of the 15 studies with regard to the use of a captive audience, the length and general quality of the film, the time intervals between test-film-retest, and the manner in which opinion was measured.

The current study differed from each of the 15 studies by utilizing a film which was developed according to a relatively objective criterion presumed to be important in mediating a change in opinion. Further, the change in opinion in the present study was substantially greater than that reported in any of the 15 studies. These two differences suggest that a film involving controversial material is likely to mediate a greater change in opinion if the film is audience tailored according to those characteristics of the audience which interact with opinion change.

This conclusion, however, is only suggested, but not proved, by the current study, for definitive conclusions cannot be drawn on the basis of results obtained from different studies. Despite the attempt to design the current study so as to be similar to many of the cited

TABLE 4—Identification Differences with Respect to the Four Measures

	E_0				
	Real	N=149	Anon	N=67	Real vs. Anon
Measure	Mean	SD	Mean	SD	t
1. Prefilm Opinion	16.23	4.48	14.25	3.66	2.39
2. Prefilm Information	2.71	1.51	2.40	1.59	.97
3. Change in Opinion	54.09	28.68	45.40	25.92	1.56
4. Change in Information	83.32	23.65	82.22	26.08	.21

	E_1				
	Real	N=93*	Anon	N=15	Real vs. Anon
Measure	Mean	SD	Mean	SD	t
1. Prefilm Opinion	14.47	4.10	12.53	4.66	1.48
2. Prefilm Information	2.48	1.60	2.20	1.37	.69
3. Change in Opinion	32.78	26.96	33.47	21.69	.11
4. Change in Information	72.10	30.74	75.67	22.86	.50

	C				
	Real	N=134	Anon	N=82	Real vs. Anon
Measure	Mean	SD	Mean	SD	t
1. Prefilm Opinion	15.16	4.47	15.07	4.21	.15
2. Prefilm Information	2.75	1.49	2.41	1.70	1.48
3. Change in Opinion	− 1.53	16.71	−3.10	18.08	.64
4. Change in Information	−12.99	39.97	−7.94	35.57	.96

* 64 of these subjects (one class) were not given option of remaining anonymous.

studies, each study has its own unique characteristics, and the results from a particular study may reflect largely these unique characteristics. For instance, in at least one of the 15 studies (7), the subjects were not aware that a study was in progress. This may have influenced the results, for it has been shown that messages tend to mediate less of an opinion change when they are presented within a naturalistic context (6).

Only one audience characteristic was utilized in the development of the film used in this study. This characteristic—prefilm opinion—is undoubtedly important enough to be considered in any attempt to change opinion, but practically any sociological or psychological characteristic is likely to interact with opinion change. Thus, it is assumed that the film would have mediated an even greater opinion change if additional characteristics, such as sex, personality, intelligence, motivation, as well as their relationships with prefilm opinion, had been taken into account. As more characteristics are considered, it becomes increasingly important to heed the suggestion of Hovland, Lumsdaine, and Sheffield (7) to the effect that films especially planned and produced are more efficient for objective study than films which have already been produced.

SUMMARY

The purpose of this study was to determine the change in opinion mediated by a film whose development was based on the prefilm opinions of a sample similar to the one used in the current study.

The subjects in the current study consisted of 540 university students, each of whom was administered a 36-item questionnaire pertaining to material presented in the film. One experimental group was shown the film a week later, and the questionnaire was readministered immediately after the film. The other experimental group was also shown the film a week later, but the questionnaire was readministered one week after the film showing. The questionnaire was readministered a week later to the control group, which did not see the film. Relative to the control group, the experimental groups showed large changes in opinion (critical ratios of 23.85 and 12.60).

These changes in opinion were substantially greater than those obtained by 15 other studies involving film-mediated opinion change, but none of which involved films which were audience-tailored according to measured psychological characteristics of the intended audience. These comparative results from unrelated studies cannot be used as the basis for definitive conclusions, but they do suggest that a film can mediate a greater opinion change if it is developed according to criteria involving those characteristics of the audience which interact with opinion change.

REFERENCES

1. Bauer, Raymond A., and Bauer, Alice H. "America, Mass Society, and Mass Media." *Journal of Social Issues* 16: 3-66; No. 3, 1960.
2. Fearing, Franklin. "Motion Pictures as a Medium of Instruction and Communication: An Experimental Analysis of the Effects of Two Films." *University of California Publications in Culture and Society* 2: 101-201; No. 3, 1950.
3. Fearing, Franklin. "Toward a Psychological Theory of Human Communication." *Journal of Personality* 22: 71-88; September 1953.
4. Harriman, B. L. *Influence of Group-Centered Therapy and Mental Health Films on Attitudes of Prisoners.* Doctor's thesis. University Park: Pennsylvania State University, 1956.
5. Hirsch, Richard S. "Moving Attitudes with Motion Pictures." *Educational Screen* 28: 446-47; December 1941.
6. Hovland, Carl I. "Reconciling Conflicting Results Derived from Experimental and Survey Studies of Attitude Change." *American Psychologist* 14: 8-17; January 1959.
7. Hovland, Carl I.; Lumsdaine, A. A.; and Sheffield, Fred D. *Experiments on Mass Communications.* Princeton, N.J.: Princeton University Press, 1949.
8. Hulett, J. E., Jr. "Estimating the Net Effect of a Commercial Motion Picture upon the Trend of Public Opinion." *American Sociological Review* 14: 263-75; August 1949.
9. Jones, Vernon. *Character and Citizenship Training in the Public School.* Chicago: University of Chicago Press, 1936.
10. Kishler, John P. *The Effects of Prestige and Identification Factors on Attitude Restructuring and Learning from Sound Films.* Technical Report No. 269-7-10. Port Washington, N.Y.: Special Devices Center, 1950.
11. Levonian, Edward. "Development of an Audience-Tailored Film." *AV Communication Review* 8: 62-68; Winter 1960.
12. Levonian, Edward. "The Use of Film in Opinion Measurement." *AV Communication Review* 10: 250-54; July-August 1962.
13. Levonian, Edward; Case, Harry W.; and Wilson, George L. "Psycho-

logical Characteristics in Relation to Sex and Driving Experience of Driver Education Students." *Traffic Safety Research Review* 6: 28-32; December 1962.

14. McFarlane, A. M. "A Study of the Influence of the Educational Geographical Film upon the Racial Attitudes of a Group of Elementary School Children." *British Journal of Educational Psychology* 15: 152-53; November 1945.

15. Mertens, Marjorie S. *The Effects of Mental Hygiene Motion Pictures on the Self-Regarding Attitudes and Self Perceptions of College Girls.* Technical Report No. 269-7-22. Port Washington, N.Y.: Special Devices Center, 1951.

16. Peterson, J. A. *The Effectiveness of Selected Motion Pictures in Changing the Beliefs of Nebraska Secondary School Students Relative to the U.N. and Its Activities.* Doctor's thesis. Lincoln: University of Nebraska, 1950.

17. Peterson, Ruth C., and Thurstone, L. L. *Motion Pictures and the Social Attitudes of Children.* New York: Macmillan Co., 1933.

18. Ramseyer, L. L. "Factors Influencing Attitudes and Attitude Changes." *Educational Research Bulletin* 18: 9-14; January 1939.

19. Rosen, I. C. "The Effect of the Motion Picture 'Gentlemen's Agreement' on the Attitudes Toward Jews." *Journal of Psychology,* 26: 525-36; October 1948.

20. Rosenthal, S. P. "Changes of Socio-Economic Attitudes Under Radical Motion Picture Propaganda." *Archives of Psychology* 25: 1-46; April 1934.

21. Spigle, Irving S. *The Cumulative Effect of Selected Educational Motion Pictures on the Attitudes of High-School Boys and the Relationship of Attitude Changes to Selected Personality and Intelligence Factors.* Doctor's thesis. Bloomington: Indiana University, 1955.

Reprinted from Journal of Abnormal and Social Psychology, 1964, Vol. 68, pp. 359–366,
by permission of L. Festinger and APA.

ON RESISTANCE TO PERSUASIVE COMMUNICATIONS [1]

LEON FESTINGER AND NATHAN MACCOBY [2]

3 separate experiments were done at different universities to test the hypothesis that a persuasive communication that argues strongly against an opinion to which the audience is committed will be more effective if the audience is somewhat distracted from the communication so that they cannot adequately counterargue while listening. 2 films were prepared, each containing the same communication arguing strongly against fraternities. One was a normal film of the speaker making a speech. The other film, with the same track, had an utterly irrelevant and highly distracting visual presentation. Fraternity men were more influenced by the distracting presentation of the persuasive communication than by the ordinary version. There was no difference between the 2 for nonfraternity men. In general, the hypothesis concerning the effect of distraction was supported.

Some time ago Allyn and Festinger (1961) reported an experiment which showed that if subjects are forewarned concerning the content of a communication arguing against an opinion they hold strongly, they tend to reject the speaker more and are influenced less than if they are not forewarned. Since the ideas which form the basis for the present article emerge in part from that experiment, it is necessary to examine it in some detail.

Allyn and Festinger, in their experiment, used high school students as subjects on the assumption that high school students, at or approaching the age at which they could obtain licenses to drive automobiles (age 16 in California), would be rather strongly committed to opinions that teen-agers were good and capable drivers. This assumption was, of course, largely correct. For the experiment a sizable number of these high school students were assembled in the high school auditorium where they heard a person, announced to them as an authority on the subject, deliver a speech denouncing teen-age drivers and arguing that the only thing

[1] The studies reported in this paper were supported by funds from Grant Number G-11255 from the National Science Foundation to Leon Festinger and by funds from Stanford University Institute for Communication Research to Nathan Maccoby.

[2] The authors wish to express their thanks and appreciation to Ernest W. Rose and Henry Breitrose for their help in planning the experiments, devising and preparing the experimental materials, and in conducting the actual experiments.

to do was to keep teen-agers off the road for as long as possible. The subjects were then asked several questions to measure their opinions about driving by teen-agers.

Two conditions were run in this experiment. As each subject entered the auditorium, he was given a booklet. For half of the subjects, the cover page on this booklet told them that they were to hear a speech against teen-age driving and that they should listen carefully since they would be asked questions about the speaker's opinions. This was the "forewarned" condition. For the other half of the subjects, the cover page told them that they would hear a person make a speech (nothing about the content of the speech) and that they should listen carefully because, afterwards, they would be asked questions about the speaker's personality.

The results of the experiment showed that in the "forewarned" condition, the students were relatively uninfluenced by the speaker and rejected him more than in the "personality" condition where the speaker successfully influenced their attitudes. The authors of the experiment interpret this result as implying that, if persons who are rather committed to a given opinion are forewarned that their opinion will be attacked, they are better able to marshal their defenses and, hence, are more successful in rejecting the speaker and in resisting his persuasions.

At first glance, this seems like a plausible interpretation of the result and fits many common-sense conceptions ̇ such as "forewarned is forearmed" and the like. Further consideration of the matter, however, produces some concern about the adequacy of this interpretation. The difference between the "forewarned" and the "personality-orientation" conditions was created by what they read on the face sheet of the booklet. After having read this, the speech commenced. Virtually the first words out of the speaker's mouth were a vigorous denunciation of teen-agers in automobiles. In other words, after the first few sentences of the speech, the personality-orientation subjects were *also* forewarned. Indeed, in terms of being forewarned, the only difference between conditions seems to have been a matter of when the forewarning took place, at the beginning of the speech or 2 to 3 minutes earlier. It does seem somewhat implausible for such a small time difference to have produced the result reported in the experiment.

But if we do not like the explanation offered by Allyn and Festinger, the problem is then created as to how one would, plausibly, explain the results they obtained. In order to arrive at such an explanation, let us first try to understand the cognitive behavior of a person who, strongly committed to an opinion, listens to a vigorous, persuasive communication that attacks that opinion. Certainly, such a listener is not passive. He does not sit there listening and absorbing what is said without any counteraction on his part. Indeed, it is most likely that under such circumstances, while he is listening to the persuasive communication, he is very actively, inside his own mind, counterarguing, derogating the points the communicator makes, and derogating the communicator himself. In other words, we can imagine that there is really an argument going on, one side being vocal and the other subvocal.

Let us imagine that one could somehow prevent the listener from arguing back while listening to the persuasive communication. If one created such a passive listener, it seems reasonable to expect that the persuasive communication would then have more of an impact. The listener, not able to counterargue, would be more influenced and would be less likely to reject the communication. And perhaps this is exactly what was really done in the experiment reported by Allyn and Festinger. The group that was not forewarned was also told to pay attention to the speaker's personality. In other words, a good deal of their attention was focused on a task which had little to do with the persuasive communication itself. It may be that, under such circumstances, they still listen to, and hear, the content of the speech that is being delivered but, with a good deal of their attention focused on something irrelevant, they are less able to counterargue while they are listening.

If this interpretation is correct, then the forewarning variable is irrelevant, at least in this particular experiment. The critical variable would be the extent to which the attention of the person was distracted from the persuasive communication while listening to it. If the attention of the listener were distracted sufficiently to make it quite difficult for him to counterargue, but not so much as to interfere with his hearing of the speech, this would represent a maximally effective influence situation.

How can we test the validity of this interpretation? The simplest procedure which suggested itself to us was to choose an issue such that we could easily identify a group of people strongly committed to a given position on that issue, devise a persuasive communication strongly attacking this committed position, and present this persuasive communication to these people under two different conditions, one where their attention was focused on the communication and one where they were distracted on a completely irrelevant basis. We decided to use attitudes toward college fraternities as the issue since fraternity members were likely to be strongly committed to a favorable opinion on this matter. We also decided to use as pure a form of distraction as we could think of so as to reduce the plausibility of alternative interpretations. We settled on a procedure whereby the subjects were visually distracted while listening to a speech.

METHOD

Experimental Materials and Procedure

A persuasive communication arguing strongly against college fraternities was prepared in the form of a color, 16-millimeter sound film. The film was about 12 minutes long. The first 2 minutes told the audience that this film was Part 4 of a series on university life, this part dealing with college fraternities. The visual showed various scenes of campus buildings and students walking on college campuses. These scenes then dissolved to a scene of a young college professor [3] who, after stating that he himself had been a member of a fraternity in college, proceeded to argue for almost 10 minutes that fraternities encouraged cheating and dishonesty, encouraged social snobbishness and racial discrimination, were antithetical to the purposes of a university and should be abolished. This film was used to present the persuasive communication to subjects in those experimental conditions in which the attention of the audience was to be focused on the communication.

A second film was prepared to present the same persuasive communication under distraction conditions. We chose to use, as the basic vehicle, an existing short color film *Day of the Painter* produced by Little Movies, Incorporated, which had sound effects and music but no dialogue or narration and which was very amusing and rather absorbing to watch. This film was edited somewhat to shorten it to match the length of the other film. It opened with the identical titles and preliminary visuals used in the original film, and the identical sound track from the persuasive-communication film superimposed over it. Thus, this film for the distraction conditions of the experiment was identical visually for the first 2 minutes with the nondistracting film. Instead of the scene shifting to the young college professor making a speech, however, the visual of this distracting film dissolved to the amusing and absorbing short film. The sound tracks on the two films were identical throughout. In short, in the distraction conditions, the subjects heard the same persuasive communication while watching a completely irrelevant and highly interesting movie.

Experiments using these film materials were conducted at three different academic institutions: the University of Minnesota, San Jose State College, and the University of Southern California. In all three institutions the procedure employed was similar. Subjects were assigned at random to a particular room. In each room the subjects were given the identical verbal introduction which told them they were to see a film about fraternities, that the presentation was a rather unusual one, and that we would appreciate their paying close attention since we would want to ask them some questions about it later. In one room they were then shown the straight film version of the persuasive communication while in the other room the subjects saw the distracting version. Following the showing of the film, the subjects were asked to answer a number of questions designed to measure their

attitudes toward fraternities and their perception of the expertness and fairness of the speaker. When the questionnaires had been completed and collected, the total procedure, its purposes and our hypotheses were explained in detail to all subjects.

After having prepared the film materials, our first step was to try them out on a preliminary basis with students at Stanford University. The results were very encouraging. We then ran the experiment at the University of Minnesota using two groups, fraternity men who saw the straight version and fraternity men who saw the distracting version of the film. The identical design was next used at San Jose State College. Finally we ran a more complete design at the University of Southern California which involved six conditions: Fraternity men and nonfraternity men, one-third of each seeing the straight version, one-third the distraction version, and one-third answering the questionnaire before seeing any film.

RESULTS

We will present the data and discuss the results separately and in the sequence in which the experiments were actually conducted for the three different academic institutions.

University of Minnesota Experiment

At the University of Minnesota [4] 65 fraternity men participated in the experiment. Thirty-three of them saw the straight film version of the persuasive communication and 32 saw the distracting version. The questionnaire which they answered after having seen the film had six questions oriented toward measuring their attitude toward fraternities. These questions were:

1. In your opinion, what should be done with American college fraternities (5-point scale from "definitely should be abolished" to "their power in university life should be increased")?

2. On the whole, how do you feel about the ways in which fraternities influence university life (5-point scale from "excellent influence" to "very poor influence")?

3. How do you personally feel about fraternities (8-point scale from "dislike fraternities strongly" to "like fraternities very much")?

4. As far as you know, how do fraternity men's grades compare with comparable independent men's grades in most universities and colleges (5-point scale from "fraternity men do much better" to "independent men do much better")?

---

[3] We wish to express our thanks to William McCord for preparing and delivering the persuasive communication in the film.

[4] We would like to thank Ben Willerman and Elliot Aronson for their help and cooperation in arranging for the conduct of the experiment at the University of Minnesota.

5. How do you feel about the nature of the contribution to American college life that fraternities make (4-point scale from "fraternities contribute nothing" to "fraternities contribute considerably")?

6. What effect, if any, do fraternities have on those students who are not chosen by them (4-point scale from "very harmful effect" to "no harmful effect")?

All answers to these questions were scored so that the larger number represented a more favorable attitude toward fraternities. The maximum profraternity score possible was 31. The more influenced they were by the persuasive communication, the lower should their score be.

The questionnaire also contained two questions to obtain a measure of the extent to which they rejected the speaker. These questions were:

1. In your opinion, how well qualified to discuss fraternities was the lecturer in this film (3-point scale from "very well qualified" to "not well qualified")?

2. In your opinion, how fair was the presentation about fraternities (4-point scale from "quite fair" to "quite biased")?

These two questions were summed to provide a rejection measure. Maximum rejection of the speaker would be represented by a score of 7.

Table 1 presents the data on attitude toward fraternities and rejection of the speaker for each of the two conditions at the University of Minnesota. It is clear from the table that the differences between conditions were negligible. The slight difference that does exist is in the direction of having been more influenced in the distraction condition and rejecting the speaker less in that condition, but the difference is disappointingly small.

One reason for continuing our investigation was an explanation offered by those familiar with the situation at the University of

TABLE 1
Average Ratings for Fraternity Men at University of Minnesota

Condition	Attitude toward fraternities	Rejection of speaker
Ordinary (N = 33)	26.2	6.0
Distraction (N = 32)	26.0	5.8

TABLE 2
Average Ratings for Fraternity Men at San Jose State College

Condition	Attitude toward fraternities	Rejection of speaker
Ordinary (N = 51)	25.7	6.0
Distraction (N = 48)	24.0	5.5

Minnesota for the failure to obtain any difference. It was suggested that the fraternity system at Minnesota is very weak and, for many years now, has been under constant attack and pressure from the University. It was suggested that the fraternity men at the University of Minnesota have already heard all the antifraternity arguments many, many times and, consequently, their counterarguments are all formed and ready. Hence, distraction may not have had the effect which we anticipated.

True or not, we proceeded to do our experiment again, this time in an institution where the fraternity system was strong and prestigeful and was *not* under attack and pressure.

San Jose State College Experiment

At San Jose State College [5] 99 fraternity men participated in the experiment. Fifty-one of them saw the straight film version and 48 saw the distracting version of the persuasive communication. The procedure and the questionnaire were identical in all respects to the experiment done at the University of Minnesota. Table 2 presents the data collected at San Jose.

An examination of the data in Table 2 shows that they clearly support our theoretical expectations. The subjects who heard the persuasive communication under distracting conditions are significantly less favorable to fraternities ($t = 3.63$, $p < .01$) and reject the speaker less ($t = 2.80$, $p < .01$).

These results are, of course, consistent with the notion that, if distracted while listening to the persuasive communication, the subject is less able to counterargue against the communication and against the speaker. As a

[5] We would like to thank Robert Martin, Dean, for his help and cooperation in arranging for the conduct of the experiment at San Jose State College.

result, under these circumstances he is less likely to reject the speaker and is more influenced by the communication than subjects who focused all their attention on the persuasive communication. However, this interpretation of the data is not quite unambiguous in the absence of a control group. It is quite conceivable, for example, that the ordinary presentation of the persuasive communication aroused so much resentment and anger in the fraternity men who were listening that a boomerang effect could have ensued. That is, in the ordinary condition they may have moved away from the position advocated by the speaker. For our interpretation to be strongly supported, it would be well to show that the distraction presentation results in effective influence which is not only significantly greater than the ordinary presentation condition but also represents significant change from a control group whose attitudes were measured before seeing any film. We thus decided to repeat the experiment once more using a more complete experimental design.

University of Southern California Experiment

The University of Southern California [6] was selected as the site for the experiment because, among other things, the fraternity system there was important on the campus, fraternities were prestigeful and had not been too much under attack in recent years. In short, we attempted to select a situation which would be comparable to San Jose State College rather than like the University of Minnesota.

The plan at the University of Southern California was to have three conditions: those who saw the straight presentation, those who saw the distracting version, and those who saw no film at all—these latter constituting a control group to give us an indication of attitudes prior to exposure to the persuasive communication. We also decided to do the experiment here using both fraternity and nonfraternity men in order to provide further clarification of the theoretical interpretation of the results. It will be recalled that the idea behind the experiment

[6] We wish to thank James Finn, Harold Gluth, Robert Heinick, Francis Joyce, and Bernard Kanter at the University of Southern California.

was that people will actively counterargue while listening to a persuasive communication which attacks an opinion to which they are committed. The distraction condition is intended to interfere with this activity of counterarguing while listening. If this is the correct interpretation, one should find that the distracting presentation is indeed more effective in influencing fraternity men but one should not find it any more effective in influencing nonfraternity men. After all, many, if not most, of the nonfraternity men will already tend to agree with the speaker and, although their opinions may not be as extreme as those represented in the persuasive communication, there is little reason to expect nonfraternity men to be motivated to counterargue while listening. Thus, the distraction version of the film should not provide any advantage in effectiveness over the straight version.

The experiment was carried out as planned with 179 fraternity men and 114 independents. In order to have the two samples as comparable as possible, the samples were restricted to sophomores, juniors, and seniors, since relatively few freshmen already belong to fraternities. Subjects were randomly assigned to one of three rooms, fraternity and nonfraternity men being mixed in each room. In one room, after the same introduction as in the previous studies, they saw the straight version of the persuasive communication; in another they saw the distracting version; and in the third room they were asked to answer the questionnaire before seeing the film.

The questionnaire was changed somewhat for this experiment. Questions 1 and 2 were extended to 6-point scales; Question 3 was contracted to a 7-point scale; Questions 5 and 6 were omitted and in their place they were asked to indicate on a 7-point scale their "overall reaction to college fraternities"; Question 4 on the original questionnaire was retained unchanged. The two questions measuring rejection of the speaker had the scales extended to 5- and 6-point scales in place of the original 3- and 4-point scales. Thus, on this revised questionnaire, the maximum profraternity attitude would be represented again by a score of 31. Maximum rejection of the speaker and the communication would be represented by a score of 11.

TABLE 3

AVERAGES FOR FRATERNITY MEN AND INDEPENDENTS AT THE UNIVERSITY OF SOUTHERN CALIFORNIA

Condition	Fraternity men		Independents	
	Attitude to fraternities	Rejection of speaker	Attitude to fraternities	Rejection of speaker
Control	24.8 (N = 59)	—	17.4 (N = 37)	—
Ordinary film version	24.6 (N = 59)	8.6	16.3 (N = 34)	7.4
Distracting film	23.5 (N = 61)	8.0	16.1 (N = 43)	7.5

Table 3 presents the results of the experiment at the University of Southern California.

Let us first examine the data from the fraternity men to see how they compare with the data collected at San Jose. It is clear that, once more, the distracting persuasive communication has resulted in a less favorable attitude toward fraternities and less rejection of the speaker than the ordinary, nondistracting version. Although the differences are not quite as significant as they were at San Jose, they are quite adequate considering the fact of replication. The difference between the two experimental conditions on attitude toward fraternities is significant at the 6% level ($t = 1.88$), and the difference in rejection of the speaker is significant at the 5% level ($t = 1.97$). In other words, we have replicated and confirmed the San Jose result.

It is also clear in Table 3 that the straight film version does not produce a boomerang effect. Rather, it produces virtually no effect at all. The difference between the control condition and the ordinary film version is negligible. On the other hand, those who saw the distracting version of the persuasive communication have indeed been influenced significantly ($t = 1.94$).

Let us now turn our attention to the results on the nonfraternity men. First of all, it is clear and not surprising that there is a huge initial difference between their attitude toward fraternities and the attitudes of fraternity men. In other words, the independents do agree more initially with the speaker in the film and should not be expected to counterargue while listening. And, indeed, it may be seen that there are only negligible differences either in attitude toward fraternities or in rejection of the speaker between those who saw the ordinary version and those who saw the distracting version of the persuasive communication. Both of these conditions seem to have been somewhat influenced although the differences from the control condition are not significant ($t = 1.17$ and $t = 1.08$).

Relation between the Attitude and Rejection Measures

It is of interest to examine the relation which exists between attitude toward fraternities after seeing the persuasive-communication film and the extent to which the speaker is rejected. It is generally accepted that the extent to which a person is influenced by a persuasive communication is related to the extent to which he accepts the speaker as trustworthy, expert, unbiased, and the like. There is, for example, a fair amount of research which shows that if the source of a communication is regarded as untrustworthy, the communication is less effective in influencing people. And in the data we have presented above, we also find that in the distraction condition, where we find more effective influence, we also find less rejection of the speaker.

In terms of the reaction of one individual to a persuasive communication, however, the direction of the empirical relation we would expect is less clear. On the one hand, we would still expect that if a person, listening to a persuasive communication, succeeds in utterly derogating and rejecting the communicator and his arguments, he would not have been influenced. On the other hand, since changing one's opinion and derogating the communicator are both modes of coping with the impact of the persuasive communication, one might expect that a person on whom the communication has a strong impact might do both of them to some extent rather than one to the exclusion of the other. Thus, if within any experimental condition one correlated the amount of change of opinion with the amount of rejection of the speaker, the size and direction of the correlation would depend on whether or not these two reactions were alternate forms of coping with the situation or whether they were both simultaneously available to the same person.

The data from our three experiments are rather interesting in this respect. Table 4 presents the correlations between attitude toward fraternities and rejection of the speaker for fraternity men in each of our two conditions in the three universities. It will be recalled that a larger number indicated greater profraternity sentiment and indicated greater rejection of the speaker. Hence, a positive correlation between these two variables indicates that the less the person was influenced by the persuasive communication, the more he rejects the speaker.

An examination of the figures in the table makes it clear that there is a consistent difference in the magnitude of the correlations between the two conditions. While all of the correlations are positive, none of them is significantly different from zero for those subjects who saw the ordinary, straight version of the film and had their attention focused on the persuasive communication. On the other hand, all of the correlations for those subjects who saw the distracting film are significantly different from zero at the 5% level or better. While none of the differences between the correlations is significant for any one of the experiments, the consistency of the result lends considerable weight to the conclusion that they are different.

We did not anticipate this finding and we must regard it as tentative but suggestive. It may be that in the distraction condition, not being able to effectively counterargue, subjects are influenced by the communication unless they are able to derogate and reject the speaker. In the condition where they are able to counterargue, the result suggests

TABLE 4

CORRELATIONS BETWEEN ATTITUDE AND REJECTION OF SPEAKER FOR FRATERNITY MEN

Academic institution	Experimental condition	
	Ordinary film	Distracting film
University of Minnesota	+.04	+.36
San Jose State College	+.18	+.37
University of Southern California	+.16	+.39

that they are able to resist influence by other means even if they do not reject the speaker. If this tentative interpretation of the magnitudes of these correlations is correct, one could perhaps summarize it by saying that, to the extent one does not counterargue while listening to a persuasive communication, there will be a positive correlation between rejecting the speaker and being able to resist influence. Such a hypothesis would, of course, suggest that one should also find such positive correlations for the nonfraternity men in the experiment at the University of Southern California. After all, there is little reason for the nonfraternity men to be motivated to counterargue even when seeing the straight, ordinary version of the film. The correlation between attitude and rejection for the independents who saw the ordinary version is, indeed, +.45, a significant correlation. Things are not, however, as clear-cut as one might like to have them. The comparable correlation for the independents who saw the distracting film is −.02, certainly not consistent with what we might expect from our tentative hypothesis. Perhaps the distracting film introduces other variables for the independent men who would not counterargue anyhow, or perhaps our suggested hypothesis to account for the correlations is not quite correct. We will leave it at this, a suggestion which may be worthwhile to explore more adequately in the future.

Possible Alternative Interpretations

An experiment can never rule out all possible alternative explanations of the findings and, perhaps, the best support for one particular interpretation is to say that the experiment was designed with that interpretation in mind and, indeed, it came out as predicted. Nevertheless, it is useful to look briefly at the plausibility of some other explanations. Two such possible explanations readily come to mind and we will examine them each.

1. It is conceivable that the so-called "distracting" version of the communication was actually not distracting. In fact, it may have produced the reverse effect, namely, because of the attempt to distract, the subjects may have concentrated harder on listening to the speech. If this did occur, it could explain the results for the fraternity men—the more closely they listened, the more they were influenced. There are two sources of data relevant to this possible explanation. In the experiment done at the University of Southern California the questionnaire contained one page on which the subjects were asked to "list the main criticisms of fraternities which the speaker made." If the greater influence among fraternity men in the distracting condition was due to *more* careful attention on their part to the verbal content, we might expect this to reveal itself on this question. Analysis of the answers to this question, however, reveals no superior retention of arguments for those viewing the distracting film. In fact, the mean number of arguments repeated by those viewing the ordinary version was slightly higher (3.9) than for those exposed to the distracting version (3.7).

Another relevant source of data comes from comments written by subjects in a space provided for "general comments." The following are some rather typical comments obtained from subjects who had seen the distracting version of the persuasive communication:

The presentation was interesting because, although I had already seen that film, and was interested in the monologue which was against something I am in favor of, I would still find myself watching the film instead of listening fully.

It was extremely difficult to pay close attention to both the audio and visual parts of the film. It would seem that attention would be determined by whether you wanted to defend fraternities or enjoy the visual part.

I could see only a slight correlation between the acting and the commentary. Trying to understand the action detracted from the commentary.

I could not see any tie in between what was being said and what was being shown. It was

very hard to concentrate on what was being said without completely looking away from the movie.

There seems to be little question but that the distracting film was really distracting.

2. It is possible that the effect obtained for the fraternity men is simply the result of reward and reinforcement. The visual portion of the distracting film was a highly amusing thing and, consequently, those in the distracting condition heard the message while they were being rewarded or entertained and, hence, were more influenced. It is difficult, of course, to marshal data relevant to such a possible explanation. There are two things which can be said, however, to indicate a lack of plausibility. No spontaneous comments were obtained which indicated that they actually enjoyed the film. Comments that dealt with the issue almost always indicated some irritation with the difficulty of both watching and listening. This is clear to anyone who has seen the film used in the distracting condition. The visual portion commands attention but the experience is not as entertaining as it would have been with its original sound track. The other point that can be made in reference to this possible interpretation is that, if it is true, it is difficult to understand why the independents at the University of Southern California do not respond in the same way to the same reinforcing mechanism. It seems difficult to believe that the distracting film would be reinforcing for fraternity men but not for independents.

We, ourselves, have not been able to think of other possible explanations which even superficially promise plausibility. For example, the experience of those subjects who see the distracting film must certainly constitute an unusual, and rather strange experience for them. There does not seem to be, however, any plausible reason for assuming that simply the unusual and strange would be more effective in influencing people in this context. The data strongly suggest that our own explanation has validity.

REFERENCE

ALLYN, JANE, & FESTINGER, L. The effectiveness of unanticipated persuasive communications. *J. abnorm. soc. Psychol.*, 1961, **62**, 35–40.

PART V

EFFECTS

How much opinion change should a communication demand for it to achieve maximum impact? How long-lasting are the effects of persuasion? What are the repercussions of a reaction to one stimulus on the effects of persuasion stimuli which may be close in time to it, or logically related to it? What are some of the principal sources of artifact and systematic bias in experimental research on attitude?

Magnitude of Impact

> All seems infected that th' infected spy,
> As all looks yellow to the jaundic'd eye.[1]

Each of us perceives the world in a uniquely different fashion. Some cues capture our attention. Others elude us. We magnify some incidents well out of proportion to their actual significance, and seem oblivious to others. In politics, for example, a staunch Republican's idea of who won the 1960 Kennedy-Nixon debates is probably just the opposite of that of an avowedly liberal Democrat.[2] Similarly, but on a grander scale and with more sobering overtones, the United States overevaluated the worth of its Cuban collaborators in the Bay of Pigs incident, but underestimated the Japanese at the beginning of World War II.[3] England and France similarly overevaluated each other in 1939, yet underestimated their common enemy Germany.[4]

Charles Solley tells of an interesting perception experiment he carried out using his friends as subjects. In 1951, there was a Cadillac model which was shorter than the Buick Roadmaster. By happenstance the two models were parked side by side when Solley asked a number of his friends which of the two was longer. Invariably they would glance at the cars and say that the Cadillac was longer. "They 'knew' that Cadillacs were longer than Buicks because they cost more. They looked at or attended to the two cars *only* long enough to identify them; they did not attend to the two objects long enough to take in the cues necessary for effective size discrimination."[5]

Similarly so in communication, perception is *selective*. Some parts of some arguments are attended to, other parts ignored. More often than not, even the very position advocated tends to be misperceived. Sears and Freedman found that supporters of Nixon in the 1960 Presi-

---

[1] Pope, A. *An essay on criticism.* Part II, 1711.

[2] Rosnow, R. L. Bias in evaluating the presidential debates: A "splinter" effect. *J. soc. Psychol.*, 1965, **67**, 211–219.

[3] Bass, B. M., & Dunteman, G. Bias in the evaluation of one's group, its allies and opponents. *J. Conflict Resolution*, 1963, **7**, 16–20.

[4] *Ibid.*

[5] Quoted from Solley, C. M., & Murphy, G. *Development of the perceptual world.* New York: Basic Books, 1960. P. 100. By permission of C. M. Solley and the publisher.

dential election reduced the dissonance they experienced resulting from his loss of the election by displacing President-elect Kennedy's position on campaign issues closer to their own.[6] Berelson, Lazarsfeld, and McPhee have observed that voters generally tend to perceive greater agreement between their own views and their party's candidates than may actually exist.[7]

When a message is perceived closer to one's own position than it actually is, we call this "assimilation." Assimilation has the effect of making the message seem fair and impartial. When a message is perceived farther from one's own position than it actually is, we call this "contrast." Contrast has the effect of making the message seem biased and propagandistic. Although a number of factors can influence assimilation and contrast, in general it has been found that positions already close to one's own tend to be displaced even closer (assimilation), while positions already far removed tend to be displaced further (contrast). With this in mind, Robert Lane and David Sears caution that we should counsel our political leaders as follows:

> People who differ from you will tend to distort your views. When you differ slightly from your friends, they will think you agree with them. Your enemies will think you disagree with them more than you actually do. Both tendencies will weaken your capacity to influence them in the way you wish to.[8]

The earliest definitive investigation of the assimilation-contrast phenomenon in communication was reported in 1957 by Carl Hovland, O. J. Harvey, and Muzafer Sherif. The study consisted of presenting communications advocating different stands on the issue of prohibition of alcohol to subjects whose own beliefs varied from "wet" to "dry."[9] Part of the results, those concerned with the assimilation and contrast of the moderate-wet appeal, are depicted in Fig. 2.

> The subject's own position is indicated on the abscissa and along the ordinate the average rating of the communication. The dots indicate the mean placement of the position of the communication for subjects who checked each

[6] Sears, D. O., & Freedman, J. L. Organizational and judgmental models of cognitive conflict resolution. *Amer. Psychologist*, 1961, **16**, 409. (Abstract) Cited in Lane, R. E. & Sears, D. O. *Public opinion*. Englewood Cliffs, N.J.: Prentice-Hall, 1964. P. 50.

[7] Berelson, B. R., Lazarsfeld, P. F., & McPhee, W. N. *Voting*. Chicago: Univer. of Chicago Press, 1954.

[8] Quoted from Lane, R. E., & Sears, D. O. *Public opinion*. Englewood Cliffs, N.J.: Prentice-Hall, 1964. P. 51. By permission of R. E. Lane and the publisher.

[9] Hovland, C. I., Harvey, O. J., & Sherif, M. Assimilation and contrast effects in reactions to communication and attitude change. *J. abnorm. soc. Psychol.*, 1957, **55**, 244–252. *Cf.* Diab, L. N. Reaction to a communication as a function of attitude-communication discrepancy. *Psychol. Rep.*, 1966, **18**, 767–774.

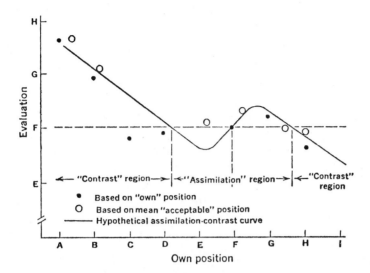

FIG. 2. Average placement of position of moderately wet communication by subjects holding various positions on the issue, with superimposed hypothetical assimilation-contrast curve.[10]

particular position as their own stand. The circles represent the mean placement of the position advocated when the subject's position is estimated from the mean of his latitude of acceptance. The dotted line indicates a hypothetical relationship in which individuals holding the same position as the communication report its position accurately (at F), those a small distance removed assimilate it to their position, and those still further removed exaggerate the distance between their own stand and the communication, revealing a contrast effect.[11]

Besides the sheer proximity of the recipient's position to the stand taken in the communication (i.e., the "communication-recipient discrepancy"), other factors also influence assimilation and contrast. For example, the more highly involved the recipient, the more he tends to exaggerate the discrepancy between his own position and the communication.[12] The more committed he is to a particular point of view,

[10]Reprinted from Sherif, M., & Hovland, C. I. *Social judgment.* New Haven, Conn.: Yale Univer. Press, 1961. P. 150. By permission of M. Sherif and the publisher.

[11]Quoted from M. Sherif and C. I. Hovland, *ibid.,* pp. 150–151, by permission of M. Sherif and the publisher. "Latitude of acceptance" is defined as the range of positions on an issue that the subject considers acceptable to him. This can be contrasted with "latitude of rejection" which refers to the range of positions the subject finds objectionable.

[12]Ward, C. D. Ego-involvement and the absolute judgment of attitude statements. *J. Pers. soc. Psychol.,* 1965, **2,** 202–208.

the more he tends to perceive others' opinions as extreme.[13] With a positive communicator, the recipient tends to minimize the difference between his own position and the communicator's. The difference is maximized, however, when the communicator is perceived negatively.[14] Time can also be an important independent variable affecting perception. When opposing messages are presented with no intervening delay, contrast results; the second message is displaced away from the first. When a 2–5-day interval separates the two messages, the second message is perceived closer to the first than it actually is (assimilation).[15]

These findings have important implications for methodology in public opinion measurement. For a long time it was believed that in constructing attitude scales of the Thurstone-type known as "equal-appearing interval,"[16] judges' own beliefs would not influence their assignment of scale values to the individual items. Since one of the goals in constructing an attitude scale is to select items which correspond to the entire range of public opinion, the assumption of impartiality of judgments is crucial. If the assumption does not hold true, then steps have to be taken to ameliorate the error which could result.[17]

Carl Hovland and Muzafer Sherif were among the first to challenge the assumption that sorting of items when constructing an attitude scale is not greatly influenced by the sorters' own attitudes toward the items' content.[18] In the years following their pioneering studies,

[13] Manis, M. The interpretation of opinion statements as a function of recipient attitude. *J. abnorm. soc. Psychol.*, 1960, **60**, 340–344. Manis, M. The interpretation of opinion statements as a function of message ambiguity and recipient attitude. *J. abnorm. soc. Psychol.*, 1961, **63**, 76–81.

[14] Kelman, H. C., & Eagly, A. H. Attitude toward the communicator, perception of communication content, and attitude change. *J. Pers. soc. Psychol.*, 1965, **1**, 63–78. This finding is consistent with an earlier one by Manis to the effect that assimilation results with prestigeful communicators: Manis, M. The interpretation of opinion statements as a function of recipient attitude and source prestige. *J. abnorm. soc. Psychol.*, 1961, **63**, 82–86.

[15] Manis, M. Immunization, delay, and the interpretation of persuasive messages. *J. Pers. soc. Psychol.*, 1965, **1**, 541–550.

[16] Thurstone, L. L., & Chave, E. J. *The measurement of attitude.* Chicago: Univer. of Chicago Press, 1929.

[17] For a more thorough discussion of this problem and suggestions regarding alternative solutions, see Edwards, A. L. *Techniques of attitude scale construction.* New York: Appleton-Century-Crofts, 1957.

[18] Hovland, C. I., & Sherif, M. Judgmental phenomena and scales of attitude measurement: Item displacement in Thurstone scales. *J. abnorm. soc. Psychol.*, 1952, **47**,

evidence in opposition to that assumption, and in support of Hovland and Sherif, has continued to accumulate.[19] Viewing the problem in the context of assimilation-contrast theory, Hovland and Sherif account for the resulting perception-judgment bias as a function of the relative distance between the judges' own attitudes and the position advocated in the message—what we have called the *communication-recipient discrepancy*. The person's stand on a reference scale is conceived as an internal anchor. The discrepancy between his stand and the communication determines what he will accept and what he will reject.[20]

> . . . The distance referred to is defined by the individual's placement of communication at some position (near or distant) relative to his own stand on the issue. We have found that the individual's own stand includes a range of acceptable positions and is accompanied by a latitude of rejection. Thus the effect of a communication depends upon the placement of communication relative to the individual's latitudes of acceptance and rejection.
>
> The latitudes of acceptance and rejection vary with degree of familiarity, the extremity of the individual's stand, and the degree of ego-involvement with the issue—whether it arouses an intense attitude or, rather, whether the individual can regard the issue with some detachment as primarily a "factual" matter.
>
> It is our contention that the distance between the position of the communication and that of the recipient can only be assessed through knowledge of the judgment scale of the recipient. What appear to be small differences in position to one individual (say the difference between the Russian and Chinese concerning the nature of communism as it appears to a typical American "democrat") may be of enormous significance to the other individual. Thus where there are small distances on a scale for one individual there may be tremendous ones for another. Combined with these distances are clear-cut differences in the intensity with which the beliefs are held, specified by latitudes of acceptance and rejection. It is on the basis of these phenomena that individuals frequently misjudge the difficulty involved in changing

---

822–832. Sherif, M., & Hovland, C. I. Judgmental phenomena and scales of attitude measurement: Placement of items with individual choice of number of categories. *J. abnorm. soc. Psychol.*, 1953, **48**, 135–141.

[19] Prothro, E. T. The effect of strong negative attitudes on the placement of items in a Thurstone scale. *J. soc. Psychol.*, 1955, **41**, 11–17. Prothro, E. T. Personal involvement and item displacement on Thurstone scales. *J. soc. Psychol.*, 1957, **45**, 191–196. Upshaw, H. S. Own attitude as an anchor in equal-appearing intervals. *J. abnorm. soc. Psychol.*, 1962, **64**, 85–96. Zavalloni, M., & Cook, S. W. Influence of judges' attitudes on ratings of favorableness of statements about a social group. *J. Pers. soc. Psychol.*, 1965, **1**, 43–54.

[20] Sherif, C. W., Sherif, M., & Nebergall, R. E. *Attitude and attitude change*. Philadelphia, Pa.: W. B. Saunders, 1965. P. 187.

another's opinion: what seems to them only a minor revision may be to the person they are attempting to influence a major shift in stand.[21, 22]

If an individual tends to assimilate positions already close to his own and to contrast those further removed, then his tolerance for a persuasive appeal (and, subsequently, the magnitude of its impact upon him) should be determined by the existing communication-recipient discrepancy. In effect, the amount of opinion change obtained would seem to depend on the amount demanded.[23] But how much? What is the optimum discrepancy? If we want to influence a staunch liberal, should we present an argument advocating an extremely conservative point of view, or should the position advocated be only slightly different from the subject's? James Whittaker addresses himself to this question when he states,

> Common sense tells us that if we take a position substantially different from that of our listener, he will reject our position completely; and perhaps he will even become more entrenched, or even more extreme in his position. There is a substantial amount of evidence from psychological warfare efforts to substantiate this common sense notion. For example, many propaganda leaflets were prepared in England during World War II as part of a continuing effort to change opinions about the conditions which prevailed in allied POW camps, the treatment prisoners received, and so on. The hope, of

---

[21] Quoted from Sherif, M., & Hovland, C. I. *Social judgment.* New Haven, Conn.: Yale Univer. Press, 1961. Pp. 191–192. By permission of M. Sherif and the publisher.

[22] Other investigators have offered somewhat different explanations for this effect. Helson's *adaptation-level* theory emphasizes the value which characterizes the center of the judge's reference scale. Volkmann and Upshaw posit a *rubber-band* theory, asserting that the anchor point is based on the values at the ends of the reference scale. ("Rubber-band" comes from the idea that the scale stretches and shrinks as a function of the stimuli being judged.) Helson, H. Current trends and issues in adaptation-level theory. *Amer. Psychologist*, 1964, **19**, 26–38. For support of Helson's proposition, see Segall, M. H. The effect of attitude and experience on judgments of controversial statements. *J. abnorm. soc. Psychol.*, 1959, **58**, 61–68. Volkmann, J. Scales of judgment and their implications for social psychology. In J. H. Rohrer & M. Sherif (Eds.), *Social psychology at the crossroads.* New York: Harper & Row, 1951. Pp. 273–294. Upshaw, H. S. The effect of variable perspectives on judgments of opinion statements for Thurstone scales: Equal-appearing intervals. *J. Pers. soc. Psychol.*, 1965, **2**, 60–69. For support of the Volkmann-Upshaw proposition, see Ostrom, T. M. Perspective as an intervening construct in the judgment of attitude statements. *J. Pers. soc. Psychol.*, 1966, **3**, 135–144.

[23] Obviously, the intensity of existing opinions is also a prime factor influencing the amount of change which can result. It has already clearly been established by Tannenbaum, Carlson, Feather, McGinnies, Donelson, Haaf, and others that extremely intense opinions are those most difficult to change. With some imagination, however, even under these circumstances a promising strategy might be developed (e.g., Vernon's prescription, p. 249). Tannenbaum, P. H. Initial attitude toward source and concept as factors in attitude change through communication. *Publ. Opin. quart.*, 1956,

course, was that if the attitudes of German soldiers toward probable treatment could be changed, more of them would surrender.

One particular leaflet contained photographs of conditions in a POW camp in Canada. These photographs showed prisoners engaged in playing cards, ping pong, and other activities, and the accompanying message included, among other things, a description of meals in the camp—for example, coffee, eggs, and toast for breakfast. An important fact relevant to this particular leaflet is that it represented the unadulterated truth. The photographs were actually taken in the Canadian camp, and the meals described were those actually provided for prisoners.

Before dropping the leaflet behind enemy lines, however, Army personnel decided to "test" it with German prisoners already in camps in Italy. These prisoners, it should be emphasized, were already captives and knew something of conditions in allied POW camps. They had discovered that actual conditions and treatment differed considerably from what they had been led to expect. Yet almost without exception, they could not accept the leaflet as truthful. It was too divergent from their own opinions concerning conditions in allied prison camps and consequently they regarded it as "propagandistic."[24]

Diametrically opposite to the commonsense notion of which Whittaker speaks is an interesting and often cited finding from an experiment conducted by Carl Hovland and Henry Pritzker. Hand-tailored items on twelve diverse topics, such as "the likelihood that electricity produced by atomic power would be available for use in American homes within five years" and "the desirability of making voting in presidential elections compulsory for all citizens over 21," were presented to three groups of subjects whose own opinions on the topics differed from those advocated either slightly, moderately, or markedly. The items advocating the most extreme change had significantly greater impact on opinions than those advocating moderate change which, in turn, had significantly greater impact than those advocating only slight change.[25] *The more opinion change asked for, the more obtained.*[26]

20, 413–425. Carlson, E. R. Attitude change through modification of attitude structure. *J. abnorm. soc. Psychol.*, 1956, **52**, 256–261. Feather, N. T. Acceptance and rejection of arguments in relation to attitude strength, critical ability, and intolerance of inconsistency. *J. abnorm. soc. Psychol.*, 1964, **69**, 127–136. McGinnies, E., Donelson, E., & Haaf, R. Level of initial attitude, active rehearsal, and instructional set as factors in attitude change. *J. abnorm. soc. Psychol.*, 1964, **69**, 437–440.

[24] Quoted by permission of Whittaker, J. O., from Resolution of the communication discrepancy issue in attitude change. Paper read at the East. Psychol. Ass., New York, April, 1966. Pp. 1–3. The study referred to is in Daugherty, W., & Janowitz, M. (Eds.), *A psychological warfare casebook.* Baltimore, Md.: Johns Hopkins Univer. Press, 1958.

[25] Hovland, C. I., & Pritzker, H. A. Extent of opinion change as a function of amount of change advocated. *J. abnorm. soc. Psychol.*, 1957, **54**, 257–261.

[26] The reader will recall that Norman Anderson's linear operator model for predicting primacy and recency was based on this assumption (pp. 105 ff.).

However, the Hovland-Pritzker finding is not without qualification. Whittaker replicated the experiment using undergraduate college students as subjects, and substituting for some of Hovland and Pritzker's topics several more ego-involving ones. More important, Whittaker extended the discrepancy continuum, using eight instead of three degrees of communication-recipient discrepancy. Where Hovland and Pritzker found a linear relationship between the amount of change demanded and the amount obtained, Whittaker found that the median opinion change for all twelve topics corresponding to eight degrees of discrepancy could best be described as curvilinear,[27] the greatest change occurring around the middle of the discrepancy continuum. However, when Whittaker's topics are roughly divided on the basis of high ego-involvement for his college student subjects (e.g., "Sororities and fraternities should be abolished" and "There should be curfews for male students") and low ego-involvement (e.g., "Likelihood of cancer cure within 5 years" and "Washington or Lincoln greater President"), the results suggest the nonmonotonic relationship only for high ego-involvement, and a linear relationship much the same as that obtained by Hovland and Pritzker for low.[28]

---

[27]Whittaker, J. O. Attitude change and communication-attitude discrepancy. *J. soc. Psychol.*, 1965, **65**, 141–147. Whittaker observed the same curvilinear relationship in other experimental situations: Whittaker, J. O. Cognitive dissonance and the effectiveness of persuasive communications. *Publ. Opin. quart.*, 1964, **28**, 547–555. Whittaker, J. O. Opinion change as a function of communication-attitude discrepancy. *Psychol. Rep.*, 1963, **13**, 763–772.

[28]Disregarding ego-involvement, both the linear and the curvilinear relationships have been derived by Festinger and Aronson from cognitive dissonance theory when the factor of source credibility interacts with discrepancy to influence opinion change. When a subject finds that an opinion advocated by a credible communicator is discrepant from his own opinion, he experiences dissonance. There are several ways open to him for reducing that dissonance. He can change his own opinion, bringing it into line with the communicator's. He can reinforce his opinion by seeking support from others who hold the same opinion. He can derogate the communicator's credibility and discount the opinion advocated. When the communicator is already established as highly credible, the last alternative is no longer open to the subject. Dissonance will probably be reduced by opinion change. The greater the discrepancy, probably the greater the change that will result. At the other extreme, when the communicator is not highly credible, the subject will probably reduce his dissonance by derogating the communicator and discounting the advocated opinion; hence, no opinion change. Where there is mild credibility, both opinion change and derogation can be used. When the discrepancy is small, dissonance can easily be reduced by a slight shift in opinion. When the discrepancy is great, dissonance can be more easily reduced by derogating the communicator. Hence, under conditions of mild credibility, the greatest amount of opinion change should occur around the middle of the discrepancy continuum. About the same

The problem becomes even more complex when the factor of cognitive dissonance is introduced. As a result of opposing predictions which can be derived from dissonance theory and from assimilation-contrast, an interesting controversy has arisen which pits against one another several leading students of social influence. Herbert Greenwald summarizes as follows this controversy concerning the effect of involvement on opinion change and, particularly, how involvement affects the relationship between discrepancy and opinion change:

> Festinger has argued that dissonance, a type of psychological discomfort, will arise when cognitive elements are inconsistent with one another, as, for example, when a person is confronted with the information that his opinion and that of a highly respected other person are discrepant. The person may try a number of things to reduce dissonance, such as changing the other's opinion, or changing his own opinion toward the other viewpoint. The theory postulates that dissonance is intensified, and, therefore, motivation to reduce dissonance is increased by such things as increased importance of the cognitive elements (involvement) and increased difference in opinion between the person and the other (discrepancy). Thus, assuming that other channels of dissonance reduction are not available to the person, Festinger's dissonance theory predicts that increases in either involvement or discrepancy should result in increased opinion change toward the discrepant position.
>
> A different set of predictions is derived from Sherif and Hovland's assimilation and contrast theory. By extension of psychophysical judgment studies on anchoring effects, this theory postulates that a person's opinion will function as does a main achor in perceptual tasks; that is, his opinion will become a highly weighted, personal reference point. On this basis, assimilation and contrast theory hypothesizes that a credible other's discrepant opinion, when

time that Aronson, Turner, and Carlsmith tested and confirmed this cognitive dissonance hypothesis, by coincidence Arthur Hill at the University of Melbourne in Australia and, even earlier, Tong-He Choo at Boston University were also investigating the relationship between source credibility and discrepancy. Neither Hill's results nor those by Choo are consistent with the complex relationship predicted by cognitive dissonance theory, although they do corroborate the Hovland-Pritzker finding. Unlike Aronson *et al.*, Hill and Choo find no significant interaction between credibility and discrepancy. Festinger, L., & Aronson, E. The arousal and reduction of dissonance in social contexts. In D. Cartwright & A. Zander (Eds.), *Group dynamics Research and theory.* (2nd ed.) Evanston, Ill.: Row, Peterson, 1960. Pp. 214–231. Aronson, E., Turner, J. A., & Carlsmith, J. M. Communicator credibility and communication discrepancy as determinants of opinion change. *J. abnorm. soc. Psychol.*, 1963, **67**, 31–36. Hill, A. H. Credibility, discrepancy and latitude of communication as dimensions of dissonance influencing attitude change. *Australian J. Psychol.*, 1963, **15**, 124–132. Choo, T. Communicator credibility and communication discrepancy as determinants of opinion change. *J. soc. Psychol.*, 1964, **64**, 65–76.

similar to the person's own opinion, will result in "assimilation" of the two opinions. That is, the person will misperceive the other opinion to lie nearer his own opinion than it actually does and/or change his opinion toward the other person. However, should the other person's opinion be highly dissimilar to his own, "contrast" is hypothesized to occur. That is, the person is expected, in the latter case, to misperceive that other's opinion as lying further from his own than it actually does and/or change only slightly toward the other opinion. In the extreme case, he may even change away from the discrepant viewpoint (a boomerang effect). Assimilation is expected to occur when the other's opinion lies within the person's range of acceptable opinions (his "latitude of acceptance"), but should the other's opinion lie within the person's range of unacceptable opinions (his "latitude of rejection"), the dissimilar opinion is expected to be contrasted. Furthermore, the deeper the other's opinion falls within the rejection area, the greater the anticipated contrast effect.

Should the person be highly ego-involved, his stand will function as an even more highly weighted anchor and therefore reduce the possibility of opinion change. Perhaps this is because ego-involvement would increase the possibility that a discrepant opinion would fall into the person's latitude of rejection. Thus, on the hypothesis that the greater the discrepancy and the greater the involvement the less the opinion change, Sherif and Hovland's assimilation and contrast theory makes contradictory predictions with those derived from Festinger's dissonance theory.[29]

There have been several attempts to resolve the "involvement controversy" which finds cognitive dissonance theory predicting greater opinion change with increased discrepancy and involvement, and assimilation-contrast predicting reduced change. Greenwald has attempted to reconcile the opposed predictions by positing two different types of involvement. He suggests that the Sherif-Hovland conception of "involvement" refers to commitment to a position, while Festinger's "involvement" constitutes attention to seeking a solution to a problem.[30] Another interesting effort to resolve the involvement controversy is the study that follows, by Jonathan L. Freedman. Like Greenwald, Freedman too differentiates between the types of involvement referred to by Festinger and by Sherif and Hovland. Freedman's results will be reminiscent of the linear-low involvement and curvilinear-high involvement relationship suggested by Whittaker's replication of the Hovland-Pritzker study.

---

[29] Quoted by permission of Greenwald, H. J., from The opinion change controversy in persuasion research. Paper read at Amer. Psychol. Ass., Los Angeles, September, 1964.

[30] Ibid.

Reprinted from Journal of Abnormal and Social Psychology, 1964, Vol. 69, pp. 290–295, by permission of Jonathan L. Freedman and APA.

INVOLVEMENT, DISCREPANCY, AND CHANGE [1]

JONATHAN L. FREEDMAN

Ss took a position under high or low involvement; were subsequently exposed to information which was slightly, moderately, or extremely discrepant from the initial position; and the amount of change in their positions was measured. Under low involvement, there was more change with greater discrepancy; but under high involvement, the relationship was nonmonotonic, with maximum change occurring at moderate discrepancy. The situation is analyzed in terms of the relative difficulty of position change and rejection of the information as alternative modes of resolution.

When a person is exposed to information that is discrepant from his own opinion, there is a tendency for him to change his position in the direction of the information. What effect does the size of the discrepancy between his initial position and the information have on the amount of change? Despite the considerable amount of research that has dealt with this basic situation, the answer to this question is not clear. A number of studies have demonstrated that in general the greater the discrepancy, the more change occurs (Fisher & Lubin, 1958; Fisher, Rubinstein, & Freeman, 1956; Goldberg, 1954; Harvey, Kelley, & Shapiro, 1957; Hovland & Pritzker, 1957; Zimbardo, 1960). It has been suggested, however (Hovland, 1959; Hovland, Harvey, & Sherif, 1957) that under conditions of high involvement in the initial position this relationship breaks down; and that extreme discrepancy may produce little or even negative change. The present paper presents an experiment designed to provide evidence bearing directly on this suggestion.

To begin with it is essential to have a clear understanding of what is meant by "involvement." Unfortunately it appears to have been used in at least two quite different ways by different authors. While probably the most common usage is to refer to interest in,

concern about, or commitment to a particular position on an issue, it has also sometimes referred to general level of interest in or concern about an issue without reference to a specific position. Since a person can be greatly interested in an issue without having yet taken a stand on it, these two meanings of the terms are clearly different. In their discussion Hovland et al. (1957) appear to be using the term in the former, more specific sense and that is how it will be used in this paper. That is, involvement will refer to degree of concern about or commitment to a specific response or position.

How has the effect of involvement and discrepancy on change been explained? Hovland et al. (1957) compared the attitude-change situation to that in psychophysics in which near or remote anchors are given. When the anchor is near, assimilation occurs and all judgments move toward the anchor; when the anchor is very far away, contrast occurs and all judgments move away from the anchor. It is suggested that a similar phenomenon occurs in attitude-change situations. Slightly or moderately discrepant information produces movement away from the initial position; but information that is so discrepant that it falls within the latitude of rejection produces no change or even produces a "boomerang" effect, with subjects moving away from the new information.

What does this imply about the relationship between discrepancy and change? In the first place, although Hovland and Sherif do not state this explicitly, it seems reasonable to assume that if assimilation occurs, there will be greater change with larger discrepancies. An

[1] This study is based on a dissertation presented to Yale University in candidacy for the degree of Doctor of Philosophy. It was conducted while the author held a United States Public Health Service research fellowship.

The author is extremely grateful for the guidance and encouragement he received from the late Carl I. Hovland who served as chairman of the dissertation committee until his death.

290

extremely close external anchor would be expected to produce very small displacements in judgments of the closest stimuli, because the displacement would be limited by the size of the discrepancy between the anchor and the stimuli. Although the relative change (that is, absolute change divided by size of the discrepancy) would be very high, the absolute change would be small. A somewhat more remote anchor, which was still close enough to cause assimilation, would be expected to produce greater absolute change, because the total amount of change possible would be greater. The various attitude-change studies cited above also lend support to this assumption. Thus, as long as the discrepant information falls within the latitude of acceptance, larger discrepancies should produce greater change. Once the information falls outside the latitude of acceptance, however, little or no change is expected to occur. Therefore, as discrepancy increases, amount of change increases up to a point and then decreases. Or, in other words, the relationship between discrepancy and change is nonmonotonic, with maximum change occurring at moderate levels of discrepancy.

This nonmonotonic relationship between discrepancy and change should hold regardless of the degree of involvement in the initial position, but involvement should be an important determinant of the level of discrepancy at which maximum change occurs. With low involvement the latitude of acceptance is relatively wide and it is consequently difficult to get beyond it into the latitude of rejection; with high involvement the latitude of acceptance is narrower and it is considerably easier to get into the latitude of rejection. Thus, with low involvement only extremely discrepant information will fall within the latitude of rejection, whereas with high involvement relatively moderate information may be rejected. Since the point at which the latitude of rejection is reached is the point of maximum change, and since this point should be more moderate for high- than for low-involvement conditions, maximum change should occur at a more moderate level of discrepancy for high than for low involvement.

The present experiment was designed to test this hypothesis. The general design was to take an issue on which the subjects initially had no opinion; have them take a position under conditions of high or low involvement; present them with information that was slightly, moderately, or highly discrepant from their initial position; and measure the amount of change. On the basis of pretesting the three levels of discrepancy were selected so that all would be more moderate than the maximal change point for the low-involvement condition, but the high discrepancy information would fall beyond the point of maximum change for the high-involvement subjects. Therefore it was predicted that within the range of discrepancies used there would be more change with greater discrepancy under conditions of low involvement; but with high involvement, maximum change would occur at the moderate level of discrepancy.

METHOD

In order to minimize the possibility that the subjects had previous opinions on the issue and to maximize the objectivity of the information, a concept formation task was employed as the "issue." A number of concept instances were presented and the subjects were required to decide what the correct concept was. This first description of the concept was considered their initial position. The instances were constructed so that only one consistent concept could be formed and only subjects who gave this response were included in the experimental analysis. Additional concept instances were then presented which were discrepant from the subjects' first response, and subjects were told that these new instances were examples of the same concept. The new instances were thus essentially discrepant information. After seeing the new instances, subjects were asked to give a final description of the concept and the amount of change from the initial concept to this last one was measured, and is considered a measure of position change.

The subjects were 119 freshmen from an introductory psychology class at the University of Bridgeport and 96 students from North Haven high school. In both samples, participation in the experiment was required by the school. Ninety-one subjects were eliminated because of failure to give the appropriate response to the first series of concept instances. An additional 14 subjects did not give any response to the second part of the test and could therefore not be included in the results. The remaining 110 subjects were divided about equally among experimental conditions, with no difference between conditions even approaching significance. Although the number of subjects eliminated was very high, this was due primarily to the difficulty of the concept formation task which was the same for all groups. This means that the remaining subjects were probably a somewhat select group (in that they were better able to cope with the concept formation task), but there is no reason to expect this selection to affect the various experimental groups differentially.

The experiment was described as a test being conducted as part of a survey of college and high school students. The subjects were run in groups ranging from four to eight. The test situation, the test booklet, and the instructions were designed to create an atmosphere which resembled a typical group intelligence test or scholastic aptitude test. When the subject entered the room he was asked to take a seat at which a booklet was placed. When all subjects had arrived, the signal to begin was given. Silence was strictly enforced.

All instructions and materials were in the test booklet which was entitled "Yale Personality Survey." It contained, in order, a personality questionnaire, the concept formation test, and a short questionnaire concerning the concept formation test. All subjects first took a 25-item personality test. This questionnaire was administered in order to increase the subjects' interest and motivation by impressing them with the fact that the survey concerned important things about themselves. It was also expected that this would make it more credible that the concept formation test was a test of intelligence and perceptiveness, as it was described.

The concept formation test was presented next. The materials and procedure were similar to those employed in standard concept formation studies (cf. Hunt & Hovland, 1960). Concept instances consisted of a rectangle containing three figures in a row. The figures varied in shape (circle, triangle, or square) and size (large or small); and additional variation was produced by the number of a particular shape or size that was included (one, two, or three) and each figure's position (first, second, or third). There were thus four dimensions: shape, size, number, and position; three with three values, and one with two.

Three concept problems were shown, with the first being the critical one and the others serving merely as buffer items to minimize the possibility that the subjects would remember the exact instances that were used. The subjects were first presented with eight instances labeled either "alpha" or "not-alpha," and they were given detailed instructions which explained that their task was to discover what characteristics defined an alpha. Responses were recorded on a separate answer sheet and consisted of verbal descriptions of the identifying characteristic (e.g., alpha is a triangle in the second position). The eight instances were chosen so that only one answer was consistent with all of them, and all subjects who did not give the correct answer were discarded from the sample.

Discrepancy Manipulation

After working on these problems, the subjects were told that they would be shown some ad-

ditional instances of each of the concepts they had just seen, beginning with the first concept. It was stressed that these new instances were examples of exactly the same concept, and that in order for a solution to be correct it had to be consistent with all instances. To be certain that all subjects remembered their first answer and to increase its salience, subjects were required to copy their answers from the separate answer sheet on to the instruction page.

Sixteen instances were then presented one at a time, with each labeled either alpha or not-alpha as in Part I. Of these 16 new instances, 5 were discrepant from the first response given by the subjects, but all were consistent with a new response. That is, by responding with the new concept subjects would be consistent with all 16 instances. Also, since it was virtually impossible for the subject to remember the first 8 instances exactly, it would appear that he was responding consistently with all instances. Thus, this new concept is essentially the position advocated by the new instances. Discrepancy was defined as the number of common elements between the initial concept and the advocated concept. In the low-discrepancy condition the two concepts shared three elements; in moderate discrepancy they shared two; and in high discrepancy they shared no elements.

These 16 instances were presented for 15 seconds each, and immediately after each, the subject was given 20 seconds to record his current guess as to the correct solution on an answer page. After the last instance, the subject gave his final description of the concept. All timing was done by having the subjects turn pages on a signal from the experimenter.

Immediately before and after the presentation of the new instances, subjects were given an objective identification test on which they were to indicate whether each of 12 unlabeled instances was an alpha or a not-alpha. After the second identification test, subjects were asked a number of questions designed to measure the success of the involvement manipulation, degree of acceptance of the instructions, and to assess the possibility that involvement groups exerted differential effort on the two parts of the test.

Involvement Manipulation

Before the concept formation test was presented, the high-involvement (HI) group was given instructions designed to emphasize the importance of their first response as an indicator of intelligence and perceptiveness; while the low-involvement (LI) subjects were led to believe that the first response was relatively unimportant as a personality indicator.

The key phrases from the high-involvement instructions were:

It is extremely important to form an impression quickly and accurately. . . . Therefore, speed of solution is the most important aspect of this test. Your score depends mainly on how close your first answer is to the correct answer.

Low-involvement instructions included the following:

The first part of the test will not be marked. . . . Your score cannot be based on these first impressions.

The rationale for this manipulation was that the subjects who thought that their score depended primarily on the first response would be more concerned about having that response be correct than those subjects who thought the second response counted more. Since involvement is defined as concern about a response, the manipulation should cause the former to be more involved in their first response than the latter.

Note that a special effort was made to equate the groups in level of interest in and concern about the test as a whole. All subjects were given the same instructions about the importance of the test and its relevance to intelligence and perceptiveness; and all were urged to work hard and concentrate on both parts of the test. The only difference between high- and low-involvement groups was in the instructions dealing with the relative significance of the initial and final responses.

The two sources of data concerning amount of change are the difference between initial and final description of the concept, and between first and last identification tests. Since the concept descriptions have more intuitive similarity to "opinions" as used in attitude-change studies, the results will be presented in terms of change from initial to final concept description. All results are virtually identical for both measures.

Scoring for amount of change in the concept descriptions was based on the assumption that perfect maintenance consists of retaining the original concept intact, with no elements subtracted or changed. In addition, it was felt that subtracting elements was a more serious change than adding new ones; and that forming a concept which included the original intact but provided for exceptions (e.g., a disjunctive concept of the form either A or B) was in essence no change at all. Rating was done on a 7-point scale, ranging from 0 (no change) to 6 (maximum change). All analyses are based on scoring done by the author, since an interrater reliability coefficient based on the scoring of 25 randomly selected protocols was .98.

RESULTS

Check on the Manipulation

The instructions were designed to produce either high or low involvement in the first concept description. A direct check on this manipulation is provided by responses to the question: "Which part of the problem was more important?" Over 90% of the subjects responded consistently with the manipulation instructions (that is, HI subjects said the

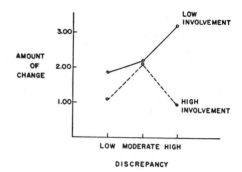

FIG. 1. Mean amount of change from initial to final response.

first part; LI subjects, the second part). The difference is highly significant. Thus, as far as this direct check indicates, the manipulation was successful in producing greater involvement in their first response for the HI group.

Another check on the manipulation is provided by the amount of change by the two groups. Since high involvement is defined as greater concern with the first response being correct, there should be greater resistance to changing the first response with high than with low involvement. As may be seen in Table 1 and Figure 1, at each level of discrepancy HI subjects changed less than LI subjects, although at moderate discrepancy the difference was slight. The overall difference between HI and LI groups is highly significant ($F = 6.95$, $p < .02$). In addition, 54% of HI subjects showed no change at all, whereas the comparable figure for LI subjects is only 32%. This difference is significant ($\chi^2 = 5.59$, $p < .02$).

A possible alternative explanation of this difference might be that LI subjects worked harder than HI subjects on the second set of instances and the former therefore changed more (see Cohen, 1959). A check on this possibility is provided by responses to a post-test question which asked subjects to rate how hard they worked on all parts of the test, with possible responses ranging from "not hard at all" to "very hard." Since there were no appreciable differences between groups in amount of effort expended on either part of the test nor in total effort, it seems unlikely that difference between groups in

TABLE 1

AMOUNT OF CHANGE FROM INITIAL
TO FINAL POSITION

Condition	Discrepancy		
	Low	Moderate	High
Low involvement	1.85	2.16	3.15
High involvement	1.14	2.12	0.94

amount of change was due to differential effort. Thus, it seems reasonable to assume that the manipulation was successful in producing differential involvement in the initial response.

Involvement and Discrepancy

The major results are presented in Table 1 and Figure 1, which show the amount of change for each involvement and discrepancy condition. The main hypothesis was that there would be more change with greater discrepancy under low involvement, but with high involvement maximum change would occur at the moderate level of discrepancy. As may be seen in the figure, the results are in line with this prediction. With low involvement change increases monotonically with discrepancy; while under conditions of high involvement, the relationship is nonmonotonic.

A trend analysis (McNemar, 1962) of the three means in each condition demonstrates that the linear trend is significant in the low-involvement condition ($F = 3.71$, $p < .07$) and the quadratic trend is significant in the high-involvement condition ($F = 4.05$, $p < .05$). Neither the quadratic component under low involvement nor the linear component under high involvement approaches significance ($F < 1$ for each). Thus, the results are consistent with the hypothesis and indicate that within the range used the relationship between discrepancy and amount of change is monotonic for low involvement and nonmonotonic for high involvement with maximum change at moderate discrepancy.

DISCUSSION

Although the present results are consistent with the suggestion by Hovland et al. (1957), the analysis these authors offer in terms of

latitudes of acceptance and rejection is more a description of the situation than an explanation. The main point of their analysis is that with high involvement extremely discrepant information is rejected and therefore does not cause position change. But the central question remains why rejection of the information occurs rather than position change. This may be answered by analyzing the effect of discrepancy and involvement on the relative difficulty of employing these two modes of resolution.

As discrepancy increases, the difficulty of changing the position also increases, because a greater change is necessary. Assuming that there is some resistance to change, it is harder to change a great deal than to change only a little. Thus, reducing the discrepancy by position change would be considerably harder when discrepancy is extreme than when it is slight. The difficulty of rejecting the information, however, does not increase with greater discrepancy. Extremely discrepant information sometimes tends to appear biased or fanatical and is consequently easier to reject. In any case, extremely discrepant information is no harder to reject than moderate information. Therefore, since position change becomes harder with increasing discrepancy and rejection does not, the difficulty of employing position change must increase relative to the difficulty of rejection.

It follows from this that at some point along the discrepancy continuum position change should become more difficult than rejection of the information. At that point, the subject will reject the information and will not change his position. Since this point will be different for different subjects, a further increase in discrepancy will result in even less change because the point will have been reached by more subjects. Thus, maximum change will occur when the discrepancy is just below the level at which change becomes easier than rejection. Less discrepancy will produce less change because subjects have less far to change; while more discrepancy will produce less change because subjects will reject the information instead.

According to this analysis the relationship between discrepancy and change is nonmonotonic regardless of the degree of involvement in the initial position. Degree of involvement is important, however, because it affects the point along the discrepancy continuum at which the downturn in amount of change occurs. This point will be determined by any factors which affect the difficulty of employing either position change or rejection of the information. Increases in difficulty of changing the initial position will decrease the discrepancy level at which the downturn occurs; while increases in the difficulty of rejecting the information will increase the level. Since an increase in involvement in the initial position will make change more difficult, it should decrease the degree of discrepancy at which the downturn occurs. This is what was found in the present experiment. On the other hand, an increase in the prestige of the communicator will make rejection more difficult and should increase the level of discrepancy. This prediction was supported by the results of a recent experiment by Aronson, Turner, and Carlsmith (1963).

Note that in both of these experiments the downturn was actually found in only one condition. It was not found in the low-involvement condition of the present study nor in the high-prestige condition of the Aronson et al. study. This may be explained by the limited range of discrepancies employed. If the discrepancy level were made extreme enough presumably the downturn would occur eventually. Thus, although the present analysis asserts that the relationship between discrepancy and change is nonmonotonic under both high and low involvement, with low involvement it may appear to be monotonic for a broad range of discrepancies.

Additional support for this analysis is provided by inspection of the amount of change by those subjects in the various conditions who did change. According to the analysis, the decrease in amount of change under high involvement and high discrepancy is caused by a shift in the method of resolution employed from position change to rejection of the information. It follows from this that those subjects who did change (that is, did not reject the information) should change more under high than moderate discrepancy (al-

though, of course, fewer should change). This is what the data show. The mean change under high involvement for those subjects who change is 4.25 for high discrepancy and 2.77 for moderate discrepancy ($t = 1.92$, $p < .06$). In other words, if they change, they change more the greater the discrepancy; but at some point fewer subjects change, thus causing a decrease in the mean amount of change. This implies (as Zimbardo, 1960, also discusses) that if all modes of resolution other than position change were eliminated, there would be a direct, positive relationship between discrepancy and change. Since it is virtually impossible to eliminate alternative modes entirely, however, the present results and analysis should generally hold.

REFERENCES

Aronson, E., Turner, Judy, & Carlsmith, J. M. Communicator credibility and communication discrepancy. *J. abnorm. soc. Psychol.*, 1963, **67**, 31–36.

Cohen, A. R. Communication discrepancy and attitude change: A dissonance theory approach. *J. Pers.*, 1959, **27**, 386–396.

Fisher, S., & Lubin, A. Distance as a determinant of influence in a two-person serial interaction situation. *J. abnorm. soc. Psychol.*, 1958, **56**, 230–238.

Fisher, S., Rubinstein, I., & Freeman, R. W. Intertrial effects of immediate self-committal in a continuous social influence situation. *J. abnorm. soc. Psychol.*, 1956, **52**, 200–207.

Goldberg, S. C. Three situational determinants of conformity to social norms. *J. abnorm. soc. Psychol.*, 1954, **49**, 325–329.

Harvey, O. J., Kelley, H. H., & Shapiro, M. M. Reactions to unfavorable evaluations of the self made by other persons. *J. Pers.*, 1957, **25**, 393–411.

Hovland, C. I. Reconciling conflicting results derived from experimental and survey studies of attitude change. *Amer. Psychologist*, 1959, **14**, 8–17.

Hovland, C. I., Harvey, O. J., & Sherif, M. Assimilation and contrast effects in reactions to communication and attitude change. *J. abnorm. soc. Psychol.*, 1957, **55**, 244–252.

Hovland, C. I., & Pritzker, H. A. Extent of opinion change as a function of amount of change advocated. *J. abnorm. soc. Psychol.*, 1957, **54**, 257–261.

Hunt, E. B., & Hovland, C. I. Order of consideration of different types of concepts. *J. exp. Psychol.*, 1960, **59**, 220–225.

McNemar, Q. *Psychological statistics*. New York: Wiley, 1962.

Zimbardo, P. G. Involvement and communication discrepancy as determinants of opinion conformity. *J. abnorm. soc. Psychol.*, 1960, **60**, 86–94.

Persistency

From the results obtained by Freedman[1] and by Whittaker,[2] in the preceding section, one can make specific predictions about the magnitude of impact of a communication under conditions of high or low commitment and under varying degrees of communication-recipient discrepancy. In summary, the more opinion change demanded when commitment is low, the more that should result. Under high commitment, the greatest amount of opinion change should result when the demand is for a moderate amount; as the communication-recipient discrepancy increases or decreases beyond this point, the magnitude of opinion change should decrease.

Thus having specified the optimum conditions of commitment and discrepancy which should maximize the impact of a communication, the next logical questions would be concerned with the persistency of the induced effects. How long will they last? And, under what conditions can they be made to last even longer?

With regard to the first question, it is a common assumption in communications research that persistency is a function of the vividness of the individual's memory of the message. A more precise statement about the relationship between memory and opinion change will be found in the study by Watts and McGuire reprinted later in this section. However, on the preliminary assumption that there is a positive relationship between the amount of forgetting (of the message) and the rate of decay of induced opinion change, a rough estimate can be made at this point of the extent to which induced change would persist over time. Referring again to the Ebbinghaus curves for forgetting used by Miller and Campbell to predict order effects in opinion change (p. 118), one observes that immediately upon presentation of the verbal stimulus there follows a period of rapid forgetting, after which time the level of forgetting appears to reach a plateau. Almost one half of the information about the stimulus is forgotten dur-

[1]Freedman, J. L. Involvement, discrepancy, and change. *J. abnorm. soc. Psychol.*, 1964, **69**, 290–295.

[2]Whittaker, J. O. Attitude change and communication-attitude discrepancy. *J. soc. Psychol.*, 1965, **65**, 141–147. See discussion of Whittaker's findings on page 406.

ing the first hour. Based on this observation, one might predict that an accelerated regression of opinions would occur shortly after exposure to the message, but that this regression would level off after a few days had passed. From what we already have learned about the influence of competing variables on opinion change, it should be obvious that this simple prediction could prove embarrassing if the experimental conditions were amenable, for instance, to a sleeper effect (pp. 10 ff.).

Furthermore, any variation in the message which affected the degree to which it was initially learned would probably also influence retention and, subsequently, the persistency of whatever change could successfully be induced. But even if all of the original information were equally well learned, some, for various reasons, might be better retained. Numerous variables could effect such differential learning or differential retention. For example, opinion change effected by unqualified, or one-sided, messages tends to persist longer than change resulting from qualified, or two-sided, messages.[3, 4] Pleasant information (e.g., receiving a high grade on a quiz) is usually retained better than unpleasant information (e.g., a low grade).[5] Memories of incomplete tasks last longer than memories of completed tasks.[6] The more meaningful[7] and well-structured[8] that material is,

---

[3] Papageorgis, D. Bartlett effect and the persistency of induced opinion change. *J. abnorm. soc. Psychol.*, 1963, **67**, 61–67. Unfortunately, since the Papageorgis experiment involved taking repeated measurements of the subjects' opinions, there is the possibility that some of this difference between one-sided and two-sided communications was a function of the measurement process itself. In a study which is reprinted in a later section (pp. 475 ff.) Robert Lana shows that while the opinion questionnaire may have an inhibitory effect on opinion change to a two-sided communication, it seems to have little effect on opinion change to one-sided communications: Lana, R. E. Inhibitory effects of a pretest on opinion change. *Educ. psychol. Measmt.*, 1966, **26**, 139–150.

[4] The exception to Papageorgis' finding would be when the recipient is exposed to a counterappeal. Lumsdaine and Janis, it may be recalled, found that in this case the two-sided communication has the greater sustained effect (pp. 255–256).

[5] Koch, H. L. The influence of some affective factors upon recall. *J. gen. Psychol.*, 1930, **4**, 171–190. Kanungo, R. N., & Dutta, S. Retention of affective material: Frame of reference or intensity? *J. Pers. soc. Psychol.*, 1966, **4**, 27–35.

[6] Zeigarnik, B. Das behalten erledigter und unerledigter handlungen. *Psychol. Forsch.*, 1927, **9**, 1–85.

[7] Dietze, A. G., & Jones, G. E. Factual memory of secondary school pupils for a short article which they read a single time. *J. educ. Psychol.*, 1931, **22**, 586–598, 667–676. Hovland, C. I. Human learning and retention. In S. S. Stevens (Ed.), *Handbook of experimental psychology.* New York: Wiley, 1951. Pp. 645–646.

[8] Koffka, K. *Principles of gestalt psychology.* New York: Harcourt-Brace, 1935. P. 496.

the better it is retained. General conclusions are remembered better than the detailed arguments used to support them.[9] Material which is purposely emphasized ("Now get this!") tends to increase retention,[10] although it is conceivable that overemphasis would result in some of the material's losing its distinctiveness. (Hovland, Janis, and Kelley remind us of the phenomenon of "remembering the joke but not what it was supposed to illustrate.")[11] Although repetition tends to facilitate learning only up to a point,[12] this facilitative effect might be further increased simply by varying the form and style of the communication, thereby alleviating the boredom which could result from overexposure.[13]

The two papers that follow elaborate upon different aspects of the problem of the persistency of induced change. The first paper is by William A. Watts and William J. McGuire. It describes various empirically derived relationships between opinion change and recall of the source, the topic, the conclusion, and the arguments of a communication designed to induce that change. The second paper is by Theodore M. Newcomb. Newcomb's nonexperimental field study of the persistency problem, altogether different in method from that of Watts and McGuire, takes its rationale from the cognitive consistency hypothesis. Newcomb postulates that new attitudes will tend to persist only as long as one expression of those attitudes is the selection of a supportive social environment. He tests this hypothesis in the results of an interesting follow-up to his earlier, often cited Bennington college study.

[9] Hovland, C. I., Janis, I. L., & Kelley, H. H. *Communication and persuasion.* New Haven, Conn.: Yale Univer. Press, 1953. P. 248.

[10] Jersild, A. Primacy, recency, frequency, and vividness. *J. exp. Psychol.,* 1929, **12,** 58–70. Ehrensberger, R. An experimental study of the relative effectiveness of certain forms of emphasis in public speaking. *Speech Monogr.,* 1945, **12,** 94–111.

[11] Hovland, C. I., Janis, I. L., & Kelley, H. H. *Communication and persuasion.* New Haven, Conn.: Yale Univer. Press, 1953. P. 247.

[12] Krueger, W. C. F. The effect of overlearning on retention. *J. exp. Psychol.,* 1929, **12,** 71–78.

[13] Hovland, C. I., Janis, I. L., & Kelley, H. H. *Communication and persuasion.* New Haven, Conn.: Yale Univer. Press, 1953. P. 247.

Reprinted from Journal of Abnormal and Social Psychology, 1964, Vol. 68, pp. 233–241, by permission of William J. McGuire and APA.

PERSISTENCE OF INDUCED OPINION CHANGE AND RETENTION OF THE INDUCING MESSAGE CONTENTS [1]

WILLIAM A. WATTS

AND WILLIAM J. McGUIRE

Induced opinion change shows a strong positive relationship to recall of the contents of the persuasive message 1 week after receipt of the communication but tends, over time, to become functionally autonomous of recall of at least some aspects of the contents of the inducing message. Induced opinion change was found to decay rectilinearly over a 6-week period, while recall of contents showed a negatively accelerated decay trend. Opinion change and recall of the message topic were positively related 1 week after the communication, but negatively related 6 weeks later. Recall of the side taken and of the specific arguments used were positively related to opinion change both 1 week and 6 weeks after the communication. Recall of source was complexly related to opinion change.

The present study was designed to investigate the persistence over time of the opinion change induced by a persuasive message, and to relate this persistence to memory for various aspects of the content of the message that induced the change. Three separate issues are involved in this question: the persistence of induced opinion change, the retention of message content, and the relation between opinion change and recall of contents. We shall review briefly the research on each of these issues.

Research on the persistence of induced opinion change yields abundant evidence that there is no such thing as *the* decay function of persuasion. Rather, there is a wide variety of such functions reflecting variations in the communication situations that induced the changes. In their classical study on the influence of commercial films on social attitudes of children, Peterson and Thurstone (1933) found that the opinion change induced by some films decayed completely within 8 months, while the persuasive effects of other films were higher after 6 months than immediately after the showing. Others who report almost complete decay within 6 months include Chen (1936) and Sims (1938). Those

[1] This study was supported by a grant from the Division of Social Sciences, National Science Foundation.

finding some decay but a still significant residual change after considerable periods include Cherrington and Miller (1933), Dietrich (1946), Janis, Lumsdaine, and Gladstone (1951), and McGuire (1960a). Almost complete persistence of the initially induced change was found by Annis and Meier (1934) and Smith (1943). Thus, the findings range from complete loss to complete persistence of induced opinion change over comparable periods of time.

Actually, the full range of findings indicate more diversity still, since a number of studies showed a delayed action persuasive effect; that is, an increase in opinion change with time since message. Lewin (1958) reported that the amount of compliance induced by group discussion was greater 3 weeks later than it was immediately after the discussion. In the World War II studies, Hovland, Lumsdaine, and Sheffield (1949) tested soldiers either 5 days or 9 weeks after they saw the *Battle of Britain* film and found that opinion change showed a net increase over that time. The experimenters named this phenomenon the "sleeper effect" and proposed various theories to account for it. One of these, the "discounting cue" theory, has been much studied subsequently (for example, Kelman & Hovland, 1953) and will be discussed below in connection with our source recall results. Delayed action effects have also been found when the persuasive message is complex or indirect (Cohen, 1957; McGuire, 1960b; Stotland, Katz, & Patchen, 1959), possibly because complex material can be fully assimilated into the cognitive system only with the passage of considerable time.

The second general question involved in the present investigation deals with retention of the content of the persuasive message. Research on this verbal learning topic has been voluminous, and competent reviews are so readily available (for example, McGeogh & Irion, 1952) that discussion is hardly needed here.

It is on the third question that the present research focuses; namely, to the extent to which the persistence of the induced opinion change is related to retention in memory of the various aspects of the persuasive content that induced it. We have found no previous study undertaken primarily to investigate this relationship directly, but a number of earlier investigators have reported incidental findings on the overall relationship. Hovland et al. (1949) found a slight negative relation between content recall and persistence of opinion change, but suggest a confounding due to postcommunication interactions among subjects of different predispositions. McGuire (1957) found a biserial r of $+.53$ ($p < .01$) between content recall and opinion change immediately after the communication. Janis and Rife (1959), studying persuasibility in mental patients, found the correlation between content recall and opinion change to be $+.21$ ($p = .06$) immediately after the message and $+.24$ ($p < .05$) after 1 week. Miller and Campbell (1959) found attitude and recall complexly related. When measured immediately after the message, they were positively related ($r = .49$ and $r = .27$), and when a week intervened, the correlation was negative ($-.51$ and $-.40$).

The present study goes beyond these previous ones by attempting to relate opinion change to recall for the separate aspects of the communication content. These aspects include the following: recall that a message on the given issue had even been received; recall of whether the pro or con side had been taken in the message; recall of the specific arguments that had been employed

to support this side; and recall of the source of the message.

It is almost tautological (ignoring without trepidation any possibility of inducing opinion change through "subliminal perception") that for the opinion change to have been induced by the message, there must have been some initial learning of the inducing content. But granting this assumption of positive relationship between initial learning and opinion change, two alternative hypotheses regarding their concurrent decay rates are a priori plausible. One hypothesis we can call the "functional dependence" view. It would say that recall of the inducing content is necessary not only to induce the opinion change, but also to maintain it so that as inducing content is forgotten, the opinion falls back to its initial position. The alternative hypothesis, which we call the "functional autonomy" view (after Allport, 1937), holds that initial learning of the inducing content is necessary for producing the opinion change; but once the change is made, it is as if a switch were thrown and the new opinion persists, regardless of the retention of the content, unless subsequently some countercontent is received, thus throwing the opinion "switch" back again. As will be discussed in detail in connection with our findings, there is reason to expect induced opinion change to be functionally dependent on recall of some aspects of the communication and functionally autonomous of the retention of other aspects.

METHOD

Since we wished to measure persistence of induced opinion change and retention for learned message content, each experimental subject took part in four sessions spaced over a 6-week interval and in each session read a persuasive message on a different issue. Then, after the fourth session, for the only time in the experiment, we measured opinion change on all four issues and retention of the contents of all four messages.

Material

Since the design required persuasive messages on four different issues, a prestudy was carried out to select appropriate issues. A group of undergraduate education students were asked to indicate, on a 15-point scale, their degree of agreement with each item in an initial pool of opinion statements. On the basis of their responses, four items were selected as the experimental issues. These four best met the criteria of homogeneous initial opinions (the four mean agreement scores ranged from 5.38 to 5.91 on the 15-point scale) and high homogeneity among subjects as regards initial opinion on each issue. The four issues selected were the following: "Puerto Rico should be admitted to the Union as the 51st State"; "Courts should deal more leniently with juvenile delinquents"; "The Secretary of State should be elected by the people, not appointed by the President"; "The State Sales tax should be abolished."

The final opinion questionnaire used in this study consisted of these four statements. Each statement was followed by a 15-point graphic scale with the left end labeled "Definitely Disagree" and the right end, "Definitely Agree." The subject was instructed to mark an "X" in whichever of the 15 categories best indicated his own stand on the statement.

Four persuasive messages were prepared, one on each issue. Each argued in favor of one of the above statements so as to push the mean agreement from the 5.00- to 6.00-point initial level toward the high agreement, 15.00-point end of the scale. Each message consisted of a title, an attributed source, and about 600 words of text divided into four paragraphs. The introductory paragraph stated that the communicator favored the statement and mentioned three arguments supporting it. Each of the following paragraphs developed in detail one of these three arguments. The messages were written in a calm, authoritative fashion with frequent citation of (purported) facts and figures bearing on the point being made.[2]

Alternate forms of each of the four messages were prepared, the pair of messages on any one issue being identical except that on one form the attribution was to a positively valenced source and on the other form to a negatively valenced source.[3] For example, on the "Sales Tax" issue, the positively valenced source was the report of a "Presidential Council for the study of the sales tax," while the corresponding negatively valenced source was "a defense argument by a man convicted of sales-tax fraud."

Recall for the various aspects of the communications was measured by a series of recall and recognition tests of increasing demandingness. The first asked the subject to recall and state, in his own words, the general topic discussed in each of the four messages he had received over the past 2 months. The second test reinstated these four topics and called upon the subject to state whether a pro or a con stand had been taken in the message on each

topic. The third test reinstated each topic and stand and listed four possible sources of each message, the subject being required to select the source to whom the message had actually been attributed. The fourth test consisted of three multiple-choice questions on each message designed to measure the subject's recall of the three specific arguments used in that message.

Opinion change was measured by the 15-point scales described above. Since we employed an after-only design, the opinion change scores were actually based on the final mean belief levels with the scales calibrated so that the messages were always pushing the person's opinion toward the 15-point end. The opinion change score in a given cell in Tables 1 through 5 is the final mean opinion level for subjects in that cell minus the final mean opinion level of the control (no message) subjects.

Subjects and Design

The subjects were 191 students enrolled in an introductory education course at the University of Illinois. Almost all of these subjects were women. They took part in all the sessions of the experiment during their usual section meeting. All 10 sections of the course were used. Four sections received the four messages from positively valenced sources; another 4 sections received them from negatively valenced sources; and a final 2 sections served as no message controls. The section size averaged 19 and ranged from 12 to 26. The precise numbers of cases serving in each condition are shown in each cell of the tables in the Results section below. The four topics were rotated around the four time intervals from section to section.

Procedure

The study was represented to the subjects as an attempt to develop instruments for measuring reading comprehension and analytic thinking ability in future teachers. The subjects were told they would be asked to read standardized passages dealing with controversial issues and that their task was to select and underline in each paragraph the shortest clause which epitomized the whole point being made in that paragraph. They were then allowed 6 minutes for reading and underlining in the prescribed manner one of the four persuasive messages.

Each subject (except those in the no message control condition) served in four experimental sessions. Each of the first three sessions was brief (lasting about 10 minutes) and consisted of receiving the general instructions and then reading and underlining one of the four persuasive messages. The fourth session was much longer, lasting about 60 minutes. It began, like the others, with the general instructions and then reading and underlining the message on a fourth issue. Immediately afterward the subjects filled out (for the only time in the experiment) the opinion questionnaire on all four issues and took the tests of retention of the various aspects of the communications as described above.

Since the opinion change and recall for all four topics were measured at the same time, namely, immediately after receipt of the message on the

---

[2] The four persuasive messages used in this study have been deposited with the American Documentation Institute. Order Document No. 7783 from ADI Auxiliary Publications Project, Photoduplication Service, Library of Congress, Washington, D. C. 20540. Remit in advance $1.25 for microfilm or $1.25 for photocopies and make checks payable to: Chief, Photoduplication Service, Library of Congress.

[3] The document referred to in Footnote 2 lists the positive and negative sources used with each of the four messages.

fourth topic, the retention interval was determined by how long prior to this last session the message on a given topic had been received. For all subjects the message on the first topic preceded the final opinion and memory measurement session by 6 weeks; the second, by 2 weeks; the third, by 1 week; and the fourth, by a few minutes. The present design was employed to achieve the statistical sensitivity obtained by using the subject as his own control while avoiding the ambiguity of using repeated measurements. But while this design allowed us to avoid repeated measurement of the same subjects at successive time intervals, there does remain the problem that the subjects were exposed to repeated messages (on different issues) which could conceivably have resulted in some kind of a progressive wariness. Such a possible effect would be troublesome since the irrelevant wariness variation would be perfectly correlated with our experimental variable of recency. However, the wariness effect would go in the opposite direction to the recency effect, and the data reported below show that there was an overwhelming recency effect in these results. Hence, this possible wariness contamination is not a major worry in interpreting the present results.

RESULTS AND DISCUSSION

Overall Decay Rates

The persuasive impact of the messages and also the recall of each of the various aspects of the message contents decayed fairly steadily over the 6-week postcommunication interval. Table 1 and Figure 1 show the shapes of these time trends when the data on the four issues and two source credibility conditions are combined.

Induced opinion change can be seen to decay progressively over time. The 69% drop from immediately after to 6 weeks after is

significant at the .01 level. (Unless otherwise specified, all p values given in this Results section for time trends and their interactions are based on analyses of variance in which the error terms consist of the residual within-subjects' variance, that is, the interactions between subjects and the treatments whose effects are being evaluated.) It would seem logical to expect this decay function to be negatively accelerated approaching an asymptote at about the 5.95-point control level. However, it can be seen in Figure 1 that the decay curve resembles very closely a straight line. An analysis using the F ratio of the deviations of means from the regression line to the within arrays shows that the obtained data do not depart significantly ($F = .09$) from the best-fitting straight line which has a slope of $-.287$. This slope is significantly different from zero ($F = 5.35$, $df = 3/575$, $p < .01$).

Recall of each of the three aspects of the communication can likewise be seen to fall over time as did the decay of induced opinion change. However, in contrast to the rectilinear decay of induced opinion change, all three of these retention curves show the negative acceleration characteristic of the forgetting curves usually reported in verbal learning studies. The fact that the function for opinion change decay has the same direction, but a different rate from the functions for retention of content, suggests that the persistence of the induced change is only partly dependent on the retention of the persuasive content of

TABLE 1

TEMPORAL DECAY OF INDUCED OPINION CHANGE AND OF RECALL FOR ASPECTS OF THE COMMUNICATION

Variable measured	Interval between message receipt and opinion measurement			
	Immediately after	1 week	2 weeks	6 weeks
Opinion change (on a 15-point scale) in the induced direction from 5.95-point no-message control level.	2.53	2.12	2.09	0.78
Percentage of subjects recalling message topic	94	60	63	61
Percentage of subjects recalling the side taken in the message (after reinstatement of topic)	93	65	65	60
Percentage of subjects recognizing message source (after reinstatement of topic)	85	44	50	34
Percentage of subjects recognizing all three arguments in the message (after reinstatement of topic and side)	72	29	24	11

Note.—Each cell score is based on 151 subjects.

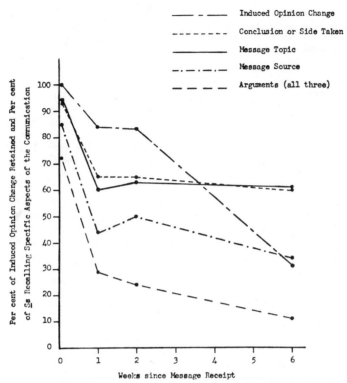

FIG. 1. Temporal decay of induced opinion change and of recall for various aspects of the persuasive communication. (Points are based on percentages in Table 1.)

the message, a point which is brought out more clearly by analyses discussed below.

Relation between Persistence of Opinion Change and Recall of the Topic Discussed

In order to determine how the persistence of the induced opinion change is related to the retention of the most basic aspect of the content of the inducing message, namely, recall of topic, we compared the opinion change on the issue in question of those who could and those who could not recall this aspect of the message received 1 week earlier with the opinion change of those who could and could not recall the topic of the message received 6 weeks earlier.[4] It can be seen from the re-

[4] It might seem strange we did not compare decay trends for the immediately-before versus 6-weeks-before issue, rather than the 1- versus 6-weeks. The reason is that the immediately-before condition yielded too asymmetrical a split, only 9 of the 151 subjects being unable to recall the topic of the message that had come immediately before the test.

sults in Table 2 that the two resulting decay functions for opinion change cross, indicating an interaction effect. One week after receipt of the message, those who remember the message topic are more influenced than those who do not remember it; while 6 weeks after the message, those remembering the topic are *less* influenced than those forgetting it. This interaction is significant above the .05 level ($F = 4.42$).[5]

This vanishing cell N made a sensitive statistical test impossible so we selected the less extreme time interval (even though this tended to weaken the magnitude of this trend difference) in order to obtain a nearer-the-median split on the basis of recall. For the sake of consistency, the same procedure was followed with respect to recall of each of the other aspects of the message. In any case, for each of the effects reported, the same trend is evident whether we compare the immediately-before or the 1-week-before condition with the 6-weeks-before condition.

[5] Partitioning the subjects on the basis of recall of the various aspects of the message contents frequently resulted in very disproportional cell Ns, as

TABLE 2

OPINION CHANGE AS RELATED TO ABILITY TO RECALL
THE TOPIC DISCUSSED IN THE MESSAGE

Recall of topic	Interval between message receipt and opinion measurement		
	1 week	6 weeks	M
Yes	2.57 (80)	0.38 (92)	1.39 (172)
No	1.45 (53)	1.41 (59)	1.43 (112)
M	2.12 (133)	0.78 (151)	1.41 (284)

Note.—Number in parentheses indicates number of scores on which cell mean is based.

While this inverse relationship after 6 weeks might seem paradoxical, it is neither unprecedented nor without a ready interpretation. Miller and Campbell (1959) found somewhat similar results: the overall relationship between attitude and recall was negligible ($r = -.10$); but when the opinion measure was taken immediately after the messages, the relationship was substantially positive ($r = .49$ and $r = .27$); while when the messages and opinion measurement were spread over a 2-week interval, substantial negative correlations ($-.51$ and $-.40$) were found.

Hence, both studies show that soon after message receipt, those subjects who recall having heard a message on the topic show more opinion change on it; while, after more time passes, more opinion change is shown by those not recalling having heard the message. (The time parameters were different in the two studies: 0 versus 2 weeks in the Miller-Campbell study and 1 versus 6 weeks in ours. However, the same trend shows up in our study also when we compare the 0—rather than 1—week interval with the 6 weeks. We did the significance test on the 1- versus 6-weeks comparison only to avoid the "vanishing cell N" problem discussed in Footnote 4.)

Our explanation for this rather unexpected, but highly significant and replicated,

can be seen in Table 2 and the following tables. Hence, in estimating the significance of the interaction effects shown in these tables we used an approximation for unequal frequencies in subclasses in analysis of variance (Walker & Lev, 1953, pp. 381–382).

interaction effect is as follows: Inability to recall so basic a point as the topic of a message soon after that message was presented indicates a high likelihood that, for some reason (such as inattention or misunderstanding), the person did not effectively receive the message in the first place and, hence, was unaffected by it. However, as time passes, there is increasing likelihood that the inability to recall the topic is due rather to forgetting of a message whose content was initially received. For the group whose inability to recall the topic after the prolonged interval due to forgetting of the specific communication situation, we would expect a sleeper effect to occur; that is, these subjects would tend to discount partially the arguments at first, while they still recalled that they heard them during a "propaganda" session. As time passed, however, and they forgot this discounting cue regarding the context in which they heard the argumentative material, the full persuasive impact of this material would tend to emerge undampened. As can be seen in Table 2, the interaction effect is due to such a delayed action effect in the no recall condition. This interpretation of the present finding is in close accord with Hovland's original interpretation of the "sleeper effect" (Hovland et al., 1949).

Regardless of the interpretation, however, the results indicate clearly that the persistence of induced opinion change tends to become, not only autonomous of recalling ever having heard a persuasive message on the issue, but actually negatively related to such recall. The significant interaction effect between persistence of induced opinion change and recall of topics has the result of canceling any first-order effect of the recall-of-topics variable. The trivial difference in opinion change between those recalling and not recalling the topic over both intervals (1 week and 6 weeks) yields an F of only .04.

Relation between Persistence of Opinion Change and Recall of the Side Taken on the Topic

The persistence of the induced opinion change was found to be related to retention of the conclusions drawn in the message. That is, when the topic was reinstated for the subject, his ability to recall which side of the topic had been supported in the message was positively related to the amount of opinion change, as can be seen in Table 3. Both of the marginals in this table are significant. The significant ($p < .01$) vertical margin indicates the overall decay of the induced opinion change which has already been discussed. The significant ($F = 5.65$, $p < .05$) horizontal margin indicates that, over both time intervals, those better able to recall the side taken in the message when the topic is reinstated are also more influenced. While there is some tendency for this positive relationship between recall of what side had been taken and amount of opinion change to lessen as time passes (see Table 3), the interaction falls short of the conventional level of significance ($F = 2.49$, $p = .12$); and, hence, we cannot conclude that persistence of opinion change becomes functionally autonomous of recognition of which side had been taken in a prior persuasive message when its topic is reinstated.

Relation between Persistence of Opinion Change and Recognizing the Specific Arguments Used

After the topics and the sides taken on them in the messages were reinstated for the subject, he was asked three multiple-choice questions designed to measure his ability to recognize the three arguments that had been used in each message. On the basis of their responses to these questions, the subjects were partitioned into those who answered correctly three or two of the questions on a given issue versus those who answered only one or none correctly (this point of partition coming

TABLE 3
OPINION CHANGE AS RELATED TO RECALL OF THE SIDE WHICH HAD BEEN TAKEN IN THE MESSAGE ON THE GIVEN TOPIC

Recall of side after message topic is reinstated	Interval between message receipt and opinion measurement		
	1 week	6 weeks	M
Yes	2.83 (86)	0.94 (91)	1.86 (177)
No	0.81 (47)	0.53 (60)	0.66 (107)

Note.—Number in parentheses indicates number of scores on which cell mean is based.

TABLE 4
OPINION CHANGE AS RELATED TO RECALL OF THE SPECIFIC ARGUMENTS USED IN A MESSAGE AFTER THE TOPIC AND THE SIDE TAKEN ARE REINSTATED

Number of arguments recognized	Interval between message receipt and opinion measurement		
	1 week	6 weeks	M
3 or 2	2.75 (86)	1.52 (68)	2.21 (154)
1 or 0	0.96 (47)	0.17 (83)	0.46 (130)

Note.—Number in parentheses indicates number of scores on which cell mean is based.

closest to yielding a median split for the 1- and 6-week intervals). The opinion scores of the resulting subsets of subjects are shown in Table 4. The main effect is significant ($F = 9.65$, $p < .01$), indicating that with the topics and the sides taken reinstated, the recall of the specific arguments contributes to the amount of opinion change. Those recalling two or more arguments show more change both 1 week after the message ($t = 2.26$, $p < .05$) and 6 weeks later, although the difference is trivial ($t = .98$) at the longer interval. The interaction effect is trivial ($F = .20$). Hence, there is evidence that opinion change is functionally dependent on the recall of the arguments originally inducing it, given that the topics and sides taken in the messages are reinstated.

Effect of Source without Regard to Recall

As shown in Figure 2, there is some evidence of a main-order source effect and of the "sleeper effect" interaction between source valence and time since communication. As regards the main effect of source valence, the mean change produced by the messages over the four intervals was 2.10 when they were attributed to the positively valenced sources and 1.54 when attributed to the negatively valenced sources ($F = 2.77$, $p = .10$). As regards the sleeper interaction effect, it can be seen that the induced change decays fairly steadily over time in both source conditions, but more rapidly in the positively valenced source condition, even to the extent that the two curves cross (see Figure 2). This sleeper-effect interaction between the source-valence variable and the immediate versus 6-week

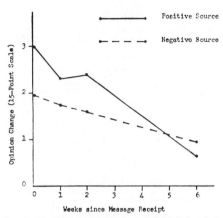

FIG. 2. Persistence of opinion change induced by positively and negatively valenced sources.

interval variable is of only borderline significance ($F = 3.71$, $p < .10$) and could be due, at least in part, to a regression effect.

Effects of Recall of Source

After the topics and sides taken in the message were reinstated, the subject's ability to recognize the source of the message on each issue was measured by a multiple-choice question that allowed him to select either the correct source or one of the incorrect sources of positive or negative valence. Hence, the subjects in the positive and those in the negative source-valence conditions could be further partitioned into those who could and those who could not recall the source. The mean opinion change of each of these four subsets is shown in Table 5 for each of the

four time intervals. Insofar as recall of source contributes to opinion change, there should be an interaction effect between source valence and source recall such that those in the positive source condition should show more opinion change when they can recognize the source, and those in the negative source condition should show less change if they can recognize the source. As can be seen in Table 5, the data for all four intervals combined show no such trend. Rather, there is a main-order effect such that those who recall better the source show more opinion change ($F = 4.09$, $p < .05$) even when the source was a negative one. An inspection of the means shows that this effect was confined almost entirely to the positive source condition. With the negative source, those recalling and not recalling the source show about equal change; while with positive sources, those recalling the source show far greater change ($t = 2.74$, $p < .01$).

The second-order interaction effect (involving source valence, source recall, and interval since message) is practically nil (see Table 5). Hence, the discounting cue theory receives no support if the theory is stated in terms of the subject's ability to recall the source. Hovland and Weiss (1951) and Kelman and Hovland (1953) have, however, already reformulated the theory in terms, not of the subject's ability to recall the source, but of his spontaneous tendency to do so.

An interesting incidental finding is that the positive sources were much better recalled than the negative. As shown in Table 6, the

TABLE 5

OPINION CHANGE AS RELATED TO SOURCE VALENCE AND RECALL OF SOURCE AFTER THE TOPICS AND SIDES TAKEN IN THE MESSAGES ARE REINSTATED

Source condition	Interval between message receipt and opinion measurement				
	Immediate	1 week	2 weeks	6 weeks	M
Positive valence	3.17	2.59	2.78	1.16	2.54
Source recalled	(76)	(48)	(56)	(46)	(226)
	1.49	1.99	1.71	0.05	1.22
Source not recalled	(9)	(37)	(29)	(39)	(114)
Negative valence	1.75	2.05	1.35	0.72	1.62
Source recalled	(53)	(10)	(20)	(6)	(89)
	2.67	1.65	1.70	0.97	1.49
Source not recalled	(13)	(38)	(46)	(60)	(157)

Note.—Number in parentheses indicates number of scores on which cell mean is based.

TABLE 6
NUMBER OF SUBJECTS WHO RECALL HIGH VALENCED AND LOW VALENCED SOURCES

Source condition	Interval between message receipt and opinion measurement			
	Immediately after	1 week	2 weeks	6 weeks
Positive valence				
Recalled	76	48	56	46
Not recalled	9	37	29	39
Negative valence				
Recalled	53	10	20	6
Not recalled	13	38	46	60
x^2 (High versus Low)	1.80	14.43*	17.42*	31.40*

* $p < .001$

positive sources are better recalled than the negative at all four time intervals and the superiority increases with the length of the interval, attaining the .001 level of significance at each of the three longer intervals (1-, 2-, and 6-weeks). This differential can be explained in terms of the more rapid forgetting of dissonant material (Festinger, 1957). The messages used in the study were designed to be reasonable and logical. The incongruous attribution of so impressive a message to a negatively valenced source may account for the more rapid forgetting of the negatively valenced sources. Alternatively, the differential recall could be attributed to some systematic difference between the sets of negative and of positive sources used here such that the positive sources were systematically more familiar, more interesting, etc., than the negative and, hence, better recalled. However, the instances used within the sets are varied enough so that this interpretation is not compelling.

REFERENCES

ALLPORT, G. W. *Personality: A psychological interpretation.* New York: Holt, 1937.
ANNIS, A. D., & MEIER, N. C. The induction of opinion change through suggestion by means of "planted content." *J. soc. Psychol.,* 1934, 5, 65–81.
CHEN, W. K. C. Retention of the effect of oral propaganda. *J. soc. Psychol.,* 1936, 7, 479–483.
CHERRINGTON, B. M., & MILLER, L. W. Changes in attitude as a result of a lecture and of reading similar materials. *J. soc. Psychol.,* 1933, 4, 479–484.
COHEN, A. R. Need for cognition and order of communication as determinants of opinion change. In

C. I. Hovland et al. (Eds.), *The order of presentation in persuasion.* New Haven: Yale Univer. Press, 1957. Pp. 79–97.
DIETRICH, J. E. The relative effectiveness of two modes of radio delivery in influencing attitudes. *Speech Monogr.,* 1946, 13, 58–65.
FESTINGER, L. *A theory of cognitive dissonance.* Evanston, Ill.: Row, Peterson, 1957.
HOVLAND, C. I., LUMSDAINE, A. A., & SHEFFIELD, F. D. *Experiments on mass communication.* Princeton: Princeton Univer. Press, 1949.
HOVLAND, C. I., & WEISS, W. The influence of source credibility on communication effectiveness. *Publ. Opin. Quart.,* 1951, 15, 635–650.
JANIS, I. L., LUMSDAINE, A. A., & GLADSTONE, A. I. Effects of preparatory communications on reactions to a subsequent news event. *Publ. Opin. Quart.,* 1951, 15, 487–518.
JANIS, I. L., & RIFE, D. Persuasibility and emotional disorder. In C. I. Hovland & I. L. Janis (Eds.), *Personality and persuasibility.* New Haven: Yale Univer. Press, 1959. Pp. 121–140.
KELMAN, H. C., & HOVLAND, C. I. "Reinstatement" of the communicator in delayed measurement of opinion change. *J. abnorm. soc. Psychol.,* 1953, 48, 327–335.
LEWIN, K. Group decision and social change. In Eleanor E. Maccoby, T. M. Newcomb, & E. L. Hartley (Eds.), *Readings in social psychology.* (3rd ed.) New York: Holt, 1958. Pp. 197–211.
McGEOGH, J. A., & IRION, A. L. *The psychology of human learning.* New York: Longmans, 1952.
McGUIRE, W. J. Order of presentation as a factor in "conditioning" persuasiveness. In C. I. Hovland et al. (Eds.), *The order of presentation in persuasion.* New Haven: Yale Univer. Press, 1957. Pp. 98–114.
McGUIRE, W. J. Cognitive consistency and attitude change. *J. abnorm. soc. Psychol.,* 1960, 60, 345–353. (a)
McGUIRE, W. J. A syllogistic analysis of cognitive relationships. In C. I. Hovland & M. I. Rosenberg (Eds.), *Attitude organization and change.* New Haven: Yale Univer. Press, 1960. Pp. 65–111. (b)
MILLER, N., & CAMPBELL, D. T. Recency and primacy in persuasion as a function of the timing of speeches and measurements. *J. abnorm. soc. Psychol.,* 1959, 59, 1–9.
PETERSON, RUTH C., & THURSTONE, L. L. *Motion pictures and the social attitudes of children.* New York: Macmillan, 1933.
SIMS, V. M. Factors influencing attitude toward the TVA. *J. abnorm. soc. Psychol.,* 1938, 33, 34–56.
SMITH, F. T. An experiment in modifying attitudes toward the Negro. *Teachers Coll. Columbia U. Contr. Educ.,* 1943, No. 887.
STOTLAND, E., KATZ, D., & PATCHEN, M. Reduction of prejudice through the arousal of self insight. *J. Pers.,* 1959, 27, 507–531.
WALKER, HELEN M., & LEV, J. *Statistical inference.* New York: Holt, Rinehart, & Winston, 1953.

Reprinted from the Journal of Social Issues, 1963, Vol. 19, No. 4, pp. 3–13, by permission of Theodore M. Newcomb and the publisher.

Persistence and Regression of Changed Attitudes: Long-Range Studies

Theodore M. Newcomb

I.

One's attitude toward something is not only a resultant of one's previous traffic with one's environment but also a determinant of selective response to present and future environments. Viewed in the latter way, existing attitudes may determine one's selection among alternative environmental settings, and these in turn may serve to

3

preserve or undermine the very attitudes that had been initially responsible for one's selection among the alternatives. Insofar as attitudes are self-preserving, such tendencies to select a supportive environment would, if empirically supported, provide an important explanation of their persistence. In its most general form, the hypothesis would run somewhat as follows: Existing attitudes are most likely to persist, other things equal, when one's environment provides most rewards for their behavioral expression. But this platitudinous proposition ("things persist when conditions are favorable to their persistence") is not very interesting, and is probably not even testable. A more interesting and more testable form of the proposition would take account of both change and persistence, both of attitudes and of environmental supportiveness. In particular, it would say something about a changed selection of environments following attitude change, about the ways in which the recently formed attitude is or is not reinforced by the new environment, and about the persistence of the attitude in both supportive and hostile environments. Such a proposition, in its simplest form, would run somewhat as follows: A recently changed attitude is likely to persist insofar as it leads to the selection of subsequent environments that provide reinforcements for the behavioral expression of the changed attitude.

Among the many possible forms of environmental reinforcements of behavioral expressions of attitudes, I shall consider a single class: behavior on the part of other people that one perceives as supportive of one's own attitudes. With few exceptions, such support comes from persons or groups toward whom one is positively attracted, according to the principles of what is perhaps most frequently known as balance theory (Cf. Heider, 1958; Brown, 1962; Newcomb, 1963). I am, in short, about to defend the limited proposition that a recently changed attitude is most likely to persist if one of its behavioral expressions is the selection of a social environment which one finds supportive of the changed attitude. This proposition differs from the one about autistic hostility primarily in that persistence of a recently acquired attitude depends upon continuing rather than cutting off sources of information about the attitude-object.

II.

There are various ways in which such a proposition might be tested in the laboratory. But insofar as one is interested, as I have been, in long-range effects, one will make use of "natural" settings. I shall therefore cite a few findings from two of my own studies, mentioning only briefly the less immediately relevant one (1961), which involved the daily observation of two populations of 17 male students, all initial strangers to one another, who lived intimately together for four-month periods. The only attitudes of these subjects that showed much change, from first to last, were their attractions toward each other—attitudes which had not even existed, of course, before their initial encounters in this research setting. Expressions of interpersonal attraction during the first week or two were highly unstable, but after about the fifth week they showed only slow and slight changes (Cf. Newcomb, 1963).

Under the conditions of this research, imposed environments (in the form of arbitrarily assigned rooms, roommates, and floors) had no consistent effects beyond the first week or two in interpersonal preferences. That is, one could predict little or nothing about interpersonal attraction from the fact of being roommates or floormates. Self-selected interpersonal environment, however, was closely associated with interpersonal attraction. At all times later than the first week or two, pairs of subjects who were reported by others to belong to the same voluntary subgroups were almost invariably pairs whose members chose each other at very high levels of attraction. If this seems to be a commonplace observation (as indeed it is), let me remind you of my reason for reporting it; interpersonal environments are not only consequences of existing attraction but also sources of future attraction. It is an everyday phenomenon that, having developed differential attitudes toward one's several acquaintances, one manipulates one's interpersonal environment, insofar as one can, to correspond with one's interpersonal preferences. And insofar as one is successful, chances are that the preferences will be further reinforced. My data, showing stability both of preferences and of voluntarily associating subgroups following the first month or so, indicate that exactly this was occurring. The fact that it is an everyday occurrence enhances rather than negates the importance of the principle involved, namely, that a recently acquired attitude will persist insofar as it results in the selection of an environment that is supportive of that attitude.

III.

I now turn to a totally different set of data, or rather to two sets of data from the same subjects, obtained over an interval of more than 20 years. The earlier responses were obtained between 1935 and 1939 at Bennington College (Newcomb, 1943); the later ones, obtained in 1960 and 1961, were from almost all of the subjects who had been studied for three or more consecutive years during the 1930's. To be specific, out of 141 former students in this category who in 1960 were alive, resident in continental United States, and not hopelessly invalided, 130 (scattered in 28 states) were interviewed, and 9 of the remaining 11 completed more or less parallel questionnaires. The interview dealt primarily with their present attitudes toward a wide range of public-affairs issues, with attitudes of their husbands and other contemporary associates, and with their histories and careers since leaving the College.

Before telling you some of the follow-up findings, I ought to report a few of the original ones. During each of four consecutive years (1935-36 through 1938-39), juniors and seniors were on the average markedly less conservative than freshmen in attitude toward many public issues of the day. Studies of the same individuals over three- and four-year intervals showed the same trend, which was not attributable to selective withdrawal from the College. Comparisons with other colleges showed almost no intercollege differences in freshmen attitudes, but much less conservatism at Bennington than at the other institutions on the part of seniors. Individual studies showed that at Bennington nonconservatism was rather closely associated with being respected by other students, with participation in college activities, and with personal involvement in the College as an institution. The relatively few malcontents were, with surprisingly few exceptions, those who held conservative attitudes toward public issues.

Given these initial findings, one of my concerns in planning the follow-up study was the following: Under what conditions would individuals who had become less conservative during their college years remain relatively nonconservative 20-odd years later, and under what conditions would they "regress" to relatively conservative positions? (As to the problem of comparing attitudes toward one set of issues in the 1930's with those toward quite different issues in the 1960's, I shall for present purposes note only that at both times we used indices of relative, not absolute standing: each subject is compared with the same set of peers.)

By way of noting the general pattern of persistence vs. regression on the part of the total population, I shall first compare one early with one later datum. In the 1940 presidential election, 51% of our interview sample who reported a preference for either major candidate chose the Democrat, F. D. Roosevelt, and 49% the Republican, W. Willkie. Twenty years later, the comparable figures were 60% for J. F. Kennedy and 40% for R. M. Nixon. No single election, of course, provides a very good test of what might be termed "general conservatism concerning public affairs," but at any rate this particular comparison does not suggest any conspicuous regression toward freshman conservatism. This conclusion is also supported by the following finding: In six consecutive presidential elections (1940 through 1960), an outright majority of our interviewees (51%) reported that they had preferred the Republican candidate either once or never, whereas only 27% of them had preferred that candidate as many as five times out of the six times.

The problem of regressive effects can also be approached by comparing relative conservatism on the part of the same individuals over the interval of 20-odd years. In terms of party or candidate preference in 1960, the degree of individual stability is startling. As shown in Table 1, individuals who were in the least conservative quartile of the total population, on graduating, preferred Kennedy by frequencies of 30 to 3, and those in the next quartile by 25 to 8;

TABLE 1

PRESIDENTIAL PREFERENCES IN 1960, ACCORDING TO QUARTILES OF PEP SCORES ON LEAVING COLLEGE IN THE LATE 1930s

PEP quartile	Nixon preferred	Kennedy preferred	Total
1 (least conservative)	3	30	33
2	8	25	33
3	18	13	31
4 (most conservative)	22	11	33
TOTAL	51	79	130

83% of this half of the population preferred Kennedy 20 years later, while 37% of the initially more conservative half preferred Kennedy after 20 years. Political party preferences, and also an index of general political conservatism, showed about the same relationship to political conservatism more than two decades earlier. These data provide no support for a prediction of general regression—either toward previous conservatism or in the statistical sense of regression toward the mean.

Other evidence concerning the general nonconservatism in this population in the early 1960's includes the following:

77% of them considered themselves "liberal" or "somewhat liberal," as compared with 17% who were "conservative" or "somewhat conservative";

76% "approved" or "strongly approved" of "Medicare" for the aged under Social Security;

61% "approved" or "strongly approved" of admitting Red China into the United Nations.

These and other data suggest that the population as a whole is now far less conservative than is to be expected in view of its demographic characteristics. Its socio-economic level may be judged from these facts: (1) 77% of the 117 respondents who were or had been married were judged by the interviewer to be at least "fairly well-to-do," with annual incomes of not less than $20,000; and (2) of 113 mothers in the population, 65% had sent at least one of their children to a private school. In religious background, about three-quarters of them were Protestants (more than half of whom were Episcopalian), and less than 10% were either Catholic or Jewish. According to

THEODORE M. NEWCOMB

information assembled for me by the Survey Research Center of the University of Michigan,* the proportion of Protestant women college graduates at the income level of this population who in 1960 expressed a preference for Kennedy over Nixon was less than 25—as compared with 60% of this alumnae population.

I shall now revert to my earlier theme: If this population is now less conservative than one might expect, to what extent is this explainable in terms of its members' selection of post-college environments that were supportive of nonconservative attitudes? It proves to be very difficult to categorize total environments from this point of view, and so for the present I shall limit myself to a single aspect of post-college environments: husbands. I am making no assumptions here except that (1) husbands were indeed a part of their wives' environments; (2) wives had had something to do with selecting this part of their environments; and (3) husbands, as environmental objects, were capable of being either supportive or nonsupportive of their wives' attitudes.

Nearly 80% of our respondents both had a husband and were able to report on his attitudes toward most of the issues with which we were concerned, during all or most of the past 20 years; one reason for placing a good deal of confidence in their reports is that they seem highly discriminating, as indicated by such responses as these: "I don't think I know how he'd feel on that particular issue," or "Now on *that* one he doesn't agree with me at all." Here are some summaries concerning all husbands whose wives were willing to attribute attitudes toward them (nearly all wives on most issues):

54% of the husbands in 1960 favored Kennedy over Nixon;

64% of them either "approved" or "strongly approved" of "Medicare" for the aged under Social Security;

57% of them either "approved" or "strongly approved" of admitting Red China into the United Nations.

And so it is almost as true of husbands as of wives that they are less conservative than is to be expected in view of their demographic characteristics: husbands' and wives' demographic characteristics are taken to be identical except for a very few couples differing in religious background, and their present attitudes are highly similar (90% of 1960 presidential preferences by pairs of spouses, for example, being reported as the same in 1960). It would hardly seem to be a matter of sheer chance that a set of men who are less conservative than is to be expected are married to a set of women of whom just the same thing is true. It seems necessary, therefore, to

---

* By my colleague Philip Converse, to whom I am most grateful.

assume that attitudes toward public affairs had something to do with husbands' and wives' reciprocal selection of one another, or with post-marital influence upon one another, or with both. Here is one statistical support for this assumption: the correlation between wives' scores on an instrument labeled Political and Economic Progressivism, as of their graduating from college in the late 1930's, with the number of Republican candidates that their subsequent husbands voted for between 1940 and 1960 was .32; this does not account for much of the variance, but its p value is $< .0005$.

Another interesting finding has to do with the number of women in our interview sample whose husbands had attended Ivy League colleges; one would expect this proportion to be high, since so many of the women's fathers and brothers had attended these colleges. The actual frequency turned out to be just 50%. These Ivy League husbands' voting preferences in 1960, however, turned out to be much more like their wives' preferences than like their classmates' preferences: 52% of husbands whose wives were able to state a preference were for Kennedy—which is to say that they did not differ at all in voting preferences from all non-Ivy League husbands. This total set of facts can best be interpreted as follows: Our Bennington graduates of the late 1930's found their husbands in the kinds of places where their families expected them to be found, but they selected somewhat atypical members of these "proper" populations of eligibles; they tended not to have conservative attitudes that were then typical of these populations.

One evidence of this atypical selection is to be seen in the occupational distribution of these womens' husbands. Only 38% of all husbands are classifiable as "in management or business," the remaining 62% representing for the most part a wide range of professions (especially college teaching, entertainment, and the arts) and public employment (especially in government). Husbands in these two general categories (management and business vs. all others) differed sharply in their voting preferences in 1960; of the 113 husbands whose wives attributed preferences to them, 26% of those in management and business preferred Kennedy, and 68% of all other husbands preferred Kennedy. In sum, these women's husbands had typically come from "the right" places but a majority of them did not have "the right" attitudes or occupational interests.

If, therefore, I were to select a single factor that contributed most to these women's maintenance of nonconservative attitudes between the late 1930's and early 1960's, I think it would be the fact of selecting husbands of generally nonconservative stripe who helped to maintain for them an environment that was supportive of their existing attributes.

IV.

Now I shall turn from the total population of interviewees to some comparisons of subpopulations. The most crucial of these, from the point of view of my proposition about supportive environments, are to be found within the population of nonconservatives on leaving college in the late 1930's: What seems to be the differences between those who do and those who do not remain nonconservative in the early 1960's? Such comparisons will have to be impressionistic, since numbers of cases are small.

Among 22 individuals previously labeled as clearly nonconservative in their third or fourth year of attendance at the College, just half belong in the same category now. Only three of them are clearly conservative today, the remaining eight being classified as intermediate. Here are these wives' descriptions of their husbands' political positions over the years:

> 3 presently conservative wives: 3 Republican husbands (100%)
> 7 presently intermediate wives: 3 Republican husbands (42%)
> 8 presently nonconservative wives: 2 Republican husbands (25%)

Of the three presently conservative women, none mentions having engaged in activities related to political or other public issues; of the eight who are intermediate, six mention some activity of this kind, but they identify their activity only in such general terms as "liberal" or "Democratic Party"; of the 11 still nonconservative women, eight mention such activities, more than half of them specifying such "causes" or organizations as labor unions, civil liberties, the ADA, or the NAACP.

Each interviewee was also asked about the general orientation of "most of your friends" toward political and other public affairs. More than half (12) of the 22 women originally labeled as clearly nonconservative described their environment of friends as "liberal," in spite of the fact that most of them lived in suburbs or other geographical areas not generally renowned for liberalism. Interestingly enough, those who are now relatively conservative answered this question in just about the same way as did those who are still relatively nonconservative. The 16 women originally labeled as clearly conservative, on leaving college, answered this question somewhat differently; more than half of them (9) described their environment of friends as predominantly "conservative," but answers differed with the present attitudes of the respondents. That is, those who are now, in fact, relatively conservative with near-unanimity describe their friends as conservative, whereas those who are now relatively nonconservative consider a substantial proportion or even most of their friends to be "liberal." Thus only those who were quite conservative in the late 1930's and who still remain so see themselves surrounded by friends who are primarily conservative.

In sum, nearly all of the still nonconservative women mention either husbands or public activities (most commonly both) that have served to support and maintain previously nonconservative attitudes, while none of the three formerly nonconservative but presently conservative women mentions either husband or public activities which have served to maintain earlier attitudes.

What about attitude persistence on the part of those who, after three or four years in college, were still relatively conservative? Sixteen of those who were then labeled conservative were interviewed in the early 1960's, ten of them being categorized as still conservative and three as now nonconservative. Only one of the nonchangers reported having a husband who was a Democrat, and in this lone case he turned out to have voted for Nixon in 1960. Two of the three changers, on the other hand, report husbands who were Democrats and Kennedy voters in 1960. Only two of the persistent conservatives mentioned public activities presumably supportive of their attitudes (in behalf of the Republican Party, in both cases); eight of the ten described most of their friends either as conservative or as Republicans. The conditions that favor the persistence of conservatism over the 20-odd years are thus about the same as those that favor the persistence of nonconservatism: supportive environments in the form of husbands, local friends, and (for the nonconservatives but not the conservatives) in the form of associates in activities related to public issues.

There is a special sub-population of students who, as of graduating in the late 1930's, were candidates for regression; that is, they became much less conservative during their college years. Of these, about one-third (9 of 28) were among the most conservative half of the same population in the early 1960's, and may be regarded as regressors, in some degree at least. Eight of these potential regressors were, for various reasons, unable to report on husbands' preferences. Among the remaining 19 respondents, five were actual regressors, four of whom reported their husbands to be Republicans or "conservative Republicans." Among 14 actual non-regressors reporting, ten described their husbands as Democrats or "liberal Democrats," two referred to them as "Republicans who have been voting Democratic," and only two call their husbands Republicans. These are highly significant differences: the actual regressors can pretty well be differentiated from the nonregressors merely by knowing their husbands' present attitudes. By this procedure only 3 of 19, or 16% of all predictions would not have been correct.

This total set of data suggests that either regression and persistence of attitudes as of leaving college are, over the years, influenced by husbands' attitudes, or early post-college attitudes had something to do with the selection of husbands, or both. In either case, both regression and persistence are facilitated by the supportiveness of husbands.

V.

If there is any very general principle that helps to account for this whole range of phenomena (both my 1946 and my 1963 versions), I believe that it is to be found in an extended version of "balance theory," as originally outlined by Heider (1946, 1958). Heider's formulations are formulated in individual and phenomenological ·terms; a balanced state is a strictly intrapersonal, psychological state. But it is also possible to conceptualize an objective, multi-person state of balance, referring to the actual relationships among different persons' attitudes, regardless of the person's awareness of each other. Such a concept is psychologically useful not only because it describes an actual, existing situation—an environment of which each person is himself a part, as suggested by Asch (1952)—but also because it describes a relationship which, given reasonably full and accurate communication, comes to be accurately perceived. My own recent work on the acquaintance process has been interesting to me primarily because it inquires into the processes by which and the conditions under which *intra*personal states of balance come to correspond with *inter*personal ones. As outlined by Heider, and subsequently by many others (Cf. Brown *et al.*, 1962), the processes by which imbalanced states serve as goals toward the attainment of balanced ones include both internal, psychological changes and external modifications of the environment. Thus, one may achieve a balanced state with the important figures in one's social environment—whether by selecting those figures, by modifying one's own attitudes, or by influencing others' attitudes—and at the same time continue to perceive that environment accurately.

According to such an extended, *inter*personal concept of balance, an imbalanced state under conditions of continued interaction is likely to be an unstable one, simply because when it is discovered it arouses *intra*personal imbalance on the part of one or more of the interactors, and this state arouses forces toward change. Given marked attitude change on the part of one but not the other member of a dyad actually in balance with respect to that attitude, imbalance results. This was what typically happened to students at Bennington College vis-à-vis their parents, in the 1930's. A common way in which they attempted to reduce imbalance was by avoidance—not necessarily of parents but of the divisive issues as related to parents. As Heider might say, unit formation between issue and parents was broken up, and psychological imbalance thus reduced. Such a "solution" resembles autistic hostility in that it involves a marked restriction of communication.

But this solution, as many of my subjects testified, was not a particularly comfortable one. Hence, it would hardly be surprising if many of them, during early post-college years, were in search of environments that would provide less uncomfortable solutions—or, better yet, more positively rewarding ones. An ideal one, of course, would be a husband who was rewarding as a supporter of one's own attitudes as well as in other ways.

And so, vis-à-vis parents and fellow-students at first, and later vis-à-vis husbands (or perhaps working associates), forces toward balance were at work. Specifically, support from important people concerning important issues came to be the rule, and its absence the exception. Support sometimes came about by changing one's own attitudes toward those of needed supporters, or, more commonly, by selecting supporters for existing attitudes. The latter stratagem represented not merely an automatic tendency for attitudes to perpetuate themselves. More significantly, I believe, it represents an adaptation to a world that includes *both* persons and issues. Such a dual adaptation can be made, of course, by sacrificing one's stand on the issues (regression). But if the dual adaptation is to be made without this sacrifice, then an interpersonal world must be selected (or created) that is supportive—in which case we can say that the attitude has been expressed by finding a supportive environment.

According to my two themes (of *1946* and *1963*) an existing attitude may be maintained by creating environments in which *either* new information can be avoided *or* in which other persons support one's own information. In either case, the fate of an attitude is mediated by the social environment in which the individual attempts to maintain or to restore balance regarding that same attitude. Insofar as that environment excludes disturbing information or provides reinforcing information, the attitude persists. And insofar as the selection or the acceptance of that environment is a consequence of holding the attitude, we have a steady-state, self-maintaining system.

REFERENCES

Asch, S. E. *Social Psychology*. New York: Prentice-Hall, 1952.
Brown, R. Models of attitude change. In Brown, R., Galanter, E., Hess, E. H., & Mandler, G. *New Directions in Psychology*. New York: Holt, Rinehart & Winston, 1962.
Heider, F. Attitudes and cognitive organization. *J. Psychol*, 1946, 21, 107-112.
———. *The Psychology of Interpersonal Relations*. New York: Wiley, 1958.
Newcomb, T. M. *Personality and Social Change*. New York: Holt, Rinehart & Winston, 1943.
———. Autistic hostility and social reality. *Human Relations*, 1947, 1, 69-86.
———. *The Acquaintance Process*. New York: Holt, Rinehart & Winston, 1961.

Irradiation Effects

When does a reaction end?

The study by Suedfeld and Vernon (pp. 251 ff.) provided an example of whiat might conveniently be thought of as a kind of *irradiation*, or diffusion,[1] of the effect of confinement to a restricted psychological environment onto persuasibility. Whatever primary effect sensory deprivation has on behavior,[2] from Suedfeld and Vernon we learned that communication is a sufficient stimulus for evoking an interesting secondary effect. Subjects deprived for a sustained period of normal perceptual stimulation give the impression that they perceive whatever verbal stimuli that are subsequently made available to them as possible remedies for the psychological discomfort they have been made to suffer. As a result, an important side effect of sensory deprivation is that it heightens the individual's susceptibility to other stimuli and thereby enhances his persuasibility. The hapless subject is left in a state of mind where he is easy prey for the propagandist.

An altogether different illustration of irradiation is suggested by the findings in two well-known studies by Razran and Murray. Razran found that subjects showed a greater preference for pictures when the pictures were shown to them during the course of a meal.[3] Presumably, there was a diffusion of the *positive affect*, or pleasant emotion, associated with the satisfying act of eating onto subjects' responses to the originally neutral pictures. Murray's findings, similar to the one by Razran, provides an example of the diffusion of *negative affect*,

---

[1] The classic use in psychology of the concept of "irradiation" is somewhat different than that proposed here. Ivan Pavlov, the Russian physiologist-psychologist, is attributed with having made the earliest experimental observations of generalized conditioned reactions. His findings were taken as providing evidence for a *principle of irradiation* of excitatory processes within the cortex. Pavlov, I. *Conditioned reflexes.* (transl. by G. V. Anrep) New York: Dover Publications, 1960.

[2] Vernon, J. *Inside the black room.* New York: Clarkson N. Potter, 1963. Schultz, D. P. *Sensory restriction: Effects on behavior.* New York: Academic Press, 1965.

[3] Razran, G. H. S. Conditioning away social bias by the luncheon technique. *Psychol. Bull.*, 1938, **35**, 693. (Abstract)

or unpleasant emotion. Murray observed that frightening children led them to make low judgments of the personalities of faces shown them during their fear.[4] And, consistent with Murray's finding, Neal Miller and Richard Bugelski report that young male campers increased their negative attitude toward Mexicans and Japanese when the children were forced to miss a highly prized social event and required instead to fill out questionnaires assessing their attitudes including those toward the two minority groups.[5]

A fascinating application of this principle in persuasion is the study by Janis, Kaye, and Kirschner, reprinted later in this section, on the effects of eating while reading. Consistent with Razran's finding, Janis *et al.* show that recipients of a persuasive communication increase their acceptance of its contents if they are given soda pop and peanuts to eat while reading the communication.[6] McGuire's succinct summary of these results is that things often do "go better with coke!"[7] Dabbs and Janis replicated the Janis, Kaye, and Kirschner study in an attempt to find out exactly why eating while reading facilitates opinion change. Their findings suggest that there is an immediate, unsustained diffusion of the "momentary mood of compliance" induced by the satisfying act of eating the preferred foods onto other temporally contiguous stimuli.[8]

The same rationale would seem to fit the results of the well-known studies on self-persuasion by William Scott, although here the affect-evoking stimulus was approval rather than food.[9] Pairs of college student subjects debated one of three controversial issues, each student required to defend a position opposite to the one he preferred. A rigged vote by the audience purportedly indicated who won the debates. Scott found that debaters who were told that they had lost

---

[4]Murray, H. A. The effect of fear upon estimates of the maliciousness of other personalities. *J. soc. Psychol.*, 1933, **4**, 310–329.

[5]Miller, N. E., & Bugelski, R. Minor studies in aggression: II. The influence of frustrations imposed by the in-group on attitudes expressed toward out-groups. *J. Psychol.*, 1948, **25**, 437–442.

[6]Janis, I. L., Kaye, D., & Kirschner, P. Facilitating effects of "eating-while-reading" on responsiveness to persuasive communications. *J. Pers. soc. Psychol.*, 1965, **1**, 181–186.

[7]McGuire, W. J. Attitudes and opinions. *Annu. Rev. Psychol.*, 1966, **17**, 482.

[8]Dabbs, J. M., Janis, I. L. Why does eating while reading facilitate opinion change?—An experimental inquiry. *J. exp. soc. Psychol.*, 1965, **1**, 133–144.

[9]Scott, W. A. Attitude change through reward of verbal behavior. *J. abnorm. soc. Psychol.*, 1957, **55**, 72–75. Scott, W. A. Cognitive consistency, response reinforcement, and attitude change. *Sociometry*, 1959, **22**, 219–229. Scott, W. A. Attitude change by response reinforcement: Replication and extension. *Sociometry*, 1959, **22**, 328–335.

experienced no significant opinion change, while debaters who were told that they had won experienced significant change in the very direction that they had defended in the debate.[10] In a follow-up study, Scott produced the same effects, but now independent of the direction of the debaters' original preferences, i.e., regardless of whether they were required to defend their own beliefs, the opposite side, or some neutral position.[11,12]

A series of experiments founded in a similar rationale are those by Rosnow and his colleagues in which the effects of both positively and negatively reinforcing stimuli have been explored. The standard procedure in these experiments was to expose subjects to arguments representing both sides of a controversial issue and immediately precede or immediately follow the arguments with reinforcements in the form of rewarding or punishing incidents. In one study, for example, the "reward" consisted of an announcement to high school students that their grades would be discounted on a quiz which they all thought they had failed.[13] In another experiment, the "punish-

---

[10] Scott, W. A. Attitude change through reward of verbal behavior. *J. abnorm. soc. Psychol.*, 1957, **55**, 72–75. A slightly different reinforcement procedure was used in a similar self-persuasion experiment by Sarbin and Allen. Positive reinforcement consisted of the audience's responding to the communicator in various contrived ways, e.g., nodding their heads in agreement, jotting down notes, smiling, looking pleasant and pleased. Negative reinforcement consisted of such responses as looking away from the speaker, shaking their heads slowly in disagreement, fidgeting and shuffling their feet, yawning. Greater attitude change was effected for negatively than for positively reinforced speakers, possibly because of the greater effort they may have felt compelled to exert (Zimbardo *et al.*, pp. 347 f.) to persuade the seemingly resistant audience, but ended up persuading themselves. Sarbin, T. R., & Allen, V. L. Role enactment, audience feedback, and attitude change. *Sociometry*, 1964, **27**, 183–193.

[11] Scott, W. A. Attitude change by response reinforcement: Replication and extension. *Sociometry*, 1959, **22**, 328–335.

[12] A more recent study, by Chester Insko, utilized only the technique of approval, but in a uniquely different fashion than was used by Scott. Insko conducted his experiment while he was at the University of Hawaii, where, in the fall, there is the annual Aloha Week Festival. Insko had his assistants telephone students at the University, read to them 14 statements concerning the creation of a Springtime Aloha Week, and ask them what their opinions were about each of the statements. Half of the males and females were reinforced with approval ("good!") whenever they gave a positive response, and the other half were similarly reinforced whenever they gave a negative response. Results of a follow-up questionnaire indicated significant differences in the expected direction between the two groups of subjects. Insko, C. A. Verbal reinforcement of attitude. *J. Pers. soc. Psychol.*, 1965, **2**, 621–623.

[13] Rosnow, R. L., & Russell, G. Spread of effect of reinforcement in persuasive communication. *Psychol. Rep.*, 1963, **12**, 731–735.

ment" consisted of a short unannounced test on material which the students had not been forewarned to study.[14] The most elaborately designed experiment in this series was one in which college students argued extemporaneously in defense of four pro and four con statements on the topic "use of nuclear weapons." At random, some of the students were told in the middle of their arguments that they were doing better than average ("reward"). Also at random, other students were told that they were doing worse than average ("punishment"). Another group of students served as nonreinforcement controls, defending the eight pro and con statements, but not receiving any feedback about their performance. Under each of these three treatment conditions, half of the students defended a pro statement first, and the other half a con. Still other students acted as "zero" controls, neither defending the eight statements nor receiving any reinforcement. The consistent finding in this investigation was that the students' opinions about the use of nuclear weapons *tended to change in whatever direction was closer in time to a reward or farther in time from a punishment.*[15]

A more recent experiment, by John Corrozi, has extended this finding to the situation where consonant and dissonant communications are the reinforcements. Earlier it had been shown by Golightly and Byrne that short consonant and dissonant attitude statements could be used in the same way as traditional verbal rewards[16] and verbal punishments to reinforce learning in a discrimination task.[17] Corrozi's clever systematic-replication consisted of presenting to high school students pro and con arguments about the personality of the artist Pablo Picasso, and preceding or following the Picasso arguments with another communication which was consonant ("reward") or dissonant ("punishment") with the students' opinions on a topic unrelated to the target issue, to wit, "Should the school week be lengthened or shortened?" Corrozi's results were consistent with Rosnow's finding. The students' opinions on the target issue (Picasso) tended to change in the direction of whichever argument (about

---

[14] Rosnow, R. L. A delay-of-reinforcement effect in persuasive communication? *J. soc. Psychol.*, 1965, **67**, 39–43.

[15] Rosnow, R. L. "Conditioning" the direction of opinion change in persuasive communication. *J. soc. Psychol.*, 1966, **69**, 291–303.

[16] Insko's use of the word "good" is an example of a traditional verbal reward; see footnote 12 in this section.

[17] Golightly, C., & Byrne, D. Attitude statements as positive and negative reinforcements. *Science*, 1964, **146**, 798–799.

Picasso) was closer to a consonant communication ("shorter school week") or farther in time from a dissonant communication ("longer school week").[18]

There is one major commonality in all of the findings cited thus far— an irradiation, or diffusion, of the effect of the principal stimulus onto responses to other *temporally contiguous*, though not necessarily logically relevant, stimuli. In the Suedfeld and Vernon experiment, there was a diffusion of the effect of confinement to a restricted psychological environment onto the factor of persuasibility. Propaganda was a sufficient stimulus for evoking this response. The investigations by Razran and by Janis and his colleagues Kaye, Kirschner, and Dabbs demonstrated the diffusion of the positive affect produced by eating onto responses to other temporally contiguous, but logically irrelevant, stimuli. Murray's study and the one by Miller and Bugelski indicated a similar diffusion effect, but now for the negative affect resulting from fear or frustration. In the studies by Scott, Rosnow, and Corrozi, there was a diffusion of the effects of reward- and punishment-producing stimuli onto responses (opinions) to other stimuli (communications) which, though only sometimes relevant to the reinforcement, in all cases were in temporal proximity to it.[19]

The study by Irving L. Janis, Donald Kaye, and Paul Kirschner is one of the two papers reprinted here. The other, by William J. McGuire, is the classic example in persuasion of a slightly different type of irradiation effect: this time, the diffusion of the effect of a target stimulus onto responses to other stimuli which are logically relevant to the target stimulus, though not necessarily close to it in

---

[18]Corrozi, J. F., & Rosnow, R. L. Consonant and dissonant communications as positive and negative reinforcements in opinion change. *J. Pers. soc. Psychol.*, in press.

[19]An impressive series of studies by Robert Weiss and his associates takes a somewhat different tack, though also based upon learning-reinforcement principles. The Weiss experiments are derived from a model based on Hullian theory. The interested reader will want to examine the following: Weiss, R. F. Persuasion and the acquisition of attitudes: Models from conditioning and selective learning. *Psychol. Rep.*, 1962, **11**, 709–732, Monogr. Supple. 4–V11. Weiss, R. F., Rawson, H. E., & Pasamanick, B. Argument strength, delay of argument and anxiety in the "conditioning" and "selective learning" of attitudes. *J. abnorm. soc. Psychol.*, 1963, **67**, 157–165. Weiss, R. F., & Pasamanick, B. Number of exposures to persuasive communication in the instrumental conditioning of attitudes. *J. soc. Psychol.*, 1964, **63**, 373–382. Weiss, R. F., Buchanan, W., & Pasamanick, B. Delay of reinforcement and delay of punishment in persuasive communication. *Psychol. Rep.*, 1965, **16**, 576.

time. In McGuire's study, this type of irradiation effect is exemplified by the finding that communication may influence opinions toward an explicit target issue as well as opinions toward derived issues not mentioned in the communication.[20] Thus, the individual can alter his opinions in response to the demands of a persuasive appeal, yet still maintain a semblance of cognitive consistency.[21]

As for the question posed earlier—"When does a reaction end?"— the answer would seem to depend on what stimuli happen to be available. A reaction may have repercussions not only affecting responses to other stimuli that are logically relevant to the target stimulus, but also responses to irrelevant stimuli whose only connection with the target stimulus is that they happen to be close to it in time.

----

[20] This finding has been replicated by Dillehay, R. C., Insko, C. A., & Smith, M. B. Logical consistency and attitude change. *J. Pers. soc. Psychol.*, 1966, 3, 646–654.

[21] Other interesting variations of this type of diffusion effect have been demonstrated by Tannenbaum based on the Osgood-Tannenbaum congruity principle *(viz.,* modification of an attitude toward one of two objects in a cognitive relationship often results in attitude change toward the other object—thus maintaining cognitive consistency): Tannenbaum, P. H., & Gengel, R. W. Generalization of attitude change through congruity principle relationships. *J. Pers. soc. Psychol.*, 1966, 3, 299–304. Tannenbaum, P. H. Mediated generalization of attitude change via the principle of congruity. *J. Pers. soc. Psychol.*, 1966, 3, 493–499. One of the best discussions of the congruity model will be found in Brown, R. W. Models of attitude change. In *New directions in psychology.* New York: Holt, Rinehart, & Winston, 1962. Pp. 14 ff. The congruity principle was originally derived by Osgood, C. E., & Tannenbaum, P. H. The principle of congruity in the prediction of attitude change. *Psychol. Rev.*, 1955, **62**, 42–55.

Reprinted from Journal of Personality and Social Psychology, 1965, Vol. 1, No. 2, pp. 181–186, by permission of Irving L. Janis and APA.

FACILITATING EFFECTS OF "EATING-WHILE-READING" ON RESPONSIVENESS TO PERSUASIVE COMMUNICATIONS [1]

IRVING L. JANIS, DONALD KAYE, AND PAUL KIRSCHNER

This experiment was designed to test the hypothesis that food, as an extraneous gratification accompanying exposure to a persuasive communication, will increase acceptance, even though the donor of the food is not the source of the communication and does not endorse it. 2 replicating experiments were carried out with 216 male college students. In both experiments there were 3 groups of Ss, assigned on a random basis to the following conditions, which involved exposure to: (a) 4 persuasive communications while eating desirable food; (b) the same 4 communications with no food present; (c) no relevant communications (control condition). Both experiments provide confirmatory evidence, indicating that more opinion change tends to be elicited under conditions where the Ss are eating while reading the communications. The theoretical implications are discussed with respect to psychological processes involved in changing attitudes.

It is commonly assumed that people are more likely to yield to persuasion at a time when they are eating or drinking than at a time when they are not engaged in any such gratifying activity. Salesmen, business promoters, and lobbyists often try to "soften up" their clients by inviting them to talk things over at a restaurant or cafe. Representatives of opposing economic or political groups, when unable to settle their disputes while seated formally around a conference table,

[1] This experimental investigation was conducted under the auspices of the Yale Studies in Attitude and Communication, which is supported by a grant from the Rockefeller Foundation.

may find themselves much more amenable to mutual influence, and hence more conciliatory, while seated comfortably around a dinner table.

Little systematic research has been done, as yet, to determine the conditions under which pleasant stimulation will augment the acceptance of persuasive communications. One might expect that when the communicator is the perceived source of the gratifying stimulation, a more favorable attitude toward him will ensue, which would tend to lower the recipient's resistance to his persuasive efforts (see Hovland, Janis, & Kelley, 1953, pp. 19–55). But a more complicated situation often arises at educational symposia, political conventions, cocktail parties, and informal dinners where: (*a*) the donor (that is, the person who is perceived as being responsible for the gratification) is *not* the communicator and (*b*) the donor does *not* endorse the persuasive communications that happen to be presented at the particular time when the recipients are being indulged. If a positive gain in effectiveness is found to occur under these conditions, where the gratifying activity is entirely extraneous to the content, source, or endorsement of the communications, a number of important theoretical questions will arise—questions concerning some of the basic processes of attitude change which will require systematic experimental analysis. For example, when eating has a facilitating effect on acceptance of persuasive messages, does it always depend entirely upon the heightened motivation of the recipients to conform with the donor's wishes? If so, a positive outcome under non-endorsement conditions will be paradoxical unless it turns out that there is a general tendency for people to assume, consciously or unconsciously, that the donor would like them to be influenced by whatever communications are presented (even though he explicitly says that he does not endorse the point of view being expressed). Or does the extraneous gratification operate as a source of reinforcement independently of the recipient's attitude toward the donor? If this is the case, we might be led to assume that the food corresponds to an "unconditioned stimulus," and its facilitating effects might be accounted for in terms of the laws of conditioning.

The latter theoretical possibility is suggested by Razran's (1940) brief research note, published 25 years ago, in which he gave a summary statement of the following two experimental observations: (*a*) an increase in ratings of "personal approval" occurred when a series of sociopolitical slogans were presented to experimental subjects while they were enjoying a free lunch and (*b*) a decrease in such ratings occurred when the slogans were presented while the subjects were being required to inhale a number of unpleasant, putrid odors. In his report, however, Razran does not mention certain important details, such as whether the experimenter was the donor of the free lunch and whether he said anything to the subjects about his personal attitude toward the slogans.

So far as the authors have been able to ascertain, no subsequent experiments have been published pertinent to checking Razran's observations. Nor has any published research been found bearing on the related questions of whether or not (and under what limiting conditions) extraneous pleasant or unpleasant stimulation can affect the degree to which a recipient will accept a series of persuasive arguments that attempt to induce him to change a personal belief or preference.

As a preliminary step toward reopening experimental research on the above-mentioned set of theoretical problems, the present study was designed to investigate the alleged phenomenon of enhanced communication effectiveness arising from "eating-while-reading." The research was designed primarily to answer the following question: If an experimenter gives the subjects desirable food and drink but states explicitly that the persuasive messages to be presented are ones with which he does not necessarily agree, will there be a significant increase in acceptance from the gratifying activity of eating that accompanies exposure to the communications?

Method and Procedure

Experimental Design

The basic design involved randomly assigning the subjects to two different experimental conditions. One was a condition in which a substantial quantity of food was offered to the subjects during the time they were engaged in reading a series of four persuasive communications. Upon entering the experimental room, the subjects found the experimenter imbibing some refreshments (peanuts and Pepsi-Cola) and they were offered the same refreshments with the simple explanation that there was plenty on hand because "I brought some along for you too." The contrasting "no-food" condition was identical in every respect except that no refreshments were in the room at any time during the session.

The same measures of opinion change were used in the two experimental groups and also in a third group of *unexposed controls*, who were included in the study in order to obtain a base line for ascertaining the effectiveness of each communication per se. The subjects randomly assigned to the control condition were given the same pre- and postcommunication questionnaires, separated by the same time interval as in the other two experimental conditions, but without being exposed to any relevant communications.

The Communications and the Opinion Measures

On the basis of extensive pretesting, we prepared four communications, each of which advocated an unpopular point of view and had been found to be capable of inducing a significant degree of opinion change. These communications were attributed to fictitious authors who were described as journalists or news commentators. The main conclusions, all of which involved quantitative predictions or preferences about future events, were as follows:

1. It will be more than 25 years before satisfactory progress can be expected in the search for a cure for cancer.

2. The United States Armed Forces do not need additional men and can be reduced to less than 85% of their present strength.

3. A round-trip expedition to the moon will be achieved within the next decade.[2]

4. Within the next 3 years, three-dimensional films will replace two-dimensional films in practically all movie theaters.

In order to assess opinion changes, four key questions were included in both the pre- and the postcommunication questionnaires, each of which asked the subject to express his opinion in the form of a quantitative estimate (for example, "How many years do you think it will be before an extremely effective cure is found for cancer so that cancer will no longer be a major cause of death? About ———— years.")

Experiments I and II: Similarities and Differences

The same experimental design, described above, was used in two separate experiments, during successive semesters at the same college. In all essential features the first (Experiment I) was identical with the second (Experiment II) in that exactly the same experimental variations were used along with the same instructions, the same communications, and the same pre- and postcommunication questionnaires. But the two experiments differed in several minor ways. The main difference was that in Experiment I the time interval between the precommunication questionnaire and exposure to the communications was about 2 months; whereas in Experiment II the precommunication questionnaire was given at the beginning of the experimental session, immediately preceding the communications.

In Experiment I, the initial questionnaire was administered in regular undergraduate class sessions. It was introduced as a "survey of student opinions" and the key questions were embedded among numerous filler questions on a variety of other controversial issues. After a period of 2 months, the subjects were contacted by telephone and asked to be unpaid volunteers for a study on reading preferences. The vast majority volunteered and each subject was seen in a private interview session, at the beginning of which he was randomly assigned to the "food with communication" condition or the "no food with communication" condition or the unexposed control condition. After answering the

[2] This study was carried out before the major developments in space flights had occurred, at a time when few people were optimistic about the rate of technical progress in this field. In response to the moon-flight question on the initial questionnaire, almost all the students gave estimates of 10 years or more before a successful round-trip flight could be expected.

final set of postcommunication questions, each subject was briefly interviewed concerning his reactions to the experimental situation.

In Experiment II, the same essential procedures were used except for the fact that the precommunication questionnaire was given at the beginning of the experimental session. Another minor difference was that the unexposed controls were given some extracts from a popular magazine on irrelevant topics, which took approximately the same reading time as the four persuasive communications. Moreover, unlike the unexposed controls in Experiment I, those in Experiment II were given the same food in the same way as in the main experimental condition, so that they too were eating while reading the (irrelevant) articles.

In addition to the three conditions that were set up to replicate the essential features of Experiment I, a fourth experimental condition was introduced in Experiment II in order to investigate a subsidiary problem, namely, the effects of extraneous *unpleasant* stimuli. The fourth experimental group, while reading the four persuasive communications, was exposed to an unpleasant odor (produced by a hidden bottle of butyric acid), for which the experimenter disclaimed any responsibility.

In both experiments, the experimenter explained that the purpose was to assess the students' reading preferences. He asserted that he did *not* endorse the communications and casually mentioned that he happened to agree with certain of the ideas expressed and not with others (without specifying which). He asked the subjects to read the articles as though they were at home reading a popular magazine. In line with the alleged purpose, the postcommunication questionnaire in both Experiments I and II included 20 filler questions asking for interest ratings of the articles (for example, ratings of how much interest they would expect the average college student to have in each topic).

Subjects

A total of 216 Yale undergraduate students were used in the two experiments. In Experiment I, 35 men were in the unexposed control group, 32 in the "no food with communication" condition, and 33 in the "food with communication" condition. In Experiment II, the corresponding numbers were 23, 31, and 31, respectively. There were also 31 subjects in the fourth experimental group exposed to the "unpleasant" condition.

RESULTS

In both experiments, observations of the subjects' eating behavior in the "food" condition showed that every one of them ate at least one handful of peanuts and drank at least one-half glass of the soft drink. The main findings concerning the effects of eating desirable food on the acceptance of the four persuasive communications are shown in Table 1. In general, the

TABLE 1

Opinion Changes Induced by Exposure to Four Persuasive Communications
under Two Different Conditions: "Food" versus "No Food"
Given by the Experimenters

Communication topic	% opinion change					
	Experiment I		Experiment II		Combined data from Experiments I and II	
	No food (N = 32)	Food (N = 33)	No food (N = 31)	Food (N = 31)	No food (N = 63)	Food (N = 64)
1. Cure for cancer						
Positive change	68.7	81.8	80.7	93.5	74.6	87.4
Negative change	21.8	12.1	3.2	0.0	12.7	6.3
No change	9.5	6.1	16.1	6.5	12.7	6.3
Total	100.0	100.0	100.0	100.0	100.0	100.0
Net change	46.9	69.7	77.5	93.5	61.9	81.1
p	= .11		< .10		< .05	
2. Preferred size of United States Armed Forces						
Positive change	65.6	81.8	29.0	51.6	47.6	67.2
Negative change	9.4	0.0	0.0	0.0	4.8	0.0
No change	25.0	18.2	71.0	48.4	47.6	32.8
Total	100.0	100.0	100.0	100.0	100.0	100.0
Net change	56.2	81.8	29.0	51.6	42.8	67.2
p	< .05		< .05		< .01	
3. Round trip to moon						
Positive change	53.2	75.9	48.4	58.0	50.8	67.2
Negative change	21.9	12.1	19.4	12.9	20.6	12.5
No change	24.9	12.0	32.2	29.1	28.6	20.3
Total	100.0	100.0	100.0	100.0	100.0	100.0
Net change	31.3	63.8	29.0	45.1	30.2	54.7
p	= .05		= .20		< .05	
4. Three dimensional movies						
Positive change	68.7	75.9	74.2	77.4	71.5	76.6
Negative change	21.8	12.1	0.0	6.5	11.1	9.4
No change	9.5	12.0	25.8	16.1	17.4	14.0
Total	100.0	100.0	100.0	100.0	100.0	100.0
Net change	46.9	63.8	74.2	70.9	60.4	67.2
p	= .20		= .40		< .20	

results indicate that "eating-while-reading" has a facilitating effect on the amount of opinion change. In Experiment I, the differences between the food and no-food conditions are consistently in the predicted direction for all four communications, two of which are significant at the .05 level. (All p values are one-tailed and were obtained on the basis of the formula for assessing the difference between two net percentage changes, given by Hovland, Lumsdaine, & Sheffield, 1949.) The results for Experiment II show differences in the same direction for three of the four communications, two of which are significant at the .10 level. There is a very small, nonsignificant difference in the reverse direction on the fourth communication.

The p values based on the combined data from both experiments, shown in the last column of Table 1, can be regarded as a satisfactory summary of the overall outcome inasmuch as: (a) the numbers of cases in each experiment are almost equal; and (b) the two experiments differed only in minor features that are irrelevant to the main comparison under investigation. The combined data show that all four communications produced differences in the predicted direction and for three of them the differences are large enough to be statistically significant. Thus, the results support the conclusion that, in general, the extraneous gratification of eating while reading a series of persuasive communications tends to increase their effectiveness.

That each communication was effective in inducing a significant degree of opinion change, whether presented under food or no-food conditions, is indicated by the comparative data from the unexposed controls. In both experiments, the control group showed very slight positive changes, if any, on each of the four key questions and the amount of change was always significantly less than the corresponding net change shown by the food and no-food experimental groups.[3] There were no consistent differences between the control group in Experiment I and the one in Experiment II, which indicates that the different time intervals between the before and after measures and the other minor procedural differences between the two experiments had no direct effect on the opinion measures.

The condition of unpleasant stimulation introduced into Experiment II had no observable effect on the amount of opinion change. The net changes obtained from the group exposed to the foul odor ($N = 31$) were as follows: cancer cure, 67.7%; size of armed forces, 25.8%; round trip to moon, 38.7%; three-dimensional movies, 64.5%. These values differ only very slightly from those obtained from the group exposed to the no-food condition in Experiment II (see Table 1); none of the differences are large enough to approach statistical significance. As expected, however, all the net changes for the unpleasant odor condition are smaller than those for the food condition and in two of the four instances the differences are statistically significant at beyond the .05 level.

[3] In all but one instance, the net change shown by the unexposed controls was not significantly different from zero. The one exception occurred in the control group in Experiment I with respect to the first issue (cancer cure), on which a significant net change of −34% was found. This change, however, was in the reverse direction from that advocated by the communication (probably as a consequence of optimistic publicity concerning new advances in cancer research that appeared in the newspapers during the months between the before and after questionnaires). Thus, on this item, as well as on the other three, the control group showed significantly less change in the expected direction than the two experimental groups.

An analysis of responses to the precommunication questionnaire from both experiments showed that initially, on each of the four key opinion questions, there were only very slight, nonsignificant differences among the experimental and control groups. None of the results in Table 1 and none of the other observed differences in amount of opinion change are attributable to initial differences.

DISCUSSION

Our finding that the extraneous gratifying activity of eating tended to increase the degree to which the accompanying persuasive messages were accepted may prove to have important implications for the psychology of attitude change, especially if subsequent research shows that the gains tend to be persistent, giving rise to sustained modifications of personal beliefs or preferences. Since the control group in Experiment II (which received food along with irrelevant communications) showed net opinion changes that were practically zero and were significantly less than those shown by the main experimental group, the food alone appears to have had no direct effect on any of the opinion measures. Hence the observed outcome seems to implicate psychological processes involved in the *acceptance* of persuasive influences.

Our results on the positive effects of food are similar to Razran's (1940) findings on the increase in favorable ratings of sociopolitical slogans induced by a free lunch. Razran has indicated that he regards his observations as evidence of Pavlovian conditioning, resulting from the contiguity of the conditioned stimuli (the slogans) and the unconditioned pleasant stimuli (food). Before accepting any such interpretation, however, further investigations are needed to check systematically on the possibility that the change in acceptability is brought about by creating a more favorable attitude toward the donor. We attempted to minimize this possibility in both Experiments I and II by having the experimenter give the subjects an introductory explanation in which he clearly stated that he was not sponsoring the persuasive communications. Despite this attempt, however, the subjects may have ignored or forgotten his remarks and assumed that he was sponsoring them. We have no evidence bearing directly on this matter, but we did note that in the informal interviews conducted at the end of each experimental session, many more favorable comments about the experimenter were made by the subjects who had been in the food condition than by those who had been in the no-food condition.

Our failure to confirm Razran's findings on the negative effects of *unpleasant* stimulation might be accounted for in terms of attitude toward the experimenter. In Razran's experiment, the experimenter "required" the subjects to sniff the putrid odors, and hence he might have been directly blamed for the unpleasant stimulation; whereas in our Experiment II, the unpleasant odor was presented as an accidental

186 BRIEF ARTICLES

occurrence for which the experimenter was not responsible. Further experimental analysis is obviously needed to determine if the effects of pleasant and unpleasant stimulation observed in our experiment are dependent upon whether or not the experimenter is perceived as the causal agent.

The fact that the experimenter himself participated in eating the food might have influenced the subjects' perceptions of the general atmosphere of the reading session and hence needs to be investigated as a possible variable, independently of the subjects' food consumption. The limiting conditions for positive effects from "eating-while-reading" also require systematic investigation, particularly in relation to unpleasant interpersonal stimuli, such as those provoking embarrassment, outbreaks of hostility, or other forms of emotional tension that could counteract the positive atmosphere created by the availability of desirable food.

It is also important to find out whether variations in the experimenter's endorsement of the communications play a crucial role in determining the facilitating effects of the proferred food. For example, if subsequent research shows that the experimenter's positive versus negative endorsements make a difference, then an explanation in terms of increased motivation to please the donor will be favored, rather than a simple conditioning mechanism, and a more complicated explanation will be required to account for the positive effects obtained under conditions where

the experimenter explicitly detaches himself from sponsorship of the communications.[4] These implications are mentioned to illustrate the new lines of research suggested by comparing the results from the present experiment with those from Razran's earlier study.

[4] The potential importance of positive versus negative endorsement by the experimenter as an interacting variable was suggested by some unexpected results obtained in a pilot study by Dabbs and Janis, which was carried out as a preliminary step toward replicating the present experiment under conditions where the experimenter indicates that he personally *disagrees* with the persuasive communications. The pilot study results led us to carry out a new experiment in which we compared the effects of eating-while-reading under two different endorsement conditions (the experimenter agreeing or disagreeing with the communications). A report on the effects of the interacting variables, as revealed by the data from the Dabbs and Janis experiment, is currently being prepared for publication.

REFERENCES

HOVLAND, C. I., JANIS, I. L., & KELLEY, H. H. *Communication and persuasion.* New Haven: Yale Univer. Press, 1953.
HOVLAND, C. I., LUMSDAINE, A. A., & SHEFFIELD, F. D. *Experiments on mass communication.* Princeton: Princeton Univer. Press, 1949.
RAZRAN, G. H. S. Conditioned response changes in rating and appraising sociopolitical slogans. *Psychological Bulletin,* 1940, 37, 481.

Reprinted from Journal of Abnormal and Social Psychology, 1960, Vol. 60, No. 3, pp. 345–353, by permission of William J. McGuire and APA.

COGNITIVE CONSISTENCY AND ATTITUDE CHANGE

WILLIAM J. McGUIRE

THERE has been a recent resurgence of interest among psychological researchers in the predictive value of a postulate that people tend to maintain logical consistency among their cognitions (and even between cognitions and more gross behavior). The most influential single source of this revived interest is probably Heider's (1946, 1958) "balance" theory, while Festinger's (1957) theory of cognitive dissonance is probably the most stimulating elaboration to date. Most of the approaches that employ this postulate recognize, implicitly or explicitly, that the tendency towards consistency is not absolute. Its expression is limited by other, potentially conflicting forces in the person and by the inadequacies of his cognitive apparatus, even in the absence of conflicting forces, to achieve full consistency. These coordinate hypotheses of cognitive consistency and its predictable limitations have been applied successfully to the prediction of behavior in many areas. The work reported here involves two applications in the area of persuasion.

The first of these applications involves what will be called the "Socratic method" of persuasion. The persuasion technique usually studied in the social sciences involves inducing a change in a person's opinion by presenting him with a persuasive message from an external source, either through a "mass" one-way communication channel or in a face-to-face reciprocal communication network. The postulate of cognitive consistency suggests that persuasion could be effected by the quite different technique of eliciting the persuasive material from the person's own cognitive repertory, rather than presenting it from outside. Specifically, this technique would involve asking the person his opinions on logically related issues, thus sensitizing him to any inconsistencies that exist among his stands on these issues and producing a change towards greater mutual consistency. The technique has an obvious affinity to the "Socratic method" used in the Platonic dialogues (Jowett, 1937).

The derivation of the foregoing hypothesis requires, besides the postulate of a tendency to maintain cognitive consistency, the assumptions that various distorting factors (of which "wishful thinking" is given primary attention in this study) have introduced inconsistency among the initially elicited set of opinions, and that the temporally contiguous elicitation of these opinions brings the tendency towards consistency more strongly to bear upon them.

Part of the study described below was designed to test the hypothesis that a person tends to change his opinions on logically related issues in the direction of greater mutual consistency when he is merely asked to state these opinions in close temporal contiguity. Several additional hypotheses regarding the focus of the Socratic effect, that is, the type of opinion most likely to be adjusted in case of inconsistency, were also tested.

The second application of the cognitive consistency postulate to the area of persuasion in the present experiment dealt with the logical repercussions of persuasive communications. The effectiveness of a persuasive message is usually gauged by the amount of change in opinion that it induces on the issue with which it explicitly deals. From the postulated consistency tendency, however, it would follow that an induced change on the explicit issue tends also to produce changes on logically related (unmentioned) issues such as would tend to maintain internal consistency among beliefs.

From the additional, limiting assumption that there is a certain amount of inertia in the person's cognitive apparatus, two additional hypotheses were derived. It was hypothesized that the consistency-maintaining change expected on remote issues is less than the amount logically required for complete consistency with the induced changes on the explicit issues. Further, it was hypothesized that inertia would also result in temporal effects, such that the impact of the message on the remote issue occurs only gradually, the opinion on the

345

remote issue continuing to change in the logically required direction for some time after receipt of the persuasive message.

Since most of these hypotheses involve predictions of fine graduations of change towards or away from a reference point of precise cognitive consistency, we need a quantitative definition of consistency. Such a definition is provided by a model combining formal logic and probability theory, the relevant aspects of which are summarized below.

Consider three issues so interrelated that a person taking Stands a and b on two of these issues would, if he were to be consistent, be logically required to take Stand c on the third. That is, the three stands are in a syllogistic relationship, with c following as a valid conclusion from the conjunction of a and b. If the person's opinions on these issues are obtained by having him indicate his adherence to each of the Stands, a, b, and c, on a probabilistic scale, we can specify that to be completely consistent, these probabilistically scaled opinions must be interrelated in the form

$$p(c) = p(a \& b) + p(k)(1 - p(a \& b))$$

[1]

where $p(k)$ is his opinion of the probability of c on bases other than the conjunction of a and b. It can also be specified that if we induce a change of opinion on a and/or b (for example, by a persuasive communication) while $p(k)$ does not change appreciably, then the required change on c necessary for maintaining logical consistency among the opinions is

$$\Delta p(c) = \Delta p(a \& b)$$

[2]

which, assuming that a and b are independent events i.e., that $p(a \& b) = p(a) p(b)$ becomes

$$\Delta p(c) = \Delta p(a)p(b) + \Delta p(b)p(a) + \Delta p(a)\Delta p(b)$$

[3]

where $p(a)$ and $p(b)$ refer to the initial opinions, before the communication induced changes. When, in the discussion below, we refer to the "logically required change on the conclusion," we are referring to the $\Delta p(c)$ value specified in Equation 3.

Method

Material. The Ss' opinions on sets of logically related issues were measured by means of a questionnaire that contained 48 statements. These statements comprised

16 sets of three syllogistically related propositions; that is, two of the propositions stated stands on a pair of issues, agreement with which would logically imply agreement with the stand taken in the proposition on the third issue.[1] The three propositions making up any one syllogism appeared in different parts of the questionnaire, being interspersed with the propositions of other syllogisms.

The Ss were asked to indicate in probabilistic terms the extent of their adherence to the stand taken in each proposition. For this purpose each proposition was followed by a graphic scale consisting of a five-inch horizontal line marked off at half-inch intervals and calibrated 0, 10, 20. . . 90, 100. To the left of the scale was written "Very improbable end," and at the right, "Very probable end." The Ss were asked to decide how probable they felt the truth of each statement to be, and to indicate this subjective probability by drawing a line through the scale at the appropriate point.

In a later section of the questionnaire the propositions were repeated, this time with a scale consisting of five boxes labelled from left to right "very desirable," "somewhat desirable,". . .," "very undesirable." The S was instructed to indicate his feeling regarding the desirability of each proposition by putting an X in the appropriate box. (As explained below, these ratings of desirability were obtained to allow identification of initial inconsistencies, due to wishful thinking, among the probability ratings.)

The questionnaires were administered during each of the three experimental sessions. Between the first and second administrations of the opinion questionnaires, a series of persuasive messages were communicated to the Ss in mimeographed booklets.[2] There were 16 such messages, each directed at one premise of each of the 16 syllogisms. Each message argued that the proposition in question was true, i.e., was aimed at increasing the S's probabilistic estimate of the statement's truth. These messages were "one-sided," 200–300 words long, employed rational appeals, and based arguments on factual evidence. They were mild in tone and attributed to a purportedly competent and dependable source.

---

[1] A complete list of all the syllogisms and persuasive messages used in the present study has been deposited with the American Documentation Institute. Order Document No. 6235, from ADI Auxiliary Publications Project, Photoduplication Service, Library of Congress, Washington 25, D. C., remitting in advance $1.25 for microfilm or $1.25 for photocopies. Make checks payable to Chief, Photoduplication Service, Library of Congress.

One of the 16 syllogisms used was as follows. Students who violate any regulation that has been made to safeguard the lives and property of other students will be expelled; the regulations against smoking in the classrooms and corridors were made to safeguard the lives and property of the student; students who violate the regulation against smoking in the classrooms and corridors will be expelled.

[2] The text of all 16 persuasive messages can be obtained in the ADI Document No. 6235, cited in Footnote 1.

Procedure. There were three 50–min. experimental sessions. In the first, the questionnaires were administered to obtain "before communication" measures of opinions on the issues. The second session, which came one week after the first, was devoted to communicating the persuasive messages and then to a second administration of the opinion questionnaires in order to measure the immediate impact of the persuasive messages. One week later, the *S*s participated in the third session during which the questionnaires were again administered (in order to ascertain the delayed effects of the persuasive messages). At this final session the *S*s were also told the purpose of the experiment and the *E* pointed out the deceits that he had employed in the experiments and his reasons for so doing.

Until this final "catharsis," an attempt was made to conceal, or at least distract attention from, the persuasion aspect of the experiment and from the investigator's interest in cognitive consistency. The study was purported to be an investigation of people's ability to understand experts' discussions of controversial topics. The persuasive messages were alleged to be excerpts from such discussions, and after each message the *S*s were required to answer a series of comprehension questions (to emphasize the contention that we were primarily interested in studying the *S*s' understanding of the material). The opinion questionnaires were explained as required to ascertain whether the issues dealt with were actually controversial in the group being studied and whether they continued to be controversial throughout the period of the experiment.

Subjects and design. A total of 120 *S*s participated in the experiment. One-fourth of these were high school seniors and the remainder, college freshman; the ratio of men to women was about 2:1 at both grade levels. To minimize the likelihood that the consistency hypotheses would receive specious confirmation by the employment of atypically rationalistic *S*s, these *S*s were selected from a group with a rather low level of intellectual attainment. Their modal high school grade average was below the 30th percentile for all high school students in their state. Each of these students reported that he had never had a course in formal logic or in probability theory.

In order that the *S*s might have time to respond thoughtfully to the opinion items and to read the persuasive messages carefully, each *S* was required to provide data on only 8 of the 16 syllogistically related sets of propositions. On only four of these eight did he receive persuasive messages, the other four serving as no-communication "control" items. These no-communication syllogisms provided the data for testing the Socratic effect hypotheses. The syllogisms on which messages were communicated provided the data for testing the hypotheses concerning logical repercussions. Specific syllogisms were alternated between message and no-message conditions from *S* to *S*.

RESULTS AND DISCUSSION

Hypotheses Concerning the Socratic Effect

Initial inconsistencies among the opinions. In order to identify initial opinion inconsistencies we employed an auxilliary hypothesis that the subjective probabilities of the propositions would be distorted in the direction of wishful thinking. Internal evidence indicates that this assumption was a valid one. The 16 syllogisms were partitioned into two subsets: the eight in which the desirability of the conclusions was low relative to that of the premises; and the eight whose conclusions had relatively high desirabilities. Wishful thinking would tend to make the subjective probabilities of the conclusions low relative to those of their (more desirable) premises in the first subset of syllogisms, while the subjective probabilities of the conclusions in the second set should be high relative to their less desirable premises. This prediction is borne out by the subjective probability ratings obtained in the first session, as shown in Table 1. (To avoid confusing them with the significance levels, the obtained subjective probability ratings given in this report are the obtained probability ratings, multiplied by 100.) The mean subjective probability of the conclusions exceeded the mean joint probability of the premises by only 2.20 points on the 100-point scale in the first eight syllogisms, while in the other eight syllogisms (the conclusions of which had relatively high desirability) the mean subjective probability of the conclusions exceeded the mean joint probability of the premises by 17.18 points. This difference between 2.20 and 17.18 points is significant beyond the .01 level. (All significance levels reported in this paper are based on analyses of variance and two-tailed tests.) Hence, the attempted manipulation of initial inconsistency by use of the tendency toward wishful thinking was successful.

The main effect. The changes in opinion obtained in the conditions in which no persuasive message was communicated on the given issues provide the test of the main Socratic hypothesis, that when the person's opinions on related issues are elicited in close temporal contiguity, his need for consistency is brought more fully to bear on them. Hence, when these opinions are again elicited on a later occasion, they will be found to have changed towards greater mutual consistency. In view of the initial distortions from consistency produced by wishful thinking, it would follow that in the no-communication conditions in the

TABLE 1
SUBJECT PROBABILITY SCORES (MULTIPLIED BY A FACTOR OF 100) IN THE NO-COMMUNICATION
CONDITIONS

	Session	Major Premises	Minor Premises	Joint of Premises	Conclu-sions	Excess of Conclu-sions over Premises
Syllogisms with conclusions less desir-able than premises	1st	62.15	54.14	33.66	35.86	2.20
	Changes, 1st to 2nd	−3.04	1.45	−0.79	5.17	5.96
Syllogisms with conclusions more de-sirable than premises	1st	55.50	55.41	30.12	47.30	17.18
	Changes, 1st to 2nd	3.96	−1.98	2.06	0.35	−1.72

present experiment initial questioning should produce an increase in the subjective proba-bilities of the conclusions relative to those of the premises in the first eight syllogisms (those with the relatively undesirable con-clusions); while for the second eight syllogisms, there would be a relative decline in the subjec-tive probabilities of the conclusions.

The results bear out this prediction. As can be seen in Table 1, the gain in probability of the conclusions over that of the premises in the first eight syllogisms averaged 5.96 points. The probabilities of the conclusions of the second eight syllogisms, on the other hand, showed a loss of 1.72 points relative to the premises. This net difference of 7.68 points between means is significant at the .02 level. Hence, simply eliciting opinions on logically related issues does tend to move those opinions toward greater mutual consistency when sub-sequent elicitation occurs one week later.

The difference obtained between the two sets of syllogisms as regards internal changes is in the direction that would be expected on the basis of a simple regression from the initially obtained difference. In order to test whether there is a Socratic effect over and above simple regression, an additional covari-ance analysis was carried out. The obtained difference in change of probability scores between the two sets of syllogisms was adjusted for the difference in initial levels by means of the obtained within-set correlation between the initial probability scores and the changes therein. Even when the obtained changes are adjusted for initial levels by this analysis of covariance, the difference in changes remains significant at the .02 level, indicative that a significant Socratic effect remains, even when the effect of regression is partialed out.

The Socratic effect tends to be produced primarily by the first contiguous elicitation of the opinions, with only slight evidence of an accumulative effect from subsequent, addi-tional elicitations. As discussed above, there was a net Socratic effect, from the first to second elicitation of the opinions, of 7.68 points. The corresponding net effect, from second to third elicitations was again in the predicted direction but amounted to only 2.62 points, which falls far short of the conventional levels of statistical significance.

Focus of the Socratic effect. An attempt was made to answer the further question of where this Socratic effect is focused; that is, which of the person's initially inconsistent opinions are most likely to be changed in bringing about the greater consistency? The present data were analyzed to ascertain whether the amount of change was related to any of three variables: the logical status of the propositions, their initial valence, or their ordinal position on the questionnaire in the first session.

As regards logical status of the proposition, we tested whether the major premise, minor, and conclusion contributed differentially to the change towards consistency. All of the syllogisms used in this study were of the "Barbara" type. Hence the major premise contained the M-P terms; the minor, the S-M terms; and the conclusion, the S-P terms (where S refers to the subject of the conclusion; P to its predicate; and M to the middle term).

Logical status of the proposition did have a significant overall impact on amount of opinion change. As can be seen in Table 1, the major premise contributed most of the change to-wards increased consistency, the mean change being 3.50 points on the 100-point scale. The conclusion showed the next greatest change towards consistency, a mean of 2.41 points; and the minor premise contributed least, in fact their mean change was slightly (1.71 points) away from consistency. These differences among the three means are significant at the .05 level by an overall analysis of variance.

The overall significance of the variance among the three means is due primarily to the greater change towards consistency (averaging 2.95 points) of the propositions with the P terms (namely, the major premises and the conclusions) than of those without these P terms (namely the minor premises), which averaged a 1.71 point change away from consistency. The difference between the two classes of propositions is significant at the .03 level. It appears to be explicable on the basis of initial distortion. In these "Barbara" syllogisms, the P terms tend to have the greatest emotional valence. Therefore, by the auxiliary hypothesis of wishful thinking, the propositions that include these emotionally-tinged terms would have been the most distorted originally. The minor premises, without the P terms, are typically statements of class inclusion ("Socrates is a man") and therefore less likely to be distorted. Hence, the greater change towards consistency of the other propositions appear to be a consequence of the fact that the others had contributed more of the original inconsistency.

Two other propositional characteristics were investigated for possible relationship to the amount of change in opinion produced by the Socratic method: initial valence and initial order of presentation. It was found that somewhat more change towards consistency occurred on the highly valenced propositions—the 12 most and the 12 least desirable propositions—than on the 24 moderately valenced ones. The direction of this outcome tends to reverse the "polarity" prediction (Osgood & Tannenbaum, 1955; Tannenbaum, 1956), but it does not approach the conventional level of statistical significance. Regarding initial order, it was found that somewhat more change toward consistency occurred on those propositions which, in the first session, appeared earlier on the questionnaire than on those that appeared towards the end, but that this difference was not statistically significant. The difference has been predicted on the

assumption that the later appearing propositions had already, on the first administration of the questionnaire, been brought into closer agreement with the opinions given on the propositions that had come earlier, so that less change remained to be made.

A number of other hypotheses, not tested in this study, regarding propositional characteristics that affect amount of change in cases of mutual inconsistency could be tested. Opinions on more familiar issues may be more stable than those on less familiar. Opinions on issues that show greater cognitive complexity and greater articulation with the rest of the person's cognitive system (as defined, for example, by Zajonc's [1954] procedures) might participate less in the change towards consistency than more isolated and undifferentiated opinions. Tannenbaum's (1956) finding (that when differently valenced sources and stands on issues are paired, the person's attitude on the issue shows less change than his attitude towards the source) is suggestive in this regard. Following Asch's (1952) thinking that persuasion involves a change of the issue being judged rather than change of judgement on the given issue, we might expect that in case of conflict, the greatest change would occur on the issues most easily redefined. Another hypothesis is that the relative proneness to readjustment of conflicting opinions is related to the bases for accepting the opinions. For example, following Kelman's (1956) terminology, we might conjecture that opinions based on internalization might be more prone to change, in case of internal conflict, than those based on identification or on compliance. These latter need not be consistent with one's other beliefs, because the adherence to them is based on extrinsic considerations.

Hypothesis Concerning Logical Repercussions

The results just reported regarding the Socratic effect hypotheses are all based on data in the no-communications conditions. The following results, which deal with the logical repercussions of persuasive messages are based on data from the conditions in which persuasive communications were received. The changes reported as due to the persuasive messages are computed from a baseline provided by the change from first to second session in the no-communication condition. Since the results concerning the Socratic effect indicate certain systematic changes in opinions occur from first to second session even in the absence of persuasive messages, the message-induced changes must be computed from a control baseline that will eliminate those other changes and also any regression trends.

Immediate postcommunication changes. The induced changes of opinion on the explicit target issues (the premises) were considerable. Each message argued that the stand taken in one of the premises of each syllogism was true and that, therefore, the receiver should increase his subjective probability regarding the truth of that proposition. As can be seen in Table 2, the mean induced increase on the 16 explicit propositions immediately after the communication was 17.56 points on the 100-point scale ($p < .001$).

In order to maintain cognitive consistency, the Ss should therefore have increased their subjective probabilities regarding the truth of the conclusions. Even though neither conclusions nor the additional premises needed for their derivation had been adverted to in the communications, a considerable immediate postcommunication increase was indeed produced on these conclusions. As can be seen in Table 2, there was an increase (as required for consistency) immediately after the messages on 14 of the 16 unmentioned conclusions, the mean increase being 5.96 points. A mean change of this magnitude is significant at the .01 level. Hence, the results do indicate a consistency tendency sufficiently strong to cause a persuasive message to have an impact on logically related issues not explicitly mentioned in the communication.

These obtained changes on the derivative issues are, however, less than the amount required for complete logical consistency as determined by substituting the amount of the obtained change on the explicit premise in Equation 3. The mean required increase on the conclusions so computed was 11.57 points, while the actually obtained increase was only 5.96 (see Table 2), a difference significant beyond the .05 level. Hence, persuasive messages, while they do produce changes on remote, unmentioned issues, produce less than the amount logically required, a finding that

supports the hypothesis of a certain amount of cognitive inertia.

Delayed postcommunication changes. A considerable amount of the immediately induced persuasion on the explicit target issues had dissipated by the end of the week following the communication. As can be seen in Table 2, almost half of the immediately induced change on these explicit issues had dissipated one week later. The mean loss of 8.43 points was significant at the .02 level. On the other hand, the 9.13 points of change remaining after one week was also significant (at the .01 level), indicating that there is still a significant amount of change of opinion on the explicit issue one week after the persuasive communication.

When this loss on the premises is substituted in Equation 3 the amount of the originally induced change on the unmentioned derived issues that should logically have dissipated during the succeeding week was computed as 6.69 points (see Table 2.) The obtained loss during the interim, however, was only a negligible 1.48 points, a gain of 5.20 points relative to the explicit premises for the week ($p = .10$). In fact, by the week after the persuasive communication, the net mean change on the conclusions from their precommunication level was an increase of 4.47 points, which was almost as much as the 4.89 points logically required in view of the net changes on the premises. The trivial extent to which the change on conclusions fell short of the required amount one week after, as compared with the significant extent to which it fell short immediately after the communication, gives some support to the hypothesis that the persuasive messages had a delayed-action effect on the derived issues. The net change on the derived issues did not actually increase with the passage of time, but it fell off less sharply than would have been expected on the basis of the usual rate of temporal decay of the immediately transmitted opinion change, suggesting that continued seepage of the impact on the explicit issue almost completely overcame the opposing decay effect on the derived, unmentioned issue.

Comparison with previous studies. One methodological artifact in the present study, the use of a before-after design, may have augmented the amount of the logical repercussions of the persuasive messages. In order to obtain each S's precommunication opinions he was required to fill out, one week prior to receipt of the persuasive messages, an opinion questionnaire containing all the issues, including the auxilliary premises and conclusions not mentioned in the message itself. It is possible that having stated his opinions on these related issues during the previous week may have somewhat increased their saliency, so that they were more affected by the message than would have been the case had they not been raised the previous week.

On the other hand, the finding of logical repercussions in the present experiment is particularly convincing in view of the fact that the method included a number of conditions that have been shown in previous studies to militate against logical repercussions. In the first place, not only was the conclusion itself unmentioned in the messages but also one of the two premises necessary for its derivation was left unmentioned. Also, the Ss employed were of a type, being below average in intelligence, that has been found (Cooper & Dinerman, 1951) to be relatively resistant to nonexplicit messages. Furthermore, no mention was made during the experiment of our interest in consistency, and the logically related propositions were widely interspersed with other propositions within the questionnaire. Finally the Ss gave their opinions on a scale with whose computational axioms they were unfamiliar, so that they could hardly have determined the extent of their inconsistencies even had they been interested in this matter.

Hence, the negative indications reported in some previous studies for the hypothesis that persuasive communications have logical repercussions require comment. While more persuasion has typically been found on a derived issue if that issue is explicitly mentioned rather than only implied, the data reported typically do show some change on the nonexplicit issue (Hovland, Lumsdaine, & Sheffield, 1949; Hovland & Mandell, 1952). Also, the relative lack of effect on the derived issue is most evident in the immediate postcommunication periods. Hovland, Lumsdaine, and Sheffield (1949, pp. 70–71) found that the "Why We Fight" films did have an impact

on more general attitudes after the passage of a greater amount of time, and have postulated that there may be need for a "sinking in" period before these derivative effects are felt. Similarly, Katz, Stotland, Patchen, and Jochen (1957) report that giving Ss case history material regarding the roots of prejudice causes little immediate effect on their own prejudice, but after the passage of several weeks, the extrapolation of the intellectual knowledge to their opinions does occur. Furthermore, the magnitude of the logically required change on the derived issue is, as shown by Equation 3, less than that on the explicit issue. This logically consistent attenuation of the persuasive impact on derived issues due to a compounding of contingencies becomes more severe as the derived issue becomes more tenuously related to the explicit issue. For example, the more premises beside the explicit one needed for its derivation, the less the logically required change on the derived conclusion. Where the derived issues are as remote from those explicitly dealt with as was the case, for example, in the Hovland, Lumsdaine, and Sheffield "Why We Fight" studies (1949), very little change on the derived issues would be logically required even in a perfectly consistent S.

However, while only a small change in opinion is logically required on the derived issue, the amount actually occurring is even less. People's opinions seem to follow a "loose-link" model such that a considerable change

TABLE 2

CHANGES IN SUBJECTIVE PROBABILITIES ON EXPLICIT ISSUE AND ON DERIVED, UNMENTIONED ISSUES IMMEDIATELY AFTER AND ONE WEEK AFTER PERSUASIVE MESSAGES

	Obtained Change on Premises	Logically Required Change on Conclusions	Obtained Change on Conclusions	Discrepancies of Obtained from Required Change on Conclusions
Changes from before to immediately after	17.56	11.57	5.96	−5.61
Changes from immediately to one week after	−8.43	−6.69	−1.48	5.20

can be induced on one cognition before any pull is exerted on related cognitions. This effect, however, is at least partially corrected by the continued seepage of change from the explicit issue to the derived one as time passes after the receipt of the communication.

The question of conscious awareness arises in connection with the psychodynamics of the present effect: to what extent is it necessary that the person be consciously aware of the inconsistencies among his beliefs in order that the effects occur? In the present study several procedures were employed in an attempt to minimize the degree of conscious awareness. (For example, no mention was made to the Ss that their consistency was being assessed; the related propositions were widely separated from one another in the questionnaire; a quantitative expression of opinion was required and the assessment of inconsistency involved a mathematical model unfamiliar to the Ss.) Hence, the present findings indicate that the effects occur even under conditions that attempt to avoid any suggestion of inconsistency.

The Ss' level of awareness of inconsistency was not systematically varied within the present experiment, but it is interesting to speculate on the results of such a manipulation. Increasing the person's awareness of his inconsistency by, say, explicitly pointing it out to him might produce greater changes towards consistency. On the other hand, such a procedure could well have the opposite effect by provoking the person's hostility or defensiveness, and so result, not in a greater change towards consistency, but in some other reaction such as the rejection of consistency, with Carlyle, as the hob-goblin of little minds; or in the repression of some of the conflicting issues.

SUMMARY

Two sets of hypotheses were derived from the postulate that people tend to maintain consistency among their opinions on logically related issues. First, it was hypothesized that opinion change would be effected by the Socratic method of simply asking the person to state contiguously his opinions on logically related issues, thus bringing the tendency towards consistency to bear on any logical

discrepancies among these opinions. Secondly, it was hypothesized that a persuasive communication directed at a person's opinion on some explicit issue tends to change also his opinions on logically related (even if unmentioned) derivative issues in a consistent direction. A procedure for quantitatively measuring the degree of logical consistency among opinions on related issues was described.

The Ss were 120 college students participating in three experimental sessions. In the first, before-communication opinions regarding the subjective probabilities and desirabilities of 16 sets of syllogistically related propositions were obtained. In the second session, 16 messages, each arguing for the truth of one premise of each syllogism, were communicated, and the immediate postcommunication opinion of the truth of each of the 48 propositions was obtained. Each S served in communication conditions with respect to some issues, and control, no-communication conditions with respect to others. In the third session, one week later, the delayed postcommunication opinions on the truth of the 48 propositions were obtained.

With respect to the Socratic effect hypothesis a significant amount of inconsistency attributable to wishful thinking was found, as postulated on the first elicitation of the opinions ($p < .01$). One week later, on a second elicitation of the opinions, there was a significant ($p = .02$) decline in the amount of this wishful thinking, indicating that the Socratic method did indeed produce the predicted change towards consistency. Several propositional variables were examined for possible relationship to the amount of change towards consistency. It was found that propositions with the predicate term (namely, major premises and conclusions) contributed significantly more ($p = .03$) of the change towards consistency than those without the predicate term.

With respect to the hypothesis concerning logical repercussions, it was found that immediately after the communication there was an induced opinion gain not only on the explicit target issues ($p < .001$) but also the derived issues ($p = .02$), even though neither the derived issues themselves nor even the auxiliary premises needed for their derivation were mentioned in the communication. This indirectly induced gain on the derived issues fell short, however, of the full amount needed for complete logical consistency ($p < .05$). One week later, there was some suggestion that the impact of the persuasive message had continued to seep down to the derived issues: immediately after the messages the opinions on the derived issues had shown only 52% of the logically required amount of change, while by one week after, this impact had risen to 91% of the required amount ($p = .10$).

REFERENCES

ASCH, S. E. Social psychology. New York: Prentice-Hall, 1952.

BAGLEY, W. C. The educative process. N. Y.: Macmillan, 1906.

COOPER, EUNICE, & DINERMAN, HELEN. Analysis of the film "Don't be a Sucker": A study in communication. Publ. opin. Quart., 1951, 15, 243–264.

FESTINGER, L. A theory of cognitive dissonance. Evanston: Roe, Peterson, 1957.

HEIDER, F. Attitudes and cognitive organization. J. Psychol., 1946, 21, 107–112.

HEIDER, F. The psychology of interpersonal relations. New York: Wiley, 1958.

HOVLAND, C. I., LUMSDAINE, A. A., & SHEFFIELD, F. D. Experiments on mass communication. Princeton: Princeton Univer. Press, 1949.

HOVLAND, C. I., & MANDELL, W. An experimental comparison of conclusion—drawing by the communicator and by the audience. J. abnorm. soc. Psychol., 1952, 47, 581–588.

JOWETT, B. (Ed.) The dialogues of Plato. New York: Random House, 1937.

KATZ, D., STOTLAND, E., PATCHEN, M., & JOCHEN J. Research in methods for changing attitudes. I. Situational and personality determinants of the reduction of prejudice through self-insight. Univer. of Michigan, 1957. (Mimeo.)

KELMAN, H. C. Three processes of acceptance of social influence: Compliance, identification and internalization. Amer. Psychol., 1956, 11, 261. (Abstract)

OSGOOD, C., & TANNENBAUM, P. The prinicple of congruity and the production of attitude change. Psychol. Rev., 1955, 62, 42–55.

TANNENBAUM, P. Initial attitude towards source and concept as factors in attitude change through communication. Publ. opin. Quart., 1956, 20, 413–425.

ZAJONC, R. B. Cognitive structure and cognitive tuning. Unpublished doctoral dissertation, Univer. Michigan, 1954.

Sources of Artifact

Earlier we briefly discussed the relevance of findings in experimental studies to "real life." We noted that one major advantage of the experimental-type investigation is that it permits fairly precise control of the circumstances under which persuasion takes place. Obviously no experimenter is infallible, and, consequently, no experiment is without some potential flaw. The important question, however, is not whether an experiment is flawless, but whether the source of any imperfection is relevant to the effects of the experimental variables. An imperfection which could not contaminate these effects is an imperfection of little consequence to the experimenter. On the other hand, an imperfection which, even though inadvertent, establishes a source of artifact or systematic error is an imperfection of major consequence.

In recent years there has been an increased interest in identifying the sources of artifact in social research. Unfortunately the analagous effort in communications research has not been as intense as one would like it to be. Nevertheless, some considerable progress has been made in identifying problem areas requisite of further investigation. As this information continues to accumulate, new insights are gained about old findings. Concomitantly, there is a continuous leveling and sharpening of the principles and theories of human behavior that have been gleaned over the years. And, as we become more aware of the potential sources of error seemingly endemic to experimental-type research we become better able to control for the artifact which could result. Karl Weick expresses the problem succinctly when he writes,

> . . . there are *NO* limitations to laboratory experiments. The limitations instead involve laboratory experimenters, their decisions and their concerns. Laboratory experiments themselves are not inherently limiting. Instead the limitations arise from the ways in which experiments have been implemented. Given this perspective, it should be apparent that there is some hope for change and improvement if we can just get to the experimenters.[1]

---

[1] Quoted by permission of Weick, K. E., and John Wiley & Sons Publishers, from Promise and limitations of laboratory experiments in the development of attitude

One of the most intriguing potential sources of error in attitude research is the factor of "awareness." It has generally been assumed that subjects who are aware of an experimenter's manipulatory intent react differently than subjects who are unaware. This, of course, is one major reason why deception techniques are so often employed in experimental social research.[2] Sometimes, however, even despite an experimenter's having taken the usual precautions dictated by common sense to disguise the purpose of his study, nevertheless subjects may become aware of his intent.

In attitude research, it is not yet clear under what conditions awareness of the communicator's persuasive intent has a facilitative effect on opinion change[3] or a depressive effect,[4] whether in two-sided communication "unawareness" leads to primacy[5] or to recency,[6] although awareness seems consistently to lead to primacy.[7]

In the typical attitude study where college students are administered pretests followed by persuasive communications which, in turn, are followed by posttests, it seems reasonable to conjecture that the students would perceive that some change is "demanded"[8]

change theory. Paper read at Sympos. on Attitude and Attitude Change, sponsored by Pennsylvania State Univer., May, 1966, p. 2. [To be published in Sherif, M., Sherif, C., & Kent, D. (Eds.) *Attitude, ego-involvement and change.* New York: Wiley.]

[2] Zimbardo *et al.*, pp. 29 ff.; Festinger and Carlsmith, pp. 309 ff.

[3] McGuire, W. J., & Papageorgis, D. Effectiveness of forewarning in developing resistance to persuasion. *Publ. Opin. quart.*, 1962, **26**, 24–34. McGuire, W. J., & Millman, S. Anticipatory belief lowering following forewarning of a persuasive attack. *J. Pers. soc. Psychol.*, 1965, **2**, 471–479. Mills, J., & Aronson, E. Opinion change as a function of the communicator's attractiveness and desire to influence. *J. Pers. soc. Psychol.*, 1965, **1**, 173–177.

[4] Kerrick, J. S., & McMillan, D. A. III. The effects of instructional set on the measurement of attitude change through communications. *J. soc. Psychol.*, 1961, **53**, 113–120. Allyn, J., & Festinger, L. The effectiveness of unanticipated persuasive communications. *J. abnorm. soc. Psychol.*, 1961, **62**, 35–40. Kiesler, C. A., & Kiesler, S. B. Role of forewarning in persuasive communications. *J. abnorm. soc. Psychol.*, 1964, **68**, 547–549. Freedman, J. L., & Sears, D. O. Warning, distraction, and resistance to influence. *J. Pers. soc. Psychol.*, 1965, **1**, 262–266.

[5] Holz, R. F. An experimental investigation of the influence of awareness of manipulatory intent on reactions to persuasive communications. Unpublished master's thesis, Boston Univer. School of Public Communication, 1965.

[6] Schultz, D. P. Time, awareness, and order of presentation in opinion change. *J. appl. Psychol.*, 1963, **47**, 280–283.

[7] *Ibid.*, and Holz, R. F. An experimental investigation of the influence of awareness of manipulatory intent on reactions to persuasive communications. Unpublished master's thesis, Boston Univer. School of Public Communication, 1965.

[8] Martin Orne refers to the sum total of the cues which communicate the experimenter's hypotheses as the "demand characteristics" of the experiment. Orne, M. T.

of them. Even when there is no explicitly verbalized forewarning to this effect, subjects may become cognizant of, or develop hypotheses about, the purpose of the study.[9] The experimenter's instructions, the setting, the procedure — all of these can furnish cues which may serve as an implicit forewarning to subjects of the communicator's persuasive intent.

More important here, however, is the possibility that subjects' reactions to an experimental communication could be influenced by their awareness of the communicator's intent. They might, for example, become suspicious of the communicator's motives and respond to his effort with hostility. This would probably lead to their increased resistance to his persuasive appeal,[10] even perhaps to a boomerang effect. On the other hand, it is possible that subjects, perhaps motivated by a need for approval,[11] would tend to go along with whatever position happened to be advocated by the communicator.[12] Rosenberg's contention, it will be recalled, was that the typical subject is likely to view the social research situation as one which has as one of its unrevealed purposes to evaluate his competence as a subject (pp. 317 ff.). What better way to ensure his positive evaluation by the experimenter than by giving precisely the response that he thinks the experimenter is looking for?[13] And, possibly, the greater a subject's desire for approval, the more submissive and suggestible he will be. Volunteer subjects, it has been observed, tend to be higher in need for social approval than nonvolunteers.[14] Does it then follow that in a persuasion experiment volunteers more than nonvolunteers would be prone to comply with the communicator's implicit demands? One

---

On the social psychology of the psychological experiment: With reference to demand characteristics and their implications. *Amer. Psychologist*, 1962, **17**, 776–783.

[9] Rosnow, R. L. One-sided vs. two-sided communication under indirect awareness of persuasive intent. *Publ. Opin. quart.*, in press.

[10] Freedman, J. L., & Sears, D. O. Warning, distraction and resistance to influence. *J. Pers. soc. Psychol.*, 1965, **1**, 262–266.

[11] Crowne, D. P., & Marlowe, D. *The approval motive.* New York: Wiley, 1964.

[12] Rosnow, R. L. One-sided vs. two-sided communication under indirect awareness of persuasive intent. *Publ. Opin. quart.*, in press.

[13] Rosenberg, M. J. When dissonance fails: On eliminating evaluation apprehension from attitude measurement. *J. Pers. soc. Psychol.*, 1965, **1**, 28–42.

[14] Marlowe, D., & Crowne, D. P. Social desirability and response to perceived situational demands. *J. Consult. Psychol.*, 1961, **25**, 109–115. Leipold, W. D., & James, R. L. Characteristics of shows and no-shows in a psychological experiment. *Psychol. Rep.*, 1962, **11**, 171–174. McDavid, J. W. Approval-seeking motivation and the volunteer subject. *J. Pers. soc. Psychol.*, 1965, **2**, 115–117.

of the studies reprinted here, by Ralph L. Rosnow and Robert Rosenthal, addresses itself to this question.

A second study, by Robert E. Lana, probes another potential source of systematic error in attitude research. Of major concern in experiments which utilize the before-after-type design is the possibility that the pretest, perhaps because it evokes awareness, "sensitizes" the subject so that his responses to the persuasive communication are different than they would have been if there were no pretest. The usual precautions to safeguard against this possibility include disguising the pretest,[15] delaying presentation of the communication for a long enough period so as to ensure that the subjects will have forgotten their responses,[16] the utilization of additional control groups,[17] etc. Lana's study is addressed to a problem of long standing in attitude research: whether pretest sensitization has a facilitative or a depressive effect on reaction to a communication.

Finally, one might ask what the empirical relationship is between verbal opinion and overt, action-type behavior. Does opinion change necessarily imply behavior change? Contrary perhaps to first impression, awareness does not necessarily preclude the possibility of sustained behavioral compliance. The reader will recall Janis and Mann's finding that emotional role-playing is effective for changing beliefs about cigarette smoking, and habits as well (pp. 361 ff.). Festinger's position in this matter, reminiscent perhaps of Newcomb's (pp. 429 ff.), is that behavior change requires environmental support.

> It is my present contention that, in order to produce a stable behavior change following opinion change, an environmental change must also be produced which, representing reality, will support the new opinion and the new behavior. Otherwise, the same factors that produced the initial opinion and the behavior will continue to operate to nullify the effect of the opinion change.[18]

---

[15] Lana, R. E., & Rosnow, R. L. Subject awareness and order effects in persuasive communications. *Psychol. Rep.*, 1963, 12, 523–529. The ideal instrument is, of course, one which measures the ongoing state of behavior without influencing that behavior; see, for example, Webb, E. J., Campbell, D. T., Schwartz, R. D., & Sechrest, L. *Unobtrusive measures: Nonreactive research in the social sciences.* Chicago: Rand-McNally, 1966.

[16] Lana, R. E. Familiarity and the order of presentation of persuasive communications. *J. abnorm. soc. Psychol.*, 1961, 62, 573–577.

[17] Solomon, R. L. An extension of control group design. *Psychol. Bull.*, 1949, 46, 137–150. Campbell, D. T., & Stanley, J. C. Experimental and quasi-experimental designs for research on teaching. In N. L. Gage (Ed.), *Handbook of research on teaching.* Chicago: Rand-McNally, 1963. Pp. 171–246.

[18] Quoted from Festinger, L. Behavioral support for opinion change. *Publ. Opin. quart.*, 1964, 28, 416. By permission of the author and the publisher.

The two remaining studies, by Anthony G. Greenwald and Lawrence S. Linn, suggest two other variables—commitment and social involvement—which seem also to ensure the desired positive relationship between opinion and behavior.

Reprinted from Psychological Reports, 1966, Vol. 19, pp. 1183–1187, by permission of Ralph L. Rosnow, Robert Rosenthal and Southern University Press.

VOLUNTEER SUBJECTS AND THE RESULTS OF OPINION CHANGE STUDIES[1]

RALPH L. ROSNOW   AND   ROBERT ROSENTHAL

Summary.—Female volunteers and nonvolunteers for a (fictitious) perception experiment participated in a study of opinion change. Opinions about college fraternities were measured before and after the receipt of pro-fraternity, anti-fraternity, or no (control) communication. Volunteers reacted differently from nonvolunteers to pro- and to anti-fraternity communications. In addition, volunteers' opinions were significantly less reliable than the opinions of nonvolunteers, i.e., volunteers were more heterogeneous in their opinion-change behavior. The present results taken together with earlier findings raise the possibility that volunteers more than nonvolunteers may more often confirm what they perceive to be *E*'s hypothesis. Therefore, the volunteer status of the subject sample might well be specified routinely in research reports.

There is a growing literature which shows that volunteers for participation in a psychological experiment differ in a number of important ways from those who do not volunteer. As a detailed summary of these differences is available elsewhere (Rosenthal, 1965), it is enough to cite a few examples. Volunteers tend to manifest greater intellectual ability, interest and motivation than do non-volunteers; they tend to be younger, less authoritarian and conventional, more sociable, and higher in need for social approval than nonvolunteers. Since many or all of these characteristics may be related to *S*'s task performance, we must be cautious in generalizing from the performance of volunteers to the performance of *S*s in general. Thus, if we were standardizing a test of need for social approval, our sample mean might be inflated if we relied on a sample of volunteers for our standardization group. That point is fairly banal, but it leaves a more important question to be asked.

Suppose that we want now to conduct an experiment comparing the effects of two treatment conditions. If we employed only volunteer *S*s would the difference between the means (i.e., the experimental effect) be affected by their volunteer status? It is entirely possible that, although volunteers may differ from nonvolunteers in a given task performance, the effects of an experimental treatment condition may remain unaltered by *S*s' volunteer status. It was to learn whether appreciable experimental effects might be influenced by *S*s' volunteer status that the present experiment was performed.

[1]This investigation, one in a series on the sources of artifact in social research, was supported by Grants GS-1375 and GS-714 from the Division of Social Sciences of the National Science Foundation. The initial exploratory research on this topic was supported in part by Grant MH-11972-01 from the National Institute of Mental Health, U. S. Public Health Service. This investigation was carried out under the auspices of the Boston University Communication Research Center. We want to express our appreciation to Robert F. Holz, John Corrozi, and Professor E. Stuart Wells for their assistance.

METHOD

Subjects

Ss were 42 female undergraduates enrolled in an introductory sociology class at Boston University's College of Liberal Arts.

Stimuli

The stimuli were pro-fraternity and anti-fraternity persuasive communications, each approximately 280 words in length. Special care was taken to ensure that the four major pro and con arguments in each communication carried equal weight.

Opinion Questionnaires

Four statements relevant to the four arguments were embedded in a pretest opinion questionnaire—disguised as a "national collegiate opinion survey" —along with 12 irrelevant items. Ss indicated on a 7-point Likert-type scale the extent of their agreement or disagreement with each statement. Hence, the range of the summed responses to the fraternity statements was from 4, strongly anti-fraternity, to 28, strongly pro-fraternity. The posttest questionnaires contained only the four fraternity items originally embedded in the pretest.

Procedure

The pretest questionnaires were administered by E during a regularly scheduled class period. (E was unfamiliar to Ss but was identifiable as a professor.) Once the questionnaires had been completed, E thanked Ss and the instructor for their cooperation and left the room. Some time later in the period, the instructor told Ss the following:

Some of you may already be familiar with the research on perception of ambiguous figures being carried out by Dr. Elton Harris at the Harvard Psychology Laboratories.

Well, Dr. Harris asked me if I would ask you whether you might be interested in volunteering to participate in one of his experiments. Although I don't know all of the details, I can tell you that Dr. Harris is planning to set up his perception apparatus here in CLA (College of Liberal Arts) during the next four weeks, and he will need subjects.

The pay will be nominal—$1.00 an hour, and he will need you for approximately two hours.[2]

If you are interested, would you please print your name, your phone number or local address, and the day (or days) of the week your schedule tends to be most free—even if it's on a weekend. I will pass the list on to Dr. Harris. He will then get in touch with you to see if he can find some time when it would be mutually convenient for both of you to get together.

I would appreciate any help you can give to Dr. Harris.

Thus, we were able to obtain a list of volunteers ($n = 20$ females)[3] for

---

[2] The "$1.00 an hour" ploy was used, because it was reasoned that payment for services would lend the fictitious Harris experiment some air of credibility; yet compensation purposely was kept small to assure that it would not serve as a major incentive, motivating students to volunteer purely for monetary gain.

[3] There were 15 males enrolled in this course which was too small a sample to include for analysis, especially so in view of the fact that, while 48% of the females volunteered only 13% of the males volunteered, a significant difference in rates ($\chi^2 = 5.49, p < .02$).

an experiment which was logically unrelated to anything mentioned in the pre-test opinion questionnaire or, subsequently, to anything in the content of the persuasive communications.

One week later, *E* returned to the class. At that time, the students were as-signed at random to one of three treatment groups. In one group, *E* read to *Ss* the pro-fraternity communication. At the same time, *Ss* read to themselves a mimeographed copy of the message. In a second group, the same procedure was used, except that the anti-fraternity communication was read to *Ss* instead. As soon as each communication was completed, *Ss* were administered the post-test opinion questionnaire. A third group, also selected at random, served as a "zero" control. *Ss* in this group completed the posttest questionnaire but re-ceived neither communication.

At the conclusion of the treatments, *Ss* were asked to tell what they thought was the purpose of the experiment. Although the responses of both volunteer and nonvolunteer *Ss* to this question implied their awareness of *E*'s persuasive intent (Rosnow, in press), not one *S* drew an association between volunteering and opinion change.

RESULTS AND DISCUSSION

Table 1 shows the mean change in favorableness of opinions about frater-nities for the two experimental groups and the control group for both the vol-unteer and nonvolunteer *Ss*. The communications led to opinion change in

TABLE 1

MEAN OPINION CHANGE OF VOLUNTEERS AND NONVOLUNTEERS

Ss	Type of Communication		
	Pro-fraternity	Control	Anti-fraternity
Volunteers	+1.67	+0.40	−3.50*
	(16.33)	(13.20)	(15.17)
Nonvolunteers	+2.50*	−0.91	−1.20
	(16.67)	(15.00)	(18.40)
M	+2.09*	−0.26	−2.35†

Note.—Means differ from their respective control group means at indicated *p* levels. Pre-test means are shown in parenthesis.
†*p* ≅ .10, two-tail. **p* ≤ .05, two-tail.

the predicted directions for all *Ss* ($F = 6.31, df = 2/36, p < .005$). The over-all magnitude of effect, while larger among volunteers ($t = 3.11, df = 36, p = .004$) as predicted, was not significantly different from the treatments' effects on nonvolunteer *Ss* ($t = 1.92, df = 36, p = .07$). Examination of Table 1 shows, however, that volunteers and nonvolunteers reacted differently to specific communications.

Thus, nonvolunteers presented with anti-fraternity communications did not change their opinions any more than did the nonvolunteer controls, but volunteers became significantly more anti-fraternity when presented with these communications. When presented with pro-fraternity communications volunteers did not change their opinions significantly in a pro-fraternity direction, but nonvolunteers did. One explanation for these results may lie in the possibility that the faculty E who provided the pro- and anti-fraternity communications was himself perceived as partial to the anti-fraternity communication.[4] In order to please such an E, the volunteers may have been more responsive to the anti-fraternity communication than the nonvolunteers. Since volunteers appear to have a higher need for social approval (Leipold & James, 1962; Marlowe & Crowne, 1961; McDavid, 1965), it could be reasoned that, where E's implicit demands (Orne, 1962) are fairly clear, volunteers should show greater effects of the experimental treatment. In experiments on opinion change, where pretests are followed by persuasive communications which, in turn, are followed by posttests, it should be fairly clear to Ss that some change is expected by E (Orne, 1962). Because of his greater need for social approval from E, the volunteer S more than the nonvolunteer may be more sensitive to and/or more responsive to those cues which tell him how he might be able better to please E. When the communication was pro-fraternity, the volunteers may have been less responsive because they felt that E himself was not really pro-fraternity, while the nonvolunteers utilized the opportunity to express their independence of E's own opinion. To examine this interpretation an experiment is needed which would vary not only the content of the communications but the presumably "real" opinion of the communicator as well. In the absence of such information, this interpretation is intended, of course, as speculation.

So far we have looked only at the effects of volunteer status on immediate changes in favorableness toward fraternities as a function of type of persuasive communication. Such changes in degree of favorableness could occur with or without any effect on the reliability of Ss' ratings of favorableness. Table 2 shows the reliability of opinions before and after the communication among volunteers and nonvolunteers in each experimental condition. There were no significant effects on reliability of the treatment conditions within Ss of either volunteer or nonvolunteer status (i.e., the ps that the reliabilities differed from

---

[4]Although the following information was gathered several months after the experiment, at least circumstantial evidence in support of this assumption is a finding from a follow-up evaluation using a comparable group of 8 female Boston University undergraduates who were asked to rate E with regard to their impressions of his attitude toward fraternities. E, who was introduced to Ss as a professor at Boston University, presented to Ss as a rationale for their rating task his interest in investigating the psychological processes involved when people form impressions of the attitudes of others. E told Ss that he wanted to determine how accurate Ss' impressions were of his attitude toward college fraternities. A 9-point graphic scale was used, anchored at the negative end by the phrase "extremely anti-fraternity," in the middle, or zero, by "neither pro- nor anti-fraternity," and at the positive end by "extremely pro-fraternity." The mean rating by these Ss was -1.12 (less than zero at $p < .04$, one-tail, $t = 2.22$, $df = 7$), the average impression of E thus being moderately anti-fraternity.

TABLE 2

OPINION RELIABILITY AS A FUNCTION OF VOLUNTEER STATUS

| Ss | Type of Communication | | | | | | M | |
| | Pro-fraternity | | Control | | Anti-fraternity | | rho | n |
	rho	n	rho	n	rho	n		
Volunteer	.49	9	−.52	5	.76	6	.35	20
Nonvolunteer	.99*	6	.95**	11	.98*	5	.97**	22

*$p < .02$.   **$p < .001$.

one another exceeded .20). However, the opinions of the volunteers were significantly less reliable than were the opinions of the nonvolunteers ($z = 4.20$, $p < .0005$, two-tail). This means that volunteers were more heterogeneous in their opinion-change behavior than were the nonvolunteers, a finding which may be attributable to their greater willingness to change their opinions in whatever direction they felt demanded by the situation (Marlowe & Crowne, 1961).

It has long been suggested that the behavior of volunteer and nonvolunteer Ss in an experiment might be different. The results of the present study raise the possibility that not only may the average performance of S depend on his volunteer status but also that the effects of experimental treatments may be a function of S's volunteer status. From the results of this study and from a survey of the literature on characteristics of the volunteer S (Rosenthal, 1965) our hypothesis is that the volunteer S as compared to the nonvolunteer may more often confirm what he perceives to be E's hypothesis. It would, therefore, be desirable for the volunteer status of the subject sample to be routinely specified in reports of research.

REFERENCES

LEIPOLD, W. D., & JAMES, R. L. Characteristics of shows and no-shows in a psychological experiment. *Psychological Reports*, 1962, 11, 171-174.

MARLOWE, D., & CROWNE, D. P. Social desirability and response to perceived situational demands. *Journal of Consulting Psychology*, 1961, 25, 109-115.

MCDAVID, J. W. Approval-seeking motivation and the volunteer subject. *Journal of Personality and Social Psychology*, 1965, 2, 115-117.

ORNE, M. T. On the social psychology of the psychological experiment: with particular reference to demand characteristics and their implications. *American Psychologist*, 1962, 17, 776-783.

ROSENTHAL, R. The volunteer subject. *Human Relations*, 1965, 18, 389-406.

ROSNOW, R. L. One-sided *vs.* two-sided communication under indirect awareness of persuasive intent. *Public Opinion Quarterly*, in press.

Reprinted by Educational and Psychological Measurement, 1966, Vol. 26, No. 1, pp. 139–150, by permission of Robert E. Lana and the publisher.

INHIBITORY EFFECTS OF A PRETEST ON OPINION CHANGE[1]

ROBERT E. LANA

In recently reported studies (Lana and Rosnow, 1963; Lana, 1964b) it has been shown that the use of a pretest and its manner of presentation can affect the direction of opinion change when two opposed arguments on the same topic are utilized. Primacy refers to the success in changing opinion of an initial argument of two opposed communications. Recency refers to a similar success of an argument presented second. When the pretest is hidden from the subject (Lana and Rosnow, 1963) or missing altogether (Lana, 1964b), in the pretest-treatment-posttest opinion change research design (Solomon, 1949), change occurs usually in the direction of the first presented of two opposed arguments (primacy). Recency, however, does not necessarily occur when the pretest is exposed.

The principal concern of this study is to examine the effect of the pretest on opinion change regardless of direction (primacy or recency). The initial focus of the studies mentioned above (Lana and Rosnow, 1963; Lana, 1964b) was on the effect of the present on the resulting directional effect (primacy-recency), but a more important consideration may be whether or not the pretest generally in-

[1] This research was supported by the National Institute of Mental Health, United States Public Health Service Grant No. MH 06926–02.

The Vivisection Questionnaire, the pro and con communications, and the familiarization talk utilized in this study have been deposited with the American Documentation Institute. Order Document No. 6765 from ADI Auxiliary Publications Project, Photoduplication Service, Library of Congress; Washington 25, D. C., remitting in advance $1.25 for microfilm or $1.25 for photocopies. Make checks payable to: Chief; Photoduplication Service, Library of Congress.

hibits or facilitates opinion change when two opposed arguments on the same topic are presented to the subject. The concept here is that the subject may "commit" himself to a particular position with respect to the topic at hand. Thus responding to a pretest should result in less opinion change, either in favor of or against a specific issue, than where an initial pretest is not used. If this is true, then using a pretest in opinion and attitude studies will reduce the effect ordinarily produced by persuasion. Solomon (1949) discovered a depressive effect of the pretest on errors in spelling using school children as subjects. Entwisle (1961) found significant interaction effects with IQ and sex in a similar training situation. Both utilized a single, unidirectional treatment.

Hovland and Mandell (1957) have shown that commitment to an attitudinal position inhibits change when commitment is elicited after an initial influence attempt but not when response to a pre-communication questionnaire constitutes the commitment. Their suggestion, however, is that there are forms of attitudinal commitment, usually made under public conditions, which inhibit opinion or attitude change as a result of materials presented later.

A subject's initial response to a questionnaire may provide a basis of comparison for further questionnaire responses and thus a positive correlation of some magnitude might be expected between the individual's first and second responses to the same questionnaire. This expectation of correlation between successive responses to some task by the same subject is the basis for methodological concern with repeated measurements in experimental design. Statistical psychologists have been concerned with the problem for years, and there seems to be little doubt about the influence of one response on another in the repeated measurement situation.

When two treatments are performed in succession, a treatment carryover may occur. The rotation design (Cochran and Cox, 1957) is specifically intended to give information on such a treatment carryover. In the experimental situation described in this paper where a pretest precedes a single treatment, the possible effects of carryover from pretest to treatment are the same as the treatment to treatment carryover. A rotation design is not possible when the first factor is a pretest since, by definition, it must precede the treatment. Consequently any examination of the confounding effects of the pretest with treatment must be made by experimentally manipulating the nature of the pretest. The major question that remains concerns the nature of the relationship. At any rate, there seems to be ample information to establish the suspicion that initial responses of a subject in the opinion and attitude situation may very well depress later changes.

In a study done in 1959, Lana found no depressive effect of the pretest (interaction between pretest and treatment) when a single, unidirectional communication was utilized. However, when two opposed communications on the same topic were presented to the same subject (Lana and Rosnow, 1963, 1964b) a pretest inhibition or depressive effect was present. Recalculation of the data of these studies was necessary, and the depressive effects were not reported at the time of publication.

In order to facilitate comparisons among the various experiments already reported in the literature and the current one, the procedure, results, and conclusions of each of the three previously published experiments are listed below. All *primacy-recency effects* are summed by taking the algebraic differences between pretest and posttest and subtracting these differences for each pro-con and con-pro group. These results have already been reported in the first three published studies cited below and, for the fourth study, in Table 2 of this report. All *opinion change effects regardless of direction* (primacy or recency), are absolute differences, taken between pre and posttest for all groups and averaged regardless of algebraic sign.

Experiment I (Lana 1959) Exposed Pretest, Unidirectional Persuasion.

One-hundred fifty-six college students were randomly assigned to four treatment conditions. Two of these groups received the pretest attitude questionnaire. One of the two groups listened to a taped pro-vivisection communication 12 days after taking the pretest. After treatment, this group (Group I) was immediately posttested with the same questionnaire. The other group (Group IV) was simply posttested 12 days later. Group II heard the pro-vivisection communication and was posttested immediately afterward without having been pretested. Group III answered the questionnaire once. Opinion change was measured as the algebraic difference from pretest to posttest.

The only significant F was that for the treatment effect, while the F ratios for the effects of the pretest and the pretest-by-treatment interaction were both less than unity. It can be concluded that the pretest and treatment did not interact, and that the pretest did not sensitize or desensitize the subjects to the communication. The main effect of pretesting was not significant.

Experiment II (Lana and Rosnow 1963) Exposed Versus Hidden Pretest, Bidirectional Persuasion

One-hundred twenty-eight students from beginning level psychology classes at the American University were used as subjects in this study. They were randomly divided into eight groups of 16 each. All S's initially received either the opinion questionnaire on nuclear weapons or one on public censorship. Four of the groups were presented the pretest during a regularly scheduled class as a separate part of the hour's activity. These were labeled the "exposed pretest" group. The remaining four groups responded to the questionnaire presented as part of their regularly scheduled hour examination in general psychology. The opinion questions appeared as a 5-question unit in the exam and were "buried" among other similar question units pertaining to the usual subject matter of an introductory psychology class. These groups were labeled the "hidden pretest" group. All groups, immediately after listening to the pro and con arguments, received the appropriate posttest, which was identical with the pretest.

Primacy-recency effects are given in the 1963 report on this experiment. Recalculation of the data indicated that the average opinion change per group (mean absolute differences from pretest to posttest) of the four groups where the pretest was hidden was 1.88 scale points as compared with an average absolute change of .41 scale points per group of those four groups where the pretest was exposed. This difference was significant beyond the .05 level (t-test for independent means).

Experiment III (Lana 1964b) Exposed versus No Pretest, Bidirectional Persuasion

One-hundred thirty-six subjects from the introductory psychology classes at Alfred University were randomly assigned to 12 experimental groups. Two of the groups were "zero" control groups which received the pretest and then the posttest either 12 or 24 days later. Neither of these groups indicated any change in opinion whatsoever and thus were dropped from any further analysis. Of the remaining 10 groups, eight were pretested with an opinion questionnaire on Nikita Khrushchev. Pretests for all groups were then analyzed for differences with a one-way analysis of variance to determine whether or not the groups could reasonably be assumed to be homogeneous with respect to initial opinion concerning Khrushchev. The F ratio was less than 1. It was concluded that the groups were homogeneous on initial opinion. It was assumed that initial opinions of the two groups not pretested were homogeneous with the eight pretested groups since they were formed randomly from the same sample from which these latter groups were selected.

Four of these eight groups, immediately after filling out the pretest, were exposed to the successive presentation of two opposed (pro and con) prose statements regarding Khrushchev. Two of these groups received the pro argument first and the other two groups the con argument first. Two of these four groups were then immediately posttested. The remaining six groups, and the two groups that were not initially pretested, were dismissed for 12 days. At the termination of this interval, all eight groups who had not as yet been given a posttest were run as follows: The two groups that had been exposed to the pro and con arguments were posttested with the identical questionnaire used as the pretest. The two groups receiving no pretest were given the pro-con or con-pro order of arguments and immediately posttested. Two of the groups having received the pretest only received the pro-con or con-pro order of arguments and were then posttested. The remaining two groups, who had received the pretest only, were exposed to the arguments as had the other groups. They were then posttested 12 days after the presentation of the arguments. Because this design is more complicated than those of the other reported studies, a summary of the experimental procedure is given in Table 1.

In the two groups receiving no pretest, the average opinion change (mean absolute difference from pretest to posttest) per group was .75 scale points as compared with an average per group change of .35 scale points for the groups receiving a pretest. These differences are significant beyond the .05 level (t-test for independent means).

TABLE 1

Experimental Design for Experiment III

GROUPS											
A	B	C	D	E	F	G	H	I	J	K	L
Pretest		Pretest				Pretest		Pretest		Pretest	
Pro	Con	Pro	Con	Pro	Con	12 days		12 days		12	24
Con	Pro	Con	Pro	Con	Pro	Pro	Con	Pro	Con	days	
12 days		Posttest₁		Posttest₁		Con	Pro	Con	Pro		
Posttest₁						12 days		Posttest₁		Posttest₁	
						Posttest₁					

3-months delay
Posttest₂

Thus, in Experiment I, with a unidirectional influence attempt, no damping of the posttest by the pretest was found. In Experiment II, with a hidden pretest and bidirectional persuasion, there was no damping effect of pretest on posttest, but there was a damping effect when the pretest was exposed. In Experiment III with bidirectional persuasion and no pretest, there was no damping effect (estimated); with an exposed pretest, there was a damping effect. For procedural details and analysis of primacy-recency effects the original publications should be examined.

Experiment IV—Current Study

The primary hypothesis is that a pretest will dampen the effect of bidirectional persuasion. A second hypothesis was also tested in this study. Previous research has shown that a subject familiar with the topic of a communication is more likely to change his opinion in the direction of the first presented of two opposed arguments (primacy effect) when that topic is concerned with some social issue. As stated above, it also seems that a primacy effect is prevalent in cases where the subject is not pretested. In combining these two conditions, high familiarity and no pretest, a pronounced primacy effect should occur.

One-hundred subjects in the introductory psychology classes at Alfred University were randomly assigned to one of eight experimental groups. All subjects were asked to answer two questions on a sheet of paper. They were: "If you know what the word, 'vivisection' refers to, describe it in one of two sentences," and "Also describe, in one or two sentences, any recent events that you know of concerning vivisection." Only about ten percent of all subjects knew to what vivisection referred. This group, and randomly chosen subjects from the unfamiliar students, were designated the "familiar group." The remainder of the subjects were designated the "unfamiliar group." Just prior to pretesting, and again just prior to posttesting, the familiar group was read a 213 word passage describing vivisection. The information presented was factual and did not represent any attitudinal point of view. Thus the familiar group, some of the members of which already possessed some knowledge of the topic, was exposed to information about the nature of vivisection. The familiar and unfamiliar groups were randomly divided, half receiving a questionnaire tapping opinions for or against the practice of vivisection. These groups were again randomly subdivided into groups receiving a pro-vivisection communication followed by a con-vivisection communication, or the con-communication and then the pro-communication. The scores on the pretest for the four groups were analyzed for differences by a one-way analysis of variance to determine whether the groups could reasonably be assumed to be homogeneous with respect to initial opinion on vivisection. The F ratio was less than one. It is concluded that the groups were homogeneous on initial opinion. It is assumed that the four remaining groups not pretested are homogeneous with the four pretested groups since they were formed randomly from the same sample as the pretested groups. In a single study such as this one, assumptions of this nature might seem tenuous. However, in other studies (Lana, 1959, 1964b) there seemed to be reasonable assurance that one could assume that unpretested groups had similar initial opinions as pretested groups. Random allocation assured homogeneity of opinion for the variously formed experimental groups over the long run. In any case, random allocation is one of the few techniques available at this time which is useful in creating the conditions necessary for making a test of the current hypothesis. One alternative to administering a pretest, and being reasonably certain of the opinion of the group on some topic, is to use groups which have been formed because of their stand on the very topic in question. Other difficulties, however, arise with this technique (Lana, 1964b).

All groups were then posttested with the identical questionnaire used as the pretest. The design is presented in Table 2.

Materials

A Likert-type, 19-item, 6-alternative questionnaire (Molnar, 1955) was utilized as both the pretest and posttest. It has been used in two previous studies by Lana (1959, 1961). High score indicates pro-vivisection opinion. The range of possible scores is 6 to 60. The pro and con communications on vivisection are about 500 words long and take about five minutes to read. They were developed by Molnar (1955) and have succeeded in changing the opinions of college students toward vivisection in other similar studies (Lana, 1959, 1961; Molnar, 1955).

Vivisection was chosen as the topic since it is generally not considered particularly controversial (Lana 1962) by most college students. Also, from the results of the initial questions asked, many students have no idea as to what the term refers. This makes it easy to familiarize the appropriate groups with the topic by providing vivisection information to them, thus increasing the probability that the familiar and unfamiliar conditions have been established in the experimental groups. Zero control groups (no communication) were not included in the design because in all similar instances (Lana, 1959, 1964b) no pretest-posttest changes were evident.

Results

The results of the experiment were analyzed by the use of the t-test for significance of average absolute differences between pre and posttest and the subtractive-difference technique, which is useful for detecting directional effects in opinion change. The groups not pretested were assigned mean pretest values based on the average of the scores of the pretested subjects. The average absolute opinion change score per unpretested group was 2.18 scale points regardless of direction (pro or con). Average absolute opinion change in the pretested groups was .95 scale points. The difference between the two groups is significant beyond the .01 level. The unpretested groups shifted 28 percent of the total distance it was possible for them to change on the opinion questionnaire continuum. The pretested groups shifted 12 percent of the maximum amount that it was possible to change.

Significant (.01) recency effects were evident in the familiar groups, and no significant directional effects of any kind resulted in the unfamiliar groups. There were no differences in significant primacy-recency effects between the pretested and unpretested groups. The results are summarized in Table 2.

TABLE 2

Experimental Design and Summary of Primacy—Recency Results

	2 Questions on Vivisection—3 Days						
	FAMILIAR INFORMATION ON VIVISECTION				UNFAMILIAR NO INFORMATION ON VIVISECTION		
NO PRETEST		PRETEST		NO PRETEST		PRETEST	
			12 DAYS				
PRO CON	CON PRO	PRO CON	CON PRO	PRO CON	CON PRO	PRO CON	CON PRO
INFORMATION ON VIVISECTION				NO INFORMATION ON VIVISECTION			
			Posttest				
(EST.)	(EST.)			(EST.)	(EST.)		
PRE 37.43	37.43	37.00	35.71	37.43	37.43	39.92	37.36
POST 36.18	39.29	36.45	38.07	40.00	40.45	39.33	37.07
GAIN −1.25	+1.86	−.55	+2.36	+2.57	+3.02	−.59	−.29
DIFF. OF DIFFERENCES −3.11		−2.91		−.45		−.30	
(recency)		(recency)		(recency)		(recency)	
n 11	14	11	14	13	11	12	14
t **3.99		**4.04		<1		<1	

** p < .01

Discussion

The results indicate that the first hypothesis has been supported. Opinion change was significantly greater under conditions where no pretest was utilized than under conditions of pretesting. Unpretested, disguised pretest, and pretest groups (Lana, 1964b; Lana and Rosnow, 1963), and groups in preliminary experiments to the current study, were examined for differential amounts of opinion change. In all cases the no-pretest and disguised pretest groups changed to a greater degree than the pretested groups. This represents observations on 520 subjects. There seems to be some support for the contention that the pretest can act as a device by which the individual commits himself to maintain his opinion in the face of opposed (bidirectional) arguments presented later. Presumably, a single, unidirectional communication allows for greater change regardless of initial pretest conditions because, if the individual is initially in favor of the position advocated by the communication his initial commitment is supported. If about half of all subjects are in favor of a given argument (assuming a normal distribution of pretest scores concerning the issue at hand, an assumption which holds true for this study) this half need not consider their initial commitment. On the other hand, when two opposed arguments are presented, there will always be one position confronting every subject which is essentially opposed to his own initial commitment. Thus, his commitment via pretest may influence his reaction to material presented later in the experiment, and this will be true for all subjects.

The pretest seems most effective in minimizing opinion change when the subject is later confronted with two opposed arguments on the topic in question rather than when he is later presented with a single, unidirectional argument. Conceivably one may speculate that the more complex and multi-sided the communicative materials, the greater the inhibitory effect of the pretest. Also it may be possible that the length, complexity and obviousness of the intent of the pretest might produce less opinion change after a communication than when a pretest is relatively simple, short and disguised.

The secondary hypothesis of the study, that the combined effects of familiarity of the subject with the topic, and the lack of a pretest, will produce a strong primacy effect was rejected. Precisely the opposite occurred. A strong recency effect was evident for the high familiar groups and no significant order effect of any kind resulted in the groups who were relatively unfamiliar with the topic. Recency effects were predicted for these latter groups. There were no differences in order effects between the pretested and the unpretested groups. In previous studies, primacy had been produced by high familiarity of the subjects with the topic and when the pretest was hidden or absent. This reversal of the predicted effects for the familiar group is surprising and no ex-post-facto interpretation of these results is entirely satisfactory. However, certain contingencies may be forwarded as possible sources of explanation.

The topic of vivisection has characteristically been rated as one of low controversy by college students. It has been shown (Lana, 1963a; 1964a) that topics of low controversy tend to produce no significant primacy-recency effects. This might have mitigated against the appearance of primacy throughout all the groups of the study. It is also obvious that the familiarity of the subjects was more important in producing order effects than the fact of having been, pretested or not. In the current experiment, unlike previous studies on familiarity (Lana, 1961; Rosnow and Lana, 1965), the familiarization talk was presented twice, once before the pretest and again before the communications. This, and the questions used to measure existing familiarity in the subjects towards vivisection, probably provide a better assurance of familiarity for the subjects of this study than for those of previous studies. Even with these differences in methodology between the present study and the others, there is no convincing reason why recency should have dominated under conditions of familiarity.

Summary and Conclusions

One-hundred subjects were exposed to various experimental conditions where familiarity-unfamiliarity and pretesting-no pretesting were manipulated to examine their influence on magnitude of, and order effects in, opinion change. The following conclusions were made:

1. The taking of a pretest in the form of an opinion questionnaire inhibits opinion change regardless of the direction of change (primacy-recency) that may be strongest when opposed arguments are utilized.
2. Familiarity of the subjects with the topic of the influence attempt does not necessarily result in a significant primacy effect as predicted.

Theoretical interpretations of primacy-recency opinion change and, perhaps, measurement methodology, need to be revised and sensitized to establish consistent, successful predictions of these effects.

REFERENCES

Cochran, W. G. and Cox, G. M. Experimental Design (2nd ed.). New York: Wiley, 1957.

Entwisle, D. R. "Interactive Effects of Pretesting." EDUCATIONAL AND PSYCHOLOGICAL MEASUREMENT, XXI (1961), 607–620.

Hovland, C. I. and Mandell, W. "Is There a 'Law of Primacy' in Persuasion." In C. I. Hovland, et al, The Order of Presentation in Persuasion. New Haven: Yale University Press, 1957.

Lana, R. E. "Pretest-Treatment Interaction Effects in Attitudinal Studies." Psychological Bulletin, LVI (1959), 293–300.

Lana, R. E. "Familiarity and the Order of Presentation of Persuasive Communications." *Journal of Abnormal and Social Psychology*, LXII (1961), 573–577.

Lana, R. E. "Order Effects in Persuasive Communications." Progress Report to the National Institute of Mental Health, United States Public Health Service, Research Grant M4830, May 1962.

Lana, R. E. "Controversy of the Topic and the Order of Presentation in Persuasive Communications." *Psychological Reports*, XII (1963), 163–170. (a)

Lana, R. E. "Interest, Media, and the Order Effects in Persuasive Communications." *Journal of Psychology*, LVI (1963), 9–13. (b)

Lana, R. E. "Three Theoretical Interpretations of Order Effects in Persuasive Communications." *Psychological Bulletin*, LXI (1964), 314–320. (a)

Lana, R. E. "The Influence of the Pretest on Order Effects in Persuasive Communications." *Journal of Abnormal and Social Psychology*, LXIX (1964), 337–341. (b)

Lana, R. E. "Order Effects in Persuasive Communications." Progress Report to the National Institute of Mental Health, United States Public Health Service, Research Grant MH 06926, May 1964. (c)

Lana, R. E. and Rosnow, R. L. "Subject Awareness and Order Effects in Persuasive Communications." *Psychological Reports*, XII (1963), 523–529.

Molnar, A. "The Effects of Styles, Speeches, and Arguments on the Attitudes and Perceptions of a Listening Audience." Unpublished master's thesis, University of Maryland, 1955.

Rosnow, R. L. and Lana, R. E. "Complementary and Competing Order Effects in Opinion Change." *Journal of Social Psychology*, LXVI (1965), 201–207.

Solomon, R. L. "An Extension of Control Group Design." *Psychological Bulletin*, XLVI (1949), 137–150.

Reprinted from Public Opinion Quarterly, 1965, Vol. 29, pp. 595–601, by permission of
Anthony G. Greenwald and the publisher.

EFFECTS OF PRIOR COMMITMENT
ON BEHAVIOR CHANGE AFTER
A PERSUASIVE COMMUNICATION*

BY ANTHONY G. GREENWALD

WHEN a smoker becomes convinced that smoking is dangerous, will he then cut down on his cigarette habit? When a neurotic achieves some understanding of his adjustment problems, will his behavioral symptoms begin to fade? More generally, when some force brings about a change in belief, will behavior relevant to the belief also change? Although psychologists have devoted much effort to studying both change of verbal beliefs and change of nonverbal behavior, relatively little attention has been given to this question about the relationship between belief change and behavior change.[1]

Festinger has recently interpreted the existing evidence as indicating that behavior change does not necessarily accompany the change of relevant beliefs.[2] More recently, however, in the author's own re-

* The study reported here was supported in part by funds from the United States Public Health Service (grant #1-TI-MH-8260-02). The author is indebted to Albert E. Myers and Lawrence J. Stricker for critical readings of an earlier drift.

[1] It should be pointed out that only a limited subset of beliefs—those about the desirability of performing some action—has a direct bearing on behavior. Because of its bearing on behavior, however, this subset is an extremely important one and includes, for instance, beliefs about the desirability of voting for a particular candidate, of going to college, of getting married, of going to war for one's country, etc.

[2] L. Festinger, "Behavioral Support for Opinion Change," *Public Opinion Quarterly,* Vol. 28, 1964, pp. 404-417.

search,[3] a communication to junior high school children advocating the importance of vocabulary learning did influence both belief (rated importance of vocabulary learning) and relevant action (learning vocabulary by doing difficult vocabulary problems). A further experiment with junior high school children suggested a possible explanation for some failures to obtain behavior change following belief change.[4] In that experiment, the subjects were required to state a preference for or against vocabulary learning prior to receiving the pro-vocabulary communication. It was found that subjects who were initially anti-vocabulary showed a temporary belief change following the communication, but *no* behavior change, while subjects who initially favored vocabulary reacted to the communication with both greater belief change and substantial behavior change. It appeared, then, that a prior commitment opposing an influence attempt could produce the pattern of belief change without behavior change. The present experiment was an attempt to reproduce this finding under conditions more specifically designed to determine the importance of the prior commitment.

METHOD

Subjects. Four eighth-grade classes in a Trenton, N. J., junior high school participated in the experiment.[5] Two classes were assigned to the Commitment condition and two to the No Commitment condition in such fashion as to match these two conditions in terms of subjects' mean I.Q. The experimenter met with each of the classes for two testing sessions, separated by nine days. Results will be given only for those subjects present at both sessions.

Procedure. The experimental procedure was, in large part, similar to that used and described in detail in the author's previous work.[6] Only the major procedural features of the present experiment will be described here.

Belief and behavior relevant to vocabulary learning were assessed at a few points during the experiment. In each case, belief scores were obtained by asking the subjects to rank eight areas of learning (including history and vocabulary) in order of importance. The belief score was the extent to which vocabulary was ranked as more important than history. This score could range, then, from $+7$, when vo-

---

[3] A. G. Greenwald, "Behavior Change Following a Persuasive Communication," *Journal of Personality*, Vol. 33, 1965, pp. 370-391.

[4] Also described in *ibid.*

[5] The author is indebted to Reynold Strunk, principal of Junior High School Four in Trenton, and to Sarah C. Christie, Assistant Superintendent of Schools in Trenton, for their generous cooperation in making arrangements for the experiment.

[6] Greenwald, *op. cit.*

cabulary was ranked first and history eighth, to —7, with history first and vocabulary eighth. To obtain behavior scores, subjects were given a series of seven choices between doing a difficult problem from which they could learn something about history and doing one from which they could learn some vocabulary. (The problems were presented as learning opportunities, with answers provided, and *not* as a test.) The behavior score was the number, ranging from 0 to 7, of vocabulary problems chosen and done.

In the No Commitment condition, session I consisted of administration of pre-test belief and behavior measures; reading of a communication (attributed to a group of college professors) strongly advocating the importance of vocabulary learning; and administration of behavior and belief post-tests—all of this taking about half an hour for each class. Nine days later, the experimenter returned to each of the classes for session II, in which delayed behavior and belief post-tests were administered.

In the Commitment condition, the procedure was identical to that for the No Commitment condition, with one exception: the Commitment subjects were not pre-tested. Instead, they were asked to state in writing—and prior to hearing the communication—a preference for learning about either history or vocabulary. In addition to naming his preferred topic, each subject was asked to write three or four brief reasons for his choice and then to work quickly through ten practice problems—five of each type.

In summary, the design called for one group of subjects to commit themselves to an initial preference for or against vocabulary, while a second group expressed belief in the importance of vocabulary and behavioral preference for vocabulary in a fashion that avoided commitment. It was predicted that the Commitment condition subjects who were initially against vocabulary would be influenced by the communication to increase their belief in the importance of vocabulary learning but would, despite this influence, not alter their vocabulary-learning behavior correspondingly. Pre-test belief and behavior levels for the anti-vocabulary subjects in the Commitment condition (who, it will be recalled, were not pre-tested) were estimated in order to test this prediction from scores of initially anti-vocabulary subjects in the No Commitment condition (who were pre-tested). For this purpose, No Commitment subjects were designated "anti-vocabulary" if they had both (1) ranked history as more important than vocabulary on the belief pre-test and (2) selected a history problem as their first choice on the behavior pre-test. The remaining No Commitment subjects were considered to be "pro-vocabulary." This method of selecting "control" subsamples was used because it yielded a proprotion of anti-vocabulary subjects in the No Commitment condition (46 per cent) that best approximated the proportion of anti-vocabulary subjects in the Commitment condition (37 per cent). Alternative procedures were possible and will be discussed below.

RESULTS

The results are summarized in the accompanying table. Column 4 shows that the predicted results were obtained; that is, the beliefs of the anti-vocabulary Commitment subjects were affected by the communication while their behavior was not. The upper half of column 4 shows that for belief both the post-test and delayed post-test were significantly higher than the estimated pre-test level, while the lower half of the column shows that there was no significant behavior change on either of the post-tests. From these data, it may be concluded (as predicted) that subjects who, before receipt of a communication, commit themselves to a position opposing it show effects of the communication on belief but not on behavior.

An incidental finding of the experiment stems from the fact that both the lowest and highest post-test scores occurred in the subsamples of the Commitment condition, while the No Commitment condition subsamples were intermediate; that is, prior commitment against the communication increased resistance to both belief and behavior change, while prior commitment in favor of the communication increased susceptibility to both types of change.[7] The significance levels of these differences are shown in columns 3 and 6 of the table. Another way of describing this finding would be to say that the elicitation of a commitment had the effect of polarizing subjects in the Commitment condition in the direction of their initial preference.[8]

DISCUSSION

Control subsample selection procedure. Some attention should be given to the procedure used to select the pro- and anti-vocabulary "control" subsamples from the No Commitment condition, since it is on the basis of the pre-test data from these subsamples that conclusions have been made about the effects of both the commitment and the communication. Note that the pre-test belief and behavior data for the

---

[7] Caution is necessary in regard to the latter part of this conclusion, since the pro-vocabulary Commitment subjects may have undergone some self-persuasion in addition to the communication persuasion. That is, their high post-test scores may reflect the effects of their own arguments in favor of vocabulary learning in addition to the effects of the communication's arguments.

[8] Cf. D. O. Sears, J. L. Freedman, and E. F. O'Connor, Jr., "The Effects of Anticipated Debate and Commitment on the Polarization of Audience Opinion," *Public Opinion Quarterly,* Vol. 28, 1964, pp. 615-627.

MEAN BELIEF AND BEHAVIOR SCORES FOR PRO- AND ANTI-VOCABULARY
SUBJECTS IN COMMITMENT AND NO COMMITMENT CONDITIONS

	Pro-vocabulary Subjects			Anti-vocabulary Subjects		
	Commitment $(N=27)$ (1)	No Commitment $(N=26)$ (2)	t (3)	Commitment $(N=16)$ (4)	No Commitment $(N=22)$ (5)	t (6)
Belief scores:						
A. Pre-test	$(-.42)$*	$-.42$		(-3.00)*	-3.00	
B. Post-test	$+2.59$	$+1.38$	2.29ᵃ	-1.63	$+.05$	2.24ᵃ
C. Delayed post-test	$+2.04$	$+1.46$	1.18	-1.69	$+.77$	3.23ᵇ
t(B-A)†	4.39ᶜ	2.94ᵇ		2.62ᵃ	6.65ᶜ	
t(C-A)†	3.74ᶜ	3.50ᵇ		2.25ᵃ	7.29ᶜ	
Behavior scores:						
D. Pre-test	(3.46)*	3.46		(2.00)*	2.00	
E. Post-test	4.37	3.65	2.03ᵃ	2.31	3.36	2.19ᵃ
F. Delayed post-test	4.81	3.38	3.42ᵇ	2.38	2.86	0.85
t(E-D)†	2.60ᵃ	0.60		0.76	3.53ᵇ	
t(F-D)†	3.32ᵇ	-0.32		0.72	2.66ᵃ	

* These are the mean pre-test scores for the corresponding subsample of the No Commitment condition. They were used to calculate the amount and significance of change in the Commitment condition subsamples.

† In the Commitment subsamples, t's are for differences between independent means; in the No Commitment subsamples, t's are for differences between correlated means. The different tests were necessitated by the fact that only subjects in the No Commitment condition had been pretested.

ᵃ $p < .05$.   ᵇ $p < .01$.   ᶜ $p < .001$, two-tailed.

pro-vocabulary No Commitment subjects are a bit puzzling, in that they indicate approximate neutrality between history and vocabulary rather than favorableness to vocabulary. Possibly, the findings mentioned above would not have resulted with other subsample selection procedures. It would have been possible, for example, to select subsamples on the basis of either belief pre-test data alone or behavior pre-test data alone instead of the combination of the two types of data that was used. These alternative subsamples were not presented, since they had two undesirable features: (1) A pro-vocabulary sample selected on the basis of the belief pre-test alone was not pro-vocabulary on the behavior pre-test, and vice versa. (2) Also, the proportion of subjects in the pro-vocabulary subsample selected on the basis of either the belief or behavior pre-test alone would have been substantially smaller than the proportion of pro-vocabulary subjects in the Commitment condition. It is reassuring, in any case, to note that when analyses similar to those in the table were done with each of these alternative subsample selecting procedures, the same pattern of results was obtained—namely, belief change but no behavior change in the anti-vocabulary Commitment subsample and more extreme reactions following the communication in the two Commitment subsamples than in the corresponding two No Commitment subsamples.

Implications. Primarily, the theoretical significance of the present findings consists in their offering a means of reconciling previously discrepant findings. It was mentioned earlier that Festinger[9] has cited a variety of evidence indicating that behavior change does not necessarily follow upon the change of relevant beliefs. It may now be suggested that such failures to obtain behavior change, *when belief change has occurred,* can result from a prior commitment opposing the influence attempt. Although the studies cited by Festinger did not explicitly require the subjects to commit themselves in any way, still the behavior changes that were demanded in those studies were definitely in opposition to established behavior patterns of the subjects. Since these established behavior patterns may have been functionally similar to the commitment procedure used in the present study, their failure to change following belief change is no longer problematic.

The present findings also have relevance to previous work in which it was found that commitment to an opinion increases that opinion's resistance to change.[10] It seems proper, now, to extend this relationship between commitment and resistance to change beyond the domain of opinions, attitudes, and beliefs and into the domain of behavior. The findings, in fact, suggest that the inertia (or tendency to resist change) of behavior following commitment is greater than the inertia of belief in the communication situation. It seems quite meaningful—returning now to the questions posed at the start of this paper—to consider the smoking habit that persists despite irrefutable evidence of its harmfulness, and the neurotic symptom that persists in the face of the patient's understanding, as instances of this sort of behavioral inertia.

We must observe, however, that when the change-inducing force is a behavioral incentive rather than a persuasive communication, a different picture may develop. Suppose, for example, that, instead of being exposed to a persuasive communication, the junior high school students in the present study had been offered a penny for each vocabulary problem they chose on the behavior post-test. Under these conditions, we would expect that a rather marked pro-vocabulary trend would be shown on the *behavior* post-test, with no change on the *belief* post-test. Unpublished data collected by the author show exactly

---

[9] *Op. cit.*

[10] E.g. J. W. Brehm and A. R. Cohen, *Explorations in Cognitive Dissonance,* New York, Wiley, 1962.

this pattern of results.[11] Thus, whereas there is behavioral inertia in the opposing-commitment-prior-to-persuasive-communication situation, there is belief inertia in the behavioral-incentive situation.[12]

We are left up in the air as to the nature of the underlying relationship between belief and behavior. It seems clear, at least, that there is no *automatic* relationship between them. The data show that the occurrence of behavior change does not depend upon the prior occurrence of belief change, and vice versa. Our safest hypothesis as to the relationship between belief and behavior is that there is, in fact, no relationship; rather, belief and behavior may be independently determined by the environment. Normally, the environment will have parallel effects on belief and behavior, so that they will appear to be correlated. However, in special situations, such as persuasion following an opposing commitment or the offering of a behavioral incentive, the environment exerts differential pressures on belief and behavior and then they appear to be uncorrelated.

At the moment, it appears that the only simple way to account for these special situations is to imagine (contrary to common sense) that belief and behavior may, indeed, be independent. In order for future research testing this "independence" hypothesis (or alternative hypotheses) to be meaningful, it will be necessary for the researcher to be quite explicit about his use of the term "belief." Ideally, one might like to distinguish "true" (unobservable) belief from "stated" (observable) belief, with the understanding that stated belief is a form of verbal behavior assumed to measure true belief. The reader will quickly appreciate that the assumption that true belief can be measured via the medium of verbal behavior rests upon the supposition that (true) belief and (verbal) behavior are *not* independent of each other! With such a conception of "true" belief, we could not test the "independence" hypothesis without assuming that it was false, nor could we test alternative ("nonindependence") hypotheses without assuming that they were (at least in part) true! It should be clear, then, that in order for future research in this area to be meaningful, it will be necessary to conceive of "belief" as a term designating a delineated set of verbal *behaviors*. The present point of view is that it would be most appropriate to use "belief" to refer specifically to the set of statements about the desirability of performing some action.

[11] A. G. Greenwald, "Value Change and Its Effects on Behavior," Cambridge, Mass., Harvard University, 1963, unpublished Ph.D. dissertation.

[12] Despite appearances, the persuasive-communication and behavioral-incentive situations are not mirror images of each other. The persuasive communication *can* produce some lasting changes in both belief and behavior, while the behavioral incentive seems to produce no lasting changes; in the author's research (*ibid.*), as soon as the behavioral incentive was withdrawn, behavior scores reverted to their original (pre-incentive) levels.

Reprinted from Social Forces, 1965, Vol. 43, pp. 353–364, by permission of Lawrence S.
Linn and University of North Carolina Press.

VERBAL ATTITUDES AND OVERT BEHAVIOR: A STUDY OF RACIAL DISCRIMINATION*

LAWRENCE S. LINN

ABSTRACT

The present study in attempting to measure the relationship between racial attitudes and overt behavior asked *Ss* to pose for a photograph with a Negro of the opposite sex. Discrepancies between verbal attitudes and subsequent overt behavior involving those attitudes was found in 59 percent of the cases. The relationship between attitude (prejudice) and behavior (discrimination) is seen to be a function of the level of social involvement with the attitude object as well as the amount of prior experience with it. One implication of the study is that statements or predictions of racial behavior based on attitude measurements have little reliability unless first validated empirically.

The present study is concerned with the relationship between verbal attitudes as expressed through response items on an attitude questionnaire and subsequent overt behavior.[1] It is incorrect to assume that the response to a verbal question (printed or oral) necessarily reveals an attitude which would become operative in the situation depicted in the question. This study will examine the utility of attitude measurements as a means for predicting future behavior. Since considerable funds are expended on attitude research each year and since such research constitutes a large bulk of the social science enterprise, it is essential to make clear what relevance such data have and what kind of restrictions must be placed on their application. This is not to say that there are no verbal attitudes which correlate highly with behavior. But, if the goal of a research project is to predict behavior on the basis of verbal attitudes, evidence must be cited showing the probability of accurate prediction and the degree of validity in generalizing from an attitude to behavior.[2]

The present study will examine the relationship between expressed racial attitudes and overt behavior, looking at the level of precision and accuracy that can be obtained in predicting behavior from attitude scores based on written verbal responses. It will also be of interest to examine how people will account for discrepancies between their expressed attitudes and their behavior if and when discrepancies exist. But, before turning to a discussion of the empirical findings of

* The author is indebted to David Mechanic for his valuable advice and criticism in the designing and carrying out of this study and to Michael Hakeem, Gerald Marwell, and William H. Sewell for their criticisms of the text. The work reported here was supported by a NIMH training program in social psychology (Grant #2N-7413).

[1] One of the most diversely defined concepts in social psychology is attitude. Not only are there vast differences concerning what properly constitutes an attitude, but there has been developing a large literature debating how attitudes should be measured. Both of these topics have been thoroughly discussed in a recent article by Melvin DeFleur and Frank Westie, "Attitude as a Scientific Concept," *Social Forces*, 42 (October 1963), pp. 17-31, so that a long theoretical analysis of the problems of defining and measuring attitudes will not be dealt with in this paper. This is not to say that they will be ignored; they will be discussed, but relevant only to issues that are raised in this research.

[2] Robert K. Merton has pointed out that it should not be assumed that overt behavior is intrinsically any "more real" than verbal behavior nor should it be considered as more "truthful." Overt actions do not necessarily reflect verbal attitudes and may deliberately conceal or disguise them. In fact, there are times when it may be valuable to know a person's verbal opinion even if it is not directly related to his behavior. . . . See Merton, "Fact and Factitiousness in Ethnic Opinionaires," *American Sociological Review*, 5, (1940).

this study, it would be beneficial to review the studies done in the past on the relationship between attitudes and action, paying particular attention to the following three variables: (1) the *method* of attitude and behavior measurement, (2) the *prevalence* of discrepant behavior between attitude and action, and (3) the *direction* of the discrepant behavior.

The first study which examined the relationship between human behavior and expressed attitudes was the classical study by LaPiere.[3] LaPiere traveled through the United States with a Chinese couple, stopping at many hotels, motels, and restaurants, but they were refused service only once. In a follow-up study, he mailed questionnaires to the proprietors of the establishments visited in order to find out if members of the Chinese race would be accepted as guests. Approximately 93 percent of the restaurants and 92 percent of the sleeping places indicated that they would not accept or accommodate Chinese people. A control group of other restaurants and hotels were also sent questionnaires, and almost identical results were obtained. This study clearly shows a large discrepancy between expressed attitudes and overt behavior but in a *positive* direction. In other words, although the hotel and restaurant owners expressed a verbal policy of discrimination, when confronted face-to-face with the situation, they did not discriminate. However, it must be pointed out that the LaPiere study has certain methodological problems which reduce the validity of the results and which make a comparison of attitudes and action less credible. First, the questionnaire which he used to measure attitudes toward the Chinese dealt with general prejudice indices and was *not* necessarily comparable to the behavioral situation in the study. Secondly, LaPiere's presence with the couple probably had a considerable biasing effect. Much different results would have been obtained had the couple gone across the country alone. Nevertheless, the study, even with its problems, does demonstrate a considerable discrepancy between expressed attitudes and overt behavior.

[3] Richard LaPiere, "Attitude vs. Action," *Social Forces*, 13 (December 1934), pp. 230-37.

A more recent study by Kutner, Wilkins, and Yarrow[4] seems to substantiate LaPiere's findings that attitude scores alone are not sufficient predictors of behavior and that racially discriminatory behavior may be less likely to occur in a face-to-face situation. In their study, two white women and one Negro woman entered 11 restaurants in a fashionable community and were served in a normal manner. Two weeks later, letters were sent to each establishment inquiring about reservations for a social affair. Included in the letter was the sentence, "Since some of them are colored, I wondered whether you would object to their coming?" Seventeen days after the letters were sent out, no replies had been received, and thus telephone calls were made repeating parts of the letters. In eight of the 11 cases, the managers denied receiving the letters. In a control phone call made a day later, no reference to the racial character of the group was made, and all but one restaurant accepted the reservation of the party. Thus, this study, like the LaPiere study, demonstrates a substantial discrepancy between verbal attitudes and subsequent overt behavior involving racial prejudice. Again, it should be noted that the discrepancy is in the *positive* direction, moving from a conservative, prejudicial attitude position to a more liberal behavioral one.

There are further lines of evidence which demonstrate the discrepancy between verbal attitudes and overt behavior. Saenger and Gilbert,[5] when testing the hypothesis that anti-Negro prejudice in white department store customers would not lead to discrimination against Negro sales personnel or the stores employing them, found that there was no tendency in prejudiced individuals to avoid dealing with Negro clerks. Minard,[6] in ex-

[4] Bernard Kutner, Carol Wilkins, and Penny Yarrow. "Verbal Attitudes and Overt Behavior Involving Racial Prejudice," *Journal of Abnormal & Social Psychology*, 47 (1952), pp. 649-52.

[5] Gerhart Saenger, and Emily Gilbert. "Customer Reactions to the Integration of Negro Sales Personnel," *International Journal of Opinion Attitude Research*, 4 (1950), pp. 57-76.

[6] R. D. Minard. "Race Relationships in the Pocahontas Coal Field," *Journal of Social Issues*, 8 (1952), pp. 29-44.

amining the attitudes and behavior of white coal miners toward Negroes within the same mine and outside it, found that racial integration and equality only existed within the work roles of the mine. Outside the job, the two races occupied different status levels in almost every situation. In the Saenger and Gilbert study, the discrepant behavior was again in the positive direction. In the Minard study the direction is less clear, but it appears that the discrepancies in behavior ran in both directions.

Fishman,[7] in his introduction to a study of the Negro's entrance into Bridgeview, a New Jersey suburb near New York City, found a clear discrepancy between expressed attitudes and actual behavior that ran in both the positive and negative directions. He found that many people who, for the most part, had negative attitudes toward the Negro nevertheless remained in an interracial community which was progressively becoming more Negro. Yet, others who had positive attitudes toward Negroes moved away.

DeFleur and Westie[8] have also studied the relationship between attitude and action. After the administration of a prejudice scale to a group of college students, those scoring high and low were recalled as subjects and given a projective test in which each was shown slides of pairs of Negro and white men and women in various social situations. At the end of the projective test session, each *S* was asked to pose with a Negro person of the opposite sex. The *Ss* were then given a standard photographic release agreement which consisted of a graded series of situations in which the photograph might be used. The *S* was asked to sign his name to each release. The relationship between the amount of prejudice expressed on the questionnaire and the level of signed agreement to be photographed with a Negro is shown below.

[7] J. Fishman, "Some Social and Psychological Determinants of Inter-Group Relations in Changing Neighborhoods: An Introduction to the Bridgeview Study," *Social Forces,* 40 (October 1961), pp. 42-51.

[8] Melvin DeFleur, and Frank Westie, "Verbal Attitudes and Overt Acts: An Experiment on the Salience of Attitudes," *American Sociological Review,* 23 (1958), pp. 667-673.

signed level of agreement	prejudiced	non-prejudiced
Below mean	18	9
Above mean	5	14

$$x^2 = 7.264$$
$$p = .01$$

Although DeFleur and Westie found the relationship between attitude and action statistically significant, it was not found to be a linear relationship. Fourteen students, about 30 percent of the sample, showed discrepant behavior. DeFleur and Westie considered these 14 cases to be too many to be attributed to measurement error and therefore suggest that the lack of a linear relationship may be explained by an intervening variable related to social involvement.

Even though the DeFleur and Westie study is methodologically superior to its predecessors, there are still problems of the reliability and validity of attitude measurement. For example, *Ss* in their study were chosen on the basis of high and low prejudice scores on Summated Difference Scales. In this technique the *S* is asked many questions which involve him in a hypothetical relationship with both a Negro and a white of the same occupation. The *Ss* are scored according to the total number of racial discrepancies for each occupational category. This method of attitude assessment actually may not measure the same attitude objects or situational variables involved in the willingness to pose for a picture with a Negro in various social situations. Therefore, in attempting to improve attitude measurement, the present study will use attitude objects (items on the questionnaire) identical to the behavior observed (the signing of photographic releases). Since all the past studies have lacked a reliable or precise attitude measurement that validly could be related to the observed behavior, it is important to see if a linear relationship might exist when direct comparisons between attitude and behavior can be made in a more credible manner. If discrepant behavior continues to exist even after refinements have been made, then, as has been suggested, it might be beneficial to look for intervening variables which would account for the *Ss* discrepancies.

A second improvement built into the design of the present study involves making the experimental situations more credible. This was, in part, accomplished by the fact that the *Ss* did *not* know that they were subjects in a psychological experiment and also by the use of Negro experimentors. The effect of their presence will be discussed later in the paper, but here it might be pointed out that besides making the situation more real, their presence should also serve to intensify the *Ss* attitudes towards Negroes.

A final advantage of the present study is the use of a post-test interview. This interview session will serve as a check on the validity of the behavior-measuring instrument (the photographic releases) and hopefully will give insight into some of the social-psychological aspects of the *Ss* behavior.

Thus, the concern of the present study is to examine the relationship between racial attitudes and overt behavior looking at (1) the level of consistency between the two phenomena, which implies (2) the ability to predict behavior accurately on the basis of attitude scores, and (3) the existence of intervening variables such as peer or family reference groups which would account for any discrepant behavior.

Therefore, the present study will examine and test the following hypothesis:

Individuals with either positive or negative verbal attitudes do not necessarily act in accord with those attitudes in an overt situation, even when the measuring instrument apparently taps the same attitude objects that are involved in the behavior.

A. This implies that attitudes may often be poor indicators of behavior and that their use in this direction must be carefully restricted.

B. The accuracy of an attitude scale as an indicator of behavior can be determined by empirical research and is necessary in determining the validity of the instrument.

METHOD

Subjects. All of the *Ss* in the present study were females enrolled in introductory courses in sociology at the University of Wisconsin. An attitude questionnaire was administered to ten discussion sections and scattered among the total number of questions were 14 items concerning attitudes toward Negroes. The 14 questions were used by the present study to construct the following two attitude scales:

Scale I

1. I would be willing to pose with a Negro of the opposite sex if the picture were to be used in laboratory experiment work where it would be seen only by professional sociologists and psychologists.

2. I would be willing to pose with a Negro of the opposite sex if the picture were to be published in a professional journal and read only by professional sociologists and psychologists.

3. I would be willing to pose with a Negro of the opposite sex if the picture would be shown to a few dozen university students in a laboratory situation.

4. I would be willing to pose with a Negro of the opposite sex if the picture were to be used as part of a projective personality test to be used widely by psychologists and sociologists to measure peoples' attitudes.

5. I would be willing to pose with a Negro of the opposite sex if the picture were to be published in the student newspaper in my own university as part of a campus-wide campaign for racial integration by an organization like the NAACP.

6. I would be willing to pose with a Negro of the opposite sex if the picture were to be published in my hometown newspaper as part of a publicity campaign by an organization like the NAACP for racial integration.

7. I would be willing to pose with a Negro of the opposite sex if the picture were to be used in a brochure of an organization like the NAACP and circulated in a nationwide campaign for racial integration.

Scale II

8. I don't mind going to a racially integrated school, Negroes and whites mixed together.

9. I wouldn't mind living in a neighborhood where there were some Negroes integrated into the community.

10. I wouldn't mind if a Negro lived next door to me in my home community.

11. I wouldn't mind if a Negro family lived in the same building in which I lived.

12. I wouldn't mind attending a party in which there were both Negro and white couples.

13. If I were unattached, I would have no objection to dating a Negro person of the opposite sex.

14. If I were in love, I would have no objections to marrying a Negro of the opposite sex.

Design and procedure. Four weeks after the administration of the attitude questionnaire, it was announced to each of the classes sampled that:

Two student representatives of the Psychological Testing Company, Boston, Mass., will be interviewing students on campus during the next ten days. They are interviewing Wisconsin students who may be interested in helping to develop a new semi-projective personality test. Participation is completely voluntary, and not all of you will be asked to take part at the same time. . . .

The interview session will take about 15 minutes. The names of those who are asked to help construct the test have been given to your teacher along with an appointment sign-up schedule. If your name is on the list, and, if you desire to participate, sign up now or after class for a time that is convenient to you.

The students who were asked to volunteer were all of the 18 and 19 year old girls who had previously responded to the attitude questionnaire. The girls who signed up for interview appointments were told to wait in chairs outside the Psychological Testing Company office until called. The white *E* greeted the *S* and ushered her into the office, introducing himself and *E'* (a light-skinned Negro) as representatives of the Psychological Testing Company. The *S* was seated directly opposite the two *Es*. In the first part of the interview, the *Es* discussed the general plans of the "Test Construction Program." The *Ss* were shown the TAT test as a model for construction and given a short lecture on the construction, purpose, and use of projective personality tests. The second phase of the interview became more specific:

(Dialogue—*E'*, light-skinned Negro) What the company is interested in developing is a set of cards which will be used similarly to the TAT that you have just seen, but with pictures of people of different races who will portray various social situations. The number of people in each picture will vary, but the focus of attention of each one will be on a racially integrated couple,

a Negro and a white. The subject matter of the pictures will be typical social scenes like playing cards or chess, studying together, dancing, or sipping a coke. . . .

(Dialogue—*E*, white). More specifically, we have asked you here today to see if you would be willing to help us with our test construction program and if you would therefore be willing to pose for a photograph with a Negro of the opposite sex of the type that has just been described to you. If you are interested in helping us construct the test, we would like you to indicate the conditions under which you will allow the pictures to be used. This is formally done by the signing of these photographic releases. The signing of a photographic release agreement is standard procedure and is necessary in any situation which a photograph of an individual is used in any professional way. You may sign some of them, all of them, or none of them as you see fit. . . .

If the *S* signed any of the releases, *E'* set up an appointment on a future date for taking the photograph. The *S* was told that the photo appointment would take only 15 minutes and that she should wear neatly-appearing school clothes.

For the final phase of the interview, the *Ss* were asked to talk to a representative of the National Association for the Advancement of Negro Right (NAANR), a dark-skinned Negro (*E"*). After introductions were made, *E"* explained to the *S* what the NAANR was and why they were interested in the photographs, explaining that they would be interested in them for various campaigns and publicity programs for racial integration. The *S* was then asked to sign three more photographic release agreements. The four photographic release agreements which *E'* presented to the *S* were identical to the first four items in Scale I which the *S* had previously completed four weeks ago. The three releases which *E"* presented to the *S* were identical to the remaining three items in Scale I.

The *Ss* who were supposedly to have their pictures taken returned individually several days later for their appointments. They were met by the white *E* at the Pyschological Testing Company office and were asked to come and sit down for a minute so that some details could be ironed out before posing for the pictures. The *S* was seated and asked if she had changed her mind about participating in the program. After answering the question, the *S* was then told that the "construction program" was an experiment, was given some explanation, and finally interviewed about the entire situation. The content of the interview and the results of the information gained from it will be reported in another section of the paper. Also, *Ss* who refused to sign any of the releases were contacted by telephone, told that the "construction program" was an experiment, and asked to return for an interview.

RESULTS AND DISCUSSION

Relationship between Attitude and Action

Degree of relationship. As has been discussed, past studies examining racial attitudes and overt behavior have found varying relationships between the two variables. For example, the studies by LaPiere, Kutner, and others have shown that, when people who have racially prejudiced attitudes are placed in a situation calling for overt action, they fail to behave in a discriminatory fashion. Although the magnitude of the results of these studies was impressive, the methodological problems inherent in each study were so large that a more careful analysis of the problem was necessary. DeFleur and Westie attempted such a study using an experimental laboratory approach in examining the problem. They found that racial attitudes were *positively* related to behavior at the .01 level of confidence. Yet, in spite of the statistical significance, almost one-third of the cases were clear instances of discrepant behavior. The present study devised a means of measuring racial attitudes (Attitude Scale I) in which direct comparison can be made from the attitude scores to the overt behavior observed. An attitude score ranging from 0-7 was compiled for each *S*, showing the degree of willingness to pose for a photograph with a Negro in a social situation. Similarly, a comparable behavior score was compiled for each person, indicating the *signed* level of agreement to pose for a photograph with the Negro. Mean

TABLE 1. THE MEAN AND MEDIAN SCORES FOR THE 34 SUBJECTS ON TWO ATTITUDE SCALES AND A BEHAVIOR SCALE

Scale	Mean	Median	N
Attitude Scale I........	4.9	5.5	34
Behavior Scale..........	2.8	2.5	34
Attitude Scale II........	4.3	5.0	34

and median scores were compiled for both attitude scales (I and II) and the scale of overt behavior. (See Table 1.) Notice that for both attitude scales, the mean and the median are considerably higher than for the behavioral scale, showing a marked difference between attitude and overt behavior. Focusing more closely on discrepant behavior, 59 percent of the total sample (N = 34) was found to have discrepant scores of *two* or more (out of a possible 7), and 65 percent of this group had scores showing *three* or more discrepancies. More significant relationships can be seen in Table 2, where the responses have been divided into three categories for each variable—low (score of 0-2), medium (score of 3-5), and high (score of 6-7) willingness to pose for a photograph with a Negro for the attitude variable and low (score of 0-2), medium (score of 3-5), and high (score of 6-7) level of signed agreement to pose for such a photograph. A chi-square test was run on Table 2, and an *r* correlation was run on the two variables. Neither test showed the variables to be significantly related, thus confirming the hypothesis that individuals with either positive or negative verbal attitudes do not necessarily act in accord with those attitudes in an overt situation even when the measuring instrument apparently taps the same attitude objects involved in the observed behavior.[9]

[9] It should be pointed out that the Chi-square test and *r* correlations are both very sensitive to sample size. The relatively small sample size in the present study probably accounts for the lack of statistical significance. Regardless, the major concern here is to point out that more than 50 percent of the *Ss* of the study showed behavior which was discrepant with their previously expressed attitudes.

TABLE 2. THE RELATIONSHIP BETWEEN THE SCORES ON ATTITUDE SCALE 1, SHOWING THE LEVEL OF WILLING-
NESS TO POSE FOR A PHOTOGRAPH WITH A NEGRO OF THE OPPOSITE SEX AND THE SIGNED LEVEL OF AGREEMENT
TO POSE FOR SUCH A PHOTOGRAPH. ($N = 34$)

	Overt Behavior				
Verbal Attitude	High level of signed agreement (6-7)	Medium level of signed agreement (3-5)	Low level of signed agreement (0-2)	Total	% of N
High level of willingness (6-7).................	7 (41%)	3 (18%)	7 (41%)	17	(50%)
Medium level of willingness (3-5).............	1 (9%)	4 (36%)	6 (55%)	11	(32%)
Low level of willingness (0-2).................	0	1 (17%)	5 (83%)	6	(18%)
Totals..	8 (24%)	8 (24%)	18 (52%)	34	(100%)

$\chi^2 = 7.26$ with 4 degrees of freedom; not significant.

Direction of discrepant behavior. Thus far, the present study has shown that there is no linear relationship between expressed attitudes and overt behavior and that, in fact, 52 percent of the Ss in the sample showed behavior which was inconsistent with previously expressed attitudes. The purpose of this section is to analyze and discuss the direction of these discrepant cases. In Table 2, the marginal totals clearly show that, whereas 50 percent of the respondents verbally expressed a high willingness to pose for a photograph with a Negro, only 24 percent of the respondents showed a high level of signed agreement to pose for such a photograph. By the same token, whereas only 18 percent of the respondents verbally expressed a low willingness to pose with a Negro, 52 percent of the respondents, when confronted with the actual situation, expressed a low level of signed agree. Of the 18 cases showing discrepant behavior in Table 2, 89 percent (16 cases) were discrepant in a "negative" direction. By negative it is meant that more liberal, less prejudiced attitudes were originally expressed, but, when the individual was confronted with the real situation, his behavior became more discriminatory than his attitudes had formerly indicated. Only *two* Ss in the present study deviated from their expressed attitudes in a "positive" direction. How can the negative direction of the discrepant behavior be accounted for in the present study? What factors might be attributed to its cause?

Some of the directional disparity—but certainly not all of it—might be due to more valid, reliable, and precise measurement of variables. Of more importance, however, in the present study is the cultural milieu of the S. That is, the Ss were college students attending a large midwestern university which has a reputation for being politically and racially liberal. Within this climate of university liberalism, it is a social and cultural norm held by most faculty and students to take a liberal position on racial integration. Liberal attitudes toward the Negro are, in most circles, not only criteria for social approval but a sign of intellectual maturity—a sign of a "liberal education." It is therefore not surprising that 50 percent (17) of the Ss expressed highly liberal racial attitudes and 32 percent (11) expressed attitudes that fell within the middle range. In other words, the skewed distribution of attitude scores toward the liberal direction is at least in part due to the students' playing, or attempting to play, their social role of the liberal college student. However, this role of "racial liberalism" with its associated constellation of attitudes is quite contradictory to the way in which most people have been socialized into our society. Contrary to the university atmosphere, most segments of American society and the norms associated with them do *not* see racial integration as being socially acceptable; in fact, integration is probably more often viewed as something either to fear or to avoid on a personal level. The present study therefore suggests that discrepant behavior in a negative direction is partially due to a breakdown of *unstable* attitudes which are part of a social role that has never been

TABLE 3. THE RELATIONSHIP BETWEEN PREJUDICE SCORES ON ATTITUDE SCALE II AND THE LEVEL OF SIGNED AGREEMENT TO POSE FOR A PHOTOGRAPH WITH A NEGRO. ($N = 34$)

Verbal Attitude	Overt Behavior				
	High level of signed agreement (6-7)	Medium level of signed agreement (3-5)	Low level of signed agreement (0-2)	Total	% of N
Low prejudice (5-7)............................	7 (30%)	6 (27%)	10 (43%)	23	(68%)
High prejudice (1-4)...........................	1 (10%)	2 (18%)	8 (72%)	11	(32%)
Totals.......................................	8 (24%)	8 (24%)	18 (52%)	34	(100%)

$\chi^2 = 3.79$ with 2 degrees of freedom; not significant.

behaviorally put to test. Further evidence for and development of this position will be presented later in the paper.

The salient effect of Negro experimenters and its effect on action. Both of the Negroes used in the present study were intelligent and impressive college graduates. However, in spite of their attractiveness, the Ss were very, conscious of their race. For many of them, the experimental situation provided the first actual face-to-face contact with a Negro. This situation became very stressful for some, producing strong feelings of uncertainty. Three of the Ss never kept their appointments to have their pictures taken even though they had signed photographic releases. These three Ss could not be recontacted, and they refused to respond to several telephone messages. Three other girls who signed release agreements refused to have their pictures taken, saying that they had changed their minds and did not want to participate.

It is interesting that on the attitude questionnaire only *two* Ss were not willing to pose for a photograph with a Negro no matter how the picture would be used, but, when confronted with the actual situation, *twelve* Ss refused to sign any of the releases. The act of refusing to sign any of the photographic releases in the presence of a Negro, while at the same time holding more liberal attitudes, appeared to be a confusing and stressful situation for the S. Several girls, at the time they were asked to sign the releases, explained in an almost remorseful tone, "I want to . . . but I can't!"

Of course, the Ss level of involvement with a Negro in the present study is much different than allowing a Negro to take a room in a motel, allowing him to eat in a restaurant, working with him in a coal mine, or buying merchandise from him in a department store. Posing for a photograph with a Negro of the opposite sex, in which the photograph would be used in the situations depicted in the present study, involves an extremely high degree of personal social involvement, much greater than that required in the situations depicted in other studies. In summary, however, it can be said that the use of Negro experimenters in the present study seems to have served its purpose. It heightened the Ss attitudes toward the Negro in general and made the situation more credible and immediate.

Attitudes as predictors of behavior. This final section discussing the relationship between attitude and action will examine the reliability and validity of the racial attitude as a predictor of behavior as found in the present study. Again looking at Table 2, which shows the relationship between scores from Attitude Scale I and the subsequently observed overt behavior, it can be said that imprecise and unreliable prediction occurs only for Ss who hold more liberal attitudes (high and medium willingness to pose). For those Ss who expressed prejudiced attitudes (low willingness to pose), their behavior in all but one case was consistent. The same trend was found when Attitude Scale II was used as a predictor of overt behavior. As shown in Table 3, a total of 70 percent of the predictions made for Ss with *low* prejudice attitudes were inaccurate. However, for *Ss* with *high* prejudice attitudes, 72 percent behaved consistently with their attitudes, making prediction of behavior for this group reasonably accurate.

Therefore, it is apparent from the findings shown in Tables 2 and 3 that *Ss* with racial prejudiced attitudes can be expected to behave in accord with those attitudes; prediction of overt behavior for *Ss* with liberal racial attitudes can be made no better than by chance; and, finally, that *Ss* who exhibit racially discriminatory behavior may actually hold to liberal attitudes as often as not.

Post-Test Interview

There were two major functions which the post-test interview session was to serve in the present study: (1) as a validity-check on the measurement of behavior and (2) as a means of gaining insight into the *Ss* perceptions and feelings about the experimental situation.

Validity check. In the present study, appearance or non-appearance for the "picture taking" session was a means of checking the precision, reliability, and validity of the photographic release agreement as a measure of behavior. That is, it is possible that, even though a *S* has signed an agreement to have her photograph released, she may refuse to have her picture taken (not keeping her appointment) or she may change her mind on how the pictures are to be used. Thus, one of the reasons for having *Ss* return for a picture posing session rather than ending the experiment immediately after signing the releases was to correct for measurement error. In fact, it was found that corrections had to be made for six cases, 18 percent of the total sample. Of these six cases, three never showed up for their appointments or responded to any subsequent phone messages. The other three changed their minds about participating.

A second means for checking the validity of the study was to ask the *Ss* if they had any knowledge that they were participating in a psychological experiment, and secondly, if the experimental situation seemed credible. Of the 29 *Ss* interviewed, only one thought that the present study was an experiment. *All 29 Ss felt that the situation was credible.*

Persuasion, salience, and the effect of Negro experimenters. One of the goals of the research design was to make the situation as credible and realistic as possible without persuading or forcing the *Ss* into behavior which was against their wishes. As has already been pointed out, all *Ss* indicated that the situation was credible, but the question still remains, had they been persuaded into making a decision to sign (or not sign) the photographic releases? Out of the 29 *Ss* interviewed, only four indicated that they had felt persuaded and not in full control over the decision to sign or not to sign the release agreements.

Yet, although most of the *Ss* did not feel that they had been persuaded, it was interesting that 38 percent of the sample (11 cases) felt that the presence of a Negro had "bothered" them. Some students indicated that the presence of the Negro had an effect on their action; others found his presence made the decision to sign the releases more "uncomfortable." For example:

I didn't know if I should sign or not. I really couldn't visualize the consequences. Yes, I was aware of the fact that there was a Negro present. I couldn't look at him but only at you (white *E*) when I told you I wouldn't sign the releases. It was really a very embarrassing type of situation. What could he (the Negro *E*) be thinking of me?

I felt a little pressured. The presence of a Negro made it a little uncomfortable. If I didn't sign, it made me not look like a good American. I thought the pictures were too much like dating, and I don't like that. I really felt guilty for not doing my part.

You *want* to say yes, but because he is a Negro there are strong social pressures. It was like I was discriminating against him to his face.

The majority (62 percent) of the *Ss* reported that they were not bothered or influenced in a negative way. In fact, some *Ss* commented that the presence of a Negro made the situation more real. For example:

The presence of a Negro really had no effect in my signing the releases, but he made the situation seem more important, just his being there. The

Negro being right there showed that he felt it was important and thus you wanted to help him.

Discrepant behavior: how the Ss explain it. As has been pointed out earlier, 59 percent of the sample were found to have two or more discrepant responses between their verbal attitudes and overt behavior. In the process of interviewing, these *Ss* were confronted with their differing attitudes and action scores and asked, "How would you account for your discrepant behavior?" Most of the responses could be classified into a single category. Essentially, this group of *Ss* saw the signing of the photographic releases as being a different, more "real" situation than answering questions on a questionnaire. Yet, the questionnaire response was also seen as representing "what I *should* or *would like* to do" and the signing of releases as being "what I *could* or *had to* do." For example:

I don't really know how I feel until I'm actually confronted with the situation. You *think* you should act one way, but you're not sure and probably won't.

In the questionnaire I wasn't faced with the real thing. It (the signing of the releases) *should* be done, but I can't. Those were my desires, but I couldn't do them. I had to think of my parents and of my hometown.

When it comes down to it, I guess I back down. I hadn't given another thought to the questionnaire, but the face-to-face situation made me back down. It was nice to think I'd be willing!

At that time (time of the questionnaire) I was thinking of what I *should* do, but when confronted with the situation, I thought more deeply about participating. I was worried about other people and what they would think. I was not worried for myself.

On the questionnaire it seemed all right but when it came to the *real* thing, it seemed "scary." It wouldn't have been so bad for a large group picture. Did anybody else do what I did?

Discrepant behavior: an analysis and its relationship to reference group theory. De-Fleur and Westie in trying to explain the lack of a straight-line relationship between attitudes and action suggest that a conscious consideration of reference groups intervenes and is responsible for making the decision to act

or not to act consistently with one's attitudes. They therefore conclude that the decision to pose or not to pose for a photograph with a Negro was a peer-directed one. The present study recognizes the importance of reference groups in the decision-making process but believes that they are more inclusive than peers alone and furthermore should be seen as antecedent rather intervening variables. In other words, reference groups influence the individual by being part of his normative system which reflects the attitudes and norms of the society in which he lives, as well as his community, family, friends, and school. Prejudice and discrimination are the products of learning the customs, beliefs, values, and norms of these various social groups and institutions. Thus, the group, whether community, family, or friendship, becomes the agent of attitude formation for the individual through the processes of interaction, identification, or association. The forces which account for an individual's behavior are far greater than just his immediate referents. In fact, quite often people will behave in ways contrary to their peers. Therefore, prejudice and discrimination as conceived by the present study are products of experience and learning which have occurred throughout one's lifetime. Several sociologists have described the process as follows:

Prejudices are generally acquired slowly and over a period of time. The child acquires his ethnic and racial attitudes as he learns other social lessons, from adults, from his peers, and from his life experiences. . . .[10]

Few parents actually teach their children to be prejudiced; however, their own attitudes and behavior, their restrictions on the playmates of their children, and the tendency to stereotype all individuals of a given racial or religious group with certain physical, behavioral, and mental characteristics results in a pattern of prejudice which their children imitate. It is not the parents' attitudes alone, but the whole home influence that is responsible for the development of prejudice.[11]

[10] M. Vosk, "Correlates of Prejudice," *Review of Educational Research*, 23 (1953), pp. 353-361.

[11] Elizabeth Hurlock, *Child Development* (3d ed.; New York: McGraw-Hill Book Co., 1956), p. 290.

Thus, for the most part, the values and norms of the general society do *not* foster the nature and degree of integration as depicted in the present study. These values, which often characterize the Negro as being dirty, dangerous, and dumb, may be learned, overtly or covertly within the context of the family, the community or the school. These values of racial prejudice and the associated norms of segregation and discrimination are part of what is taught and what is learned in our society.

On the other hand, within the university community there exists a "subculture" in which the prevailing values and norms appear to be quite opposite of those of the general society. As has already been mentioned, in this "subculture" it is the social norm to take a liberal position on racial integration. Figure 1 shows this skewed distribution of attitude

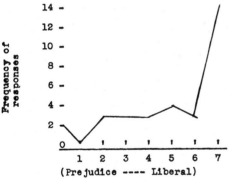

FIG. 1. FREQUENCY OF RESPONSES TO
ATTITUDE SCALE [1]

scores toward the liberal direction, quite contrary to what might be expected from society in general.

Thus far, two antecedent variables have been introduced which are thought to explain the lack of a straight-line relationship between verbal attitudes and overt actions: (1) that racial prejudice and/or racial discrimination have been either overtly or covertly the prevailing norm in the general society and (2) that the social norm in the "university subculture" is one advocating racial liberalism, a norm which conflicts with the norms of the general society. But a third and most

crucial variable which must be added in order to account for the behavior in the present study as well as in the past ones is the concept of social involvement. The level of social involvement is determined by the amount of interaction with the attitude object, the degree of visibility of this interaction, who views it, and what consequences, positive or negative, might arise.

Hopefully, by relating these three variables together, it will be possible to arrive at one possible explanation for discrepant behavior in both a positive and negative direction.

The *Ss* in the present study as well as in the DeFleur and Westie study were young college girls who had only recently been exposed to the norms and values of the liberal university subculture. As has been shown, a large number of them, when asked to indicate their attitudes toward Negroes in a questionnaire, had already begun to play their university social role as a racial liberal. The questions asked the *Ss* if they would be willing to pose for a photograph with a Negro of the opposite sex which would be used in situations with varying degrees of visibility, seen by various kinds of audiences, and having different kinds of potential consequences. Posing for a picture with a Negro which eventually will be published is a situation with a high degree of social involvement, especially when compared with the situations depicted in other studies, such as serving a Negro in northern restaurants or working with Negroes in a coal mine.

However, for many of the *Ss*, the role of a racial liberal had been discussed or thought about only on a symbolic or hypothetical level and had rarely, if ever, been put to empirical test. Most of the *Ss* had no chance to test their attitudes with overt action in real situations. Thus, they had no way of reinforcing, modifying, or possibly even rejecting the validity or stability of their attitudinal position. The present study provided a very clear opportunity for *Ss* with racially liberal attitudes to act overtly in the direction of their convictions, but it was interesting, yet not unusual, to find that a large number of girls were unable to act in this way. The explanation offered by the present study suggests that the *Ss* were confronted with two sets of conflicting roles; that the overt behavior which resulted (various degrees of discrimination) was due to the stronger role, the more stable and comfortable role, the more imprinted, tested, and experienced role · becoming operative and dominant over the weaker one. But, this process of the "differential association" between two opposing sets of norms and associated roles was dependent upon the required level of social involvement with the attitude object. Therefore, the following hypothetical statement can be made in explaining when and why discrepant behavior occurs: The level of consistency between racial attitudes and racial behavior is a function of the stability of the attitude position and of the degree of social involvement required between the individual and the attitude object. Therefore, the following types of propositions can be made:

1. Discrepant behavior in a negative direction (racially liberal attitudes which are inconsistent with subsequent discriminatory behavior) will increase if the liberal attitudes represent an *un*stable position (the lacking of actual experience and reality-testing) and if the level of social involvement with the attitude object is high.

2. Discrepant behavior in a positive direction (racially prejudiced attitudes which are inconsistent with subsequent behavior which is non-discriminatory) will increase if the level of social involvement is low and if the prejudiced attitudes have not been overtly tested. Both of these propositions assume that the measurements of attitude and behavior can be validly compared.

Author Index

Numbers in parentheses are reference numbers and are included to assist in locating references in which authors' names are not mentioned in the text. Numbers in *italics* refer to pages on which the complete references are listed.

AUTHOR INDEX

Campbell, E. H., *xviii, 101,* 117, 124, *125,* 260, *294*
Cannell, C., 361, *367*
Cantril, H., 265, *294*
Carlsmith, J. M., 29, *50, 304,* 320, 321, *331,* 333, 334, 338, 339, *345, 407, 414*
Carlson, E. R., 262, *294,* 319, *330, 405*
Carment, D. W., *198*
Carter, R. F., *374*
Cartwright, D., *191, 299*
Carver, M. E., *372*
Casey, R. D., *xvii*
Cervin, V. B., *198*
Chapanis, A., *300, 305, 330*
Chapanis, N. P., *300, 305, 330*
Charters, W. W., 263, *294*
Chave, E. J., *402*
Chen, W. K. C., 419, *427*
Cherrington, B. M., *372,* 419, *427*
Child, I. L., 240, *244*
Choo, T., 25, *407*
Chu, G. C., *150*
Citron, A. F., 266, *294*
Clausen, J. A., *69*
Clemens, T. L., *375*
Clore, G. L., Jr., *53*
Cochran, W. G., 476, *485*
Cofer, C. N., *297*
Cohen, A. R., *xviii,* 26, *101, 102,* 117, 124, *125,* 169, 186, *191,* 195 (1), *196, 199,* 226, 241, *244,* 260, 261, 284, *294, 297, 300, 301, 305, 306,* 319, 320, 327, *330,* 334, 336, 337, 344, *345,* 412, *414,* 420, *427,* 492
Cohler, J., *197, 201*
Coleman, J. F., *226*
Collier, R. M., 266, *294*
Collins, B. E., *306*
Conn, L. K., *199*
Converse, P. E., *299*
Cook, S. W., *403*
Cooper, E., 265, 294, *297,* 459, *461*
Corrozi, J. F., *102, 445*
Corsini, R., 362, *367*
Corwin, R., *375*
Cottingham, D. R., *150,* 264, *293*
Cottrell, L. S., Jr., *69*
Cox, D. F., *229*
Cox, G. M., 476, *485*

Crockett, W. H., *103*
Cromwell, H., *101*
Cronbach, L. J., 48, *50*
Crowne, D. P., *199, 200,* 319, *330,* 465, *472, 473*
Crutchfield, R. S., 2, 172, *192, 200,* 265, *294*
Culbertson, F. M., 319, *331,* 362, *367*

Dabbs, J. M., *199,* 241, *244, 442*
Das, J. P., 266, *294*
Das, R. S., 266, *294*
Davidson, H. H., *7,* 55, *66*
Davison, L. A., *375*
DeFleur, M., *495, 497*
Deutsch, M., *234,* 260, *294, 301,* 307
DeVinney, L. C., *69*
DeWolfe, A. S., *150*
Dexter, L. A., *376*
Diab, L. N., *298, 400*
DiCicco, L., *192*
Dietrich, J. E., 419, *427*
Dietze, A. G., *416*
Dillehay, R. C., *446*
Dinerman, H., 265, *294,* 459, *461*
Dittes, J. E., 240, 241, *244, 247,* 263, *294*
Dollard, J., 154 (2), 165 (2), *167*
Donelson, E., *405*
Driver, M. J., 251, *254*
Duncker, R., 5
Dunteman, G., *399*
Dutta, S., *416*

Eagly, A. H., *402*
Ebbinghaus, H., 117, *125*
Edwards, A. L., 319, *331,* 356, *358, 402*
Ehrensberger, R., *417*
Ehrlich, D., *298*
Eindhoven, J., 36, 49, *51*
Ekman, P., 3
Elms, A., 335, 343, *345*
English, A. C., *xv*
English, H. B., *xv*
Entwisle, D. R., 476, *485*
Ericksen, C. W., 174, *192*
Eron, L. D., *375*
Ewing, T. N., 4

Fearing, F., 379 (2, 3), *387*

Subject Index

A

Active participation, 261
  need for approval and, 350
  passive participation vs., 285 *ff.*, 333 *ff.*,
    347 *ff.*
  "saying is believing," 302
Advertising, 255, *see also* Attitude,
    modification
  American Cancer Society, 128, 148
    cigarette, xiv *f.*
  political, 127, 132, 148
Anxiety, 128, 151, 153, 240, 263
  realistic fear vs., 175 *ff.*
Approval
  need for, 199, 350
    volunteering and, 469
Artifact, 32
  sources of, 463 *ff.*
    awareness of intent, 464 *ff.*
    evaluation apprehension, 317 *ff.*, 465
    experimenter expectancy, 337, 473
    neighbor effect, 120
    noncommitment, 487 *ff.*
    noninvolvement, 495 *ff.*
    pretest sensitization, 45, 78, 475 *ff.*
    volunteer subject, 465 *f.*, 469 *ff.*
Assimilation, 400 *ff.*
Attitude, *see also* Cognitive dissonance,
    Forgetting, Information
  components of
    affect, xvi, 375
    cognition, xvi, 297, 375
    behavior, xvi, 375
  defined, xv *f.*
  magnitude of change, 190, 399 *ff.*
    optimum discrepancy and, 404 *ff.*
  modification regarding
    arithmetic, 30, 59 *ff.*
    atomic electricity, 405
    atomic power for submarines, 11 *ff.*,
      55

boring task, 310 *ff.*, 333 *ff.*
cancer
  cure for, 207 *ff.*, 406, 449 *ff.*
  research, 242 *ff.*
  smoking and, 173, 361 *ff.*
censorship, 478
civil defense, 207 *ff.*
classical music on radio, 207 *ff.*
comic books, 303, 334
compulsory ROTC, 354 *ff.*
concept formation, 411 *ff.*
courtroom proceedings
  bigamy, 107 *ff.*
  suit for damages, 119 *ff.*
curfew for college students, 406
dental hygiene, 154 *ff.*, 267
drugs, 11 *ff.*
  penicillin, effects of, 267
fraternities, 391 *ff.*, 406, 470 *ff.*
grasshoppers, 26, 32 *f.*, 34 *ff.*
health insurance, 55
Hindenburg, General von, 207 *ff.*
India, 380 *ff.*
Islam, 249
Japan, war with, 72 *ff.*
juvenile delinquency, 55, 196 *f.*,
    421 *ff.*
Krushchev, 479
mental illness, 267
moon, travel to, 449 *ff.*
movie theaters, 11 *ff.*
nuclear weapons, 444, 478
Picasso, 444
police, 320 *f.*, 334
preventive health practices, 168 *ff.*
Puerto Rico statehood, 421 *ff.*
Rose Bowl, participation in, 322 *ff.*,
    336
Russia's producing atomic bombs,
    255 *f.*
sales tax, abolishment of, 421 *ff.*
smoking, 173, 361 *ff.*

SUBJECT INDEX

steel shortage, 11 ff.
stockings, 227
student exchange with Russia, 333
television show, 207 ff.
tetanus inoculation, 182 ff.
3-D films, 449 ff.
tuition, increased or decreased, 355 ff.
Turkey, 252
U.S. Armed Forces, reduction of,
449 ff.
vivisection, 477, 480 f.
vocabulary learning, 488 ff.
voting behavior, 432 ff.
compulsory voting, 405
election of Sect. of State, 421 ff.
Socialist Party, 132 ff.
Washington vs. Lincoln, 406
X-ray examination, 173, 267
opinion vs., xv f.
Audience, see Recipient(s)
Audience-tailored film, 379 ff.
Authoritarianism, 199
volunteering and, 469

B

Balance theory, 430, 453
Bay of Pigs, 399
Beliefs
relevance of shared beliefs, 4, 53
similarity of, 4
Bennington College study, 431 ff.
Boomerang effect, 41 f., 195 f., 408, 409
Brainwashing, 249, 264

C

Channel(s), 370 ff.
comparative potency of, 372 ff.
seductive quality of, 370
typology, 371 ff.
face-to-face confrontation, public vs.
private, 372
mass media, 7, 264, 361
specialized channels
audience-tailored film, 379 ff.
technical vs. nontechnical, 371 f.
Civil rights, 53, 375
Coercion, see Fear appeals
Cognitive complexity, 103

Cognitive consistency, see Consistency
hypothesis
Cognitive dissonance theory, 300 ff., 453,
see also Consistency hypothesis
active vs. passive participation and, 347
controversy concerning, 297 ff., 407 ff.
counterattitudinal act and, 34 ff.
criticisms of, 304 ff.
forced compliance and, 304 ff.
magnitude of reward or punishment
and, 303 ff.
opinion/attitude change and, 40 ff., 147,
407 ff.
prestige suggestion and, 5, 26 ff.
self-persuasion and, 297 ff.
Commitment, 30, 260 ff., 328, 375, 389,
487 ff.
communication-recipient discrepancy
and, 409 ff.
initial opinion and persuasibility, 82 f.
audience-tailored film, 379 ff.
Communication, see Message
Communication-recipient discrepancy,
401 ff.
defined, 403
magnitude of attitude change and,
404 ff.
involvement and, 409 ff.
Communicator, see Source
Conformity, 29 ff., 151, 169, 200, 230
score, 105
Congruity, principle of, 299
Consistency hypothesis, 3, 4, 298 ff., see
also Cognitive dissonance theory
cognitive consistency and attitude
change, 453 ff.
Contagion effects, 39
neighbor effect, 120
Counterattitudinal act
persuasiveness of communicator and,
3 f.
relation to self-persuasion, 297 ff.
Contrast, 400 ff.
Credibility, see Source

D

Discounting cue theory, 419
Dissonant, see Cognitive dissonance

SUBJECT INDEX

Message, 68 *ff.*, *see also* Forgetting, Order
of presentation
emotional vs. rational, 127 *ff.*, 147 *f.*
fear appeals, 147 *ff.*, 205
source credibility and, 149
one-sided vs. two-sided, 71 *ff.*, 99, 255,
416
perception of, 15
primacy-recency, 99 *ff.*
Methodology, *see* Experimental methodology, Pretest sensitization
Momentary mood of compliance, 442
Motivation, 147, 153, 206, *see also*
Persuasibility
volunteering and, 469

N

Nonmonotonic relationship, 151, 202 *ff.*,
352, 406, 409 *ff.*

O

One-sided message, *see* Message
Open- and closed-mindedness, *see*
Dogmatism
Opinion, *see also* Attitude, Cognitive dissonance, Information
attitude vs., xv *f.*
defined, xv *f.*
Order of presentation
law of primacy, 100
primacy vs. recency, 99 *ff.*, 475, 477
Ebbinghaus curves and, 104, 117 *ff.*
free variables, 101
strength, 102
reinforcement, 102
primacy-bound variables, 101
awareness, 464
controversialism, 101
familiarity, 101, 485
interestingness, 101
nonsalience, 101
recency-bound variables, 101
salience, 102
unfamiliarity, 102
uninterestingness, 102
Overheard communication, 352 *ff.*

P

Passive, *see* Active participation

Perception
of communication, 15
assimilation vs. contrast, 400 *ff.*
two-sided messages, 99
of source credibility, 3
verbal and nonverbal cues, 3
selective, 399 *f.*
subliminal, 420
Persistence, *see* Effects, long range
Personality variables, *see* Persuasibility,
inherent factors
Persuasibility, *see also* Active participation; Recipient(s)
general factor of, 201, 205 *ff.*
induced factors, 247 *ff.*
inherent factors, 195 *ff.*
aggressiveness, 199
authoritarianism, 199
cognitive need, 199
dogmatism, 199
ego-defensiveness, 199, 226
extrapunitiveness, 197
free vs. bound, 195 *f.*
hostility, 197
intelligence, 55, 198, 202 *f.*, 206
need for affiliation, 200
need for social approval, 199, 350
self-esteem, 199, 203, 225 *ff.*, 239 *ff.*
sex, 198 *f.*, 206, 384
test for, 242 *ff.*
typology, 195 *f.*
abstract vs. concrete, 251 *ff.*
clarifiers vs. simplifiers, 197
copers vs. avoiders, 197
Persuasion, defined, xv
Preconditioning, 264
Prejudice, 62 *ff.*, 495 *ff.*
Prestige suggestion
cognitive dissonance and, 5
defined, 2
Pretest sensitization, 45, 78, 475 *ff.*
Primacy, *see* Order of presentation
Psychodrama, 302 *f.*
Psychotherapy, 154, 302 *f.*
Punishment, *see* Reinforcement

Q

Qualified vs. unqualified messages, *see*
Message, one-sided vs. two-sided

SUBJECT INDEX

R

Race of communicator and persuasiveness, 30, 53 ff.
Rational communication, see Message
Recall, see Forgetting
Recency, see Order of presentation
Receptivity, 202
    active vs. passive participation and, 348
    selection of channel and, 374
    theory of social influence and, 150 f.
Recipient(s), 194 ff., see also Persuasibility
    audience-tailored film, 379 ff.
    captive audience, 164
    perception of message, 15
    persuasibility
        heightening, 247 ff., 389 ff.
        reducing, 257 ff.
Reinforcement, 102, 103, 251, see also Incentive
    diffusion of reinforcement, 443 f.
    rewards and punishments, 31, 147, 170
    cognitive dissonance and, 303 ff.
Resistance, see Recipient(s), persuasibility of
Reward, see Reinforcement
Role-playing, 302, 333 ff., 361 ff., see also Counterattitudinal act, Self-persuasion
Rotation design, 476

S

Saying is believing, 302
Selective exposure, 266, 297 ff.
Self-persuasion, 297 ff., see also Counterattitudinal act
Sensitization, see Pretest sensitization
Sensory deprivation, 249, 251 ff., 255
Sensory variation theory, 103
Sex
    persuasibility and, 198 f., 206, 384
    persuasiveness and, 8
    volunteering and, 470
Sleeper effect, 10 ff., 25
    discounting cue and, 419
    forgetting source and, 19 ff.
Social influence, see also Persuasibility
    personality variables in, 197 ff.
    theory of, 150 f., 200 ff.

Socratic method, 453 ff.
Source, 2 ff., see also Race, Sleeper effect
    credibility, 2 ff.
        fear arousal and, 149
        perception of, 3, 47
        prestige suggestion, 7 ff.
            defined, 2
        relevant vs. irrelevant aspects of, 7, 29 ff., 55 ff.
    persuasiveness, 2 ff.
        physical attractiveness and, 2
        physical stature and, 2
        positiveness-negativeness and, 29 ff.
Spontaneous recovery, 123
S-R, 201
Strong's law, 132
Subliminal perception, 420

T

Threat, see Fear appeals
Thurstone scale, underlying assumption, 402
Trustworthiness, see Source, credibility
Two-sided message, see also Order of presentation
    one-sided vs., 71 ff., 99, 255, 416
    perception of, 99
Two-step flow, 376 f.

U

Unintentional communication, 352 ff.

V

Volunteers vs. nonvolunteers, 465 f., 469 ff.
Voting behavior, 30, 127, 133 ff., 147, 405
    Bennington College study and, 432 ff.

W

World War I, 207
World War II, xviii, 69, 404 f., 419

Y

Yale Communication Research Program, xviii, 69
Yielding, 202
    selection of channel and, 374
    theory of social influence and, 150 f.